HISTORY OF THE CHRISTIAN CHURCH

WICLIF

HISTORY

OF THE

CHRISTIAN CHURCH

BY

PHILIP SCHAFF

Christianus sum. Christiani nihil a me alienum puto

VOLUME VI

THE MIDDLE AGES

FROM BONIFACE VIII., 1294, TO THE PROTESTANT REFORMATION, 1517

BY

DAVID S. SCHAFF, D.D.

WM. B. EERDMANS PUBLISHING COMPANY

GRAND RAPIDS   MICHIGAN

Reprinted 1995

ISBN 0-8028-8052-5

PHOTOLITHOPRINTED BY EERDMANS PRINTING COMPANY
GRAND RAPIDS, MICHIGAN, UNITED STATES OF AMERICA

To the

RECTOR AND THEOLOGICAL FACULTY

OF THE

UNIVERSITY OF GENEVA

FOUNDED BY

JOHN CALVIN

AND ADMINISTERED BY

THÉODORE DE BÈZE

AS ITS FIRST RECTOR

NOMINA PRAECLARA

IN GRATEFUL ACKNOWLEDGMENT OF THE DEGREE OF DOCTOR

OF DIVINITY CONFERRED UPON THE AUTHOR AT THE THREE

HUNDRED AND FIFTIETH ANNIVERSARY OF THIS DISTIN-

GUISHED SEAT OF LEARNING, JULY 7–10, 1909, AND

IN THE HOPE OF A YET FULLER REALIZATION

OF THE VENERABLE GENEVAN MOTTO

POST TENEBRAS LUX

PREFACE

This volume completes the history of the Church in the Middle Ages. Dr. Philip Schaff on one occasion spoke of the Middle Ages as a *terra incognita* in the United States, — a territory not adequately explored. These words would no longer be applicable, whether we have in mind the instruction given in our universities or theological seminaries. In Germany, during the last twenty years, the study of the period has been greatly developed, and no period at the present time, except the Apostolic age, attracts more scholarly and earnest attention and research.

The author has had no apologetic concern to contradict the old notion, perhaps still somewhat current in our Protestant circles, that the Middle Ages were a period of superstition and worthy of study as a curiosity rather than as a time directed and overruled by an all-seeing Providence. He has attempted to depict it as it was and to allow the picture of high religious purpose to reveal itself side by side with the picture of hierarchical assumption and scholastic misinterpretation. Without the mediæval age, the Reformation would not have been possible. Nor is this statement to be understood in the sense in which we speak of reaching a land of sunshine and plenty after having traversed a desert. We do well to give to St. Bernard and Francis d'Assisi, St. Elizabeth and St. Catherine of Siena, Gerson, Tauler and Nicolas of Cusa a high place in our list of religious personalities, and to pray for men to speak to our generation as well as they spoke to the generations in which they lived.

Moreover, the author has been actuated by no purpose to disparage Christians who, in the alleged errors of Protestantism, find an insuperable barrier to Christian fellowship. Where he has passed condemnatory judgments on personalities, as on the popes of the last years of the 15th and the earlier years of the 16th century, it is not because they occupied the papal throne, but because they were personalities who in any walk of life would call for the severest reprobation. The unity of the Christian faith and the promotion of fellowship between Christians of all names and all ages are considerations which should make us careful with pen or spoken word lest we condemn, without properly taking into consideration that interior devotion to Christ and His kingdom which seems to be quite compatible with divergencies in doctrinal statement or ceremonial habit.

On the pages of the volume, the author has expressed his indebtedness to the works of the eminent mediæval historians and investigators of the day, Gregorovius, Pastor, Mandell Creighton, Lea, Ehrle, Denifle, Finke, Schwab, Haller, Carl Mirbt, K. Müller, Kirsch, Loserth, Janssen, Valois, Burckhardt-Geiger, Seebohm and others, Protestant and Roman Catholic, and some no more among the living.

It is a pleasure to be able again to express his indebtedness to the Rev. David E. Culley, his colleague in the Western Theological Seminary, whose studies in mediæval history and accurate scholarship have been given to the volume in the reading of the manuscript, before it went to the printer, and of the printed pages before they received their final form.

Above all, the author feels it to be a great privilege that he has been able to realize the hope which Dr. Philip Schaff expressed in the last years of his life, that his *History of the Christian Church* which, in four volumes, had traversed the first ten centuries and, in the sixth and seventh, set forth the progress of the German and Swiss Reformations, might be carried through the fruitful period from 1050–1517.

DAVID S. SCHAFF.

THE WESTERN THEOLOGICAL SEMINARY,
    PITTSBURG.

CONTENTS.

CHAPTER X. THE CLOSE OF THE MIDDLE AGES.

ILLUSTRATIONS

Julius II

THE MIDDLE AGES.

THE DECLINE OF THE PAPACY AND THE PREPARATION FOR MODERN CHRISTIANITY.

FROM BONIFACE VIII. TO MARTIN LUTHER.
A.D. 1294–1517.

THE SIXTH PERIOD OF CHURCH HISTORY.

§ 1. *Introductory Survey.*

THE two centuries intervening between 1294 and 1517, between the accession of Boniface VIII. and the nailing of Luther's Ninety-five Theses against the church door in Wittenberg, mark the gradual transition from the Middle Ages to modern times, from the universal acceptance of the papal theocracy in Western Europe to the assertion of national independence, from the supreme authority of the priesthood to the intellectual and spiritual freedom of the individual. Old things are passing away ; signs of a new order increase. Institutions are seen to be breaking up.   The scholastic systems of theology lose their compulsive hold on men's minds, and even become the subject of ridicule.   The abuses of the earlier Middle Ages call forth voices demanding reform on the basis of the Scriptures and the common well-being of mankind.   The inherent vital energies in the Church seek expression in new forms of piety and charitable deed.

The power of the papacy, which had asserted infallibility of judgment and dominion over all departments of human life, was undermined by the mistakes, pretensions, and worldliness of the papacy itself, as exhibited in the policy of Boni-

1

face VIII., the removal of the papal residence to Avignon, and the disastrous schism which, for nearly half a century, gave to Europe the spectacle of two, and at times three, popes reigning at the same time and all professing to be the vicegerents of God on earth.

The free spirit of nationality awakened during the crusades grew strong and successfully resisted the papal authority, first in France and then in other parts of Europe. Princes asserted supreme authority over the citizens within their dominions and insisted upon the obligations of churches to the state. The leadership of Europe passed from Germany to France, with England coming more and more into prominence.

The tractarian literature of the fourteenth century set forth the rights of man and the principles of common law in opposition to the pretensions of the papacy and the dogmatism of the scholastic systems. Lay writers made themselves heard as pioneers of thought, and a practical outlook upon the mission of the Church was cultivated. With unexampled audacity Dante assailed the lives of popes, putting some of St. Peter's successors into the lowest rooms of hell.

The Reformatory councils of Pisa, Constance, and Basel turned Europe for nearly fifty years, 1409–1450, into a platform of ecclesiastical and religious discussion. Though they failed to provide a remedy for the disorders prevailing in the Church, they set an example of free debate, and gave the weight of their eminent constituency to the principle that not in a select group of hierarchs does supreme authority in the Church rest, but in the body of the Church.

The hopelessness of expecting any permanent reform from the papacy and the hierarchy was demonstrated in the last years of the period, 1460–1517, when ecclesiastical Rome offered a spectacle of moral corruption and spiritual fall which has been compared to the corrupt age of the Roman Empire.

The religious unrest and the passion for a better state of affairs found expression in Wyclif, Huss, and other leaders who, by their clear apprehension of truth and readiness to stand by their public utterances, even unto death, stood far above their own age and have shone in all the ages since.

While coarse ambition and nepotism, a total perversion of the ecclesiastical office and violation of the fundamental virtues of the Christian life held rule in the highest place of Christendom, a pure stream of piety was flowing in the Church of the North, and the mystics along the Rhine and in the Lowlands were unconsciously fertilizing the soil from which the Reformation was to spring forth.

The Renaissance, or the revival of classical culture, unshackled the minds of men. The classical works of antiquity were once more, after the churchly disparagement of a thousand years, held forth to admiration. The confines of geography were extended by the discoveries of the continent in the West.

The invention of the art of printing, about 1440, forms an epoch in human advancement, and made it possible for the products of human thought to be circulated widely among the people, and thus to train the different nations for the new age of religious enfranchisement about to come, and the sovereignty of the intellect.

To this generation, which looks back over the last four centuries, the discovery of America and the pathways to the Indies was one of the remarkable events in history, a surprise and a prophecy. In 1453, Constantinople easily passed into the hands of the Turk, and the Christian empire of the East fell apart. In the far West the beginnings of a new empire were made, just as the Middle Ages were drawing to a close.

At the same time, at the very close of the period, under the direction and protection of the Church, an institution was being prosecuted which has scarcely been equalled in the history of human cruelty, the Inquisition, — now papal, now Spanish, — which punished heretics unto death in Spain and witches in Germany.

Thus European society was shaking itself clear of long-established customs and dogmas based upon the infallibility of the Church visible, and at the same time it held fast to some of the most noxious beliefs and practices the Church had allowed herself to accept and propagate. It had not the original genius or the conviction to produce a new system of theology. The great Schoolmen continued to rule doctrinal thought. It established no new ecclesiastical institution of an abiding character like the canon law. It exhibited no consuming passion such as went out in the preceding period in the crusades and the activity of the Mendicant Orders. It had no transcendent ecclesiastical characters like St. Bernard and Innocent III. The last period of the Middle Ages was a period of intellectual discontent, of self-introspection, a period of intimation and of preparation for an order which it was itself not capable of begetting.

CHAPTER I.

THE DECLINE OF THE PAPACY AND THE AVIGNON EXILE.
A.D. 1294-1377.

§ 2. *Sources and Literature.*

For works covering the entire period, see V. 1. 1–3, such as the collections of MANSI, MURATORI, and the Rolls Series; Friedberg's *Decretum Gratiani*, 2 vols., Leipzig, 1879–1881; HEFELE-KNÖPFLER: *Conciliengeschichte;* MIRBT: *Quellen zur Geschichte des Papstthums*, 2d ed., 1901; the works of GREGOROVIUS and BRYCE, the General Church and Doctrinal Histories of GIESELER, HEFELE, FUNK, HERGENRÖTHER-KIRSCH, KARL MÜLLER, HARNACK, LOOFS, and SEEBERG; the Encyclopædias of HERZOG, WETZER-WELTE, LESLIE STEPHEN, POTTHAST, and CHÉVALIER; the Atlases of F. W. PUTZGER, Leipzig, HEUSSI and MULERT, Tübingen, 1905, and LABBERTON, New York. L. PASTOR: *Geschichte der Päpste*, etc., 4 vols., 4th ed., 1901–1906, and MANDELL CREIGHTON: *History of the Papacy*, etc., London, 1882–1894, also cover the entire period in the body of their works and their Introductory Chapters. There is no general collection of ecclesiastical authors for this period corresponding to Migne's *Latin Patrology*.

For §§ 3, 4. BONIFACE VIII. *Regesta Bonifatii* in POTTHAST: *Regesta pontificum rom.*, II., 1923–2024, 2133 sq. — *Les Registres de Boniface VIII.*, ed. DIGARD, FAUÇON ET THOMAS, 7 Fasc., Paris, 1884–1903. — *Hist. eccles.* of Ptolemæus of Lucca, *Vitæ Pontif.* of Bernardus Guidonis, *Chron. Pontif.* of Amalricus Auger, *Hist. rerum in Italia gestarum* of Ferretus Vicentinus, and *Chronica universale* of Villani, all in MURATORI: *Rerum Ital. Scriptores*, III. 670 sqq., X. 690 sqq., XI. 1202 sqq., XIII. 348 sqq. — *Selections from Villani*, trans. by ROSE E. SELFE, ed. by P. H. WICKSTEED, Westminster, 1897. — FINKE: *Aus den Tagen Bonifaz VIII.*, Münster, 1902. Prints valuable documents, pp. i–ccxi. Also *Acta Aragonensia. Quellen . . . zur Kirchen und Kulturgeschichte aus der diplomatischen Korrespondenz Jayme II., 1291-1327*, 2 vols., Berlin, 1908. — DÖLLINGER: *Beiträge zur politischen, kirchlichen und Culturgeschichte der letzten 6 Jahrh.*, 3 vols., Vienna, 1862–1882. Vol. III., pp. 347–353, contains a *Life of Boniface drawn from the Chronicle of Orvieto* by an eye-witness, and other documents. — DENIFLE: *Die Denkschriften der Colonna gegen Bonifaz VIII.*, etc., in *Archiv für Lit. und Kirchengeschichte des M.A.*, 1892, V. 493 sqq. — DANTE: *Inferno*, XIX. 52 sqq., XXVII. 85 sqq.; *Paradiso*, IX. 132, XXVII. 22, XXX. 147. MODERN WORKS. — J. RUBEUS: *Bonif. VIII. e familia Cajetanorum*, Rome, 1651. Magnifies Boniface as an ideal pope. — P. DUPUY: *Hist. du différend entre le Pape Bon. et Philip le Bel*, Paris, 1655. — BAILLET (a Jansenist): *Hist. des désmelez du Pape Bon. VIII. avec Philip le Bel*, Paris, 1718. —

L. Tosti : *Storia di Bon. VIII. e de' suoi tempi*, 2 vols., Rome, 1846. A glorification of Boniface.—W. Drumann : *Gesch. Bonifatius VIII.*, 2 vols., Königsberg, 1852.—Cardinal Wiseman : *Pope Bon. VIII.* in his *Essays*, III. 161–222. Apologetic. — Boutaric : *La France sous Philippe le Bel*, Paris, 1861.—R. Holtzmann : *W. von Nogaret*, Freiburg, 1898.—E. Renan : *Guil. de Nogaret*, in *Hist. Litt. de France*, XXVII. 233 sq. ; also *Études sur la politique rel. du règne de Phil. le Bel*, Paris, 1899.—Döllinger : *Anagni in Akad. Vorträge*, III. 223–244.—Heinrich Finke (prof. in Freiburg) : as above. Also *Papsttum und Untergang des Tempelordens*, 2 vols., Münster, 1907.—J. Haller : *Papsttum und Kirchenreform*, Berlin, 1903. — Rich. Scholz : *Die Publizistik zur Zeit Philipps des Schönen und Bonifaz VIII.*, Stuttgart, 1903. — The *Ch. Histt.* of Gieseler, Hergenröther-Kirsch, 4th ed., 1904, II. 582–598, F. X. Funk, 4th ed., 1902, Hefele, 3d ed., 1902, K. Müller, Hefele-Knöpfler : *Conciliengeschichte*, VI. 281–364.—Ranke : *Univers. Hist.*, IX. — Gregorovius : *History of the City of Rome*, V. — Wattenbach : *Gesch. des röm. Papstthums*, 2d ed., Berlin, 1876, pp. 211–225. — G. B. Adams : *Civilization during the Middle Ages*, New York, 1894, ch. XIV. —Art. *Bonifatius* by Hauck in Herzog, III. 291–300.

For § 5. Literary Attacks upon the Papacy. Dante Allighieri : *De monarchia*, ed. by Witte, Vienna, 1874 ; Giuliani, Florence, 1878 ; Moore, Oxford, 1894. Eng. trans. by F. C. Church, together with the essay on Dante by his father, R. W. Church, London, 1878 ; P. H. Wicksteed, Hull, 1896 ; Aurelia Henry, Boston, 1904. — Dante's *De monarchia*, Valla's *De falsa donatione Constantini*, and other anti-papal documents are given in *De jurisdictione, auctoritate et præeminentia imperiali*, Basel, 1566. Many of the tracts called forth by the struggle between Boniface VIII. and Philip IV. are found in Melchior Goldast : *Monarchia S. Romani imperii, sive tractatus de jurisdictione imperiali seu regia et pontificia seu sacerdotali*, etc., Hanover, 1610, pp. 756, Frankfurt, 1668. With a preface dedicated to the elector, John Sigismund of Brandenburg ; in Dupuy : *Hist. du Différend*, etc., Paris, 1655, and in Finke and Scholz. See above.— E. Zeck : *De recuperatione terræ Sanctæ, Ein Traktat d. P. Dubois*, Berlin, 1906. For summary and criticism, S. Riezler : *Die literarischen Widersacher der Päpste zur Zeit Ludwig des Baiers*, pp. 131–155. Leipzig, 1874. —R. L. Poole : *Opposition to the Temporal Claims of the Papacy*, in his *Illustrations of the Hist. of Med. Thought*, pp. 256–281, London, 1884. — Finke : *Aus den Tagen Bonifaz VIII.*, pp. 159 sqq., etc. — Denifle : *Chartularium Un. Parisiensis*, 4 vols.— Haller : *Papsttum.*—Artt. in Wetzer-Welte, *Colonna*, III. 667–671, and *Johann von Paris*, VI. 1744–1746, etc. — Renan : *Pierre Dubois in Hist. Litt. de France*, XXVI. 471–536.— Hergenröther-Kirsch : *Kirchengesch.*, II. 754 sqq.

For § 6. Transfer of the Papacy to Avignon. Benedict XI. : *Registre de Benoît XI.*, ed. C. Grandjean. —For Clement V., *Clementis papæ V. regestum ed. cura et studio monachorum ord. S. Benedicti*, 9 vols., Rome, 1885–1892.—Etienne Baluze : *Vitæ paparum Avenoniensium 1305–1394*, dedicated to Louis XIV. and placed on the Index, 2 vols., Paris, 1693. Raynaldus : *ad annum*, 1304 sqq., for original documents. — W. H. Bliss : *Calendar of Entries in the Papal Registries relating to Great Britain and*

Ireland, I.-IV., London, 1896–1902. — GIOVANNI and MATTEO VILLANI: *Hist. of Florence sive Chronica universalis*, bks. VIII. sq. — M. TANGL: *Die päpstlichen Regesta von Benedict XII.-Gregor XI.*, Innsbruck, 1898. MANSI: *Concil.*, XXV. 368 sqq., 389 sqq. — J. B. CHRISTOPHE: *Hist. de la papauté pendant le XIVe siècle*, 2 vols., Paris, 1853. — C. VON HÖFLER: *Die avignonesischen Päpste*, Vienna, 1871. — FAUÇON: *La libraire des papes d'Avignon*, 2 vols., Paris, 1886 sq. — M. SOUCHON: *Die Papstwahlen von Bonifaz VIII.-Urban VI.*, Braunschweig, 1888. — A. EITEL: *D. Kirchenstaat unter Klemens V.*, Berlin, 1905. — CLINTON LOCKE: *Age of the Great Western Schism*, pp. 1–99, New York, 1896. — J. H. ROBINSON: *Petrarch*, New York, 1898. — SCHWAB: *J. Gerson*, pp. 1–7. — DÖLLINGER-FRIEDRICH: *Das Papstthum*, Munich, 1892. — PASTOR: *Geschichte der Päpste seit dem Ausgang des M.A.*, 4 vols., 3d and 4th ed., 1901 sqq., I. 67–114. — STUBBS: *Const. Hist. of England.* — CAPES: *The English Church in the 14th and 15th Centuries*, London, 1900. — WATTENBACH: *Röm. Papstthum*, pp. 226–241. — HALLER: *Papsttum*, etc. — HEFELE-KNÖPFLER: VI. 378–936. — RANKE: *Univers. Hist.*, IX. — GREGOROVIUS: VI. — The *Ch. Histt.* of GIESELER, HERGENRÖTHER-KIRSCH, II. 737–776, MÜLLER, II. 16–42. — EHRLE: *Der Nachlass Clemens V.* in *Archiv für Lit. u. Kirchengesch.*, V. 1–150. For the fall of the Templars, see for lit. V. 1. p. 301 sqq., and especially the works of BOUTARIC, PRUTZ, SCHOTTMÜLLER, DÖLLINGER. — FUNK in Wetzer-Welte, XI. 1311–1345. — LEA: *Inquisition*, III. FINKE: *Papsttum und Untergang des Tempelordens*, 2 vols., 1907. Vol. II. contains Spanish documents, hitherto unpublished, bearing on the fall of the Templars, especially letters to and from King Jayme of Aragon. They are confirmatory of former views.

For § 7. THE PONTIFICATE OF JOHN XXII. *Lettres secrètes et curiales du pape Jean XXII. relative à la France*, ed. AUG. COULON, 3 Fasc., 1900 sq. *Lettres communes de p. Jean XXII.*, ed. MOLLAT, 3 vols., Paris, 1904–1906. — J. GUÉRARD: *Documents pontificeaux sur la Gascogne. Pontificat de Jean XXII.*, 2 vols., Paris, 1897–1903. — BALUZE: *Vitæ paparum.* — V. VELARQUE: *Jean XXII. sa vie et ses œuvres*, Paris, 1883. — J. SCHWALM, *Appellation d. König Ludwigs des Baiern v. 1324*, 1906. — RIEZLER: *D. lit. Widersacher.* Also *Vatikanische Akten zur deutschen Gesch. zur Zeit Ludwigs des Bayern*, Innsbruck, 1891. — K. MÜLLER: *Der Kampf Ludwigs des Baiern mit der römischen Curie*, 2 vols., Tübingen, 1879 sq. — EHRLE: *Die Spirituallen, ihr Verhältniss zum Franciskanerorden*, etc., in *Archiv für Lit. und Kirchengesch.*, 1885, p. 509 sqq., 1886, p. 106 sqq., 1887, p. 553 sqq., 1890. Also *P. J. Olivi: S. Leben und s. Schriften*, 1887, pp. 409–540. — DÖLLINGER: *Deutschlands Kampf mit dem Papstthum unter Ludwig dem Bayer* in *Akad. Vorträge*, I. 119–137. — HEFELE: VI. 546–579. — LEA: *Inquisition*, I. 242–304. — The Artt. in Wetzer-Welte, *Franziskanerorden*, IV. 1650–1683, and *Armut*, I. 1394–1401. Artt. *John XXII.* in Herzog, IX. 267–270, and Wetzer-Welte, VIII. 828 sqq. — HALLER: *Papsttum*, p. 91 sqq. — STUBBS: *Const. Hist. of England.* — GREGOROVIUS, VI. — PASTOR: I. 80 sqq.

For § 8. THE PAPAL OFFICE ASSAILED. Some of the tracts may be found in GOLDAST: *Monarchia*, Hanover, 1610, *e.g. Marsiglius of Padua*, II. 154–312 ; Ockam's *Octo quæstionum decisiones super potestate ac dignitate papali*, II. 740 sqq., and *Dialogus inter magistrum et discipulum*, etc.,

II., 399 sqq.   Special edd. are given in the body of the chap. and may be
found under Alvarus Pelagius, Marsiglius, etc., in POTTHAST: *Bibl. med. œvi.*—
Un trattato inedito di Egidio Colonna: De ecclesiæ potestate, ed. G. U. OXILIA
et G. BOFFITO, Florence, 1908, pp. lxxxi, 172.— SCHWAB: *Gerson,* pp. 24–
28.— MÜLLER: *D. Kampf Ludwigs des Baiern.*— RIEZLER: *Die lit. Widersacher der Päpste,* etc., Leipzig, 1874.— MARCOUR: *Antheil der Minoriten am
Kampf zwischen Ludwig dem Baiern und Johann XXII.,* Emmerich, 1874.—
POOLE: *The Opposition to the Temporal Claims of the Papacy,* in *Illust. of
the Hist. of Med. Thought,* pp. 256–281.— HALLER: *Papsttum,* etc., pp. 73–
89.   English trans. of *Marsiglius of Padua, The Defence of Peace,* by W.
MARSHALL, London, 1535.— M. BIRCK: *Marsilio von Padua und Alvaro
Pelayo über Papst und Kaiser,* Mühlheim, 1868.— B. LABANCA, Prof. of
Moral Philos. in the Univ. of Rome: *Marsilio da Padova, riformatore polit-
ico e religioso,* Padova, 1882, pp. 235.— L. JOURDAN: *Étude sur Marsile de
Padoue,* Montauban, 1892.— J. SULLIVAN: *Marsig. of Padua,* in *Engl. Hist.
Rev.,* 1905, pp. 293–307.   An examination of the MSS.   See also DÖLLINGER-
FRIEDRICH: *Papstthum*; Pastor, I. 82 sqq.; Gregorovius, VI. 118 sqq., the
Artt. in Wetzer-Welte, *Alvarus Pelagius,* I. 667 sq., *Marsiglius,* VIII.,
907–911, etc., and in Herzog, XII. 368–370, etc.— N. VALOIS: *Hist. Litt.,*
Paris, 1900, XXIII., 528–623, an Art. on the authors of the *Defensor.*

For § 9.   THE FINANCIAL SYSTEM OF THE AVIGNON POPES.   EHRLE:
Schatz, Bibliothek und Archiv der Päpste im 14ten Jahrh., in *Archiv für
Lit. u. Kirchengesch.,* I. 1–49, 228–365, also *D. Nachlass Clemens V. und der
in Betreff desselben von Johann XXII. geführte Process,* V. 1–166.— PH.
WOKER: *Das kirchliche Finanzwesen der Päpste,* Nördlingen, 1878.— M.
TANGL: *Das Taxenwesen der päpstlichen Kanzlei vom 13ten bis zur Mitte
des 15ten Jahrh.,* Innsbruck, 1892.— J. P. KIRSCH: *Die päpstl. Kollektorien
in Deutschland im XIVten Jahrh.,* Paderborn, 1894; *Die Finanzverwal-
tung des Kardinalkollegiums im XIII. u. XIV.ten Jahrh.,* Münster, 1896;
*Die Rückkehr der Päpste Urban V. und Gregor XI. von Avignon nach
Rom. Auszüge aus den Kameralregistern des Vatikan. Archivs,* Pader-
born, 1898; *Die päpstl. Annaten in Deutschland im XIV. Jahrh. 1323–1360,*
Paderborn, 1903.— P. M. BAUMGARTEN: *Untersuchungen und Urkunden
über die Camera Collegii Cardinalium, 1295–1437,* Leipzig, 1898.— A. GOTT-
LOB: *Die päpstl. Kreuzzugsteuern des 13ten Jahrh.,* Heiligenstadt, 1892;
Die Servitientaxe im 13ten Jahrh., Stuttgart, 1903.— EMIL GOELLER:
*Mittheilungen u. Untersuchungen über das päpstl. Register und Kanzlei-
wesen im 14ten Jahrh.,* Rome, 1904; *D. Liber Taxarum d. päpstl. Kammer.
Eine Studie zu ihrer Entstehung u. Anlage,* Rome, 1905, pp. 105.—
HALLER: *Papsttum u. Kirchenreform; also Aufzeichnungen über den päpstl.
Haushalt aus Avignonesischer Zeit; die Vertheilung der Servitia minuta u.
die Obligationen der Praelaten im 13ten u. 14ten Jahrh.; Die Ausfertigung
der Provisionen,* etc., all in *Quellen u. Forschungen,* ed. by the Royal Prus-
sian Institute in Rome, Rome, 1897, 1898.— C. LUX: *Constitutionum apos-
tolicarum de generali beneficiorum reservatione, 1265–1378,* etc., Wratislav,
1904.— A. SCHULTE: *Die Fugger in Rom, 1495–1523,* 2 vols., Leipzig, 1904.—
C. SAMARIN and G. MOLLAT: *La Fiscalité pontif. en France au XIV* siècle,*
Paris, 1905.— P. THOMAN: *Le droit de propriété des laïques sur les églises*

et le patronat laïque au moy. âge, Paris, 1906.   Also the work on Canon
Law by T. HINSCHIUS, 6 vols., Berlin, 1869–1897, and E. FRIEDBERG, 5th ed.,
Leipzig, 1903.

For § 10.   LATER AVIGNON POPES.   *Lettres des papes d'Avignon se rap-
portant à la France*, viz.   *Lettres communes de Benoît XII.*, ed. J. M.
VIDAL, Paris, 1905; *Lettres closes, patentes et curiales*, ed. G. DAUMET,
Paris, 1890; *Lettres . . . de Clement VI.*, ed. E. DEPREZ, Paris, 1901; *Ex-
cerpta ex registr. de Clem. VI. et Inn. VI.*, ed. WERUNSKY, Innsbruck, 1885;
Lettres . . . de Pape Urbain V., ed. P. LECACHEUX, Paris, 1902.—J. H.
ALBANS: *Actes anciens et documents concernant le bienheureux Urbain V.*,
ed. by U. CHEVALIER, Paris, 1897.   Contains the fourteen early lives of
Urban.—BALUZE: *Vitæ paparum Avenionensium, 1693;*—MURATORI: in
Rer. ital. scripp, XIV. 9–728.—CERRI: *Innocenzo VI., papa*, Turin, 1873.
MAGNAN: *Hist. d' Urbain V.*, 2d ed., Paris, 1863.—WERUNSKY: *Gesch.
Karls IV. u. seiner Zeit*, 3 vols., Innsbruck, 1880–1892.—GEO. SCHMIDT: *Der
hist. Werth der 14 alten Biographien des Urban V.*, Breslau, 1907.—KIRSCH:
Rückkehr der Päpste, as above.   In large part, documents for the first time
published.—LECHNER: *Das grosse Sterben in Deutschland, 1348–1351*, 1884.—
C. CREIGHTON: *Hist. of Epidemics in England*, CAMBRIDGE, 1891.   F. A.
GASQUET: *The Great Pestilence*, London, 1893, 2d ed., entitled *The Black
Death*, 1908.—A. JESSOPP: *The Black Death in East Anglia* in *Coming of
the Friars*, pp. 166–261.—VILLANI, WATTENBACH, p. 226 sqq.; PASTOR, I.,
GREGOROVIUS, VI.—WURM: *Cardinal Albornoz*, Paderborn, 1892.

For § 11.   THE RE-ESTABLISHMENT OF THE PAPACY IN ROME.   *The Lives
of Gregory XI. in Baluz*, I. 425 sqq., and MURATORI, III. 2, 645.—KIRSCH:
Rückkehr, etc., as above.—LÉON MIROT: *La politique pontif. et le rétour du
S. Siège à Rome, 1376*, Paris, 1899.—F. HAMMERICH: *St. Brigitta, die nordische
Prophetin u. Ordenstifterin*, Germ. ed., Gotha, 1872.   For further lit. on St.
Brigitta, see HERZOG, III. 239.   For works on Catherine of Siena, see
ch. III.   Also GIESELER, II., 3, pp. 1–131; PASTOR, I. 101–114; GREGO-
ROVIUS, VI.   Lit. under § 10.

§ 3.   *Pope Boniface VIII.*   1294–1303.

The pious but weak and incapable hermit of Murrhone, Cœlestine V., who abdicated the papal office, was followed by Benedict Gaetani, — or Cajetan, the name of an ancient family of
Latin counts, — known in history as Boniface VIII.   At the
time of his election he was on the verge of fourscore,[1] but like
Gregory IX. he was still in the full vigor of a strong intellect

---

[1] Drumann, p. 4, Gregorovius, etc.   Setting aside the testimony of the contemporary Ferretus of Vicenza, and on the ground that it would be well-nigh
impossible for a man of Boniface's talent to remain in an inferior position till
he was sixty, when he was made cardinal, Finke, p. 3 sq., makes Boniface fifteen years younger when he assumed the papacy.

and will.   If Cœlestine had the reputation of a saint, Boniface
was a politician, overbearing, implacable, destitute of spiritual
ideals, and controlled by blind and insatiable lust of power.

Born at Anagni, Boniface probably studied canon law, in
which he was an expert, in Rome.[1]   He was made cardinal in
1281, and represented the papal see in France and England
as legate.   In an address at a council in Paris, assembled
to arrange for a new crusade, he reminded the mendicant
monks that he and they were called not to court glory or
learning, but to secure the salvation of their souls.[2]

Boniface's election as pope occurred at Castel Nuovo, near
Naples, Dec. 24, 1294, the conclave having convened the day
before.   The election was not popular, and a few days later,
when a report reached Naples that Boniface was dead, the people celebrated the event with great jubilation.   The pontiff was
accompanied on his way to Rome by Charles II. of Naples.[3]

The coronation was celebrated amid festivities of unusual
splendor.   On his way to the Lateran, Boniface rode on a white
palfrey, a crown on his head, and robed in full pontificals.
Two sovereigns walked by his side, the kings of Naples and
Hungary.   The Orsini, the Colonna, the Savelli, the Conti and
representatives of other noble Roman families followed in a
body.   The procession had difficulty in forcing its way through
the kneeling crowds of spectators.   But, as if an omen of the
coming misfortunes of the new pope, a furious storm burst
over the city while the solemnities were in progress and extin-
guished every lamp and torch in the church.   The following
day the pope dined in the Lateran, the two kings waiting
behind his chair.

While these brilliant ceremonies were going on, Peter of
Murrhone was a fugitive.   Not willing to risk the possible
rivalry of an anti-pope, Boniface confined his unfortunate

[1] Not at Paris, as Bulæus, without sufficient authority, states.   See Finke,
p. 6.

[2] Finke discovered this document and gives it pp. iii–vii.

[3] There is no doubt about the manifestation of popular joy over the rumor
of the pope's death.   Finke, p. 45.   At the announcement of the election, the
people are said to have cried out, " Boniface is a heretic, bad all through,
and has in him nothing that is Christian."

predecessor in prison, where he soon died.   The cause of his death was a matter of uncertainty.   The Cœlestine party ascribed it to Boniface, and exhibited a nail which they declared the unscrupulous pope had ordered driven into Cœlestine's head.

With Boniface VIII. began the decline of the papacy.   He found it at the height of its power.   He died leaving it humbled and in subjection to France.   He sought to rule in the proud, dominating spirit of Gregory VII. and Innocent III.; but he was arrogant without being strong, bold without being sagacious, high-spirited without possessing the wisdom to discern the signs of the times.[1]   The times had changed.   Boniface made no allowance for the new spirit of nationality which had been developed during the crusading campaigns in the East, and which entered into conflict with the old theocratic ideal of Rome.   France, now in possession of the remaining lands of the counts of Toulouse, was in no mood to listen to the dictation of the power across the Alps.   Striving to maintain the fictitious theory of papal rights, and fighting against the spirit of the new age, Boniface lost the prestige the Apostolic See had enjoyed for two centuries, and died of mortification over the indignities heaped upon him by France.

French enemies went so far as to charge Boniface with downright infidelity and the denial of the soul's immortality. The charges were a slander, but they show the reduced confidence which the papal office inspired.   Dante, who visited Rome during Boniface's pontificate, bitterly pursues him in all parts of the *Divina Commedia*.   He pronounced him "the prince of modern Pharisees," a usurper "who turned the Vatican hill into a common sewer of corruption."   The poet assigned the pope a place with Nicholas III. and Clement V. among the simoniacs in "that most afflicted shade," one of the lowest circles of hell.[2]   Its floor was perforated with holes into which the heads of these popes were thrust.

[1] Gregorovius, V. 597, calls Boniface "an unfortunate reminiscence" of the great popes.

[2] "Where Simon Magus hath his curst abode
     To depths profounder thrusting Boniface." — *Paradiso*, xxx. 147 sq.

> " The soles of every one in flames were wrapt — [1]
> . . . whose upper parts are thrust below
> Fixt like a stake, most wretched soul
> *   *   *   *   *   *
> Quivering in air his tortured feet were seen."

Contemporaries comprehended Boniface's reign in the description, "He came in like a fox, he reigned like a lion, and he died like a dog, *intravit ut vulpes, regnavit ut leo, mortuus est sicut canis.*

In his attempt to control the affairs of European states, he met with less success than failure, and in Philip the Fair of France he found his match.

In Sicily, he failed to carry out his plans to secure the transfer of the realm from the house of Aragon to the king of Naples.

In Rome, he incurred the bitter enmity of the proud and powerful family of the Colonna, by attempting to dictate the disposition of the family estates. Two of the Colonna, James and Peter, who were cardinals, had been friends of Cœlestine, and supporters of that pope gathered around them. Of their number was Jacopone da Todi, the author of the *Stabat Mater*, who wrote a number of satirical pieces against Boniface. Resenting the pope's interference in their private matters, the Colonna issued a memorial, pronouncing Cœlestine's abdication and the election of Boniface illegal.[2] It exposed the haughtiness of Boniface, and represented him as boasting that he was supreme over kings and kingdoms, even in temporal affairs, and that he was governed by no law other than his own will.[3] The document was placarded on the churches and a copy left in St. Peter's. In 1297 Boniface deprived the Colonna of their dignity, excommunicated them, and proclaimed a crusade against them. The two cardinals appealed to a general council, the resort in the next centuries of so many who found themselves out of accord with the papal plans. Their strongholds fell one after another. The last of them, Palestrina, had a melancholy fate. The two car-

---

[1] *Inferno*, xix. 45 sq. 118.   [2] Dupuy, pp. 225–227.
[3] *Super reges et regna in temporalibus etiam presidere se glorians*, etc., Scholz, p. 338.

dinals with ropes around their necks threw themselves at the
pope's feet and secured his pardon, but their estates were
confiscated and bestowed upon the pope's nephews and the
Orsini.   The Colonna family recovered in time to reap a
bitter vengeance upon their insatiable enemy.

The German emperor, Albrecht, Boniface succeeded in
bringing to an abject submission.   The German envoys were
received by the haughty pontiff seated on a throne with a
crown upon his head and sword in his hand, and exclaiming,
" I, I am the emperor."   Albrecht accepted his crown as a
gift, and acknowledged that the empire had been transferred
from the Greeks to the Germans by the pope, and that the
electors owed the right of election to the Apostolic See.

In England, Boniface met with sharp resistance.   Edward
I., 1272–1307, was on the throne.   The pope attempted to
prevent him from holding the crown of Scotland, claiming it
as a papal fief from remote antiquity.[1]   The English parliament, 1301, gave a prompt and spirited reply.   The English
king was under no obligation to the papal see for his temporal acts.[2]   The dispute went no further.   The conflict
between Boniface and France is reserved for more prolonged
treatment.

An important and picturesque event of Boniface's pontificate was the Jubilee Year, celebrated in 1300.   It was a fortunate conception, adapted to attract throngs of pilgrims to
Rome and fill the papal treasury.   An old man of 107 years
of age, so the story ran, travelled from Savoy to Rome, and
told how his father had taken him to attend a Jubilee in the
year 1200 and exhorted him to visit it on its recurrence a century after.   Interesting as the story is, the Jubilee celebration
of 1300 seems to have been the first of its kind.[3]   Boniface's
bull, appointing it, promised full remission to all, being penitent and confessing their sins, who should visit St. Peter's

---

[1] Tytler, *Hist. of Scotland*, I. 70 sqq.

[2] Edward removed from Scone to Westminster the sacred stone on which
Scotch kings had been consecrated, and which, according to the legend, was
the pillow on which Jacob rested at Bethel.

[3] So Hefele VI. 315, and other Roman Catholic historians.

during the year 1300.[1]   Italians were to prolong their sojourn 30 days, while for foreigners 15 days were announced to be sufficient.   A subsequent papal deliverance extended the benefits of the indulgence to all setting out for the Holy City who died on the way.   The only exceptions made to these gracious provisions were the Colonna, Frederick of Sicily, and the Christians holding traffic with Saracens.   The city wore a festal appearance.   The handkerchief of St. Veronica, bearing the imprint of the Saviour's face, was exhibited.   The throngs fairly trampled upon one another.   The contemporary historian of Florence, Giovanni Villani, testifies from personal observation that there was a constant population in the pontifical city of 200,000 pilgrims, and that 30,000 people reached and left it daily.   The offerings were so copious that two clerics stood day and night by the altar of St. Peter's gathering up the coins with rakes.

So spectacular and profitable a celebration could not be allowed to remain a memory.   The Jubilee was made a permanent institution.   A second celebration was appointed by Clement VI. in 1350.   With reference to the brevity of human life and also to the period of our Lord's earthly career, Urban VI. fixed its recurrence every 33 years.   Paul II., in 1470, reduced the intervals to 25 years.   The twentieth Jubilee was celebrated in 1900, under Leo XIII.[2]   Leo extended the

---

[1] Potthast, 24917.   The bull is reprinted by Mirbt, *Quellen*, p. 147 sq.   The indulgence clause runs: *non solum plenam sed largiorem immo plenissimam omnium suorum veniam peccatorum concedimus.*   Villani, VIII. 36, speaks of it as " a full and entire remission of all sins, both the guilt and the punishment thereof."

[2] Leo's bull, dated May 11, 1899, offered indulgence to pilgrims visiting the basilicas of St. Peter, the Lateran, and St. Maria Maggiore.   A portion of the document runs as follows: " Jesus Christ the Saviour of the world, has chosen the city of Rome alone and singly above all others for a dignified and more than human purpose and consecrated it to himself."   The Jubilee was inaugurated by the august ceremony of opening the *porta santa*, the sacred door, into St. Peter's, which it is the custom to wall up after the celebration. The special ceremony dates from Alexander VI. and the Jubilee of 1500.   Leo performed this ceremony in person by giving three strokes upon the door with a hammer, and using the words *aperite mihi*, open to me.   The door symbolizes Christ, opening the way to spiritual benefits.

offered benefits to those who had the will and not the ability to make the journey to Rome.

For the offerings accruing from the Jubilee and for other papal moneys, Boniface found easy use.   They enabled him to prosecute his wars against Sicily and the Colonna and to enrich his relatives.   The chief object of his favor was his nephew, Peter, the second son of his brother Loffred, the Count of Caserta.   One estate after another was added to this favorite's possessions, and the vast sum of more than $5,000,000 was spent upon him in four years.[1]   Nepotism was one of the offences for which Boniface was arraigned by his contemporaries.

§ 4. *Boniface VIII. and Philip the Fair of France.*

The overshadowing event of Boniface's reign was his disastrous conflict with Philip IV. of France, called Philip the Fair.   The grandson of Louis IX., this monarch was wholly wanting in the high spiritual qualities which had distinguished his ancestor.   He was able but treacherous, and utterly unscrupulous in the use of means to secure his ends.   Unattractive as his character is, it is nevertheless with him that the first chapter in the history of modern France begins.   In his conflict with Boniface he gained a decisive victory.   On a smaller scale the conflict was a repetition of the conflict between Gregory VII. and Henry IV., but with a different ending.   In both cases the pope had reached a venerable age, while the sovereign was young and wholly governed by selfish motives.   Henry resorted to the election of an anti-pope. Philip depended upon his councillors and the spirit of the new French nation.

The heir of the theocracy of Hildebrand repeated Hildebrand's language without possessing his moral qualities.   He claimed for the papacy supreme authority in temporal as well

---

[1] See Gregorovius, V. 299, 584, who gives an elaborate list of the estates which passed by Boniface's grace into the hands of the Gaetani. Adam of Usk, *Chronicon*, 1377–1421, 2d ed., London, 1904, p. 259, " the fox, though ever greedy, ever remaineth thin, so Boniface, though gorged with simony, yet to his dying day was never filled."

as spiritual matters.   In his address to the cardinals against
the Colonna he exclaimed: "How shall we assume to judge
kings and princes, and not dare to proceed against a worm!
Let them perish forever, that they may understand that the
name of the Roman pontiff is known in all the earth and that
he alone is most high over princes." [1]   The Colonna, in one of
their proclamations, charged Boniface with glorying that he is
exalted above all princes and kingdoms in temporal matters,
and may act as he pleases in view of the fulness of his power
— *plenitudo potestatis*.   In his official recognition of the emperor, Albrecht, Boniface declared that as "the moon has no
light except as she receives it from the sun, so no earthly power
has anything which it does not receive from the ecclesiastical
authority."   These claims are asserted with most pretension
in the bulls Boniface issued during his conflict with France.
Members of the papal court encouraged him in these haughty
assertions of prerogative.   The Spaniard, Arnald of Villanova,
who served Boniface as physician, called him in his writings
lord of lords — *deus deorum*.

On the other hand, Philip the Fair stood as the embodiment
of the independence of the state.   He had behind him a unified
nation, and around him a body of able statesmen and publicists
who defended his views. [2]

The conflict between Boniface and Philip passed through
three stages: (1) the brief tilt which called forth the bull
Clericis laicos; (2) the decisive battle, 1301–1303, ending in
Boniface's humiliation at Anagni; (3) the bitter controversy
which was waged against the pope's memory by Philip, ending
with the Council of Vienne. [3]

---

[1] *Quomodo presumimus judicare reges et principes orbis terrarum et vermi-
culum aggredi non audemus*, etc.; Denifle, *Archiv*, etc., V. 521. For these and
other quotations, see Finke, *Aus den Tagen Bon.*, etc., p. 152 sqq.

[2] Contemporary writers spoke of the modern or recent French nation as
opposed to the nation of a preceding period.   So the author of the Tractate
of 1308 in defence of Boniface VIII., Finke, p. lxxxvi.   He said "the kings of
the modern French people do not follow in the footsteps of their predecessors"
— *reges moderni gentis Francorum*, etc.   The same writer compared Philip
to Nebuchadnezzar rebelling against the higher powers.

[3] See Scholz, *Publizistik*, VIII. p. 3 sqq.

The conflict originated in questions touching the war between France and England.   To meet the expense of his armament against Edward I., Philip levied tribute upon the French clergy.   They carried their complaints to Rome, and Boniface justified their contention in the bull *Clericis laicos*, 1296. This document was ordered promulged in England as well as in France.   Robert of Winchelsea, archbishop of Canterbury, had it read in all the English cathedral churches.   Its opening sentence impudently asserted that the laity had always been hostile to the clergy.   The document went on to affirm the subjection of the state to the papal see.   Jurisdiction over the persons of the priesthood and the goods of the Church in no wise belongs to the temporal power.   The Church may make gratuitous gifts to the state, but all taxation of Church property without the pope's consent is to be resisted with excommunication or interdict.

Imposts upon the Church for special emergencies had been a subject of legislation at the third and fourth Lateran Councils.   In 1260 Alexander IV. exempted the clergy from special taxation, and in 1291 Nicolas IV. warned the king of France against using for his own schemes the tenth levied for a crusade.   Boniface had precedent enough for his utterances. But his bull was promptly met by Philip with an act of reprisal prohibiting the export of silver and gold, horses, arms, and other articles from his realm, and forbidding foreigners to reside in France.   This shrewd measure cut off French contributions to the papal treasury and cleared France of the pope's emissaries.   Boniface was forced to reconsider his position, and in conciliatory letters, addressed to the king and the French prelates, pronounced the interpretation put upon his deliverance unjust.   Its purpose was not to deny feudal and freewill offerings from the Church.   In cases of emergency, the pope would also be ready to grant special subsidies.   The document was so offensive that the French bishops begged the pope to recall it altogether, a request he set aside.   But to appease Philip, Boniface issued another bull, July 22, 1297, according thereafter to French kings, who had reached the age of 20, the right to judge whether a tribute from the clergy was

a case of necessity or not.   A month later he canonized Louis
IX., a further act of conciliation.

Boniface also offered to act as umpire between France and
England in his personal capacity as Benedict Gaetanus.   The
offer was accepted, but the decision was not agreeable to the
French sovereign.   The pope expressed a desire to visit
Philip, but again gave offence by asking Philip for a loan of
100,000 pounds for Philip's brother, Charles of Valois, whom
Boniface had invested with the command of the papal forces.

In 1301 the flame of controversy was again started by a
document, written probably by the French advocate, Pierre
Dubois,[1] which showed the direction in which Philip's mind
was working, for it could hardly have appeared without his
assent.   The writer summoned the king to extend his dominions to the walls of Rome and beyond, and denied the pope's
right to secular power.   The pontiff's business is confined to
the forgiving of sins, prayer, and preaching.   Philip continued
to lay his hand without scruple on Church property; Lyons,
which had been claimed by the empire, he demanded as a part
of France.   Appeals against his arbitrary acts went to Rome,
and the pope sent Bernard of Saisset, bishop of Pamiers, to
Paris, with commission to summon the French king to apply
the clerical tithe for its appointed purpose, a crusade, and for
nothing else.   Philip showed his resentment by having the
legate arrested.   He was adjudged by the civil tribunal a
traitor, and his deposition from the episcopate demanded.

Boniface's reply, set forth in the bull *Ausculta fili* — Give
ear, my son — issued Dec. 5, 1301, charged the king with
high-handed treatment of the clergy and making plunder
of ecclesiastical property.   The pope announced a council
to be held in Rome to which the French prelates were
called and the king summoned to be present, either in person or by a representative.   The bull declared that God
had placed his earthly vicar above kings and kingdoms.   To
make the matter worse, a false copy of Boniface's bull was
circulated in France known as *Deum time*, — Fear God, —

----

[1] *Summaria brevis et compendiosa · doctrina felicis expeditionis et abbre-
viationis guerrarum ac litium regni Francorum.*   See Scholz, p. 415.

which made the statements of papal prerogative still more exasperating. This supposititious document, which is supposed to have been forged by Pierre Flotte, the king's chief councillor, was thrown into the flames Feb. 11, 1302.[1] Such treatment of a papal brief was unprecedented. It remained for Luther to cast the genuine bull of Leo X. into the fire. The two acts had little in common.

The king replied by calling a French parliament of the three estates, the nobility, clergy and representatives of the cities, which set aside the papal summons to the council, complained of the appointment of foreigners to French livings, and asserted the crown's independence of the Church. Five hundred years later a similar representative body of the three estates was to rise against French royalty and decide for the abolition of monarchy. In a letter to the pope, Philip addressed him as "your infatuated Majesty,"[2] and declined all submission to any one on earth in temporal matters.

The council called by the pope convened in Rome the last day of October, 1302, and included 4 archbishops, 35 bishops, and 6 abbots from France. It issued two bulls. The first pronounced the ban on all who detained prelates going to Rome or returning from the city. The second is one of the most notable of all papal documents, the bull *Unam sanctam*, the name given to it from its first words,

---

[1] See Scholz, p. 357. The authenticity of the bull *Ausculta* was once called in question, but is now universally acknowledged. The copy in the Vatican bears the erasure of Clement V., who struck out the passages most offensive to Philip. Hefele gives the copy preserved in the library of St. Victor.

[2] *Sciat maxima tua fatuitas in temporalibus nos alicui non subesse*, etc. Hefele, VI. 332, calls in question the authenticity of this document, at the same time recognizing that it was circulated in Rome in 1302, and that the pope himself made reference to it. The original phrase is ascribed to Pierre Flotte, Scholz, p. 357. Flotte was an uncompromising advocate of the king's sovereignty and independence of the pope. He made a deep impression by an address at the parliament called by Philip, 1302. He was probably the author of the anti-papal tract beginning *Antequam essent clerici*, the text of which is printed by Dupuy, pp. 21–23. Here he asserts that the Church consists of laymen as well as clerics, Scholz, p. 361, and that taxes levied upon Church property are not extortions.

" We are forced to believe in one holy Catholic Church." It
marks an epoch in the history of the declarations of the
papacy, not because it contained anything novel, but because
it set forth with unchanged clearness the stiffest claims of the
papacy to temporal and spiritual power. It begins with the
assertion that there is only one true Church, outside of which
there is no salvation. The pope is the vicar of Christ, and
whoever refuses to be ruled by Peter belongs not to the fold
of Christ. Both swords are subject to the Church, the spiritual and the temporal. The temporal sword is to be wielded
for the Church, the spiritual *by* it. The secular estate may
be judged by the spiritual estate, but the spiritual estate by
no human tribunal. The document closes with the startling
declaration that for every human being the condition of salvation is obedience to the Roman pontiff.

There was no assertion of authority contained in this bull
which had not been before made by Gregory VII. and his
successors, and the document leans back not only upon the
deliverances of popes, but upon the definitions of theologians
like Hugo de St. Victor, Bernard and Thomas Aquinas.
But in the *Unam sanctam* the arrogance of the papacy finds
its most naked and irritating expression.

One of the clauses pronounces all offering resistance to
the pope's authority Manichæans. Thus Philip was made a
heretic. Six months later the pope sent a cardinal legate,
John le Moine of Amiens, to announce to the king his excommunication for preventing French bishops from going to
Rome. The bearer of the message was imprisoned and the
legate fled. Boniface now called upon the German emperor,
Albrecht, to take Philip's throne, as Innocent III. had called
upon the French king to take John's crown, and Innocent IV.
upon the count of Artois to take the crown of Frederick II.
Albrecht had wisdom enough to decline the empty gift.
Philip's seizure of the papal bulls before they could be
promulged in France was met by Boniface's announcement
that the posting of a bull on the church doors of Rome was
sufficient to give it force.

The French parliament, June, 1303, passed from the negative attitude of defending the king and French rights to an attack upon Boniface and his right to the papal throne. In 20 articles it accused him of simony, sorcery, immoral intercourse with his niece, having a demon in his chambers, the murder of Cœlestine, and other crimes. It appealed to a general council, before which the pope was summoned to appear in person. Five archbishops and 21 bishops joined in subscribing to this document. The university and chapter of Paris, convents, cities, and towns placed themselves on the king's side.[1]

One more step the pope was about to take when a sudden stop was put to his career. He had set the eighth day of September as the time when he would publicly, in the church of Anagni, and with all the solemnities known to the Church, pronounce the ban upon the disobedient king and release his subjects from allegiance. In the same edifice Alexander III. had excommunicated Barbarossa, and Gregory IX., Frederick II. The bull already had the papal signature, when, as by a storm bursting from a clear sky, the pope's plans were shattered and his career brought to an end.

During the two centuries and a half since Hildebrand had entered the city of Rome with Leo IX., popes had been imprisoned by emperors, been banished from Rome by its citizens, had fled for refuge and died in exile, but upon no one of them had a calamity fallen quite so humiliating and complete as the calamity which now befell Boniface. A plot, formed in France to checkmate the pope and to carry him off to a council at Lyons, burst Sept. 7 upon the peaceful population of Anagni, the pope's country seat. William of Nogaret, professor of law at Montpellier and councillor of the king, was the manager of the plot and was probably its inventor. According to the chronicler, Villani,[2] Nogaret's parents were Cathari, and suffered for heresy in the flames in Southern France. He stood as a representative of a new class of men, laymen, who were able to compete in culture with the best-trained

---

[1] The university declared in favor of a general council June 21, 1303, *Chartul. Univ. Par.* II. 101 sq.

[2] VIII. 63. See Scholz, pp. 363–375, and Holtzmann: *W. von Nogaret.*

ecclesiastics, and advocated the independence of the state. With him was joined Sciarra Colonna, who, with other members of his family, had found refuge in France, and was thirsting for revenge for their proscription by the pope. With a small body of mercenaries, 300 of them on horse, they suddenly appeared in Anagni. The barons of the Latium, embittered by the rise of the Gaetani family upon their losses, joined with the conspirators, as also did the people of Anagni. The palaces of two of Boniface's nephews and several of the cardinals were stormed and seized by Sciarra Colonna, who then offered the pope life on the three conditions that the Colonna be restored, Boniface resign, and that he place himself in the hands of the conspirators. The conditions were rejected, and after a delay of three hours, the work of assault and destruction was renewed. The palaces one after another yielded, and the papal residence itself was taken and entered. The supreme pontiff, according to the description of Villani,[1] received the besiegers in high pontifical robes, seated on a throne, with a crown on his head and a crucifix and the keys in his hand. He proudly rebuked the intruders, and declared his readiness to die for Christ and his Church. To the demand that he resign the papal office, he replied, " Never; I am pope and as pope I will die." Sciarra was about to kill him, when he was intercepted by Nogaret's arm. The palaces were looted and the cathedral burnt, and its relics, if not destroyed, went to swell the booty. One of the relics, a vase said to have contained milk from Mary's breasts, was turned over and broken. The pope and his nephews were held in confinement for three days, the

---

[1] VIII. 63. ·Döllinger, whose account is very vivid, depends chiefly upon the testimony of three eye-witnesses, a member of the curia, the chronicler of Orvieto and Nogaret himself. He sets aside much of Villani's report, which Reumont, Wattenbach, Gregorovius, and other historians adopt. Dante and Villani, who both condemn the pope's arrogance and nepotism, resented the indignity put upon Boniface at Anagni, and rejoiced over his deliverance as of one who, like Christ, rose from the dead. Dante omits all reference to Sciarra Colonna and other Italian nobles as participants in the plot. Dante's description is given in *Paradiso*, xx. 86 sqq.

" I see the flower-de-luce Alagna [Anagni] enter,
And Christ in his own vicar captive made."

captors being undecided whether to carry Boniface away to
Lyons, set him at liberty, or put him to death.   Such was the
humiliating counterpart to the proud display made at the
pope's coronation nine years before!

In the meantime the feelings of the Anagnese underwent
a change.   The adherents of the Gaetani family rallied their
forces and, combining together, they rescued Boniface and
drove out the conspirators.   Seated at the head of his palace
stairway, the pontiff thanked God and the people for his deliverance.   "Yesterday," he said, "I was like Job, poor and
without a friend.   To-day I have abundance of bread, wine,
and water."   A rescuing party from Rome conducted the unfortunate pope to the Holy City, where he was no longer his
own master.[1]   A month later, Oct. 11, 1303, his earthly career closed.   Outside the death-chamber, the streets of the
city were filled with riot and tumult, and the Gaetani and Colonna were encamped in battle array against each other in the
Campagna.

Reports agree that Boniface's death was a most pitiable one.
He died of melancholy and despair, and perhaps actually insane.   He refused food, and beat his head against the wall.
"He was out of his head," wrote Ptolemy of Lucca,[2] and believed that every one who approached him was seeking to put
him in prison.

Human sympathy goes out for the aged man of fourscore
years and more, dying in loneliness and despair.   But judgment comes sooner or later upon individuals and institutions
for their mistakes and offences.   The humiliation of Boniface

---

[1] Ferretus of Vicenza, Muratori: *Scriptores*, IX. 1002, reports that Boniface wanted to be removed from St. Peter's to the Lateran, but the Colonna
sent word he was in custody.

[2] *Extra mentem positus.*   Ferretus relates that Boniface fell into a rage and,
after gnawing his staff and striking his head against the wall, hanged himself.
Villani, VIII. 63, speaks of a "strange malady" begotten in the pope so that
he gnawed at himself as if he were mad.   The chronicler of Orvieto, see Döllinger: *Beiträge*, etc., III. 353, says Boniface died weighed down by despon-
dency and the infirmities of age, *ubi tristitia et senectutis infirmitate gravatus
mortuus est.*   It is charitable to suppose that the pope's old enemy, the stone,
returned to plague him, the malady from which the Spanish physician Arnald
of Villanova had given him relief.   See Finke, p. 200 sqq.

was the long-delayed penalty of the sacerdotal pride of his
predecessors and himself.   He suffered in part for the hierarchical arrogance of which he was the heir and in part for
his own presumption.   Villani and other contemporaries represent the pope's latter end as a deserved punishment for his
unblushing nepotism, his pompous pride, and his implacable
severity towards those who dared to resist his plans, and for
his treatment of the feeble hermit who preceded him.   One
of the chroniclers reports that seamen plying near the Liparian
islands, the reputed entrance to hell, heard evil spirits rejoicing and exclaiming, " Open, open; receive pope Boniface into
the infernal regions."

Catholic historians like Hergenröther and Kirsch, bound to
the ideals of the past, make a brave attempt to defend Boniface, though they do not overlook his want of tact and his
coarse violence of speech.   It is certain, says Cardinal
Hergenröther,[1] " that Boniface was not ruled by unworthy
motives and that he did not deviate from the paths of his
predecessors or overstep the legal conceptions of the Middle
Ages."   Finke, also a Catholic historian, the latest learned
investigator of the character and career of Boniface, acknowledges the pope's intellectual ability, but also emphasizes his
pride and arrogance, his depreciation of other men, his disa-
greeable spirit and manner, which left him without a personal
friend, his nepotism and his avarice.   He hoped, said a contemporary, to live till " all his enemies were suppressed."

In strong contrast to the common judgment of Catholic
historians is the sentence passed by Gregorovius.   " Boniface
was devoid of every apostolical virtue, a man of passionate
temper, violent, faithless, unscrupulous, unforgiving, filled
with ambitions and lust of worldly power."   And this will
be the judgment of those who feel no obligation to defend
the papal institution.

---

[1] *Kirchengesch.*, II. 597 sq. Boniface called the French "dogs" and
Philip *garçon*, which had the meaning of street urchin.   A favorite expression with him was *ribaldus*, rascal, and he called Charles of Naples "meanest
of rascals," *vilissimus ribaldus*.   See Finke, p. 292 sq.   Finke's judgment is
based in part upon new documents he found in Barcelona and other libraries.

In the humiliation of Boniface VIII., the state gained a signal triumph over the papacy.   The proposition, that the papal pretension to supremacy over the temporal power is inconsistent with the rights of man and untaught by the law of God, was about to be defended in bold writings coming from the pens of lawyers and poets in France and Italy and, a half century later, by Wyclif.   These advocates of the sovereign independence of the state in its own domain were the real descendants of those jurisconsults who, on the plain of Roncaglia, advocated the same theory in the hearing of Frederick Barbarossa.   Two hundred years after the conflict between Boniface and Philip the Fair, Luther was to fight the battle for the spiritual sovereignty of the individual man.   These two principles, set aside by the priestly pride and theological misunderstanding of the Middle Ages, belong to the foundation of modern civilization.

Boniface's Bull, Unam Sanctam.

The great importance of Boniface's bull, Unam Sanctam, issued against Philip the Fair, Nov. 18, 1302, justifies its reproduction both in translation and the original Latin.   It has rank among the most notorious deliverances of the popes and is as full of error as was Innocent VIII.'s bull issued in 1484 against witchcraft.   It presents the theory of the supremacy of the spiritual power over the temporal, the authority of the papacy over princes, in its extreme form.   The following is a translation : —

Boniface, Bishop, Servant of the servants of God.   For perpetual remembrance : —

Urged on by our faith, we are obliged to believe and hold that there is one holy, catholic, and apostolic Church.   And we firmly believe and profess that outside of her there is no salvation nor remission of sins, as the bridegroom declares in the Canticles, "My dove, my undefiled, is but one; she is the only one of her mother; she is the choice one of her that bare her."   And this represents the one mystical body of Christ, and of this body Christ is the head, and God is the head of Christ.   In it there is one Lord, one faith, one baptism.   For in the time of the Flood there was the single ark of Noah, which prefigures the one Church, and it was finished according to the measure of one cubit and had one Noah for pilot and captain, and outside of it every living creature on the earth, as we read, was destroyed.   And this Church we revere as the only one, even as the Lord saith by the prophet, "Deliver my soul from the sword, my darling from the power of the dog."   He prayed for his soul, that is, for himself, head and body.   And this body he called one body, that is, the Church, because of the single bridegroom, the unity of the faith, the sacraments, and the love of the Church.   She is that seamless shirt of the Lord which was not rent but was allotted by the casting of lots. Therefore, this one and single Church has one head and not two heads, — for had she two heads, she would be a monster, — that is, Christ and Christ's vicar, Peter and Peter's successor.   For the Lord said unto Peter, "Feed my sheep."   "My," he said, speaking generally and not particularly, "these and those," by which it is to be understood that all the sheep are committed unto him.   So, when the Greeks or others say that they were not committed to the care of Peter and his successors, they must confess that they are not of Christ's sheep, even as the Lord says in John, "There is one fold and one shepherd."

That in her and within her power are two swords, we are taught in the Gospels, namely, the spiritual sword and the temporal sword.   For when the Apostles said, "Lo, here," — that is, in the Church, — are two swords, the Lord did not reply to the Apostles "it is too much," but "it is enough."   It is certain that whoever denies that the temporal sword is in the power of Peter, hearkens ill to the words of the Lord which he spake, "Put up thy sword into its sheath."   Therefore, both are in the power of the Church, namely, the spiritual sword and the temporal sword ; the latter is to be used for the Church, the former by the Church ; the former by the hand of the priest, the latter by the hand of princes and kings, but at the nod and sufferance of the priest.   The one sword must of necessity be subject to the other, and the temporal authority to the spiritual.   For the Apostle said, "There is no power but of God, and the powers that be are ordained of God" ; and they would not have been ordained unless one sword had been made subject to the other, and even as the lower is subjected by the other for higher things. For, according to Dionysius, it is a divine law that the lowest things are made by mediocre things to attain to the highest.   For it is not according to the law of the universe that all things in an equal way and immediately should reach their end, but the lowest through the mediocre and the lower through the higher.   But that the spiritual power excels the earthly power in dignity and worth, we will the more clearly acknowledge just in proportion as the spiritual is higher than the temporal.   And this we perceive quite distinctly from the donation of the tithe and functions of benediction and sanctification, from the mode in which the power was received, and the government of the subjected realms.   For truth being the witness, the spiritual power has the functions of establishing the temporal power and sitting in judgment on it if it should prove to be not good.[1]   And to the Church and the Church's power the prophecy of Jeremiah attests: "See, I have set thee this day over the nations and the kingdoms to pluck up and to break down and to destroy and to overthrow, to build and to plant."

And if the earthly power deviate from the right path, it is judged by the spiritual power ; but if a minor spiritual power deviate from the right path, the lower in rank is judged by its superior ; but if the supreme power [the papacy] deviate, it can be judged not by man but by God alone.   And so the

---

[1] This passage is based almost word for word upon Hugo de St. Victor, *De Sacramentis*, II. 2, 4.

Apostle testifies, "He which is spiritual judges all things, but he himself is judged by no man." But this authority, although it be given to a man, and though it be exercised by a man, is not a human but a divine power given by divine word of mouth to Peter and confirmed to Peter and to his successors by Christ himself, whom Peter confessed, even him whom Christ called the Rock. For the Lord said to Peter himself, " Whatsoever thou shalt bind on earth," etc. Whoever, therefore, resists this power so ordained by God, resists the ordinance of God, unless perchance he imagine two principles to exist, as did Manichæus, which we pronounce false and heretical. For Moses testified that God created heaven and earth not in the beginnings but " in the beginning."

Furthermore, that every human creature is subject to the Roman pontiff, — this we declare, say, define, and pronounce to be altogether necessary to salvation.

Bonifatius, Episcopus, Servus servorum Dei. Ad futuram rei memoriam.[1]
Unam sanctam ecclesiam catholicam et ipsam apostolicam urgente fide credere cogimur et tenere, nosque hanc firmiter credimus et simpliciter confitemur, extra quam nec salus est, nec remissio peccatorum, sponso in Canticis proclamante : Una est columba mea, perfecta mea. Una est matris suæ, electa genetrici suæ [Cant. 6 : 9]. *Quæ unum corpus mysticum repræsentat, cujus caput Christus, Christi vero Deus. In qua unus Dominus, una fides, unum baptisma. Una nempe fuit diluvii tempore arca Noë, unam ecclesiam præfigurans, quæ in uno cubito consummata unum, Noë videlicet, gubernatorem habuit et rectorem, extra quam omnia subsistentia super terram legimus fuisse deleta.*

Hanc autem veneramur et unicam, dicente Domino in Propheta : Erue a framea, Deus, animam meam et de manu canis unicam meam. [Psalm 22 : 20.] *Pro anima enim, id est, pro se ipso, capite simul oravit et corpore. Quod corpus unicam scilicet ecclesiam nominavit, propter sponsi, fidei, sacramentorum et caritatis ecclesiæ unitatem. Hæc est tunica illa Domini inconsutilis, quæ scissa non fuit, sed sorte provenit.* [John 19.]

Igitur ecclesiæ unius et unicæ unum corpus, unum caput, non duo capita, quasi monstrum, Christus videlicet et Christi vicarius, Petrus, Petrique successor, dicente Domino ipsi Petro: Pasce oves meas. [John 21 : 17.] *Meas, inquit, generaliter, non singulariter has vel illas : per quod commisisse sibi intelligitur universas. Sive ergo Græci sive alii se dicant Petro ejusque successoribus non esse commissos : fateantur necesse est, se de ovibus Christi non esse, dicente Domino in Joanne, unum ovile et unicum esse pastorem.* [John 10: 16.]

In hac ejusque potestate duos esse gladios, spiritualem videlicet et temporalem, evangelicis dictis instruimur. Nam dicentibus Apostolis : Ecce gladii duo hic [Luke 22 : 38], *in ecclesia scilicet, cum apostoli loquerentur, non respondit Dominus, nimis esse, sed satis. Certe qui in potestate Petri temporalem gladium esse negat, male verbum attendit Domini proferentis : Converte gladium tuum in vaginam.* [Matt. 26 : 52.] *Uterque ergo est in potestate*

---

[1] The text is taken from W. Römer: *Die Bulle, unam sanctam*, Schaffhausen, 1889. See also Mirbt: *Quellen*, p. 148 sq.

ecclesiæ, spiritualis scilicet gladius et materialis.   Sed is quidem pro ecclesia, ille vero ab ecclesia exercendus, ille sacerdotis, is manu regum et militum, sed ad nutum et patientiam sacerdotis.

Oportet autem gladium esse sub gladio, et temporalem auctoritatem spirituali subjici potestati.   Nam cum dicat Apostolus : Non est potestas nisi a Deo ; quæ autem sunt, a Deo ordinata sunt [Rom. 13 : 1], *non autem ordinata essent, nisi gladius esset sub gladio, et tanquam inferior reduceretur per alium in suprema.   Nam secundum B. Dionysium lex divinitatis est, infima per media in suprema reduci. . . .   Sic de ecclesia et ecclesiastica potestate verificatur vaticinium Hieremiæ* [Jer. 1 : 10]: *Ecce constitui te hodie super gentes et regna et cetera, quæ sequuntur.*

Ergo, si deviat terrena potestas, judicabitur a potestate spirituali ; sed, si deviat spiritualis minor, a suo superiori ; si vero suprema, a solo Deo, non ab homine poterit judicari, testante Apostolo : Spiritualis homo judicat omnia, ipse autem a nemine judicatur.   [1 Cor. 2 : 15.]   *Est autem hæc auctoritas, etsi data sit homini, et exerceatur per hominem, non humana, sed potius divina potestas, ore divino Petro data, sibique suisque successoribus in ipso Christo, quem confessus fuit, petra firmata, dicente Domino ipsi Petro : Quodcunque ligaveris, etc.*   [Matt. 16 : 19.]   *Quicunque igitur huic potestati a Deo sic ordinatæ resistit, Dei ordinationi resistit, nisi duo, sicut Manichæus, fingat esse principia, quod falsum et hæreticum judicamus, quia, testante Moyse, non in principiis, sed in principio cœlum Deus creavit et terram.*   [Gen. 1 : 1.]

Porro subesse Romano Pontifici omni humanæ creaturæ declaramus dicimus, definimus et pronunciamus omnino esse de necessitate salutis.

The most astounding clause of this deliverance makes subjection to the pope an essential of salvation for every creature.   Some writers have made the bold attempt to relieve the language of this construction, and refer it to princes and kings.   So fair and sound a Roman Catholic writer as Funk[1] has advocated this interpretation, alleging in its favor the close connection of the clause with the previous statements through the particle *porro,* furthermore, and the consideration that the French people would not have resented the assertion that obedience to the papacy is a condition of salvation.   But the overwhelming majority of Catholic historians take the words in their natural meaning.[2]   The expression "every human creature" would be a

[1] In his *Kirchengeschichtliche Abhandlungen,* I. 483–489.   This view is also taken by J. Berchtold : *Die Bulle Unam sanctam ihre wahre Bedeutung und Tragweite für Staat und Kirche,* Munich, 1887.   An attempt was made by Abbé Mury, *La Bulle Unam sanctam,* in *Rev. des questions histor.* 1879, on the ground of the bull's stinging affirmations and verbal obscurities to detect the hand of a forger, but Cardinal Hergenröther, *Kirchengesch.,* II. 594, pronounces the genuineness to be above dispute.

[2] So Hergenröther-Kirsch, Hefele-Knöpfler : *Kirchengesch.,* p. 380, and *Conciliengesch.,* VI. 349 sq.   Every writer on Boniface VIII. and Philip the Fair discusses the meaning of Boniface's deliverance.   Among the latest is W. Joos : *Die Bulle Unam sanctam,* Schaffhausen, 1896.   Finke : *Aus den Tagen Bonifaz VIII.,* p. 146 sqq., C–CXLVI.   Scholz : *Publizistik,* p. 197 sqq.

most unlikely one to be used as synonymous with temporal rulers.   Boniface
made the same assertion in a letter to the duke of Savoy, 1300, when he
demanded submission for every mortal, — *omnia anima*.   Ægidius Colonna
paraphrased the bull in these words, " the supreme pontiff is that authority
to which every soul must yield subjection." [1]   That the mediæval Church
accepted this construction is vouched for by the Fifth Lateran Council,
1516, which, in reaffirming the bull, declared " it necessary to salvation
that all the faithful of Christ be subject to the Roman pontiff." [2]

§ 5.   *Literary Attacks against the Papacy.*

Nothing is more indicative of the intellectual change going on in Western Europe in the fourteenth century than the
tractarian literature of the time directed against claims made
by the papacy.   Three periods may be distinguished.   In the
first belong the tracts called forth by the struggle of Philip
the Fair and Boniface VIII., with the year 1302 for its centre.
Their distinguishing feature is the attack made upon the
pope's jurisdiction in temporal affairs.   The second period
opens during the pontificate of John XXII. and extends from
1320–1340.   Here the pope's spiritual supremacy was attacked.   The most prominent writer of the time was Marsiglius of Padua.   The third period begins with the papal
schism toward the end of the fourteenth century.   The
writers of this period emphasized the need of reform in the
Church and discussed the jurisdiction of general councils as
superior to the jurisdiction of the pope. [3]

The publicists of the age of Boniface VIII. and Philip the
Fair now defended, now openly attacked the mediæval theory
of the pope's lordship over kings and nations.   The body of
literature they produced was unlike anything which Europe

---

[1] *Summus pontifex . . . est illa potestas cui omnis anima debet esse
subjecta.*

[2] *De necessitate esse salutis omnes Christi fideles romani pontifici subesse.*
The writer in Wetzer-Welte, XII. 229 sqq., pronounces the view impossible
which limits the meaning of the clause to temporal rulers.

[3] I have followed closely in this chapter the clear and learned presentations
of Richard Scholz and Finke and the documents they print as well as the
documents given by Goldast.   See below.   A most useful contribution to the
study of the age of Boniface VIII. and the papal theories current at the time
would be the publication of the tracts mentioned in this section and others
in a single volume.

had seen before.   In the conflict between Gregory IX. and
Frederick II., Europe was filled with the epistolary appeals of
pope and emperor, who sought each to make good his case
before the court of European public opinion, and more especially of the princes and prelates.   The controversy of this
later time was participated in by a number of writers who
represented the views of an intelligent group of clerics and
laymen.   They employed a vigorous style adapted to make
an impression on the public mind.

Stirred by the haughty assertions of Boniface, a new class
of men, the jurisconsults, entered the lists and boldly called
in question the old order represented by the policy of Hildebrand and Innocent III.   They had studied in the universities, especially in the University of Paris, and some of them,
like Dubois, were laymen.   The decision of the Bologna
jurists on the field of Roncaglia was reasserted with new
arguments and critical freedom, and a step was taken far in
advance of that decision which asserted the independence of
the emperor.   The empire was set aside as an antiquated institution, and France and other states were pronounced sovereign
within their own limits and immune from papal dominion over
their temporal affairs.   The principles of human law and the
natural rights of man were arrayed against dogmatic assertions based upon unbalanced and false interpretations of
Scripture.   The method of scholastic sophistry was largely
replaced by an appeal to common sense and regard for the
practical needs of society.   The authorities used to establish
the new theory were Aristotle, the Scriptures and historic
facts.   These writers were John the Baptists preparing the
way for the more clearly outlined and advanced views of Marsiglius of Padua and Ockam, who took the further step of
questioning or flatly denying the pope's spiritual supremacy,
and for the still more advanced and more spiritual appeals of
Wyclif and Luther.   A direct current of influence can be
traced back from the Protestant Reformation to the anti-papal
tracts of the first decade of the fourteenth century.

The tract writers of the reign of Philip the Fair, who defended the traditional theory of the pope's absolute suprem-

acy in all matters, were the Italians Ægidius Colonna, James of Viterbo, Henry of Cremona, and Augustinus Triumphus. The writers who attacked the papal claim to temporal power are divided into two groups. To the first belongs Dante, who magnified the empire and the station of the emperor as the supreme ruler over the temporal affairs of men. The men of the second group were associated more or less closely with the French court and were, for the most part, Frenchmen. They called in question the authority of the emperor. Among their leaders were John of Paris and Peter Dubois. In a number of cases their names are forgotten or uncertain, while their tracts have survived. It will be convenient first to take up the theory of Dante, and then to present the views of papal and anti-papal writings which were evidently called forth by the struggle started by Boniface.

Dante was in nowise associated with the court of Philip the Fair, and seems to have been moved to write his treatise on government, the *De monarchia*, by general considerations and not by any personal sympathy with the French king. His theory embodies views in direct antagonism to those promulged in Boniface's bull *Unam sanctam*, and Thomas Aquinas, whose theological views Dante followed, is here set aside.[1] The independence and sovereignty of the civil estate is established by arguments drawn from reason, Aristotle, and the Scriptures. In making good his position, the author advances three propositions, devoting a chapter to each: (1) Universal monarchy or empire, for the terms are used synonymously, is necessary. (2) This monarchy belongs to the Roman people. (3) It was directly bequeathed to the Romans by God, and did not come through the mediation of the Church.

[1] The date of the *De monarchia* is a matter of uncertainty. There are no references in the treatise to Dante's own personal affairs or the contemporary events of Europe to give any clew. Witte, the eminent Dante student, put it in 1301; so also R. W. Church, on the ground that Dante makes no reference to his exile, which began in 1801. The tendency now is to follow Boccaccio, who connected the treatise with the election of Henry VII. or Henry's journey to Rome, 1311. The treatise would then be a manifesto for the restoration of the empire to its original authority. For a discussion of the date, see Henry: *Dante's de monarchia*, XXXII. sqq.

The interests of society, so the argument runs, require an impartial arbiter, and only a universal monarch bound by no local ties can be impartial. A universal monarchy will bring peace, the peace of which the angels sang on the night of Christ's birth, and it will bring liberty, God's greatest gift to man.[1] Democracy reduces men to slavery. The Romans are the noblest people and deserve the right to rule. This is evident from the fine manhood of Æneas, their progenitor,[2] from the evident miracles which God wrought in their history and from their world-wide dominion. This right to rule was established under the Christian dispensation by Christ himself, who submitted to Roman jurisdiction in consenting to be born under Augustus and to suffer under Tiberius. It was attested by the Church when Paul said to Festus, " I stand at Cæsar's judgment seat, where I ought to be judged," Acts 25 : 10. There are two governing agents necessary to society, the pope and the emperor. The emperor is supreme in temporal things and is to guide men to eternal life in accordance with the truths of revelation. Nevertheless, the emperor should pay the pope the reverence which a first-born son pays to his father, such reverence as Charlemagne paid to Leo III.[3]
In denying the subordination of the civil power, Dante rejects the figure comparing the spiritual and temporal powers to the sun and moon,[4] and the arguments drawn from the alleged precedence of Levi over Judah on the ground of

[1] *Libertus est maximum donum humanæ naturæ a Deo collatum*, I. 14.   It is a striking coincidence that Leo XIII. began his encyclical of June 20, 1888, with these similar words, *libertas præstantissimum naturæ donum*, " liberty, the most excellent gift of nature."
[2] ii. 3. Dante appeals to the testimony of Virgil, his guide through hell and purgatory. He also quotes Virgil's proud lines : —

> "*Tu regere imperii populos, Romane, memento.*
> *Hæc tibi erunt artes, pacisque imponere morem*
> *Parcere subjectis et debellare superbos.*"

Roman, remember that it was given to thee to rule the nations. Thine it is to establish peace, spare subject peoples and war against the proud.
[3] ii. 12, 13 ; iii. 13, 16.
[4] This last section of the book has the heading *auctoritatem imperii immediate dependere a Deo.*

the priority of Levi's birth ; from the oblation of the Magi
at the manger and from the sentence passed upon Saul by
Samuel.   He referred the two swords both to spiritual functions.   Without questioning the historical occurrence, he set
aside Constantine's donation to Sylvester on the ground that
the emperor no more had the right to transfer his empire in
the West than he had to commit suicide.   Nor had the pope
a right to accept the gift.[1]   In the *Inferno* Dante applied to
that transaction the oft-quoted lines : [2]—

> " Ah, Constantine, of how much ill was cause,
> Not thy conversion, but those rich domains
> Which the first wealthy pope received of thee."

The Florentine poet's universal monarchy has remained an
ideal unrealized, like the republic of the Athenian philosopher.[3]   Conception of popular liberty as it is conceived in this
modern age, Dante had none.   Nevertheless, he laid down the
important principle that the government exists for the people, and not the people for the government.[4]

The treatise *De monarchia* was burnt as heretical, 1329, by
order of John XXII. and put on the Index by the Council of
Trent.   In recent times it has aided the Italian patriots in
their work of unifying Italy and separating politics from the
Church according to Cavour's maxim, " a free Church in a free
state."

In the front rank of the champions of the temporal power
of the papacy stood Ægidius Colonna, called also Ægidius
Romanus, 1247–1316.[5]   He was an Augustinian, and rose to

---

[1] iii. 10, *Constantinus alienare non poterat imperii dignitatem nec ecclesia
recipere.*

[2] xix. 115 sqq.   *Ahi, Constantin, di quanto mal fu matre,*
> *Non la tua conversion, ma quella dote*
> *Che da te prese il primo ricco padre !*

In the *Purgatorio*, xvi. 106–112, Dante deplores the union of the crozier
and the sword.

[3] With reference to the approaching termination of the emperor's influence
in Italian affairs, Bryce, ch. XV., sententiously says that Dante's *De monarchia* was an epitaph, not a prophecy.

[4] *Non cives propter consules nec gens propter regem sed e converso consules propter cives, rex propter gentem*, iii. 14.

[5] Scholz, pp. 32–129.

be general of his order.   He became famous as a theological teacher and, in 1287, his order placed his writings in all its schools.[1]   In 1295 he was made archbishop of Bourges, Boniface setting aside in his favor the cleric nominated by Cœlestine.   Ægidius participated in the council in Rome, 1301, which Philip the Fair forbade the French prelates to attend. He was an elaborate writer, and in 1304 no less than 12 of his theological works and 14 of his philosophical writings were in use in the University of Paris.

The tract by which Ægidius is chiefly known is his Power of the Supreme Pontiff — *De ecclesiastica sive de summi pontificis potestate.*   It was the chief work of its time in defence of the papacy, and seems to have been called forth by the Roman Council and to have been written in 1301.[2]   It was dedicated to Boniface VIII.   Its main positions are the following : —

The pope judges all things and is judged by no man, 1 Cor. 2 : 15.   To him belongs plenary power, *plenitudo potestatis.*   This power is without measure, without number, and without weight.[3]   It extends over all Christians.   The pope is above all laws and in matters of faith infallible.   He is like the sea which fills all vessels, like the sun which, as the universally active principle, sends his rays into all things.   The priesthood existed before royalty.   Abel and Noah, priests, preceded Nimrod, who was the first king.   As the government of the world is one and centres in one ruler, God, so in the affairs of the militant Church there can be only one source of power, one supreme government, one head to whom belongs

[1] *Chartul. Univ. Paris.*, II. 12.

[2] Jourdain, in 1858, was the first to call attention to the manuscript, and Kraus the first to give a summary of its positions in the *Œsterr. Vierteljahrsschrift*, Vienna, 1862, pp. 1–33.   Among Ægidius' other tracts is the "Rule of Princes," — *De regimine principum* — 1285, printed 1473.   It was at once translated into French and Italian and also into Spanish, Portuguese, English, and even Hebrew.   The "Pope's Abdication" — *De renunciatione papæ sive apologia pro Bonifacio VIII.* — 1297, was a reply to the manifesto of the Colonna, contesting a pope's right to resign his office.   For a list of Ægidius' writings, see art. *Colonna Ægidius*, in Wetzer-Welte, III. 667–671. See Scholz, pp. 46, 126.

[3] Ægidius quotes the Wisdom of Solomon, 2 : 21.

the plenitude of power. This is the supreme pontiff. The priesthood and the papacy are of immediate divine appointment. Earthly kingdoms, except as they have been established by the priesthood, owe their origin to usurpation, robbery, and other forms of violence.[1] In these views Ægidius followed Augustine: *De civitate*, IV. 4, and Gregory VII. The state, however, he declared to be necessary as a means through which the Church works to accomplish its divinely appointed ends.

In the second part of his tract, Ægidius proves that, in spite of Numb. 18 : 20, 21, and Luke 10 : 4, the Church has the right to possess worldly goods. The Levites received cities. In fact, all temporal goods are under the control of the Church.[2] As the soul rules the body, so the pope rules over all temporal matters. The tithe is a perpetual obligation. No one has a right to the possession of a single acre of ground or a vineyard without the Church's permission and unless he be baptized.

The fulness of power, residing in the pope, gives him the right to appoint to all benefices in Christendom, but, as God chooses to rule through the laws of nature, so the pope rules through the laws of the Church, but he is not bound by them. He may himself be called the Church. For the pope's power is spiritual, heavenly and divine. Ægidius was used by his successors, James of Viterbo, Augustinus Triumphus and Alvarus, and also by John of Paris and Gerson who contested some of his main positions.[3]

The second of these writers, defending the position of Boniface VIII., was James of Viterbo,[4] d. 1308. He also was an Italian, belonged to the Augustinian order, and gained prominence as a teacher in Paris. In 1302 he was appointed by Boniface archbishop of Beneventum, and a few months later archbishop of Naples. His Christian Government — *De regimine christiano* — is, after the treatise of Ægidius, the most

---

[1] See Scholz, p. 96 sqq. This author says the *de regimine principum* of Ægidius presents a different view, and following Aristotle, derives the state from the social principle.   [2] *Sub dominio et potestate ecclesiæ.*
[3] Scholz, p. 124.   [4] See Finke, pp. 163–166; Scholz, pp. 129–153.

comprehensive of the papal tracts. It also was dedicated to Boniface VIII., who is addressed as "the holy lord of the kings of the earth." The author distinctly says he was led to write by the attacks made upon the papal prerogative.

To Christ's vicar, James says, royalty and priesthood, *regnum et sacerdotium*, belong. Temporal authority was not for the first time conferred on him when Constantine gave Sylvester the dominion of the West. Constantine did nothing more than confirm a previous right derived from Christ, when he said, "whatsoever ye shall bind on earth shall be bound in heaven." Priests are kings, and the pope is the king of kings, both in mundane and spiritual matters.[1] He is the bishop of the earth, the supreme lawgiver. Every soul must be subject to him in order to salvation.[2] By reason of his fulness of power, the supreme pontiff can act according to law or against it, as he chooses.[3]

Henry of Cassaloci, or Henry of Cremona, as he is usually called from his Italian birthplace, d. 1312, is mentioned, contrary to the custom of the age, by name by John of Paris, as the author of the tract, The Power of the Pope — *De potestate papæ*.[4] He was a distinguished authority in canon law and consulted by Boniface. He was appointed, 1302, a member of the delegation to carry to Philip the Fair the two notorious bulls, *Salvator mundi* and *Ausculta fili*. The same year he was appointed bishop of Reggio.[5] The papal defenders were well paid.

Henry began his tract with the words of Matt. 27 : 18, "All power is given unto me," and declared the attack

---

[1] Scholz, pp. 135, 145, 147. These two prerogatives are called *potestas ordinis* and *potestas jurisdictionis*.　　　　　　[2] Scholz, p. 148.

[3] *Potest agere et secundum leges quas ponit et præter illas, ubi opportunum esse judicaverit.* Finke, p. 166.

[4] Finke, pp. 166–170 ; Scholz, pp. 152–165. Finke was the first to use this tract. Scholz describes two MSS. in the National Library of Paris, and gives the tract entire, pp. 459–471.

[5] A contemporary notes that the consistory was reminded that the nominee was the author of the *De potestate papæ*, " a book which proves that the pope was overlord in temporal as well as spiritual matters." Scholz, p. 155. The tract was written, as Scholz thinks, not later than 1301, or earlier than 1298, as it quotes the *Liber sextus.*

against the pope's temporal jurisdiction over the whole earth
a matter of recent date, and made by " sophists " who deserved death.   Up to that time no one had made such denial.
He attempts to make out his fundamental thesis from Scripture, the Fathers, canon law, and reason.   God at first ruled
through Noah, the patriarchs, Melchizedec, and Moses, who
were priests and kings at the same time.   Did not Moses
punish Pharaoh?   Christ carried both swords.   Did he not
drive out the money-changers and wear the crown of thorns ?
To him the power was given to judge the world.   John 5 : 22.
The same power was entailed upon Peter and his successors.
As for the state, it bears to the Church the relation of the
moon to the sun, and the emperor has only such power as the
pope is ready to confer.   Henry also affirms that Constantine's
donation established no right, but confirmed what the pope
already possessed by virtue of heavenly gift.[1]   The pope transferred the empire to Charlemagne, and Innocent IV. asserted
the papal supremacy over kings by deposing Frederick II.
If in early and later times the persons of popes were abused,
this was not because they lacked supreme authority in the
earth [2] or were in anywise subject to earthly princes.   No
emperor can legally exercise imperial functions without papal
consecration.   When Christ said, " my kingdom is not of this
world," he meant nothing more than that the world refused
to obey him.   As for the passage, " render to Cæsar the things
which are Cæsar's," Christ was under no obligation to give
tribute to the emperor, and the children of the kingdom are
free, as Augustine, upon the basis of Matt. 27 : 26 sq., said.

The main work of another defender of the papal prerogatives, Augustinus Triumphus, belongs to the next period.[3]

An intermediate position between these writers and the
anti-papal publicists was taken by the Cardinals Colonna and
their immediate supporters.[4]   In their zeal against Boniface

---

[1] *Constantinus non dedit sed recognovit ab ecclesia se tenere — confitetur
se ab ecclesia illud tenere.*   See Scholz, p. 467.

[2] *Non defectus juris, sed potentiæ.*

[3] Four of his smaller tracts are summarized by Scholz, pp. 172–189. See § 8.

[4] Scholz, pp. 198–207.

VIII. they questioned the absolute power of the Church in temporal concerns, and placed the supreme spiritual authority in the college of cardinals, with the pope as its head.

Among the advanced writers of the age was William Durante, d. 1331, an advocate of Gallicanism.[1] He was appointed bishop of Mende before he had reached the canonical age. He never came under the condemnation of the Church. In a work composed at the instance of Clement V. on general councils and the reformation of Church abuses, *De modo generalis concilii celebrandi et corruptelis in ecclesiis reformandis*, he demanded a reformation of the Church in head and members,[2] using for the first time this expression which was so often employed in a later age. He made the pope one of the order of bishops on all of whom was conferred equally the power to bind and to loose.[3] The bishops are not the pope's assistants, the view held by Innocent III., but agents directly appointed by God with independent jurisdiction. The pope may not act out of harmony with the canons of the early Church except with the approval of a general council. When new measures are contemplated, a general council should be convened, and one should be called every ten years.[4]

Turning now to the writers who contested the pope's right to temporal authority over the nations, we find that while the most of them were clerics, all of them were jurists. It is characteristic that besides appealing to Aristotle, the Scriptures, and the canon law, they also appealed to the Roman law. We begin with several pamphlets whose authorship is a matter of uncertainty.

The Twofold Prerogative — *Quæstio in utramque partem* — was probably written in 1302, and by a Frenchman.[5] The

---

[1] Scholz, pp. 208–223.

[2] *Tam in capite quam in membris.* Scholz, pp. 211, 220. The tract was reprinted at the time of the Council of Trent and dedicated to Paul III.

[3] The words Matt. 16 : 19, were addressed to the whole Church, he says, and not to Peter alone.

[4] Scholz, p. 214.

[5] This date is made very probable by Scholz, p. 225 sqq. Riezler, p. 141, wrongly put it down to 1364–1380. Scheffer-Boichorst showed that the author spoke of the canonization of Louis IX., 1297, as having occurred " in

tract clearly sets forth that the two functions, the spiritual and the temporal, are distinct, and that the pope has plenary power only in the spiritual realm.   It is evident that they are not united in one person, from Christ's refusal of the office of king and from the law prohibiting the Levites holding worldly possessions.   Canon law and Roman law recognized the independence of the civil power.   Both estates are of God.   At best the pope's temporal authority extends to the patrimony of Peter.   The empire is one among the powers, without authority over other states.   As for the king of France, he would expose himself to the penalty of death if he were to recognize the pope as overlord.[1]

The same positions are taken in the tract,[2] The Papal Power, — *Quœstio de potestate papœ.*   The author insists that temporal jurisdiction is incompatible with the pope's office. He uses the figure of the body to represent the Church, giving it a new turn.   Christ is the head.   The nerves and veins are officers in the Church and state.   They depend directly upon Christ, the head.   The heart is the king.   The pope is not even called the head.   The soul is not mentioned.   The old application of the figure of the body and the soul, representing respectively the *regnum* and the *sacerdotium,* is set aside.   The pope is a spiritual father, not the lord over Christendom.   Moses was a temporal ruler and Aaron was priest.   The functions and the functionaries were distinct. At best, the donation of Constantine had no reference to France, for France was distinct from the empire.   The deposition of Childerich by Pope Zacharias established no right, for all that Zacharias did was, as a wise counsellor, to give the barons advice.

A third tract, one of the most famous pieces of this litera-

our days," and that he quoted the *Liber sextus,* 1298, as having recently appeared.   The tract is given in Goldast: *Monarchia,* II. 195 sqq.

[1] Scholz, p. 239.   On Feb. 23, 1302, Philip made his sons swear never to acknowledge any one but God as overlord.

[2] It is bound up in MS. with the former tract and with the work of John of Paris.   It is printed in Dupuy, pp. 663–683.   It has been customary to regard Peter Dubois as the author, but Scholz, p. 257, gives reasons against this view.

ture, the Disputation between a Cleric and a Knight,[1] was written to defend the sovereignty of the state and its right to levy taxes upon Church property.   The author maintains that the king of France is in duty bound to see that Church property is administered according to the intent for which it was given.   As he defends the Church against foreign foes, so he has the right to put the Church under tribute.

In the publicist, John of Paris, d. 1306, we have one of the leading minds of the age.[2]   He was a Dominican, and enjoyed great fame as a preacher and master.   On June 26, 1303, he joined 132 other Parisian Dominicans in signing a document calling for a general council, which the university had openly favored five days before.[3]   His views of the Lord's Supper brought upon him the charge of heresy, and he was forbidden to give lectures at the university.[4]   He appealed to Clement V., but died before he could get a hearing.

John's chief writing was the tract on the Authority of the Pope and King, — *De potestate regia et papali*,[5] — which almost breathes the atmosphere of modern times.

John makes a clear distinction between the " body of the faithful," which is the Church, and the " body of the clergy." [6]

---

[1] *Disputatio inter clericum et militem.*   It was written during the conflict between Boniface and Philip, and not by Ockam, to whom it was formerly ascribed.   Recently Riezler, p. 145, has ascribed it to Peter Dubois.   It was first printed, 1475, and is reprinted in Goldast: *Monarchia*, I. 13 sqq.   MSS. are found in Paris, Oxford, Cambridge, and Prag.   See Scholz, p. 336 sqq. An English translation appeared with the following title : *A dialogue betwene a knight and a clerke concerning the Power Spiritual and temporal*, by William Ockham, the great philosopher, in English and Latin, London, 1540.

[2] Finke, pp. 170–177 ; Scholz, pp. 275–333.

[3] *Chartul. Univ. Paris.*, II. 102.

[4] *De modo existendi corporis Christi in sacramento altaris.   Chartul.* II. 120.

[5] First printed in Paris, 1506, and is found in Goldast, II. 108 sqq.   For the writings ascribed to John, see Scholz, p. 284 sq.   Finke, p. 172, says, *ein gesundes beinahe modernes Empfinden zeichnet ihn aus.*   His tract belongs to 1302–1303.   So Scholz and Finke.   John writes as though Boniface were still living.   He quotes " the opinions of certain moderns " and Henry of Cremona by name.   The last chapter of John's tract is largely made up of excerpts from Ægidius' *De renuntiatione papæ.*   Scholz, p. 291, thinks it probable that Dante used John's tract.

[6] *Congregatio fidelium . . . congregatio clericorum.*

The Church has its unity in Christ, who established the two estates, spiritual and temporal.   They are the same in origin, but distinguished on earth.   The pope has the right to punish moral offences, but only with spiritual punishments.   The penalties of death, imprisonment, and fines, he has no right to impose.   Christ had no worldly jurisdiction, and the pope should keep clear of " Herod's old error." [1]   Constantine had no right to confer temporal power on Sylvester.   John adduced 42 reasons urged in favor of the pope's omnipotence in temporal affairs and offers a refutation for each of them.

As for the pope's place in the Church, the pope is the representative of the ecclesiastical body, not its lord.   The Church may call him to account.   If the Church were to elect representatives to act with the supreme pontiff, we would have the best of governments.   As things are, the cardinals are his advisers and may admonish him and, in case he persists in his error, they may call to their aid the temporal arm.   The pope may be deposed by an emperor, as was actually the case when three popes were deposed by Henry III.   The final seat of ecclesiastical authority is the general council.   It may depose a pope.   Valid grounds of deposition are insanity, heresy, personal incompetence and abuse of the Church's property.

Following Aristotle and Thomas Aquinas, John derived the state from the family and not from murder and other acts of violence.[2]   It is a community organized for defence and bodily well-being.   With other jurists, he regarded the empire as an antiquated institution and, if it continues to exist, it is on a par with the monarchies, not above them.   Climate and geographical considerations make different monarchies necessary, and they derive their authority from God.   Thus John and Dante, while agreeing as to the independence of the state, differ as to the seat where secular power resides.   Dante placed it in a universal empire, John of Paris in separate monarchies.

The boldest and most advanced of these publicists, Pierre Dubois,[3] was a layman, probably a Norman, and called him-

---

[1] Scholz, p. 315.   [2] Finke, p. 72 ; Scholz, p. 324.
[3] See Renan : *Hist. Litt.* XXVI. 471–536 ; Scholz, pp. 374–444.

self a royal attorney.[1]   As a delegate to the national council
in Paris, April, 1302, he represented Philip's views.   He was
living as late as 1321.   In a number of tracts he supported the
contention of the French monarch against Boniface VIII.[2]
France is independent of the empire, and absolutely sovereign
in all secular matters.   The French king is the successor of
Charlemagne.   The pope is the moral teacher of mankind,
" the light of the world," but he has no jurisdiction in temporal affairs.   It is his function to care for souls, to stop
wars, to exercise oversight over the clergy, but his jurisdiction extends no farther.

The pope and clergy are given to worldliness and self-indulgence.   Boniface is a heretic.   The prelates squander the
Church's money in wars and litigations, prefer the atmosphere
of princely courts, and neglect theology and the care of souls.
The avarice of the curia and the pope leads them to scandalous
simony and nepotism.[3]   Constantine's donation marked the
change to worldliness among the clergy.   It was illegal, and
the only title the pope can show to temporal power over the
patrimony of Peter is long tenure.   The first step in the direction of reforms would be for clergy and pope to renounce
worldly possessions altogether.   This remedy had been prescribed by Arnold of Brescia and Frederick II.

Dubois also criticised the rule and practice of celibacy.
Few clergymen keep their vows.   And yet they are retained,
while ordination is denied to married persons.   This is in the
face of the fact that the Apostle permitted marriage to all.
The practice of the Eastern church is to be preferred.   The
rule of single life is too exacting, especially for nuns.   Durante had proposed the abrogation of the rule, and Arnald
of Villanova had emphasized the sacredness of the marriage
tie, recalling that it was upon a married man, Peter, that
Christ conferred the primacy.[4]

---

[1] *Advocatus regalium causarum.*

[2] For these tracts, see Renan, p. 476 sq. ; Scholz, p. 385 sqq.

[3] Scholz, p. 398.

[4] *Contulit conjugato scilicet beato Petro primatum ecclesiæ,* Finke, p.
clxxiii.   Arnald is attacking the Minorites and Dominicans for publicly teach-

Dubois showed the freshness of his mind by suggestions of a practical nature.   He proposed the colonization of the Holy Land by Christian people, and the marriage of Christian women to Saracens of station as a means of converting them.   As a measure for securing the world's conversion, he recommended to Clement the establishment of schools for boys and girls in every province, where instruction should be given in different languages.   The girls were to be taught Latin and the fundamentals of natural science, and especially medicine and surgery, that they might serve as female physicians among women in the more occult disorders.

A review of the controversial literature of the age of Philip the Fair shows the new paths along which men's thoughts were moving.[1]   The papal apologists insisted upon traditional interpretations of a limited number of texts, the perpetual validity of Constantine's donation, and the transfer of the empire.   They were forever quoting Innocent's famous bull, *Per venerabilem*.[2]   On the other hand, John of Paris, and the publicists who sympathized with him, as also Dante, corrected and widened the vision of the field of Scripture, and brought into prominence the common rights of man.   The resistance which the king of France offered to the demands of Boniface encouraged writers to speak without reserve.

The pope's spiritual primacy was left untouched.   The attack was against his temporal jurisdiction.   The fiction of the two swords was set aside.   The state is as supreme in its sphere as the Church in its sphere, and derives its authority immediately from God.   Constantine had no right to confer the sovereignty of the West upon Sylvester, and his gift constitutes no valid papal claim.   Each monarch is supreme in his own realm, and the theory of the overlordship of the emperor is abandoned as a thing out of date.

The pope's tenure of office was made subject to limitation.

ing that the statements of married people in matters of doctrine are not to be believed, *conjugato non est credendum super veritate divina*.

[1] See the summary of Scholz, pp. 444–458.

[2] It is quoted again and again by Henry of Cremona.   See the text in Scholz, p. 464 sq., etc.   For the text of the bull, see Mirbt: *Quellen*, pp. 127–130.

He may be deposed for heresy and incompetency. Some writers went so far as to deny to him jurisdiction over Church property. The advisory function of the cardinals was emphasized and the independent authority of the bishops affirmed. Above all, the authority residing in the Church as a body of believers was discussed, and its voice, as uttered through a general council, pronounced to be superior to the authority of the pope. The utterances of John of Paris and Peter Dubois on the subject of general councils led straight on to the views propounded during the papal schism at the close of the fourteenth century.[1] Dubois demanded that laymen as well as clerics should have a voice in them. The rule of clerical celibacy was attacked, and attention called to its widespread violation in practice. Pope and clergy were invoked to devote themselves to the spiritual well-being of mankind, and to foster peaceable measures for the world's conversion.

This freedom of utterance and changed way of thinking mark the beginning of one of the great revolutions in the history of the Christian Church. To these publicists the modern world owes a debt of gratitude. Principles which are now regarded as axiomatic were new for the Christian public of their day. A generation later, Marsiglius of Padua defined them again with clearness, and took a step still further in advance.

§ 6. *The Transfer of the Papacy to Avignon.*

The successor of Boniface, Benedict XI., 1303–1304, a Dominican, was a mild-spirited and worthy man, more bent on healing ruptures than on forcing his arbitrary will. Departing from the policy of his predecessor, he capitulated to the state and put an end to the conflict with Philip the Fair. Sentences launched by Boniface were recalled or modified, and the interdict pronounced by that pope upon Lyons was revoked. Palestrina was restored to the Colonna. Only Sciarra Colonna and Nogaret were excepted from the act of immediate clemency and ordered to appear at Rome. Benedict's death, after a brief reign of eight months, was ascribed

[1] Scholz, p. 322 ; Schwab : *Life of Gerson*, p. 133.

to poison secreted in a dish of figs, of which the pope partook freely.[1]

The conclave met in Perugia, where Benedict died, and was torn by factions. After an interval of nearly eleven months, the French party won a complete triumph by the choice of Bertrand de Got, archbishop of Bordeaux, who took the name of Clement V. At the time of his election, Bertrand was in France. He never crossed the Alps. After holding his court at Bordeaux, Poictiers, and Toulouse, he chose, in 1309, Avignon as his residence.

Thus began the so-called Babylonian captivity, or Avignon exile, of the papacy, which lasted more than seventy years and included seven popes, all Frenchmen, Clement V., 1305–1314 ; John XXII., 1316–1334 ; Benedict XII., 1334–1342 ; Clement VI., 1342–1352 ; Innocent VI., 1352–1362 ; Urban V., 1362–1370 ; Gregory XI., 1370–1378. This prolonged absence from Rome was a great shock to the papal system. Transplanted from its maternal soil, the papacy was cut loose from the hallowed and historical associations of thirteen centuries. It no longer spake as from the centre of the Christian world.

The way had been prepared for the abandonment of the Eternal City and removal to French territory. Innocent II. and other popes had found refuge in France. During the last half of the thirteenth century the Apostolic See, in its struggle with the empire, had leaned upon France for aid. To avoid Frederick II., Innocent IV. had fled to Lyons, 1245. If Boniface VIII. represents a turning-point in the history of the papacy, the Avignon residence shook the reverence of Christendom for it. It was in danger of becoming a French institution. Not only were the popes all Frenchmen, but the large majority of the cardinals were of French birth. Both were reduced to a station little above that of court prelates subject to the nod of the French sovereign. At the same

---

[1] Ferretus of Vicenza, Muratori, IX. 1013. Villani, VIII. 80. As an example of Benedict's sanctity it was related that after he was made pope he was visited by his mother, dressed in silks, but he refused to recognize her till she had changed her dress, and then he embraced her.

time, the popes continued to exercise their prerogatives over
the other nations of Western Christendom, and freely hurled
anathemas at the German emperor and laid the interdict
upon Italian cities. The word might be passed around,
"where the pope is, there is Rome," but the wonder is that
the grave hurt done to his œcumenical character was not
irreparable.[1]

The morals of Avignon during the papal residence were
notorious throughout Europe. The papal household had all
the appearance of a worldly court, torn by envies and
troubled by schemes of all sorts. Some of the Avignon
popes left a good name, but the general impression was bad
— weak if not vicious. The curia was notorious for its
extravagance, venality, and sensuality. Nepotism, bribery, and simony were unblushingly practised. The financial operations of the papal family became oppressive to
an extent unknown before. Indulgences, applied to all
sorts of cases, were made a source of increasing revenue.
Alvarus Pelagius, a member of the papal household and a
strenuous supporter of the papacy, in his De planctu ecclesiæ,
complained bitterly of the peculation and traffic in ecclesiastical places going on at the papal court. It swarmed with
money-changers, and parties bent on money operations.
Another contemporary, Petrarch, who never uttered a word
against the papacy as a divine institution, launched his sat-
ires against Avignon, which he called "the sink of every
vice, the haunt of all iniquities, a third Babylon, the Babylon
of the West." No expression is too strong to carry his biting invectives. Avignon is the "fountain of afflictions, the

---

[1] See Pastor, I. 75–80. He calls Clement's decision to remain in France
der unselige Entschluss, " the unholy resolve," and says the change to Avignon had the meaning of a calamity and a fall, die Bedeutung einer Katastrophe, eines Sturzes. Hefele-Knöpfler, Kirchengeschichte, p. 458, pronounces
it " a move full of bad omen." Baur, Kirchengesch. d. M.A., p. 265, said,
"The transference of the papal chair to Avignon was the fatal turning-point
from which the papacy moved on to its dramatic goal with hasty step." See
also Haller, p. 23. Pastor, p. 62, making out as good a case as he can for the
Avignon popes, lays stress upon the support they gave to missions in Asia
and Africa. Clement VI., 1342–1352, appointed an archbishop for Japan.

refuge of wrath, the school of errors, a temple of lies, the awful prison, hell on earth."[1] But the corruption of Avignon was too glaring to make it necessary for him to invent charges. This ill-fame gives Avignon a place at the side of the courts of Louis XIV. and Charles II. of England.

During this papal expatriation, Italy fell into a deplorable condition. Rome, which had been the queen of cities, the goal of pilgrims, the centre towards which the pious affections of all Western Europe turned, the locality where royal and princely embassies had sought ratification for ambitious plans —Rome was now turned into an arena of wild confusion and riot. Contending factions of nobles, the Colonna, Orsini, Gaetani, and others, were in constant feud,[2] and strove one with the other for the mastery in municipal affairs and were often themselves set aside by popular leaders whose low birth they despised. The source of her gains gone, the city withered away and was reduced to the proportions, the poverty, and the dull happenings of a provincial town, till in 1370 the population numbered less than 20,000. She had no commerce to stir her pulses like the young cities in Northern and Southern Germany and in Lombardy. Obscurity and melancholy settled upon her palaces and public places, broken only by the petty attempts at civic displays, which were like the actings of the circus ring compared with the serious manœuvres of a military campaign. The old monuments were neglected or torn down. A papal legate sold the stones of the Colosseum to be burnt in lime-kilns, and her marbles were transported to other cities, so that it was said she was drawn upon more than Carrara.[3] Her churches became

[1] Petrarch speaks of it "as filled with every kind of confusion, the powers of darkness overspreading it and containing everything fearful which had ever existed or been imagined by a disordered mind." Robinson : *Petrarch*, p. 87. Pastor, I. p. 76, seeks to reduce the value of Petrarch's testimony on the ground that he spoke as a poet, burning with the warm blood of his country, who, notwithstanding his charges, preferred to live in Avignon.

[2] The children did not escape the violence of this mad frenzy. The little child, Agapito Colonna, was found in the church, where it had been taken by the servant, strangled by the Orsini.

[3] Pastor, p. 78, with note.

roofless. Cattle ate grass up to the very altars of the Lateran
and St. Peter's.   The movement of art was stopped which
had begun with the arrival of Giotto, who had come to Rome
at the call of Boniface VIII. to adorn St. Peter's.   No product of architecture is handed down from this period except
the marble stairway of the church of St. Maria, Ara Cœli,
erected in 1348 with an inscription commemorating the deliverance from the plague, and the restored Lateran church
which was burnt, 1308.[1] Ponds and débris interrupted the
passage of the streets and filled the air with offensive and
deadly odors.   At Clement V.'s death, Napoleon Orsini assured Philip that the Eternal City was on the verge of destruction and, in 1347, Cola di Rienzo thought it more fit to
be called a den of robbers than the residence of civilized men.

The Italian peninsula, at least in its northern half, was a
scene of political division and social anarchy.   The country
districts were infested with bands of brigands.   The cities
were given to frequent and violent changes of government.
High officials of the Church paid the price of immunity from
plunder and violence by exactions levied on other personages
of station.   Such were some of the immediate results of the
exile of the papacy. Italy was in danger of succumbing to the
fate of Hellas and being turned into a desolate waste.

Avignon, which Clement chose as his residence, is 460 miles
southeast of Paris and lies south of Lyons.   Its proximity to
the port of Marseilles made it accessible to Italy.   It was purchased by Clement VI., 1348, from Naples for 80,000 gold florins, and remained papal territory until the French Revolution.
As early as 1229, the popes held territory in the vicinity, the
duchy of Venaissin, which fell to them from the domain of
Raymond of Toulouse.   On every side this free papal home
was closely confined by French territory.   Clement was urged
by Italian bishops to go to Rome, and Italian writers gave as
one reason for his refusal fear lest he should receive meet punishment for his readiness to condemn Boniface VIII.[2]

---

[1] John XXII. paid off the cost incurred for this restoration with the price of
silver vessels left by Clement V. for the relief of the churches in Rome.
See Ehrle, V. 131.   [2] See Finke : *Quellen*, p. 92.

Clement's coronation was celebrated at Lyons, Philip and
his brother Charles of Valois, the Duke of Bretagne and representatives of the king of England being present. Philip
and the duke walked at the side of the pope's palfrey. By
the fall of an old wall during the procession, the duke, a
brother of the pope, and ten other persons lost their lives.
The pope himself was thrown from his horse, his tiara rolled
in the dust, and a large carbuncle, which adorned it, was lost.
Scarcely ever was a papal ruler put in a more compromising
position than the new pontiff. His subjection to a sovereign
who had defied the papacy was a strange spectacle. He owed
his tiara indirectly, if not immediately, to Philip the Fair.
He was the man Philip wanted.[1] It was his task to appease
the king's anger against the memory of Boniface, and to meet
his brutal demands concerning the Knights Templars. These,
with the Council of Vienne, which he called, were the chief
historic concerns of his pontificate.

The terms on which the new pope received the tiara were
imposed by Philip himself, and, according to Villani, the price
he made the Gascon pay included six promises. Five of them
concerned the total undoing of what Boniface had done in his
conflict with Philip. The sixth article, which was kept secret,
was supposed to be the destruction of the order of the Templars. It is true that the authenticity of these six articles has
been disputed, but there can be no doubt that from the very
outset of Clement's pontificate, the French king pressed their
execution upon the pope's attention.[2] Clement, in poor position to resist, confirmed what Benedict had done and went

[1] Döllinger says Clement passed completely into the service of the king, *er
trat ganz in den Dienst des Königs*. *Akad. Vorträge*, III. 254.

[2] Mansi was the first to express doubts concerning these articles, reported by
Villani, VIII. 80. Döllinger: *Akad. Vorträge*, III. 254, and Hefele, following
Bouteric, deny them altogether. Hefele, in a long and careful statement, VI.
394–403, gives reasons for regarding them as an Italian invention. Clement
distinctly said that he knew nothing of the charges against the Templars till
the day of his coronation. On the other hand, Villani's testimony is clear and
positive, and at any rate shows the feeling which prevailed in the early part of
the fourteenth century. Archer is inclined to hold on to Villani's testimony,
Enc. Brit., XXIII. 164. The character of pope and king, and the circumstances under which Clement was elected, make a compact altogether probable.

farther.   He absolved the king; recalled, Feb. 1, 1306, the
offensive bulls *Clericis laicos* and *Unam sanctam*, so far as they
implied anything offensive to France or any subjection on
the part of the king to the papal chair, not customary before
their issue, and fully restored the cardinals of the Colonna
family to the dignities of their office.

The proceedings touching the character of Boniface VIII.
and his right to a place among the popes dragged along for
fully six years.   Philip had offered, among others, his brother,
Count Louis of Evreux, as a witness for the charge that Boniface had died a heretic.   There was a division of sentiment
among the cardinals.   The Colonna were as hostile to the
memory of Boniface as they were zealous in their writings
for the memory of Cœlestine V.   They pronounced it to be
contrary to the divine ordinance for a pope to abdicate.   His
spiritual marriage with the Church cannot be dissolved.   And
as for there being two popes at the same time, God was himself not able to constitute such a monstrosity.   On the other
hand, writers like Augustinus Triumphus defended Boniface
and pronounced him a martyr to the interests of the Church
and worthy of canonization.[1]   In his zeal against his old enemy
Philip had called, probably as early as 1305, for the canonization of Cœlestine V.[2]   A second time, in 1307, Boniface's condemnation was pressed upon Clement by the king in person.
But the pope knew how to prolong the prosecution on all sorts
of pretexts.   Philip represented himself as concerned for the
interests of religion, and Nogaret and the other conspirators
insisted that the assault at Avignon was a religious act, *negotium
fidei*.   Nogaret sent forth no less than twelve apologies defending himself for his part in the assault.[3]   In 1310 the formal

---

[1] Dupuy, pp. 448–465. See Finke and Scholz, pp. 198–207. Among those who
took sides against the pope was Peter Dubois.   In his *Deliberatio super agen-
dis a Philippo IV.* (Dupuy, pp. 44–47), he pronounced Boniface a heretic.
This tract was probably written during the sessions of the National Assembly
in Paris, April, 1302.   See Scholz, p. 386.   In another tract Dubois (Dupuy,
pp. 214–19) called upon the French king to condemn Boniface as a heretic.

[2] This is upon the basis of a tractate found and published by Finke, *Aus
den Tagen Bon. VIII.*, pp. lxix–c, and which he puts in the year 1308.   See
pp. lxxxv, xcviii.   Scholz, p. 174, ascribes this tract to Augustinus Triumphus.

[3] Holtzmann: *W. von Nogaret*, p. 202 sqq.

trial began.   Many witnesses appeared to testify against Boniface,—laymen, priests and bishops.   The accusations were that
the pope had declared all three religions false, Mohammedanism, Judaism and Christianity, pronounced the virgin birth
a tale, denied transubstantiation and the existence of hell and
heaven and that he had played games of chance.

Clement issued one bull after another protesting the innocency of the offending parties concerned in the violent measures against Boniface.   Philip and Nogaret were declared
innocent of all guilt and to have only pure motives in prefer-
ring charges against the dead pope.[1]   The bull, *Rex gloriæ*,
1311, addressed to Philip, stated that the secular kingdom
was founded by God and that France in the new dispensation
occupied about the same place as Israel, the elect people, occupied under the old dispensation.   Nogaret's purpose in entering into the agreement which resulted in the affair at Anagni
was to save the Church from destruction at the hands of Boniface, and the plundering of the papal palace and church was
done against the wishes of the French chancellor.   In several
bulls Clement recalled all punishments, statements, suspen-
sions and declarations made against Philip and his kingdom,
or supposed to have been made.   And to fully placate the
king, he ordered all Boniface's pronouncements of this character effaced from the books of the Roman Church.   Thus in
the most solemn papal form did Boniface's successor undo all
that Boniface had done.[2]   When the Œcumenical Council of
Vienne met, the case of Boniface was so notorious a matter
that it had to be taken up.   After a formal trial, in which the
accused pontiff was defended by three cardinals, he was adjudged not guilty.   To gain this point, and to save his predecessor from formal condemnation, it is probable Clement

---

[1] The tract of 1308 attempts to prove some of the charges against Boniface
untrue, or that true sayings attributed to him did not make him a heretic.
For example, it takes up the charges that Boniface had called the Gauls dogs,
and had said he would rather be a dog than a Gaul.   The argument begins by
quoting Eccles. 3 : 19, p. lxx. sqq.

[2] The condemned clauses were in some cases erased, but Boniface's friends
succeeded in keeping some perfect copies of the originals.   See Hefele-
Knöpfler, VI. 460.

had to surrender to Philip unqualifiedly in the matter of the Knights of the Temple.

After long and wearisome proceedings, this order was formally legislated out of existence by Clement in 1312.   Founded in 1119 to protect pilgrims and to defend the Holy Land against the Moslems, it had outlived its mission.   Sapped of its energy by riches and indulgence, its once famous knights might well have disbanded and no interest been the worse for it.   The story, however, of their forcible suppression awakens universal sympathy and forms one of the most thrilling and mysterious chapters of the age.   Döllinger has called it "a unique drama in history."[1]

The destruction of the Templar order was relentlessly insisted upon by Philip the Fair, and accomplished with the reluctant co-operation of Clement V.   In vain did the king strive to hide the sordidness of his purpose under the thin mask of religious zeal.   At Clement's coronation, if not before, Philip brought charges against it.   About the same time, in the insurrection called forth by his debasement of the coin, the king took refuge in the Templars' building at Paris.   In 1307 he renewed the charges before the pope.   When Clement hesitated, he proceeded to violence, and on the night of Oct. 13, 1307, he had all the members of the order in France arrested and thrown into prison, including Jacques de Molay, the grand-master.   Döllinger applies to this deed the strong language that, if he were asked to pick out from the whole history of the world the accursed day, — dies nefastus, — he would be able to name none other than Oct. 13, 1307.   Three days later, Philip announced he had taken this action as the defender of the faith and called upon Christian princes to follow his example.   Little as the business was to Clement's taste, he was not man enough to set himself in opposition to the king, and he gradually became complai-

---

[1] Döllinger's treatment, *Akad. Vorträge*, III. 244–274, was the last address that distinguished historian made before the Munich Academy of the Sciences. In his zeal to present a good case for the Templars, he suggests that if they had been let alone they might have done good service by policing the Mediterranean, with Cyprus as a base.

sant.[1] The machinery of the Inquisition was called into use.
The Dominicans, its chief agents, stood high in Philip's
favor, and one of their number was his confessor. In 1308
the authorities of the state assented to the king's plans to
bring the order to trial. The constitution of the court was
provided for by Clement, the bishop of each diocese and two
Franciscans and two Dominicans being associated together.
A commission invested with general authority was to sit in
Paris.[2]

In the summer of 1308 the pope ordered a prosecution of
the knights wherever they might be found.[3] The charges set
forth were heresy, spitting upon the cross, worshipping an idol,
Bafomet — the word for Mohammed in the Provençal dialect
— and also the most abominable offences against moral decency
such as sodomy and kissing the posterior parts and the navel of
fellow knights. The members were also accused of having
meetings with the devil who appeared in the form of a black
cat and of having carnal intercourse with female demons.
The charges which the lawyers and Inquisitors got together
numbered 127 and these the pope sent through France and
to other countries as the basis of the prosecution.

Under the strain of prolonged torture, many of the unfortunate men gave assent to these charges, and more particularly

[1] In the bull *Pastoralis præeminentiæ*, 1307. Augustinus Triumphus, in his
tract on the Templars, *de facto Templarorum*, without denying the charges of
heresy, denied the king's right to seize and try persons accused of heresy on
his own initiative and without the previous consent of the Church. See the
document printed by Scholz, pp. 508–516.

[2] It consisted of the archbishop of Narbonne, the bishops of Mende, Bayeux,
and Limoges and four lesser dignitaries. The place of sitting was put at Paris
at the urgency of Philip.

[3] In the bull *Faciens misericordiam*. In this document the pope made
the charge that the grand-master and the officers of the order were in the habit
of granting absolution, a strictly priestly prerogative. It was to confirm the
strict view of granting absolution that Alexander III. provided for the admission of priests to the Military Orders. See Lea's valuable paper, *The
Absolution Formula of the Templars*. See also on this subject Finke I. 395–
397. Funk, p. 1330, says *der Pabst kam von jetzt an dem König mehr und
mehr entgegen und nachdem er sich von dem gewaltigsten und rücksichtsosig-
sten Fürsten seiner Zeit hatte ungarnen lassen, war ein Entkommen aus
seiner Gewalt kaum mehr möglich.*

to the denial of Christ and the spitting upon the cross.   The Templars seem to have had no friends in high places bold enough to take their part.   The king, the pope, the Dominican order, the University of Paris, the French episcopacy were against them.   Many confessions once made by the victims were afterwards recalled at the stake.   Many denied the charges altogether.[1]   In Paris 36 died under torture, 54 suffered there at one burning, May 10, 1310, and 8 days later 4 more.   Hundreds of them perished in prison.   Even the bitterest enemies acknowledged that the Templars who were put to death maintained their innocence to their dying breath.[2]

In accordance with Clement's order, trials were had in Germany, Italy, Spain, Portugal, Cyprus and England.   In England, Edward II. at first refused to apply the torture, which was never formally adopted in that land, but later, at Clement's demand, he complied.   Papal inquisitors appeared.   Synods in London and York declared the charges of heresy so serious that it would be impossible for the knights to clear themselves. English houses were disbanded and the members distributed among the monasteries to do penance.   In Italy and Germany, the accused were, for the most part, declared innocent.   In Spain and Portugal, no evidence was forthcoming of guilt and the synod of Tarragona, 1310, and other synods favored their innocence.

The last act in these hostile proceedings was opened at the Council of Vienne, called for the special purpose of taking action upon the order.   The large majority of the council were

[1] These practices have been regarded by Prutz, Loiscleur (*La doctrine secrète des Templiers*, Paris, 1872) and others as a part of a secret code which came into use in the thirteenth century.   But the code has not been forthcoming and was not referred to in the trials.   Frederick II. declared that the Templars received Mohammedans into their house at Jerusalem and preferred their religious rites.   This statement must be taken with reserve, in view of Frederick's hostility to the order for its refusal to help him on his crusade.   See M. Paris, *an.* 1244.

[2] At the trial before the bishop of Nismes in 1309, out of 32, all but three denied the charges.   At Perpignan, 1310, the whole number, 25, denied the charges.   At Clermont 40 confessed the order guilty, 28 denied its guilt.   With such antagonistic testimonies it is difficult, if at all possible, to decide the question of guilt or innocence.

in favor of giving it a new trial and a fair chance to prove its innocence. But the king was relentless. He reminded Clement that the guilt of the knights had been sufficiently proven, and insisted that the order be abolished. He appeared in person at the council, attended by a great retinue. Clement was overawed, and by virtue of his apostolic power issued his decree abolishing the Templars, March 22, 1312.[1] Clement's reasons were that suspicions existed that the order held to heresies, that many of the Templars had confessed to heresies and other offences, that thereafter reputable persons would not enter the order, and that it was no longer necessary for the defence of the Holy Land. Directions were given for the further procedure. The guilty were to be put to death ; the innocent to be supported out of the revenues of the order. With this action the famous order passed out of existence.

The end of Jacques de Molay, the 22d and last grand-master of the order of Templars, was worthy of its proudest days. At the first trial he confessed to the charges of denying Christ and spitting upon the cross, and was condemned, but afterwards recalled his confession. His case was reopened in 1314. With Geoffrey de Charney, grand-preceptor of Normandy, and others, he was led in front of Notre Dame Cathedral, and sentenced to perpetual imprisonment. Molay then stood forth and declared that the charges against the order were false, and that he had confessed to them under the strain of torture and instructions from the king. Charney said the same. The commission promised to reconsider the case the next day. But the king's vengeance knew no bounds, and that night, March 11, 1314, the prisoners were burned. The story ran that while the flames were doing their grewsome work, Molay summoned pope and king to meet him at the judgment bar within a year. The former died, in a little more than a month, of a loathsome dis-

---

[1] *Per viam provisionis seu ordinationis apostolicæ* is the language of the bull, that is, as opposed to *de jure* or as a punishment for proven crimes. This bull, *Vox clamantis*, was found by the Benedictine, Dr. Gams, in Spain, in 1865. See Hefele-Knöpfler, VI. 525 sqq. It is found in Mirbt : *Quellen*, p. 149 sq. Clement asserts he issued the order of abolition " not without bitterness and pain of heart," *non sine cordis amaritudine et dolore*. Two other bulls on the Templars and the disposition of their property followed in May.

ease, though penitent, as it was reported, for his treatment of
the order, and the king, by accident, while engaged in the chase,
six months later.   The king was only 46 years old at the time
of his death, and 14 years after, the last of his direct descendants was in his grave and the throne passed to the house of
Valois.

As for the possessions of the order, papal decrees turned
them over to the Knights of St. John, but Philip again intervened and laid claim to 260,000 pounds as a reimbursement
for alleged losses to the Temple and the expense of guard-
ing the prisoners.[1]   In Spain, they passed to the orders of
San Iago di Compostella and Calatrava.   In Aragon, they
were in part applied to a new order, Santa Maria de Montesia,
and in Portugal to the Military Order of Jesus Christ, *ordo
militiæ Jesu Christi*.   Repeated demands made by the pope
secured the transmission of a large part of their possessions to
the Knights of St. John.   In England, in 1323, parliament
granted their lands to the Hospitallers, but the king appropriated a considerable share to himself.   The Temple in London
fell to the Earl of Pembroke, 1313.[2]

The explanation of Philip's violent animosity and persistent persecution is his cupidity.   He coveted the wealth of
the Templars.   Philip was quite equal to a crime of this
sort.[3]   He robbed the bankers of Lombardy and the Jews of

[1] The wealth of the Templars has been greatly exaggerated.   They were
not richer in France than the Hospitallers.   About 1300, the possessions of
each of these orders in that country were taxed at 6000 pounds.   See Döllinger,
p. 267 sq.   Thomas Fuller, the English historian, quaintly says, " Philip would
never have taken away the Templars' lives if he might have taken away their
lands without putting them to death.   He could not get the honey without
burning the bees."   The Spanish delegation to the Council of Vienne wrote
back to the king of Aragon that the chief concern at the council and with the
king in regard to the Templars was the disposition of their goods, Finke, I.
350, 374.   Finke, I. 111, 115, etc., ascribes a good deal of the animosity against
the order to the revelations made by Esquin de Floyran to Jayme of Aragon
in 1305.   But the charges he made were already current in France.

[2] In 1609 the benchers of the Inner and Middle Temple received the buildings for a small annual payment to the Crown, into whose possession they had
passed under Henry VIII.

[3] Dante and Villani agree that the Templars were innocent.   In this judgment most modern historians concur.   Funk declares the sentence of inno-

France, and debased the coin of his realm.   A loan of 500,000 pounds which he had secured for a sister's dowry had involved him in great financial straits.   He appropriated all the possessions of the Templars he could lay his hands upon.   Clement V.'s subserviency it is easy to explain.   He was a creature of the king.   When the pope hesitated to proceed against the unfortunate order, the king beset him with the case of Boniface VIII.   To save the memory of his predecessor, the pope surrendered the lives of the knights.[1]   Dante, in representing the Templars as victims of the king's avarice, compares Philip to Pontius Pilate.

> " I see the modern Pilate, whom avails
> No cruelty to sate and who, unbidden,
> Into the Temple sets his greedy sails."
>
> *Purgatory*, xx. 91.

The house of the Templars in Paris was turned into a royal residence, from which Louis XVI., more than four centuries later, went forth to the scaffold.

The Council of Vienne, the fifteenth in the list of the œcumenical councils, met Oct. 16, 1311, and after holding three sessions adjourned six months later, May 6, 1312.   Clement opened it with an address on Psalm 111 : 1, 2, and designated three subjects for its consideration, the case of the order of the Templars, the relief of the Holy Land and Church reform.   The documents bearing on the council are defective.[2]   In addition

cence to be " without question the right one," p. 1341.   Döllinger, with great emphasis, insists that nowhere did a Templar make a confession of guilt except under torture, p. 257.   More recently, 1907, Finke (I. p. ix. 326 sq. 337) insists upon their innocence and the untrustworthiness of the confessions made by the Templars.   He declares that he who advocates their guilt must accept the appearances of the devil as a tom-cat.   Prutz, in his earlier works, decided for their guilt.   Schottmüller, Döllinger, Funk, and our own Dr. Lea strongly favor their innocence.   Ranke : *Univ. Hist.*, VIII. 622, wavers and ascribes to them the doctrinal standpoint of Frederick II. and Manfred.   In France, Michelet was against the order ; Michaud, Guizot, Renan and Boutaric for it.   Hallam : *Middle Ages*, I. 142–146, is undecided.

[1] See Döllinger, p. 255, and Gregorovius.   Lea gives as excuse for the length at which he treats the trial and fate of the unfortunate knights, their helplessness before the Inquisition.

[2] Ehrle, *Archiv für Lit. und Kirchengesch.* IV. 361–470, published a fragmentary report which he discovered in the National Library in Paris.   For the best account of the proceedings, see Hefele-Knöpfler, VI. 514–554.

to the decisions concerning the Templars and Boniface VIII., it condemned the Beguines and Beghards and listened to charges made against the Franciscan, Peter John Olivi (d. 1298). Olivi belonged to the Spiritual wing of the order. His books had been ordered burnt, 1274, by one Franciscan general, and a second general of the order, Bonagratia, 1279, had appointed a commission which found thirty-four dangerous articles in his writings. The council, without pronouncing against Olivi, condemned three articles ascribed to him bearing on the relation of the two parties in the Franciscan order, the Spirituals and Conventuals.

The council has a place in the history of biblical scholarship and university education by its act ordering two chairs each, of Hebrew, Arabic, and Chaldee established in Paris, Oxford, Bologna, and Salamanca.

While the proceedings against Boniface and the Templars were dragging on in their slow course in France, Clement was trying to make good his authority in Italy. Against Venice he hurled the most violent anathemas and interdicts for venturing to lay hands on Ferrara, whose territory was claimed by the Apostolic See. A crusade was preached against the sacrilegious city. She was defeated in battle, and Ferrara was committed to the administration of Robert, king of Naples, as the pope's vicar.

All that he could well do, Clement did to strengthen the hold of France on the papacy. The first year of his pontificate he appointed 9 French cardinals, and of the 24 persons whom he honored with the purple, 23 were Frenchmen. He granted to the insatiable Philip a Church tithe for five years. Next to the fulfilment of his obligations to this monarch, Clement made it his chief business to levy tributes upon ecclesiastics of all grades and upon vacant Church livings.[1] He was prodigal with offices to his relatives. This was a leading feature of his pontificate. Five of his kin were made cardinals, three being still in their youth. His brother he made rector of Rome, and other members of his family received Ancona, Ferrara, the duchy of Spoleto, and the duchy of Venaissin, and

---

[1] Haller, p. 45 sqq.

other territories within the pope's gift.[1]   The administration
and disposition of his treasure occupied a large part of Clement's time and have offered an interesting subject to the pen
of the modern Jesuit scholar, Ehrle.   The papal treasure left
by Clement's predecessor, after being removed from Perugia
to France, was taken from place to place and castle to castle,
packed in coffers laden on the backs of mules.   After Clement's death, the vast sums he had received and accumulated
suddenly disappeared.   Clement's successor, John XXII., instituted a suit against Clement's most trusted relatives to
account for the moneys.   The suit lasted from 1318–1322, and
brought to light a great amount of information concerning
Clement's finances.[2]

His fortune Clement disposed of by will, 1312, the total
amount being 814,000 florins; 300,000 were given to his
nephew, the viscount of Lomagne and Auvillars, a man otherwise known for his numerous illegitimate offspring.   This
sum was to be used for a crusade ; 314,000 were bequeathed to
other relatives and to servants.   The remaining 200,000 were
given to churches, convents, and the poor.   A loan of 160,000
made to the king of France was never paid back.[3]

Clement's body was by his appointment buried at Uzeste.
His treasure was plundered.   At the trial instituted by John
XXII., it appeared that Clement before his death had set apart
70,000 florins to be divided in equal shares between his successor and the college of cardinals.   The viscount of Lomagne
was put into confinement by John, and turned over 300,000
florins, one-half going to the cardinals and one-half to the
pope.   A few months after Clement's death, the count made
loans to the king of France of 110,000 florins and to the king
of England of 60,000.

Clement's relatives showed their appreciation of his liberality by erecting to his memory an elaborate sarcophagus at

[1] Ehrle, V. 139 sq.

[2] Ehrle, p. 147, calculates that Clement's yearly income was between 200,000
and 250,000 gold florins, and that of this amount he spent 100,000 for the expenses of his court and saved the remainder, 100,000 or 150,000.   Ehrle, p. 149,
gives Clement's family tree.   [3] Ehrle, pp. 126, 135.

Uzeste, which cost 50,000 gold florins. The theory is that the pope administers moneys coming to him by virtue of his papal office for the interest of the Church at large. Clement spoke of the treasure in his coffers as his own, which he might dispose of as he chose.[1]

Clement's private life was open to the grave suspicion of unlawful intimacy with the beautiful Countess Brunissenda of Foix. Of all the popes of the fourteenth century, he showed the least independence. An apologist of Boniface VIII., writing in 1308, recorded this judgment : [2] "The Lord permitted Clement to be elected, who was more concerned about temporal things and in enriching his relatives than was Boniface, in order that by contrast Boniface might seem worthy of praise where he would otherwise have been condemned, just as the bitter is not known except by the sweet, or cold except by heat, or the good except by evil." Villani, who assailed both popes, characterized Clement " as licentious, greedy of money, a simoniac, who sold in his court every benefice for gold." [3]

By a single service did this pope seem to place the Church in debt to his pontificate. The book of decretals, known as the Clementines, and issued in part by him, was completed by his successor, John XXII.

§ 7. *The Pontificate of John XXII.* 1316–1334.

Clement died April 20, 1314. The cardinals met at Carpentras and then at Lyons, and after an interregnum of twenty-seven months elected John XXII., 1316–1334, to the papal throne. He was then seventy-two, and cardinal-bishop of

---

[1] Clement's grave is reported to have been opened and looted by the Calvinists in 1568 or 1577. See Ehrle, p. 139.

[2] Finke : *Aus den Tagen Bon. VIII.*, p. lxxxviii.

[3] *Chronicle*, IX. 59. Villani tells the story that at the death of one of Clement's nephews, a cardinal, Clement, in his desire to see him, consulted a necromancer. The master of the dark arts had one of the pope's chaplains conducted by demons to hell, where he was shown a palace, and in it the nephew's soul laid on a bed of glowing fire, and near by a place reserved for the pope himself. He also relates that the coffin, in which Clement was laid, was burnt, and with it the pope's body up to the waist.

Porto.[1] Dante had written to the conclave begging that it elect an Italian pope, but the French influence was irresistible.

Said to be the son of a cobbler of Cahors, short of stature,[2] with a squeaking voice, industrious and pedantic, John was, upon the whole, the most conspicuous figure among the popes of the fourteenth century, though not the most able or worthy one. He was a man of restless disposition, and kept the papal court in constant commotion. The Vatican Archives preserve 59 volumes of his bulls and other writings. He had been a tutor in the house of Anjou, and carried the preceptorial method into his papal utterances. It was his ambition to be a theologian as well as pope. He solemnly promised the Italian faction in the curia never to mount an ass except to start on the road to Rome. But he never left Avignon. His devotion to France was shown at the very beginning of his reign in the appointment of eight cardinals, of whom seven were Frenchmen.

The four notable features of John's pontificate are his quarrel with the German emperor, Lewis the Bavarian, his condemnation of the rigid party of the Franciscans, his own doctrinal heresy, and his cupidity for gold.

The struggle with Lewis the Bavarian was a little afterplay compared with the imposing conflicts between the Hohenstaufen and the notable popes of preceding centuries. Europe looked on with slight interest at the long-protracted dispute, which was more adapted to show the petulance and weakness of both emperor and pope than to settle permanently any great principle. At Henry VII.'s death, 1313, five of the electors gave their votes for Lewis of the house of Wittelsbach, and two for Frederick of Hapsburg. Both appealed to the new pope, about to be elected. Frederick was crowned by

---

[1] Villani, IX : 81, gives the suspicious report that the cardinals, weary of their inability to make a choice, left it to John. Following the advice of Cardinal Napoleon Orsini, he grasped his supreme chance and elected himself. He was crowned at Lyons.

[2] Villani's statement that he was the son of a cobbler is doubted. Ferretus of Vicenza says he was "small like Zaccheus."

the archbishop of Treves at Bonn, and Lewis by the archbishop
of Mainz at Aachen.   In 1317 John declared that the pope
was the lawful vicar of the empire so long as the throne was
vacant, and denied Lewis recognition as king of the Romans on
the ground of his having neglected to submit his election to
him.

The battle at Mühldorf, 1322, left Frederick a prisoner in
his rival's hands.   This turn of affairs forced John to take
more decisive action, and in 1323 was issued against Lewis
the first of a wearisome and repetitious series of complaints
and punishments from Avignon.   The pope threatened him
with the ban, claiming authority to approve or set aside an
emperor's election.[1]   A year later he excommunicated Lewis
and all his supporters.

In answer to this first complaint of 1323, Lewis made a
formal declaration at Nürnberg in the presence of a notary
and other witnesses that he regarded the empire as independent of the pope, charged John with heresy, and appealed
to a general council.   The charge of heresy was based on the
pope's treatment of the Spiritual party among the Franciscans.   Condemned by John, prominent Spirituals, Michael
of Cesena, Ockam and Bonagratia, espoused Lewis' cause,
took refuge at his court, and defended him with their pens.
The political conflict was thus complicated by a recondite ecclesiastical problem.   In 1324 Lewis issued a second appeal,
written in the chapel of the Teutonic Order in Sachsen-
hausen, which again renewed the demand for a general council
and repeated the charge of heresy against the pope.

The next year, 1325, Lewis suffered a severe defeat from
Leopold of Austria, who had entered into a compact to put
Charles IV. of France on the German throne.   He went so
far as to express his readiness, in the compact of Ulm, 1326,
to surrender the German crown to Frederick, provided he
himself was confirmed in his right to Italy and the imperial
dignity.   At this juncture Leopold died.

By papal appointment Robert of Naples was vicar of Rome.

---

[1] See Müller: *Kampf Ludwigs*, etc., I. 61 sqq.   *Examinatio, approbatio ac
admonitio, repulsio quoque et reprobatio.*

But Lewis had no idea of surrendering his claims to Italy, and, now that he was once again free by Leopold's death, he marched across the Alps and was crowned, January 1327, emperor in front of St. Peter's. Sciarra Colonna, as the representative of the people, placed the crown on his head, and two bishops administered unction. Villani [1] expresses indignation at an imperial coronation conducted without the pope's consent as a thing unheard of. Lewis was the first mediæval emperor crowned by the people. A formal trial was instituted, and "James of Cahors, who calls himself John XXII." was denounced as anti-christ and deposed from the papal throne and his effigy carried through the streets and burnt.[2] John of Corbara, belonging to the Spiritual wing of the Franciscans, was elected to the throne just declared vacant, and took the name of Nicolas V. He was the first anti-pope since the days of Barbarossa. Lewis himself placed the crown upon the pontiff's head, and the bishop of Venice performed the ceremony of unction. Nicolas surrounded himself with a college of seven cardinals, and was accused of having forthwith renounced the principles of poverty and abstemiousness in dress and at the table which the day before he had advocated.

To these acts of violence John replied by pronouncing Lewis a heretic and appointing a crusade against him, with the promise of indulgence to all taking part in it. Fickle Rome soon grew weary of her lay-crowned emperor, who had been so unwise as to impose an extraordinary tribute of 10,000 florins each upon the people, the clergy, and the Jews of the city. He retired to the North, Nicolas following him with his retinue of cardinals. At Pisa, the emperor being present, the anti-pope excommunicated John and summoned a general council to Milan. John was again burnt in effigy, at the cathedral, and condemned to death for heresy. In 1330

[1] X. 55.

[2] The grounds on which John was deposed were his decisions against the Spirituals, the use of money and ships, intended for a crusade, to reduce Genoa, appropriation of the right of appointment to clerical offices, and his residence away from Rome. The document is found in Muratori, XIV., 1167-1173. For a vivid description of the enthronement and character of John of Corbara, see Gregorovius, VI. 153 sqq.

Lewis withdrew from Italy altogether, while Nicolas, with a cord around his neck, submitted to John.   He died in Avignon three years later.   In 1334, John issued a bull which, according to Karl Müller, was the rudest act of violence done up to that time to the German emperor by a pope.[1]   This fulmination separated Italy from the crown and kingdom — *imperium et regnum* — of Germany and forbade their being reunited in one body.   The reason given for this drastic measure was the territorial separation of the two provinces. Thus was accomplished by a distinct announcement what the diplomacy of Innocent III. was the first to make a part of the papal policy, and which figured so prominently in the struggle between Gregory IX. and Frederick II.

With his constituency completely lost in Italy, and with only an uncertain support in Germany, Lewis now made overtures for peace.   But the pope was not ready for anything less than a full renunciation of the imperial power. John died 1334, but the struggle was continued through the pontificate of his successor, Benedict XII.   Philip VI. of France set himself against Benedict's measures for reconciliation with Lewis, and in 1337 the emperor made an alliance with England against France.   Princes of Germany, making the rights of the empire their own, adopted the famous constitution of Rense, — a locality near Mainz, which was confirmed at the Diet of Frankfurt, 1338.   It repudiated the pope's extravagant temporal claims, and declared that the election of an emperor by the electors was final, and did not require papal approval.   This was the first representative German assembly to assert the independence of the empire.

The interdict was hanging over the German assembly when Benedict died, 1342.   The battle had gone against Lewis, and his supporters were well-nigh all gone from him.   A submission even more humiliating than that of Henry IV. was the only thing left.   He sought the favor of Clement VI., but in vain.   In a bull of April 12, 1343, Clement enumerated the emperor's many crimes, and anew ordered him to renounce the imperial dignity.   Lewis wrote, yielding sub-

[1] 336 sqq., 376 sqq., 406.

mission, but the authenticity of the document was questioned at Avignon, probably with the set purpose of increasing the emperor's humiliation.   Harder conditions were laid down. They were rejected by the diet at Frankfurt, 1344.   But Germany was weary, and listened without revulsion to a final bull against Lewis, 1346, and a summons to the electors to proceed to a new election.   The electors, John of Bohemia among them, chose Charles IV., John's son.   The Bohemian king was the blind warrior who met his death on the battle-field of Crécy the same year.   Before his election, Charles had visited Avignon, and promised full submission to the pope's demands.   His continued complacency during his reign justified the pope's choice.   The struggle was ended with Lewis' death a year later, 1347, while he was engaged near Munich in a bear-hunt.   It was the last conflict of the empire and papacy along the old lines laid down by those ecclesiastical warriors, Hildebrand and Innocent III. and Gregory IX.

To return to John XXII., he became a prominent figure in the controversy within the Franciscan order over the tenure of property, a controversy which had been going on from the earliest period between the two parties, the Spirituals, or Observants, and the Conventuals.   The last testament of St. Francis, pleading for the practice of absolute poverty, and suppressed in Bonaventura's Life of the saint, 1263, was not fully recognized in the bull of Nicolas III., 1279, which granted the Franciscans the right to use property as tenants, while forbidding them to hold it in fee simple.   With this decision the strict party, the Spirituals, were not satisfied, and the struggle went on.   Cœlestine V. attempted to bring peace by merging the Spiritual wing with the order of Hermits he had founded, but the measure was without success.

Under Boniface VIII. matters went hard with the Spirituals.   This pope deposed the general, Raymond Gaufredi, putting in his place John of Murro, who belonged to the laxer wing.   Peter John Olivi (d. 1298), whose writings were widely circulated, had declared himself in favor of Nicolas' bull, with the interpretation that the use of property and goods was to be the "use of necessity,"— *usus pauper*,— as opposed to the more liberal use advocated by the Conventuals and called *usus moderatus*. Olivi's personal fortunes were typical of the fortunes of the Spiritual branch. After his death, the attack made against his memory was, if possible, more determined, and culminated in the charges preferred at Vienne. Murro adopted violent measures, burning Olivi's writings, and casting his sympathizers into prison. Other prominent Spirituals fled. Angelo Clareno found refuge for a time in Greece, returning to Rome, 1305, under the protection of the Colonna.

The case was formally taken up by Clement V., who called a commission to Avignon to devise measures to heal the division, and gave the Spirituals temporary relief from persecution. The proceedings were protracted till the meeting of the council in Vienne, when the Conventuals brought up the case in the form of an arraignment of Olivi, who had come to be regarded almost as a saint. Among the charges were that he pronounced the *usus pauper* to be of the essence of the Minorite rule, that Christ was still living at the time the lance was thrust into his side, and that the rational soul has not the form of a body. Olivi's memory was defended by Ubertino da Casale, and the council passed no sentence upon his person.

In the bull *Exivi de paradiso*,[1] issued 1313, and famous in the history of the Franciscan order, Clement seemed to take the side of the Spirituals. It forbade the order or any of its members to accept bequests, possess vineyards, sell products from their gardens, build fine churches, or go to law. It permitted only " the use of necessity," *usus arctus* or *pauper*, and nothing beyond. The Minorites were to wear no shoes, ride only in cases of necessity, fast from Nov. 1 until Christmas, as well as every Friday, and possess a single mantle with a hood and one without a hood. Clement ordered the new general, Alexander of Alessandra, to turn over to Olivi's followers the convents of Narbonne, Carcas-

---

[1] It is uncertain whether this bull was made a part of the proceedings of the Œcumenical Council of Vienne. See Hefele, VI. 550, who decides for it, and Ehrle, *Archiv*, 1885, p. 540 sqq.

sonne and Béziers, but also ordered the Inquisition to punish
the Spirituals who refused submission.

In spite of the papal decree, the controversy was still being
carried on within the order with great heat, when John XXII.
came to the throne.   In the decretal *Quorumdam exegit*, and in
the bull *Sancta romana et universalis ecclesia*, Dec. 30, 1317,
John took a positive position against the Spirituals.   A few
weeks later, he condemned a formal list of their errors and
abolished all the convents under Spiritual management.
From this time on dates the application of the name
Fraticelli [1] to the Spirituals.   They refused to submit, and
took the position that even a pope had no right to modify the
Rule of St. Francis.   Michael of Cesena, the general of the
order, defended them.   Sixty-four of their number were summoned to Avignon.   Twenty-five refused to yield, and
passed into the hands of the Inquisition.   Four were burnt
as martyrs at Marseilles, May 7, 1318.   Others fled to Sicily.[2]

The chief interest of the controversy was now shifted to
the strictly theological question whether Christ and his
Apostles observed complete poverty.   This dispute threatened
to rend the wing of the Conventuals itself.   Michael of Cesena,
Ockam, and others, took the position that Christ and his
Apostles not only held no property as individuals, but held
none in common.   John, opposing this view, gave as arguments
the gifts of the Magi, that Christ possessed clothes and bought
food, the purse of Judas, and Paul's labor for a living.   In the
bull *Cum inter nonnullos*, 1323, and other bulls, John declared
it heresy to hold that Christ and the Apostles held no possessions.   Those who resisted this interpretation were pronounced,
1324, rebels and heretics.   John went farther, and gave back to
the order the right of possessing goods in fee simple, a right
which Innocent IV. had denied, and he declared that in things
which disappear in the using, such as eatables, no distinction
can be made between their use and their possession.   In 1326
John pronounced Olivi's commentary on the Apocalypse

---

[1] Hefele, VI. 581.   Ehrle: *Die Spiritualen* in *Archiv*, 1885, pp. 509–514.
[2] Ehrle : *Archiv*, pp. 156–158.   He adduces acts of Inquisition against the
Spirituals in Umbria, in the vicinity of Assisi, as late as 1341.

heretical.   The three Spiritual leaders, Cesena, Ockam, and Bonagratia were seized and held in prison until 1328, when they escaped and fled to Lewis the Bavarian at Pisa.   It was at this time that Ockam was said to have used to the emperor the famous words, " Do thou defend me with the sword and I will defend thee with the pen" — *tu me defendes gladio, ego te defendam calamo.*   They were deposed from their offices and included in the ban fulminated against the anti-pope, Peter of Corbara.   Later, Cesena submitted to the pope, as Ockam is also said to have done shortly before his death. Cesena died at Munich, 1342.   He committed the seal of the order to Ockam.   On his death-bed he is said to have cried out : " My God, what have I done ?   I have appealed against him who is the highest on the earth.   But look, O Father, at the spirit of truth that is in me which has not erred through the lust of the flesh but from great zeal for the seraphic order and out of love for poverty." Bonagratia also died in Munich.[1]

Later in the fourteenth century the Regular Observance grew again to considerable proportions, and in the beginning of the fifteenth century its fame was revived by the flaming preachers Bernardino of Siena and John of Capistrano.   The peace of the Franciscan order continued to be the concern of pope after pope until, in 1517, Leo X. terminated the struggle of three centuries by formally recognizing two distinct societies within the Franciscan body.   The moderate wing was placed under the Master-General of the Conventual Minorite Brothers, and was confirmed in the right to hold property.   The strict or Observant wing was placed under a Minister-General of the Whole Order of St. Francis.[2]   The latter takes precedence in processions and at other great functions, and holds his office for six years.

[1] See Riezler, p. 124.

[2] *Magister-generalis fratrum minorum conventualium* and *minister-generalis totius ordinis S. Francesci.*   The Capuchins, who are Franciscans, were recognized as a distinct order by Paul V., 1619.   Among the other schismatic Franciscan orders are the Recollect Fathers of France, who proceeded from the Recollect Convent of Nevers, and were recognized as a special body by Clement VIII., 1602.   These monks were prominent in mission work among the Indians in North America.

If the Spiritual Franciscans had been capable of taking secret delight in an adversary's misfortunes, they would have had occasion for it in the widely spread charge that John was a heretic.   At any rate, he came as near being a heretic as a pope can be.   His heresy concerned the nature of the beatific vision after death.   In a sermon on All Souls', 1331, he announced that the blessed dead do not see God until the general resurrection.   In at least two more sermons he repeated this utterance.   John, who was much given to theologizing, Ockam declared to be wholly ignorant in theology.[1] This Schoolman, Cesena, and others pronounced the view heretical.   John imprisoned an English Dominican who preached against him, and so certain was he of his case that he sent the Franciscan general, Gerardus Odonis, to Paris to get the opinion of the university.

The King, Philip VI., took a warm interest in the subject, opposed the pope, and called a council of theologians at Vincennes to give its opinion.   It decided that ever since the Lord descended into hades and released souls from that abode, the righteous have at death immediately entered upon the vision of the divine essence of the Trinity.[2]   Among the supporters of this decision was Nicolas of Lyra.   When official announcement of the decision reached the pope, he summoned a council at Avignon and set before it passages from the Fathers for and against his view.   They sat for five days, in December, 1333.   John then made a public announcement, which was communicated to the king and queen of France, that he had not intended to say anything in conflict with the Fathers and the orthodox Church and, if he had done so, he retracted his utterances.

The question was authoritatively settled by Benedict XII. in the bull *Benedictus deus*, 1336, which declared that the blessed dead — saints, the Apostles, virgins, martyrs, confessors who need no purgatorial cleansing — are, after death and before the resurrection of their bodies at the general

---

[1] In *facultate theologiæ omnino fuit ignarus.*   See Müller: *Kampf*, etc., I. 24, note.

[2] Mansi, XXV. 982–984.

judgment, with Christ and the angels, and that they behold the divine essence with naked vision.[1] Benedict declared that John died while he was preparing a decision.

The financial policy of John XXII. and his successors merits a chapter by itself. Here reference may be made to John's private fortune. He has had the questionable fame of not only having amassed a larger sum than any of his predecessors, but of having died possessed of fabulous wealth. Gregorovius calls him the Midas of Avignon. According to Villani, he left behind him 18,000,000 gold florins and 7,000,000 florins' worth of jewels and ornaments, in all 25,-000,000 florins, or $60,000,000 of our present coinage. This chronicler concludes with the remark that the words were no longer remembered which the Good Man in the Gospels spake to his disciples, "Lay up for yourselves treasure in heaven."[2] Recent investigations seem to cast suspicion upon this long-held view as an exaggeration. John's hoard may have amounted to not more than 750,000 florins, or $2,000,-000[3] of our money. If this be a safe estimate, it is still true that John was a shrewd financier and perhaps the richest man in Europe.

When John died he was ninety years old.

[1] *Divinam essentiam immediate, se bene et clare et aperte illis ostendentem.* *Mansi*, XXV. 986.

[2] XI. 20. Another writer, Galvaneus de La Flamma, Muratori, XII. 1009 (quoted by Haller, *Papsttum*, p. 104), says, John left 22,000,000 florins besides other "unrecorded treasure." This writer adds, the world did not have a richer Christian in it than John XXII.

[3] This is the figure reached by Ehrle, *Die 25 Millionen im Schatz Johann XXII.*, *Archiv*, 1889, pp. 155-166. It is based upon the contents of 15 coffers, opened in the year 1342 at the death of Benedict XII. These coffers contained John's treasure, and at that time yielded 750,000 florins. But it is manifestly uncertain how far John's savings had been reduced by Benedict, or whether these coffers were all that were left by John. For example, at his consecration, Benedict gave 100,000 florins to his cardinals, and 150,000 to the churches at Rome, and it is quite likely he drew upon John's hoard. The gold mitres, rings, and other ornaments which John's thrift amassed, were stored in other chests. Villani got his report from his brother, a Florentine banker in the employ of the curia at Avignon. It is difficult to understand how, in making his statement, he should have gone so wide of the truth as Ehrle suggests.

§ 8. *The Papal Office Assailed.*

To the pontificate of John XXII. belongs a second group of literary assailants of the papacy.   Going beyond Dante and John of Paris, they attacked the pope's spiritual functions.   Their assaults were called forth by the conflict with Lewis the Bavarian and the controversy with the Franciscan Spirituals.   Lewis' court became a veritable nest of anti-papal agitation and the headquarters of pamphleteering. Marsiglius of Padua was the cleverest and boldest of these writers, Ockam — a Schoolman rather than a practical thinker — the most copious.   Michael of Cesena[1] and Bona-gratia also made contributions to this literature.

Ockam sets forth his views in two works, *The Dialogue* and the *Eight Questions.*   The former is ponderous in thought and a monster in size.[2]   It is difficult, if at times possible, to detect the author's views in the mass of cumbersome disputation.   These views seem to be as follows : The papacy is not an institution which is essential to the being of the Church. Conditions arise to make it necessary to establish national churches.[3]   The pope is not infallible.   Even a legitimate pope may hold to heresy.   So it was with Peter, who was judaizing, and had to be rebuked by Paul, Liberius, who was an Arian, and Leo, who was arraigned for false doctrine by Hilary of Poictiers.   Sylvester II. made a compact with the devil.   One or the other, Nicolas III. or John XXII., was a heretic, for the one contradicted the other.   A general council may err just as popes have erred.   So did the second Council of Lyons and the Council of Vienne, which condemned the true Minorites.   The pope may be pronounced a heretic by a council or, if a council fails in its duty, the cardinals

---

[1] Riezler, p. 247 sq.   Three of these writings are in Goldast's *Monarchia* II., 1236 sqq.   Riezler's work, *Die literarischen Widersacher der Päpste* is the best treatment of the subject of this chapter.

[2] *The Dialogue,* which is printed in Goldast, is called by Riezler an almost unreadable monster, *ein kaum übersehbares Monstrum.*

[3] *Quod non est necesse, ut sub Christo sit unus rector totius ecclesiæ sed sufficit quod sint plures diversas regentes provincias.*   Quoted by Haller, p. 80.

may pronounce the decision.   In case the cardinals fail, the right to do so belongs to the temporal prince.   Christ did not commit the faith to the pope and the hierarchy, but to the Church, and somewhere within the Church the truth is always held and preserved.   Temporal power did not originally belong to the pope.   This is proved by Constantine's donation, for what Constantine gave, he gave for the first time. Supreme power in temporal and spiritual things is not in a single hand.   The emperor has full power by virtue of his election, and does not depend for it upon unction or coronation by the pope or any earthly confirmation of any kind.

More distinct and advanced were the utterances of Marsiglius of Padua.   His writings abound in incisive thrusts against the prevailing ecclesiastical system, and lay down the principles of a new order.   In the preparation of his chief work, the Defence of the Faith, — *Defensor pacis*, — he had the help of John of Jandun.[1]   Both writers were clerics, but neither of them monks.   Born about 1270 in Padua, Marsiglius devoted himself to the study of medicine, and in 1312 was rector of the University of Paris.   In 1325 or 1326 he betook himself to the court of Lewis the Bavarian.   The reasons are left to surmisal. He acted as the emperor's physician.   In 1328 he accompanied the emperor to Rome, and showed full sympathy with the measures taken to establish the emperor's authority.   He joined in the ceremonies of the emperor's coronation, the deposition of John XXII. and the elevation of the anti-pope, Peter of Corbara.   The pope had already denounced Marsiglius and John of Jandun[2] as " sons of perdition, the sons of Belial, those pestiferous individuals, beasts from the abyss," and summoned the Romans to make them prisoners.   Marsiglius was made

---

[1] Müller, I. 368, upon the basis of a note in a MS. copy in Vienna, places its composition before June 24, 1324 ; Riezler between 1324–1326.   John of Jandun's name is associated with the composition of the book in the papal bulls. However, the first person singular, *ego*, is used throughout.   According to Innocent VI., Marsiglius was much influenced by Ockam, then the leading teacher in France. This is inherently probable from their personal association in Paris and at the emperor's court and the community of many of their views.   See Haller, p. 78.   John of Jandun died probably 1328.   See Riezler, p. 56.   [2] See the bull of Oct. 23, 1327, Mirbt, *Quellen*, p. 152.

vicar of Rome by the emperor, and remained true to the principles stated in his tract, even when the emperor became a suppliant to the Avignon court.   Lewis even went so far as to
express to John XXII. his readiness to withdraw his protection from Marsiglius and the leaders of the Spirituals.   Later,
when his position was more hopeful, he changed his attitude
and gave them his protection at Munich.   But again, in his
letter submitting himself to Clement VI., 1343, the emperor
denied holding the errors charged against Marsiglius and
John, and declared his object in retaining them at his court
had been to lead them back to the Church.   The Paduan
died before 1343.[1]

The personal fortunes of Marsiglius are of small historical
concern compared with his book, which he dedicated to the
emperor.   The volume, which was written in two months,[2] was
as audacious as any of the earlier writings of Luther.   For
originality and boldness of statement the Middle Ages has
nothing superior to offer.   To it may be compared in modern
times Janus' attack on the doctrine of papal infallibility at
the time of the Vatican Council.[3]   Its Scriptural radicalism
was in itself a literary sensation.

In condemning the work, John XXII., 1327, pronounced as
contrary " to apostolic truth and all law " its statements that
Christ paid the stater to the Roman government as a matter

---

[1] In that year Clement spoke of Marsiglius as dead, Riezler, p. 122.   With
Ockam, Marsiglius defended the marriage of Lewis' son to Margaret of
Maultasch, in spite of the parties being within the bounds of consanguinity
forbidden by the Church.   His defence is found in Goldast, II. 1383–1391.
For Ockam's tract, see Riezler, p. 254.

[2] Riezler, p. 36.   It contains 150 folio pages in Goldast.   Riezler, 193 sq.,
gives a list of MS. copies.   Several French translations appeared.   Gregory
XI. in 1376 complained of one of them.   An Italian translation of 1363 is
found in a MS. at Florence, *Engl. Hist. Rev.*, 1905, p. 302.   The work was
translated into English under the title *The Defence of Peace translated out
of Latin into English* by Wyllyam Marshall, London, R. Wyer, 1535.

[3] Hergenröther-Kirsch, II. 755, says : *Unerhört in der christlichen Welt
waren die kühnen Behauptungen die sie zu Gunsten ihres Beschützers auf-
stellten.*   Pastor, I. 85, says that Marsiglius' theory of the omnipotence of
the state cut at the root of all individual and Church liberty and surpassed
in boldness, novelty, and keenness all the attacks which the position claimed
by the Church in the world had been called upon to resist up to that time.

of obligation, that Christ did not appoint a vicar, that an emperor has the right to depose a pope, and that the orders of the hierarchy are not of primitive origin.   Marsiglius had not spared epithets in dealing with John, whom he called "the great dragon, the old serpent."   Clement VI. found no less than 240 heretical clauses in the book, and declared that he had never read a worse heretic than Marsiglius.   The papal condemnations were reproduced by the University of Paris, which singled out for reprobation the statements that Peter is not the head of the Church, that the pope may be deposed, and that he has no right to inflict punishments without the emperor's consent.[1]

The *Defensor pacis* was a manifesto against the spiritual as well as the temporal assumptions of the papacy and against the whole hierarchical organization of the Church.   Its title is shrewdly chosen in view of the strifes between cities and states going on at the time the book was written, and due, as it claimed, to papal ambition and interference.   The peace of the Christian world would never be established so long as the pope's false claims were accepted.   The main positions are the following : [2] —

The state, which was developed out of the family, exists that men may live well and peaceably.   The people themselves are the source of authority, and confer the right to exercise it upon the ruler whom they select.   The functions of the priesthood are spiritual and educational.   Clerics are called upon to teach and to warn.   In all matters of civil misdemeanor they are responsible to the civil officer as other men are.   They should follow their Master by self-denial.   As St. Bernard said, the pope needs no wealth or outward display to be a true successor of Peter.

The function of binding and loosing is a declarative, not a judicial, function.   To God alone belongs the power to for-

---

[1] *Chartul. Univ. Paris.*, II. 301.

[2] Mirbt : *Quellen*, pp. 150–152, presents a convenient summary of Part III. of the *Defensor*. In this part a resumé is given by the author of the preceding portion of the work.   Marsiglius quotes Aristotle and other classic writers, Augustine and other Fathers, Hugo of St. Victor and other Schoolmen, but he ignores Thomas Aquinas, and never even mentions his name.

give sins and to punish.   No bishop or priest has a right to excommunicate or interdict individual freedom without the consent of the people or its representative, the civil legislator. The power to inflict punishments inheres in the congregation " of the faithful " — *fidelium.*   Christ said, " if thy brother offend against thee, tell it to the Church."   He did not say, tell it to the priest.   Heresy may be detected as heresy by the priest, but punishment for heresy belongs to the civil official and is determined upon the basis of the injury likely to be done by the offence to society.   According to the teaching of the Scriptures, no one can be compelled by temporal punishment and death to observe the precepts of the divine law.[1]

General councils are the supreme representatives of the Christian body, but even councils may err.   In them laymen should sit as well as clerics.   Councils alone have the right to canonize saints.

As for the pope, he is the head of the Church, not by divine appointment, but only as he is recognized by the state.   The claim he makes to fulness of power, *plenitudo potestatis,* contradicts the true nature of the Church.   To Peter was committed no greater authority than was committed to the other Apostles.[2]   Peter can be called the Prince of the Apostles only on the ground that he was older than the rest or more steadfast than they.   He was the bishop of Antioch, not the founder of the Roman bishopric.   Nor is his presence in Rome susceptible of proof.   The pre-eminence of the bishop of Rome depends upon the location of his see at the capital of the empire.   As for sacerdotal power, the pope has no more of it than any other cleric, as Peter had no more of it than the other Apostles.[3]

The grades of the hierarchy are of human origin.   Bishops

---

[1] *Ad observanda præcepta divinæ legis poena vel supplicio temporali nemo evangelica scriptura compelli præcipitur,* Part III. 3.

[2] *Nullam potestatem eoque minus coactivam jurisdictionem habuit Petrus a Deo immediate super apostolos reliquos,* II. 15.   This is repeated again and again.

[3] *Non plus sacerdotalis auctoritatis essentialis habet Rom. episcopus, quam alter sacerdos quilibet sicut neque beatus Petrus amplius ex hac habuit ceteris apostolis,* II. 14.

and priests were originally equal. Bishops derive their authority immediately from Christ.

False is the pope's claim to jurisdiction over princes and
nations, a claim which was the fruitful source of national
strifes and wars, especially in Italy. If necessary, the emperor may depose a pope. This is proved by the judgment
passed by Pilate upon Christ. The state may, for proper
reasons, limit the number of clerics. The validity of Constantine's donation Marsiglius rejected, as Dante and John of Paris
had done before, but he did not surmise that the Isidorean
decretals were an unblushing forgery, a discovery left for
Laurentius Valla to make a hundred years later.

As for the Scriptures, Marsiglius declares them to be the ultimate source of authority. They do not derive that authority
from the Church. The Church gets its authority from them.
In cases of disputed interpretation, it is for a general council
to settle what the true meaning of Scripture is.[1] Obedience
to papal decretals is not a condition of salvation. If that
were so, how is it that Clement V. could make the bull *Unam
sanctam* inoperative for France and its king ? Did not that
bull declare that submission to the pope is for every creature
a condition of salvation ! Can a pope set aside a condition
of salvation? The case of Liberius proves that popes may be
heretics. As for the qualifications of bishops, archbishops,
and patriarchs, not one in ten of them is a doctor of theology.
Many of the lower clergy are not even acquainted with grammar. Cardinals and popes are chosen not from the ranks of
theologians, but lawyers, *causidici.* Youngsters are made cardinals who love pleasure and are ignorant in studies.

Marsiglius quotes repeatedly such passages as " My kingdom is not of this world," John 17 : 36, and " Render unto
Cæsar the things which are Cæsar's ; and to God the things
which are God's," Matt. 22 : 21. These passages and others,
such as John 6 : 15, 19 : 11, Luke 12 : 14, Matt. 17 : 27, Rom.
13, he opposes to texts which were falsely interpreted to the
advantage of the hierarchy, such as Matt. 16 : 19, Luke 22 : 38,
John 21 : 15–17.

---

[1] *Interpretatio ex communi concilio fidelium facta,* etc., Part III. 1.

If we overlook his doctrine of the supremacy of the state over the Church, the Paduan's views correspond closely with those held in Protestant Christendom to-day.   Christ, he said, excluded his Apostles, disciples, and bishops or presbyters from all earthly dominion, both by his example and his words.[1] The abiding principles of the *Defensor* are the final authority of the Scriptures, the parity of the priesthood and its obligation to civil law, the human origin of the papacy, the exclusively spiritual nature of priestly functions, and the body of Christian people in the state or Church as the ultimate source of authority on earth.

Marsiglius has been called by Catholic historians the forerunner of Luther and Calvin.[2] He has also been called by one of them the "exciting genius of modern revolution."[3] Both of these statements are not without truth.   His programme was not a scheme of reform.   It was a proclamation of complete change such as the sixteenth century witnessed. A note in a Turin manuscript represents Gerson as saying that the book is wonderfully well grounded and that the author was most expert in Aristotle and also in theology, and went to the roots of things.[4]

The tractarian of Padua and Thomas Aquinas were only 50 years apart.   But the difference between the searching epigrams of the one and the slow, orderly argument of the other is as wide as the East is from the West, the directness of mod-

[1] *Exclusit se ipsum et app. ac discipulos etiam suos ipsorumque successores, consequenter episcopos seu presbyteros, ab omni principatu seu mundano regimine exemplo et sermone,* II. 4.

[2] Döllinger: *Kirchengesch.* II. 259, 2d ed., 1843, says, "In the *Defensor* the Calvinistic system was, in respect to Church power and constitution, already marked out." Pastor, 1. 85, says, "If Calvin depended upon any of his predecessors for his principles of Church government, it was upon the keen writer of the fourteenth century."

[3] Pastor, I. 84, shifts this notoriety from Huss to Marsiglius. Riezler, p. 232, and Haller, p. 77, compare Marsiglius' keenness of intellect with the Reformers', but deny to him their religious warmth.

[4] *Est liber mirabiliter bene fundatus. Et fuit homo multum peritus in doctrina Aristoteleia,* etc., *Engl. Hist. Rev.,* p. 298.   The Turin MS. dates from 1416, that is, contemporary with Gerson.   In this MS. John of Paris' *De potestate* is bound up with the *Defensor.*

ern thought from the cumbersome method of mediæval scholasticism.   It never occurred to Thomas Aquinas to think out beyond the narrow enclosure of Scripture interpretation built up by other Schoolmen and mediæval popes.   He buttressed up the régime he found realized before him.   He used the old misinterpretations of Scripture and produced no new idea on government.   Marsiglius, independent of the despotism of ecclesiastical dogma, went back to the free and elastic principles of the Apostolic Church government.   He broke the moulds in which the ecclesiastical thinking of centuries had been cast, and departed from Augustine in claiming for heretics a rational and humane treatment.   The time may yet come when the Italian people will follow him as the herald of a still better order than that which they have, and set aside the sacerdotal theory of the Christian ministry as an invention of man.[1]

Germany furnished a strong advocate of the independent rights of the emperor, in Lupold of Bebenburg, who died in 1363.   He remained dean of Würzburg until he was made bishop of Bamberg in 1353.   But he did not attack the spiritual jurisdiction of the Apostolic See.   Lupold's chief work was The Rights of the Kingdom and Empire — *de juribus regni et imperii*, — written after the declarations of Rense.   It has been called the oldest attempt at a theory of the rights of the German state.[2]   Lupold appeals to the events of history.

In defining the rights of the empire, this author asserts that an election is consummated by the majority of the electors and that the emperor does not stand in need of confirmation by the pope.   He holds his authority independently from God.   Charlemagne exercised imperial functions before he was

---

[1] Compared with Wyclif, a pamphleteer as keen as he, Marsiglius did not enter into the merits of distinctly theological doctrine nor see the deep connection between the dogma of transubstantiation and sacramental penance and papal tyranny as the English reformer did.   But so far as questions of government are concerned, he went as far as Wyclif or farther.   See the comparison, as elaborated by Poole, p. 275.

[2] *Der älteste Versuch einer Theorie des deutschen Staatsrechts*, Riezler, p. 180.   Two other works by Lupold have come down to us.   See Riezler, pp. 180–192.

anointed and crowned by Leo.   The oath the emperor takes
to the pope is not the oath of fealty such as a vassal renders,
but a promise to protect him and the Church.   The pope has
no authority to depose the emperor.   His only prerogative is
to announce that he is worthy of deposition.   The right to
depose belongs to the electors.   As for Constantine's donation, it is plain Constantine did not confer the rule of the
West upon the bishop of Rome, for Constantine divided both
the West and the East among his sons.   Later, Theodosius
and other emperors exercised dominion in Rome.   The notice
of Constantine's alleged gift to Sylvester has come through
the records of Sylvester and has the appearance of being
apocryphal.

The papal assailants did not have the field all to themselves.   The papacy also had vigorous literary champions.
Chief among them were Augustinus Triumphus and Alvarus Pelagius.[1]   The first dedicated his leading work to John
XXII., and the second wrote at the pope's command.   The
modern reader will find in these tracts the crassest exposition of the extreme claims of the papacy, satisfying to the
most enthusiastic ultramontane, but calling for apology from
sober Catholic historians.[2]

[1] For the papal tracts by Petrus de Palude and Konrad of Megenberg, d.
1374, see Riezler, p. 287 sqq.   The works are still unpublished.   Konrad's
Planctus ecclesiæ is addressed to Benedict in these lines, which make the
pope out to be the summit of the earth, the wonder of the world, the door-
keeper of heaven, a treasury of delights, the only sun for the world.

> " *Flos et apex mundi, qui totius esse rotundi*
> *Nectare dulcorum conditus aromate morum*
> *Orbis papa stupor, clausor cœli et reserator,*
> *Tu sidus clarum, thesaurus deliciarum*
> *Sedes sancta polus, tu mundo sol modo solus.*"

[2] Pastor, I. 85.   Hergenröther-Kirsch, II. 757, complains that these two
authors push matters beyond the limits of truth, "making the pope a semi-
god, the absolute ruler of the world."   See Haller, p. 82 sq.   Haller says it
is a common thing among the common people in Italy for a devout man to
call the pope a god upon earth, *un Dio in terra.*   One of the smaller tracts
already referred to is printed by Finke in *Aus den Tagen*, etc., LXIX–XCIX,
and three others by Scholz, *Publizistik*, pp. 486–516.   See Scholz's criticism,
pp. 172–189.   Finke, p. 250, is in doubt about the authorship.

Triumphus, an Italian, born in Ancona, 1243, made archbishop of Nazareth and died at Naples, 1328, was a zealous advocate of Boniface VIII.   His leading treatise, **The Power of the Church,** — *Summa de potestate ecclesiastica,* — vindicates John XXII. for his decision on the question of evangelical poverty and for his opposition to the emperor's dominion in Italy.[1]   The pope has unrestricted power on the earth.   It is so vast that even he himself cannot know fully what he is able to do.[2]   His judgment is the judgment of God. Their tribunals are one.[3]   His power of granting indulgences is so great that, if he so wished, he could empty purgatory of its denizens provided that conditions were complied with.[4]

In spiritual matters he may err, because he remains a man, and when he holds to heresy, he ceases to be pope.   Council cannot depose him nor any other human tribunal, for the pope is above all and can be judged by none.   But, being a heretic, he ceases, *ipso facto*, to be pope, and the condition then is as it would be after one pope is dead and his successor not yet elected.

The pope himself may choose an emperor, if he so please, and may withdraw the right of election from the electors or depose them from office.   As vicar of God, he is above all kings and princes.

The Spanish Franciscan, Alvarus Pelagius, was not always as extravagant as his Augustinian contemporary.[5]   He was professor of law at Perugia.   He fled from Rome at the approach of Lewis the Bavarian, 1328, was then appointed papal peni-

---

[1] For edd. of Triumphus' tract, see Potthast, *Bibl. Hist.* under Triumphus.   Riezler, p. 286, dates the tract 1324–1328, Haller, p. 83, 1322, Scholz, p. 172, 1320.   See Poole, 252 sq.

[2] *Nec credo, quod papa possit scire totum quod potest facere per potentiam suam,* 32. 3, quoted by Döllinger, Papstthum, p. 433.

[3] This famous passage runs *sententia papæ sententia Dei una sententia est, quia unum consistorium est ipsius papæ et ipsius Dei . . . cujus consistorii claviger et ostiarius est ipse papa.*   See Schwab, *Gerson,* p. 24.

[4] *Totum purgatorium evacuare potest,* 3. 23.   Döllinger, p. 451, says of Triumphus' tract that on almost every page the Church is represented as a dwarf with the head of a giant, that is, the pope.

[5] He incorporated into his work entire sections from James of Viterbo, *De regimine christiano,* Scholz, p. 151.

tentiary at Avignon, and later bishop of the Portuguese diocese of Silves.   His Lament over the Church, — *de planctu
ecclesiæ*,[1] — while exalting the pope to the skies, bewails the
low spiritual estate into which the clergy and the Church had
fallen.   Christendom, he argues, which is but one kingdom,
can have but one head, the pope.   Whoever does not accept
him as the head does not accept Christ.   And whosoever,
with pure and believing eye, sees the pope, sees Christ himself.[2] Without communion with the pope there is no salvation.   He wields both swords as Christ did, and in him the
passage of Jer. 1:10 is fulfilled, "I have this day set thee
over the nations and over the kingdoms to pluck up
and to break down, to destroy and to overthrow, to build
and to plant."   Unbelievers, also, Alvarus asserts to be legally under the pope's jurisdiction, though they may not be
so in fact, and the pope may proceed against them as God
did against the Sodomites.   Idolaters, Jews, and Saracens are
alike amenable to the pope's authority and subject to his
punishments.   He rules, orders, disposes and judges all
things as he pleases.   His will is highest wisdom, and what
he pleases to do has the force of law.[3] Wherever the supreme pontiff is, there is the Roman Church, and he cannot
be compelled to remain in Rome.[4] He is the source of all
law and may decide what is the right.   To doubt this means
exclusion from life eternal.

As the vicar of Christ, the pope is supreme over the state.
He confers the sword which the prince wields.   As the body
is subject to the soul, so princes are subject to the pope.
Constantine's donation made the pope, in fact, monarch over
the Occident.   He transferred the empire to Charlemagne in
trust.   The emperor's oath is an oath of fealty and homage.

---

[1] Döllinger, p. 433, places its composition in 1329, Riezler, 1331, Haller, between 1330–1332.   Alvarus issued three editions, the third at Santiago, 1340.

[2] *Vere papa representat Christum in terris, ut qui videt cum oculo contem-
plativo et fideli videat et Christum*, I. 13.

[3] *Apud eum est pro ratione voluntas, et quod ei placet legis habet vigorem*,
I. 45.

[4] *Unum est consistorium et tribunal Christi et papæ*, I. 29. *Ubicunque est
papa, ibi est eccles. Rom.* . . . .   *Non cogitur stare Romæ*, I. 31.

The views of Augustinus Triumphus and Alvarus followed the papal assertion and practice of centuries, and the assent or argument of the Schoolmen.   Marsiglius had the sanction of Scripture rationally interpreted, and his views were confirmed by the experiences of history.   After the lapse of nearly 500 years, opinion in Christendom remains divided, and the most extravagant language of Triumphus and Alvarus is applauded, and Marsiglius, the exponent of modern liberty and of the historical sense of Scripture, continues to be treated as a heretic.

§ 9. *The Financial Policy of the Avignon Popes.*

The most notable feature of the Avignon period of the papacy, next to its subserviency to France, was the development of the papal financial system and the unscrupulous traffic which it plied in spiritual benefits and ecclesiastical offices. The theory was put into practice that every spiritual favor has its price in money.   It was John XXII.'s achievement to reduce the taxation of Christendom to a finely organized system.

The papal court had a proper claim for financial support on all parts of the Latin Church, for it ministered to all.   This just claim gave way to a practice which made it seem as if Christendom existed to sustain the papal establishment in a state of luxury and ease.   Avignon took on the aspect of an exchange whose chief business was getting money, a vast bureau where privileges, labelled as of heavenly efficacy, were sold for gold.   Its machinery for collecting moneys was more extensive and intricate than the machinery of any secular court of the age.   To contemporaries, commercial transactions at the central seat of Christendom seemed much more at home than services of religious devotion.

The mind of John XXII. ran naturally to the counting-house and ledger system.[1]   He came from Cahors, the town noted for its brokers and bankers.   Under his favor the seeds of com-

---

[1] Haller says, p. 103, the characteristic of John's pontificate was finance, *der Fiskalismus.*   Tangl, p. 40, compares his commercial instincts to the concern for high ideals which animated Gregory VII., Alexander III., and Innocent III.   See vol. V, I., pp. 787, sqq.

mercialism in the dispensation of papal appointments sown
in preceding centuries grew to ripe fruitage.   Simony was
an old sin.   Gregory VII. fought against it.   John legalized
its practice.

Freewill offerings and Peter's pence had been made to
popes from of old.   States, held as fiefs of the papal chair, had
paid fixed tribute.   For the expenses of the crusades, Innocent III. had inaugurated the system of taxing the entire
Church.   The receipts from this source developed the love of
money at the papal court and showed its power, and, no matter how abstemious a pope might be in his own habits, greed
grew like a weed in his ecclesiastical household.   St. Bernard, d. 1153, complained bitterly of the cupidity of the
Romans, who made every possible monetary gain out of the
spiritual favors of which the Vatican was the dispenser.   By
indulgence, this appetite became more and more exacting, and
under John and his successors the exploitation of Christendom
was reduced by the curia to a fine art.

The theory of ecclesiastical appointments, held in the Avignon period, was that, by reason of the fulness of power
which resides in the Apostolic See, the pope may dispense all
the dignities and benefices of the Christian world.   The pope
is absolute in his own house, that is, the Church.

This principle had received its full statement from Clement
IV., 1265.[1]   Clement's bull declared that the supreme pontiff
is superior to any customs which were in vogue of filling
Church offices and conflicted with his prerogative.   In particular he made it a law that all offices, dignities, and benefices
were subject to papal appointment which became vacant *apud
sedem apostolicam* or *in curia*, that is, while the holders were
visiting the papal court.   This law was modified by Gregory
X. at the Council of Lyons, 1274, in such a way as to restore
the right of election, provided the pope failed to make an appointment within a month.[2]   Boniface VIII., 1295, again ex-

---

[1] *Licet ecclesiarum.*   See *Lib. sextus*, III. 4, 2.   Friedberg's ed., II. 102,
Lux, p. 5, says *romanus pontifex supremus collator, ad quem plenaria de
omnibus totius orbis beneficiis eccles. dispositio jure naturo pertinet*, etc.

[2] Lux, p. 12 ; Hefele : *Conciliengesch.* VI. 151.

tended the enactment by putting in the pope's hands all livings
whose occupants died within two days' journey of the curia,
wherever it might at the time be.[1] Innocent IV. was the
first pope to exercise the right of reservation or collation on
a large scale.   In 1248, out of 20 places in the cathedral of
Constance, 17 were occupied by papal appointees, and there
were 14 "expectants" under appointment in advance of the
deaths of the occupants.   In 1255, Alexander IV. limited the
number of such expectants to 4 for each church.   In 1265,
Clement IV forbade all elections in England in the usual way
until his commands were complied with, and reserved them to
himself. The same pontiff, on the pretext of disturbances going
on in Sicily, made a general reservation of all appointments in
the realm, otherwise subject to episcopal or capitular choice.
Urban IV. withdrew the right of election from the Ghibelline
cities of Lombardy; Martin IV. and Honorius IV. applied the
same rule to the cathedral appointments of Sicily and Aragon;
Honorius IV. monopolized all the appointments of the Latin
Church in the East; and Boniface VIII., in view of Philip IV.'s
resistance, reserved to himself the appointments to all "cathedral and regular churches" in France. Of 16 French sees which
became vacant, 1295–1301, only one was filled in the usual way
by election.[2]

With the haughty assumption of Clement IV.'s bull and
the practice of later popes, papal writers fell in.   Augustinus
Triumphus, writing in 1324, asserted that the pope is above
all canon law and has the right to dispose of all ecclesiastical
places.[3]   The papal system of appointments included provisions, expectances, and reservations.[4]

[1] Lux, p. 13 ; Friedberg: *Reservationen* in Herzog, XVI. 672.

[2] Lux, p. 17 sqq., and Haller, p. 38, with authorities.

[3] *Verum super ipsum jus, potest dispensare*, etc.   Quoted by Gieseler,
II. 123.

[4] A provision, that is, *providere ecclesiæ de episcopo* signified in the
first instance a promotion, and afterwards the papal right to supersede appointments made in the usual way by the pope's own arbitrary appointment.
The methods of papal appointment are given in *Liber sextus*, I. 16, 18 ;
Friedberg's ed., II. 959. See Stubbs, *Const. Hist.*, III. 320. "Collations"
was also used as a general term to cover this papal privilege. The formulas

In setting aside the vested rights of chapters and other electors, the pope often joined hands with kings and princes. In the Avignon period a regular election by a chapter was the exception.[1]   The Chronicles of England and France teem with usurped cases of papal appointment. In 1322 the pope reserved to himself all the appointments in episcopal, cathedral, and abbey churches, and of all priors in the sees of Aquileja, Ravenna, Milan, Genoa, and Pisa.[2]   In 1329 he made such reservation for the German dioceses of Metz, Toul, and Verdun, and in 1339 for Cologne.[3]   There was no living in Latin Christendom which was safe from the pope's hands.   There were not places enough to satisfy all the favorites of the papal household and the applicants pressed upon the pope's attention by kings and princes.   The spiritual and administrative qualities of the appointees were not too closely scrutinized.   Frenchmen were appointed to sees in England, Germany, Denmark, and other countries, who were utterly unfamiliar with the languages of those countries.   Marsiglius complains of these " monstrosities " and, among other unfit appointments, mentions the French bishops of Winchester and Lund, neither of whom knew English or Danish.   The archbishop of Lund, after plundering his diocese, returned to Southern France.

To the supreme right of appointment was added the supreme right to tax the clergy and all ecclesiastical property. The supreme right to exercise authority over kings, the supreme right to set aside canonical rules, the supreme right to make appointments in the Church, the supreme right to tax Church property, these were, in their order, the rights asserted by the popes of the Middle Ages.   The scandal growing out

of this period commonly ran *de apostol. potestatis plenitudine reservamus.* See John's bull of July 30, 1322, Lux, p. 62 sq.   *Rogare, monere, precipere* are the words generally used by pope Innocent III., 1198–1216, see Hinschius, II. 114 sq.   Alexander III. used the expression *ipsum commendamus rogantes et rogando mandantes* and others like it.   Hinschius, III. 116, dates insistence on reservations as a right from the time of Lucius III., 1181–1185.

[1] Haller, p. 107.

[2] Lux, p. 61 sq.   This author, pp. 59–106, gives 57 documents not before published, containing reservations by John XXII. and his successors.

[3] Kirsch : *Kollektorien*, p. xxv sq.

of this unlimited right of taxation called forth the most vigorous complaints from clergy and laity, and was in large part the cause which led to the summoning of the three great Reformatory councils of the fifteenth century.[1]

Popes had acted upon this theory of jurisdiction over the property of the Church long before John XXII. They levied taxes for crusades in the Orient, or to free Italy from rebels for the papal state. They gave their sanction to princes and kings to levy taxes upon the Church for secular purposes, especially for wars.[2] In the bull *Clericis laicos*, Boniface did not mean to call in question the propriety of the Church's contributing to the necessities of the state. What he demanded was that he himself should be recognized as arbiter in such matters, and it was this demand which gave offence to the French king and to France itself. The question was much discussed whether the pope may commit simony. Thomas Aquinas gave an affirmative answer. Alvarus Pelagius[3] thought differently, and declared that the pope is exempt from the laws and canons which treat of simony. Augustinus Triumphus took the same ground.[4] The pope is not bound by laws. He is above laws. Simony is not possible to him.

In estimating the necessities of the papal court, which justified the imposition of customs, the Avignon popes were no longer their own masters. They were the creatures of the camera and the hungry horde of officials and sycophants

[1] See Hergenröther-Kirsch, II. 762. K. Müller: *Kirchengesch.*, II. 45. Kirsch: *Finanzverwaltung*, p. 70. Pastor, in the 1st ed. of his *Hist. of the Popes*, I. 63, said *das unheilvolle System der Annaten, Reservationen und Expektanzen hat seit Johann XXII. zur Ausbildung gelangt.*

[2] The course of Clement V., in allowing grants to Philip the Fair, Charles of Valois, and other princes, was followed by John. In 1316 he granted to the king of France a tenth and annates for four years, in 1326 a tenth for two years, and in 1333 a tenth for six years. The English king, in 1317, was given a share of the tenth appointed by the Council of Vienne for a crusade and at the same time one-half of the annates. Again, in the years 1319, 1322, 1330, a tenth was accorded to the same sovereign. See Haller, p. 116 sq.

[3] *De planctu eccles.*, II. 14, *papa legibus loquentibus de simonia et canonibus solutus est.*

[4] V. 3, *certum est, summum pontificem canonicam simoniam a jure positivo prohibitam non posse committere, quia ipse est supra jus et eum jura positiva non ligant.*

whose clamor filled the papal offices day and night. These retainers were not satisfied with bread. Every superior office in Christendom had its value in terms of gold and silver. When it was filled by papal appointment, a befitting fee was the proper recognition. If a favor was granted to a prince in the appointment of a favorite, the papal court was pretty sure to seize some new privilege as a compensation for itself. Precedent was easily made a permanent rule. Where the pope once invaded the rights of a chapter, he did not relinquish his hold, and an admission fee once fixed was not renounced. We may not be surprised at the rapacity which was developed at the papal court. That was to be expected. It grew out of the false papal theory and the abiding qualities of human nature.[1]

The details governing the administration of the papal finances John set forth in two bulls of 1316 and 1331. His scheme fixed the financial policy of the papacy and sacred college.[2] The sources from which the papacy drew its revenues in the fourteenth century were: (1) freewill offerings, so called, given for ecclesiastical appointments and other papal favors, called visitations, annates, *servitia*; and (2) tributes from feudal states such as Naples, Sicily, Sardinia, and England, and the revenues from the papal state in Italy.[3] The moneys so received were apportioned between four parties, the pope, the college of cardinals, and their two households. Under John XXII. the freewill offerings, so called, came to be regarded as obligatory fees. Every papal gift had its compensation. There was a list of prices, and it remained in force till changed on the basis of new estimates of the incomes of benefices. To answer objections, John XXII., in his bull of 1331, insisted that the prices set upon such favors were not a charge for the grace imparted, but a charge for the labor required for writing the pertinent documents.[4] But the declaration did

---

[1] Kirsch : *Kollektorien*, p. xii sq. and other Catholic writers make some defence of John's financial measures on the ground that the sources of income from the State of the Church dried up when the papacy was transferred to Avignon.

[2] For the details, see Tangl, p. 20 sqq.   [3] See vol. V. 1, p. 787 sqq.

[4] *Non habita consideratione ad valorem beneficii, de quo fiet gratia sed ad laborem scripturæ dumtaxat.* See Tangl, p. 21.

not remove the ill odor of the practice.   The taxes levied were
out of all proportion to the actual cost of the written documents, and the privileges were not to be had without money.

These payments were regularly recorded in registers or
ledgers kept by the papal secretaries of the camera.   The details of the papal exchequer, extant in the Archives of the
Vatican, have only recently been subjected to careful investigation through the liberal policy of Leo XIII., and have made
possible a new chapter in works setting forth the history
of the Church in this fourteenth century.[1]

These studies confirm the impression left by the chroniclers
and tract-writers of the fourteenth century.   The money
dealings of the papal court were on a vast scale, and the
transactions were according to strict rules of merchandise.[2]
Avignon was a great money centre.   Spiritual privileges were
vouched for by carefully worded and signed contracts and
receipts.   The papal commercial agents went to all parts of
Europe.

Archbishop, bishop, and abbot paid for the letters confirming their titles to their dignities.   The appointees to lower
clerical offices did the same.   There were fees for all sorts of
concessions, dispensations and indulgences, granted to layman
and to priest.   The priest born out of wedlock, the priest
seeking to be absent from his living, the priest about to be

[1] Woker took up the study in 1878, and has been followed by a number of
scholars such as Tangl, Gottlob, Goeller, Haller, Baumgarten, Schulte, and
especially Dr. Kirsch, professor of church history in the Catholic University
of Freiburg, Switzerland.   See, for a full description, Baumgarten, pp. v-
xxiii.   The subject involves a vast array of figures and commercial briefs of
all kinds, and includes the organization of the camera, the system of collection, the graduated scales of prices, the transmission of moneys to Avignon,
the division of the receipts between the pope and the cardinals, the values of
the numerous coins, etc.   Garampi, a keeper of the Vatican Archives, in the
eighteenth century arranged these registers according to countries.   See
Kirsch, *Kollektorien*, [p. vii, and *Rückkehr*, p. xli-l; Tangl, vi sqq. ; Baumgarten, viii, x sqq.

[2] Kirsch: *Kollektorien*, p. vii, note, gives four different headings under
which the moneys were recorded, namely: (1) census and visitations ;
(2) bulls ; (3) *servitia communia;* (4) sundry sources.   He also gives the
entries under which disbursements were entered, such as the kitchen, books
and parchments, palfreys, journeys, wars, etc.

ordained before the canonical age, all had to have a dispensation, and these cost money.[1] The larger revenues went directly
into the papal treasury and the treasury of the camera.   The
smaller fees went to notaries, doorkeepers, to individual cardinals, and other officials.   These intermediaries stood in a long
line with palms upturned.   To use a modern term, it was an
intricate system of graft.   The beneficiaries were almost endless.   The large body of lower officials are usually designated
in the ledgers by the general term "familiars" of the pope or
camera.[2] The notaries, or copyists, received stipulated sums
for every document they transcribed and service they performed.   However exorbitant the demands might seem, the
petitioners were harried by delays and other petty annoyances
till in sheer weariness they yielded.

The taxes levied upon the higher clergy were usually paid
at Avignon by the parties in person. For the collection of the
annates from the lower clergy and of tithes and other general
taxes, collectors and subcollectors were appointed.   We find
these officials in different parts of Europe.   They had their
fixed salaries, and sent periodical reckonings to the central
bureau at Avignon.[3] The transmission of the moneys they collected was often a dangerous business.   Not infrequently the
carriers were robbed on their way, and the system came into
vogue of employing merchant and banking houses to do this
business, especially Italian firms, which had representatives in
Northern and Central Europe.   The ledgers show a great
diversity in the names and value of the coins.   And it was a
nice process to estimate the values of these moneys in the
terms of the more generally accepted standards.[4]

[1] Tangl, 74 sq.

[2] As an example of the host of these officials who had to be fed, see Tangl,
pp. 64–67. He gives a list of the fees paid by agents of the city of Cologne,
which was seeking certain bulls in 1393. The title "secretary" does not
occur till the reign of Benedict XII., 1338. Goeller, p. 46.

[3] One of the allowances made by John XXII. for collectors was 5 gold florins
a day. Kirsch : *Kollektorien*, VII. sqq., XLIX. sqq. Kirsch gives the official
ledgers of papal collectors in Basel, pp. 4–32, and other sees of Germany.
Sometimes the bishop acted as collector in his diocese, Goeller, p. 71.

[4] For elaborate comparisons of the value of the different coins of the fourteenth century, see Kirsch, *Kollektorien*, LXXVIII. and *Rückkehr*, p. xli sqq.

The offerings made by prelates at their visits to the papal
see, called *visitationes*,[1] were divided equally between the papal
treasury and the cardinals.   From the lists it appears that the
archbishops of York paid every three years " 300 marks sterling, or 1200 gold florins."   Every two years the archbishops
of Canterbury paid " 300 marks sterling, or 1500 gold florins";
the archbishop of Tours paid 400 pounds Tournois; of Rheims,
500 pounds Tournois; of Rouen, 1000 pounds Tournois.[2]   The
archbishop of Armagh, at his visitation in 1301, paid 50 silver
marks, or 250 gold florins.   In 1350 the camera claimed from
Armagh back payments for fifty years.[3]   Presumably no
bishop of that Irish diocese had made a visit in that interval.
Whether the claim was honored or not, is not known.

The *servitia communia*, or payments made by archbishops,
bishops, and abbots on their confirmation to office, were also
listed, according to a fixed scale.   The voluntary idea had
completely disappeared before a fixed assessment.[4]   Such a
dignitary was called an *electus* until he had paid off the

Gottlob, pp. 133, 174 sq., etc.   Baumgarten, CCXI sqq.   The silver mark, the
gold florin, and the pound Tournois were among the larger coins most current.
One mark was worth 4 or 5 gold florins, or 8 pounds Tournois.   The *grossus
Turonensis* was equal to about 25 cents of our value.   See Tangl, 14.   For the
different estimates of marks in florins, see Baumgarten, CXXI.   The gold
florin had the face value of $2.50 of our money, or nearly 10 marks German
coinage.   See Kirsch, *Kollektorien*, p. lxx; *Rückkehr*, p. xlv; Gottlob,
Servitientaxe, p. 176 ; Baumgarten, p. ccxiii ; Tangl, 14, etc.   Kirsch gives the
purchasing price of money in the fourteenth century as four times what it now
is, *Finanzverwaltung*, p. 56.   The gold mark in 1370 was worth 62 gold florins,
the silver mark 5 florins, Kirsch : *Rückkehr*, p. xlv.   Kirsch : *Rückkehr*,
pp. l-lxi, gives a very elaborate and valuable list of the prices of commodities and wages in 1370 from the Vatican ledger accounts.   Urban V.'s agents
bought two horses for 117 florins gold and two mules for 90 florins.   They
paid 1 gold florin for 12 pairs of shoes and 1 pair of boots.   A salma of wheat
— equal to 733 loaves of bread — cost 4 florins, or $10 in our money.   The
keeper of the papal stables received 120 gold florins a year.   The senator of
Rome received from Gregory XI. 500 gold florins a month.   A watchman of
the papal palace, 7 gold florins a month.   Carpenters received from 12-18
shillings *Provis*, or 60-80 cents, 47 of these coins being equal to 1 gold florin.

[1] *Visitationes ad limina apostolorum*, that is, visits to Rome.

[2] See Baumgarten, CXXI.; Kirsch : *Finanzverwaltung*, p. 22 sq.

[3] Baumgarten, p. cxxii.

[4] Gottlob, *Servitien*, p. 30 sqq., 75-93 ; Baumgarten, p. xcvii sqq.

tax.[1] In certain cases the tax was remitted on account of the poverty of the ecclesiastic, and in the ledgers the entry was made, " not taxed on account of poverty," *non taxata propter paupertatem*. The amount of this tax seems to have varied, and was sometimes one-third of the income and sometimes a larger portion.[2] In the fourteenth century the following sees paid *servitia* as follows : Mainz, 5,000 gold florins; Treves, 7,000; Cologne, 10,000; Narbonne, 10,000. On the basis of a new valuation, Martin V. in 1420 raised the taxation of the sees of Mainz and Treves to 10,000 florins each, or $25,000 of our money, so that they corresponded to the assessment made from of old upon Cologne.[3] When an incumbent died without having met the full tax, his successor made up the deficit in addition to paying the assessment for his own confirmation.[4]

The following cases will give some idea of the annoyances to which bishops and abbots were put who travelled to Avignon to secure letters of papal confirmation to their offices. In 1334, the abbot-elect of St. Augustine, Canterbury, had to wait in Avignon from April 22 to Aug. 9 to get his confirmation, and it cost him 148 pounds sterling.   John IV., abbot-elect of St. Albans, in 1302 went for consecration to Rome, accompanied by four monks.   He arrived May 6, presented his case to Boniface VIII. in person at Anagni, May 9, and did not get back to London till Aug. 1, being all the while engaged in the process of getting his papers properly prepared and cer-

<hr>

[1] Gottlob, p. 130.

[2] Kirsch : *Finanzverwaltung*, and Baumgarten, p. xcvii, make it one-third. Gottlob, p. 120, says it was sometimes more.

[3] Baumgarten, p. cvi, Schulte, p. 97 sq. Cases are also reported of the reduction of the assessment upon a revaluation of the property. In 1326 the assessment of the see of Breslau was reduced from 4,000 to 1,785 gold florins. Kirsch : *Finanzverwaltung*, p. 8.

[4] For cases, see Baumgarten, p. cviii. Attempts to get rid of this assessment were unavailing. The bishop of Bamberg, in 1335, left Avignon without a bull of confirmation because he had not made the prescribed payment. The reason is not recorded, but the statement is spread on the ledger entry that episcopal confirmation should not be granted to him till the Apostolic letters pertaining to it were properly registered and delivered by the Apostolic camera. Goeller, p. 69.

tified to.[1]   The expense of getting his case through was 2,585
marks, or 10,340 gold florins, or $25,000 of our money.   The
ways in which this large sum was distributed are not a matter
of conjecture.   The exact itemized statement is extant: 2,258
marks, or 9,032 florins, went to " the Lord pope and the cardinals."   Of this sum 5,000 florins, or 1,250 marks, are entered
as a payment for the *visitatio*, and the remainder in payment
of the *servitium* to the cardinals.   The remaining 327 marks,
or 1,308 florins, were consumed in registration and notarial
fees and gifts to cardinals.   To Cardinal Francis of St. Maria
in Cosmedin, a nephew of Boniface, a gift was made costing
more than 10 marks, or 40 florins.

Another abbot-elect of St. Albans, Richard II., went to
Avignon in 1326 accompanied by six monks, and was well
satisfied to get away with the payment of 3,600 gold florins.
He was surprised that the tax was so reasonable.   Abbot
William of the diocese of Autun, Oct. 22, 1316, obligated
himself to pay John XXII., as confirmation tax, 1,500 gold
florins, and to John's officials 170 more.[2]

The fees paid to the lower officials, called *servitia minuta*,
were classified under five heads, four of them going to the
officials, *familiares* of the pontiff, and one to the officials of the
cardinals.[3]   The exact amounts received on account of *servitia*
or confirmation fees by the pope and the college of cardinals,
probably will never be known.   From the lists that have been
examined, the cardinals between 1316-1323 received from this
source 234,047 gold florins, or about 39,000 florins a year.   As
the yield from this tax was usually, though not always, divided
in equal shares between the pope and the cardinals, the full
sum realized from this source was double this amount.[4]

The annates, so far as they were the tax levied by the pope
upon appointments made by himself to lower clerical offices

---

[1] *Gesta Abb. monaster. S. Albani*, II. 55 sq.   See Gottlob, *Servitien*, p. 174
sqq. for the full list of his expenses.

[2] The contract is printed entire by Kirsch, *Finanzverwaltung*, pp. 73-77,
and Gottlob, p. 162 sqq.

[3] See Gottlob, pp. 102-118; Schulte, p. 13 sqq.

[4] Baumgarten, p. cxx.

and livings, went entirely into the papal treasury, and seem to
have been uniformly one-half of the first year's income.[1] They
were designated as livings " becoming vacant in curia," which
was another way of saying, places which had been reserved
by the pope.   The popes from time to time extended this tax
through the use of the right of reservation to all livings becoming vacant in a given district during a certain period.   In
addition to the annate tax, the papal treasury also drew an
income during the period of their vacancy from the livings reserved for papal appointment and during the period when an
incumbent held the living without canonical right.   These
were called the "intermediate fruits " — *medii fructus*.[2]

Special indulgences were an uncertain but no less important
source of revenue.   The prices were graded according to the
ability of the parties to pay and the supposed inherent value
of the papal concession.   Queen Johanna of Sicily paid 500
grossi Tournois, or about $150, for the privilege of taking the
oath to the archbishop of Naples, who acted as the pope's representative.   The bull readmitting to the sacraments of the
Church Margaret of Maultasch and her husband, Lewis of Brandenburg, the son of Lewis the Bavarian, cost the princess 2000
grossi Tournois.   The king of Cyprus was poor, and secured
for his subjects indulgence to trade with the Egyptians for
the modest sum of 100 pounds Tournois, but had to pay 50
pounds additional for a ship sent with cargo to Egypt.[3]
There was a graduated scale for papal letters giving persons
liberty to choose their confessor without regard to the parish
priests.

[1] John XXII., 1316, Benedict XII., 1335, Clement VI., 1342, and Boniface
IX., 1392, issued bulls requiring such appointees to pay one-half the first year's
income into the papal treasury. See, on this subject, Kirsch, *Kollektorien*, p.
xxv sqq. He mentions the papal collector, Gerardus, who gives a continuous
list for the years 1343–1360, of such payments of annates, *fructus beneficiorum vacantium ad Cameram Apostolicam pertinentes.* The annates, or
annalia, were originally given to the bishops when livings became vacant, but
were gradually reserved for the papal treasury. See Friedberg, *Kirchliche
Abgaben*, in Herzog, I. 95.

[2] Kirsch : *Kollektorien*, p. xxvi. Benedict, 1335, appropriated these payments to the papal treasury.

[3] Tangl, pp. 31, 32, 37.

To these sources of income were added the taxes for the relief of the Holy Land — *pro subsidio terræ sanctæ*. The Council of Vienne ordered a tenth for six years for this purpose. John XXII., 1333, repeated the substance of Clement's bull. The expense of clearing Italy of hostile elements and reclaiming papal territory as a preliminary to the pope's return to Rome was also made the pretext for levying special taxes. For this object Innocent VI. levied a three-years' tax of a tenth upon the Church in Germany, and in 1366 Urban V. levied another tenth upon all the churches of Christendom.[1]

It would be a mistake to suppose that the Church always responded to these appeals, or that the collectors had easy work in making collections. The complaints, which we found so numerous in England in the thirteenth century, we meet with everywhere during the fourteenth century. The resistance was determined, and the taxes were often left unpaid for years or not paid at all.

The revenues derived from feudal states and princes, called *census*, were divided equally between the cardinals and the pope's private treasury. Gregory X., in 1272, was the first to make such a division of the tribute from Sicily, which amounted to 8000 ounces of gold, or about $90,000.[2] In the pontificate of John XXII. there is frequent mention of the amounts contributed by Sicily and their equal partition. The sums varied from year to year, and in 1304 it was 3000 ounces of gold. The tribute of Sardinia and Corsica was fixed in 1297 at the annual sum of 2000 marks, and was divided between the two treasuries.[3] The papal state and Ferrara yielded uncertain sums, and the tribute of 1000 marks, pledged by John of England, was paid irregularly, and finally abrogated altogether. Peter's pence, which belongs in this category, was an irregular source of papal income.[4]

[1] Kirsch : *Kollektorien*, pp. xx, xxi.

[2] Kirsch : *Finanzverwaltung*, p. 3; *Rückkehr*, p. xv. The payment to Urban V. in 1367 and its division into equal shares is a matter of record. In a ledger account begun in 1317, and now in the Vatican, an ounce of gold was estimated at 5 florins, a pound of gold at 96 florins. See Kirsch, *Finanzverwaltung*, p. 71 ; Baumgarten, p. ccxi.

[3] Baumgarten, p. cxlii sq.   [4] Baumgarten, CXXVI. sqq.

The yearly income of the papal treasury under Clement V. and John XXII. has been estimated at from 200,000 to 250,000 gold florins.[1] In 1353 it is known to have been at least 260,000 florins, or more than $600,000 of our money.

These sources of income were not always sufficient for the expenses of the papal household, and in cases had to be anticipated by loans. The popes borrowed from cardinals, from princes, and from bankers. Urban V. got a loan from his cardinals of 30,000 gold florins. Gregory XI. got loans of 30,000 florins from the king of Navarre, and 60,000 from the duke of Anjou. The duke seems to have been a ready lender, and on another occasion loaned Gregory 40,000 florins.[2] It was a common thing for bishops and abbots to make loans to enable them to pay the expense of their confirmation. The abbot of St. Albans, in 1290, was assessed 1300 pounds for his *servitium*, and borrowed 500 of it.[3] The habit grew until the time of the Reformation, when the sums borrowed, as in the case of Albrecht, archbishop of Mainz, were enormous.

The transactions of the Avignon chancellory called forth loud complaints, even from contemporary apologists for the papacy. Alvarus Pelagius, in his *Lament over the Church*, wrote : " No poor man can approach the pope. He will call and no one will answer, because he has no money in his purse to pay. Scarcely is a single petition heeded by the pope until it has passed through the hands of middlemen, a corrupt set, bought with bribes, and the officials conspire together to extort more than the rule calls for." In another place he said that whenever he entered into the papal chambers he always found the tables full of gold, and clerics counting

---

[1] Ehrle: *Process über d. Nachlass Klemens V.*, in *Archiv*, etc., V. 147. The revenue of Philip the Fair amounted in 1301 to 267,900 pounds. See Gottlob, *Servitien*, 133. Gottlob, p. 134, says the cardinals received as much more as their share.

[2] Haller, p. 138.

[3] Walter de Gray, bishop of Worcester, is said to have borrowed 10,000 pounds at his elevation, 1215. Roger de Wendover, as quoted by Gottlob, p. 136. The passage runs *obligatus in curia Romana de decem millibus libris*, etc. Gottlob understands this to refer to Roman bankers, not to the Roman curia.

and weighing florins.[1] Of the Spanish bishops he said that
there was scarcely one in a hundred who did not receive
money for ordinations and the gift of benefices. Matters
grew no better, but rather worse as the fourteenth century
advanced.   Dietrich of Nieheim, speaking of Boniface IX.,
said that " the pope was an insatiable gulf, and that as for
avarice there was no one to compare with him."[2] To effect
a cure of the disease, which was a scandal to Christendom,
the popes would have been obliged to cut off the great army
of officials who surrounded them.   But this vast organized
body was stronger than the Roman pontiff. The fundamental theory of the rights of the papal office was at fault.
The councils made attempts to introduce reforms, but in vain.
Help came at last and from an unexpected quarter, when
Luther and the other leaders openly revolted against the
mediæval theory of the papacy and of the Church.

§ 10.   *The Later Avignon Popes.*

The bustling and scholastic John XXII. was followed by
the scholarly and upright Benedict XII., 1334-1342.   Born
in the diocese of Toulouse, Benedict studied in Paris, and
arose to the dignity of bishop and cardinal before his elevation to the papal throne. If Villani is to be trusted, his
election was an accident.   One cardinal after another who
voted for him did so, not dreaming he would be elected.   The
choice proved to be an excellent one. The new pontiff at
once showed interest in reform. The prelates who had no
distinct duties at Avignon he sent home, and to his credit it
was recorded that, when urged to enrich his relatives, he replied that the vicar of Christ, like Melchizedek, must be without father or mother or genealogy. To him belongs the honor
of having begun the erection of the permanent papal palace
at Avignon, a massive and grim structure, having the features

---

[1] *De planctu eccl.* II. 7, *quum sœpe intraverim in cameram camerarii
domni papœ, semper ibi vidi nummularios et mensas plenas auro, et clericos
computantes et trutinantes florenos.* See Döllinger-Friedrich, pp. 86, 420.

[2] *Insatiabilis vorago et in avaricia nullus ei similis.   De schismate,* Erler's
ed., p. 119. The *sacra auri fames* prevailed at Avignon.

of a fortress rather than a residence.   Its walls and towers were built of colossal thickness and strength to resist attack. Its now desolated spaces are a speechless witness to perhaps the most singular of the episodes of papal history.   The cardinals followed Benedict's example and built palaces in Avignon and its vicinity.

Clement VI., 1342–1352, who had been archbishop of Rouen, squandered the fortune amassed by John XXII. and prudently administered by Benedict.   He forgot his Benedictine train- ing and vows and was a fast liver, carrying into the papal office the tastes of the French nobility from which he sprang. Horses, a sumptuous table, and the company of women made the papal palace as gay as a royal court.[1]   Nor were his rela- tives allowed to go uncared for.   Of the twenty-five cardinals' hats which he distributed, twelve went to them, one a brother and one a nephew.   Clement enjoyed a reputation for elo- quence and, like John XXII., preached after he became pope. Early in his pontificate the Romans sent a delegation, which included Petrarch, begging him to return to Rome.   But Clement, a Frenchman to the core, preferred the atmosphere of France.   Though he did not go to Rome, he was gracious enough to comply with the delegation's request and appoint a Jubilee for the deserted and impoverished city.

During Clement's rule, Rome lived out one of the pictur- esque episodes of its mediæval history, the meteoric career of the tribune Cola (Nicolas) di Rienzo.   Of plebeian birth, this visionary man was stirred with the ideals of Roman inde- pendence and glory by reading the ancient classics.   His oratory flattered and moved the people, whose cause he espoused against the aristocratic families of the city.   Sent to Avignon at the head of a commission, 1343, to confer the highest municipal authority upon the pope, he won Clement's attention by his frank manner and eloquent speech.   Return-

---

[1] Pastor, I. 76, says, "Luxury and fast living prevailed to the most flagrant degree under Clement's rule."   For detailed description of Avignon and the papal palace, see A. Penjon, *Avignon, la ville et le palais des papes*, pp. 134, Avignon, 1878 ; F. Digonnet: *Le palais des papes en Avignon*, Avignon, 1907.

ing to Rome, he fascinated the people with visions of freedom
and dominion.   They invested him on the Capitol with the
signiory of the city, 1347.   Cola assumed the democratic title
of tribune.   Writing from Avignon, Petrarch greeted him
as the man whom he had been looking for, and dedicated to
him one of his finest odes.   The tribune sought to extend
his influence by enkindling the flame of patriotism throughout
all Italy and to induce its cities to throw off the yoke of their
tyrants.   Success and glory turned his head.   Intoxicated with
applause, he had the audacity to cite Lewis the Bavarian and
Charles IV. before his tribunal, and headed his communications with the magnificent superscription, "In the first year
of the Republic's freedom."   His success lasted but seven
months.   The people had grown weary of their idol.   He
was laid by Clement under the ban and fled, to appear again
for a brief season under Innocent V.

Avignon was made papal property by Clement, who paid
Joanna of Naples 80,000 florins for it.   The low price may have
been in consideration of the pope's services in pronouncing the
princess guiltless of the murder of her cousin and first husband, Andreas, a royal Hungarian prince, and sanctioning her
second marriage with another cousin, the prince of Tarentum.

This pontiff witnessed the conclusion of the disturbed career of Lewis the Bavarian, in 1347.   The emperor had sunk
to the depths of self-abasement when he swore to the 28 articles Clement laid before him, Sept. 18, 1343, and wrote to
the pope that, as a babe longs for its mother's breast, so his
soul cried out for the grace of the pope and the Church.
But, if possible, Clement intensified the curses placed upon
him by his two predecessors.   The bull, which he announced
with his own lips, April 13, 1346, teems with rabid execra-
tions.   It called upon God to strike Lewis with insanity,
blindness, and madness.   It invoked the thunderbolts of
heaven and the flaming wrath of God and the Apostles Peter
and Paul both in this world and the next.   It called all the
elements to rise in hostility against him ; upon the universe
to fight against him, and the earth to open and swallow him
up alive.   It blasphemously damned his house to desolation

and his children to exclusion from their abode. It invoked upon him the curse of beholding with his own eyes the destruction of his children by their enemies.[1]

During Clement's pontificate, 1348–1349, the Black Death swept over Europe from Hungary to Scotland and from Spain to Sweden, one of the most awful and mysterious scourges that has ever visited mankind. It was reported by all the chroniclers of the time, and described by Boccaccio in the introduction to his novels. According to Villani, the disease appeared as carbuncles under the armpits or in the groin, sometimes as big as an egg, and was accompanied with devouring fever and vomiting of blood. It also involved a gangrenous inflammation of the lungs and throat and a fetid odor of the breath. In describing the virulence of the infection, a contemporary said that one sick person was sufficient to infect the whole world.[2] The patients lingered at most a day or two. Boccaccio witnessed the progress of the plague as it spread its ravages in Florence.[3] Such measures of sanitation as were then known were resorted to, such as keeping the streets of the city clean and posting up elaborate rules of health. Public religious services and processions were appointed to stay death's progress. Boccaccio tells how he saw the hogs dying from the deadly contagion which they caught in rooting amongst cast-off clothing. In England all sorts of cattle were affected, and Knighton speaks of 5000 sheep dying in a single district.[4] The mortality was appalling. The figures, though they differ in different accounts, show a vast loss of life.

---

[1] This awful denunciation runs : *Veniat ei laqueus quem ignorat, et cadat in ipsum. Sit maledictus ingrediens, sit maledictus egrediens. Percutiat eum dominus amentia et cæcitate ac mentis furore. Cælum super eum fulgura mittat. Omnipotentis dei ira et beatorum Petri et Pauli . . . in hoc et futuro seculo exardescat in ipsum. Orbis terrarum pugnet contra eum, aperiatur terra et ipsum absorbeat vivum.* ·Mirbt: *Quellen*, p. 153. See Müller: *Kampf Ludwigs*, etc., II. 214.

[2] Quoted by Gasquet, *Black Death*, p. 46.

[3] Whitcomb, *Source Book of the Renaissance*, pp. 15–18, gives a translation.

[4] Knighton's account, *Chronicon*, Rolls Series II. 58–65.

A large per cent of the population of Western Europe fell
before the pestilence.   In Siena, 80,000 were carried off ; in
Venice, 100,000 ; in Bologna, two-thirds of the population ;
and in Florence, three-fifths.   In Marseilles the number who
died in a single month is reported as 57,000.   Nor was the
papal city on the Rhone exempt.   Nine cardinals, 70 prelates,
and 17,000 males succumbed.   Another writer, a canon writing from the city to a friend in Flanders, reports that up to the
date of his writing one-half of the population had died.   The
very cats, dogs, and chickens took the disease.[1]   At the pre-
scription of his physician, Guy of Chauliac, Clement VI.
stayed within doors and kept large fires lighted, as Nicolas
IV. before him had done in time of plague.

No class was immune except in England, where the higher
classes seem to have been exempt.   The clergy yielded in great
numbers, bishops, priests, and monks.   At least one archbishop of Canterbury, Bradwardine, was carried away by it.
The brothers of the king of Sweden, Hacon and Knut, were
among the victims.   The unburied dead strewed the streets
of Stockholm.   Vessels freighted with cargoes were reported
floating on the high seas with the last sailor dead.[2]   Convents
were swept clear of all their inmates.   The cemeteries were
not large enough to hold the bodies, which were thrown into
hastily dug pits.[3]   The danger of infection and the odors
emitted by the corpses were so great that often there was no
one to give sepulture to the dead.   Bishops found cause in this
neglect to enjoin their priests to preach on the resurrection
of the body as one of the tenets of the Catholic Church, as
did the bishop of Winchester.[4]   In spite of the vast mortality, many of the people gave themselves up without restraint to revelling and drinking from tavern to tavern and
to other excesses, as Boccaccio reports of Florence.

In England, it is estimated that one-half of the population,

[1] Quoted by Gasquet, p. 46 sqq.   [2] Gasquet, p. 40.
[3] Thorold Rogers saw the remains of a number of skeletons at the digging
for the new divinity school at Cambridge, and pronounced the spot the plague-
pit of this awful time.   *Six Centuries of Work and Wages*, I. 157.
[4] Gasquet, p. 128.

or 2,500,000 people, fell victims to the dread disease.[1] According to Knighton, it was introduced into the land through Southampton. As for Scotland, this chronicler tells the grewsome story that some of the Scotch, on hearing of the weakness of the English in consequence of the malady, met in the forest of Selfchyrche — Selkirk — and decided to fall upon their unfortunate neighbors, but were suddenly themselves attacked by the disease, nearly 5000 dying. The English king prorogued parliament. The disaster that came to the industries of the country is dwelt upon at length by the English chroniclers. The soil became " dead," for there were no laborers left to till it. The price per acre was reduced one-half, or even much more. The cattle wandered through the meadows and fields of grain, with no one to drive them in. " The dread fear of death made the prices of live stock cheap." Horses were sold for one-half their usual price, 40 solidi, and a fat steer for 4 solidi. The price of labor went up, and the cost of the necessaries of life became " very high." [2] The effect upon the Church was such as to interrupt its ministries and perhaps check its growth. The English bishops provided for the exigencies of the moment by issuing letters giving to all clerics the right of absolution. The priest could now make his price, and instead of 4 or 5 marks, as Knighton reports, he could get 10 or 20 after the pestilence had spent its course. To make up for the scarcity of ministers, ordination was granted before the canonical age, as when Bateman, bishop of Norwich, set apart by the sacred rite 60 clerks, " though only shavelings " under 21. In another direction the evil effects of the plague were seen. Work was stopped

[1] These are the figures of Jessopp, *Coming of the Friars*, Gasquet, p. 226, and Cunningham, *Growth of English Industries and Commerce*, p. 275. Thorold Rogers, however, in *Six Centuries of Work*, etc., and *England before and after the Black Death, Fortnightly Review*, VIII. 190 sqq. reduces the number. Jessopp bases his calculations upon local documents and death lists of the diocese of Norwich and finds that in some cases nine-tenths of the population died. The Augustinians at Heveringland, prior and canons, died to a man. At Hickling only one survived. Whether this fell mortality among the clergy, especially the orders, points to luxuriant living and carelessness in habits of cleanliness, we will not attempt to say.

[2] Knighton, II. 62, 65.

on the Cathedral of Siena, which was laid out on a scale of almost unsurpassed size, and has not been resumed to this day.[1]

The Black Death was said to have invaded Europe from the East, and to have been carried first by Genoese vessels.[2] Its victims were far in excess of the loss of life by any battles or earthquakes known to European history, not excepting the Sicilian earthquake of 1908.

In spite of the plague, and perhaps in gratitude for its cessation, the Jubilee Year of 1350, like the Jubilee under Boniface at the opening of the century, brought thousands of pilgrims to Rome.   If they left scenes of desolation in the cities and villages from which they came, they found a spectacle of desolation and ruin in the Eternal City which Petrarch, visiting the same year, said was enough to move a heart of stone. Matthew Villani[3] cannot say too much in praise of the devotion of the visiting throngs.   Clement's bull extended the benefits of his promised indulgence to those who started on a pilgrimage without the permission of their superiors, the cleric without the permission of his bishop, the monk without the permission of his abbot, and the wife without the permission of her husband.

Of the three popes who followed Clement, only good can be said.   Innocent VI., 1352–1362, a native of the see of Limoges, had been appointed cardinal by Clement VI.   Following in the

[1] Gasquet, p. 253. This author, pp. viii, 8, compares the ravages of the bubonic plague in India, 1897–1905, to the desolations of the Black Death. He gives the mortality in India in this period as 3,250,000 persons. He emphasizes the bad effects of the plague in undoing the previous work of the Church and checking its progress.

[2] Ralph, bishop of Bath and Wells, in a pastoral letter warned against the "pestilence which had come into a neighboring kingdom from the East." Knighton refers its origin to India, Thomas Walsingham, *Hist. Angl.*, Rolls Series I. 273, thus speaks of it: "Beginning in the regions of the North and East it advanced over the world and ended with so great a destruction that scarcely half of the people remained. Towns once full of men became destitute of inhabitants, and so violently did the pestilence increase that the living were scarcely able to bury the dead. In certain houses of men of religion, scarcely two out of twenty men survived. It was estimated by many that scarcely one-tenth of mankind had been left alive."

[3] Muratori, XV. 56.

footsteps of Benedict XII., he reduced the ostentation of the Avignon court, dismissed idle bishops to their sees, and instituted the tribunal of the *rota*, with 21 salaried auditors for the orderly adjudication of disputed cases coming before the papal tribunal.   Before Innocent's election, the cardinals adopted a set of rules limiting the college to 20 members, and stipulating that no new members should be appointed, suspended, deposed, or excommunicated without the consent of two-thirds of their number, and that no papal relative should be assigned to a high place.   Innocent no sooner became pontiff than he set it aside as not binding.

Soon after the beginning of his reign, Innocent released Cola di Rienzo from confinement[1] and sent him and Cardinal Ægidius Alvarez of Albernoz to Rome in the hope of establishing order. Cola was appointed senator, but only a few months afterwards was put to death in a popular uprising, Oct. 8, 1354.   He dreamed of a united Italy, 500 years before the union of its divided states was consummated, but his name remains a powerful impulse to popular freedom and national unity in the peninsula.

Tyrants and demagogues infested Italian municipalities and were sucking their life-blood.   The State of the Church had been parcelled up into petty principalities ruled by rude nobles, such as the Polentas in Ravenna, the Malatestas in Rimini, the Montefeltros in Urbino.   The pope was in danger of losing his territory in the peninsula altogether.   Soldiers of fortune from different nations had settled upon it and spread terror as leaders of predatory bands.   In no part was anarchy more wild than in Rome itself, and in the Campagna. Albernoz had fought in the wars against the Moors, and had administered the see of Toledo.   He was a statesman as well as a soldier.   He was fully equal to his difficult task and restored the papal government.[2]

---

[1] Cola had roamed about till he went to Prag, where Charles IV. seized him and sent him to Avignon in 1352.   Petrarch, who corresponded with him, speaks of seeing him in Avignon, attended by two guards.   See Robinson, *Petrarch*, pp. 341–343 sqq.

[2] The full term of Albernoz' service in Italy extended from 1353–1368.   By his code, called the Ægidian Constitutions, he became the legislator of the

In 1355, Albernoz, as administrator of Rome, placed the crown of the empire on the head of Charles IV.   To such a degree had the imperial dignity been brought that Charles was denied permission by the pope to enter the city till the day appointed for his coronation.   His arrival in Italy was welcomed by Petrarch as Henry VII.'s arrival had been welcomed by Dante.   But the emperor disappointed every expectation, and his return from Italy was an inglorious retreat.   He placed his own dominion of Bohemia in his debt by becoming the founder of the University of Prag.[1]   It was he also who, in 1356, issued the celebrated Golden Bull, which laid down the rules for the election of the emperor.   They placed this transaction wholly in the hands of the electors, a majority of whom was sufficient for a choice.   The pope is not mentioned in the document.   Frankfurt was made the place of meeting.   The electors designated were the archbishops of Mainz, Treves, and Cologne, the Count Palatine, the king of Bohemia, the margrave of Brandenburg, and the duke of Saxony.[2]

Urban V., 1362–1370, at the time of his election abbot of the Benedictine convent of St. Victor in Marseilles, developed merits which secured for him canonization by Pius IX., 1870. He was the first of the Avignon popes to visit Rome.   Petrarch, as he had written before to Benedict XII. and Clement VI., now, in his old age, wrote to the new pontiff rebuking the curia for its vices and calling upon him to be faithful to his part as Roman bishop.   Why should Urban hide himself away in a corner of the earth?   Italy was fair, and Rome, hallowed by history and legend of empire and Church, was the theocratic capital of the world.   Charles IV. visited Avignon and offered to escort the pontiff.   But the French

State of the Church for centuries. For text, see Mansi, XXVI. 299–307. Gregorovius, VI. 430, calls him " the most gifted statesman who ever sat in the college of cardinals," and Wurm, his biographer, " the second founder of the State of the Church."

[1] In 1334 Clement had set off the diocese of Prag from the diocese of Mainz and made it an archbishopric.

[2] Bryce, ch. XIV., says well that the Golden Bull completed the Germanization of the Holy Roman Empire by separating the imperial power from the papacy. See Mirot, *La politique pontificale*, p. 2.

king opposed the plan and was supported by the cardinals in
a body.   Only three Italians were left in it.   Urban started
for the home of his spiritual ancestors in April, 1367.   A fleet
of sixty vessels furnished by Naples, Genoa, Venice, and Pisa
conducted the distinguished traveller from Marseilles to
Genoa and Corneto, where he was met by envoys from Rome,
who put into his hands the keys of the castle of St. Angelo, the symbol of full municipal power.   All along the way
transports of wine, fish, cheese, and other provisions, sent on
from Avignon, met the papal party, and horses from the
papal stables on the Rhone were in waiting for the pope at
every stage of the journey.[1]

At Viterbo, a riot was called forth by the insolent manners
of the French, and the pope launched the interdict against
the city.   The papal ledgers contain the outlay by the apothecary for medicines for the papal servants who were wounded
in the mêlée.   Here Albernoz died, to whom the papacy
owed a large debt for his services in restoring order to Rome.
The legend runs that, when he was asked by the pope for an
account of his administration, he loaded a car with the keys
of the cities he had recovered to the papal authority, and sent
them to him.

Urban chose as his residence the Vatican in preference to
the Lateran.   The preparations for his advent included the
restoration of the palace and its gardens.   A part of the
garden was used as a field, and the rest was overgrown with
thorns.   Urban ordered it replanted with grape-vines and
fruit trees.   The papal ledger gives the cost of these improvements as 6,621 gold florins, or about $15,000.   Roofs,
floors, doors, walls, and other parts of the palace had to be
renewed.   The expenses from April 27, 1367, to November,

---

[1] Kirsch : *Rückkehr*, etc., pp. xii, 74–90.   During the stop of five days at
Genoa, Urban received timely help in the payment of the feoffal tax of Naples,
8000 ounces of gold.   Kirsch, in his interesting and valuable treatment, pub-
lishes the ledger entries made in the official registers, deposited in Rome and
Avignon and giving in detail the expenses incurred on the visits of Urban and
Gregory XI.   Gregorovius, VI. 430 sqq., gives an account of Urban's pilgrimage in his most brilliant style.

1368, as shown in the report of the papal treasurer, Gaucelin de Pradello, were 15,559 florins, or $39,000.[1]

During the sixty years that had elapsed since Clement V. fixed the papal residence in France, Rome had been reduced almost to a museum of Christian monuments, as it had before been a museum of pagan ruins. The aristocratic families had forsaken the city. The Lateran had again fallen a prey to the flames in 1360. St. Paul's was desolate. Rubbish or stagnant pools filled the streets. The population was reduced to 20,000 or perhaps 17,000.[2] The return of the papacy was compared by Petrarch to Israel returning out of Egypt.

Urban set about the restoration of churches. He gave 1000 florins to the Lateran and spent 5000 on St. Paul's. Rome showed signs of again becoming the centre of European society and politics. Joanna, queen of Naples, visited the city, and so did the king of Cyprus and the emperor, Charles IV. In 1369 John V. Palæologus, the Byzantine emperor, arrived, a suppliant for aid against the Turks, and publicly made solemn abjuration of his schismatic tenets.

The old days seemed to have returned, but Urban was not satisfied. He had not the courage nor the wide vision to sacrifice his own pleasure for the good of his office. Had he so done, the disastrous schism might have been averted. He turned his face back towards Avignon, where he arrived "at the hour of vespers," Sept. 27, 1370. He survived his return scarcely two months, and died Dec. 19, 1370, universally beloved and already honored as a saint.

§ 11. *The Re-establishment of the Papacy in Rome.* 1377.

Of the nineteen cardinals who entered the conclave at the death of Urban V., all but four were Frenchmen. The choice immediately fell on Gregory XI., the son of a French count. At 17 he had been made cardinal by his uncle, Clement VI.

---

[1] The accounts are published entire by Kirsch, pp. ix sqq. xxx, 109–165.

[2] Döllinger, *The Church and the Churches*, Engl. trans., 1862, p. 353, puts the population at 17,000. Gregorovius, VI. 438, makes the estimate somewhat higher.

His contemporaries praised him for his moral purity, affability, and piety.   He showed his national sympathies by appointing 18 Frenchmen cardinals and filling papal appointments in Italy with French officials.   In English history he is known for his condemnation of Wyclif.   His pontificate extended from 1370–1378.

With Gregory's name is associated the re-establishment of the papacy in its proper home on the Tiber.   For this change the pope deserves no credit.   It was consummated against his will.   He went to Rome, but was engaged in preparations to return to Avignon, when death suddenly overtook him.

That which principally moved Gregory to return to Rome was the flame of rebellion which filled Central and Northern Italy, and threatened the papacy with the permanent loss of its dominions.   The election of an anti-pope was contemplated by the Italians, as a delegation from Rome informed him.   One remedy was open to crush revolt on the banks of the Tiber.   It was the presence of the pope himself.[1]

Gregory had carried on war for five years with the disturbing elements in Italy.   In the northern parts of the peninsula, political anarchy swept from city to city.   Soldiers of fortune, the most famous of whom was the Englishman, John Hawkwood, spread terror wherever they went. In Milan, the tyrant Bernabo was all-powerful and truculent. In Florence, the revolt was against the priesthood itself, and a red flag was unfurled, on which was inscribed the word "Liberty."   A league of 80 cities was formed to abolish the pope's secular power.   The interdict hurled against the Florentines, March 31, 1376, for the part they were taking in the sedition, contained atrocious clauses, giving every one the right to plunder the city and to make slaves of her people wherever they might be found.[2]   Genoa and Pisa

---

[1] Pastor, Hergenröther-Kirsch, Kirsch, *Rückkehr*, p. xvii ; Mirot, p. viii, 7 sq., and other Catholic historians agree that this was Gregory's chief motive. Mirot, pp. 10–18, ascribes to Gregory three controlling ideas — the reform of the Church, the re-establishment of peace with the East as a preliminary to a new crusade against the Turks, and the return of the papacy to Rome.

[2] Baluz, I. 435, Gieseler, IV. 1, p. 90 sq., give the bull.

followed Florence and incurred a like papal malediction. The papal city, Bologna, was likewise stirred to rebellion in 1376 by its sister city on the Arno.

Florence fanned the flames of rebellion in Rome and the other papal towns, calling upon them to throw off the yoke of tyranny and return to their pristine liberty. What Italian, its manifesto proclaimed, " can endure the sight of so many noble cities, serving barbarians appointed by the pope to devour the goods of Italy ? "[1]   But Rome remained true to the pope, as did Ancona.   On the other hand, Perugia, Narni, Viterbo, and Ferrara, in 1375, raised the banner of rebellion until revolt threatened to spread over the whole of the papal patrimony.   The bitter feeling against the French officials was intensified by a detachment of 10,000 Breton mercenaries which the pope sent to crush the revolution. They were under the leadership of Cardinal Robert of Geneva, — afterward Clement VII., — an iron-hearted soldier and pitiless priest.   It was as plain as day, Pastor says, that Gregory's return was the only thing that could save Rome to the papacy.

To the urgency of these civil commotions were added the pure voices of prophetesses, which rose above the confused sounds of revolt and arms, the voices of Brigitta of Sweden and Catherine of Siena, both canonized saints.

Petrarch, who for nearly half a century had been urging the pope's return, now, in his last days, replied to a French advocate who compared Rome to Jericho, the town to which the man was going who fell among thieves, and stigmatized Avignon as the sewer of the earth.   He died 1374, without seeing the consuming desire of his life fulfilled.   Guided by patriotic instincts, he had carried into his appeals the feeling of an Italian's love of his country.   Brigitta and Catherine made their appeals to Gregory on higher than national grounds, the utility of Christendom and the advantage of the king-dom of God.   Emerging from visions and ecstatic moods of devotion, they called upon the Church's chief bishop to be faithful to the obligations of his holy office.

[1] Quoted by Mirot, p. 48, and Gregorovius, VI. 466 sqq.

On the death of her husband, St. Brigitta left her Scandinavian home and joined the pilgrims whose faces were set towards Rome in the Jubilee year of 1350.[1] Arriving in the papal city, the hope of seeing both the emperor and the pope once more in that centre of spiritual and imperial power moved her to the devotions of the saint and the messages of the seer. She spent her time in going from church to church and ministering to the sick, or sat clad in pilgrim's garb, begging. Her revelations, which were many, brought upon her the resentment of the Romans. She saw Urban enter the city and, when he announced his purpose to return again to France, she raised her voice in prediction of his speedy death, in case he persisted in it. When Gregory ascended the throne, she warned him that he would die prematurely if he kept away from the residence divinely appointed for the supreme pontiff. But to her, also, it was not given to see the fulfilment of her desire. The worldliness of the popes stirred her to bitter complaints. Peter, she exclaimed, "was appointed pastor and minister of Christ's sheep, but the pope scatters them and lacerates them. He is worse than Lucifer, more unjust than Pilate, more cruel than Judas. Peter ascended the throne in humility, Boniface in pride." To Gregory she wrote, "in thy curia arrogant pride rules, insatiable cupidity and execrable luxury. It is the very deepest gulf of horrible simony.[2] Thou seizest and tearest from the Lord innumerable sheep." And yet she was worthy to be declared a saint. She died in 1373. Her daughter Catherine took the body to Sweden.

Catherine of Siena was more fortunate. She saw the papacy re-established in Italy, but she also witnessed the unhappy beginnings of the schism. This Tuscan prophetess, called by a sober Catholic historian, "one of the most wonderful appearances in history,"[3] wrote letter after letter to

[1] Brigitta was born near Upsala, 1303. See Gardner, *St. Catherine of Siena*, p. 44 sqq. Döllinger has called attention to the failure of her prophecies to be fulfilled, *Fables and Prophecies of the Middle Ages*, trans. by Prof. Henry B. Smith, pp. 331, 398.

[2] *Vorago pessima horribilis symoniae*, Brigitta's *Revelationes*, as quoted by Gieseler, Haller, p. 88, and Gardner, p. 78 sq.

[3] Pastor, I. 103.

Gregory XI. whom she called " sweet Christ on earth," appealing to him and admonishing him to do his duty as the head
of the Church, and to break away from his exile, which she
represented as the source of all the evils with which Christendom was afflicted.   " Be a true successor of St. Gregory," she
wrote.   " Love God.   Do not bind yourself to your parents
and your friends.   Do not be held by the compulsion of
your surroundings.   Aid will come from God."   His return to
Rome and the starting of a new crusade against the Turks,
she represented as necessary conditions of efficient measures
to reform the Church.   She bade him return " swiftly like a
gentle lamb.   Respond to the Holy Spirit who calls you.   I
tell you, Come, come, come, and do not wait for time,
since time does not wait for you.   Then you will do like
the Lamb slain, whose place you hold, who, without weapons
in his hands, slew our foes.   Be manly in my sight, not fearful.   Answer God, who calls you to hold and possess the seat
of the glorious shepherd, St. Peter, whose vicar you are."[1]

Gregory received a letter purporting to come from a man
of God, warning him of the poison which awaited him at Rome
and appealing to his timidity and his love of his family.   In
a burning epistle, Catherine showed that only the devil or one
of his emissaries could be the author of such a communication,
and called upon him as a good shepherd to pay more honor to
God and the well-being of his flock than to his own safety, for
a good shepherd, if necessary, lays down his life for the sheep.
The servants of God are not in the habit of giving up a
spiritual act for fear of bodily harm.[2]

In 1376, Catherine saw Gregory face to face in Avignon,
whither she went as a commissioner from Florence to arrange
a peace between the city and the pope.   The papal residence
she found not a paradise of heavenly virtues, as she expected,
but in it the stench of infernal vices.[3]   The immediate object

---

[1] Scudder : *Letters of St. Catherine*, p. 132 sq.; Gardner, pp. 158, 176, etc.
[2] Scudder, p. 182 sqq.
[3] This was Catherine's deposition to her confessor. See Mirbt: *Quellen*,
p. 154, *in romana curia, ubi deberet paradisus esse cœlicarum virtutum, in-
veniebat fœtorem infernalium vitiarum.*

of the mission was not accomplished; but her unselfish appeals confirmed Gregory in his decision to return to Rome — a decision he had already formed before Catherine's visit, as the pope's own last words indicate.[1]

As early as 1374, Gregory wrote to the emperor that it was his intention to re-establish the papacy on the Tiber.[2] A member of the papal household, Bertrand Raffini, was sent ahead to prepare the Vatican for his reception. The journey was delayed. It was hard for the pope to get away from France. His departure was vigorously resisted by his relatives as well as by the French cardinals and the French king, who sent a delegation to Avignon, headed by his brother, the duke of Anjou, to dissuade Gregory from his purpose.

The journey was begun Sept. 13, 1376. Six cardinals were left behind at Avignon to take care of the papal business. The fleet which sailed from Marseilles was provided by Joanna of Naples, Peter IV. of Aragon, the Knights of St. John, and the Italian republics, but the vessels were not sufficient to carry the large party and the heavy cargo of personal baggage and supplies. The pope was obliged to rent a number of additional galleys and boats. Fernandez of Heredia, who had just been elected grand-master of the Knights of St. John, acted as admiral. A strong force of mercenaries was also required for protection by sea and at the frequent stopping places along the coast, and for service, if necessary, in Rome itself. The expenses of this peaceful Armada — vessels, mercenaries, and cargo — are carefully tabulated in the ledgers preserved in Avignon and the Vatican.[3] The first entries of

[1] Mirot, p. 101, is quite sure Catherine had no influence in bringing Gregory to his original decision.   So also Pastor and Gardner.

[2] Later biographers tell of a vow made by Gregory at the opening of his pontificate to return to Rome, but no contemporary writer has any reference to it, Mirot, p. 52.

[3] Kirsch, pp. 169–264, gives a copy of these ledger entries.   One set contains the expenses of preparation, one set the expenses from Marseilles to Rome, and a third set, the expenses after arriving in Rome.   Still another gives the expenses of repairing the Vatican — the wages of workmen and the prices paid for lumber, lead, iron, keys, etc.   On the back of this last volume, which is in the Vatican, are written the words, " *Expensæ palatii apostolici*, 1370–1380."

expense are for the large consignments of Burgundy and other
wines which were to be used on the way, or stored away in
the vaults of the Vatican.[1] The cost of the journey was heavy,
and it should occasion no surprise that the pope was obliged
to increase the funds at his control at this time by borrowing
30,000 gold florins from the king of Navarre.[2] The papal
moneys, amounting to 85,713 florins, were carried from Avignon to Marseilles in twelve chests on pack horses and mules,
and in boats.   To this amount were added later 41,527 florins,
or, in all, about $300,000 of our present coinage.   The cost
of the boats and mercenaries was very large, and several times
the boatmen made increased demands for their services and
craft to which the papal party was forced to accede.   Raymund
of Turenne, who was in command of the mercenaries, received
700 florins a month for his " own person," each captain with
a banner 24 florins, and each lance with three men under him
18 florins monthly.   Nor were the obligations of charity to be
overlooked.   Durandus Andreas, the papal eleemosynary, received 100 florins to be distributed in alms on the journey,
and still another 100 to be distributed after the party's arrival
at Rome.[3]

The elements seemed to war with the expedition.   The fleet
had no sooner set sail from Marseilles than a fierce storm arose
which lasted several weeks and made the journey tedious. Urban
V. was three days in reaching Genoa, Gregory sixteen.   From
Genoa, the vessels continued southwards the full distance to
Ostia, anchorage being made every night off towns.   From
Ostia, Gregory went up the Tiber by boat, landing at Rome
Dec. 16, 1377.   The journey was made by night and the banks
were lit up by torches, showing the feverish expectation of the
people.   Disembarking at St. Paul's, the pope proceeded the
next day, Jan. 17, to St. Peter's, accompanied by rejoicing

[1] Kirsch, pp. xviii, 171, Mirot, p. 112 sq., says, *Les vins paraissent avoir
tenu une grande place dans le rétour, et, à la veille du départ, on s'occupa tant
d'assurer le service de la bouteillerie durant le voyage, que de garnir en prévi-
sion de l'arrivée, les caves du Vatican.*

[2] Kirsch, p. 184.   For other loans made by Gregory, *e.g.* 30,000 florins in
1374 and 60,000 in 1376, see Mirot, p. 36.

[3] Kirsch, pp. xx, xxii, 179.

throngs.   In the procession were bands of buffoons who
added to the interest of the spectacle and afforded pastime
to the populace.   The pope abode in the Vatican and,
from that time till this day, it has continued to be the papal
residence.

Gregory survived his entrance into the Eternal City a single
year.   He spent the warmer months in Anagni, where he must
have had mixed feelings as he recalled the experiences of his
predecessor Boniface VIII., which had been the immediate
cause of the transfer of the papal residence to French soil.
The atrocities practised at Cesena by Cardinal Robert cast a
dark shadow over the events of the year.   An uprising of the
inhabitants in consequence of the brutality of his Breton troops
drove them and the cardinal to seek refuge in the citadel.
Hawkwood was called in, and, in spite of the cardinal's pacific
assurances, the mercenaries fell upon the defenceless people
and committed a butchery whose shocking details made the
ears of all Italy to tingle.   Four thousand were put to death,
including friars in their churches, and still other thousands
were sent forth naked and cold to find what refuge they could
in neighboring towns.   But, in spite of this barbarity, the
pope's authority was acknowledged by an enlarging circle of
Italian commonwealths, including Bologna.   Florence, even,
sued for peace.

When Gregory died, March 27, 1378, he was only 47 years
old.   By his request, his body was laid to rest in S. Maria
Nuova on the Forum.   In his last hours, he is said to have
regretted having given his ear to the voice of Catherine of
Siena, and he admonished the cardinals not to listen to prophecies as he had done.[1]   Nevertheless, the monument erected
to Gregory at Rome two hundred years later is true to history
in representing Catherine of Siena walking at the pope's side
as if conducting him back to Rome.   The Babylonian captivity of the papacy had lasted nearly three-quarters of a century.   The wonder is that with the pope virtually a vassal of

---

[1] So Gerson, *De examinatione doctrinarum*, I. 16, as quoted by Gieseler,
*ut caverent ab hominibus sive viris sive mulieribus, sub specie religionis lo-
quentibus visiones . . . quia per tales ipse reductus.*   See Pastor, I. 113.

France, Western Christendom remained united.   Scarcely
anything in history seems more unnatural than the voluntary
residence of the popes in the commonplace town on the Rhone
remote from the burial-place of the Apostles and from the
centres of European life.

CHAPTER II.

THE PAPAL SCHISM AND THE REFORMATORY COUNCILS.

1378–1449.

§ 12. *Sources and Literature.*

For §§ 13, 14. THE PAPAL SCHISM. — Orig. documents in RAYNALDUS: *Annal. eccles.*— C. E. BULÆUS, d. 1678 : *Hist. univer. Parisiensis*, 6 vols., Paris, 1665–1673, vol. IV. — VAN DER HARDT, see § 15. — H. DENIFLE and A. CHATELAIN : *Chartul. universitatis Paris.*, 4 vols., Paris, 1889–1897, vols. III., IV., especially the part headed *de schismate*, III. 552–639. — THEODERICH OF NIEHEIM (Niem) : *de Schismate inter papas et antipapas*, Basel, 1566, ed. by GEO. ERLER, Leipzig, 1890. Nieheim, b. near Paderborn, d. 1417, had exceptional opportunities for observing the progress of events. He was papal secretary — *notarius sacri palatii* — at Avignon, went with Gregory XI. to Rome, was there at the breaking out of the schism, and held official positions under three of the popes of the Roman line. In 1408 he joined the Livorno cardinals, and supported Alexander V. and John XXIII. — See H. V. SAUERLAND : *D. Leben d. Dietrich von Nieheim nebst einer Uebersicht über dessen Schriften*, Göttingen, 1875, and G. ERLER : *Dietr. von Nieheim, sein Leben u. s. Schriften*, Leipzig, 1887. — ADAM OF USK : *Chronicon, 1377–1421*, 2d ed. by E. M. THOMPSON, with Engl. trans., London, 1904. — MARTIN DE ALPARTILS : *Chronica actitatorum temporibus Domini Benedicti XIII.* ed. Fr. Ehrle, S.J., vol. I., Paderborn, 1906. — WYCLIF's writings, *Lives of Boniface IX. and Innocent VII.* in Muratori, III. 2, pp. 830 sqq., 968 sq. — P. DUPUY : *Hist. du schisme 1378–1420*, Paris, 1654. — P. L. MAIMBOURG (Jesuit): *Hist. du grand schisme d' Occident*, Paris, 1678. — EHRLE : *Neue Materialien zur Gesch. Peters von Luna* (Benedict XIII.), in *Archiv für Lit. und Kirchengesch.*, VI. 139 sqq., VII. 1 sqq. — L. GAYET : *Le grand schisme d' Occident*, 2 vols., Florence and Berlin, 1889. — C. LOCKE : *Age of the Great Western Schism*, New York, 1896. — PAUL VAN DYKE : *Age of the Renascence, an Outline of the Hist. of the Papacy, 1377–1527*, New York, 1897. — L. SALEMBIER : *Le grand schisme d' Occident*, Paris, 1900, 3d ed., 1907. Engl. trans., London, 1907. — N. VALOIS : *La France et le grand schisme d' Occident*, 4 vols., Paris, 1896–1901. — E. GOELLER : *König Sigismund's Kirchenpolitik vom Tode Bonifaz IX. bis zur Berufung d. Konstanzer Concils*, Freiburg, 1902. — M. JANSEN : *Papst Bonifatius IX. u. s. Beziehungen zur deutschen Kirche*, Freiburg, 1904. — H. BRUCE : *The Age of Schism*, New York, 1907. — E. J. KITTS : *In the Days of the Councils. A Sketch of the Life and Times of Baldassare Cossa, John XXIII.*, London, 1908. — HEFELE-KNÖPFLER : *Conciliengesch.*, VI. 727–936.

— HERGENRÖTHER-KIRSCH, II. 807-833. — GREGOROVIUS, VI. 494-611. — PAS-
TOR, I. 115-175. — CREIGHTON, I. 55-200.

For §§ 15, 16. THE COUNCILS OF PISA AND CONSTANCE. — MANSI : *Concilia,*
XXVI., XXVII. — LABBÆUS : *Concilia,* XI., XII. 1-259. — HERMANN VAN
DER HARDT, Prof. of Hebrew and librarian at Helmstädt, d. 1746 : *Magnum
œcumenicum Constantiense Concilium de universali ecclesiæ reformatione,
unione et fide,* 6 vols., Frankfurt and Leipzig, 1696-1700. A monumental
work, noted alike as a mine of historical materials and for its total lack of
order in their arrangement. In addition to the acts and history of the Council of Constance, it gives many valuable contemporary documents, *e.g.* the
De corrupto statu eccles., also entitled *De ruina eccles.,* of NICOLAS OF CLA-
MANGES ; the *De modis uniendi et reformandi eccles. in concilio universali ;
De difficultate reformationis ;* and *Monita de necessitate reformationis eccles.
in capite et membris,* — all probably by NIEHEIM ; and a *Hist. of the Council,*
by DIETRICH VRIE, an Augustinian, finished at Constance, 1417. These
are all in vol. I. Vol. II. contains Henry of Langenstein's *Consilium
pacis : De unione ac reformatione ecclesiæ,* pp. 1-60 ; a *Hist. of the c. of Pisa,*
pp. 61-156 ; NIEHEIM'S *Invectiva in diffugientem Johannem XXIII.* and *de
vita Johan. XXIII. usque ad fugam et carcerem ejus,* pp. 296-459, etc. The
vols. are enriched with valuable illustrations. Volume V. contains a stately
array of pictures of the seals and escutcheons of the princes and prelates
attending the council in person or by proxy, and the fourteen universities
represented. The work also contains biogg. of D'Ailly, Gerson, Zarabella,
etc. — LANGENSTEIN'S *Consilium pacis* is also given in Du Pin's ed. of Gerson's
Works, ed. 1728, vol. II. 809-839. The tracts *De difficultate reformationis* and
Monita de necessitate, etc., are also found in Du Pin, II. 867-875, 885-902,
and ascribed to Peter D'Ailly. The tracts *De reformatione* and *De eccles.,
concil. generalis, romani pontificis et cardinalium auctoritate,* also ascribed
to D'Ailly in Du Pin, II. 903-915, 925-960. — ULRICH VON RICHENTAL : *Das
Concilium so ze Costenz gehalten worden,* ed. by M. R. BUCK, Tübingen,
1882. — Also MARMION : *Gesch. d. Conc. von Konstanz nach Ul. von Richental,*
Constance, 1860. Richental, a resident of Constance, wrote from his own
personal observation a quaint and highly interesting narrative. First publ.,
Augsburg, 1483. The MS. may still be seen in Constance. — *H. FINKE :
Forschungen u. Quellen zur Gesch. des Konst. Konzils,* Paderborn, 1889.
Contains the valuable diary of Card. Fillastre, etc. — *FINKE : Actæ conc. Con-
stanciensis, 1410-1414,* Münster, 1906. — J. L'ENFANT (Huguenot refugee
in Berlin, d. 1728) : *Hist. du conc. de Constance,* Amsterdam, 1714 ; also *Hist.
du conc. de Pisa,* Amsterdam, 1724, Engl. trans., 2 vols., London, 1780. —
B. HÜBLER : *Die Konstanzer Reformation u. d. Konkordate von 1418,* Leipzig,
1867. — U. LENZ : *Drei Traktate aus d. Schriftencyclus d. Konst. Konzils,*
Marburg, 1876. Discusses the authorship of the tracts *De modis, De necessi-
tate,* and *De difficultate,* ascribing them to Nieheim. — B. BESS : *Studien zur
Gesch. d. Konst. Konzils,* Marburg, 1891. — J. H. WYLIE : *The Counc. of
Const. to the Death of J. Hus,* London, 1900. — *J. B. SCHWAB : J. Gerson,*
Würzburg, 1858. — *P. TSCHACKERT : Peter von Ailli,* Gotha, 1877. — DÖL-
LINGER-FRIEDRICH : *D. Papstthum,* new ed., Munich, 1892, pp. 154-164. —
F. X. FUNK : *Martin V. und d. Konzil von Konstanz in Abhandlungen u.*

Untersuchungen, 2 vols., Paderborn, 1897, I. 489–498. — The works cited in
§ 1, especially, Creighton, I. 200–420, Hefele, VI. 992–1043, VII. 1–375,
Pastor, I. 188–279, Valois, IV., Salembier, 250 sqq.; *Eine Invektive
gegen Gregor xii.*, *Nov. 1, 1408*, in *Ztschr. f. Kirchengesch.*, 1907, p. 188 sq.
For § 17. The Council of Basel. — *Lives of Martin V. and Eugenius IV.*
in Mansi : XXVIII. 975 sqq., 1171 sqq.; in Muratori : *Ital. Scripp.*, and
Platina : *Hist. of the Popes*, Engl. trans., II. 200–235. — Mansi, XXIX.-
XXXI.; Labbæus, XII. 454–XIII. 1280.— For *C. of Siena*, Mansi : XXVIII.
1058–1082.—*Monum. concil. general. sæc. XV.*, ed. by Palacky, 3 vols., Vienna, 1857–1896. Contains an account of C. of Siena by John Stojkoric of
Ragusa, a delegate from the Univ. of Paris. — John de Segovia : *Hist. gest.
gener. Basil. conc.*, new ed., Vienna, 1873. Segovia, a Spaniard, was a
prominent figure in the Basel Council and one of Felix V.'s cardinals. For
his writings, see Haller's *Introd.* — *Concil. Basiliense. Studien und Quellen
zur Gesch. d. Concils von Basel*, with *Introd.* ed. by T. Haller, 4 vols.,
Basel, 1896–1903. — Æneas Sylvius Piccolomini : *Commentarii de gestis
concil. Basil.*, written 1440 to justify Felix's election, ed. by Fea, Rome, 1823 ;
also *Hist. Frederici III.*, trans. by T. Ilgen, 2 vols., Leipzig. No date.
Æneas, afterward Pius II., "did not say and think the same thing at all
times," says Haller, *Introd.*, p. 12. — See Voigt : *Enea Sylvio de' Piccolomini*, etc., 3 vols., Berlin, 1856–1863. — Infessura : *Diario della città di
Roma*, Rome, 1890, pp. 22–42. — F. P. Abert : *Eugenius IV.*, Mainz, 1884.
— Wattenbach : *Röm. Papstthum*, pp. 271–284. — Hefele-Knöpfler, VII.
375–849. — Döllinger-Friedrich : *Papstthum*, 160 sqq.—Creighton, II. 3-
273. — Pastor, I. 209–306. — Gregorovius, VI.-VII. — M. G. Perouse :
Louis Aleman et la fin du grand schisme, Paris, 1905. A detailed account
of the C. of Basel.

For § 18. The Ferrara-Florence Council. — Abram of Crete : *His-
toria*, in Latin trans., Rome, 1521 ; the Greek original by order of Gregory
XIII., Rome, 1577 ; new Latin trans., Rome, 1612. — Sylv. Syropulos : *Vera
hist. unionis non veræ inter Græcos et Latinos*, ed. by Creyghton, Haag, 1660.
— Mansi, XXXI., contains the documents collected by Mansi himself, and
also the *Acts* published by Horatius Justinian, XXXI. 1355–1711, from a
Vatican MS., 1638. The Greek and Latin texts are printed side by side. —
Labbæus and Harduin also give Justinian's *Acts* and their own collections. —
T. Frommann : *Krit. Beiträge zur Gesch. d. florentinischen Kircheneinigung*,
Halle, 1872. Knöpfler, art. *Ferrara-Florenz*, in Wetzer-Welte : IV. 1363–
1380. Tschackert, art. *Ferrara-Florenz*, in Herzog, VI. 45–48. — Döl-
linger-Friedrich : *Papstthum*, pp. 166–171.

§ 13. *The Schism Begun.* 1378.

The death of Gregory XI. was followed by the schism of
Western Christendom, which lasted forty years, and proved to
be a greater misfortune for the Church than the Avignon captivity. Anti-popes the Church had had, enough of them since

the days of Gregory VII., from Wibert of Ravenna chosen by
the will of Henry IV. to the feeble Peter of Corbara, elected
under Lewis the Bavarian. Now, two lines of popes, each
elected by a college of cardinals, reigned, the one at Rome, the
other in Avignon, and both claiming to be in the legitimate
succession from St. Peter.

Gregory XI. foresaw the confusion that was likely to follow
at his death, and sought to provide against the catastrophe of
a disputed election, and probably also to insure the choice of
a French pope, by pronouncing in advance an election valid, no
matter where the conclave might be held. The rule that the
conclave should convene in the locality where the pontiff died,
was thus set aside. Gregory knew well the passionate feeling
in Rome against the return of the papacy to the banks of the
Rhone. A clash was almost inevitable. While the pope lay
a-dying, the cardinals at several sittings attempted to agree
upon his successor, but failed.

On April 7, 1378, ten days after Gregory's death, the conclave met in the Vatican, and the next day elected the Neapolitan, Bartholomew Prignano, archbishop of Bari. Of the
sixteen cardinals present, four were Italians, eleven Frenchmen, and one Spaniard, Peter de Luna, who later became famous as Benedict XIII. The French party was weakened by
the absence of the six cardinals, left behind at Avignon, and
still another was absent. Of the Italians, two were Romans,
Tebaldeschi, an old man, and Giacomo Orsini, the youngest
member of the college. The election of an Italian not a member of the curia was due to factions which divided the French
and to the compulsive attitude of the Roman populace, which
insisted upon an Italian for pope.

The French cardinals were unable to agree upon a candidate
from their own number. One of the two parties into which
they were split, the Limousin party, to which Gregory XI. and
his predecessors had belonged, numbered six cardinals. The
Italian mob outside the Vatican was as much a factor
in the situation as the divisions in the conclave itself. A
scene of wild and unrestrained turbulence prevailed in the
square of St. Peter's. The crowd pressed its way into the

very spaces of the Vatican, and with difficulty a clearing was made for the entrance of all the cardinals. To prevent the exit of the cardinals, the Banderisi, or captains of the thirteen districts into which Rome was divided, had taken possession of the city and closed the gates. The mob, determined to keep the papacy on the Tiber, filled the air with angry shouts and threats. " We will have a Roman for pope or at least an Italian." — *Romano, romano, lo volemo, o almanco Italiano* was the cry. On the first night soldiers clashed their spears in the room underneath the chamber where the conclave was met, and even thrust them through the ceiling. A fire of combustibles was lighted under the window. The next morning, as their excellencies were saying the mass of the Holy Spirit and engaged in other devotions, the noises became louder and more menacing. One cardinal, d'Aigrefeuille, whispered to Orsini, " better elect the devil than die."

It was under such circumstances that the archbishop of Bari was chosen. After the choice had been made, and while they were waiting to get the archbishop's consent, six of the cardinals dined together and seemed to be in good spirits. But the mob's impatience to know what had been done would brook no delay, and Orsini, appearing at the window, cried out " go to St. Peter." This was mistaken for an announcement that old Tebaldeschi, cardinal of St. Peter's, had been chosen, and a rush was made for the cardinal's palace to loot it, as the custom was when a cardinal was elected pope. The crowd surged through the Vatican and into the room where the cardinals had been meeting and, as Valois puts it, " the pillage of the conclave l ad begun." To pacify the mob, two of the cardinals, half beside themselves with fright, pointed to Tebaldeschi, set him up on a chair, placed a white mitre on his head, and threw a red cloak over his shoulders. The old man tried to indicate that he was not the right person. But the throngs continued to bend down before him in obeisance for several hours, till it became known that the successful candidate was Prignano.

In the meantime the rest of the cardinals forsook the building and sought refuge, some within the walls of St. Angelo, and four by flight beyond the walls of the city.   The real pope was waiting for recognition while the members of the electing college were fled.   But by the next day the cardinals had sufficiently regained their self-possession to assemble again,— all except the four who had put the city walls behind them, — and Cardinal Peter de Vergne, using the customary formula, proclaimed to the crowd through the window : " I announce to you a great joy.   You have a pope, and he calls himself Urban VI."   The new pontiff was crowned on April 18, in front of St. Peter's, by Cardinal Orsini.

The archbishop had enjoyed the confidence of Gregory XI. He enjoyed a reputation for austere morals and strict conformity to the rules of fasting and other observances enjoined by the Church.   He wore a hair shirt, and was accustomed to retire with the Bible in his hand.   At the moment of his election no doubt was expressed as to its validity.   Nieheim, who was in the city at the time, declared that Urban was canonical pope-elect.   "This is the truth," he wrote, "and no one can honestly deny it."[1]   All the cardinals in Rome yielded Urban submission, and in a letter dated May 8 they announced to the emperor and all Christians the election and coronation.   The cardinals at Avignon wrote acknowledging him, and ordered the keys to the castle of St. Angelo placed in his hands.   It is probable that no one would have thought of denying Urban's rights if the pope had removed to Avignon, or otherwise yielded to the demands of the French members of the curia.   His failure to go to France, Urban declared to be the cause of the opposition to him.

Seldom has so fine an opportunity been offered to do a worthy thing and to win a great name as was offered to Urban VI.   It was the opportunity to put an end to the disturbance in the Church by maintaining the residence of the papacy in its ancient seat, and restoring to it the dignity which it had lost by its long exile.   Urban, however, was not equal to the occasion, and made an utter failure.   He violated all the laws of common prudence and tact.   His head seemed to be completely turned.   He estranged and insulted his cardinals.   He

[1] Erler's ed., p. 16.

might have made provision for a body of warm supporters by the prompt appointment of new members to the college, but even this measure he failed to take till it was too late.   The French king, it is true, was bent upon having the papacy return to French soil, and controlled the French cardinals.   But a pope of ordinary shrewdness was in position to foil the king. This quality Urban VI. lacked, and the sacred college, stung by his insults, came to regard him as an intruder in St. Peter's chair.

In his concern for right living, Urban early took occasion in a public allocution to reprimand the cardinals for their worldliness and for living away from their sees.   He forbade their holding more than a single appointment and accepting gifts from princes.   To their demand that Avignon continue to be the seat of the papacy, Urban brusquely told them that Rome and the papacy were joined together, and he would not separate them.   As the papacy belonged not to France but to the whole world, he would distribute the promotions to the sacred college among the nations.

Incensed at the attack made upon their habits and perquisites, and upon their national sympathies, the French cardinals, giving the heat of the city as the pretext, removed one by one to Anagni, while Urban took up his summer residence at Tivoli.   His Italian colleagues followed him, but they also went over to the French.   No pope had ever been left more alone.   Forming a compact body, the French members of the curia demanded the pope's resignation.   The Italians, who at first proposed the calling of a council, acquiesced.   The French seceders then issued a declaration, dated Aug. 2, in which Urban was denounced as an apostate, and his election declared void in view of the duress under which it was accomplished.[1]   It asserted that the cardinals at the time were in mortal terror from the Romans.   Now that he would not resign, they anathematized him.   Urban replied in a document called the *Factum*, insisting upon the validity of his election.   Retiring to Fondi, in Neapolitan territory, the French cardinals proceeded to a new election,

[1] The document is given by Hefele, VI. 730–734.

Sept. 20, 1378, the choice falling upon one of their number, Robert of Geneva, the son of Amadeus, count of Geneva. He was one of those who, four months before, had pointed out Tebaldeschi to the Roman mob. The three Italian cardinals, though they did not actively participate in the election, offered no resistance. Urban is said to have received the news with tears, and to have expressed regret for his untactful and self-willed course. Perhaps he recalled the fate of his fellow-Neapolitan, Peter of Murrhone, whose lack of worldly wisdom a hundred years before had lost him the papal crown. To establish himself on the papal throne, he appointed 29 cardinals. But it was too late to prevent the schism which Gregory XI. had feared and a wise ruler would have averted.

Robert of Geneva, at the time of his election 36 years old, came to the papal honor with his hands red from the bloody massacre of Cesena. He had the reputation of being a politician and a fast liver. He was consecrated Oct. 31 under the name of Clement VII. It was a foregone conclusion that he would remove the papal seat back to Avignon. He first attempted to overthrow Urban on his own soil, but the attempt failed. Rome resisted, and the castle of St. Angelo, which was in the hands of his supporters, he lost, but not until its venerable walls were demolished, so that at a later time the very goats clambered over the stones. He secured the support of Joanna, and Louis of Anjou whom she had chosen as the heir of her kingdom, but the war which broke out between Urban and Naples fell out to Urban's advantage. The duke of Anjou was deposed, and Charles of Durazzo, of the royal house of Hungary, Joanna's natural heir, appointed as his successor. Joanna herself fell into Charles' hands and was executed, 1382, on the charge of having murdered her first husband. The duke of Brunswick was her fourth marital attempt. Clement VII. bestowed upon the duke of Anjou parts of the State of the Church and the high-sounding but empty title of duke of Adria. A portion of Urban's reward for crowning Charles, 1381, was the lordship over Capria, Amalfi, Fondi, and other localities, which he bestowed upon his unprincipled and worthless

nephew, Francis Prignano. In the war over Naples, the pope
had made free use of the treasure of the Roman churches.

Clement's cause in Italy was lost, and there was nothing for
him to do but to fall back upon his supporter, Charles V. He
returned to France by way of the sea and Marseilles.

Thus the schism was completed, and Western Europe had
the spectacle of two popes elected by the same college of
cardinals without a dissenting voice, and each making full
claims to the prerogative of the supreme pontiff of the Christian world. Each pope fulminated the severest judgments of
heaven against the other. The nations of Europe and its universities were divided in their allegiance or, as it was called,
their "obedience." The University of Paris, at first neutral,
declared in favor of Robert of Geneva,[1] as did Savoy, the
kingdoms of Spain, Scotland, and parts of Germany. England, Sweden, and the larger part of Italy supported Urban.
The German emperor, Charles IV., was about to take the same
side when he died, Nov. 29, 1378. Urban also had the vigorous
support of Catherine of Siena. Hearing of the election which
had taken place at Fondi she wrote to Urban : " I have heard
that those devils in human form have resorted to an election.
They have chosen not a vicar of Christ, but an anti-christ.
Never will I cease, dear father, to look upon you as Christ's
true vicar on earth."

The papal schism which Pastor has called "the greatest
misfortune that could be thought of for the Church "[2] soon
began to call forth indignant protests from the best men of the
time. Western Christendom had never known such a scandal. The seamless coat of Christ was rent in twain, and Solomon's words could no longer be applied, " My dove is but

[1] The full documentary accounts are given in the *Chartularium*, III. 561–
575. Valois gives a very detailed treatment of the allegiance rendered to the
two popes, especially in vol. II. Even in Sweden and Ireland Clement had
some support, but England, in part owing to her wars with France, gave un-
divided submission to Urban.

[2] Pastor, p. 143 sqq., quotes a German poem which strikingly sets forth the
evils of the schism, and Pastor himself says that nothing did so much as the
schism to prepare the way for the defection from the papacy in the sixteenth
century.

one."[1]   The divine claims of the papacy itself began to be matter of doubt.   Writers like Wyclif made demands upon the pope to return to Apostolic simplicity of manners in sharp language such as no one had ever dared to use before.   Many sees had two incumbents; abbeys, two abbots; parishes, two priests.   The maintenance of two popes involved an increased financial burden, and both papal courts added to the old practices new inventions to extract revenue.   Clement VII.'s agents went everywhere, striving to win support for his obedience, and the nations, taking advantage of the situation, magnified their authority to the detriment of the papal power.

The following is a list of the popes of the Roman and Avignon lines, and the Pisan line whose legitimacy has now no advocates in the Roman communion.

ROMAN LINE	AVIGNON LINE
Urban VI., 1378–1389.	Clement VII., 1378–1394.
Boniface IX., 1389–1404.	Benedict XIII., 1394–1409.
Innocent VII., 1404–1406.	*Deposed at Pisa, 1409, and at*
Gregory XII., 1406–1415.	*Constance, 1417, d. 1424.*
Deposed at Pisa, 1409. Resigned	
at Constance, 1415, d. 1417.	

PISAN LINE

Alexander V., 1409–1410.

John XXIII., 1410–1415.

Martin V., 1417–1431.

Acknowledged by the whole Latin Church.

The question of the legitimacy of Urban VI.'s pontificate is still a matter of warm dispute.   As neither pope nor council has given a decision on the question, Catholic scholars feel no constraint in discussing it.   French writers have been inclined to leave the matter open.   This was the case with Bossuet, Mansi, Martène, as it is with modern French writers.   Valois hesitatingly, Salembier positively, decides for Urban.   Historians, not moved by French sympathies, pronounce strongly in favor of the Roman line, as do Hefele, Funk, Hergenröther-Kirsch, Denifle, and Pastor.   The formal recognition of Urban by all the cardinals and their official announcement of

---

[1] Adam of Usk, p. 218, and other writers.

his election to the princes would seem to put the validity of his election beyond doubt. On the other hand, the *declaratio* sent forth by the cardinals nearly four months after Urban's election affirms that the cardinals were in fear of their lives when they voted; and according to the theory of the canon law, constraint invalidates an election as constraint invalidated Pascal II.'s concession to Henry V. It was the intention of the cardinals, as they affirm, to elect one of their number, till the tumult became so violent and threatening that to protect themselves they precipitately elected Prignano. They state that the people had even filled the air with the cry, "let them be killed," *moriantur*. A panic prevailed. When the tumult abated, the cardinals sat down to dine, and after dinner were about to proceed to a re-election, as they say, when the tumult again became threatening, and the doors of the room where they were sitting were broken open, so that they were forced to flee for their lives.

To this testimony were added the depositions of individual cardinals later. Had Prignano proved complaisant to the wishes of the French party, there is no reason to suspect that the validity of his election would ever have been disputed. Up to the time when the vote was cast for Urban, the cardinals seem not to have been under duress from fear, but to have acted freely. After the vote had been cast, they felt their lives were in danger.[1] If the cardinals had proceeded to a second vote, as Valois has said, Urban might have been elected. The constant communications which passed between Charles V. and the French party at Anagni show him to have been a leading factor in the proceedings which followed and the reconvening of the conclave which elected Robert of Geneva.[2]

[1] This is the judgment of Pastor, I. 119.

[2] Valois, I. 144, devotes much space to the part Charles took in preparing the way for the schism, and declares he was responsible for the part France took in it and in rejecting Urban VI. Hergenröther says all the good he can of the Roman line and all the evil he can of the Avignon line. Clement he pronounces a man of elastic conscience, and Benedict XIII., his successor, as always ready in words for the greatest sacrifices, and farthest from them when it came to deeds.

On the other hand, the same body of cardinals which elected Urban deposed him, and, in their capacity as princes of the Church, unanimously chose Robert as his successor. The question of the authority of the sacred college to exercise this prerogative is still a matter of doubt. It received the abdication of Cœlestine V. and elected a successor to him while he was still living. In that case, however, the papal throne became vacant by the supreme act of the pope himself.

§ 14. *Further Progress of the Schism.* 1378–1409.

The territory of Naples remained the chief theatre of the conflict between the papal rivals, Louis of Anjou, who had the support of Clement VII., continuing to assert his claim to the throne. In 1383 Urban secretly left Rome for Naples, but was there held in virtual confinement till he had granted Charles of Durazzo's demands. He then retired to Nocera, which belonged to his nephew. The measures taken by the cardinals at Anagni had taught him no lesson. His insane severity and self-will continued, and brought him into the danger of losing the papal crown. Six of his cardinals entered into a conspiracy to dethrone him, or at least to make him subservient to the curia. The plot was discovered, and Urban launched the interdict against Naples, whose king was supposed to have been a party to it. The offending cardinals were imprisoned in an old cistern, and afterwards subjected to the torture.[1] Forced to give up the town and to take refuge in the fortress, the relentless pontiff is said to have gone three or four times daily to the window, and, with candles burning and to the sound of a bell, to have solemnly pronounced the formula of excommunication against the besieging troops. Allowed to depart, and proceeding with the members of his household across the country, Urban reached Trani and embarked on a Genoese ship which finally landed him at Genoa, 1386. On the way, the crew threatened to carry him to Avignon, and had to be bought off by the un-

---

[1] Nieheim, p. 91. See also pp. 103 sq., 110, for the further treatment of the cardinals, which was worthy of Pharaoh.

fortunate pontiff.   Was ever a ruler in a worse predicament, beating about on the Mediterranean, than Urban!   Five of the cardinals who had been dragged along in chains now met with a cruel end.   Adam Aston, the English cardinal, Urban had released at the request of the English king.   But towards the rest of the alleged conspirators he showed the heartless relentlessness of a tyrant.   The chronicler Nieheim, who was with the pope at Naples and Nocera, declares that his heart was harder than granite.   Different rumors were afloat concerning the death the prelates were subjected to, one stating they had been thrown into the sea, another that they had their heads cut off with an axe; another report ran that their bodies were buried in a stable after being covered with lime and then burnt.

In the meantime, two of the prelates upon whom Urban had conferred the red hat, both Italians, went over to Clement VII. and were graciously received.

Breaking away from Genoa, Urban went by way of Lucca to Perugia, and then with another army started off for Naples. Charles of Durazzo, who had been called to the throne of Hungary and murdered in 1386, was succeeded by his young son Ladislaus (1386–1414), but his claim was contested by the heir of Louis of Anjou (d. 1384).   The pontiff got no farther than Ferentino, and turning back was carried in a carriage to Rome, where he again entered the Vatican, a few months before his death, Oct. 15, 1389.

Bartholomew Prignano had disappointed every expectation. He was his own worst enemy.   He was wholly lacking in common prudence and the spirit of conciliation.   It is to his credit that, as Nieheim urges, he never made ecclesiastical preferment the object of sale.   Whatever were his virtues before he received the tiara, he had as pope shown himself in every instance utterly unfit for the responsibilities of a ruler.

Clement VII., who arrived in Avignon in June, 1379, stooped before the kings of France, Charles V. (d. 1380) and Charles VI.   He was diplomatic and versatile where his rival was impolitic and intractable.   He knew how to entertain at his table with elegance.[1] The distinguished preacher, Vincent Ferrer, gave him his support. Among the new cardinals he appointed was the young prince of Luxemburg, who enjoyed a great reputation for saintliness. At the prince's death, in 1387, miracles were said to be performed at his tomb, a circumstance which seemed to favor the claims of the Avignon pope.

Clement's embassy to Bohemia for a while had hopes of securing a favorable declaration from the Bohemian king, Wenzil, but was disappointed.[2] The national pride of the French was Clement's chief dependence, and for the king's support he was obliged to pay a humiliating price by granting the royal demands to bestow ecclesiastical offices and tax Church property. As a means of healing the schism, Clement proposed a general council, promising, in case it decided in his favor, to recognize Urban as leading cardinal. The first schismatic pope died suddenly of apoplexy, Sept. 16, 1394, having outlived Urban VI. five years.

Boniface IX., who succeeded Urban VI., was, like him, a Neapolitan, and only thirty-five at the time of his election. He was a man of fine presence, and understood the art of ruling, but lacked the culture of the schools, and could not even write, and was poor at saying the services.[3] He had the satisfaction of seeing the kingdom of Naples yield to the Roman obedience. He also secured from the city of Rome full submission, and the document, by which it surrendered to him its republican liberties, remained for centuries the foundation of the relations of the municipality to the Apostolic See.[4] Bologna, Perugia, Viterbo, and other towns of Italy which had acknowledged Clement, were brought into submission to him, so that before his death the entire peninsula was under his obedience except Genoa, which Charles VI. had reduced. All men's eyes began again to turn to Rome.

In 1390, the Jubilee Year which Urban VI. had appointed attracted streams of pilgrims to Rome from Germany, Hun-

---

[1] Nieheim, p. 124.   [2] Valois, II. 282, 299 sqq.
[3] *Nesciens scribere etiam male cantabat*, Nieheim, p. 130.
[4] Gregorovius, VI. 547 sqq. ; Valois, II. 162, 166 sqq.

gary, Bohemia, Poland, and England and other lands, as did
also the Jubilee of 1400, commemorating the close of one and
the beginning of another century.   If Rome profited by these
celebrations, Boniface also made in other ways the most of
his opportunity, and his agents throughout Christendom returned with the large sums which they had realized from the
sale of dispensations and indulgences.   Boniface left behind
him a reputation for avarice and freedom in the sale of ecclesiastical concessions.[1]   He was also notorious for his nepotism,
enriching his brothers Andrew and John and other relatives
with offices and wealth.   Such offences, however, the Romans
could easily overlook in view of the growing regard throughout Europe for the Roman line of popes and the waning influence of the Avignon line.

The preponderant influence of Ladislaus secured the election of still another Neapolitan, Cardinal Cosimo dei Miglio-
rati, who took the name of Innocent VII.   He also was only
thirty-five years old at the time of his elevation to the papal
chair, a doctor of both laws and expert in the management of
affairs.   The members of the conclave, before proceeding to
an election, signed a document whereby each bound himself,
if elected pope, to do all in his power to put an end to the
schism.   The English chronicler, Adam of Usk, who was
present at the coronation, concludes the graphic description
he gives of the ceremonies[2] with a lament over the desolate
condition of the Roman city.   How much is Rome to be
pitied!   he exclaims, "for, once thronged with princes and
their palaces, she is now a place of hovels, thieves, wolves,
worms, full of desert spots and laid waste by her own citizens
who rend each other in pieces.   Once her empire devoured

---

[1] *Erat insatiabilis vorago et in avaricia nullus similis ei*, Nieheim, p. 119.
Nieheim, to be sure, was disappointed in not receiving office under Boniface, but
other contemporaries say the same thing.   Adam of Usk, p. 259, states that,
"though gorged with simony, Boniface to his dying day was never filled."

[2] *Chronicle*, p. 262 sqq.   This is one of the most full and interesting accounts extant of the coronation of a mediæval pope.   Usk describes the conclave as well as the coronation, and he mentions expressly how, on his way
from St. Peter's to the Lateran, Innocent purposely turned aside from St.
Clement's, near which stood the bust of Pope Joan and her son.

the world with the sword, and now her priesthood devours it with mummery.   Hence the lines —

"'The Roman bites at all, and those he cannot bite, he hates.
Of rich he hears the call, but 'gainst the poor he shuts his gates.'"

Following the example of his two predecessors, Innocent excommunicated the Avignon anti-pope and his cardinals, putting them into the same list with heretics, pirates, and brigands.   In revenge for his nephew's cold-blooded slaughter of eleven of the chief men of the city, whose bodies he threw out of a window, he was driven from Rome, and after great hardships he reached Viterbo.   But the Romans soon found Innocent's rule preferable to the rule of Ladislaus, king of Naples and papal protector, and he was recalled, the nephew whose hands were reeking with blood making public entry into the Vatican with his uncle.

The last pope of the Roman line was Gregory XII.   Angelo Correr, cardinal of St. Marks, Venice, elected 1406, was surpassed in tenacity as well as ability by the last of the Avignon popes, elected 1394, and better known as Peter de Luna of Aragon, one of the cardinals who joined in the revolt against Urban VI. and in the election of Clement VII. at Fondi.

Under these two pontiffs the controversy over the schism grew more and more acute and the scandal more and more intolerable.   The nations of Western Europe were weary of the open and flagitious traffic in benefices and other ecclesiastical privileges, the fulminations of one pope against the other, and the division of sees and parishes between rival claimants.   The University of Paris took the leading part in agitating remedial measures, and in the end the matter was taken wholly out of the hands of the two popes.   The cardinals stepped into the foreground and, in the face of all canonical precedent, took the course which ultimately resulted in the reunion of the Church under one head.

Before Gregory's election, the Roman cardinals, numbering fourteen, again entered into a compact stipulating that the successful candidate should by all means put an end to the schism, even, if necessary, by the abdication of his office.

Gregory was fourscore at the time, and the chief consideration which weighed in his choice was that in men arrived at
his age ambition usually runs low, and that Gregory would
be more ready to deny himself for the good of the Church
than a younger man.

Peter de Luna, one of the most vigorous personalities who
have ever claimed the papal dignity, had the spirit and much
of the ability of Hildebrand and his namesake, Gregory IX.
But it was his bad star to be elected in the Avignon and not
in the Roman succession.   Had he been in the Roman line,
he would probably have made his mark among the great
ruling pontiffs.   His nationality also was against him.   The
French had little heart in supporting a Spaniard and, at
Clement's death, the relations between the French king and
the Avignon pope at once lost their cordiality.   Peter was
energetic of mind and in action, a shrewd observer, magnified his office, and never yielded an inch in the matter of
papal prerogative.   Through the administrations of three
Roman pontiffs, he held on firmly to his office, outlived the
two Reformatory councils of Pisa and Constance, and yielded
not up this mortal flesh till the close of the first quarter of
the fifteenth century, and was still asserting his claims and
maintaining the dignity of pope at the time of his death.   Before his election, he likewise entered into a solemn compact with his cardinals, promising to bend every effort to
heal the unholy schism, even if the price were his own abdication.

The professions of both popes were in the right direction.
They were all that could be desired, and all that remained was
for either of them or for both of them to resign and make
free room for a new candidate.   The problem would thus
have been easily settled, and succeeding generations might
have canonized both pontiffs for their voluntary self-abnega-
tion.   But it took ten years to bring Gregory to this state of
mind, and then almost the last vestige of power had been
taken from him.   Peter de Luna never yielded.

Undoubtedly, at the time of the election of Gregory XII.,
the papacy was passing through one of the grave crises in its

history.   There were not wanting men who said, like Langenstein, vice-chancellor of the University of Paris, that perhaps
it was God's purpose that there should be two popes indefi-
nitely, even as David's kingdom was divided under two
sovereigns.[1]   Yea, and there were men who argued publicly
that it made little difference how many there were, two or
three, or ten or twelve, or as many as there were nations.[2]

At his first consistory Gregory made a good beginning,
when he asserted that, for the sake of the good cause of
securing a united Christendom, he was willing to travel by
land or by sea, by land, if necessary, with a pilgrim's staff,
by sea in a fishing smack, in order to come to an agreement
with Benedict.   He wrote to his rival on the Rhone, declaring that, like the woman who was ready to renounce
her child rather than see it cut asunder, so each of them
should be willing to cede his authority rather than be responsible for the continuance of the schism.   He laid his
hand on the New Testament and quoted the words that
"he who exalteth himself shall be abased, and he that
humbleth himself shall be exalted."   He promised to
abdicate, if Benedict would do the same, that the cardinals
of both lines might unite together in a new election; and he
further promised not to add to the number of his cardinals,
except to keep the number equal to the number of the
Avignon college.

Benedict's reply was shrewd, if not equally demonstrative.
He, too, lamented the schism, which he pronounced detestable,
wretched, and dreadful,[3] but gently setting aside Gregory's
blunt proposal, suggested as the best resort the *via discussionis*,
or the path of discussion, and that the cardinals of both lines
should meet together, talk the matter over, and see what
should be done, and then, if necessary, one or both popes
might abdicate.   Both popes in their communications called

[1] Du Pin, II. 821.

[2] Letter of the Univ. of Paris to Clement VII., dated July 17, 1394. *Chartul.*
III. 633, *nihil omnino curandum quot papae sint, et non modo duos aut tres,
sed decem aut duodecim immo et singulis regnis singulos prefici posse,* etc.

[3] *Hæc execranda et detestanda, diraque divisio,* Nieheim, pp. 209-213,
gives both letters entire.

themselves "servant of the servants of God."   Gregory addressed Benedict as "Peter de Luna, whom some peoples in
this wretched — *miserabili* — schism call Benedict XIII.";
and Benedict addressed the pope on the Tiber as "Angelus
Correr, whom some, adhering to him in this most destructive
— *pernicioso* — schism, call Gregory XII."   "We are both old
men," wrote Benedict.   "Time is short; hasten, and do not
delay in this good cause.   Let us both embrace the ways of
salvation and peace."

Nothing could have been finer, but it was quickly felt that
while both popes expressed themselves as ready to abdicate,
positive as the professions of both were, each wanted to have
the advantage when the time came for the election of the
new pontiff to rule over the reunited Church.

As early as 1381, the University of Paris appealed to the
king of France to insist upon the calling of a general council
as the way to terminate the schism.   But the duke of Anjou
had the spokesman of the university, Jean Ronce, imprisoned,
and the university was commanded to keep silence on the
subject.

Prior to this appeal, two individuals had suggested the
same idea, Konrad of Gelnhausen, and Henry of Langenstein,
otherwise known as Henry of Hassia.   Konrad, who wrote
in 1380,[1] and whose views led straight on to the theory of
the supreme authority of councils,[2] affirmed that there were
two heads of the Church, and that Christ never fails it, even
though the earthly head may fail by death or error.   The
Church is not the pope and the cardinals, but the body of
the faithful, and this body gets its inner life directly from
Christ, and is so far infallible.   In this way he answers those
who were forever declaring that in the absence of the pope's
call there would be no council, even if all the prelates were
assembled, but only a conventicle.

In more emphatic terms, Henry of Langenstein, in 1381,
justified the calling of a council without the pope's interven-

---

[1] Gelnhausen's tract, *De congregando concilio in tempore schismatis*, in
Martène-Durand, *Thesaurus nov. anecd.*, II. 1200–1226.

[2] So Pastor, I. 185.   See also, Schwab, *Gerson*, p. 124 sqq.

tion.[1] The institution of the papacy by Christ, he declared, did not involve the idea that the action of the pope was always necessary, either in originating or consenting to legislation. The Church might have instituted the papacy, even had Christ not appointed it. If the cardinals should elect a pontiff not agreeable to the Church, the Church might set their choice aside. The validity of a council did not depend upon the summons or the ratification of a pope. Secular princes might call such a synod. A general council, as the representative of the entire Church, is above the cardinals, yea, above the pope himself. Such a council cannot err, but the cardinals and the pope may err.

The views of Langenstein, vice-chancellor of the University of Paris, represented the views of the faculties of that institution. They were afterwards advocated by John Gerson, one of the most influential men of his century, and one of the most honored of all the centuries. Among those who took the opposite view was the English Dominican and confessor of Benedict XIII., John Hayton. The University of Paris he called "a daughter of Satan, mother of error, sower of sedition, and the pope's defamer," and declared the pope was to be forced by no human tribunal, but to follow God and his own conscience.

In 1394, the University of Paris proposed three methods of healing the schism[2] which became the platform over which the issue was afterwards discussed, namely, the *via cessionis*, or the abdication of both popes, the *via compromissi*, an adjudication of the claims of both by a commission, and the *via synodi*, or the convention of a general council to which the settlement of the whole matter should be left. No act in the whole history of this famous literary institution has given it wider fame than this proposal, coupled with the activity it displayed to bring the schism to a close. The method preferred by its faculties was the first, the abdication of both popes, which it regarded as the simplest remedy. It was

---

[1] *Consilium pacis de unione et reformatione ecclesiæ in concilio universali quærenda*, Van der Hardt, II. 3–60, and Du Pin, *Opp. Gerson*, II. 810 sqq. [2] *Chartul.* III. p. 608 sqq.

suggested that the new election, after the popes had abdicated, should be consummated by the cardinals in office at the time of Gregory XI.'s decease, 1378, and still surviving, or by a union of the cardinals of both obediences.

The last method, settlement by a general council, which the university regarded as offering the most difficulty, it justified on the ground that the pope is subject to the Church as Christ was subject to his mother and Joseph. The authority of such a council lay in its constitution according to Christ's words, "where two or three are gathered together in my name, there am I in the midst of them." Its membership should consist of doctors of theology and the laws taken from the older universities, and deputies of the orders, as well as bishops, many of whom were uneducated, — *illiterati*.[1]

Clement VII. showed his displeasure with the university by forbidding its further intermeddling, and by condemning his cardinals who, without his permission, had met and recommended him to adopt one of the three ways. At Clement's death the king of France called upon the Avignon college to postpone the election of a successor, but, surmising the contents of the letter, they prudently left it unopened until they had chosen Benedict XIII. Benedict at once manifested the warmest zeal in the healing of the schism, and elaborated his plan for meeting with Boniface IX., and coming to some agreement with him. These friendly propositions were offset by a summons from the king's delegates, calling upon the two pontiffs to abdicate, and all but two of the Avignon cardinals favored the measure. But Benedict declared that such a course would seem to imply constraint, and issued a bull against it.

The two parties continued to express deep concern for the healing of the schism, but neither would yield. Benedict gained the support of the University of Toulouse, and strengthened himself by the promotion of Peter d'Ailly, chancellor of the University of Paris, to the episcopate. The famous inquisitor, Nicolas Eymericus, also one of his cardinals, was a firm advocate of Benedict's divine claims. The difficulties

---

[1] *Chartul.*, I. 620.

were increased by the wavering course of Charles VI., 1380–1412, a man of feeble mind, and twice afflicted with insanity, whose brothers and uncles divided the rule of the kingdom amongst themselves.   French councils attempted to decide upon a course for the nation to pursue, and a third council, meeting in Paris, 1398, and consisting of 11 archbishops and 60 bishops, all theretofore supporters of the Avignon pope, decided upon the so-called subtraction of obedience from Benedict.   In spite of these discouragements, Benedict continued loyal to himself.   He was forsaken by his cardinals and besieged by French troops in his palace and wounded.   The spectacle of his isolation touched the heart and conscience of the French people, and the decree ordering the subtraction of obedience was annulled by the national parliament of 1403, which professed allegiance anew, and received from him full absolution.

When Gregory XII. was elected in 1406, the controversy over the schism was at white heat.   England, Castile, and the German king, Wenzil, had agreed to unite with France in bringing it to an end.   Pushed by the universal clamor, by the agitation of the University of Paris, and especially by the feeling which prevailed in France, Gregory and Benedict saw that the situation was in danger of being controlled by other hands than their own, and agreed to meet at Savona on the Gulf of Genoa to discuss their differences.   In October, 1407, Benedict, attended by a military guard, went as far as Porto Venere and Savona.   Gregory got as far as Lucca, when he declined to go farther, on the plea that Savona was in territory controlled by the French and on other pretexts.   Nieheim represents the Roman pontiff as dissimulating during the whole course of the proceedings and as completely under the influence of his nephews and other favorites, who imposed upon the weakness of the old man, and by his doting generosity were enabled to live in luxury.   At Lucca they spent their time in dancing and merry-making.   This writer goes on to say that Gregory put every obstacle in the way of union.[1]   He is

---

[1] Nieheim, pp. 237, 242, 274, etc., *manifeste impedire modis omnibus conabantur.*

represented by another writer as having spent more in bonbons than his predecessors did for their wardrobes and tables, and as being only a shadow with bones and skin.[1]

Benedict's support was much weakened by the death of the king's brother, the duke of Orleans, who had been his constant supporter.   France threatened neutrality, and Benedict, fearing seizure by the French commander at Genoa, beat a retreat to Perpignan, a fortress at the foot of the Pyrenees, six miles from the Mediterranean.   In May of the same year France again decreed "subtraction," and a national French assembly in 1408 approved the calling of a council.   The last stages of the contest were approaching.

Seven of Gregory's cardinals broke away from him, and, leaving him at Lucca, went to Pisa, where they issued a manifesto appealing from a poorly informed pope to a better informed one, from Christ's vicar to Christ himself, and to the decision of a general council.   Two more followed.   Gregory further injured his cause by breaking his solemn engagement and appointing four cardinals, May, 1408, two of them his nephews, and a few months later he added ten more.   Cardinals of the Avignon obedience joined the Roman cardinals at Pisa and brought the number up to thirteen.   Retiring to Livorno on the beautiful Italian lake of that name, and acting as if the popes were deposed, they as rulers of the Church appointed a general council to meet at Pisa, March 25, 1409.

As an offset, Gregory summoned a council of his own to meet in the territory either of Ravenna or Aquileja.   Many of his closest followers had forsaken him, and even his native city of Venice withdrew from him its support.   In the meantime Ladislaus had entered Rome and been hailed as king. It is, however, probable that this was with the consent of Gregory himself, who hoped thereby to gain sympathy for his cause.   Benedict also exercised his sovereign power as pontiff and summoned a council to meet at Perpignan, Nov. 1, 1408.

The word "council," now that the bold initiative was taken, was hailed as pregnant with the promise of sure relief from

[1] *Vita*, Muratori, III., II., 838, *solum spiritus cum ossibus et pelle.*

the disgrace and confusion into which Western Christendom
had been thrown and of a reunion of the Church.

§ 15. *The Council of Pisa.*

The three councils of Pisa, 1409, Constance, 1414, and
Basel, 1431, of which the schism was the occasion, are known
in history as the Reformatory councils. Of the tasks they
set out to accomplish, the healing of the schism and the institution of disciplinary reforms in the Church, the first they accomplished, but with the second they made little progress.
They represent the final authority of general councils in the
affairs of the Church — a view, called the conciliary theory—
in distinction from the supreme authority of the papacy.

The Pisan synod marks an epoch in the history of Western
Christendom not so much on account of what it actually accomplished as because it was the first revolt in council against
the theory of papal absolutism which had been accepted for
centuries. It followed the ideas of Gerson and Langenstein,
namely, that the Church is the Church even without the
presence of a pope, and that an œcumenical council is legitimate which meets not only in the absence of his assent but
in the face of his protest. Representing intellectually the
weight of the Latin world and the larger part of its constituency, the assembly was a momentous event leading in the
opposite direction from the path laid out by Hildebrand,
Innocent III., and their successors. It was a mighty blow
at the old system of Church government.

While Gregory XII. was tarrying at Rimini, as a refugee,
under the protection of Charles Malatesta, and Benedict XIII.
was confined to the seclusion of Perpignan, the synod was
opened on the appointed day in the cathedral of Pisa.   There
was an imposing attendance of 14 cardinals, — the number
being afterwards increased to 24, — 4 patriarchs, 10 archbishops, 79 bishops and representatives of 116 other bishops,
128 abbots and priors and the representatives of 200 other
abbots.   To these prelates were added the generals of the
Dominican, Franciscan, Carmelite, and Augustinian orders,

the grand-master of the Knights of St. John, who was accompanied by 6 commanders, the general of the Teutonic order, 300 doctors of theology and the canon law, 109 representatives of cathedral and collegiate chapters, and the deputies of many princes, including the king of the Romans, Wenzil, and the kings of England, France, Poland, and Cyprus. A new and significant feature was the representation of the universities of learning, including Paris,[1] Bologna, Oxford and Cambridge, Montpellier, Toulouse, Angers, Vienna, Cracow, Prag, and Cologne. Among the most important personages was Peter d'Ailly, though there is no indication in the acts of the council that he took a prominent public part. John Gerson seems not to have been present.

The second day, the archbishop of Milan, Philargi, himself soon to be elected pope, preached from Judg. 20: 7: "Behold ye are all children of Israel. Give here your advice and counsel," and stated the reasons which had led to the summoning of the council. Guy de Maillesec, the only cardinal surviving from the days prior to the schism, presided over the first sessions. His place was then filled by the patriarch of Alexandria, till the new pope was chosen.

One of the first deliverances was a solemn profession of the Holy Trinity and the Catholic faith, and that every heretic and schismatic will share with the devil and his angels the burnings of eternal fire unless before the end of this life he make his peace with the Catholic Church.[2]

The business which took precedence of all other was the healing of the schism, the *causa unionis*, as it was called, and disposition was first made of the rival popes. A formal trial was instituted, which was opened by two cardinals and two archbishops proceeding to the door of the cathedral and solemnly calling Gregory and Benedict by name and summoning them to appear and answer for themselves. The formality

---

[1] Schwab, p. 223 sq. The address which Gerson is said to have delivered and which Mansi includes in the acts of the council was a rhetorical composition and never delivered at Pisa.   Schwab, p. 243.

[2] Mansi, XXVII. 358.

was gone through three times, on three successive days, and the offenders were given till April 15 to appear.

By a series of declarations the synod then justified its existence, and at the eighth session declared itself to be " a general council representing the whole universal Catholic Church and lawfully and reasonably called together." [1] It thought along the lines marked out by D'Ailly and Gerson and the other writers who had pronounced the unity of the Church to consist in oneness with her divine Head and declared that the Church, by virtue of the power residing in herself, has the right, in response to a divine call, to summon a council. The primitive Church had called synods, and James, not Peter, had presided at Jerusalem.

D'Ailly, in making definite announcement of his views at a synod, meeting at Aix, Jan. 1, 1409, had said that the Church's unity depends upon the unity of her head, Christ. Christ's mystical body gets its authority from its divine head to meet in a general council through representatives, for it is written, " where two or three are gathered together in my name, there am I in the midst of them."   The words are not " in Peter's name," or " in Paul's name," but " in my name." And when the faithful assemble to secure the welfare of the Church, there Christ is in their midst.

Gerson wrote his most famous tract bearing on the schism and the Church's right to remove a pope — *De auferibilitate papæ ab ecclesia* — while the council of Pisa was in session.[2] In this elaborate treatment he said that, in the strict sense, Christ is the Church's only bridegroom. The marriage between the pope and the Church may be dissolved, for such a spiritual marriage is not a sacrament. The pope may choose to separate himself from the Church and resign. The Church has a similar right to separate itself from the pope by removing him. All Church officers are appointed for the Church's welfare and, when the pope impedes its welfare, it may remove him. It is bound to defend itself. This it may do through a general council, meeting by general consent and without papal appointment. Such a council depends immediately upon Christ

[1] Mansi, XXVII. 366.   [2] See Schwab, p. 250 sqq.

for its authority.   The pope may be deposed for heresy or schism.   He might be deposed even where he had no personal guilt, as in case he should be taken prisoner by the Saracens, and witnesses should testify he was dead.   Another pope would then be chosen and, if the reports of the death of the former pope were proved false, and he be released from captivity, he or the other pope would have to be removed, for the Church cannot have more than one pontiff.

Immediately after Easter, Charles Malatesta appeared in the council to advocate Gregory's cause.   A commission, appointed by the cardinals, presented forty reasons to show that an agreement between the synod and the Roman pontiff was out of the question.   Gregory must either appear at Pisa in person and abdicate, or present his resignation to a commission which the synod would appoint and send to Rimini.

Gregory's case was also represented by the rival king of the Romans, Ruprecht,[1] through a special embassy made up of the archbishop of Riga, the bishops of Worms and Verden, and other commissioners.   It presented twenty-four reasons for denying the council's jurisdiction.   The paper was read by the bishop of Verden at the close of a sermon preached to the assembled councillors on the admirable text, " Peace be unto you."   The most catching of the reasons was that, if the cardinals questioned the legitimacy of Gregory's pontificate, what ground had they for not questioning the validity of their own authority, appointed as they had been by Gregory or Benedict.

In a document of thirty-eight articles, read April 24, the council presented detailed specifications against the two popes, charging them both with having made and broken solemn promises to resign.

The argument was conducted by Peter de Anchorano, professor of both laws in Bologna, and by others.   Peter argued that, by fostering the schism, Gregory and his rival had forfeited jurisdiction, and the duty of calling a representative council of Christendom devolved on the college of cardinals.

[1] The electors deposed Wenzil in 1400 for incompetency, and elected Ruprecht of the Palatinate.

In certain cases the cardinals are left no option whether they shall act or not, as when a pope is insane or falls into heresy or refuses to summon a council at a time when orthodox doctrine is at stake.   The temporal power has the right to expel a pope who acts illegally.

In an address on Hosea 1: 11, "and the children of Judah and the children of Israel shall be gathered together and shall appoint themselves one head," Peter Plaoul, of the University of Paris, clearly placed the council above the pope, an opinion which had the support of his own university as well as the support of the universities of Toulouse, Angers, and Orleans. The learned canonist, Zabarella, afterwards appointed cardinal, took the same ground.

The trial was carried on with all decorum and, at the end of two months, on June 5, sentence was pronounced, declaring both popes "notorious schismatics, promoters of schism, and notorious heretics, errant from the faith, and guilty of the notorious and enormous crimes of perjury and violated oaths." [1]

Deputies arriving from Perpignan a week later, June 14, were hooted by the council when the archbishop of Tarragona, one of their number, declared them to be "the representatives of the venerable pope, Benedict XIII." Benedict had a short time before shown his defiance of the Pisan fathers by adding twelve members to his cabinet.   When the deputies announced their intention of waiting upon Gregory, and asked for a letter of safe conduct, Balthazar Cossa, afterwards John XXIII., the master of Bologna, is said to have declared, "Whether they come with a letter or without it, he would burn them all if he could lay his hands upon them."

The rival popes being disposed of, it remained for the council to proceed to a new election, and it was agreed to leave the matter to the cardinals, who met in the archiepiscopal palace of Pisa, June 26, and chose the archbishop of Milan, Philargi, who took the name of Alexander V.   He was about seventy,

---

[1] *Eorum utrumque fuisse et esse notorios schismaticos et antiqui schismatis nutritores . . . necnon notorios hæreticos et a fide devios, notoriisque criminibus enormibus perjuriis et violationis voti irretitos*, etc., Mansi, XXVI. 1147, 1225 sq.   Hefele, VI. 1025 sq., also gives the judgment in full.

a member of the Franciscan order, and had received the red
hat from Innocent VII.   He was a Cretan by birth, and the first
Greek to wear the tiara since John VII., in 705.   He had never
known his father or mother and, rescued from poverty by the
Minorites, he was taken to Italy to be educated, and later sent
to Oxford.   After his election as pope, he is reported to have
said, "as a bishop I was rich, as a cardinal poor, and as pope
I am a beggar again." [1]

In the meantime Gregory's side council at Cividale, near
Aquileja, was running its course.   There was scarcely an at-
tendant at the first session.   Later, Ruprecht and king Ladislaus were represented by deputies.   The assumption of the
body was out of all proportion to its size.   It pronounced the
pontiffs of the Roman line the legitimate rulers of Christendom, and appointed nuncios to all the kingdoms.   However,
not unmindful of his former professions, Gregory anew expressed his readiness to resign if his rivals, Peter of Luna and
Peter of Candia (Crete), would do the same.   Venice had declared for Alexander, and Gregory, obliged to flee in the disguise of a merchant, found refuge in the ships of Ladislaus.

Benedict's council met in Perpignan six months before, November, 1408.   One hundred and twenty prelates were in
attendance, most of them from Spain.   The council adjourned
March 26, 1409, after appointing a delegation of seven to proceed to Pisa and negotiate for the healing of the schism.

After Alexander's election, the members lost interest in the
synod and began to withdraw from Pisa, and it was found impossible to keep the promise made by the cardinals that there
should be no adjournment till measures had been taken to
reform the Church "in head and members."   Commissions
were appointed to consider reforms, and Alexander prorogued
the body, Aug. 7, 1409, after appointing another council for
April 12, 1412. [2]

---

[1] Nieheim, p. 320 sqq., gives an account of Alexander's early life.

[2] Creighton is unduly severe upon Alexander and the council for adjourn-
ing, without carrying out the promise of reform.   Hefele, VI. 1042, treats the
matter with fairness, and shows the difficulty involved in a disciplinary reform where the evils were of such long standing.

At the opening of the Pisan synod there were two popes ; at its close, three.   Scotland and Spain still held to Benedict, and Naples and parts of Central Europe continued to acknowledge the obedience of Gregory.   The greater part of Christendom, however, was bound to the support of Alexander.   This pontiff lacked the strength needed for the emergency, and he aroused the opposition of the University of Paris by extending the rights of the Mendicant orders to hear confessions.[1]   He died at Bologna, May 3, 1410, without having entered the papal city.   Rumor went that Balthazar Cossa, who was about to be elected his successor, had poison administered to him.

As a rule, modern Catholic historians are inclined to belittle the Pisan synod, and there is an almost general agreement among them that it lacked œcumenical character.   Without pronouncing a final decision on the question, Bellarmin regarded Alexander V. as legitimate pope.   Gerson and other great contemporaries treated it as œcumenical, as did also Bossuet and other Gallican historians two centuries later. Modern Catholic historians treat the claims of Gregory XII. as not affected by a council which was itself illegitimate and a high-handed revolt against canon law.[2]

But whether the name œcumenical be given or be withheld matters little, in view of the general judgment which the summons and sitting of the council call forth.   It was a desperate measure adopted to suit an emergency, but it was also the product of a new freedom of ecclesiastical thought, and

[1] The number of ecclesiastical gifts made by Alexander in his brief pontificate was large, and Nieheim pithily says that when the waters are confused, then is the time to fish.

[2] Pastor, I. 192, speaks of the unholy Pisan synod — *segenslose Pisaner Synode*.   All ultramontane historians disparage it, and Hergenröther-Kirsch uses a tone of irony in describing its call and proceedings.   They do not exonerate Gregory from having broken his solemn promise, but they treat the council as wholly illegitimate, either because it was not called by a pope or because it had not the universal support of the Catholic nations.   Hefele, I. 67 sqq., denies to it the character of an œcumenical synod, but places it in a category by itself.   Pastor opens his treatment with a discourse on the primacy of the papacy, dating from Peter, and the sole right of the pope to call a council.   The cardinals who called it usurped an authority which did not belong to them.

so far a good omen of a better age.   The Pisan synod demonstrated that the Church remained virtually a unit in spite of
the double pontifical administration.   It branded by their
right names the specious manœuvres of Gregory and Peter de
Luna.   It brought together the foremost thinkers and literary
interests of Europe and furnished a platform of free discussion.
Not its least service was in preparing the way for the imposing council which convened in Constance five years later.

§ 16. *The Council of Constance*. 1414–1418.

At Alexander's death, seventeen cardinals met in Bologna
and elected Balthazar Cossa, who took the name of John
XXIII.   He was of noble Neapolitan lineage, began his
career as a soldier and perhaps as a corsair,[1] was graduated
in both laws at Bologna and was made cardinal by Boniface
IX.   He joined in the call of the council of Pisa.   A man of
ability, he was destitute of every moral virtue, and capable of
every vice.

Leaning for support upon Louis of Anjou, John gained
entrance to Rome.   In the battle of Rocca Secca, May 14,
1411, Louis defeated the troops of Ladislaus.   The captured
battle-flags were sent to Rome, hung up in St. Peter's, then
torn down in the sight of the people, and dragged in the dust
in the triumphant procession through the streets of the city,
in which John participated.   Ladislaus speedily recovered
from his defeat, and John, with his usual faithlessness, made
terms with Ladislaus, recognizing him as king, while Ladislaus,
on his part, renounced his allegiance to Gregory XII.   That
pontiff was ordered to quit Neapolitan territory, and embark-
ing in Venetian vessels at Gaeta, fled to Dalmatia, and finally
took refuge with Charles Malatesta of Rimini, his last political ally.

The Council of Constance, the second of the Reformatory
councils, was called together by the joint act of Pope John
XXIII. and Sigismund, king of the Romans.   It was not till
he was reminded by the University of Paris that John paid

---

[1] Nieheim, in *Life of John*, in Van der Hardt, II. 339.

heed to the action of the Council of Pisa and called a council to meet at Rome, April, 1412.   Its sessions were scantily attended, and scarcely a trace of it is left.[1]   After ordering Wyclif's writings burnt, it adjourned Feb. 10, 1413.   John had strengthened the college of cardinals by adding fourteen to its number, among them men of the first rank, as D'Ailly, Zabarella of Florence, Robert Hallum, bishop of Salisbury, and Fillastre, dean of Rheims.

Ladislaus, weary of his treaty with John and ambitious to create a unified Latin kingdom, took Rome, 1413, giving the city over to sack.   The king rode into the Lateran and looked down from his horse on the heads of St. Peter and St. Paul, which he ordered the canons to display.   The very churches were robbed, and soldiers and their courtesans drank wine out of the sacred chalices.   Ladislaus left Rome, struck with a vicious disease, rumored to be due to poison administered by an apothecary's daughter of Perugia, and died at Naples, August, 1414.   He had been one of the most prominent figures in Europe for a quarter of a century and the chief supporter of the Roman line of pontiffs.

Driven from Rome, John was thrown into the hands of Sigismund, who was then in Lombardy.   This prince, the grandson of the blind king, John, who was killed at Crécy, had come to the throne of Hungary through marriage with its heiress.   At Ruprecht's death he was elected king of the Romans, 1411.   Circumstances and his own energy made him the most prominent sovereign of his age and the chief political figure in the Council of Constance.   He lacked high aims and moral purpose, but had some taste for books, and spoke several languages besides his own native German. Many sovereigns have placed themselves above national statutes, but Sigismund went farther and, according to the story, placed himself above the rules of grammar.   In his first address at the Council of Constance, so it is said, he treated the Latin word *schisma*, schism, as if it were feminine.[2]   When Pris-

---

[1] Finke : *Forschungen*, p. 2 ; *Acta conc.*, p. 108 sqq.

[2] *Date operam*, the king said, *ut ista. nefanda schisma eradicetur.* See Wylie, p. 18.

cian and other learned grammarians were quoted to him to show it was neuter, he replied, " Yes ; but I am emperor and above them, and can make a new grammar. " The fact that Sigismund was not yet emperor when the mistake is said to have been made — for he was not crowned till 1433 — seems to prejudice the authenticity of the story, but it is quite likely that he made mistakes in Latin and that the bon-mot was humorously invented with reference to it.

Pressed by the growing troubles in Bohemia over John Huss, Sigismund easily became an active participant in the measures looking towards a new council. Men distrusted John XXIII. The only hope of healing the schism seemed to rest with the future emperor. In many documents, and by John himself, he was addressed as " advocate and defender of the Church " [1] — *advocatus et defensor ecclesiæ*.[1]

Two of John's cardinals met Sigismund at Como, Oct. 13, 1413, and discussed the time and place of the new synod. John preferred an Italian city, Sigismund the small Swabian town of Kempten ; Strassburg, Basel, and other places were mentioned, but Constance, on German territory, was at last fixed upon. On Oct. 30 Sigismund announced the approaching council to all the prelates, princes, and doctors of Christendom, and on Dec. 9 John attached his seal to the call. Sigismund and John met at Lodi the last of November, 1413, and again at Cremona early in January, 1414, the pope being accompanied by thirteen cardinals. Thus the two great luminaries of this mundane sphere were again side by side.[2] They ascended together the great Torazzo, close to the cathedral of Cremona, accompanied by the lord of the town, who afterwards regretted that he had not seized his opportunity and pitched them both down to the street. Not till the following August was a formal announcement of the impending

---

[1] See Finke, *Forschungen*, p. 28. Sigismund gives himself the same title. See his letter to Gregory, Mansi, XXVIII. 3.

[2] Sigismund, in his letter to Charles VI. of France, announcing the council, had used the mediæval figure of the two lights, *duo luminaria super terram, majus videlicet minus ut in ipsis universalis ecclesiæ consistere firmamentum in quibus pontificalis auctoritas et regalis potentia designantur, unaquæ spiritualia et altera qua corporalia regerentur.* Mansi, XXVIII. 4.

council sent to Gregory XII., who recognized Sigismund as king of the Romans.[1] Gregory complained to Archbishop Andrew of Spalato, bearer of the notice, of the lateness of the invitation, and that he had not been consulted in regard to the council. Sigismund promised that, if Gregory should be deposed, he would see to it that he received a good life position.[2]

The council, which was appointed for Nov. 1, 1414, lasted nearly four years, and proved to be one of the most imposing gatherings which has ever convened in Western Europe. It was a veritable parliament of nations, a convention of the leading intellects of the age, who pressed together to give vent to the spirit of free discussion which the Avignon scandals and the schism had developed, and to debate the most urgent of questions, the reunion of Christendom under one undisputed head."[3]

Following the advice of his cardinals, John, who set his face reluctantly towards the North, reached Constance Oct. 28, 1414.   The city then contained 5500 people, and the beauty of its location, its fields, and its vineyards, were praised by Nieheim and other contemporaries.   They also spoke of the salubriousness of the air and the justice of the municipal laws for strangers.   It seemed to be as a field which the Lord had blessed.[4] As John approached Constance, coming by way of the Tirol, he is said to have exclaimed, " Ha, this is the place where foxes are trapped." He entered the town in great style, accompanied by nine cardinals and sixteen hundred mounted horsemen.   He rode a white horse, its back covered with a red rug.   Its bridles were held by the count of Montferrat and an Orsini of Rome.   The city council sent to the

---

[1] There is some evidence that a report was abroad in Italy that Sigismund intended to have all three popes put on trial at Constance, but that a gift of 50,000 gulden from John at Lodi induced him to support that pontiff.   Finke: *Acta*, p. 177 sq.

[2] Sigismund's letters are given by Hardt, VI. 5, 6 ; Mansi, XXVIII. 2–4. See Finke, *Forschungen*, p. 23.

[3] Funk, *Kirchengesch.*, p. 470, calls it *eine der grossartigsten Kirchenversammlungen welche die Geschichte kennt, gewissermassen ein Kongress des ganzen Abendlandes.*   [4] Hardt, II. 308.

The Kaufhaus, Constance

pope's lodgings four large barrels of Elsass wine, eight of native wine, and other wines.[1]

The first day of November, John attended a solemn mass at the cathedral. The council met on the 5th, with fifteen cardinals present. The first public session was held Nov. 16. In all, forty-five public sessions were held, the usual hour of assembling being 7 in the morning. Gregory XII. was represented by two delegates, the titular patriarch of Constantinople and Cardinal John Dominici of Ragusa, a man of great sagacity and excellent spirit.

The convention did not get into full swing until the arrival of Sigismund on Christmas Eve, fresh from his coronation, which occurred at Aachen, Nov. 8, and accompanied by his queen, Barbara, and a brilliant suite. After warming themselves, the imperial party proceeded to the cathedral and, at cock-crowing Christmas morning, were received by the pope. Services were held lasting eight, or, according to another authority, eleven hours without interruption. Sigismund, wearing his crown and a dalmatic, exercised the functions of deacon and read the Gospel, and the pope conferred upon him a sword, bidding him use it to protect the Church.

Constance had become the most conspicuous locality in Europe. It attracted people of every rank, from the king to the beggar. A scene of the kind on so great a scale had never been witnessed in the West before. The reports of the number of strangers in the city vary from 50,000 to 100,000. Richental, the indefatigable Boswell of the council, himself a resident of Constance, gives an account of the arrival of every important personage, together with the number of his retainers. One-half of his *Chronicle* is a directory of names. He went from house to house, taking a census, and to the thousands he mentions by name, he adds 5000 who

---

[1] Richental, *Chronik*, pp. 25–28, gives a graphic description of John's entry into the city. This writer, who was a citizen of Constance, the office he filled being unknown, had unusual opportunities for observing what was going on and getting the official documents. He gives copies of several of John's bulls, and the most detailed accounts of some of the proceedings at which he was present. See p. 129.

rode in and out of the town every day.   He states that 80,000
witnessed the coronation of Martin V.   The lodgings of the
more distinguished personages were marked with their coats
of arms.   Bakers, beadles, grooms, scribes, goldsmiths, mer-
chantmen of every sort, even to traffickers from the Orient,
flocked together to serve the dukes and prelates and the
learned university masters and doctors.   There were in attendance on the council, 33 cardinals, 5 patriarchs, 47 archbishops, 145 bishops, 93 titular bishops, 217 doctors of
theology, 361 doctors in both laws, 171 doctors of medicine,
besides a great number of masters of arts from the 37 universities represented, 83 kings and princes represented by envoys,
38 dukes, 173 counts, 71 barons, more than 1500 knights,
142 writers of bulls, 1700 buglers, fiddlers, and players on
other musical instruments.   700 women of the street practised their trade openly or in rented houses, while the
number of those who practised it secretly was a matter of
conjecture.[1]   There were 36,000 beds for strangers.   500 are
said to have been drowned in the lake during the progress
of the council.   Huss wrote, "This council is a scene of foulness, for it is a common saying among the Swiss that a generation will not suffice to cleanse Constance from the sins which
the council has committed in this city."[2]

The English and Scotch delegation, which numbered less
than a dozen persons, was accompanied by 700 or 800 mounted
men, splendidly accoutred, and headed by fifers and other
musicians, and made a great sensation by their entry into the
city.   The French delegation was marked by its university
men and other men of learning.[3]

---

[1] *Offene Huren in den Hurenhäusern und solche, die selber Häuser gemie-
thet hatten und in den Ställen lagen und wo sie mochten, doren waren über
700 und die heimlichen, die lass ich belibnen.* Richental, p. 215. The numbers
above are taken from Richental, whose account, from p. 154 to 215, is taken
up with the lists of names. See also Van der Hardt, V. 50-53, who gives
18,000 prelates and priests and 80,000 laymen. A later hand has attached to
Richental's narrative the figures 72,460.

[2] Workman : *Letters of Huss*, p. 263.

[3] Usk, p. 304 ; Rymer, *Fœder.*, IX. 167; Richental, p. 34, speaks of the
French as *die Schulpfaffen und die gelehrten Leute aus Frankreich.*

The streets and surroundings presented the spectacle of a merry fair. There were tournaments, dances, acrobatic shows, processions, musical displays. But in spite of the congestion, good order seems to have been maintained. By order of the city council, persons were forbidden to be out after curfew without a light. Chains were to be stretched across some of the streets, and all shouting at night was forbidden. It is said that during the council's progress only two persons were punished for street brawls. A check was put upon extortionate rates by a strict tariff. The price of a white loaf was fixed at a penny, and a bed for two persons, with sheets and pillows, at a gulden and a half a month, the linen to be washed every two weeks. Fixed prices were put upon grains, meat, eggs, birds, and other articles of food.[1] The bankers present were a great number, among them the young Cosimo de' Medici of Florence.

Among the notables in attendance, the pope and Sigismund occupied the chief place. The most inordinate praise was heaped upon the king. He was compared to Daniel, who rescued Susanna, and to David. He was fond of pleasure, very popular with women, always in debt and calling for money, but a deadly foe of heretics, so that whenever he roared, it was said, the Wyclifites fled.[2] There can be no doubt that to Sigismund were due the continuance and success of the council. His queen, Barbara, the daughter of a Styrian count, was tall and fair, but of questionable reputation, and her gallantries became the talk of the town.

The next most eminent persons were Cardinals D'Ailly, Zabarella, Fillastre, John of Ragusa, and Hallum, bishop of Salisbury, who died during the session of the council, and was

---

[1] Richental, p. 39 sqq., gives an elaborate list of these regulations.

[2] So de Vrie, the poet-historian of the council, Hardt, I. 193. The following description is from the accomplished pen of Æneas Sylvius, afterwards Pius II: " He was tall, with bright eyes, broad forehead, pleasantly rosy cheeks, and a long, thick beard. He was witty in conversation, given to wine and women, and thousands of love intrigues are laid to his charge. He had a large mind and formed many plans, but was changeable. He was prone to anger, but ready to forgive. He could not keep his money, but spent lavishly. He made more promises than he kept, and often deceived."

buried in Constance, the bishop of Winchester, uncle to the English king, and John Gerson, the chief representative of the University of Paris. Zabarella was the most profound authority on civil and canon law in Europe, a professor at Bologna, and in 1410 made bishop of Florence. He died in the midst of the council's proceedings, Sept. 26, 1417. Fillastre left behind him a valuable daily journal of the council's proceedings. D'Ailly had been for some time one of the most prominent figures in Europe. Hallum is frequently mentioned in the proceedings of the council. Among the most powerful agencies at work in the assemblies were the tracts thrown off at the time, especially those of Diedrich of Nieheim, one of the most influential pamphleteers of the later Middle Ages.[1]

The subjects which the council was called together to discuss were the reunion of the Church under one pope, and Church reforms.[2] The action against heresy, including the condemnation of John Huss and Jerome of Prag, is also conspicuous among the proceedings of the council, though not treated by contemporaries as a distinct subject. From the start, John lost support. A sensation was made by a tract, the work of an Italian, describing John's vices both as man and pope. John of Ragusa and Fillastre recommended the resignation of all three papal claimants, and this idea became more and more popular, and was, after some delay, adopted by Sigismund, and was trenchantly advocated by Nieheim, in his tract on the Necessity of a Reformation in the Church.

From the very beginning great plainness of speech was used, so that John had good reason to be concerned for the tenure of his office. December 7, 1414, the cardinals passed propositions binding him to a faithful performance of his papal

[1] Finke, p. 133, calls him the "greatest journalist of the later Middle Ages." The tracts *De modis uniendi, De difficultate reformationis, De necessitate reformationis* are now all ascribed to Nieheim by Finke, p. 133, who follows Lenz, and with whom Pastor concurs as against Erler.

[2] *In hoc generali concilio agendum fuit de pace et unione perfecta ecclesiæ, secundo de reformatione illius*, Fillastre's *Journal*, in Finke, p. 164. *Hæc synodus . . . pro exstirpatione præsentis schismatis et unione ac reformatione ecclesiæ Dei in capite et membris* is the council's own declaration, Mansi, XXVII. 585.

duties and abstinence from simony. D'Ailly wrote against the infallibility of councils, and thus furnished the ground for setting aside the papal election at Pisa.

From November to January, 1415, a general disposition was manifested to avoid taking the initiative — the *noli me tangere* policy, as it was called.[1] The ferment of thought and discusssion became more and more active, until the first notable principle was laid down early in February, 1415; namely, the rule requiring the vote to be by nations. The purpose was to overcome the vote of the eighty Italian bishops and doctors who were committed to John's cause. The action was taken in the face of John's opposition, and followed the precedent set by the University of Paris in the government of its affairs. By this rule, which no council before or since has followed, except the little Council of Siena, 1423, England, France, Italy, and Germany had each a single vote in the affairs of the council. In 1417, when Aragon, Castile, and Scotland gave in their submission to the council, a fifth vote was accorded to Spain. England had the smallest representation. In the German nation were included Scandinavia, Poland, and Hungary. The request of the cardinals to have accorded to them a distinct vote as a body was denied. They met with the several nations to which they belonged, and were limited to the same rights enjoyed by other individuals. This rule seems to have been pressed from the first with great energy by the English, led by Robert of Salisbury. Strange to say, there is no record that this mode of voting was adopted by any formal conciliar decree.[2]

The nations met each under its own president in separate places, the English and Germans sitting in different rooms in the convent of the Grey Friars. The vote of the majority of the nations carried in the public sessions of the council. The right to vote in the nations was extended so as to include the doctors of both kinds and princes. D'Ailly advocated this course, and Fillastre argued in favor of including rectors

---

[1] *Apud aliquos erat morbus "noli me tangere,"* Fillastre's *Journal*, p. 164.
[2] See Finke, *Forschungen*, p. 31. Richental, pp. 50–53, gives a quaint account of the territorial possessions of the five nations.

and even clergymen of the lowest rank. Why, reasoned D'Ailly, should a titular bishop have an equal voice with a bishop ruling over an extensive see, say the archbishopic of Mainz, and why should a doctor be denied all right to vote who has given up his time and thought to the questions under discussion? And why, argued Fillastre, should an abbot, having control over only ten monks, have a vote, when a rector with a cure of a thousand or ten thousand souls is excluded? An ignorant king or prelate he called a "crowned ass." Doctors were on hand for the very purpose of clearing up ignorance.

When the Italian tract appeared, which teemed with charges against John, matters were brought to a crisis. Then it became evident that the scheme calling for the removal of all three popes would go through, and John, to avoid a worse fate, agreed to resign, making the condition that Gregory XII. and Benedict should also resign. The formal announcement, which was read at the second session, March 2, 1415, ran: " I, John XXIII., pope, promise, agree, and obligate myself, vow and swear before God, the Church, and this holy council, of my own free will and spontaneously, to give peace to the Church by abdication, provided the pretenders, Benedict and Gregory, do the same." [1] At the words "vow and swear," John rose from his seat and knelt down at the altar, remaining on his knees till he finished the reading. The reading being over, Sigismund removed his crown, bent before John, and kissed his feet. Five days after, John issued a bull confirming his oath.

Constance was wild with joy. The bells rang out the glad news. In the cathedral, joy expressed itself in tears. The spontaneity of John's self-deposition may be questioned, in view of the feeling which prevailed among the councillors and the report that he had made an offer to cede the papacy for 30,000 gulden. [2]

A most annoying, though ridiculous, turn was now given to affairs by John's flight from Constance, March 20. Ru-

---

[1] Hardt, II. 240, also IV. 44 ; Mansi, XXVII. 568. Also Richental, p. 56.
[2] According to a MS. found at Vienna by Finke, *Forschungen*, p. 148.

mors had been whispered about that he was contemplating
such a move.   He talked of transferring the council to Rizza,
and complained of the unhealthiness of the air of Constance.
He, however, made the solemn declaration that he would not
leave the town before the dissolution of the council.   To be
on the safe side, Sigismund gave orders for the gates to be
kept closed and the lake watched.   But John had practised
dark arts before, and, unmindful of his oath, escaped at
high noon on a " little horse," in the disguise of a groom,
wrapped in a gray cloak, wearing a gray cap, and having a
crossbow tied to his saddle.[1]   The flight was made while the
gay festivities of a tournament, instituted by Frederick, duke
of Austria, were going on, and with two attendants.   The
pope continued his course without rest till he reached Schaffhausen.   This place belonged to the duke, who was in the
secret, and on whom John had conferred the office of commander of the papal troops, with a yearly grant of 6000 gulden.
John's act was an act of desperation.   He wrote back to the
council, giving as the reason of his flight that he had been in
fear of Sigismund, and that his freedom of action had been
restricted by the king.[2]

So great was the panic produced by the pope's flight that
the council would probably have been brought to a sudden
close by a general scattering of its members, had it not been
for Sigismund's prompt action.   Cardinals and envoys despatched by the king and council made haste to stop the
fleeing pope, who continued on to Laufenburg, Freiburg, and
Breisach.   John wrote to Sigismund, expressing his regard
for him, but with the same pen he was addressing communications to the University of Paris and the duke of Orleans,
seeking to awaken sympathy for his cause by playing upon
the national feelings of the French.   He attempted to make
it appear that the French delegation had been disparaged
when the council proceeded to business before the arrival
of the twenty-two deputies of the University.   France and

---

[1] Richental, pp. 62–72, gives a vivid account of John's flight and seizure.

[2] Fillastre ; Finke, *Forschungen*, p. 169, *papa dicebat quod pro timore regis
Romanorum recesserat.*

Italy, with two hundred prelates, had each only a single vote, while England, with only three prelates, had a vote. God, he affirmed, dealt with individuals and not with nations. He also raised the objection that married laymen had votes at the side of prelates, and John Huss had not been put on trial, though he had been condemned by the University of Paris.

To the envoys who found John at Breisach, April 23, he gave his promise to return with them to Constance the next morning ; but with his usual duplicity, he attempted to escape during the night, and was let down from the castle by a ladder, disguised as a peasant. He was soon seized, and ultimately handed over by Sigismund to Louis III., of the Palatinate, for safe-keeping.

In the meantime the council forbade any of the delegates to leave Constance before the end of the proceedings, on pain of excommunication and the loss of dignities. Its fourth and fifth sessions, beginning April 6, 1415, mark an epoch in the history of ecclesiastical statement. The council declared that, being assembled legitimately in the Holy Spirit, it was an œcumenical council and representing the whole Church, had its authority immediately from Christ, and that to it the pope and persons of every grade owed obedience in things pertaining to the faith and to the reformation of the Church in head and members. It was superior to all other ecclesiastical tribunals.[1] This declaration, stated with more precision than the one of Pisa, meant a vast departure from the papal theory of Innocent III. and Boniface VIII.

Gerson, urging this position in his sermon before the council, March 23, 1415, said[2] the gates of hell had prevailed against popes, but not against the Church. Joseph was set to guard his master's wife, not to debauch her, and when the

---

[1] Hardt, IV. 89 sq., and Mansi, XXVII. 585–590. The deliverance runs : *hæc sancta synodus Constantiensis primo declarat ut ipsa synodus in S. Spiritu legitime congregata, generale concilium faciens, eccles. catholicam militantem representans, potestatem a Christo immediate habeat, cui quilibet cujusmodi status vel dignitatis, etiamsi papalis existat, obedire tenetur in his quæ pertinent ad fidem et exstirpationem præsentis schismatis et reformationem eccles. in capite et membris.*

[2] Hardt, II. 265–273 ; Du Pin, II. 201 sqq.

pope turned aside from his duty, the Church had authority to punish him. A council has the right by reason of the vivifying power of the Holy Spirit to prolong itself, and may, under certain conditions, assemble without call of pope or his consent.

The conciliar declarations reaffirmed the principle laid down by Nieheim on the eve of the council in the tract entitled the Union of the Church and its Reformation, and by other writers.[1] The Church, Nieheim affirmed, whose head is Christ, cannot err, but the Church as a commonwealth, — *respublica*, — controlled by pope and hierarchy, may err. And as a prince who does not seek the good of his subjects may be deposed, so may the pope, who is called to preside over the whole Church. . . . The pope is born of man, born in sin — clay of clay — *limus de limo*. A few days ago the son of a rustic, and now raised to the papal throne, he is not become an impeccable angel. It is not his office that makes him holy, but the grace of God. He is not infallible; and as Christ, who was without sin, was subject to a tribunal, so is the pope. It is absurd to say that a mere man has power in heaven and on earth to bind and loose from sin. For he may be a simoniac, a liar, a fornicator, proud, and worse than the devil — *pejor quam diabolus*. As for a council, the pope is under obligation to submit to it and, if necessary, to resign for the common good — *utilitatem communem*. A general council may be called by the prelates and temporal rulers, and is superior to the pope. It may elect, limit, and depose a pope — and from its decision there is no appeal — *potest papam eligere, privare et deponere. A tali concilio nullus potest appellare.* Its canons are immutable, except as they may be set aside by another œcumenical council.

These views were revolutionary, and show that Marsiglius of Padua, and other tractarians of the fourteenth century, had not spoken in vain.

Having affirmed its superiority over the pope, the council pro-

---

[1] Hardt, vol. I., where it occupies 175 pp. Du Pin, II., 162-201. This tract, formerly ascribed to Gerson, Lenz and Finke give reason for regarding as the work of Nieheim.

ceeded to try John XXIII. on seventy charges, which included almost every crime known to man. He had been unchaste from his youth, had been given to lying, was disobedient to his parents. He was guilty of simony, bought his way to the cardinalate, sold the same benefices over and over again, sold them to children, disposed of the head of John the Baptist, belonging to the nuns of St. Sylvester, Rome, to Florence, for 50,000 ducats, made merchandise of spurious bulls, committed adultery with his brother's wife, violated nuns and other virgins, was guilty of sodomy and other nameless vices.[1] As for doctrine, he had often denied the future life.

When John received the notice of his deposition, which was pronounced May 29, 1415, he removed the papal cross from his room and declared he regretted ever having been elected pope. He was taken to Gottlieben, a castle belonging to the bishop of Constance, and then removed to the castle at Heidelberg, where two chaplains and two nobles were assigned to serve him. From Heidelberg the count Palatine transferred him to Mannheim, and finally released him on the payment of 30,000 gulden. John submitted to his successor, Martin V., and in 1419 was appointed cardinal bishop of Tusculum, but survived the appointment only six months. John's accomplice, Frederick of Austria, was deprived of his lands, and was known as Frederick of the empty purse — *Friedrich mit der leeren Tasche*. A splendid monument was erected to John in the baptistery in Florence by Cosimo de' Medici, who had managed the pope's money affairs.

While John's case was being decided, the trial of John Huss was under way. The proceedings and the tragedy of Huss' death are related in another place.

John XXIII. was out of the way. Two popes remained,

---

[1] Hardt, IV. 196–208 ; Mansi, XXVIII. 662–673,715. Adam of Usk, p. 306, says, Our pope, John XXIII., false to his promises of union, and otherwise guilty of perjuries and murders, adulteries, simonies, heresy, and other excesses, and for that he twice fled in secret, and cowardly, in vile raiment, by way of disguise, was delivered to perpetual imprisonment by the council.

Gregory XII. and Benedict XIII., who were facetiously called in tracts and addresses *Errorius*, a play on Gregory's patronymic, Angelo Correr,[1] and *Maledictus*. Gregory promptly resigned, thus respecting his promise made to the council to resign, provided John and Benedict should be set aside. He also had promised to recognize the council, provided the emperor should preside. The resignation was announced at the fourteenth session, July 4, 1415, by Charles Malatesta and John of Ragusa, representing the Roman pontiff. Gregory's bull, dated May 15, 1414, which was publicly read, " convoked and authorized the general council so far as Balthazar Cossa, John XXIII., is not present and does not preside." The words of resignation ran, " I resign, in the name of the Lord, the papacy, and all its rights and title and all the privileges conferred upon it by the Lord Jesus Christ in this sacred synod and universal council representing the holy Roman and universal Church.[2] Gregory's cardinals now took their seats, and Gregory himself was appointed cardinal-bishop of Porto and papal legate of Ancona. He died at Recanati, near Ancona, Oct. 18, 1417. Much condemnation as Angelo Correr deserves for having temporized about renouncing the papacy, posterity has not withheld from him respect for his honorable dealing at the close of his career. The high standing of his cardinal, John of Ragusa, did much to make men forget Gregory's faults.

Peter de Luna was of a different mind. Every effort was made to bring him into accord with the mind of the councilmen in the Swiss city, but in vain. In order to bring all the influence possible to bear upon him, Sigismund, at the council's instance, started on the journey to see the last of the Avignon popes face to face. The council, at its sixteenth session, July 11, 1415, appointed doctors to accompany the king, and eight days afterwards he broke away from Constance, accompanied by a troop of 4000 men on horse.

Sigismund and Benedict met at Narbonne, Aug. 15, and at Perpignan, the negotiations lasting till December. The

---

[1] This name is given to Gregory constantly by Nieheim in his *De schismate*.
[2] The document is given in Hardt, IV. 380. See, for the various documents, Hardt, IV. 192 sq., 346–381 ; Mansi, XXVII. 733–745.

decree of deposition pronounced at Pisa, and France's withdrawal of allegiance, had not broken the spirit of the old
man. His dogged tenacity was worthy of a better cause.[1]
Among the propositions the pope had the temerity to make
was that he would resign provided that he, as the only surviving cardinal from the times before the schism, should have
liberty to follow his abdication by himself electing the new
pontiff. Who knows but that one who was so thoroughly
assured of his own infallibility would have chosen himself.
Benedict persisted in calling the Council of Constance the
"congregation," or assembly. On Nov. 14 he fled to Peñiscola, a rocky promontory near Valencia, again condemned
the Swiss synod, and summoned a legitimate one to meet in
his isolated Spanish retreat. His own cardinals were weary
of the conflict, and Dec. 13, 1415, declared him deposed.
His long-time supporter, Vincent Ferrer, called him a perjurer. The following month the kingdom of Aragon, which
had been Benedict's chief support, withdrew from his obedience and was followed by Castile and Scotland.

Peter de Luna was now as thoroughly isolated as any mortal
could well be. The council demanded his unconditional abdication, and was strengthened by the admission of his old
supporters, the Spanish delegates. At the thirty-seventh session, 1417, he was deposed. By Sigismund's command the
decision was announced on the streets of Constance by trum-
peters. But the indomitable Spaniard continued to defy the
synod's sentence till his death, nine years later, and from the
lonely citadel of Peñiscola to sit as sovereign of Christendom.
Cardinal Hergenröther concludes his description of these
events by saying that Benedict " was a pope without a church
and a shepherd without sheep. This very fact proves the
emptiness of his claims." Benedict died, 1423,[2] leaving behind him four cardinals. Three of these elected the canon,
Gil Sanduz de Munoz of Barcelona, who took the name of
Clement VIII. Five years later Gil resigned, and was ap-

---

[1] Pastor, Hefele, and Hergenröther call it stubbornness, *Hartnäckigkeit.*
Döllinger is more favorable, and does not withhold his admiration from Peter.
[2] Valois, IV. 450–454, gives strong reasons for this date as against 1424.

pointed by Martin V. bishop of Majorca, on which island he was a pope with insular jurisdiction.[1] The fourth cardinal, Jean Carrier, elected himself pope, and took the name of Benedict XIV. He died in prison, 1433.

It remained for the council to terminate the schism of years by electing a new pontiff and to proceed to the discussions of Church reforms. At the fortieth session, Oct. 30, 1417, it was decided to postpone the second item until after the election of the new pope. In fixing this order of business, the cardinals had a large influence. There was a time in the history of the council when they were disparaged. Tracts were written against them, and the king at one time, so it was rumored, proposed to seize them all.[2] But that time was past; they had kept united, and their influence had steadily grown.

The papal vacancy was filled, Nov. 11, 1417, by the election of Cardinal Oddo Colonna, who took the name of Martin V. The election was consummated in the Kaufhaus, the central commercial building of Constance, which is still standing. Fifty-three electors participated, 6 deputies from each of the 5 nations, and 23 cardinals. The building was walled up with boards and divided into cells for the electors. Entrance was had by a single door, and the three keys were given, one to the king, one to the chapter of Constance, and one to the council. When it became apparent that an election was likely to be greatly delayed, the Germans determined to join the Italians in voting for an Italian to avoid suspicion that advantage was taken of the synod's location on German soil. The Germans then secured the co-operation of the English, and finally the French and Spaniards also yielded.[3] The pope-elect was thus the creature of the council.

[1] Mansi, XXVIII. 1117 sqq., gives Clement's letter of abdication. For an account of Benedict's two successors and their election, see Valois, IV. 455–478.

[2] Fillastre's *Journal*, p. 224. For the tracts hostile to the cardinals, see Finke, *Forschungen*, p. 81 sq.

[3] Richental, p. 116 sqq., gives a detailed account of the walling up of the Kaufhaus and the election, and of the ceremonies attending Martin's coronation. He also, p. 123, tells the pretty story that, before the electors met, ravens, jackdaws, and other birds of the sort gathered in great numbers on the

The Western Church was again unified under one head. But for the deep-seated conviction of centuries, the office of the universal papacy would scarcely have survived the strain of the schism.[1]   Oddo Colonna, the only member of his distinguished house who has worn the tiara, was a subdeacon at the time of his election.   Even more hastily than Photius, patriarch of Constantinople, was he rushed through the ordination of deacon, Nov. 12, of priest, Nov. 13, and bishop, Nov. 14.   He was consecrated pope a week later, Nov. 21, Sigismund kissing his toe.   In the procession, the bridles of Martin's horse were held by Sigismund and Frederick the Hohenzollern, lately created margrave of Brandenburg.   The margrave had paid Sigismund 250,000 marks as the price of his elevation, a sum which the king used to defray the expenses of his visit to Benedict.

Martin at once assumed the presidency of the council which since John's flight had been filled by Cardinal Viviers. Measures of reform were now the order of the day and some headway was made.   The papal right of granting indulgences was curtailed.   The college of cardinals was limited to 24, with the stipulation that the different parts of the church should have a proportionate representation, that no monastic order should have more than a single member in the college, and that no cardinal's brother or nephew should be raised to the curia so long as the cardinal was living. Schedules and programmes enough were made, but the question of reform involved abuses of such long standing and so deeply intrenched that it was found impossible to reconcile the differences of opinion prevailing in the council and bring it to promptness of action.   After sitting for more than three years, the delegates were impatient to get away.

As a substitute for further legislation, the so-called con-

roof of the Kaufhaus, but that as soon as Martin was elected, thousands of greenfinches and other little birds took their places and chattered and sang and hopped about as if approving what had been done.

[1] Catholic historians regard the survival of the papacy as a proof of its divine origin.   Salembier, p. 395, says, "The history of the great Schism would have dealt a mortal blow to the papacy if Christ's promises had not made it immortal."

cordats were arranged. These agreements were intended to regulate the relations of the papacy and the nations one with the other. There were four of these distinct compacts, one with the French, and one with the German nations, each to be valid for five years, one with the English to be perpetual, dated July 21, 1418, and one with the Spanish nation, dated May 13, 1418.[1] These concordats set forth rules for the appointment of the cardinals and the restriction of their number, limited the right of papal reservations and the collection of annates and direct taxes, determined what causes might be appealed to Rome, and took up other questions. They were the foundation of the system of secret or open treaties by which the papacy has since regulated its relations with the nations of Europe. Gregory VII. was the first pope to extend the system of papal legates, but he and his successors had dealt with nations on the arbitrary principle of papal supremacy and infallibility.

The action of the Council of Constance lifted the state to some measure of equality with the papacy in the administration of Church affairs. It remained for Louis XIV., 1643–1715, to assert more fully the Gallican theory of the authority of the state to manage the affairs of the Church within its territory, so far as matters of doctrine were not touched. The first decisive step in the assertion of Gallican liberties was the synodal action of 1407, when France withdrew from the obedience of Benedict XIII. By this action the chapters were to elect their own bishops, and the pope was restrained from levying taxes on their sees. Then followed the compact of the Council of Constance, the Pragmatic Sanction adopted at Bourges, 1438, and the concordat agreed upon between Francis I. and Leo X. at the time of the Reformation. In 1682 the French prelates adopted four propositions, restricting the pope's authority to spirituals, a power which is limited by the decision of the Council of Constance, and by the precedents of the Gallican Church, and declaring that even in matters of faith the pope is not infallible. Although Louis,

[1] See Mirbt, art. *Konkordat*, in Herzog, X. 705 sqq. Hardt gives the concordats with Germany and England, I. 1056-1083, and France, IV. 155 sqq. Mansi, XXVII. 1189 sqq., 1193 sqq.

who gave his authority to these articles, afterwards revoked them, they remain a platform of Gallicanism as against the ultramontane theory of the infallibility and supreme authority of the pope, and may furnish in the future the basis of a settlement of the papal question in the Catholic communion.[1]

In the deliverance known as *Frequens*, passed Oct. 9, 1417, the council decreed that a general council should meet in five years, then in seven years, and thereafter perpetually every ten years.[2] This action was prompted by Martin in the bull *Frequens*, Oct. 9, 1417. On completing its forty-fifth session it was adjourned by Martin, April 22, 1418. The Basel-Ferrara and the Tridentine councils sat a longer time, as did also the Protestant Westminster Assembly, 1643–1648. Before breaking away from Constance, the pope granted Sigismund a tenth for one year to reimburse him for the expense he had been to on account of the synod.

The Council of Constance was the most important synod of the Middle Ages, and more fairly represented the sentiments of Western Christendom than any other council which has ever sat. It furnished an arena of free debate upon interests whose importance was felt by all the nations of Western Europe, and which united them. It was not restricted by a programme prepared by a pope, as the Vatican council of 1870 was. It had freedom and exercised it. While the dogma of transubstantiation enacted by the 4th Lateran, 1215, and the dogma of papal infallibility passed by the Vatican council injected elements of permanent division into the Church, the Council of Constance unified Latin Christendom and ended the schism which had been a cause of scandal for forty years. The validity of its decree putting an œcumenical council above the pope, after being disputed for centuries, was officially set aside by the conciliar vote of 1870. For Protestants the decision at Constance is an onward step

---

[1] See art. *Gallikanismus*, in Herzog, and *Der Ursprung der gallikan. Freiheiten*, in *Hist. Zeitschrift*, 1903, pp. 194-215.

[2] Creighton, I. 393, after giving the proper citation from Hardt, IV. 1432, makes the mistake of saying that the next council was appointed for seven years, and the succeeding councils every five years thereafter.

towards a right definition of the final seat of religious authority. It remained for Luther, forced to the wall by Eck at Leipzig, and on the ground of the error committed by the Council of Constance, in condemning the godly man, John Huss, to deny the infallibility of councils and to place the seat of infallible authority in the Scriptures, as interpreted by conscience.

Note on the Œcumenical Character of the Council of Constance.

Modern Roman Catholic historians deny the œcumenical character and authority of the Council of Constance, except its four last, 42d–45th sessions, which were presided over by Pope Martin V., or at least all of it till the moment of Gregory XII.'s bull giving to the council his approval, that is, after John had fled and ceased to preside. Hergenröther-Kirsch, II. 862, says that before Gregory's authorization the council was without a head, did not represent the Roman Church, and sat against the will of the cardinals, by whom he meant Gregory's cardinals. Salembier, p. 317, says, *Il n'est devenu œcuménique qu'après la trente-cinquième session, lorsque Grégoire XII. eut donné sa démission*, etc. Pastor, I. 198 sq., warmly advocates the same view, and declares that when the council in its 4th and 5th sessions announced its superiority over the pope, it was not yet an œcumenical gathering. This dogma, he says, was intended to set up a new principle which revolutionized the old Catholic doctrine of the Church. Philip Hergenröther, in *Katholisches Kirchenrecht*, p. 344 sq., expresses the same judgment. The council was not a legitimate council till after Gregory's resignation.

The wisdom of the council in securing the resignation of Gregory and deposing John and Benedict is not questioned. The validity of its act in electing Martin V., though the papal regulation limiting the right of voting to the cardinals was set aside, is also acknowledged on the ground that the council at the time of Martin's election was sitting by Gregory's sanction, and Gregory was true pope until he abdicated.

A serious objection to the view, setting aside this action of the 4th and 5th sessions, is offered by the formal statement made by Martin V. At the final meeting of the council and after its adjournment had been pronounced, a tumultuous discussion was precipitated over the tract concerning the affairs of Poland and Lithuania by the Dominican, Falkenberg, which was written in defence of the Teutonic Knights, and justified the killing of the Polish king and all his subjects. It had been the subject of discussion in the nations, and its heresies were declared to be so glaring that, if they remained uncondemned by the council, that body would go down to posterity as defective in its testimony for orthodoxy. It was during the tumultuous debate, and after Martin had adjourned the council, that he uttered the words which, on their face, sanction whatever was done in council in a conciliar way. Putting an end to the tumult, he announced he would maintain all the decrees passed by the council in matters of faith in a conciliar way — *omnia et singula*

*determinata et conclusa et decreta in materiis fidei per præsens sacrum con-
cilium generale Constantiense conciliariter tenere et inviolabiliter observare
volebat et nunquam contravenire quoquomodo.* Moreover, he announced that
he sanctioned and ratified acts made in a " conciliar way and not made otherwise or in any other way." *Ipsaque sic conciliariter facta approbat papa
et ratificat et non aliter nec alio modo.* Funk, *Martin V. und das Konzil zu
Konstanz in Abhandlungen,* I. 489 sqq., Hefele, *Conciliengesch.,* I. 52, and
Küpper, in Wetzer-Welte, VII. 1004 sqq., restrict the application of these
words to the Falkenberg incident. Funk, however, by a narrow interpretation of the words " in matters of faith," excludes the acts of the 4th and 5th
sessions from the pope's approval. Döllinger (p. 464), contends that the expression *conciliariter,* " in a conciliar way," is opposed to *nationaliter,* " in
the nations." The expression is to be taken in its simple meaning, and refers
to what was done by the council as a council.

The only other statement made by Martin bearing upon the question
occurs in his bull *Frequens,* of Feb. 22, 1418, in which he recognized the
council as œcumenical, and declared its decrees binding which pertained to
faith and the salvation of souls — *quod sacrum concilium Constant., univer-
salem ecclesiam representans approbavit et approbat in favorem fidei et salu-
tem animarum, quod hoc est ab universis Christi fidelibus approbandum et
tenendum.* Hefele and Funk show that this declaration was not meant to
exclude matters which were not of faith, for Martin expressly approved
other matters, such as those passed upon in the 39th session. There is no
record that Martin at any time said anything to throw light upon his meaning in these two utterances.

In the latter part of the fifteenth century, as Raynaldus, *an.* 1418, shows,
the view came to expression that Martin expressly intended to except the
action of the 4th and 5th sessions from his papal approval.

Martin V.'s successor, Eugenius IV., in 1446, thirty years after the synod,
asserted that its decrees were to be accepted so far as they did not prejudice
the law, dignity, and pre-eminence of the Apostolic See — *absque tamen præ-
judicio juris et dignitatis et præeminentiæ Apost. sedis.* The papacy had at
that time recovered its prestige, and the supreme pontiff felt himself strong
enough to openly reassert the superiority of the Apostolic See over œcumenical councils. But before that time, in a bull issued Dec. 13, 1443, he formally accepted the acts of the Council of Basel, the most explicit of which
was the reaffirmation of the acts of the Council of Constance in its 4th and
5th sessions.

It occurs to a Protestant that the Council of Constance would hardly have
elected Oddo Colonna pope if he had been suspected of being opposed to the
council's action concerning its own superiority. The council would have
stultified itself in appointing a man to undo what it had solemnly done. And
for him to have denied its authority would have been, as Döllinger says
(p. 159), like a son denying his parentage. The emphasis which recent
Catholic historians lay upon Gregory's authorization of the synod as giving
it for the first time an œcumenical character is an easy way out of the difficulty, and this view forces the recognition of the Roman line of popes as
the legitimate successors of St. Peter during the years of the schism.

§ 17. *The Council of Basel.* 1431–1449.

Martin V. proved himself to be a capable and judicious ruler, with courage enough when the exigency arose. He left Constance May 16, 1418. Sigismund, who took his departure the following week, offered him as his papal residence Basel, Strassburg, or Frankfurt. France pressed the claims of Avignon, but a Colonna could think of no other city than Rome, and proceeding by the way of Bern, Geneva, Mantua, and Florence, he entered the Eternal City Sept. 28, 1420.[1] The delay was due to the struggle being carried on for its possession by the forces of Joanna of Naples under Sforza, and the bold chieftain Braccio.[2] Martin secured the withdrawal of Joanna's claims by recognizing that princess as queen of Naples, and pacified Braccio by investing him with Assisi, Perugia, Jesi, and Todi.

Rome was in a desolate condition when Martin reached it, the prey of robbers, its streets filled with refuse and stagnant water, its bridges decayed, and many of its churches without roofs. Cattle and sheep were herded in the spaces of St. Paul's. Wolves attacked the inhabitants within the walls.[3] With Martin's arrival a new era was opened. This pope rid the city of robbers, so that persons carrying gold might go with safety even beyond the walls. He restored the Lateran, and had it floored with a new pavement. He repaired the porch of St. Peter's, and provided it with a new roof at a cost of 50,000 gold gulden. Revolutions within the city ceased. Martin deserves to be honored as one of Rome's leading benefactors. His pontificate was an era of peace after years of constant strife and bloodshed due to factions within the walls and invaders from without. With him its mediæval history closes, and an age of restoration and progress begins. The inscription on Martin's tomb in the Lateran, " the Felicity of his Times," — *temporum suorum felicitas*, — expresses the debt Rome owes to him.

---

[1] Richental, pp. 149 sqq.   [2] *Infessura*, p. 21.
[3] Five large wolves were killed in the Vatican gardens, Jan. 23, 1411. Gregorovius, VI. 618.

Among the signs of Martin's interest in religion was his order securing the transfer to Rome of some of the bones of Monica, the mother of Augustine, and his bull canonizing her. On their reception, Martin made a public address in which he said, " Since we possess St. Augustine, what do we care for the shrewdness of Aristotle, the eloquence of Plato, the reputation of Pythagoras? These men we do not need. Augustine is enough. If we want to know the truth, learning, and religion, where shall we find one more wise, learned, and holy than St. Augustine? "

As for the promises of Church reforms made at Constance, Martin paid no attention to them, and the explanation made by Pastor, that his time was occupied with the government of Rome and the improvement of the city, is not sufficient to exculpate him. The old abuses in the disposition and sale of offices continued. The pope had no intention of yielding up the monarchical claims of the papal office. Nor did he forget his relatives. One brother, Giordano, was made duke of Amalfi, and another, Lorenzo, count of Alba. One of his nephews, Prospero, he invested with the purple, 1426. He also secured large tracts of territory for his house.[1]

The council, appointed by Martin at Constance to meet in Pavia, convened April, 1423, was sparsely attended, adjourned on account of the plague to Siena, and, after condemning the errors of Wyclif and Huss, was dissolved March 7, 1424. Martin and his successors feared councils, and it was their policy to prevent, if possible, their assembling, by all sorts of excuses and delays. Why should the pope place himself in a position to hear instructions and receive commands? However, Martin could not be altogether deaf to the demands of Christendom, or unmindful of his pledge given at Constance. Placards were posted up in Rome threatening him if he summoned a council. Under constraint and not of free will, he appointed the second

---

[1] Pastor, I. 227, Martin's warm admirer, passes lightly over the pope's nepotism with the remark that in this regard he overstepped the line of propriety — *er hat das Mass des Erlaubten überschritten.*

council, which was to meet in seven years at Basel, 1431, but he died the same year, before the time set for its assembling.

Eugenius IV., the next occupant of the papal throne, 1431–1447, a Venetian, had been made bishop of Siena by his maternal uncle, Gregory XII., at the age of twenty-four, and soon afterwards was elevated to the curia.   His pontificate was chiefly occupied with the attempt to assert the supremacy of the papacy against the conciliar theory.   It also witnessed the most notable effort ever made for the union of the Greeks with the Western Church.

By an agreement signed in the conclave which elevated Eugenius, the cardinals promised that the successful candidate should advance the interests of the impending general council, follow the decrees of the Council of Constance in appointing cardinals, consult the sacred college in matters of papal administration, and introduce Church reforms. Such a compact had been signed by the conclave which elected Innocent VI., 1352, and similar compacts by almost every conclave after Eugenius down to the Reformation, but all with no result, for, as soon as the election was consummated, the pope set the agreement aside and pursued his own course.

On the day set for the opening of the council in Basel, March 7, 1431, only a single prelate was present, the abbot of Vezelay. The formal opening occurred July 23, but Cardinal Cesarini, who had been appointed by Martin and Eugenius to preside, did not appear till Sept. 9. He was detained by his duties as papal legate to settle the Hussite insurrection in Bohemia. Sigismund sent Duke William of Bavaria as protector, and the attendance speedily grew. The number of doctors present was larger in comparison to the number of prelates than at Constance. A member of the council said that out of 500 members he scarcely saw 20 bishops. The rest belonged to the lower orders of the clergy, or were laymen.   "Of old, bishops had settled the affairs of the Church, but now the common herd does it."[1] The most interesting personage in the convention was Æneas Sylvius

---

[1] Traversari, as quoted by Creighton, I. 128.

Piccolomini, who came to Basel as Cardinal Capranica's secretary.   He sat on some of its important commissions.

The tasks set before the council were the completion of the work of Constance in instituting reforms,[1] and a peaceful settlement of the Bohemian heresy.   Admirable as its effort was in both directions, it failed of papal favor, and the synod was turned into a constitutional battle over papal absolutism and conciliar supremacy.   This battle was fought with the pen as well as in debate.   Nicolas of Cusa, representing the scholastic element, advocated, in 1433, the supremacy of councils in his *Concordantia catholica*.   The Dominican, John of Turrecremata, took the opposite view, and defended the doctrine of papal infallibility in his *Summa de ecclesia et ejus auctoritate*.   For years the latter writing was the classical authority for the papal pretension.

The business was performed not by nations but by four committees, each composed of an equal number of representatives from the four nations and elected for a month.   When they agreed on any subject, it was brought before the council in public session.

It soon became evident that the synod acknowledged no earthly authority above itself, and was in no mood to hear the contrary principle defended.   On the other hand, Eugenius was not ready to tolerate free discussion and the synod's self-assertion, and took the unfortunate step of proroguing the synod to Bologna, making the announcement at a meeting of the cardinals, Dec. 18, 1431.   The bull was made public at Basel four weeks later, and made an intense sensation.   The synod was quick to give its answer, and decided to continue its sittings.   This was revolution, but the synod had the nations and public opinion back of it, as well as the decrees of the Council of Constance.   It insisted upon the personal presence of Eugenius, and on Feb. 15, 1432, declared for its own sovereignty and that a general council might not be prorogued or transferred by a pope without its own consent.

In the meantime Sigismund had received the iron crown at

---

[1] *Ob reformationem eccles. Dei in capite et membris specialiter congregatur*, Mansi, XXIX. 165, etc.

Milan, Nov. 25, 1431. He was at this period a strong supporter of the council's claims. A French synod, meeting at Bourges early in 1432, gave its sanction to them, and the University of Paris wrote that Eugenius' decree transferring the council was a suggestion of the devil. Becoming more bold, the council, at its third session, April 29, 1432, called upon the pope to revoke his bull and be present in person. At its fourth session, June 20, it decreed that, in case the papal office became vacant, the election to fill the vacancy should be held in Basel and that, so long as Eugenius remained away from Basel, he should be denied the right to create any more cardinals. The council went still farther, proceeded to arraign the pope for contumacy, and on Dec. 18 gave him 60 days in which to appear, on pain of having formal proceedings instituted against him.

Sigismund, who was crowned emperor in Rome the following Spring, May 31, 1433, was not prepared for such drastic action. He was back again in Basel in October, but, with the emperor present or absent, the council continued on its course, and repeatedly reaffirmed its superior authority, quoting the declarations of the Council of Constance at its fourth and fifth sessions. The voice of Western Christendom was against Eugenius, as were the most of his cardinals. Under the stress of this opposition, and pressed by the revolution threatening his authority in Rome, the pope gave way, and in the decree of Dec. 13, 1433, revoked his three bulls, beginning with Dec. 18, 1431, which adjourned the synod. He asserted he had acted with the advice of the cardinals, but now pronounced and declared the "General Council of Basel legitimate from the time of its opening." Any utterance or act prejudicial to the holy synod or derogatory to its authority, which had proceeded from him, he revoked, annulled, and pronounced utterly void.[1] At the same time the pope appointed legates to pre-

[1] *Decernimus et declaramus generale concil. Basileense a tempore inchoationis suæ legitime continuatum fuisse et esse . . . quidquid per nos aut nostro nomine in prejudicium et derogationem sacri concil. Basiliensis seu contra ejus auctoritatem factum et attentatum seu assertum est, cassamus, revocamus, irritamus et annullamus, nullas, irritas fuisse et esse declaramus,* Mansi, XXIX. 78.

side, and they were received by the synod. They swore in their own names to accept and defend its decrees.

No revocation of a former decree could have been made more explicit. The Latin vocabulary was strained for words. Catholic historians refrain from making an argument against the plain meaning of the bull, which is fatal to the dogma of papal inerrancy and acknowledges the superiority of general councils. At best they pass the decree with as little comment as possible, or content themselves with the assertion that Eugenius had no idea of confirming the synod's reaffirmation of the famous decrees of Constance, or with the suggestion that the pope was under duress when he issued the document.[1] Both assumptions are without warrant. The pope made no exception whatever when he confirmed the acts of the synod " from its opening." As for the explanation that the decree was forced, it needs only to be said that the revolt made against the pope in Rome, May, 1434, in which the Colonna took a prominent part, had not yet broken out, and there was no compulsion except that which comes from the judgment that one's case has failed. Cesarini, Nicolas of Cusa, Æneas Sylvius, John, patriarch of Antioch, and the other prominent personages at Basel, favored the theory of the supreme authority of councils, and they and the synod would have resented the papal deliverance if they had surmised its utterances meant something different from what they expressly stated. Döllinger concludes his treatment of the subject by saying that Eugenius' bull was the most positive and unequivocal recognition possible of the sovereignty of the council, and that the pope was subject to it.

Eugenius was the last pope, with the exception of Pius IX., who has had to flee from Rome. Twenty-five popes had been obliged to escape from the city before him. Disguised in the garb of a Benedictine monk, and carried part

---

[1] So Hergenröther-Kirsch, II. 919, Pastor, I. 288, etc. Funk, *Kirchengesch.*, p. 374, with his usual fairness, says that Eugenius in his bull gave unconditional assent to the council. *So verstand er sich endlich zur unbedingten Annahme der Synode.*

of the way on the shoulders of a sailor, he reached a boat on the Tiber, but was recognized and pelted with a shower of stones, from which he escaped by lying flat in the boat, covered with a shield. Reaching Ostia, he took a galley to Livorno. From there he went to Florence. He remained in exile from 1434 to 1443.

In its efforts to pacify the Hussites, the synod granted them the use of the cup, and made other concessions. The causes of their opposition to the Church had been expressed in the four articles of Prag. The synod introduced an altogether new method of dealing with heretics in guaranteeing to the Hussites and their representatives full rights of discussion. Having settled the question of its own authority, the synod took up measures to reform the Church "in head and members." The number of the cardinals was restricted to 24, and proper qualifications insisted upon, a measure sufficiently needed, as Eugenius had given the red hat to two of his nephews. Annates, payments for the pallium, the sale of church dignities, and other taxes which the Apostolic See had developed, were abolished. The right of appeal to Rome was curtailed. Measures of another nature were the reaffirmation of the law of priestly celibacy,[1] and the prohibition of theatricals and other entertainments in church buildings and churchyards. In 1439 the synod issued a decree on the immaculate conception, by which Mary was declared to have always been free from original and actual sin.[2] The interference with the papal revenues affecting the entire papal household was, in a measure, atoned for by the promise to provide other sources. From the monarchical head of the Church, directly appointed by God, and responsible to no human tribunal, the supreme pontiff was reduced to an official of the council. Another class of measures sought to clear Basel of the offences attending a large and promiscuous gathering, such as gambling, dancing, and the arts of prostitutes, who were enjoined from showing themselves on the streets.

[1] *De concubinariis*, Mansi, XXIX. 101 sq.

[2] *Immunem semper fuisse ab omni originali et actuali culpa*, etc., Mansi, XXIX. 183.

Eugenius did not sit idly by while his prerogatives were being tampered with and an utterly unpapal method of dealing with heretics was being pursued. He communicated with the princes of Europe, June 1, 1436, complaining of the high-handed measures, such as the withdrawal of the papal revenues, the suppression of the prayer for the pope in the liturgy, and the giving of a vote to the lower clergy in the synod. At that juncture the union with the Greeks, a question which had assumed a place of great prominence, afforded the pope the opportunity for reasserting his authority and breaking up the council in the Swiss city.

Overtures of union, starting with Constantinople, were made simultaneously through separate bodies of envoys sent to the pope and the council. The one met Eugenius at Bologna ; the other appeared in Basel in the summer of 1434. In discussing a place for a joint meeting of the representatives of the two communions, the Greeks expressed a preference for some Italian city, or Vienna. This exactly suited Eugenius, who had even suggested Constantinople as a place of meeting, but the synod sharply informed him that the city on the Bosphorus was not to be considered. In urging Basel, Avignon, or a city in Savoy, the Basel councilmen were losing their opportunity. Two delegations, one from the council and one from the pope, appeared in Constantinople, 1437, proposing different places of meeting.

When the matter came up for final decision, the council, by a vote of 355 to 244, decided to continue the meeting at Basel, or, if that was not agreeable to the Greeks, then at Avignon. The minority, acting upon the pope's preference, decided in favor of Florence or Udine. In a bull dated Sept. 18, 1437, and signed by eight cardinals, Eugenius condemned the synod for negotiating with the Greeks, pronounced it prorogued, and, at the request of the Greeks, as it alleged, transferred the council to Ferrara.[1]

---

[1] "Transfer" is the word used by the pope — *transferendo hoc sacrum concilium in civitatem Ferrarensium*, Mansi, XXIX. 166. Reasons for the transfer to an Italian city and an interesting statement of the discussion over the place of meeting are given in Haller, *Conc. Bas.*, I. 141–159.

The synod was checkmated, though it did not appreciate its situation. The reunion of Christendom was a measure of overshadowing importance, and took precedence in men's minds of the reform of Church abuses. The Greeks all went to Ferrara. The prelates, who had been at Basel, gradually retired across the Alps, including Cardinals Cesarini and Nicolas of Cusa. The only cardinal left at Basel was d'Aleman, archbishop of Arles. It was now an open fight between the pope and council, and it meant either a schism of the Western Church or the complete triumph of the papacy. The discussions at Basel were characterized by such vehemence that armed citizens had to intervene to prevent violence. The conciliar theory was struggling for life. At its 28th session, October, 1437, the council declared the papal bull null and void, and summoned Eugenius within sixty days to appear before it in person or by deputy. Four months later, Jan. 24, 1438, it declared Eugenius suspended, and, June 25, 1439, at its 34th session, "removed, deposed, deprived, and cast him down," as a disturber of the peace of the Church, a simoniac and perjurer, incorrigible, and errant from the faith, a schismatic, and a pertinacious heretic.[1] Previous to this, at its 33d session, it had again solemnly declared for the supreme jurisdiction of councils, and denied the pope the right to adjourn or transfer a general council. The holding of contrary views, it pronounced heresy.

In the meantime the council at Ferrara had been opened, Jan. 8, 1438, and was daily gaining adherents. Charles VII. took the side of Eugenius, although the French people, at the synod of Bourges in the summer of 1438, accepted, substantially, the reforms proposed by the council of Basel.[2] This action, known as the Pragmatic Sanction, decided for the superiority of councils, and that they should be held every

---

[1] *Eugenium fuisse et esse notorium et manifestum contumacem, violatorem assiduum atque contemptorem sacrorum canonum synodalium, pacis et unitatis eccles. Dei perturbatorem notorium . . . simoniacum, perjurum, incorrigibilem, schismaticum, a fide devium, pertinacem hæreticum, dilapidatorem jurium et bonorum ecclesiæ, inutilem et damnosum ad administrationem romani pontificii*, etc., Mansi, XXIX. 180.

[2] Mirbt gives it in part, *Quellen*, p. 160.

ten years, abolished annates and first-fruits, ordered the large benefices filled by elections, and limited the number of cardinals to twenty-four. These important declarations, which went back to the decrees of the Council of Constance, were the foundations of the Gallican liberties.

The attitude of the German princes and ecclesiastics was one of neutrality or of open support of the council at Basel. Sigismund died at the close of the year 1437, and, before the election of his son-in-law, Albrecht II., as his successor, the electors at Frankfurt decided upon a course of neutrality. Albrecht survived his election as king of the Romans less than two years, and his uncle, Frederick III., was chosen to take his place. Frederick, after observing neutrality for several years, gave his adhesion to Eugenius.

Unwilling to be ignored and put out of life, the council at Basel, through a commission of thirty-two, at whose head stood d'Aleman, elected, 1439, Amadeus, duke of Savoy, as pope.[1] After the loss of his wife, 1435, Amadeus formed the order of St. Mauritius, and lived with several companions in a retreat at Ripaille, on the Lake of Geneva. He was a man of large wealth and influential family connections. He assumed the name of Felix V., and appointed four cardinals. A year after his election, and accompanied by his two sons, he entered Basel, and was crowned by Cardinal d'Aleman. The tiara is said to have cost 30,000 crowns. Thus Western Christendom again witnessed a schism. Felix had the support of Savoy and some of the German princes, of Alfonso of Aragon, and the universities of Paris, Vienna, Cologne, Erfurt, and Cracow. Frederick III. kept aloof from Basel and declined the offer of marriage to Margaret, daughter of Felix and widow of Louis of Anjou, with a dowry of 200,000 ducats.

The papal achievement in winning Frederick III., king of the Romans, was largely due to the corruption of Frederick's chief minister, Caspar Schlick, and the treachery of Æneas Sylvius, who deserted one cause and master after another as

[1] H. Manger, *D. Wahl Amadeos v. Savoyen zum Papste*, Marburg, 1901, p. 94. Sigismund, in 1416, raised the counts of Savoy to the dignity of dukes.

it suited his advantage.   From being a vigorous advocate of the council, he turned to the side of Eugenius, to whom he made a most fulsome confession, and, after passing from the service of Felix, he became secretary to Frederick, and proved himself Eugenius' most shrewd and pliable agent.   He was an adept in diplomacy and trimmed his sails to the wind.

The archbishops of Treves and Cologne, who openly supported the Basel assembly, were deposed by Eugenius, 1446. The same year six of the electors offered Eugenius their obedience, provided he would recognize the superiority of an œcumenical council, and within thirteen months call a new council to meet on German soil.   Following the advice of Æneas Sylvius, the pope concluded it wise to show a conciliatory attitude.   Papal delegates appeared at the diet, meeting September, 1446, and Æneas was successful in winning over the margrave of Brandenburg and other influential princes. The following January he and other envoys appeared in Rome as representatives of the archbishop of Mainz, Frederick III., and other princes.   The result of the negotiations was a concordat, — the so-called princes' concordat, — *Fürsten Konkordat*, — by which the pope restored the two deposed archbishops, recognized the superiority of general councils, and gave to Frederick the right during his lifetime to nominate the incumbents of the six bishoprics of Trent, Brixen, Chur, Gurk, Trieste, and Pilsen, and to him and his successors the right to fill, subject to the pope's approval, 100 Austrian benefices.   These concessions Eugenius ratified in four bulls, Feb. 5–7, 1447, one of them, the bull *Salvatoria*, declaring that the pope in the previous three bulls had not meant to disparage the authority of the Apostolic See, and if his successors found his concessions out of accord with the doctrine of the fathers, they were to be regarded as void. The agreement was celebrated in Rome with the ringing of bells, and was confirmed by Nicolas V. in the so-called Vienna Concordat, Feb. 17, 1448.[1]

Eugenius died Feb. 23, 1447, and was laid at the side of Eugenius III. in St. Peter's.   He had done nothing to intro-

[1] Given in Mirbt, p. 165 sqq.

duce reforms into the Church. Like Martin V., he was fond of art, a taste he cultivated during his exile in Florence. He succeeded in perpetuating the mediæval view of the papacy, and in delaying the reformation of the Church which, when it came, involved the schism in Western Christendom which continues to this day.

The Basel council continued to drag on a tedious and uneventful existence. It was no longer in the stream of noticeable events. It stultified itself by granting Felix a tenth. In June, 1448, it adjourned to Lausanne. Reduced to a handful of adherents, and weary of being a synonym for innocuous failure, it voted to accept Nicolas V., Eugenius' successor, as legitimate pope, and then quietly breathed its last, April 25, 1449. After courteously revoking his bulls anathematizing Eugenius and Nicolas, Felix abdicated. He was not allowed to suffer, much less obliged to do penance, for his presumption in exercising papal functions. He was made cardinal-bishop of Sabina, and Apostolic vicar in Savoy and other regions which had recognized his "obedience." Three of his cardinals were admitted to the curia, and d'Aleman forgiven. Felix died in Geneva, 1451.[1]

The Roman Church has not since had an anti-pope. The Council of Basel concluded the series of the three councils, which had for their chief aims the healing of the papal schism and the reformation of Church abuses. They opened with great promise at Pisa, where a freedom of discussion prevailed unheard of before, and where the universities and their learned representatives appeared as a new element in the deliberations of the Church. The healing of the schism was accomplished, but the abuses in the Church went on, and under the last popes of the fifteenth century became more infamous than they had been at any time before. And yet even in this respect these councils were not in vain, for they afforded a warning to the Protestant reformers not to put their trust

---

[1] In his bull *Ut pacis*, 1449, recognizing the Lausanne act in his favor, Nicolas V. called Amadeus " his venerable and most beloved brother," and spoke of the Basel-Lausanne synod as being held under the name of an œcumenical council, *sub nomine generalis concilii*, Labbæus, XII. 663, 665.

even in ecclesiastical assemblies. As for the theory of the
supremacy of general councils which they had maintained
with such dignity, it was proudly set aside by later popes in
their practice and declared fallacious by the Fifth Lateran in
1516,[1] and by the dogma of papal infallibility announced at
the Council of the Vatican, 1870.

§ 18. *The Council of Ferrara-Florence.* 1438–1445.

The council of Ferrara witnessed the submission of the
Greeks to the Roman see. It did not attempt to go into the
subject of ecclesiastical reforms, and thus vie with the synod
at Basel. After sixteen sessions held at Ferrara, Eugenius
transferred the council, February, 1439, to Florence. The reason given was the unhealthy conditions in Ferrara, but the real
grounds were the offer of the Florentines to aid Eugenius
in the support of his guests from the East and, by getting
away from the seaside, to lessen the chances of the Greeks
going home before the conclusion of the union. In 1442 the
council was transferred to Rome, where it held two sessions in
the Lateran. The sessions at Ferrara, Florence, and Rome are
listed with the first twenty-five sessions of the council of Basel,
and together they are counted as the seventeenth œcumenical
council.[2]

The schism between the East and the West, dating
from the middle of the ninth century, while Nicolas I. and
Photius were patriarchs respectively of Rome and Constantinople, was widened by the crusades and the conquest of Constantinople, 1204. The interest in a reunion of the two
branches of the Church was shown by the discussion at Bari,
1098, when Anselm was appointed to set forth the differences
with Greeks, and by the treatments of Thomas Aquinas and
other theologians. The only notable attempt at reunion was

---

[1] *Sess.* XI. *romanum pontificem tanquam super omnia concilia auctoritatem habentem, conciliorum indicendorum transferendorum ac dissolvendorum
plenum jus et potestatem habere.* This council at the same time pronounced
the Council of Basel a "little council," *conciliabulum,* "or rather a conventicle," *conventicula.* Mansi, XXXII. 967.

[2] Hefele-Knöpfler, *Kirchengesch.*, p. 477.

made at the second council of Lyons, 1274, when a deputation
from the East accepted articles of agreement which, however,
were rejected by the Eastern churches.   In 1369, the emperor John visited Rome and abjured the schism, but his
action met with unfavorable response in Constantinople.
Delegates appeared at Constance, 1418, sent by Manuel
Palæologus and the patriarch of Constantinople,[1] and, in
1422, Martin V. despatched the Franciscan, Anthony Mas-
sanus, to the Bosphorus, with nine articles as a basis of union.
These articles led on to the negotiations conducted at Ferrara.

Neither Eugenius nor the Greeks deserve any credit for the
part they took in the conference.   The Greeks were actuated
wholly by a desire to get the assistance of the West against
the advance of the Turks, and not by religious zeal.   So far
as the Latins are concerned, they had to pay all the expenses
of the Greeks on their way to Italy, in Italy, and on their
way back as the price of the conference.   Catholic historians
have little enthusiasm in describing the empty achievements
of Eugenius.[2]

The Greek delegation was large and inspiring, and included
the emperor and the patriarch of Constantinople.   In Venetian vessels rented by the pope, the emperor John VI., Palæologus, reached Venice in February, 1438.[3]   He was accorded
a brilliant reception, but it is fair to suppose that the pleasure he may have felt in the festivities was not unmixed with
feelings of resentment, when he recalled the sack and pillage
of his capital, in 1204, by the ancestors of his entertainers.
John reached Ferrara March 6.   The Greek delegation comprised 700 persons.   Eugenius had arrived Jan. 27.   In his
bull, read in the synod, he called the emperor his most beloved
son, and the patriarch his most pious brother.[4]   In a public

[1] Richental, *Chronik*, p. 113, has a notice of their arrival.

[2] So Hefele-Knöpfler, *Kirchengesch.*, p. 476 ; Hergenröther-Kirsch, II. 949 ;
Funk, *Kirchengesch.*, p. 377.   Pastor, II. 307, says, " *Die politische Nothlage
brachte endlich die Griechen zum Nachgeben.*"

[3] An account of the emperor's arrival and entertainment at Venice is
given in Mansi, XXXI. 463 sqq.

[4] *Dilectissimus filius noster Romæorum imperator cum piissimmo fratre
nostro, Josepho Const. patriarcha*, Mansi, XXXI. 481.

address delivered by Cardinal Cesarini, the differences dividing the two communions were announced as four, — the mode of the procession of the Holy Spirit, the use of unleavened bread in the eucharist, the doctrine of purgatory, and the papal primacy.   The discussions exhibit a mortifying spectacle of theological clipping and patchwork.   They betray no pure zeal for the religious interests of mankind.   The Greeks interposed all manner of dilatory tactics while they lived upon the hospitality of their hosts.   The Latins were bent upon asserting the supremacy of the Roman bishop.   The Orientals, moved by considerations of worldly policy, thought only of the protection of their enfeebled empire.

Among the more prominent Greeks present were Bessarion, bishop of Nice, Isidore, archbishop of Russian Kief, and Mark Eugenicus, archbishop of Ephesus.   Bessarion and Isidore remained in the West after the adjournment of the council, and were rewarded by Eugenius with the red hat.   The archbishop of Ephesus has our admiration for refusing to bow servilely to the pope and join his colleagues in accepting the articles of union.   The leaders among the Latins were Cardinals Cesarini and Albergati, and the Spaniard Turrecremata, who was also given the red hat after the council adjourned.

The first negotiations concerned matters of etiquette.   Eugenius gave a private audience to the patriarch, but waived the ceremony of having his foot kissed.   An important question was the proper seating of the delegates, and the Greek emperor saw to it that accurate measurements were taken of the seats set apart for the Greeks, lest they should have positions of less honor than the Latins.[1]   The pope's promise to support his guests was arranged by a monthly grant of thirty florins to the emperor, twenty-five to the patriarch, four each to the prelates, and three to the other visitors.   What possible respect could the more high-minded Latins have for ecclesiastics, and an emperor, who, while engaged on the mission of Church reunion, were willing to be the pope's pensioners, and live upon his dole!

---

[1] So Syrophulos.   See Hefele, *Conciliengesch.*, VII. 672.

The first common session was not held till Oct. 8, 1438. Most of it was taken up with a long address by Bessarion, as was the time of the second session by a still longer address by another Greek. The emperor did his share in promoting delay by spending most of his time hunting. At the start the Greeks insisted there could be no addition to the original creed. Again and again they were on the point of withdrawing, but were deterred from doing so by dread of the Turks and empty purses.[1]

A commission of twenty, ten Greeks and ten Latins, was appointed to conduct the preliminary discussion on the questions of difference.

The Greeks accepted the addition made to the Constantinopolitan creed by the synod of Toledo, 589, declaring that the Spirit proceeds from the Father *and the Son*, but with the stipulation that they were not to be required to introduce the *filioque* clause when they used the creed. They justified their course on the ground that they had understood the Latins as holding to the procession from the Father and the Son as from two principles. The article of agreement ran : " The Spirit proceeds from the Father and the Son eternally and substantially as it were from one source and cause."[2]

In the matter of purgatory, it was decided that immediately at death the blessed pass to the beatific vision, a view the Greeks had rejected. Souls in purgatory are purified by pain and may be aided by the suffrages of the living. At the insistence of the Greeks, material fire as an element of purification was left out.

The use of leavened bread was conceded to the Greeks.

In the matter of the eucharist, the Greeks, who, after the words, "this is my body," make a petition that the Spirit may turn the bread into Christ's body, agreed to the view that transubstantiation occurs at the use of the priestly words,

---

[1] Hergenröther-Kirsch, II. 949, lays stress upon the Greek readiness to accept alms.

[2] *Æternaliter et substantialiter tanquam ab uno principio et causa.* The statement *ex patre et filio* and *ex patre per filium* were declared to be identical in meaning.

but stipulated that the confession be not incorporated in the written articles.

The primacy of the Roman bishop offered the most serious difficulty. The article of union acknowledged him as "having a primacy over the whole world, he himself being the successor of Peter, and the true vicar of Christ, the head of the whole Church, the father and teacher of all Christians, to whom, in Peter, Christ gave authority to feed, govern and rule the universal Church."[1] This remarkable concession was modified by a clause in the original document, running, "according as it is defined by the acts of the œcumenical councils and by the sacred canons."[2] The Latins afterwards changed the clause so as to read, "even as it is defined by the œcumenical councils and the holy canons." The Latin falsification made the early œcumenical councils a witness to the primacy of the Roman pontiff.

The articles of union were incorporated in a decree[3] beginning *Lætentur cœli et exultat terra*, "Let the heavens rejoice and the earth be glad." It declared that the middle wall of partition between the Occidental and Oriental churches has been taken down by him who is the cornerstone, Christ. The black darkness of the long schism had passed away before the ray of concord. Mother Church rejoiced to see her divided children reunited in the bonds of peace and love. The union was due to the grace of the Holy Ghost. The articles were signed July 5 by 115 Latins and

[1] *Diffinimus sanctam apostol. sedem et Romanam pontificem in universum orbem tenere primatum et ipsum pontificem Romanum successorem esse B. Petri principis apostolorum, et verum Christi vicarium, totiusque ecclesiæ caput, et omnium Christianorum patrem et doctorem existere*, etc. Mansi, XXXI. 1697.

[2] *Quemadmodum et in gestis œcumenicorum conciliorum et in sacris canonibus continetur.* The change placed an *etiam* in the place of the first *et*, so that the clause ran *quemadmodum etiam in gestis*, etc. See Döllinger-Friedrich, *D. Papstthum*, pp. 170, 470 sq. Döllinger says that in the Roman ed. of 1626 the Ferrara council was called the 8th œcumenical.

[3] The document, together with the signatures, is given in Mansi, pp. 1028–1036, 1695–1701. Hefele-Knöpfler, *Conciliengesch.*, VII. 742–753, has regarded it of such importance as to give the Greek and Latin originals in full, and also a German translation.

33 Greeks, of whom 18 were metropolitans.   Archbishop
Mark of Ephesus was the only one of the Orientals who refused to sign.   The patriarch of Constantinople had died a
month before, but wrote approving the union.   His body lies
buried in S. Maria Novella, Florence.   His remains and the
original manuscript of the articles, which is preserved in the
Laurentian library at Florence, are the only relics left of
the union.

On July 6, 1439, the articles were publicly read in the
cathedral of Florence, the Greek text by Bessarion, and the
Latin by Cesarini.   The pope was present and celebrated the
mass.   The Latins sang hymns in Latin, and the Greeks followed them with hymns of their own.   Eugenius promised
for the defence of Constantinople a garrison of three hundred
and two galleys and, if necessary, the armed help of Western
Christendom.   After tarrying for a month to receive the five
months of arrearages of his stipend, the emperor returned by
way of Venice to his capital, from which he had been absent
two years.

The Ferrara agreement proved to be a shell of paper, and
all the parade and rejoicing at the conclusion of the proceedings were made ridiculous by the utter rejection of its articles
in Constantinople.

On their return, the delegates were hooted as Azymites, the
name given in contempt to the Latins for using unleavened
bread in the eucharist.   Isidore, after making announcement
of the union at Ofen, was seized and put into a convent, from
which he escaped two years later to Rome.   The patriarchs
of Jerusalem, Antioch, and Alexandria issued a letter from
Jerusalem, 1443, denouncing the council of Florence as a synod
of robbers and Metrophanes, the Byzantine patriarch as a
matricide and heretic.

It is true the articles were published in St. Sophia, Dec.
14, 1452, by a Latin cardinal, but six months later, Constantinople was in the hands of the Mohammedans.   A Greek
council, meeting in Constantinople, 1472, formally rejected
the union.

On the other hand, the success of the Roman policy was

announced through Western Europe. Eugenius' position was strengthened by the empty triumph, and in the same proportion the influence of the Basel synod lessened. If cordial relations between churches of the East and the West were not promoted at Ferrara and Florence, a beneficent influence flowed from the council in another direction by the diffusion of Greek scholarship and letters in the West.

Delegations also from the Armenians and Jacobites appeared at Florence respectively in 1439 and 1442. The Copts and Ethiopians also sent delegations, and it seemed as if the time had arrived for the reunion of all the distracted parts of Christendom.[1] A union with the Armenians, announced Nov. 22, 1439, declared that the Eastern delegates had accepted the procession of the Holy Spirit from the Son and the Chalcedon Council giving Christ two natures and by implication two wills. The uniate Armenians have proved true to the union. The Armenian catholicos, Gregory IX., who attempted to enforce the union, was deposed, and the Turks, in 1461, set up an Armenian patriarch, with seat at Constantinople. The union of the Jacobites, proclaimed in 1442, was universally disowned in the East. The attempts to conciliate the Copts and Ethiopians were futile. Eugenius sent envoys to the East to apprise the Maronites and the Nestorians of the efforts at reunion. The Nestorians on the island of Cyprus submitted to Rome, and a century later, during the sessions of the Fifth Lateran, 1516, the Maronites were received into the Roman communion.

On Aug. 7, 1445, Eugenius adjourned the long council which had begun its sittings at Basel, continued them at Ferrara and Florence, and concluded them in the Lateran.

[1] See Mansi, XXXI. 1047 sqq.; Hefele-Knöpfler, VII. 788 sqq. The only meeting since between Greeks and Western ecclesiastics of public note was at the Bonn Conference, 1875, in which Döllinger and the Old-Catholics took the most prominent part. Dr. Philip Schaff and several Anglican divines also participated. See *Creeds of Christendom*, II. 545–554, and *Life of Philip Schaff*, pp. 277–280.

CHAPTER III.

LEADERS OF CATHOLIC THOUGHT.

§ 19. *Literature.*

For § 20. Оскам and the Decay of Scholasticism. — No complete ed. of Ockam's works exists. The fullest lists are given by Riezler, see below, Little: *Grey Friars of Oxford*, pp. 225–234, and Potthast: II. 871–873. Goldast's *Monarchia*, II. 313–1296, contains a number of his works, *e.g. opus nonaginta dierum, Compendium errorum Johannis XXII., De utili dominio rerum eccles. et abdicatione bonorum temporalium, Super potestatem summi pontificis, Quæstionum octo decisiones, Dial. de potestate papali et imperiali in tres partes distinctus*, (1) *de hæreticis*, (2) *de erroribus Joh. XXII.*, (3) *de potestate papæ, conciliorum et imperatoris* (first publ. 2 vols., Paris, 1476). — Other works: *Expositio aurea super totam artem veterem*, a com. on Porphyry's *Isagoge*, and Aristotle's *Elenchus*, Bologna, 1496. — *Summa logices*, Paris, 1488. — *Super IV. libros sententiarum*, Lyons, 1483. — *De sacramento altaris*, Strassburg, 1491. — *De prædestinatione et futuris contingentibus*, Bologna, 1496. — *Quodlibeta septem*, Paris, 1487. — Riezler: *D. antipäpstlichen und publizistischen Schriften Occams* in his *Die literar. Widersacher*, etc., 241–277. — Haureau: *La philos. scolastique.* — Werner: *Die Scholastik des späteren M.A.*, II., Vienna, 1883, and *Der hl. Thos. von Aquino*, III. — Stöckl: *Die Philos. des M.A.*, II. 986–1021, and art. *Nominalismus* in Wetzer-Welte, IX. — Baur: *Die christl. Kirche d. M.A.*, p. 377 sqq. — Müller: *Der Kampf Ludwigs des Baiern.* — R. L. Poole in *Dict. of Natl. Biog.*, XLI. 357–362. — R. Seeberg in Herzog, XIV. 260–280. — A. Dorner; *D. Verhältniss von Kirche und Staat nach Occam in Studien und Kritiken*, 1885, pp. 672–722. — F. Kropatscheck: *Occam und Luther* in *Beitr. zur Förderung christl. Theol.*, Gütersloh, 1900. — Art. *Nominalismus*, by Stöckl in Wetzer-Welte, IX. 423–427.

For § 21. Catherine of Siena. — Her writings. *Epistole ed orazioni della seraphica vergine s. Catterina da Siena*, Venice, 1500, etc. — Best ed. 5 vols., Siena, 1707–1726. — Engl. trans. of the *Dialogue of the Seraphic Virgin Cath. of Siena*, by Algar Thorold, London, 1896. — Her *Letters*, ed. by N. Tommaseo: *Le lettere di S. Caterina da Siena*, 4 vols., Florence, 1860. — *Engl. trans. by Vida D. Scudder: *St. Cath. of Siena as seen in her Letters*, London, 1905, 2d ed., 1906. — Her biography is based upon the *Life* written by her confessor, Raymundo de Vineis sive de Capua, d. 1399: *vita s. Cath. Senensis*, included in the Siena ed. of her works and in the *Acta Sanctt.* III. 853–959. — Ital. trans. by Catherine's secretary, Neri de Landoccio, Fr. trans. by E. Cartier, Paris, 1853, 4th ed., 1877. — An abbreviation of Raymund's work, with annotations, *Leggenda della Cat. da Siena*, usually called

La Leggenda minore, by TOMMASO D'ANTONIO NACCI CAFFARINI, 1414. —K.
HASE : *Caterina von Siena, Ein Heiligenbild*, Leipzig, 1864, new ed., 1892. —
J. E. BUTLER: *Cath. of Siena*, London, 1878, 4th ed., 1895.—AUGUSTA T.
DRANE, Engl. Dominican : *The Hist. of Cath. of Siena*, compiled from the
orig. sources, London, 1880, 3d ed., 1900, with a trans. of the *Dialogue.* —
St. Catherine of Siena and her Times, by the author of *Mademoiselle Mori*
(Margaret D. Roberts), New York, 1906, pays little attention to the miracu-
lous element, and presents a full picture of Catherine's age.—*E. G. GARDNER :
*St. Catherine of Siena : A Study in the Religion, Literature, and History of
the fourteenth century in Italy*, London, 1907.

For § 22. PETER D'AILLY. — PAUL TSCHACKERT : *Peter von Ailli. Zur
Gesch. des grossen abendländischen Schismas und der Reformconcilien von
Pisa und Constanz*, Gotha, 1877, and Art. in HERZOG, I. 274–280.—SALEM-
BIER : *Petrus de Alliaco*, Lille, 1886. — LENZ : *Drei Traktate aus d. Schriftencyclus d. Konst. Konz.*, Marburg, 1876.—BESS : *Zur Gesch. des Konst. Konzils*,
Marburg, 1891.—FINKE : *Forschungen und Quellen*, etc., pp. 103–132. —For
a list of D'Ailly's writings, See TSCHACKERT, pp. 348–365. —Some of them
are given in VAN DER HARDT and in DU PIN's ed. of Gerson's *Works*, I. 489–
804, and the *De difficultate reform. eccles.*, and the *De necessitate reform.
eccles.*, II. 867–903.

For § 23. JOHN GERSON. —*Works.* Best ed. by L. E. DU PIN, Prof. of
Theol. in Paris, 5 vols., Antwerp, 1706 ; 2d ed., Hague Com., 1728. The
2d ed. has been consulted in this work and is pronounced by Schwab "indispensable." It contains the materials of Gerson's life and the contents of his
works in an introductory essay, *Gersoniana*, I. i–cxlv, and also writings
by D'AILLY, LANGENSTEIN, ALEMAN and other contemporaries. A number
of Gerson's works are given in GOLDAST's *Monarchia* and VAN DER HARDT. —
A *Vita Gersonis* is given in HARDT's *Conc. Const.*, IV. 26–57. — *Chartul. Univ.
Paris.*, III., IV., under *John Arnaud* and *Gerson.* —J. B. SCHWAB : *Johannes
Gerson, Prof. der Theologie und Kanzler der Universität Paris*, Würzburg,
1858, an exhaustive work, giving also a history of the times, one of the most
thorough of biographies and to be compared with HURTER'S *Innocent III.*
— A. MASSON : *J. Gerson, sa vie, son temps et ses œuvres*, Lyons, 1894. —
A. LAMBON : *J. Gerson, sa réforme de l'enseigement theol. et de l'éducation
populaire*, Paris, 1888. — BESS : *Zur Gesch. d. Konstanz. Konzils;* art.
Gerson in HERZOG, VI. 612–617. —LAFONTAINE : *Jehas Gerson, 1363–1429*,
Paris, 1906, pp. 340. —J. SCHWANE : *Dogmengesch.*—WERNER: *D. Scholastik
d. späteren M.A.*, IV., V.

For § 24. NICOLAS OF CLAMANGES. —*Works*, ed. by J. M. LYDIUS, 2 vols.,
Leyden, 1613, with *Life.* —The *De ruina ecclesiæ*, with a *Life*, in VAN DER
HARDT: *Conc. Constan.*, vol. I., pt. III. — Writings not in Lydius are given
by BULÆUS in *Hist. univ. Paris.* — BALUZIUS : *Miscellanea*, and D'ACHERY :
Spicilegium. — *Life* in DU PIN's *Works of Gerson*, I., p. xxxix sq. — A. MÜNTZ:
Nic. de Clem., sa vie et ses écrits, Strassburg, 1846. —J. SCHWAB : *J. Gerson*,
pp. 493–497.—Artt. by BESS in HERZOG, IV. 138–147, and by KNÖPFLER in
Wetzer-Welte, IX. 298–306. —G. SCHUBERT: *Nic. von Clem. als Verfasser
der Schrift de corrupto ecclesiæ statu*, Grossenhain, 1888.

For § 25. NICOLAS OF CUSA. —Edd. of his *Works*, 1476 (place not given),

as ed. by Faber Stapulensis, 3 vols., 1514, Basel.—German trans. of a
number of the works by F. A. Schrapff, Freiburg, 1862.—Schrapff: *Der
Cardinal und Bischof Nic. von Cusa*, Mainz, 1843; *Nic. von Cusa als Reformator in Kirche, Reich und Philosophie des 15ten Jahrh.*, Tübingen, 1871.—
J. M. Düx: *Der deutsche Card. Nic. von Cusa und die Kirche seiner Zeit*,
2 vols., Regensburg, 1847.—J. Uebinger: *D. Gotteslehre des Nic. von Cusa*,
Münster, 1888.—J. Marx: *Nik. von Cues und seine Stiftungen zu Cues und
Deventer*, Treves, 1906, pp. 115.—C. Schmitt: *Card. Nic. Cusanus*, Coblenz,
1907.   Presents him as astronomer, geographer, mathematician, historian, homilete, orator, philosopher, and theologian. — Stöckl, III. 23–84.—
Schwane, pp. 98–102. — Art. by Funk in Wetzer-Welte, IX. 306–315.

§ 20. *Ockam and the Decay of Scholasticism.*

Scholasticism had its last great representative in Duns
Scotus, d. 1308. After him the scholastic method gradually
passed into disrepute. New problems were thrust upon the
mind of Western Europe, and new interests were engaging its
attention. The theologian of the school and the convent gave
way to the practical theological disputant setting forth his
views in tracts and on the floor of the councils. Free discussion broke up the hegemony of dogmatic assertion. The
authority of the Fathers and of the papacy lost its exclusive hold, and thinkers sought another basis of authority in
the general judgment of contemporary Christendom, in the
Scriptures alone or in reason. The new interest in letters and
the natural world drew attention away from labored theological systems which were more adapted to display the ingenuity
of the theologian than to be of practical value to society. The
use of the spoken languages of Europe in literature was fitted
to force thought into the mould of current exigencies. The
discussions of Roger Bacon show that at the beginning of the
fourteenth century men's minds, sated with abstruse metaphysical solutions of theological questions, great and trivial,
were turning to a world more real and capable of proof.

The chief survivors of the dialectical Schoolmen were Durandus and William Ockam. Gabriel Biel of Tübingen, who
died just before the close of the fifteenth century, is usually
called the last of the Schoolmen.[1] Such men as D'Ailly, Ger-

[1] Seeberg gives a good deal of attention to Biel in his *Dogmengeschichte*.
Stöckl carries the history of scholasticism down to Cardinal Cajetan, who wrote

son and Wyclif, sometimes included under the head of mediæval scholastics, evidently belong to another class.

A characteristic feature of the scholasticism of Durandus
and Ockam is the sharper distinction they made between
reason and revelation. Following Duns Scotus, they declared
that doctrines peculiar to revealed theology are not susceptible of proof by pure reason. The body of dogmatic truth,
as accepted by the Church, they did not question.

A second characteristic is the absence of originality. They
elaborated what they received. The Schoolmen of former
periods had exhausted the list of theological questions and
discussed them from every standpoint.

The third characteristic is the revival and ascendency of
nominalism, the principle Roscellinus advocated more than
two hundred years before. The Nominalists were also called
Terminists, because they represent words as terms which do
not necessarily have ideas and realities to correspond to them.
A universal is simply a symbol or term for a number of things
or for that which is common to a number of things.[1] Univer-
sality is nothing more than a mode of mental conception. The
University of Paris resisted the spread of nominalism, and in
1339 the four nations forbade the promulgation of Ockam's
doctrine or listening to its being expounded in private or
public.[2] In 1473, Louis XI. issued a mandate forbidding the
doctors at Paris teaching it, and prohibiting the use of the
writings of Ockam, Marsiglius and other writers. In 1481
the law was rescinded.

Durandus, known as *doctor resolutissimus*, the resolute doctor, d. 1334, was born at Pourçain, in the diocese of Clermont,
entered the Dominican order, was appointed by John XXII.
bishop of Limoux, 1317, and was later elevated to the sees of
Puy and Meaux. He attacked some of the rules of the Fran-

a commentary on Thomas Aquinas' *Summa theologica*, and includes the German
mystics, Eck, Luther, etc., who clearly belong in another category. Professor
Seth, in art. *Scholasticism* in the *Enc. Brit.*, and Werner, close the history with
Francis Suarez, 1617. The new age had begun a hundred years before that time.

[1] *Terminus prolatus vel scriptus nihil significat nisi secundum voluntariam
institutionem.* Ockam, as quoted by Stöckl, II. 962.

[2] *Chartul.* II. 485. Also p. 507, etc.

ciscans and John XXII.'s theory of the beatific vision, and in
1333 was declared by a commission guilty of eleven errors.
His theological views are found in his commentary on the
Lombard, begun when he was a young man and finished in his
old age.   He showed independence by assailing some of the
views of Thomas Aquinas.   He went beyond his predecessors
in exalting the Scriptures above tradition and pronouncing
their statements more authoritative than the dicta of Aristotle
and other philosophers.[1]   All real existence is in the individual.   The universal is not an entity which can be divided
as a chunk of wood is cut into pieces.   The universal, the
unity by which objects are grouped together as a class, is deduced from individuals by an act of the mind.   That which
is common to a class has, apart from the individuals of the
class, no real existence.

On the doctrine of the eucharist Durandus seems not to
have been fully satisfied with the view held by the Church, and
suggested that the words "this is my body," may mean "contained under" — *contentum sub hoc.* This marks an approach
to Luther's view of consubstantiation.   This theologian was
held in such high esteem by Gerson that he recommended him,
together with Thomas Aquinas, Bradwardine and Henry of
Ghent, to the students of the college of Navarre.[2]

The most profound scholastic thinker of the fourteenth century was the Englishman, William Ockam, d. 1349, called
doctor invincibilis, the invincible doctor, or, with reference to
his advocacy of nominalism, *venerabilis inceptor,* the venerable
inaugurator.   His writings, which were more voluminous than
lucid, were much published at the close of the fifteenth century, but have not been put into print for several hundred
years.   There is no complete edition of them.   Ockam's
views combined elements which were strictly mediæval, and
elements which were adopted by the Reformers and modern

---

[1] *Naturalis philosophiæ non est scire quid Aristoteles vel alii philosophi
senserunt sed quid habet veritas rerum,* quoted by Deutsch, p. 97.   Durandus'
commentary on the sentences of the Lombard was publ. Paris, 1508, 1515,
etc. See *Deutsch,* art. *Durandus,* in Herzog, V. 95–104.

[2] Schwab: *J. Gerson,* p. 312.

philosophy. His identification with the cause of the Spiritual Franciscans involved him in controversy with two popes, John XXII. and Benedict XII. His denial of papal infallibility has the appearance not so much of a doctrine proceeding from theological conviction as the chance weapon laid hold of in time of conflict to protect the cause of the Spirituals.

Of the earlier period of Ockam's life, little is known. He was born in Surrey, studied at Oxford, where he probably was a student of Duns Scotus, entered the Franciscan order, and was probably master in Paris, 1315–1320. For his advocacy of the doctrine of Christ's absolute poverty he was, by order of John XXII., tried and found guilty and thrown into confinement.[1] With the aid of Lewis the Bavarian, he and his companions, Michael of Cesena and Bonagratia, escaped in 1328 to Pisa. From that time on, the emperor and the Schoolman, as already stated, defended one another. Ockam accompanied the emperor to Munich and was excommunicated. At Cesena's death the Franciscan seal passed into his hands, but whatever authority he possessed he resigned the next year into the hands of the acknowledged Franciscan general, Farinerius. Clement VI. offered him absolution on condition of his abjuring his errors. Whether he accepted the offer or not is unknown. He died at Munich and is buried there. The distinguished Englishman owes his reputation to his revival of nominalism, his political theories and his definition of the final seat of religious authority.

His theory of nominalism was explicit, and offered no toleration to the realism of the great Schoolmen from Anselm on. Individual things alone have factual existence. The universals are mere terms or symbols, fictions of the mind — *fictiones, signa mentalia, nomina, signa verbalia*. They are like images in a mirror. A universal stands for an intellectual act — *actus intelligenda* — and nothing more. Did ideas exist in God's mind as distinct entities, then the visible world would have been created out of them and not out of nothing.[2]

---

[1] It lasted four years, Müller, *Ludwig der Baier*, p. 208.

[2] *Nullum universale est aliqua substantia extra animam existens*, quoted by Seeberg, in Herzog, p. 269. *Quoddam fictum existens objective in mente.*

Following Duns Scotus, Ockam taught determinism. God's absolute will makes things what they are. Christ might have become wood or stone if God had so chosen. In spite of Aristotle, a body might have different kinds of motion at the same time. In the department of morals, what is now bad might have been good, if God had so willed it.

In the department of civil government, Ockam, advocating the position taken by the electors at Rense, 1338, declared the emperor did not need the confirmation of the pope. The imperial office is derived immediately from God.[1] The Church is a priestly institution, administers the sacraments and shows men the way of salvation, but has no civil jurisdiction,[2] *potestas coactiva*.

The final seat of authority, this thinker found in the Scriptures. Truths such as the Trinity and the incarnation cannot be deduced by argument. The being of God cannot be proven from the so-called idea of God. A plurality of gods may be proven by the reason as well as the existence of the one God. Popes and councils may err. The Bible alone is inerrant. A Christian cannot be held to believe anything not in the Scriptures.[3]

The Church is the community of the faithful — *communitas*, or *congregatio fidelium*.[4] The Roman Church is not identical with it, and this body of Christians may exist independently of the Roman Church. If the pope had plenary power, the law of the Gospel would be more galling than the law of Moses.

Werner, III. 115.   The expression *objective in mente* is equivalent to our word subjective.

[1] *Imperialis dignitas et potestas est immediate a solo Deo.*   Goldast, IV. 99, Frankf. ed.   See also Dorner, p. 675.

[2] Kropatscheck, p. 55 sq., Matt. 30 : 25 sqq.   Clement VI. declared Ockam had sucked his political heresies from Marsiglius of Padua.

[3] See Riezler, p. 273, and Seeberg, pp. 271, 278, *Christianus de necessitate salutis non tenetur ad credendum nec credere quod nec in biblia continetur nec ex solis contentis in biblia potest consequentia necessaria et manifesta inferri.*

[4] *Romana ecclesia est distincta a congregatione fidelium et potest contra fidem errare.   Ecclesia autem universalis errare non potest.*   See Kropatscheck, p. 65 sqq., and also Dorner, p. 696.

All would then be the pope's slaves.[1] The papacy is not a necessary institution.

In the doctrine of the eucharist, Ockam represents the traditional view as less probable than the view that Christ's body is at the side of the bread.   This theory of impanation, which Rupert of Deutz taught, approached Luther's theory of consubstantiation.   However, Ockam accepted the Church's view, because it was the less intelligible and because the power of God is unlimited.   John of Paris, d. 1308, had compared the presence of Christ in the elements to the co-existence of two natures in the incarnation and was deposed from his chair at the University of Paris, 1304.   Gabriel Biel took a similar view.[2]

Ockam's views on the authority of the civil power, papal errancy, the infallibility of the Scriptures and the eucharist are often compared with the views of Luther.[3] The German reformer spoke of the English Schoolman as " without doubt the leader and most ingenious of the Schoolmen " — *scholasticorum doctorum sine dubio princeps et ingeniosissimus.* He called him his " dear teacher," and declared himself to be of Ockam's party — *sum Occamicæ factionis.*[4] The two men were, however, utterly unlike. Ockam was a theorist, not a reformer, and in spite of his bold sayings, remained a child of the mediæval age. He started no party or school in theological matters. Luther exalted personal faith in the living Christ. He discovered new principles in the Scriptures, and made them the active forces of individual and national belief and practice. We might think of Luther as an Ockam if he had lived in the fourteenth century. We cannot think of Ockam as a reformer in the sixteenth century. He would scarcely have renounced monkery. Ockam's merit consists in this that, in common with Marsiglius and other leaders of

---

[1] See Werner, III. 120, who quotes Scaliger as saying of Ockam, *omnium mortalium subtillissimus, cujus ingenium vetera subvertit, nova ad invictas insanias et incomprehensibiles subtilitates fabricavit et conformavit.*

[2] See Werner, *D. hl. Thomas,* III. 111; Harnack, *Dogmengesch.,* III. 494; Seeberg, 276.

[3] For example, Kropatscheck, especially p. 66 sqq., and Seeberg, p. 289.

[4] Weimar, ed. VI. 183, 195, 600, as quoted by Seeberg.

thought, he imbibed the new spirit of free discussion, and was bold enough to assail the traditional dogmas of his time. In this way he contributed to the unsettlement of the pernicious mediæval theory of the seat of authority.

§ 21. *Catherine of Siena, the Saint.*

Next to Francis d'Assisi, the most celebrated of the Italian saints is Catherine of Siena — Caterina da Siena — 1347-1380. With Elizabeth of Thuringia, who lived more than a century before her, she is the most eminent of the holy women of the Middle Ages whom the Church has canonized.   Her fame depends upon her single-hearted piety and her efforts to advance the interests of the Church and her nation.   She left no order to encourage the reverence for her name.   She was the most public of all the women of the Middle Ages in Italy, and yet she passed unscathed and without a taint through streets and in courts.   Now, as the daughter of an humble citizen of Siena, she ministers to the poor and the sick: now, as the prophetess of heaven, she appeals to the conscience of popes and of commonwealths.   Her native Sienese have sanctified her with the fragrant name *la beata poplana*, the blessed daughter of the people.   Although much in her career, as it has been handed down by her confessor and biographer, may seem to be legendary, and although the hysterical element may not be altogether wanting from her piety, she yet deserves and will have the admiration of all men who are moved by the sight of a noble enthusiasm.   It would require a fanatical severity to read the account of her unwearied efforts and the letters, into which she equally poured the fire of her soul, without feeling that the Sienese saint was a very remarkable woman, the Florence Nightingale of her time or more, " one of the most wonderful women that have ever lived," as her most recent English biographer has pronounced her.   Or, shall we join Gregorovius, the thorough student of mediæval Rome, in saying, " Catherine's figure flits like that of an angel: through the darkness of her time, over which her gracious genius sheds a soft radiance.   Her life is more worthy and assuredly a more human subject for history than the lives of the popes of her age." [1]

Catherine Benincasa was the twenty-third of a family of twenty-five children. Her twin sister, Giovanna, died in infancy. Her father was a dyer in prosperous circumstances. Her mother, Monna Lapa, survived the daughter. Catherine treated her with filial respect, wrote her letters, several of which are extant, and had her with her on journeys and in Rome during her last days there. Catherine had no school training, and her knowledge of reading and writing she acquired after she was grown up.

As a child she was susceptible to religious impressions, and frequented the Dominican church near her father's home. The miracles of her earlier childhood were reported by her confessor and biographer, Raymund of Capua. At twelve her parents arranged for her a marriage, but to avoid it Catherine cut off her beautiful hair. She joined the tertiary order of the Dominicans, the women adherents being called the *mantellate* from their black mantles. Raymund declares "that nature had not given her a face over-fair," and her personal appearance was marred by the marks of the smallpox. And yet she had a winning expression, a fund of good spirits, and sang and laughed heartily. Once devoted to a religious life, she practised great austerities, flagellating herself three times a day, — once for herself, once for the living and once for the dead. She wore a hair undergarment and an iron chain. During one Lenten season she lived on the bread taken in communion. These asceticisms were performed in a chamber in her father's house. She was never an inmate of a convent. Such extreme asceticisms as she practised upon herself she disparaged at a later period.

At an early age Catherine became the subject of visions and revelations. On one of these occasions and after hours of dire temptation, when she was tempted to live like other girls, the Saviour appeared to her stretched on the cross and said : " My own daughter, Catherine, seest thou how much I

---

[1] Gardner, p. vii; Gregorovius, VI. 521 sqq.

have suffered for thee? Let it not be hard for thee to suffer for me." Thrilled with the address, she asked: "Where wert thou, Lord, when I was tempted with such impurity?" and He replied, "In thy heart." In 1367, according to her own statement, the Saviour betrothed himself to her, putting a ring on her finger. The ring was ever afterwards visible to herself though unseen by others. Five years before her death, she received the stigmata directly from Christ. Their impression gave sharp pain, and Catherine insisted that, though they likewise were invisible to others, they were real to her.

In obedience to a revelation, Catherine renounced the retired life she had been living, and at the age of twenty began to appear in public and perform the active offices of charity. This was in 1367. She visited the poor and sick, and soon became known as the ministering angel of the whole city. During the plague of 1374, she was indefatigable by day and night, healed those of whom the physicians despaired, and she even raised the dead. The lepers outside the city walls she did not neglect.

One of the remarkable incidents in her career which she vouches for in one of her letters to Raymund was her treatment of Niccolo Tuldo, a young nobleman condemned to die for having uttered words disrespectful of the city government. The young man was in despair, but under Catherine's influence he not only regained composure, but became joyful in the prospect of death. Catherine was with him at the block and held his head. She writes, "I have just received a head into my hands which was to me of such sweetness as no heart can think, or tongue describe." Before the execution she accompanied the unfortunate man to the mass, where he received the communion for the first time. His last words were "naught but Jesus and Catherine. And, so saying," wrote his benefactress, "I received his head in my hands." She then saw him received of Christ, and as she further wrote, "When he was at rest, my soul rested in peace, in so great fragrance of blood that I could not bear to remove the blood which had fallen on me from him."

The fame of such a woman could not be held within the

walls of her native city. Neighboring cities and even the
pope in Avignon heard of her deeds of charity and her revelations. The guide of minds seeking the consolations of
religion, the minister to the sick and dying, Catherine now
entered into the wider sphere of the political life of Italy and
the welfare of the Church. Her concern was divided between
efforts to support the papacy and to secure the amelioration
of the clergy and establish peace. With the zeal of a prophet,
she urged upon Gregory XI. to return to Rome. She sought
to prevent the rising of the Tuscan cities against the Avignon
popes and to remove the interdict which was launched against
Florence, and she supported Urban VI. against the anti-pope,
Clement VII. With equal fervor she urged Gregory to institute a reformation of the clergy, to allow no weight to considerations of simony and flattery in choosing cardinals and pastors
and " to drive out of the sheep-fold those wolves, those demons
incarnate, who think only of good cheer, splendid feasts and su-
perb liveries." She also was zealous in striving to stir up the
flames of a new crusade. To Sir John Hawkwood, the free-
lance and terror of the peninsula, she wrote, calling upon him
that, as he took such pleasure in fighting, he should thenceforth
no longer direct his arms against Christians, but against the
infidels. She communicated to the Queen of Cyprus on the
subject. Again and again she urged it upon Gregory XI.,
and chiefly on the grounds that he " might minister the blood
of the Lamb to the wretched infidels," and that converted, they
might aid in driving pride and other vices out of the Christian
world.[1]

Commissioned by Gregory, she journeyed to Pisa to influence the city in his favor. She was received with honors by
the archbishop and the head of the republic, and won over two
professors who visited her with the purpose of showing her
she was self-deceived or worse. She told them that it was
not important for her to know how God had created the world,
but that "it was essential to know that the Son of God had
taken our human nature and lived and died for our salvation." One of the professors, removing his crimson velvet

[1] Scudder, *Letters*, pp. 100, 121, 136, 179, 184, 234, etc.

cap, knelt before her and asked for forgiveness.   Catherine's cures of the sick won the confidence of the people.   On this visit she was accompanied by her mother and a group of like-minded women.

A large chapter in Catherine's life is interwoven with the history of Florence.   The spirit of revolt against the Avignon régime was rising in upper Italy and, when the papal legate in Bologna, in a year of dearth, forbade the transportation of provisions to Florence, it broke out into war.   At the invitation of the Florentines, Catherine visited the city, 1375 and, a year later, was sent as a delegate to Avignon to negotiate terms of peace.   She was received with honor by the pope, but not without hesitancy.   The other members of the delegation, when they arrived, refused to recognize her powers and approve her methods.   The cardinals treated her coolly or with contempt, and women laid snares at her devotions to bring ridicule upon her.   Such an attempt was made by the pope's niece, Madame de Beaufort Turenne, who knelt at her side and ran a sharp knife into her foot so that she limped from the wound.

The dyer's daughter now turned her attention to the task of confirming the supreme pontiff in his purpose to return to Rome and counteract the machinations of the cardinals against its execution.   Seeing her desire realized, she started back for Italy and, met by her mother at Leghorn, went on to Florence, carrying a commission from the pope.   Her effort to induce the city to bow to the sentence of interdict, which had been laid upon it, was in a measure successful.   Her reverence for the papal office demanded passive obedience.   Gregory's successor, Urban VI., lifted the ban.   Catherine then returned to Siena where she dictated the Dialogue, a mystical treatise inculcating prayer, obedience, discretion and other virtues.   Catherine declared that God alone had been her guide in its composition.

In the difficulties, which arose soon after Urban's election, that pontiff looked to Siena and called its distinguished daughter to Rome.   They had met in Avignon.   Accompanied by her mother and other companions, she reached the holy city in the Autumn of 1378. They occupied a house by themselves and lived upon alms.[1] Her summons to Urban "to battle only with the weapons of repentance, prayer, virtue and love" were not heeded. Her presence, however, had a beneficent influence, and on one occasion, when the mob raged and poured into the Vatican, she appeared as a peacemaker, and the sight of her face and her words quieted the tumult.

She died lying on boards, April 29, 1380. To her companions standing at her side, she said: "Dear children, let not my death sadden you, rather rejoice to think that I am leaving a place of many sufferings to go to rest in the quiet sea, the eternal God, and to be united forever with my most sweet and loving Bridegroom. And I promise to be with you more and to be more useful to you, since I leave darkness to pass into the true and everlasting light." Again and again she whispered, "I have sinned, O Lord; be merciful to me." She prayed for Urban, for the whole Church and for her companions, and then she departed, repeating the words, "Into thy hands I commit my spirit."

At the time of her death Catherine of Siena was not yet thirty-three years old. A magnificent funeral was ordered by Urban. A year after, her head, enclosed in a reliquary, was sent to her native Siena, and in 1461 she was canonized by the city's famous son, pope Pius II., who uttered the high praise "that none ever approached her without going away better." In 1865 when Santa Maria sopra Minerva in Rome was reopened, her ashes were carried through the streets, the silver urn containing them being borne by four bishops. Lamps are kept ever burning at the altar dedicated to her in the church. In 1866 Pius IX. elevated the dyer's daughter to the dignity of patron saint and protectress of Rome, a dignity she shares with the prince of the Apostles. With Petrarch she had been the most ardent advocate of its claims as the papal residence, and her zeal was exclusively religious.

[1] Gardner, p. 298, says one of the two houses is still shown where they dwelt.

In her correspondence and Dialogue we have the biography of Catherine's soul.   Nearly four hundred of her letters are extant.[1]   Not only have they a place of eminence as the revelations of a saintly woman's thoughts and inner life, but are, next to the letters written by Petrarch, the chief specimens of epistolary literature of the fourteenth century.   She wrote to persons of all classes, to her mother, the recluse in the cloister, her confessor, Raymund of Capua, to men and women addicted to the pleasures of the world, to the magistrates of cities, queens and kings, to cardinals, and to the popes, Gregory XI. and Urban VI., gave words of counsel, set forth at length measures and motives of action, used the terms of entreaty and admonition, and did not hesitate to employ threats of divine judgment, as in writing to the Queen of Naples.   They abound in wise counsels.

The correspondence shows that Catherine had some acquaintance with the New Testament from which she quotes the greater precepts and draws descriptions from the miracle of the water changed into wine and the expulsion of the moneychangers from the temple and such parables as the ten virgins and the marriage-feast.   One of her most frequent expressions is the blood of Christ, and in truly mystical or conventual manner she bids her correspondents, even the pope and the cardinals, bathe and drown and inebriate themselves in it, yea, to clothe and fill themselves with it, " for Christ did not buy us with gold or silver or pearls or other precious stones, but with his own precious blood." [2]

To Catherine the religious life was a subjection of the will to the will of God and the outgoing of the soul in exercises of prayer and the practice of love.   " I want you to wholly destroy your own will that it may cling to Christ crucified." So she wrote to a mother bereft of her children.   Writing to the recluse, Bartolomea della Seta, she represented the Saviour as saying, " Sin and virtue consist in the consent of the will, there is no sin or virtue unless voluntarily wrought."

[1] None of these are in her own hand, but six of them are originals as they were written down at her dictation.   Gardner, p. xii., 373 sqq.

[2] *Letters*, pp. 54, 65, 75, 110, 158, 164, 226, 263, 283, etc.

To another she wrote, " I have already seen many penitents who have been neither patient nor obedient because they have studied to kill their bodies but not their wills." [1]

Her sound religious philosophy showed itself in insisting again and again that outward discipline is not the only or always the best way to secure the victory of the spirit. If the body is weak or fallen into illness, the rule of discretion sets aside the exercises of bodily discipline. She wrote, " Not only should fasting be abandoned but flesh be eaten and, if once a day is not enough, then four times a day." Again and again she treats of penance as an instrument. "The little good of penance may hinder the greater good of inward piety. Penance cuts off," so she wrote in a remarkable letter to Sister Daniella of Orvieto, "yet thou wilt always find the root in thee, ready to sprout again, but virtue pulls up by the root."

Monastic as Catherine was, yet no evangelical guide-book could write more truly than she did in most particulars. And at no point does this noble woman rise higher than when she declined to make her own states the standard for others, and condemned those "who, indiscreetly, want to measure all bodies by one and the same measure, the measure by which they measure themselves." Writing to her niece, Nanna Benincasa, she compared the heart to a lamp, wide above and narrow below. A bride of Christ must have lamp and oil and light. The heart should be wide above, filled with holy thoughts and prayer, bearing in memory the blessings of God, especially the blessing of the blood by which we are bought. And like a lamp, it should be narrow below, " not loving or desiring earthly things in excess nor hungering for more than God wills to give us."

To the Christian virtues of prayer and love she continually returns. Christian love is compared to the sea, peaceful and profound as God Himself, for " God is love." This passage throws light upon the unsearchable mystery of the Incarnate Word who, constrained by love, gave Himself up in all humility. We love because we are loved. He loves

[1] *Letters*, pp. 43, 162, 152, 149.

of grace, and we love Him of duty because we are bound to do so; and to show our love to Him we ought to serve and love every rational creature and extend our love to good and bad, to all kinds of people, as much to one who does us ill as to one who serves us, for God is no respecter of persons, and His charity extends to just men and sinners. Peter's love before Pentecost was sweet but not strong. After Pentecost he loved as a son, bearing all tribulations with patience. So we, too, if we remain in vigil and continual prayer and tarry ten days, shall receive the plenitude of the Spirit. More than once in her letters to Gregory, she bursts out into a eulogy of love as the remedy for all evils. "The soul cannot live without love," she wrote in the Dialogue, "but must always love something, for it was created through love. Affection moves the understanding, as it were, saying, 'I want to love, for the food wherewith I am fed is love.'"[1]

Such directions as these render Catherine's letters a valuable manual of religious devotion, especially to those who are on their guard against being carried away by the underlying quietistic tone. Not only do they have a high place as the revelation of a pious woman's soul. They deal with unconcealed boldness and candor with the low conditions into which the Church was fallen. Popes are called upon to institute reforms in the appointment of clergymen and to correct abuses in other directions. As for the pacification of the Tuscan cities, a cause which lay so close to Catherine's heart, she urged the pontiff to use the measures of peace and not of war, to deal as a father would deal with a rebellious son, — to put into practice clemency, not the pride of authority. Then the very wolves would nestle in his bosom like lambs.[2]

As for the pope's return to Rome, she urged it as a duty he owed to God who had made him His vicar. In view of the opposition on the Rhone, almost holding him as by physical force, she called upon him "to play the man," "to be a manly man, free from fear and fleshly love towards himself or towards any creature related to him by kin," "to be stable

---

[1] Scudder, *Letters*, pp. 81, 84, 126 sq.; Gardner, *Life*, p. 377.
[2] *Letters*, p. 133.

in his resolution and to believe and trust in Christ in spite
of all predictions of the evil to follow his return to Rome." [1]
To this impassioned Tuscan woman, the appointment of unworthy shepherds and bad rectors was responsible for the
rebellion against papal authority, shepherds who, consumed
by self-love, far from dragging Christ's sheep away from the
wolves, devoured the very sheep themselves.   It was because
they did not follow the true Shepherd who has given His life
for the sheep.   Likening the Church to a garden, she invoked
the pope to uproot the malodorous plants full of avarice,
impurity and pride, to throw them away that the bad priests
and rulers who poison the garden might no longer have rule.
To Urban VI. she addressed burning words of condemnation.   "Your sons nourish themselves on the wealth they
receive by ministering the blood of Christ, and are not
ashamed of being money-changers.   In their great avarice
they commit simonies, buying benefices with gifts or flat-
teries or gold."   And to the papal legate of Bologna, Cardinal d'Estaing, she wrote, "make the holy father consider the
loss of souls more than the loss of cities, for God demands
souls."

The stress Catherine laid upon the pope's responsibility
to God and her passionate reproof of an unworthy and hire-
ling ministry, inclined some to give her a place among
the heralds of the Protestant Reformation.   Flacius Illyricus included her in the list of his witnesses for the truth
— *Catalogus testium veritatis*.[2]   With burning warmth she
spoke of a thorough-going reformation which was to come
upon the Church.   "The bride, now all deformed and clothed
in rags," she exclaimed, "will then gleam with beauty and
jewels, and be crowned with the diadem of all virtues.   All
believing nations will rejoice to have excellent shepherds,
and the unbelieving world, attracted by her glory, will be

---

[1] *Letters*, pp. 66, 185, 232, etc.

[2] Döllinger, *Fables and Prophecies of the Middle Ages*, p. 330, calls attention to the failure of Catherine's predictions to reach fulfilment. " How little
have these longings of the devout maiden of Siena been transformed into
history ! "

converted unto her." Infidel peoples would be brought into the Catholic fold, — *ovile catholicum*, — and be converted unto the true pastor and bishop of souls. But Catherine, admirable as these sentiments were, moved within the limits of the mediæval Church. She placed piety back of penitential exercises in love and prayer and patience, but she never passed beyond the ascetic and conventual conception of the Christian life into the open air of liberty through faith. She had the spirit of Savonarola, the spirit of fiery self-sacrifice for the well-being of her people and the regeneration of Christendom, but she did not see beyond the tradition of the past. Living a hundred years and more before the Florentine prophet, she was excelled by none in her own age and approached by none of her own nation in the century between her and Savonarola, in passionate effort to save her people and help spread righteousness. Hers was the voice of the prophet, crying in the wilderness, " Prepare ye the way of the Lord."

In recalling the women of the century from 1350 to 1450, the mind easily associates together Catherine of Siena and Joan of Arc, 1411–1431, one the passionate advocate of the Church, the other of the national honor of France. The Maid of Orleans, born of peasant parentage, was only twenty when she was burnt at the stake on the streets of Rouen, 1431. Differing from her Italian sister by comeliness of form and robustness of constitution, she also, as she thought, was the subject of angelic communications and divine guidance. Her unselfish devotion to her country at first brought it victory, but, at last, to her capture and death. Her trial by the English on the charges of heresy and sorcery and her execution are a dark sheet among the pages of her century's history. Twenty-five years after her death, the pope revoked the sentence, and the French heroine, whose standard was embroidered with lilies and adorned with pictures of the creation and the annunciation, was beatified, 1909, and now awaits the crown of canonization from Rome. The exalted passion of these two women, widely as they differ in methods and ideals and in the close of their careers, diffuses a bright light over the selfish pursuits of their time, and makes the aims of many of its courts look low and grovelling.

§ 22.   *Peter d'Ailly, Ecclesiastical Statesman.*

One of the most prominent figures in the negotiations for the healing of the papal schism, as well as one of the foremost personages of his age, was Peter d'Ailly, born in Compiègne 1350, died in Avignon 1420.   His eloquence, which reminds us of Bossuet and other French orators of the court of Louis XIV., won for him the title of the Eagle of France — *aquila Francia.*[1]

In 1372 he entered the College of Navarre as a theological student, prepared a commentary on the Sentences of the Lombard three years later, and in 1380 reached the theological doctorate.   He at once became involved in the measures for the healing of the schism, and in 1381 delivered a celebrated address in the name of the university before the French regent, the duke of Anjou, to win the court for the policy of settling the papal controversy through a general council. His appeal not meeting with favor, he retired to Noyon, from which he wrote a letter purporting to come from the devil, a satire based on the continuance of the schism, in which the prince of darkness called upon his friends and vassals, the prelates, to follow his example in promoting division in the Church.   He warned them as their overlord that the holding of a council might result in establishing peace and so bring eternal shame upon them.   He urged them to continue to make the Church a house of merchandise and to be careful to tithe anise and cummin, to make broad the borders of their garments and in every other way to do as he had given them an example.[2]

In 1384 D'Ailly was made head of the College of Navarre, where he had Gerson for a pupil, and in 1389 chancellor of the university.

---

[1] Tschackert, Salembier and Finke consider D'Ailly under the three aspects of theologian, philosopher and ecclesiastical diplomatist.   Lenz and Bess emphasize the part he played as an advocate of French policy against England.

[2] *Epistola diaboli Leviathan.* Tschackert gives the text, Appendix, pp. 15–21.

When Benedict XIII. was chosen successor to Clement VII., he was sent by the French king on a confidential mission to Avignon.   Benedict won his allegiance and appointed him successively bishop of Puy, 1395, and bishop of Cambray, 1397.   D'Ailly was with Benedict at Genoa, 1405, and Savona, 1407, but by that time seems to have come to the conclusion that Benedict was not sincere in his profession of readiness to resign, and returned to Cambray.   In his absence Cambray had decided for the subtraction of its allegiance from Avignon.   D'Ailly was seized and taken to Paris, but protected by the king, who was his friend.   Thenceforth he favored the assemblage of a general council.

At Pisa and at Constance, D'Ailly took the position that a general council is superior to the pope and may depose him.   Made a cardinal by John XXIII., 1411, he attended the council held at Rome the following year and in vain tried to have a reform of the calendar put through.   At Constance, he took the position that the Pisan council, though it was called by the Spirit and represented the Church universal, might have erred, as did other councils reputed to be general councils.   He declared that the three synods of Pisa, Rome and Constance, though not one body, yet were virtually one, even as the stream of the Rhine at different points is one and the same.   It was not necessary, so he held, for the Council of Constance to pass acts confirming the Council of Pisa, for the two were on a par.[1]

In the proceedings against John XXIII., the cardinal took sides against him.   He was the head of the commission which tried Huss in matters of faith, June 7, 8, 1415, and was present when the sentence of death was passed upon that Reformer. At the close of the council he appears as one of the three candidates for the office of pope, and his defeat was a disappointment to the French.[2]   He was appointed legate by

---

[1] These judgments are expressed in the *Capita agendorum*, a sort of programme for the guidance of the council prepared by D'Ailly, 1414.   Finke, *Forschungen*,. pp. 102–132, has no doubt that they proceeded from D'Ailly's pen, a view confirmed by MSS. in Vienna and Rome.   Finke gives a résumé of the articles, the original of which is given by van der Hardt., II. 201 sqq. and Mansi, XXVII. 547.   [2] Tschackert, p. 295.

Martin V., with his residence at Avignon, and spent his last days there.

D'Ailly followed Ockam as a nominalist.   To his writings in the departments of philosophy, theology and Church government he added works on astronomy and geography and a much-read commentary on Aristotle's meteorology.[1]   His work on geography, *The Picture of the World*, — *imago mundi*, — written 1410, was a favorite book with Columbus.   A printed copy of it containing marginal notes in the navigator's own hand is preserved in the *biblioteca Colombina*, Seville.   This copy he probably had with him on his third journey to America, for, in writing from Hayti, 1498, he quoted at length the eighth chapter.   Leaning chiefly upon Roger Bacon, the author represented the coast of India or Cathay as stretching far in the direction of Europe, so that, in a favorable wind, a ship sailing westwards would reach it in a few days.   This idea was in the air, but it is possible that it was first impressed upon the mind of the discoverer of the New World by the reading of D'Ailly's work.   Humboldt was the first to show its value for the history of discovery.[2]

§ 23.   *John Gerson, Theologian and Church Leader.*

In John Gerson, 1363–1429, we have the most attractive and the most influential theological leader of the first half of the fifteenth century.   He was intimately identified with the University of Paris as professor and as its chancellor in the period of its most extensive influence in Europe.   His voice carried great weight in the settlement of the questions rising out of the papal schism.

Jean Charlier Gerson, born Dec. 14, 1363, in the village of Gerson, in the diocese of Rheims, was the oldest of twelve children.   In a letter to him still extant,[3] his mother, a godly woman, pours out her heart in the prayer that her children may live in unity with each other and with God.   Two of John's brothers became ecclesiastics.   In 1377 Gerson went

---

[1] Tschackert gives an estimate of D'Ailly's writings, pp. 303–335.
[2] See Fiske, *Discovery of America*, I. 372.　　　　　[3] Schwab, p. 51.

to Paris, entering the College of Navarre. This college was founded by Johanna, queen of Navarre, 1304, who provided for 3 departments, the arts with 20 students, philosophy with 30 and theology with 20 students. Provision was made also for their support, 4 Paris sous weekly for the artists, 6 for the logicians and 8 for the theologians. These allowances were to continue until the graduates held benefices of the value respectively of 30, 40 and 60 pounds. The regulations allowed the theological students a fire, daily, from November to March after dinner and supper for one half-hour. The luxury of benches was forbidden by a commission appointed by Urban V. in 1366. On the festival days, the theologians were expected to deliver a collation to their fellow-students of the three classes. The rector at the head of the college, originally appointed by the faculty of the university, was now appointed by the king's confessor. The students wore a special dress and the tonsure, spoke Latin amongst themselves and ate in common.

Gerson, perhaps the most distinguished name the University of Paris has on its list of students, was a faithful and enthusiastic son of his alma mater, calling her "his mother," "the mother of the light of the holy Church," "the nurse of all that is wise and good in Christendom," "a prototype of the heavenly Jerusalem," "the fountain of knowledge, the lamp of our faith, the beauty and ornament of France, yea, of the whole world."[1]

In 1382, at the age of nineteen, he passed into the theological department, and a year later came under the guidance of D'Ailly, the newly appointed rector, remaining under him for seven years. Gerson was already a marked man, and was chosen in 1383 procurator of the French "nation," and in 1387 one of the delegation to appear before Clement VII. and argue the case against John of Montson. This Dominican, who had been condemned for denying the immaculate conception of Mary, refused to recant on the plea that in being condemned Thomas Aquinas was condemned, and he appealed to the pope. The University of Paris took up the case, and

[1] Schwab, p. 59.

D'Ailly in two addresses before the papal consistory took the ground that Thomas, though a saint, was not infallible. The case went against De Montson; and the Dominicans, who refused to bow to the decision, left the university and did not return till 1403.

Gerson advocated Mary's exemption from original as well as actual sin, and made a distinction between her and Christ, Christ being exempt by nature, and Mary — *domina nostra* — by an act of divine grace. This doctrine, he said, cannot be immediately derived from the Scriptures,[1] but, as the Apostles knew more than the prophets, so the Church teachers know some things the Apostles did not know.

At D'Ailly's promotion to the episcopate, 1395, his pupil fell heir to both his offices, the offices of professor of theology and chancellor of the university. In the discussion over the healing of the schism in which the university took the leading part, he occupied a place of first prominence, and by tracts, sermons and public memorials directed the opinion of the Church in this pressing matter. The premise from which he started out was that the peace of the Church is an essential condition to the fulfilment of its mission. This view he set forth in a famous sermon, preached in 1404 at Tarascon before Benedict XIII. and the duke of Orleans. Princes and prelates, he declared, both owe obedience to law. The end for which the Church was constituted is the peace and well-being of men. All Church authority is established to subserve the interests of peace. Peace is so great a boon that all should be ready to renounce dignities and position for it. Did not Christ suffer shame? Better for a while to be without a pope than that the Church should observe the canons and not have peace, for there can be salvation where there is no pope.[2] A general council should be convened, and it was pious to believe that in the treatment of the schism it

---

[1] *In scriptura sacra neque continetur explicite neque in contentis eadem educitur evidenter,* Du Pin's ed. III. 1350. For sermons on the conception, nativity and annunciation of the Virgin, vol. III. 1317–1377. Also III. 941, and Du Pin's *Gersoniana,* I. cviii. sq.

[2] *Potest absque papa mortali stare salus,* Du Pin, II. 72. The Tarascon sermon is given by Du Pin, II. 54–72. Schwab's analysis, pp. 171–178.

would not err — *pium est credere non erraret.* As Schwab
has said, no one had ever preached in the same way to a pope
before. The sermon caused a sensation.

Gerson, though not present at the council of Pisa, contributed to its discussions by his important tracts on the Unity
of the Church — *De unitate ecclesiastica* — and the Removal of
a Pope — *De auferbilitate papæ ab ecclesia.* The views set forth
were that Christ is the head of the Church, and its monarchical constitution is unchangeable. There must be one pope,
not several, and the bishops are not equal in authority with
him. As the pope may separate himself from the Church,
so the Church may separate itself from the pope. Such action might be required by considerations of self-defence. The
papal office is of God, and yet the pope may be deposed even
by a council called without his consent. All Church offices
and officials exist for the good of the Church, that is, for the
sake of peace which comes through the exercise of love. If
a pope has a right to defend himself against, say, the charge
of unchastity, why should not the Church have a like right
to defend itself? A council acts under the immediate authority of Christ and His laws. The council may pronounce
against a pope by virtue of the power of the keys which is
given not only to one but to the body — *unitati.* Aristotle declared that the body has the right, if necessary, to depose its
prince. So may the council, and whoso rejects a council of
the Church rejects God who directs its action. A pope may
be deposed for heresy and schism, as, for example, if he did not
bend the knee before the sacrament, and he might be deposed
when no personal guilt was chargeable against him, as in the
case already referred to, when he was a captive of the Saracens and was reported dead.

At the Council of Constance, where Gerson spoke as the
delegate of the French king, he advocated these positions
again and again with his voice, as in his address March 23,
1415, and in a second address July 21, when he defended the
decree which the synod had passed at its fifth session. He
reasserted that the pope may be forced to abdicate, that general councils are above the popes and that infallibility only

belongs to the Church as a body or its highest representative, a general council.[1]

A blot rests upon Gerson's name for the active part he took in the condemnation of John Huss. He was not above his age, and using the language of Innocent III. called heresy a cancer.[2] He declares that he was as zealous in the proceedings against Huss and Wyclif as any one could be.[3] He pronounced the nineteen errors drawn from Huss' work on the Church "notoriously heretical." Heresy, he declared, if it is obstinate, must be destroyed even by the death of its professors.[4] He denied Huss' fundamental position that nothing is to be accepted as divine truth which is not found in Scripture. Gerson also condemned the appeal to conscience, explicitly assuming the old position of Church authority and canon law as final. The opinions of an individual, however learned he may be in the Scriptures, have no weight before the judgment of a council.[5]

In the controversy over the withdrawal of the cup from the laity, involved in the Bohemian heresy, Gerson also took an extreme position, defending it by arguments which seem to us altogether unworthy of a genuine theology. In a tract on the subject he declared that, though some passages of Scripture and of the Fathers favored the distribution of both wine and bread, they do not contain a definite command, and in the cases where an explicit command is given it must be understood as applying to the priests who are obliged to commune under both kinds so as to fully represent Christ's sufferings and death. But this is not required of the laity who commune for the sake of the effect of Christ's death and not to set it forth. Christ commanded only the Apostles to partake of both kinds.[6] The custom of lay communion was never universal, as is proved by Acts 2: 42, 46. The essence of

---

[1] See Schwab, pp. 520 sqq., 668.

[2] In a sermon before the Council of Constance, Du Pin, II. 207.

[3] *Dialog. apologet.*, Du Pin, II. 387.

[4] *Ad punitionem et exterminationem errantium*, Du Pin, II. 277.

[5] See Schwab, pp. 599, 601.

[6] *Contra heresin de communione laicorum sub utraque specie*, Du Pin, I. 457–468. See Schwab, p. 604 sqq.

the sacrament of the body and blood is more important than the elements, John 6 : 54.   But the whole Christ is in either element, and, if some of the doctors take a different view, the Church's doctrine is to be followed, and not they.   From time immemorial the Church has given the communion only in one form.   The Council of Constance was right in deciding that only a single element is necessary to a saving participation in the sacrament.   The Church may make changes in the outward observance when the change does not touch the essence of the right in question.   The use of the two elements, once profitable, is now unprofitable and heretical.

To these statements Gerson added practical considerations against the distribution of the cup to laymen, such as the danger of spilling the wine, of soiling the vessels from the long beards of laymen, of having the wine turn to vinegar, if it be preserved for the sick and so it cease to be the blood of Christ — *et ita desineret esse sanguis Christi* — and from the impossibility of consecrating in one vessel enough for 10,000 to 20,000 communicants, as at Easter time may be necessary. Another danger was the encouragement such a practice would give to the notions that priest and layman are equal, and that the chief value of the sacrament lies in the participation and not in the consecration of the elements.[1]   Such are some of the " scandals " which this renowned teacher ascribed to the distribution of the cup to the laity.

A subject on which Gerson devoted a great deal of energy for many years was whether the murder of tyrants or of a traitorous vassal is justifiable or not.   He advocated the negative side of the case, which he failed to win before the Council of Constance.   The question grew out of the treatment of the half-insane French king, Charles VI. (1380–1422), and the attempt of different factions to get control of the government.

On Nov. 23, 1407, the king's cousin, Louis, duke of Orleans, was murdered at the command of the king's uncle, John, duke of Burgundy.   The duke's act was defended by the

---

[1] *Quod virtus hujus sacramenti non est principalius in consecratione quam in sumptione*, Du Pin, I. 467.

Franciscan and Paris professor, John Petit, — Johannes Par-
vus, — in an address delivered before the king March 8, 1408.
Gerson, who at an earlier time seems to have advocated the
murder of tyrants, answered Petit in a public address, and
called upon the king to suppress Petit's nine propositions.[1]
The University of Paris made Gerson's cause its own.   Petit
died in 1411, but the controversy went on.   Petit's theory
was this, that every vassal plotting against his lord is deserving of death in soul and body.   He is a tyrant, and according to the laws of nature and God any one has the right to
put him out of the way.   The higher such a person is in rank,
the more meritorious is the deed.   He based his argument
upon Thomas Aquinas, John of Salisbury, Aristotle, Cicero
and other writers, and referred to Moses, Zambri and St.
Michael who cast Lucifer out of heaven, and other examples.
The duke of Orleans was guilty of treason against the king,
and the duke of Burgundy was justified in killing him.

The bishop of Paris, supported by a commission of the Inquisition and at the king's direction, condemned Petit and his
views.   In February, 1414, Gerson made a public address defending the condemnation, and two days later articles taken
from Petit's work were burnt in front of Notre Dame.   The
king ratified the bishop's judgment, and the duke of Burgundy
appealed the case to Rome.[2]

The case was now transferred to the council, which at its
fifteenth session, July 6, 1415, passed a compromise measure
condemning the doctrine that a tyrant, in the absence of a
judicial sentence, may and ought to be put to death by any
subject whatever, even by the use of treacherous means, and
in the face of an oath without committing perjury.   Petit was
not mentioned by name.   It was this negative and timid action, which led Gerson to say that if Huss had had a defender,
he would not have been found guilty.   It was rumored that

---

[1] Vol. V. of Gerson's works is taken up with documents bearing on this
subject. Gerson's addresses, bearing upon it at Constance, are given in vol. II.
See Schwab, p. 609 sqq., and Bess, *Zur Geschichte*, etc. The *Chartularium*,
IV. 261–285, 325 sqq., gives the nine propositions in French, with Gerson's
reply, and other matter pertaining to the controversy.   [2] Schwab, p. 620.

the commission which was appointed to bring in a report, by sixty-one out of eighty votes, decided for the permissibility of Petit's articles declaring that Peter meant to kill the high priest's servant, and that, if he had known Judas' thoughts at the Last Supper, he would have been justified in killing him.   The duke of Burgundy's gold is said to have been freely used.[1]   The party led by the bishop of Arras argued that the tyrant who takes the sword is to be punished with the sword.   Gerson, who was supported by D'Ailly replied that then the command "thou shalt not kill" would only forbid such an act as murder, if there was coupled with it an inspired gloss, "without judicial authority."   The command means, "thou shalt not kill the innocent, or kill out of revenge."   Gerson pressed the matter for the last time in an address delivered before the council, Jan. 17, 1417, but the council refused to go beyond the decree of the fifteenth session.

The duke of Burgundy got possession of Paris in 1418, and Gerson found the doors of France closed to him.   Under the protection of the duke of Bavaria he found refuge at Rattenberg and later in Austria.   On the assassination of the duke of Burgundy himself, with the connivance of the dauphin, Sept. 10, 1419, he returned to France, but not to Paris.   He went to Lyons, where his brother John was, and spent his last years there in monastic seclusion.   The dauphin is said to have granted him 200 livres in 1420 in recognition of his services to the crown.

It remains to speak of Gerson as a theologian, a preacher and a patriot.

In the department of theology proper Gerson has a place among the mystics.[2]   Mysticism he defines as "the art of love," the "perception of God through experience."   Such experience is reached by humility and penance more than through the path of speculation.   The contemplative life is most desirable, but,

---

[1] Mansi, XXVII. 765, *Quilibet tyrannus potest et debet licite et meritorie occidi per quemcumque . . . non expectata sententia vel mandato judicis cuiuscumque.*   For D'Ailly's part, see Tschackert, pp. 235–247.

[2] Gerson's mysticism is presented in such tracts as *De vita spirituali animæ* and *De monte contemplationis,* Du Pin, III. 1–77, 541–579.

following Christ's example, contemplation must be combined
with action.   The contemplation of God consists of knowledge
as taught in John 17 : 3, " This is life eternal, to know Thee
and Jesus Christ whom Thou hast sent."   Such knowledge is
mingled with love.   The soul is one with God through love.
His mysticism was based, on the one hand, on the study of the
Scriptures and, on the other, on the study of Bonaventura and
the St. Victors.   He wrote a special treatise in praise of Bonaventura and his mystical writings.   Far from having any conscious affinity with the German mystics, he wrote against John
of Ruysbroeck and Ruysbroeck's pupil, John of Schönhofen,
charging them with pantheism.

While Gerson emphasized the religious feelings, he was far
from being a religious visionary and wrote treatises against the
dangers of delusion from dreams and revelations.   As coins
must be tested by their weight, hardness, color, shape and
stamp, so visions are to be tested by the humility and honesty
of those who profess to have them and their readiness to teach
and be taught.   He commended the monk who, when some one
offered to show him a figure like Christ, replied, " I do not want
to see Christ on the earth.   I am contented to wait till I see
him in heaven."

When the negotiations were going on at the Council of Constance for the confirmation of the canonization of St. Brigitta,
Gerson laid down the principle that, if visions reveal what is
already in the Scriptures,[1] then they are false, for God does
not repeat Himself, Job 33 : 14.   People have itching ears for
revelations because they do not study the Bible.   Later he
warned[2] against the revelations of women, as women are more
open to deception than men.

The Scriptures, Gerson taught, are the Church's rule and
guide to the end of the world.   If a single statement should
be proved false, then the whole volume is false, for the Holy
Spirit is author of the whole.   The letter of the text, however,
is not sufficient to determine their meaning, as is proved from

---

[1] In his *De probatione spirituum*, Du Pin, I. 37–43; and *De distinctione
verarum visionum a falsis*, Du Pin, I. 43–59.

[2] *De examinatione doctrinarum*, Du Pin, I. 7–22.

the translations of the Waldenses, Beghards and other sectaries.[1] The text needs the authority of the Church, as Augustine indicated when he said, " I would not believe the Gospel
if the authority of the Church did not compel me."

Great as Gerson's services were in other departments, it was,
to follow his sympathetic and scholarly biographer, Schwab,
from the pulpit that he exercised most influence on his generation.[2] He preached in French as well as Latin, and his sermons had, for the most part, a practical intent, being occupied
with ethical themes such as pride, idleness, anger, the commandments of the Decalogue, the marital state.   He held that the
ordinary priest should confine himself to a simple explanation
of the Decalogue, the greater sins and the articles of faith.

During the last ten years of his life, spent in seclusion at
Lyons, he continued his literary activity, writing more particularly in the vein of mystical theology.   His last work was
on the Canticles.

The tradition runs that the great teacher in his last years
conducted a catechetical school for children in St. Paul's at
Lyons, and that he taught them to offer for himself the daily
prayer, " God, my creator, have pity upon Thy poor servant,
Jean Gerson " — *Mon Dieu, mon Createur, ayez pitié de vostre
pauvre serviteur, Jean Gerson*.[3] It was for young boys and perhaps for boys spending their first years in the university that
he wrote his tractate entitled Leading Children to Christ.[4] It
opens with an exposition of the words, " Suffer little children
to come unto me " and proceeds to show how much more seemly
it is to offer to God our best in youth than the dregs of sickly

---

[1] *Si propositio aliqua s. scripturæ posita assertive per auctorem suum,
qui est Sp. sanctus, esset falsa, tota s. scripturæ vacillaret auctoritas,* quoted
by Schwab, p. 314.

[2] *Gerson hatte seine einflussreiche Stellung vorzugsweise dem Rufe zu
danken den er als Prediger genoss,* Schwab, p. 376.

[3] See Schwab, p. 773, who neither accepts nor rejects the tradition. Dr.
Philip Schaff used to bring the last literary activity of President Theodore D.
Wolsey, of Yale College, into comparison with the activity of Gerson. In his
last years Dr. Wolsey wrote the expositions of the Sunday school lessons for
the *Sunday School Times.*

[4] *De parvulis ad Christum trahendis,* written according to Schwab, 1409–
1412, Du Pin, III. 278–291.

old age.   The author takes up the sins children should be admonished to avoid, especially unchastity, and holds up to reprobation the principle that vice is venial if it is kept secret, the
principle expressed in the words *si non caste tamen caute*.

In a threefold work, giving a brief exposition of the Ten
Commandments, a statement of the seven mortal sins and some
short meditations on death and the way to meet it, Gerson
gives a sort of catechism, although it is not thrown into the
form of questions and answers.   As the author states, it was
intended for the benefit of poorly instructed curates who heard
confessions, for parents who had children to instruct, for persons not interested in the public services of worship and for
those who had the care of the sick in hospitals.[1]

The title, most Christian doctor — *doctor christianissimus* —
given to John Gerson is intended to emphasize the evangelical temper of his teaching.   To a clear intellect, he added warm
religious fervor.   With a love for the Church, which it would
be hard to find excelled, he magnified the body of Christian
people as possessing the mind and immediate guidance of Christ
and threw himself into the advocacy of the principle that the
judgment of Christendom, as expressed in a general council,
is the final authority of religious matters on the earth.

He opposed some of the superstitions inherited from another
time.   He emphasized the authority of the sacred text.   In
these views as in others he was in sympathy with the progressive spirit of his age.   But he stopped short of the principles of
the Reformers.   He knew nothing of the principles of individual sovereignty and the rights of conscience.   His thinking
moved along churchly lines.   He had none of the bold original
thought of Wyclif and little of that spirit which sets itself
against the current errors of the times in which we live.   His
vote for Huss' burning proves sufficiently that the light of
the new age had not dawned upon his mind.   He was not,
like them, a forerunner of the movement of the sixteenth
century.

---

[1] *Opusculum tripartitum: de preceptis decalogi, de confessione, et de arte
moriendi*, Du Pin, I., 425–450. Bess, in Herzog, VI. 615, calls it " the first
catechism."

The chief principle for which Gerson contended, the supremacy of general councils, met with defeat soon after the great chancellor's death, and was set aside by popes and later by the judgment of a general council.   His writings, however, which were frequently published remain the chief literary monuments in the department of theology of the first half of the fourteenth century.[1]   Separated from the Schoolmen in spirit and method, he stands almost in a class by himself, the most eminent theologian of his century.   This judgment is an extension of the judgment of the eminent German abbot and writer, Trithemius, at the close of the fifteenth century: " He was by far the chief divine of his age " [2]— *Theologorum sui temporis longe princeps.*

§ 24. *Nicolas of Clamanges, the Moralist.*

The third of the great luminaries who gave fame to the University of Paris in this period, Nicolas Poillevillain de Clamanges, was born at Clamengis,[3] Champagne, about 1367 and died in Paris about 1437.   Shy by nature, he took a less prominent part in the settlement of the great questions of the age than his contemporaries, D'Ailly and Gerson.   Like them, he was identified with the discussions called forth by the schism, and is distinguished for the high value he put on the study of the Scriptures and his sharp exposition of the corruption of the clergy.   He entered the College of Navarre at twelve, and had D'Ailly and Gerson for his teachers.   In theology he did not go beyond the baccalaureate.   It is probable he was chosen rector of the university 1393.   With Peter of Monsterolio, he was the chief classical scholar of the university and was able to write that in Paris, Virgil, Terence and Cicero were often read in public and in private.[4]

In 1394, Clamanges took a prominent part in preparing the

---

[1] The first complete edition of Gerson's writings appeared from the press of John Koelhoff.   4 vols. Cologne, 1483, 1484.   The celebrated preacher, Geiler of Strassburg, edited a second edition 1488.   [2] Schwab, p. 779, note.

[3] The spelling given by Denifle in the *Chartularium.*

[4] *Chartul.* III. pp. 5, xi.   In the *Chartularium* Clamanges always appears as a member of the faculty of the arts, III. 606, etc.

paper, setting forth the conclusions of the university in regard to the healing of the schism.[1]   It was addressed to the "most Christian king, Charles VI., most zealous of religious orthodoxy by his daughter, the university."   This, the famous document suggesting the three ways of healing the schism, — by abdication, arbitration and by a general council, — is characterized by firmness and moderation, two of the elements prominent in Clamanges' character.   It pronounced the schism pestiferous, and in answer to the question who would give the council its authority, it answered : " The communion of all the faithful will give it; Christ will give it, who said : 'Where two or three are gathered together in my name there am I in the midst of them.' "

The Paris professor was one of the men whom the keen-eyed Peter de Luna picked out, and when he was elected pope, Clamanges supported him and wrote appealing to him, as the one who no longer occupied the position of one boatman among others, but stood at the rudder of the ship, to act in the interest of all Christendom.   He was called as secretary to the Avignon court, but became weary of the commotion and the vices of the palace and the town.[2]   In 1406, he seems to have withdrawn from Benedict at Genoa and retired to Langres, where he held a canon's stall.   He did not, however, break with the pope, and, when Benedict in 1408 issued the bull threatening the French court with excommunication, Clamanges was charged with being its author.   He denied the charge, but the accusation of want of patriotism had made a strong impression, and he withdrew to the Carthusian convent, Valprofonds, and later to Fontaine du Bosc.   His seclusion he employed in writing letters and treatises and in the study of the Bible which he now expressed regret for having neglected in former years for classical studies.

To D'Ailly he wrote on the advantages of a secluded life. — *De fructu eremi.*   In another tract — *De fructu rerum adversarum* — he presented the advantages of adversity.   One of

---

[1] *Chartul.*, III. 617—624.

[2] *Tædebat me vehementer curiæ, tædebat turbæ, tædebat tumultus, tædebat ambitionis et morum in plerisque vitiosorum*, he wrote.   Quoted by Knöpfler.

more importance complained of the abuse of the Lord's Day and of the multiplication of festivals as taking the workman from his work while the interests of piety were not advanced. In still another tract — *De studio theologico* — addressed to a theologian at Paris who had inquired whether it was better for him to continue where he was or to retire to a pastorate, he emphasized the importance and delicacy of caring for souls, but advised the inquirer to remain at the university and to concern himself chiefly with the study of the Scriptures. He ascribed the Church's decline to their neglect, and pronounced the mass, processionals and festivals as of no account unless the heart be purified by faith.

During the sessions of the Council of Constance, which he did not attend, Clamanges sent a letter to that body urging unity of thought and action. He expressed doubt whether general councils were always led by the Holy Spirit. The Church, which he defined as infallible, is only there where the Holy Spirit is, and where the Church is, can be only known to God Himself. In 1425 he returned to Paris and lectured on rhetoric and theology.

Clamanges' reputation rests chiefly upon his sharp criticism of the corrupt morals of the clergy. His residence in Avignon gave him a good opportunity for observation. His tract on the prelates who were practising simony — *De præsulibus simoniacis* — is a commentary on the words, "But ye have made it a den of thieves," Matt. 21: 13. A second tract on the downfall of the Church — *De ruina ecclesiæ* — is one of the most noted writings of the age. Here are set forth the simony and private vices practised at Avignon where all things holy were prostituted for gold and luxury. Here is described the corruption of the clergy from the pope down to the lowest class of priests. The author found ideal conditions in the first century, when the minds of the clergy were wholly set on heavenly things. With possessions and power came avarice and ambition, pride and luxury. The popes themselves were guilty of pride in exalting their authority above that of the empire and by asserting for themselves the right of appointing all prelates, yea of filling all the benefices of Christendom. The evils aris-

ing from annates and expectances surpass the power of statement. The cardinals followed the popes in their greed and
pride, single cardinals having as many as 500 livings. In order
to perpetuate their "tyranny," pope and curia had entered into
league with princes, which Clamanges pronounces an abominable fornication. Many of the bishops drew large incomes from
their sees which they administered through others, never visiting them themselves. Canons and vicars followed the same
course and divided their time between idleness and sensual
pleasure. The mendicant monks corresponded to the Phari-
sees of the synagogue. Scarcely one cleric out of a thousand
did what his profession demanded. They were steeped in
ignorance and given to brawling, drinking, playing with dice
and fornication. Priests bought the privilege of keeping concubines. As for the nuns, Clamanges said, he dared not speak
of them. Nunneries were not the sanctuaries of God, but
shameful brothels of Venus, resorts of unchaste and wanton
youth for the sating of their passions, and for a girl to put on
the veil was virtually to submit herself to prostitution.[1] The
Church was drunken with the lust of power, glory and pleasures.
Judgment was sure to come, and men should bow humbly before God who alone could rectify the evils and put an end to
the schism. Descriptions such as these must be used with discrimination, and it would be wrong to deduce from them that
the entire clerical body was corrupt. The diseases, however,
must have been deep-seated to call forth such a lament from a
man of Clamanges' position.

The author did not call to open battle like the German Reformer at a later time, but suggested as a remedy prayers, processions and fasts. His watchword was that the Church must
humble itself before it can be rebuilt.[2] It was, however, a

---

[1] *Quid aliud sunt hoc tempore puellarum monasteria, nisi quædam, non
dico Dei sanctuaria sed execranda prostibula Veneris . . . ut idem hodie sit
puellam velare quod ad publice scortandum exponere*, Hardt, I. 38.

[2] *Eccles. prius humilianda quam erigenda.* The authorship of the *De ruina*
has been made a matter of dispute. Müntz denied it to Clamanges chiefly on
the ground of its poor Latin and Knöpfler is inclined to follow him. On the
other hand Schuberth and Schwab, followed somewhat hesitatingly by Bess,
accept the traditional view. Schwab brings out the similarity between the *De*

bold utterance and forms an important part of that body of
literature which so powerfully moulded opinion at the time of
the Reformatory councils.

The loud complaints against the state of morals at the papal
court and beyond during the Avignon period increased, if possible, in strength during the time of the schism.   The list of
abuses to be corrected which the Council of Constance issued,
Oct. 30, 1417, includes the official offences of the curia, such
as reservations, annates, the sale of indulgences and the unrestricted right of appeals to the papal court.   The subject of
chastity it remained for individual writers to press.   In describing the third Babylon, Petrarch was even more severe than
Clamanges who wrote of conditions as they existed nearly a
century later and accused the papal household of practising
adultery, rape and all manners of fornication.[1]   Clamanges
declared that many parishes insisted upon the priests keeping
concubines as a precaution in defence of their own families.
Against all canonical rules John XXIII. gave a dispensation
to the illegitimate son of Henry IV. of England, who was only
ten years old, to enter orders.[2]   The case of John XXIII. was
an extreme one, but it must be remembered, that in Bologna
where he was sent as cardinal-legate, his biographer, Dietrich
of Nieheim, says that two hundred matrons and maidens, including some nuns, fell victims to the future pontiff's amours.
Dietrich Vrie in his *History of the Council of Constance* said:
" The supreme pontiffs, as I know, are elected through avarice
and simony and likewise the other bishops are ordained for

---

ruina and Clamanges' other writings and takes the view that, while the tract
was written in 1401 or 1402, it was not published till 1409.

[1] *Mitto stuprum, raptus, incestus, adulteria, qui jam pontificalis lasciviae
ludi sunt*, quoted by Lea.   *Sacerd. Celibacy*, I. 426.   Gillis li Muisis, abbot of
St. Martin di Tournai, d. 1352, in the *Recollections of his Life* written a year
before his death, speaks of good wines, a good table, fine attire and above all
holidays as in his day the chief occupations of monks.   Curés and chaplains had girls and women as valets, a troublesome habit over which there
was murmuring, and it had to be kept quiet.   See C. V. Langlois, *La vie en
France au moyen âge d'après quelques moralistes du temps*, Paris, 1908, pp.
320, 336, etc.

[2] Jan. 15, 1412.   Under the name of E. Leboorde.   For the document,
see *English Historical Review*, 1904, p. 96 sq.

gold. The old proverb 'Freely give, for freely ye have received' is now most vilely perverted and runs 'Freely I have not received and freely I will not give, for I have bought my bishopric with a great price and must indemnify myself impiously for my outlay.' . . . If Simon Magus were now alive he might buy with money not only the Holy Ghost but God the Father and Me, God the Son."[1] But bad as was the moral condition of the hierarchy and papacy at the time of the schism, it was not so bad as during the last half century of the Middle Ages. The Reformatory councils are the best, though by no means the only, proof that a deep moral vitality existed in the Church. Their very summons and assembling were a protest against clerical corruption and hypocrisy "in head and members," — from the pope down to the most obscure priest, — and at the same time a most hopeful sign of future betterment.

§ 25. *Nicolas of Cusa, Scholar and Churchman.*

Of the theologians of the generation following Gerson and D'Ailly none occupies a more conspicuous place than the German Nicolas of Cusa, 1401–1464. After taking a prominent part in the Basel council in its earlier history, he went into the service of Eugenius IV. and distinguished himself by practical efforts at Church reform and by writings in theology and other departments of human learning.

Born at Cues near Treves, the son of a boatman, he left the parental home on account of harsh treatment. Coming under the patronage of the count of Manderscheid, he went to Deventer, where he received training in the school conducted by the Brothers of the Common Life. He studied law in Padua, and reached the doctorate, but exchanged law for theology because, to follow the statement of his opponent, George of Heimburg, he had failed in his first case. At Padua he had for one of his teachers Cesarini, afterwards cardinal and a prominent figure in the Council of Basel.

In 1432 he appeared in Basel as the representative of Ulrich of Manderscheid, archbishop-elect of Treves, to advocate Ulrich's

---

[1] Hardt, I. 104 sqq. The lament is put into the mouth of Christ.

cause against his rival, Rabanus of Helmstatt, bishop of Spires, whom the pope had appointed archbishop of the Treves diocese. Identifying himself closely with the conciliar body, Nicolas had a leading part in the proceedings with the Hussites and went with the majority in advocating the superiority of the council over the pope.   His work on Catholic Unity, — *De concordantia catholica*, — embodying his views on this question and dedicated to the council 1433, followed the earlier treatments of Langenstein, Nieheim and Gerson.   A general council, being inspired by the Holy Spirit, speaks truly and infallibly. The Church is the body of the faithful — *unitas fidelium* — and is represented in a general council.   The pope derives his authority from the consent of the Church, a council has power to dethrone him for heresy and other causes and may not be prorogued or adjourned without its own consent.   Peter received no more authority from Christ than the other Apostles. Whatever was said to Peter was likewise said to the others. All bishops are of equal authority and dignity, whether their jurisdiction be episcopal, archiepiscopal, patriarchal or papal, just as all presbyters are equal.[1]

In spite of these views, when the question arose as to the place of meeting the Greeks, Nicolas sided with the minority in favor of an Italian city, and was a member of the delegations appointed by the minority which visited Eugenius IV. at Bologna and went to Constantinople.   This was in 1437 and from that time forward he was a ready servant of Eugenius and his two successors.   Æneas Sylvius, afterwards Pius II., called him the Hercules of the Eugenians.   Æneas also pronounced him a man notable for learning in all branches of knowledge and on account of his godly life.[2]

---

[1] John of Turrecremata, d. 1468, whose tract on the seat of authority in the Church — *Summa de eccles. et ejus auctoritate* — 1450 has already been referred to, took the extreme ultramontane position.   The papal supremacy extends to all Christians throughout the world and includes the appointment of all bishops and right to depose them, the filling of all prelatures and benefices whatsoever and the canonizing of saints.   As the vicar of Christ, he has full jurisdiction in all the earth in temporal as well as spiritual matters because all jurisdiction of secular princes is derived from the pope *quod omnium principum sæcularium jurisdictionalis potestas a papa in eos derivata sit.*   Quoted from Gieseler, III. 5, pp. 219–227.   [2] *Hist. of Fred. III.*, 409, Germ. transl. II. 227.

Eugenius employed his new supporter as legate to arrange terms of peace with the German Church and princes, an end he saw accomplished in the concordat of Vienna, 1447. He was rewarded by promotion to the college of cardinals, and in 1452 was made bishop of Brixen in the Tyrol. Here he sought to introduce Church reforms, and he travelled as the papal legate in the same interest throughout the larger part of Germany.

By attempting to assert all the mediæval feoffal rights of his diocese, the bishop came into sharp conflict with Siegmund, duke of Austria. Even the interdict pronounced by two popes did not bring the duke to terms. He declared war against the bishop and, taking him prisoner, forced from him a promise to renounce the old rights which his predecessors for many years had not asserted. Once released, the bishop treated his oath as null, on the ground that it had been forced from him, and in this he was supported by Pius II. In 1460 he went to Rome and died at Todi, Umbria, a few years later.

Nicolas of Cusa knew Greek and Hebrew, and perhaps has claim to being the most universal scholar of Germany up to his day since Albertus Magnus. He was interested in astronomy, mathematics and botany, and, as D'Ailly had done before, he urged, at the Council of Basel, the correction of the calendar. The literary production on which he spent most labor was a discussion of the problems of theology — *De docta ignorantia*. Here he attacked the scholastic method and showed the influence upon his mind of mysticism, the atmosphere of which he breathed at Deventer. He laid stress upon the limitations of the human mind and the inability of the reason to find out God exhaustively. Faith, which he defined as a state of the soul given of God's grace, finds out truths the intellect cannot attain to.[1] His views had an influence upon Faber Stapulensis who edited the Cusan's works and was himself a French forerunner of Luther in the doctrine of justification by faith.

His last labors, in connection with the crusade against the

---

[1] *Fides est habitus bonus, per bonitatem data a deo, ut per fidem restaurentur illæ veritates objectivæ, quas intellectus attingere non potest*, quoted by Schwane, p. 100.

Turks pushed by Pius II., led him to studies in the Koran and the preparation of a tract, — *De cribatione Alcoran*, — in which he declared that false religions have the true religion as their basis.

It is as an ecclesiastical mediator, and as a reformer of clerical and conventual abuses that the cardinal has his chief place in history.   He preached in the vernacular.   In Bamberg he secured the prohibition of new brotherhoods, in Magdeburg the condemnation of the sale of indulgences for money.   In Salzburg and other places he introduced reforms in convents, and in connection with other members of his family he founded the hospital at Cues with beds for 33 patients.   He showed his interest in studies by providing for the training of 20 boys in Deventer.   He dwelt upon the rotation of the earth on its axis nearly a century before Copernicus.   He gave reasons for regarding the donation of Constantine spurious, and he also called in question the genuineness of other parts of the Isidorian Decretals.

On the other hand, the cardinal was a thorough churchman and obedient child of the Church.   As the agent of Nicolas V. he travelled in Germany announcing the indulgence of the Jubilee Year, and through him, it is said, indulgences to the value of 200,000 gulden were sold for the repair of St. Peter's.

This noble and many-sided man has been coupled together with Gutenberg by Janssen, — the able and learned apologist of the Catholic Church in the closing years of the Middle Ages, — the one as the champion of clerical and Church discipline, the other the inventor of the printing-press.   It is no disparagement of the impulses and work of Nicolas to say that he had not the mission of the herald of a new age in thought and religion as it was given to Gutenberg to promote culture and civilization by his invention.[1]   He did not possess the gift of

[1] Janssen, I. 2–6.   Here we come for the first time into contact with this author whose work has gone through 20 editions and made such a remarkable sensation.   Its conclusions and methods of treatment will be referred to at length farther on.   Here it is sufficient to call attention to the seductive plausibility of the work, whose purpose it is to show that an orderly reformation was going on in the Church in Germany when Luther appeared and by his revolutionary and immoral tendency brutally rived the unity of the

moral and doctrinal conviction and foresight which made the
monk of Wittenberg the exponent and the herald of a radical,
religious reformation whose permanent benefits are borne witness to by a large section of Christendom.

§ 26.   *Popular Preachers.*

During the century and a half closing with 1450, there were
local groups of preachers as well as isolated pulpit orators who
exercised a deep influence upon congregations.   The German
mystics with Eckart and John Tauler at their head preached
in Strassburg, Cologne and along the Rhine.   D'Ailly and
Gerson stood before select audiences, and give lustre to the
French pulpit.   Wyclif, at Oxford, and John Huss in Bohemia,
attracted great attention by their sermons and brought down
upon themselves ecclesiastical condemnation.   Huss was one
of a number of Bohemian preachers of eminence.   Wyclif
sought to promote preaching by sending out a special class of
men, his "pore preachers."

The popular preachers constitute another group, though the
period does not furnish one who can be brought into comparison with the field-preacher, Berthold of Regensburg, the Whitefield of his century, d. 1272.   Among the popular preachers
of the time the most famous were Bernardino and John of
Capistrano, both Italians, and members of the Observant wing
of the Franciscan order, and the Spanish Dominican, Vincent
Ferrer.   To a later age belong those bright pulpit luminaries,
Savonarola of Florence and Geiler of Strassburg.

Bernardino of Siena, 1380–1444, was praised by Pius II. as
a second Paul.   He made a marked impression upon Italian
audiences and was a favorite with pope Martin V.   His voice,

Church and checked the orderly reformation.   Such a conclusion is a result
of the manipulation of historic materials and the use of superlatives in describing men and influences which were like rills in the history of the onward
progress of religion and civilization.   The initial comparison between Gutenberg and Nicolas of Cusa begs the whole conclusion which Janssen had in
view in writing his work.   Of the permanent consequence of the work of the
inventor of the printing-press, no one has any doubt.   The author makes a
great jump when he asserts a like permanent influence for Nicolas in the
department of religion.

weak and indistinct at first, was said to have been made strong and clear through the grace of Mary, to whom he turned for help.   He was the first vicar-general of the Observants, who numbered only a few congregations in Italy when he joined them, but increased greatly under his administration.   In 1424 he was in Rome and, as Infessura the Roman diarist reports,[1] so influenced the people that they brought their games and articles of adornment to the Capitol and made a bonfire of them.   Wherever he went to preach, a banner was carried before him containing the monogram of Christ, IHS, with twelve rays centring in the letters.   He urged priests to put the monogram on the walls of churches and public buildings, and such a monogram may still be seen on the city building of Siena.[2]   The Augustinians and Dominicans and also Poggio attacked him for this practice.   In 1427, he appeared in Rome to answer the charges.   He was acquitted by Martin V., who gave him permission to preach everywhere, and instructed him to hold an eighty-days' mission in the papal city itself.   In 1419, he appeared in the Lombard cities, where the people were carried away by his exhortations to repentance, and often burned their trinkets and games in the public squares.   His body lies in Aquila, and he was canonized by Nicolas V., 1450.

John of Capistrano, 1386–1456, a lawyer, and at an early age intrusted with the administration of Perugia, joined the Observants in 1416 and became a pupil of Bernardino.   He made a reputation as an inquisitor in Northern Italy, converting and burning heretics and Jews.   No one could have excelled him in the ferocity of his zeal against heresy.   His first appointment as inquisitor was made in 1426, and his fourth appointment 23 years later in 1449.[3]

As a leader of his order, he defended Bernardino in 1427, and was made vicar-general in 1443.   He extended his preaching

[1] *Diario*, p. 25.   For Bernardino, see Thureau-Dangin, *St. Bernardin de Sienne.   Un prédicateur populaire*, Paris, 1896.   Several edd. of his sermons have appeared, including the ed. of Paris, 1650, 5 vols., by De la Haye.

[2] See Pastor, I. 231–233.

[3] Jacob, I. 30 sq.   For John's life, see E. Jacob, *John of Capistrano.   His Life and Writings*, 2 vols., Breslau, 1906, 1907.   Pastor, I. 463–468, 691–698; Lempp's art. in Herzog, III. 713 sqq.; Lea, *Inquisition*, II. 552 sqq.

to Vienna and far up into Germany, from Nürnberg to Dresden, Leipzig, Magdeburg and Breslau, making everywhere a tremendous sensation. He used the Latin or Italian, which had to be interpreted to his audiences. These are reported to have numbered as many as thirty thousand.[1] He carried relics of Bernardino with him, and through them and his own instrumentality many miracles were said to have been performed. His attendants made a note of the wonderful works on the spot.[2] The spell of his preaching was shown by the burning of pointed shoes, games of cards, dice and other articles of pleasure or vanity. Thousands of heretics are also reported to have yielded to his persuasions. He was called by Pius II. to preach against the Hussites, and later against the Turks. He was present at the siege of Belgrade, and contributed to the successful defence of the city and the defeat of Mohammed II. He was canonized in 1690.

The life of Vincent Ferrer, d. 1419, the greatest of Spanish preachers, fell during the period of the papal schism, and he was intimately identified with the controversies it called forth. His name is also associated with the gift of tongues and with the sect of the Flagellants. This devoted missionary, born in Valencia, joined the Dominican order, and pursued his studies in the universities of Barcelona and Lerida. He won the doctorate of theology by his tract on the Modern Schism in the Church— *De moderno ecclesiæ schismate*. Returning to Valencia, he gained fame as a preacher, and was appointed confessor to the queen of Aragon, Iolanthe, and counsellor to her husband, John I. In 1395, Benedict XIII. called him to be chief penitentiary in Avignon and master of the papal palace. Two years later he returned to Valencia with the title of papal legate. He at first defended the Avignon obedience with great warmth, but later, persuaded that Benedict was not sincere in his professions looking to the healing of the schism, withdrew from him his support and supported the Council of Constance.

---

[1] Yea, 60,000 at Erfurt. Jacob, I. 74.

[2] See Jacob, I. 50 sqq., etc. Æneas Sylvius said he had not seen any of John's miracles, but would not deny them. In Jena alone John healed thirty lame persons. Jacob, I. 69.

Ferrer's apostolic labors began in 1399.   He itinerated through Spain, Northern Italy and France, preaching two and three times a day on the great themes of repentance and the nearness of the judgment.   He has the reputation of being the most successful of missionaries among the Jews and Moham- medans.   Twenty-five thousand Jews and eight thousand Mo- hammedans are said to have yielded to his persuasions.   Able to speak only Spanish, his sermons, though they were not in- terpreted, are reported to have been understood in France and Italy.   The gift of tongues was ascribed to him by his contem- poraries as well as the gift of miracles.   Priests and singers accompanied him on his tours, and some of the hymns sung were Vincent's own compositions.   His audiences are given as high as 70,000, an incredible number, and he is said to have preached twenty thousand times.   He also preached to the Waldenses in their valleys and to the remnant of the Cathari, and is said to have made numerous converts.   He himself was not above the suspicion of heresy, and Eymerich made the charge against him of declaring that Judas Iscariot hanged himself because the people would not permit him to live, and that he found pardon with God.[1]   He was canonized by Calixtus III., 1455. The tale is that Ferrer noticed this member of the Borgia fam- ily as a young priest in Valencia, and made the prediction that one day he would reach the highest office open to mortal man.[2]

On his itineraries Ferrer was also accompanied by bands of Flagellants.   He himself joined in the flagellations, and the scourge with which he scourged himself daily, consisting of six thongs, is said still to be preserved in the Carthusian con- vent of Catalonia, *scala cœli*.   Both Gerson and D'Ailly at- tacked Ferrer for his adoption of the Flagellant delusion.   In a letter addressed to the Spanish preacher, written during the sessions of the Council of Constance, Gerson took the ground that both the Old Testament and the New Testament forbid

[1] Lea: *Inquisition*, II. 156, 176, 258, 264.

[2] Razanno, a fellow-Dominican, wrote the first biography of Ferrer, 1455. The Standard Life is by P. Fages, *Hist. de s. Vinc. Ferrer apôtre de l'Eu- rope*, 2 vols., 2d ed., Louvain, 1901.   The best ife written by a Protestant is by L. Heller, Berlin, 1830.   It is commended in Wetzer-Welte, XII. 978-983.

violence done to the body, quoting in proof Deut. 14 : 1,
"Ye shall not cut yourselves." He invited him to come to
Constance, but the invitation was not accepted.[1]

[1] For German preaching in the fourteenth century, other than that of the
mystics, see Linsenmeyer, *Gesch. der Predigt in Deutschland bis zum Aus-
gange d. 14ten Jahrh.*, Munich, 1886, pp. 391–470 ; Cruel : *Gesch. d. deutschen
Predigt im M. A.*, p. 414 sqq.; A. Franz : *Drei deutsche Minoritenprediger des
XIIten und XIVten Jahrh.*, Freiburg, 1907, pp. 160. The best-known
German preachers were the Augustinians Henry of Frimar, d. 1340, and
Jordan of Quedlinburg, d. about 1375.   See for the fifteenth century, ch. IX.

CHAPTER IV.

THE GERMAN MYSTICS.

§ 27. *Sources and Literature.*

GENERAL WORKS. — * FRANZ PFEIFFER : *Deutsche Mystiker*, 2 vols., Leipzig, 1857, 2d ed. of vol. I., Göttingen, 1906. — * R. LANGENBERG : *Quellen und Forschungen zur Gesch. der deutschen Mystik*, Bonn, 1902. — F. GALLE : *Geistliche Stimmen aus dem M.A., zur Erbauung*, Halle, 1841. — MRS. F. BEVAN : *Three Friends of God, Trees planted by the River*, London. — * W. R. INGE : *Light, Life and Love*, London, 1904. Selections from ECKART, TAULER, SUSO, RUYSBROECK, etc. — The works given under Eckart, etc., in the succeeding sections. — R. A. VAUGHAN : *Hours with the Mystics.* For a long time the chief English authority, offensive by the dialogue style it pursues, and now superseded. — * W. PREGER : *Gesch. der deutschen Mystik im Mittelalter*, 3 vols., Leipzig, 1874–1893. — G. ULLMANN : *Reformatoren vor der Reformation*, vol. II., Hamburg, 1841. — * INGE : *Christian Mysticism*, pp. 148 sqq., London, 1899. — ELEANOR C. GREGORY : *An Introd. to Christ. Mysticism*, London, 1901. — W. R. NICOLL : *The Garden of Nuts*, London, 1905. The first four chapp. give a general treatment of mysticism. — P. MEHLHORN : *D. Blüthezeit d. deutschen Mystik*, Freiburg, 1907, pp. 64. — * S. M. DEUTSCH : *Mystische Theol.* in Herzog, XIX. 631 sqq. — CRUEL : *Gesch. d. deutschen Predigt im M.A.*, pp. 370–414. — A. RITSCHL : *Gesch. d. Pietismus*, 3 vols., Bonn, 1880–1886. — HARNACK : *Dogmengesch.*, III. 376 sqq. — LOOFS : *Dogmengesch.*, 4th ed., Halle, 1906, pp. 621–633. — W. JAMES : *The Varieties of Relig. Experience*, chs. XVI., XVII.

For § 29. MEISTER ECKART. — *German Sermons* bound in a vol. with TAULER'S *Sermons*, Leipzig, 1498, Basel, 1521. — PFEIFFER : *Deutsche Mystiker*, etc., vol. II., gives 110 German sermons, 18 tracts, and 60 fragments. — * DENIFLE : *M. Eckehart's Lateinische Schriften und die Grundanschauung seiner Lehre*, in *Archiv für Lit. und Kirchengesch.*, II. 416–652. Gives excerpts from his Latin writings. — F. JOSTES : *M. Eckehart und seine Jünger, ungedruckte Texte zur Gesch. der deutschen Mystik*, Freiburg, 1895. — * H. BÜTTNER : *M. Eckehart's Schriften und Predigten aus dem Mittelhochdeutschen übersetzt*, Leipzig, 1903. Gives 18 German sermons and writings. — G. LANDAUER : *Eckhart's mystische Schriften in unsere Sprache übertragen*, Berlin, 1903. — H. MARTENSEN : *M. Eckart*, Hamburg, 1842. — A. LASSON : *M. E. der Mystiker*, Berlin, 1868. Also the section on Eckart by LASSON in Ueberweg's *Hist. of Phil.* — A. JUNDT : *Essai sur le mysticisme spéculatif d. M.E.*, Strassburg, 1871 ; also *Hist. du panthéisme populaire au moyen âge*, 1875. Gives 18 of Eckart's sermons. — PREGER, I. 309-

232

458. — H. Delacroix : *Le mysticisme spéculatif en Allemagne au 14ᵉ siècle*, Paris, 1900. — Deutsch's art. *Eckart* in Herzog, V. 142–154. — Denifle : *Die Heimath M. Eckehart's* in *Archiv für Lit. und K. Gesch. des M.A.*, V. 349–364, 1889. — Stöckl : *Gesch. der Phil.*, etc., III. 1095–1120. — Pfleiderer : *Religionsphilosophie*, Berlin, 2d ed., 1883, p. 3 sqq. — Inge. — L. Ziegler : *D. Phil. und relig. Bedeutung d. M. Eckehart* in *Preuss. Jahrbücher*, Heft 3, 1904. — See a trans. of Eckart's sermon on John 6 : 44, by D. S. Schaff, in *Homiletic Rev.*, 1902, pp. 428–431.

Note. — Eckart's German sermons and tracts, published in 1498 and 1521, were his only writings known to exist till Pfeiffer's ed., 1857. Denifle was the first to discover Eckart's Latin writings, in the convent of Erfurt, 1880, and at Cusa on the Mosel, 1886. These are fragments on Genesis, Exodus, Ecclesiastes and the Book of Wisdom. John Trithemius, in his *De scripp. eccles.*, 1492, gives a list of Eckart's writings which indicates a literary activity extending beyond the works we possess. The list catalogues four books on the *Sentences*, commentaries on Genesis, Exodus, the Canticles, the Book of Wisdom, St. John, on the Lord's Prayer, etc.

For § 30. John Tauler. — Tauler's *Works*, Leipzig, 1498 (84 sermons printed from MSS. in Strassburg) ; Augsburg, 1508 ; Basel, 1521 (42 new sermons) and 1522 ; Halberstadt, 1523 ; Cologne, 1543 (150 sermons, 23 being publ. for the first time, and found in St. Gertrude's convent, Cologne); Frankfurt, 1565 ; Hamburg, 1621 ; Frankfurt, 3 vols., 1826 (the edition used by Miss Winkworth) ; ed. by J. Hamberger, 1864, 2d ed., Prag, 1872. The best. Hamberger substituted modern German in the text and used a Strassburg MS. which was destroyed by fire at the siege of the city in 1870 ; ed. by Kuntze und Biesenthal containing the Introdd. of Arndt and Spener, Berlin, 1842. — *Engl. trans., Susanna Winkworth : *The History and Life of Rev. John Tauler with 25 Sermons*, with Prefaces by Canon Kingsley and Roswell D. Hitchcock, New York, 1858. — * *The Inner Way, 36 Sermons for Festivals, by John Tauler*, trans. with Introd. by A. W. Hutton, London, 1905. — C. Schmidt : *J. Tauler von Strassburg*, Hamburg, 1841, and *Nicolas von Basel, Bericht von der Bekehrung Taulers*, Strassburg, 1875. — Denifle : *D. Buch von geistlicher Armuth*, etc., Munich, 1877, and *Tauler's Bekehrung*, Münster, 1879. — A. Jundt : *Les amis de Dieu au 14ᵉ siècle*, Paris, 1879. — Preger, III. 1–244. — F. Cohrs : Art. *Tauler* in Herzog, XIX. 451–459.

Note. — Certain writings once ascribed to Tauler, and printed with his works, are now regarded as spurious. They are (1) *The Book of Spiritual Poverty*, ed. by Denifle, Munich, 1877, and previously under the title *Imitation of Christ's Life of Poverty*, by D. Sudermann, Frankfurt, 1621, etc. Denifle pointed out the discord between its teachings and the teachings of Tauler's sermons. (2) *Medulla animæ*, consisting of 77 chapters. Preger decides some of them to be genuine. (3) Certain hymns, including *Es kommt ein Schiff geladen*, which even Preger pronounces spurious, III. 86. They are publ. by Wackernagel.

For § 31. Henry Suso. — Ed. of his works, Augsburg, 1482, and 1512. — *M. Diepenbrock : *H. Suso's, genannt Amandus, Leben und Schriften*, Regensburg, 1829, 4th ed., 1884, with *Preface* by J. Görres. — H. Seuse

DENIFLE : *D. deutschen Schriften des seligen H. Seuse*, Munich, 1880. —*H.
SEUSE : *Deutsche Schriften*, ed. K. BIHLMEYER, Stuttgart, 1907. The first
complete edition, and based upon an examination of many MSS. — A Latin
trans. of Suso's works by L. SURIUS, Cologne, 1555. — French trans. by
THIROT : *Ouvrages mystiques du bienheureux H. Suso*, 2 vols., Paris, 1899.
Engl. extracts in *Light, Life and Love*, pp. 66–100. — PREGER : *D. Briefe
H. Suso's nach einer Handschrift d. XV. Jahrh.*, Leipzig, 1867.— C. SCHMIDT :
Der Mystiker, H. Suso in Stud. und Kritiken, 1843, pp. 835 sqq. — PREGER :
Deutsche Mystik, II. 309–419. — L. KÄRCHER : *H. Suso aus d. Predigerorden*,
in *Freiburger Diöcesenarchiv*, 1868, p. 187 sqq.— CRUEL : *Gesch. d. deutschen
Predigt*, 396 sqq. — Art. in WETZER-WELTE, H. SEUSE, V. 1721–1729.

For § 32. THE FRIENDS OF GOD. — The works of ECKART, TAULER, SUSO,
RUYSBRŒCK. — JUNDT : *Les Amis de Dieu*, Paris, 1879. — KESSEL : Art.
Gottesfreunde in WETZER-WELTE, V. 893–900. — The writings of RULMAN
MERSWIN : *Von den vier Jahren seines anfahenden Lebens*, ed. by SCHMIDT,
in Reuss and Cunitz, *Beiträge zu den theol. Wissenschaften*, V., Jena, 1854. —
His *Bannerbüchlein* given in Jundt's *Les Amis*. — *Das Buch von den neun
Felsen*, ed. from the original MS. by C. SCHMIDT, Leipzig, 1859, and in ab-
breviated form by PREGER, III. 337–407, and DIEPENBROCK : *Heinrich Suso*,
pp. 505–572. — P. STRAUCH : Art. *Rulman Merswin* in Herzog, XVII. 20–27.
— For the "Friend of God of the Oberland" and his writings. K. SCHMIDT :
Nicolas von Basel : Leben und ausgewählte Schriften, Vienna, 1866, and
Nic. von Basel, Bericht von der Bekehrung Taulers, Strassburg, 1875. — F.
LAUCHERT : *Des Gottesfreundes im Oberland Buch von den zwei Mannen*,
Bonn, 1896. — C. SCHMIDT : *Nic. von Basel und die Gottesfreunde*, Basel,
1856. — DENIFLE : *Der Gottesfreund im Oberland und Nic. von Basel. Eine
krit. Studie*, Munich, 1875. — JUNDT : *Rulman Merswin et l'Ami de Dieu de
l'Oberland*, Paris, 1890. — PREGER, III. 290–337. — K. RIEDER : *Der Gottesfreund vom Oberland. Eine Erfindung des Strassburger Johanniterbruders
Nicolaus von Löwen*, Innsbruck, 1905.

For § 33. JOHN OF RUYSBROECK. — *Vier Schriften*, ed. by ARNSWALDT,
with Introd. by ULLMANN, Hanover, 1848. — Superseded by J. B. DAVID
(prof. in Louvaine), 6 vols., Ghent, 1857–1868. Contains 12 writings. — Lat.
trans. by SURIUS, Cologne, 1549. — *F. A. LAMBERT : *Drei Schriften des
Mystikers J. van Ruysb., Die Zierde der geistl. Hochzeit, Vom glänzenden
Stein* and *Das Buch von der höchsten Wahrheit*, Leipzig. No date ; about
1906. Selections from Ruysbroeck in *Light, Life and Love*, pp. 100–196. —
*J. G. V. ENGELHARDT : *Rich. von St. Victor u. J. Ruysbroeck*, Erlangen,
1838. — ULLMANN : *Reformatoren*, etc., II. 35 sqq. — W. L. DE VREESE :
Bijdrage tot de kennis van het leven en de werken van J. van Ruusbroec, Ghent,
1896. — *M. MAETERLINCK : *Ruysbr. and the Mystics, with Selections from
Ruysb.*, London, 1894. A trans. by JANE T. STODDART of Maeterlinck's essay
prefixed to his *L'Ornement des noces spirituelles de Ruysb.*, trans. by him
from the Flemish, Brussels, 1891. — Art. *Ruysbroeck* in HERZOG, XVII. 267–
273, by VAN VEEN.

For § 34. GERRIT DE GROOTE AND THE BROTHERS OF THE COMMON LIFE.
— *Lives* of Groote, Florentius and their pupils, by THOMAS À KEMPIS : *Opera
omnia*, ed. by SOMMALIUS, Antwerp, 1601, 3 vols., Cologne, 1759, etc., and

in unpubl. MSS. — J. Busch, d. 1479: *Liber de viris illustribus,* a collection of 24 biographies of Windesheim brethren, Antwerp, 1621; also *Chronicon Windeshemense,* Antwerp, 1621, both ed. by Grube, Halle, 1886. — G. H. M. Delprat: *Verhandeling over de broederschap van Geert Groote en over den invloed der fraterhuizen,* Arnheim, etc., 1856. — J. G. R. Acquoy (prof. in Leyden): *Gerhardi Magni epistolæ XIV.,* Antwerp, 1857. — G. Bonet-Maury: *Gerhard de Groot d'après des documents inédites,* Paris, 1878. — * G. Kettlewell: *Thomas à Kempis and the Brothers of the Common Life,* 2 vols., New York, 1882. — * K. Grube: *Johannes Busch, Augustinerpropst in Hildesheim. Ein kathol. Reformator im 15ten Jahrh.,* Freiburg, 1881. Also *G. Groote und seine Stiftungen,* Cologne, 1883. — R. Langenberg: *Quellen und Forschungen,* etc., Bonn, 1902. — Boerner: *Die Annalen und Akten der Brüder des Gemeinsamen Lebens im Lichtenhofe zu Hildesheim, eine Grundlage der Gesch. d. deutschen Brüderhäuser und ein Beitrag zur Vorgesch. der Reformation,* Fürstenwalde, 1905. — The artt. by K. Hirsche in Herzog, 2d ed., II. 678–760, and L. Schulze, Herzog, 3d ed., III., 474–507, and P. A. Thijm in Wetzer-Welte, V. 1286–1289. — Ullmann: *Reformatoren,* II. 1–201. — Lea: *Inquisition,* II. 360 sqq. — Uhlhorn: *Christl. Liebesthätigkeit im M.A.,* Stuttgart, 1884, pp. 350–375.

Note. — A few of the short writings of Groote were preserved by Thomas à Kempis. To the sermons edited by Acquoy, Langenberg, pp. 3–33, has added Groote's tract on simony, which he found in the convent of Frenswegen, near Nordhorn. He has also found Groote's Latin writings. The tract on simony — *de simonia ad Beguttas* — is addressed to the Beguines in answer to the question propounded to him by some of their number as to whether it was simony to purchase a place in a Beguine convent. The author says that simony "prevails very much everywhere," and that it was not punished by the Church. He declares it to be simony to purchase a place which involves spiritual exercises, and he goes on to apply the principle to civil offices, pronouncing it simony when they are bought for money. The work is written in Low German, heavy in style, but interesting for the light it throws on practices current at that time.

For § 35. The Imitation of Christ. — Edd. of à Kempis' works, Utrecht, 1473 (15 writings, and omitting the *Imitation of Christ*); Nürnberg, 1494 (20 writings), ed. by J. Badius, 1520, 1521, 1523; Paris, 1549; Antwerp, 1574; Dillingen, 1576; ed. by H. Sommalius, 3 vols., Antwerp, 1599, 3d ed. 1615; ed. by M. J. Pohl, 8 vols. promised; thus far 5 vols., Freiburg im Br., 1903 sqq. Best and only complete ed. — Thomas à Kempis' hymns in Blume and Dreves: *Analecta hymnica,* XLVIII. pp. 475–514. — For biograph. and critical accounts. — Joh. Busch: *Chron. Windesemense.* — H. Rosweyde: *Chron. Mt. S. Agnetis,* Antwerp, 1615, and *cum Rosweydii vindiciis Kempensibus,* 1622. — J. B. Malou: *Recherches historiq. et critiq. sur le véritable auteur du livre de l'Imitat. de Jesus Chr.,* Tournay, 1848; 3d ed., Paris, 1858. — * K. Hirsche: *Prologomena zu einer neuen Ausgabe de imitat. Chr.* (with a copy of the Latin text of the MS. dated 1441), Berlin, 1873, 1883, 1894. — C. Wolfsgruber: *Giovanni Gersen sein Leben und sein Werk de Imitat. Chr.,* Augsburg, 1880. — * S. Kettlewell: *Th. à Kempis and the Brothers of the Common Life,* 2 vols., London, 1882. Also *Authorship of* *the de imitat. Chr.*, London, 1877, 2d ed., 1884. — F. R. Cruise : *Th. à Kempis, with Notes of a visit to the scenes in which his life was spent, with some account of the examination of his relics*, London, 1887. — L. A. Wheatley : *Story of the Imitat. of Chr.*, London, 1891. — Dom Vincent Scully : *Life of the Venerable Th. à Kempis*, London, 1901. — J. E. G. De Montmorency : *Th. à Kempis, His Age and Book*, London, 1906. — *C. Bigg in ·Wayside Sketches in Eccles. Hist.*, London, 1906, pp. 134-154. — D. B. Butler, *Thos. à Kempis, a Rel. Study*, London, 1908. — Art. *Thos. à Kempis* in London *Quarterly Review*, April, 1908, pp. 254-263.

First printed ed. of the Latin text of the *Imitat. of Christ*, Augsburg, 1472. Bound up with Jerome's *de viris illust.* and writings of Augustine and Th. Aquinas. — Of the many edd. in Engl. the first was by W. Atkynson, and Margaret, mother of Henry VII., London, 1502, reprinted London, 1828, new ed. by J. K. Ingram, London, 1893. — *The Imitat. of Chr., being the autograph MS. of Th. à Kempis de Imitat. Chr. reproduced in facsimile from the orig. in the royal libr. at Brussels*. With Introd. by C. Ruelens, London, 1879. — *The Imitat. of Chr. Now for the first time set forth in Rhythm and Sentences*. With Pref. by Canon Liddon, London, 1889. — *Facsimile Reproduction of the 1st ed. of 1471*, with Hist. Introd. by C. Knox-Little, London, 1894. — *The Imitat. of Chr.*, trans. by Canon W. Benham, with 12 photogravures after celebrated paintings, London, 1905. — An ed. issued 1881 contains a Pref. by Dean Farrar. — R. P. A. de Backer : *Essai bibliograph. sur le livre de imitat. Chr.*, Liège, 1864. — For further lit. on the *Imitat. of Chr.*, see the Note at the end of § 35.

§ 28. *The New Mysticism.*

In joy of inward peace, or sense
  Of sorrow over sin,
He is his own best evidence —
  His witness is within.
                — Whittier, *Our Master.*

At the time when the scholastic method was falling into disrepute and the scandals of the Avignon court and the papal schism were shaking men's faith in the foundations of the Church, a stream of pure pietism was watering the regions along the Rhine, from Basel to Cologne, and from Cologne to the North Sea.   North of the Alps, voices issuing from convents and from the ranks of the laity called attention to the value of the inner religious life and God's immediate communications to the soul.

To this religious movement has recently been given the name, the Dominican mysticism, on account of the large

number of its representatives who belonged to the Dominican order. The older name, German mysticism, which is to
be preferred, points to the locality where it manifested itself,
and to the language which the mystics for the most part
used in their writings. Like the Protestant Reformation,
the movement had its origin on German soil, but, unlike
the Reformation, it did not spread beyond Germany and the
Lowlands. Its chief centres were Strassburg and Cologne;
its leading representatives the speculative Meister Eckart, d.
1327, John Tauler, d. 1361, Henry Suso, d. 1366, John Ruysbroeck, d. 1381, Gerrit Groote, d. 1384, and Thomas à Kempis,
d. 1471. The earlier designation for these pietists was
Friends of God. The Brothers of the Common Life, the
companions and followers of Groote, were of the same type,
but developed abiding institutions of practical Christian
philanthropy. In localities the Beguines and Beghards also
breathed the same devotional and philanthropic spirit. The
little book called the *German Theology*, and the *Imitation of
Christ*, were among the finest fruits of the movement. Gerson
and Nicolas of Cusa also had a strong mystical vein, but
they are not to be classed with the German mystics. With
them mysticism was an incidental, not the distinguishing,
quality.

The mystics along the Rhine formed groups which, however,
were not bound together by any formal organization. Their
only bond was the fellowship of a common religious purpose.

Their religious thought was not always homogeneous in its
expression, but all agreed in the serious attempt to secure
purity of heart and life through union of the soul with God.
Mysticism is a phase of Christian life. It is a devotional
habit, in contradistinction to the outward and formal practice
of religious rules. It is a religious experience in contrast to
a mere intellectual assent to tenets. It is the conscious effort
of the soul to apprehend and possess God and Christ, and expresses itself in the words, "I live, and yet not I but Christ
liveth in me." It is essentially what is now called in some
quarters "personal religion." Perhaps the shortest definition of mysticism is the best. It is the love of God shed

abroad in the heart.[1]   The element of intuition has a large
place, and the avenues through which religious experience
is reached are self-detachment from the world, self-purga-
tion, prayer and contemplation.

Without disparaging the sacraments or disputing the authority of the Church, the German mystics sought a better way.
They laid stress upon the meaning of such passages as "he
that believeth in me shall never hunger and he that cometh
unto me shall never thirst," " he that loveth me shall be loved
of my Father " and " he that followeth me shall not walk in
darkness."   The word love figures most prominently in their
writings.   Among the distinctive terms in vogue among them
were *Abgeschiedenheit*, Eckart's word for self-detachment from
the world and that which is temporal, and *Kehr*, Tauler's
oft-used word for conversion.   They laid stress upon the
new birth, and found in Christ's incarnation a type of the
realization of the divine in the soul.

German mysticism had a distinct individuality of its own.
On occasion, its leaders quoted Augustine's *Confessions* and
other works, Dionysius the Areopagite, Bernard and Thomas
Aquinas, but they did not have the habit of referring back to
human authorities as had the Schoolmen, bulwarking every
theological statement by patristic quotations, or statements
taken from Aristotle.   The movement arose like a root out
of a dry ground at a time of great corruption and distraction
in the Church, and it arose where it might have been least expected to arise.   Its field was the territory along the Rhine
where the heretical sects had had representation.   It was a
fresh outburst of piety, an earnest seeking after God by other
paths than the religious externalism fostered by sacerdotal

---

[1] See Inge, *Engl. Mystics*, p. 37.   This author, in his *Christian Mysticism*,
p. 5, gives the definition that mysticism is "the attempt to realize in the
thought and feeling the immanence of the temporal in the eternal and of the
eternal in the temporal."   His statements in another place, *The Inner Way*,
pp. xx–xxii, are more simple and illuminating.   The mystical theology is
that knowledge of God and of divine things which is derived not from observation or from argument but from conscious experience.   The difficulty of
giving a precise definition of mysticism is seen in the definitions Inge cites,
Christian Mysticism, Appendix A.   Comp. Deutsch, p. 632 sq.

prescriptions and scholastic dialectics.   The mystics led the people back from the clangor and tinkling of ecclesiastical symbolisms to the refreshing springs of water which spring up into everlasting life.

Compared with the mysticism of the earlier Middle Ages and the French quietism of the seventeenth century, represented by Madame Guyon, Fénelon and their predecessor the Spaniard Miguel de Molinos, German mysticism likewise has its own distinctive features.   The religion of Bernard expressed itself in passionate and rapturous love for Jesus. Madame Guyon and Fénelon set up as the goal of religion a state of disinterested love, which was to be reached chiefly by prayer, an end which Bernard felt it scarcely possible to reach in this world.

The mystics along the Rhine agreed with all genuine mystics in striving after the direct union of the soul with God.   They sought, as did Eckart, the loss of our being in the ocean of the Godhead, or with Tauler the undisturbed peace of the soul, or with Ruysbroeck the impact of the divine nature upon our nature at its innermost point, kindling with divine love as fire kindles.   With this aspiration after the complete apprehension of God, they combined a practical tendency.   Their silent devotion and meditation were not final exercises.   They were moved by warm human sympathies, and looked with almost reverential regard upon the usual pursuits and toil of men.   They approached close to the idea that in the faithful devotion to daily tasks man may realize the highest type of religious experience.

By preaching, by writing and circulating devotional works, and especially by their own examples, they made known the secret and the peace of the inner life.   In the regions along the lower Rhine, the movement manifested itself also in the care of the sick, and notably in schools for the education of the young.   These schools proved to be preparatory for the German Reformation by training a body of men of wider outlook and larger sympathies than the mediæval convent was adapted to rear.

For the understanding of the spirit and meaning of German mysticism, no help is so close at hand as the comparison between it and mediæval scholasticism.   This religious movement was the antithesis of the theology of the Schoolmen; Eckart and Tauler of Thomas Aquinas, the German Theology of the endless argumentation of Duns Scotus, the *Imitation of Christ* of the cumbersome exhaustiveness of Albertus Magnus.   Roger Bacon had felt revulsion from the hairsplitting casuistries of the Schoolmen, and given expression to it before Eckart began his activity at Cologne.   Scholasticism had trodden a beaten and dusty highway.   The German mystics walked in secluded and shady pathways.   For a catalogue of dogmatic maxims they substituted the quiet expressions of filial devotion and assurance.   The speculative element is still prominent in Eckart, but it is not indulged for the sake of establishing doctrinal rectitude, but for the nurture of inward experience of God's operations in the soul. Godliness with these men was not a system of careful definitions, it was a state of spiritual communion; not an elaborate construction of speculative thought, but a simple faith and walk with God.   Not processes of logic but the insight of devotion was their guide.[1]   As Loofs has well said, German mysticism emphasized above all dogmas and all external works the necessity of the new birth.[2]

It also had its dangers.   Socrates had urged men not to rest hopes upon the Delphian oracle, but to listen to the voice in their own bosoms.   The mystics, in seeking to hear the voice of God speaking in their own hearts, ran peril of magnifying individualism to the disparagement of what was common to all and of mistaking states of the overwrought imagination for revelations from God.[3]

Although the German mystical writers have not been

---

[1] It is quite in keeping with this contrast that Pfleiderer, in his *Religionsphilosophie*, excludes the German mystics from a place in the history of German philosophy on the ground that their thinking was not distinctly systematic.   He, however, gives a brief statement to Eckart, but excludes Jacob Boehme.   [2] *Dogmengesch.*, p. 631.

[3] Nicoll, *Garden of Nuts*, p. 31, says, "We study the mystics to learn from them.   It need not be disguised that there are great difficulties in the way. The mystics are the most individual of writers," etc.

quoted in the acts of councils or by popes as have been the theologies of the Schoolmen, they represented, if we follow the testimonies of Luther and Melanchthon, an important stage in the religious development of the German people, and it is certainly most significant that the Reformation broke out on the soil where the mystics lived and wrought, and their piety took deep root.   They have a perennial life for souls who, seeking devotional companionship, continue to go back to the leaders of that remarkable pietistic movement.

The leading features of the mysticism of the fourteenth and fifteenth centuries may be summed up in the following propositions.

1. Its appeals were addressed to laymen as well as to clerics.

2. The mystics emphasized instruction and preaching, and, if we except Suso, withdrew the emphasis which had been laid upon the traditional ascetic regulations of the Church. They did not commend buffetings of the body.   The distance between Peter Damiani and Tauler is world-wide.

3. They used the New Testament more than they used the Old Testament, and the words of Christ took the place of the Canticles in their interpretations of the mind of God.   The *German Theology* quotes scarcely a single passage which is not found in the New Testament, and the *Imitation of Christ* opens with the quotation of words spoken by our Lord. Eckart and Tauler dwell upon passages of the New Testament, and Ruysbroeck evolves the fulness of his teaching from Matthew 25: 6, " Behold the Bridegroom cometh, go ye out to meet him."

4. In the place of the Church, with its sacraments and priesthood as a saving institution, is put Christ himself as the mediator between the soul and God, and he is offered as within the reach of all.

5. A pure life is taught to be a necessary accompaniment of the higher religious experience, and daily exemplification is demanded of that humility which the Gospel teaches.

6. Another notable feature was their use of the vernacular in sermon and treatise.   The mystics are among the very earliest masters of German and Dutch prose.   In the Intro-

duction to his second edition of the *German Theology*,
Luther emphasized this aspect of their activity when he said,
" I thank God that I have heard and find my God in the German tongue as neither I nor they [the adherents of the old
way] have found Him in the Latin and Hebrew tongues."
In this regard also the mystics of the fourteenth and fifteenth
centuries were precursors of the evangelical movement of the
sixteenth century.   Their practice was in plain conflict with
the judgment of that German bishop who declared that the
German language was too barbarous a tongue to be a proper
vehicle of religious truth.

The religious movement represented by German and Dutch
mysticism is an encouraging illustration that God's Spirit
may be working effectually in remote and unthought-of
places and at times when the fabric of the Church seems to be
hopelessly undermined with formalism, clerical corruption and
hierarchical arrogance and worldliness.   It was so at a later
day when, in the little and remote Moravian town of Herrnhut, God was preparing the weak things of the world, and
the things which were apparently foolish, to confound the
dead orthodoxy of German Protestantism and to lead the
whole Protestant Church into the way of preaching the Gospel in all the world.   No organized body survived the mystics
along the Rhine, but their example and writings continue to
encourage piety and simple faith toward God within the pale
of the Catholic and Protestant churches alike.

A classification of the German mystics on the basis of
speculative and practical tendencies has been attempted, but
it cannot be strictly carried out.[1]   In Eckart and Ruysbroeck,
the speculative element was in the ascendant; in Tauler, the

---

[1] See Preger, I. 8, and Ullmann, *Reformatoren*, II. 203.   Harnack goes far
when he denies all originality to the German mystics.   Of Eckart he says,
Dogmengesch., III. 378, " I give no extracts from his writings because I do
not wish to seem to countenance the error that the German mystics expressed
anything we cannot read in Origen, Plotinus, the Areopagite, Augustine,
Erigena, Bernard and Thomas Aquinas, or that they represented a stage of
religious progress."   The message they announced was certainly a fresh one
to their generation, even if all they said had been said before.   They spoke
from the living sources of their own spiritual experience.   They were not

devotional; in Suso, the emotional; in Groote and other men
of the Lowlands, the practical.

§ 29. *Meister Eckart.*

Meister Eckart, 1260–1327, the first in the line of the German mystics, was excelled in vigor of thought by no religious
thinker of his century, and was the earliest theologian who
wrote in German.[1] The philosophical bent of his mind won
for him from Hegel the title, " father of German philosophy."
In spite of the condemnation passed upon his writings by the
pope, his memory was regarded with veneration by the succeeding generation of mystics. His name, however, was almost forgotten in later times. Mosheim barely mentions it,
and the voluminous historian, Schroeckh, passes it by altogether. Baur, in his *History of the Middle Ages*, devotes to
Eckart and Tauler only three lines, and these under the head
of preaching, and makes no mention at all of German mysticism. His memory again came to honor in the last century,
and in the German church history of the later Middle Ages
he is now accorded a place of pre-eminence for his freshness of thought, his warm piety and his terse German style.[2]
With Albertus Magnus and Rupert of Deutz he stands out
as the earliest prominent representative in the history of
German theology.

imitators. Harnack, however, goes on to give credit to the German mystics
for fulfilling a mission when he says they are of invaluable worth for the
history of doctrine and the church history of Germany. In the same connection he denies the distinction between mysticism and scholastic theology.
" Mysticism," he asserts, " cannot exist in the Protestant Church, and the
Protestant who is a mystic and does not become a Roman Catholic is a
dilettante." This condemnation is based upon the untenable premise that
mysticism is essentially conventual, excluding sane intellectual criticism and
a practical out-of-doors Christianity.

[1] Eckart's name is written in almost every conceivable way in the documents. See Büttner, p. xxii, as Eckardus, Eccardus, Egghardus ; Deutsch
and Delacroix, Eckart ; Pfeiffer, Preger, Inge and Langenberg, Eckhart ;
Denifle and Büttner, Eckehart. His writings give us scarcely a single clew to
his fortunes. Quiétif-Echard was the first to lift the veil from portions of his
career. See Preger, I. 325.

[2] Deutsch, Herzog, V. 149, says that parts of Eckart's sermons might serve
as models of German style to-day.

During the century before Eckart, the German church
also had its mystics, and in the twelfth century the godly
women, Hildegard of Bingen and Elizabeth of Schönau, added
to the function of prophecy a mystical element.   In the
thirteenth century the Benedictine convent of Helfta, near
Eisleben, Luther's birthplace, was a centre of religious warmth.
Among its nuns were several by the names of Gertrude and
Mechthild, who excelled by their religious experiences, and
wrote on the devotional life.   Gertrude of Hackeborn, d.
1292, abbess of Helfta, and Gertrude the Great, d. 1302,
professed to have immediate communion with the Saviour
and to be the recipients of divine revelations.   When one of
the Mechthilds asked Christ where he was to be found, the
reply was, " You may seek me in the tabernacle and in Gertrude's heart."   From 1293 Gertrude the Great recorded her
revelations in a work called the Communications of Piety —
Insinuationes divinæ pietatis.   Mechthild of Magdeburg, d.
1280, and Mechthild of Hackeborn, d. 1310, likewise nuns of
Helfta, also had visions which they wrote out.   The former,
who for thirty years had been a Beguine, Deutsch calls " one
of the most remarkable personalities in the religious history
of the thirteenth century."   Mechthild of Hackeborn, a younger
sister of the abbess Gertrude, in her book on special grace, —
Liber specialis gratiæ, — sets forth salvation as the gift of
grace without the works of the law.   These women wrote in
German.[1]

David of Augsburg, d. 1271, the inquisitor who wrote on the
inquisition, — *De inquisitione hæreticorum,* — also wrote on the
devotional life.   These writings were intended for monks, and
two of them [2] are regarded as pearls of German prose.

---

[1] Flacius Illyricus includes the second Mechthild in his *Catal. veritatis.*
For the lives of these women and the editions of their works, see Preger, I.
71–132, and the artt. of Deutsch and Zöckler in Herzog.   Some of the elder
Mechthild's predictions and descriptions seem to have been used by Dante.
See Preger, p. 103 sq.   Mechthild v. Magdeburg : *D. fliessende Licht der
Gottheit,* Berlin, 1907.

[2] *Die sieben Vorregeln der Tugend* and *der Spiegel der Tugend,* both given
by Pfeiffer, together with other tracts, the genuineness of some of which is
doubted.   See Preger, I. 268–283, and Lempp in Herzog, IV. 503 sq.

In the last years of the thirteenth century, the Franciscan Lamprecht of Regensburg wrote a poem entitled "Daughter of Zion" (Cant. III. 11), which, in a mystical vein, depicts the soul, moved by the impulse of love, and after in vain seeking its satisfaction in worldly things, led by faith and hope to God. The Dominicans, Dietrich of Freiburg and John of Sterngassen, were also of the same tendency.[1]   The latter labored in Strassburg.

Eckart broke new paths in the realm of German religious thought.   He was born at Hochheim, near Gotha, and died probably in Cologne.[2]   In the last years of the thirteenth century he was prior of the Dominican convent of Erfurt, and provincial of the Dominicans in Thuringia, and in 1300 was sent to Paris to lecture, taking the master's degree, and later the doctorate.   After his sojourn in France he was made prior of his order in Saxony, a province at that time extending from the Lowlands to Livland.   In 1311 he was again sent to Paris as a teacher.   Subsequently he preached in Strassburg, was prior in Frankfurt, 1320, and thence went to Cologne.

Charges of heresy were preferred against him in 1325 by the archbishop of Cologne, Henry of Virneburg.   The same year the Dominicans, at their general chapter held in Venice, listened to complaints that certain popular preachers in Germany were leading the people astray, and sent a representative to make investigations.   Henry of Virneburg had shown himself zealous in the prosecution of heretics.   In 1322, Walter, a Beghard leader, was burnt, and in 1325 a number of Beghards died in the flames along the Rhine.   It is possible that Eckart was quoted by these sectaries, and in this way was exposed to the charge of heresy.

The archbishop's accusations, which had been sent to Rome, were set aside by Nicolas of Strassburg, Eckart's friend, who at the time held the position of inquisitor in Germany. In 1327, the archbishop again proceeded against the suspected preacher and also against Nicolas.   Both appealed from the

[1] Denifle, *Archiv*, etc., II. 240, 529.

[2] Till the investigations of Denifle, his place of birth was usually given as Strassburg.   See Denifle, p. 355.

archbishop's tribunal to the pope.   In February, Eckart made
a public statement in the Dominican church at Cologne,
declaring he had always eschewed heresy in doctrine and
declension in morals, and expressed his readiness to retract
errors, if such should be found in his writings.[1]

In a bull dated March 27, 1329, John XXII. announced
that of the 26 articles charged against Eckart, 15 were heretical and the remaining 11 had the savor of heresy.   Two other
articles, not cited in the indictment, were also pronounced
heretical.   The papal decision stated that Eckart had acknowledged the 17 condemned articles as heretical.   There
is no evidence of such acknowledgment in the offender's
extant writing.[2]

Among the articles condemned were the following.   As
soon as God was, He created the world. — The world is
eternal. — External acts are not in a proper sense good and
divine. — The fruit of external acts does not make us good,
but internal acts which the Father works in us. — God loves
the soul, not external acts.   The two added articles charged
Eckart with holding that there is something in the soul
which is uncreated and uncreatable, and that God is neither
good nor better nor best, so that God can no more be called
good than white can be called black.

Eckart merits study as a preacher and as a mystic theologian.

---

[1] *Ego magister Ekardus, doctor sac. theol., protestor ante omnia, quod
omnem errorem in fide et omnem deformitatem in moribus semper in quantum
mihi possibile fuit, sum detestatus,* etc.   Preger, I. 475–478.   Preger, I. 471
sqq., gives the Latin text of Eckart's statement of Jan. 24, 1327, before the
archiepiscopal court, his public statement of innocence in the Dominican
church and the document containing the court's refusal to allow his appeal
to Rome.

[2] The 26 articles, as Denifle has shown, were based upon Eckart's Latin
writings.   John's bull is given by Preger, I. 479–482, and by Denifle, *Archiv*,
II. 636–640.   Preger, I. 365 sqq., Delacroix, p. 238 and Deutsch, V. 145, insist
that Eckart made no specific recantation.   The pope's reference must have
been to the statement Eckart made in the Dominican church, which contained the words, " I will amend and revoke in general and in detail, as often
as may be found opportune, whatever is discovered to have a less wholesome
sense, *intellectum minus sane.*

As a Preacher. — His sermons were delivered in churches and at conferences within cloistral walls. His style is graphic and attractive, to fascination. The reader is carried on by the progress of thought. The element of surprise is prominent. Eckart's extant sermons are in German, and the preacher avoids dragging in Latin phrases to explain his meaning, though, if necessary, he invents new German terms. He quotes the Scriptures frequently, and the New Testament more often than the Old, the passages most dwelt upon being those which describe the new birth, the sonship of Christ and believers, and love. Eckart is a master in the use of illustrations, which he drew chiefly from the sphere of daily observation, — the world of nature, the domestic circle and the shop. Although he deals with some of the most abstruse truths, he betrays no ambition to make a show of speculative subtlety. On the contrary, he again and again expresses a desire to be understood by his hearers, who are frequently represented as in dialogue with himself and asking for explanations of difficult questions. Into the dialogue are thrown such expressions as " in order that you may understand, " and in using certain illustrations he on occasion announces that he uses them to make himself understood.[1]

The following is a resumé of a sermon on John 6 : 44, " No man can come unto me except the Father draw him." [2] In drawing the sinner that He may convert him, God draws with more power than he would use if He were to make a thousand heavens and earths. Sin is an offence against nature, for it breaks God's image in us. For the soul, sin is death, for God is the soul's true life. For the heart, it is restlessness, for a thing is at rest only when it is in its natural state. Sin is a disease and blindness, for it blinds men to the brief duration of time, the evils of fleshly lust and the long duration of the pains of hell. It is bluntness to all grace. Sin is the prison-house of hell. People say they intend to turn away from their sins. But how can one who is dead make himself alive again? And by one's own powers to turn from sin unto God is much less possible than it would be for the

[1] Büttner, p. 14 ; Pfeiffer, p. 192, etc.   [2] Pfeiffer, 216.

dead to make themselves alive.   God himself must draw.
Grace flows from the Father's heart continually, as when He
says, " I have loved thee with an everlasting love."

There are three things in nature which draw, and these
three Christ had on the cross.   The first was his fellow-like-
ness to us.   As the bird draws to itself the bird of the same
nature, so Christ drew the heavenly Father to himself, so that
the Father forgot His wrath in contemplating the sufferings
of the cross.   Again Christ draws by his self-emptiness.   As
the empty tube draws water into itself, so the Son, by empty-
ing himself and letting his blood flow, drew to himself all the
grace from the Father's heart.   The third thing by which he
draws is the glowing heat of his love, even as the sun with its
heat draws up the mists from the earth.

The historian of the German mediæval pulpit, Cruel, has
said,[1] "Eckart's sermons hold the reader by the novelty and
greatness of their contents, by their vigor of expression and
by the genial frankness of the preacher himself, who is felt
to be putting his whole soul into his effort and to be giving
the most precious things he is able to give."   He had his
faults, but in spite of them "he is the boldest and most
profound thinker the German pulpit has ever had, — a
preacher of such original stamp of mind that the Church in
Germany has not another like him to offer in all the centuries."

ECKART AS A THEOLOGICAL THINKER. — Eckart was still
bound in part by the scholastic method.   His temper, however, differed widely from the temper of the Schoolmen.
Anselm, Hugo of St. Victor, Thomas Aquinas and Bonaventura, who united the mystical with the scholastic element,
were predominantly Schoolmen, seeking to exhaust every
supposable speculative problem.   No purpose of this kind
appears in Eckart's writings.   He is dominated by a desire
not so much to reach the intellect as to reach the soul and to
lead it into immediate fellowship with God.   With him the
weapons of metaphysical dexterity are not on show; and in
his writings, so far as they are known, he betrays no inclination to bring into the area of his treatment those remoter

[1] p. 384.

topics of speculation, from the constitution of the angelic
world to the motives and actions which rule and prevail in
the regions of hell.   God and the soul's relation to Him are
the engrossing subjects.[1]

The authorities upon whom Eckart relied most, if we are
to judge by his quotations, were Dionysius the Areopagite,
and St. Bernard, though he also quotes from Augustine,
Jerome and Gregory the Great, from Plato, Avicenna and
Averrhoes.   His discussions are often introduced by such expressions as "the masters say," or "some masters say."   As
a mystical thinker he has much in common with the mystics
who preceded him, Neo-Platonic and Christian, but he was
no servile reproducer of the past.   Freshness characterizes
his fundamental principles and his statement of them.   In
the place of love for Jesus, the precise definitions of the stages
of contemplation emphasized by the school of St. Victor and
the hierarchies and ladders and graduated stairways of Dionysius, he magnifies the new birth in the soul, and sonship.[2]

As for God, He is absolute being, *Deus est esse.*   The
Godhood is distinct from the persons of the Godhead, — a
conception which recalls Gilbert of Poictiers, or even the qua-
ternity which Peter the Lombard was accused of setting up.

[1] Denifle lays down the proposition that Eckart is above all a Schoolman, and that whatever there is of good in him is drawn from Thomas
Aquinas.   These conclusions are based upon Eckart's Latin writings.   Deutsch,
V. 15, says that the form of Eckart's thought in the Latin writings is scholastic,
but the heart is mystical.   Delacroix, p. 277 sqq., denies that Eckart was a
scholastic and followed Thomas.   Wetzer-Welte, IV. 11, deplores as Eckart's
defect that he departed from "the solid theology of Scholasticism" and took
up Neo-Platonic vagaries.   If Eckart had been a servile follower of Thomas, it
is hard to understand how he should have laid himself open in 28 propositions
to condemnation for heresy.

[2] Harnack and, in a modified way, Delacroix and Loofs, regard Eckart's
theology as a reproduction of Erigena, Dionysius and Plotinus.   Delacroix,
p. 240, says, *sur tous les points essentiels, il est d'accord avec Plotin et Pro-
clus.*   But, in another place, p. 260, he says Eckart took from Neo-Platonism
certain leading conceptions and "elaborated, transformed and transmuted
them."   Loofs, p. 630, somewhat ambiguously says, *Die ganze Eckehartsche
Mystik ist verständlich als eine Erfassung der thomistischen und augus-
tinischen Tradition unter dem Gesichtswinkel des Areopagiten.*

The Trinity is the method by which this Godhood reveals itself by a process which is eternal. Godhood is simple essence having in itself the potentiality of all things.[1] God has form, and yet is without form; is being, and yet is without being. Great teachers say that God is above being. This is not correct, for God may as little be called a being, *ein Wesen*, as the sun may be called black or pale.[2]

All created things were created out of nothing, and yet they were eternally in God. The master who produces pieces of art, first had all his art in himself. The arts are master within the master. Likewise the first Principle, which Eckart calls *Erstigkeit*, embodied in itself all images, that is, God in God. Creation is an eternal act. As soon as God was, He created the world. Without creatures, God would not be God. God is in all things and all things are God — *Nu sint all Ding gleich in Gott und sint Got selber*.[3] Thomas Aquinas made a clear distinction between the being of God and the being of created things. Eckart emphasized their unity. What he meant was that the images or universals exist in God eternally, as he distinctly affirmed when he said, " In the Father are the images of all creatures."[4]

As for the soul, it can be as little comprehended in a definition as God Himself.[5] The soul's kernel, or its ultimate essence, is the little spark, *Fünkelein*, a light which never goes out, which is uncreated and uncreatable.[6] Notwithstanding these statements, the German theologian affirms that God created the soul and poured into it, in the first instance, all His own purity. Through the spark the soul is brought into union with God, and becomes more truly one with Him than

---

[1] Pfeiffer, pp. 254, 540.

[2] Pfeiffer, p. 268. The following passage is an instance of Eckart's abstruseness in definition. He says God's *einveltigin Natur ist von Formen formelos, von Werdenen werdelos, von Wesenen weselos, und ist von Sachen sachelos.* Pfeiffer, p. 497.   [3] Pfeiffer, pp. 282, 311, 579.

[4] *In dem Vater sind Bilde aller Creaturen*, Pfeiffer, pp. 269, 285, etc.

[5] *Die Seele in ihrem Grunde ist so unsprechlich als Gott unsprechlich ist.* Pfeiffer, p. 89.

[6] pp. 39, 113, 193, 286, etc. Pfleiderer, p. 6, calls this the soul's spirit, — *der Geist der Seele*, — and Deutsch, p. 152, *der innerst Seelengrund.*

food does with the body. The soul cannot rest till it returns
to God, and to do so it must first die to itself, that is, completely submit itself to God.[1] Eckart's aim in all his sermons,
as he asserts, was to reach this spark.

It is one of Eckart's merits that he lays so much stress upon
the dignity of the soul. Several of his tracts bear this title.[2]
This dignity follows from God's love and regenerative operation.

Passing to the incarnation, it is everywhere the practical
purpose which controls Eckart's treatment, and not the metaphysical. The second person of the Trinity took on human
nature, that man might become partaker of the divine nature.
In language such as Gregory of Nyssa used, he said, God became man that we might become God. *Gott ist Mensch worden
dass wir Gott wurden.* As God was hidden within the human
nature so that we saw there only man, so the soul is to be
hidden within the divine nature, that we should see nothing
but God.[3] As certainly as God begets the Son from His own
nature, so certainly does He beget Him in the soul. God is
in all things, but He is in the soul alone by birth, and nowhere else is He so truly as in the soul. No one can know
God but the only begotten Son. Therefore, to know God,
man must through the eternal generation become Son. It
is as true that man becomes God as that God was made man.[4]

The generation of the eternal Son in the soul brings joy
which no man can take away. A prince who should lose his
kingdom and all worldly goods would still have fulness of
joy, for his birth outweighs everything else.[5] God is in the
soul, and yet He is not the soul. The eye is not the piece
of wood upon which it looks, for when the eye is closed, it is
the same eye it was before. But if, in the act of looking, the
eye and the wood should become one, then we might say the
eye is the wood and the wood is the eye. If the wood were
a spiritual substance like the eyesight, then, in reality, one

---

[1] pp. 113, 152, 286, 497, 530.

[2] *Die Edelkeit der Seele, Von der Würdigkeit der Seele, Von dem Adel
der Seele.* Pfeiffer, pp. 382–448.

[3] p. 540.   [4] pp. 158, 207, 285, 345.   [5] pp. 44, 478–483.

might say eye and wood are one substance.[1]   The fundament
of God's being is the fundament of my being, and the fundament of my being is the fundament of God's being.   Thus I
live of myself even as God lives of Himself.[2]   This begetment
of the Son of God in the soul is the source of all true life and
good works.

One of the terms which Eckart uses most frequently, to de-
note God's influence upon the soul, is *durchbrechen*, to break
through, and his favorite word for the activity of the soul, as
it rises into union with God, is *Abgeschiedenheit*, the soul's
complete detachment of itself from all that is temporal and
seen.   Keep aloof, *abgeschieden*, he says, from men, from yourself, from all that cumbers.   Bear God alone in your hearts,
and then practise fasting, vigils and prayer, and you will come
unto perfection.   This *Abgeschiedenheit*, total self-detachment from created things,[3] he says in a sermon on the subject, is "the one thing needful."   After reading many writings by pagan masters and Christian teachers, Eckart came to
consider it the highest of all virtues, — higher than humility,
higher even than love, which Paul praises as the highest;
for, while love endures all things, this quality is receptive-
ness towards God.   In the person possessing this quality, the
worldly has nothing to correspond to itself.   This is what
Paul had reference to when he said, "I live and yet not I,
for Christ liveth in me."   God is Himself perfect *Abgeschiedenheit*.

In another place, Eckart says that he who has God in
his soul finds God in all things, and God appears to him out
of all things.   As the thirsty love water, so that nothing
else tastes good to them, even so it is with the devoted
soul.   In God and God alone is it at rest.   God seeks rest,
and He finds it nowhere but in such a heart.   To reach this

---

[1] Pfeiffer, p. 139.

[2] *Hier ist Gottes Grund mein Grund und mein Grund Gottes Grund.   Hier
lebe ich aus meinem Eigenen, wie Gott aus seinem Eigenen lebt.*   Büttner,
p. 100.

[3] *Lautere, alles Erschaffenen ledige Abgeschiedenheit.*   For the sermon, see
Büttner, p. 9 sqq.

condition of *Abgeschiedenheit*, it is necessary for the soul first to meditate and form an image of God, and then to allow itself to be transformed by God.[1]

What, then, some one might say, is the advantage of prayer and good works?   In eternity, God saw every prayer and every good work, and knew which prayer He could hear. Prayers were answered in eternity.   God is unchangeable and cannot be moved by a prayer.   It is we who change and are moved.   The sun shines, and gives pain or pleasure to the eye, according as it is weak or sound.   The sun does not change.   God rules differently in different men.   Different kinds of dough are put into the oven; the heat affects them differently, and one is taken out a loaf of fine bread, and another a loaf of common bread.

Eckart is emphatic when he insists upon the moral obligation resting on God to operate in the soul that is ready to receive Him.   God *must* pour Himself into such a man's being, as the sun pours itself into the air when it is clear and pure.   God would be guilty of a great wrong — *Gebrechen* — if He did not confer a great good upon him whom He finds empty and ready to receive Him.   Even so Christ said of Zaccheus, that He must enter into his house.   God first works this state in the soul, and He is obliged to reward it with the gift of Himself.   " When I am blessed, *selig*, then all things are in me and in God, and where I am, there is God, and where God is, there I am."[2]

Nowhere does Eckart come to a distinct definition of justification by faith, although he frequently speaks of faith as a heavenly gift.   On the other hand, he gives no sign of laying stress on the penitential system.   Everywhere there are symptoms in his writings that his piety breathed a different atmosphere from the pure mediæval type.   Holy living is with him the product of holy being.   One must first be righteous before he can do righteous acts.   Works do not sanctify.   The righteous soul sanctifies the works.   So long as one does good works for the sake of the kingdom of heaven or for the sake of God or for the sake of salvation or for any

[1] Pfeiffer, II. 484.   [2] Pfeiffer, pp. 27, 32, 479 sq., 547 sq.

external cause, he is on the wrong path.   Fastings, vigils,
asceticisms, do not merit salvation.[1]   There are places in
the mystic's writings where we seem to hear Luther himself
speaking.

The stress which Eckart lays upon piety, as a matter of
the heart and the denial to good works of meritorious virtue,
gave plausible ground for the papal condemnation, that
Eckart set aside the Church's doctrine of penance, affirming
that it is not outward acts that make good, but the disposition
of the soul which God abidingly works in us.   John XXII.
rightly discerned the drift of the mystic's teaching.

In his treatment of Mary and Martha, Eckart seems to make
a radical departure from the mediæval doctrine of the superior
value of pure contemplation.   From the time of Augustine,
Rachel and Mary of Bethany had been regarded as the representatives of the contemplative and higher life.   In his sermon
on Mary, the German mystic affirmed that Mary was still at
school.   Martha had learned and was engaged in good works,
serving the Lord.   Mary was only learning.   She was striving to be as holy as her sister.   Better to feed the hungry and
do other works of mercy, he says, than to have the vision of
Paul and to sit still.   After Christ's ascension, Mary learned
to serve as fully as did Martha, for then the Holy Spirit was
poured out.   One who lives a truly contemplative life will
show it in active works.   A life of mere contemplation is a
selfish life.   The modern spirit was stirring in him.   He saw
another ideal for life than mediæval withdrawal from the
world.   The breath of evangelical freedom and joy is felt in
his writings.[2]

Eckart's speculative mind carried him to the verge of pantheism, and it is not surprising that his hyperbolical expressions subjected him to the papal condemnation.   But his
pantheism was Christian pantheism, the complete union of

---

[1] Pfeiffer, II. 546, 564, 633, *Niht endienent unserin were dar zuo dass uns
Got iht gebe oder tuo.*

[2] *Es geht ein Geist evangelischer Freiheit durch Eckart's Sittenlehre
welcher zugleich ein Geist der Freudigkeit ist,* Preger, I. 452.   See the sermon
on Mary, Pfeiffer, pp. 47-53.   Also pp. 18-21, 607.

the soul with God.   It was not absorption in the divine being
involving the loss of individuality, but the reception of Godhood, the original principle of the Deity.   What language
could better express the idea that God is everything, and
everything God, than these words, words adopted by Hegel
as a sort of motto: " The eye with which I see God is the
same eye with which God sees me.   My eye and God's eye
are the same, and there is but one sight, one apprehension,
one love." [1]   And yet such language, endangering, as it might
seem, the distinct personality of the soul, was far better than
the imperative insistence laid by accredited Church teachers
on outward rituals and conformity to sacramental rites.

Harnack and others have made the objection that the Cologne divine does not dwell upon the forgiveness of sins.   This
omission may be overlooked, when we remember the prominence given in his teaching to regeneration and man's divine
sonship.   His most notable departure from scholasticism
consists in this, that he did not dwell upon the sacraments
and the authority of the Church.   He addressed himself to
Christian individuals, and showed concern for their moral and
spiritual well-being.   Abstruse as some of his thinking is,
there can never be the inkling of a thought that he was setting forth abstractions of the school and contemplating matters chiefly with a scientific eye.   He makes the impression
of being moved by strict honesty of purpose to reach the
hearts of men. [2]   His words glow with the *Minne*, or love, of
which he preached so often.   In one feature, however, he
differed widely from modern writers and preachers.   He did
not dwell upon the historical Christ.   With him Christ in us is
the God in us, and that is the absorbing topic.   With all his
high thinking he felt the limitations of human statement and,
counselling modesty in setting forth definitions of God, he

[1] *Das Auge das da inne ich Gott sehe, das ist selbe Auge da inne mich Gott
sieht.   Mein Auge und Gottes Auge, das ist ein Auge, und ein Erkennen und
ein Gesicht und ein Minnen*, Pfeiffer, p. 312.
[2] This is well expressed by Lasson in Ueberweg, I. 471. Inge says, p. 150,
Eckart's transparent honesty and his great power of thought, combined with
deep devoutness and purity of soul, make him one of the most interesting figures in the history of Christian philosophy.

said, " If we would reach the depth of God's nature, we must
humble ourselves.   He who would know God must first know
himself." [1]

Not a popular leader, not professedly a reformer, this early
German theologian had a mission in preparing the way for
the Reformation.   The form and contents of his teaching had
a direct tendency to encourage men to turn away from the
authority of the priesthood and ritual legalism to the realm
of inner experience for the assurance of acceptance with God.
Pfleiderer has gone so far as to say that Eckart's " is the spirit
of the Reformation, the spirit of Luther, the motion of whose
wings we already feel, distinctly enough, in the thoughts of
his older German fellow-citizen." [2]   Although he declared his
readiness to confess any heretical ideas that might have crept
into his sermons and writings, the judges at Rome were right
in principle.   Eckart's spirit was heretical, provoking revolt
against the authority of the mediæval Church and a restate-
ment of some of the forgotten verities of the New Testament.

§ 30.   *John Tauler of Strassburg.*

To do Thy will is more than praise,
    As words are less than deeds ;
And simple trust can find Thy ways
    We miss with chart of creeds.
                    — WHITTIER, *Our Master.*

Among the admirers of Eckart, the most distinguished were
John Tauler and Heinrich Suso.   With them the speculative
element largely disappears and the experimental and practical
elements predominate.   They emphasized religion as a matter
of experience and the rule of conduct.   Without denying any
of the teachings or sacraments of the Church, they made prominent immediate union with Christ, and dwelt upon the Christian
graces, especially patience, gentleness and humility.   Tauler
was a man of sober mind, Suso poetical and imaginative.

---

[1] Pfeiffer, II. 155, 390.
[2] p. 7.   Preger concludes his treatment of Eckart by saying, I. 458, that it
was he who really laid the foundations of Christian philosophy.   *Er erst hat
die christliche Philosophie eigentlich begründet.*

John Tauler, called *doctor illuminatus*, was born in Strassburg about 1300, and died there, 1361. Referring to his father's
circumstances, he once said, "If, as my father's son, I had once
known what I know now, I would have lived from my paternal
inheritance instead of resorting to alms."[1] Probably as early
as 1315, he entered the Dominican order. Sometime before
1330, he went to Cologne to take the usual three-years' course
of study. That he proceeded from there to Paris for further
study is a statement not borne out by the evidence. He,
however, made a visit in the French capital at one period of
his career. Nor is there sufficient proof that he received the
title doctor or master, although he is usually called Dr. John
Tauler.

He was in his native city again when it lay under the interdict fulminated against it in 1329, during the struggle between John XXII. and Lewis the Bavarian. The Dominicans
offered defiance, continuing to say masses till 1339, when they
were expelled for three years by the city council. We next
find Tauler at Basel, where he came into close contact with
the Friends of God, and their leader, Henry of Nördlingen.
After laboring as priest in Bavaria, Henry went to the Swiss
city, where he was much sought after as a preacher by the
clergy and laymen, men and women. In 1357, Tauler was
in Cologne, but Strassburg was the chief seat of his activity.
Among his friends were Christina Ebner, abbess of a convent
near Nürnberg, and Margaret Ebner, a nun of the Bavarian
convent of Medingen, women who were mystics and recipients of visions.[2] Tauler died in the guest-chamber of a nunnery in Strassburg, of which his sister was an inmate.

Tauler's reputation in his own day rested upon his power
as a preacher, and it is probable that his sermons have been

---

[1] Preger, III. 131. The oldest Strassburg MS. entitles Tauler *erluhtete beg-
nodete Lerer*. See Schmidt, p. 159. Preger, III. 93, gives the names of a
number of persons by the name of Taweler, or Tawler, living in Strassburg.

[2] Christina wrote a book entitled *Von der Gnaden Ueberlast*, giving an account of the tense life led by the sisters in her convent. She declared that the
Holy Spirit played on Tauler's heart as upon a lute, and that it had been revealed to her in a vision that his fervid tongue would set the earth on fire.
See Strauch's art. in Herzog, V. 129 sq. Also Preger, II. 247-251, 277 sqq.

more widely read in the Protestant Church than those of other mediæval preachers.   The reason for this popularity is the belief that the preacher was controlled by an evangelical spirit which brought him into close affinity with the views of the Reformers.   His sermons, which were delivered in German, are plain statements of truth easily understood, and containing little that is allegorical or fanciful.   They attempt no display of learning or speculative ingenuity.   When Tauler quotes from Augustine, Gregory the Great, Dionysius, Anselm or Thomas Aquinas, as he sometimes does, though not as frequently as Eckart, he does it in an incidental way.   His power lay in his familiarity with the Scriptures, his knowledge of the human heart, his simple style and his own evident sincerity.[1]   He was a practical every-day preacher, intent on reaching men in their various avocations and trials.

If we are to follow the *History of Tauler's Life and Conscience*, which appeared in the first published edition of his works, 1498, Tauler underwent a remarkable spiritual change when he was fifty.[2]   Under the influence of Nicolas of Basel, a Friend of God from the Oberland, he was then led into a higher stage of Christian experience.   Already had he achieved the reputation of an effective preacher when Nicolas, after hearing him several times, told him that he was bound in the letter and that, though he preached sound doctrine, he did not feel the power of it himself.   He called Tauler a Pharisee.   The rebuked man was indignant, but his monitor replied that he lacked humility and that, instead of seeking God's honor, he was seeking his own.   Feeling the justice of the criticism, Tauler confessed he had been told his sins and faults for the first time.   At Nicolas' advice he desisted from preaching for two years, and led a retired life.   At the end of that time Nicolas visited him again, and bade him resume his sermons. Tauler's first attempt, made in a public place and before a

---

[1] Specklin, the Strassburg chronicler, says Tauler spoke "in clear tones, with real fervor.   His aim was to bring men to feel the nothingness of the world.   He condemned clerics as well as laymen."

[2] A translation of the book is given by Miss Winkworth, pp. 1–73.   It calls Tauler's monitor *der grosse Gottesfreund im Oberlande*.   See § 32.

large concourse of people, was a failure.   The second sermon
he preached in a nunnery from the text, Matt. 25: 6, "Behold
the bridegroom cometh, go ye out to meet him," and so powerful was the impression that 50 persons fell to the ground like
dead men.   During the period of his seclusion, Tauler had
surrendered himself entirely to God, and after it he continued
to preach with an unction and efficiency before unknown in
his experience.

Some of Tauler's expressions might give the impression
that he was addicted to quietistic views, as when he speaks of
being "drowned in the Fatherhood of God," of "melting in
the fire of His love," of being "intoxicated with God."   But
these tropical expressions, used occasionally, are offset by the
sober statements in which he portrays the soul's union with
God.   To urge upon men to surrender themselves wholly to
God and to give a practical exemplification of their union with
Him in daily conduct was his mission.

He emphasized the agency of the Holy Spirit, who enlightens
and sanctifies, who rebukes sin and operates in the heart to
bring it to self-surrender.[1]   The change effected by the Spirit,
which he called *Kehr* — conversion — he dwelt upon continually.   The word, which frequently occurs in his sermons,
was almost a new word in mediæval sermonic vocabulary.
Tauler also insisted upon the Eckartian *Abgeschiedenheit*, detachment from the world, and says that a soul, to become
holy, must become "barren and empty of all created things,"
and rid of all that "pertains to the creature."   When the
soul is full of the creature, God must of necessity remain apart
from it, and such a soul is like a barrel that has been filled
with refuse or decaying matter.   It cannot thereafter be
used for good, generous wine or any other pure drink.[2]

As for good works, if done apart from Christ, they are of
no avail.   Tauler often quoted the words of Isaiah 64: 6.
"All our righteousnesses are as a polluted garment."   By

---

[1] One of the sermons, bringing out the influence of the Spirit, based on
John 16: 7–11, is quoted at length by Archdeacon Hare in his *Mission of the
Comforter*.   See also Miss Winkworth, pp. 350–358.

[2] *Inner Way*, pp. 81, 113, 128, 130.

his own power, man cannot come unto God.   Those who
have never felt anxiety on account of their sins are in the
most dangerous condition of all.[1]

The sacraments suffer no depreciation at Tauler's hands,
though they are given a subordinate place.   They are all
of no avail without the change of the inward man.   Good
people linger at the outward symbols, and fail to get at
the inward truth symbolized.   Yea, by being unduly concerned about their movements in the presence of the Lord's
body, they miss receiving him spiritually.   Men glide, he
says, through fasting, prayer, vigils and other exercises, and
take so much delight in them that God has a very small
part in their hearts, or no part in them at all.[2]

In insisting upon the exercise of a simple faith, it seems
almost impossible to avoid the conclusion that Tauler took
an attitude of intentional opposition to the prescient and self-
confident methods of scholasticism.   It is better to possess
a simple faith — *einfaltiger Glaube* — than to vainly pry into
the secrets of God, asking questions about the efflux and re-
flux of the Aught and Nought, or about the essence of the
soul's spark.   The Arians and Sabellians had a marvellous
intellectual understanding of the Trinity, and Solomon and
Origen interested the Church in a marvellous way, but what
became of them we know not.   The chief thing is to yield
oneself to God's will and to follow righteousness with
sincerity of purpose.   " Wisdom is not studied in Paris, but
in the sufferings of the Lord," Tauler said.   The great
masters of Paris read large books, and that is well.   But
the people who dwell in the inner kingdom of the soul
read the true Book of Life.   A pure heart is the throne of
the Supreme Judge, a lamp bearing the eternal light, a
treasury of divine riches, a storehouse of heavenly sweetness,
the sanctuary of the only begotten Son.[3]

A distinctly democratic element showed itself in Tauler's
piety and preaching which is very attractive.   He put honor

---

[1] Miss Winkworth, pp. 353, 475, etc.

[2] *Inner Way*, p. 200.   Miss Winkworth, pp. 345, 360 sqq.

[3] Preger, III. 132 ; Miss Winkworth, p. 348.

upon all legitimate toil, and praised good and faithful work as an expression of true religion.   One, he said, "can spin, another can make shoes, and these are the gifts of the Holy Ghost; and I tell you that, if I were not a priest, I should esteem it a great gift to be able to make shoes, and would try to make them so well as to become a pattern to all." Fidelity in one's avocation is more than attendance upon church. He spoke of a peasant whom he knew well for more than forty years.   On being asked whether he should give up his work and go and sit in church, the Lord replied no, he should win his bread by the sweat of his brow, and thus he would honor his own precious blood.   The sympathetic element in his piety excluded the hard spirit of dogmatic complacency.   "I would rather bite my tongue," Tauler said, "till it bleed, than pass judgment upon any man. Judgment we should leave to God, for out of the habit of sitting in judgment upon one's neighbor grow self-satisfaction and arrogance, which are of the devil."[1]

It was these features, and especially Tauler's insistence upon the religious exercises of the soul and the excellency of simple faith, that won Luther's praise, first in letters to Lange and Spalatin, written in 1516.   To Spalatin he wrote that he had found neither in the Latin nor German tongue a more wholesome theology than Tauler's, or one more consonant with the Gospel.[2]

The mood of the heretic, however, was furthest from Tauler.   Strassburg knew what heresy was, and had proved her orthodoxy by burning heretics.   Tauler was not of their number. He sought to call a narrow circle away from the formalities of ritual to close communion with God, but the Church was to him a holy mother.   In his reverence for the Virgin, he stood upon mediæval ground.   Preaching on

[1] Preger, III. 131; Miss Winkworth, p. 355.
[2] Köstlin, *Life of M. Luther*, I. 117 sq., 126.   Melanchthon, in the Preface to the Franf. ed. of Tauler said : "Among the moderns, Tauler is easily the first. I hear, however, that there are some who dare to deny the Christian teaching of this highly esteemed man."   Beza was of a different mind, and called Tauler a visionary. See Schmidt, p. 160. Preger, III. 194, goes so far as to say that Tauler clearly taught the evangelical doctrine of justification.

the Annunciation, he said that in her spirit was the heaven
of God, in her soul His paradise, in her body His palace.
By becoming the mother of Christ, she became the daughter
of the Father, the mother of the Son, the Holy Spirit's bride.
She was the second Eve, who restored all that the first Eve
lost, and Tauler does not hesitate to quote some of Bernard's
passionate words pronouncing Mary the sinner's mediator
with Christ.   He himself sought her intercession.   If any
one could have seen into her heart, he said, he would have
seen God in all His glory.[1]

Though he was not altogether above the religious perver-
sions of the mediæval Church, John Tauler has a place
among the godly leaders of the Church universal, who have
proclaimed the virtue of simple faith and immediate communion with God and the excellency of the unostentatious practice of righteousness from day to day.   He was an expounder
of the inner life, and strikes the chord of fellowship in all who
lay more stress upon pure devotion and daily living than upon
ritual exercises.   A spirit congenial to his was Whittier, whose
undemonstrative piety poured itself out in hearty appreciation
of his unseen friend of the fourteenth century.   The modern
Friend represents the mysterious stranger, who pointed out to
Tauler the better way, as saying : —

> What hell may be, I know not.   This I know,
> I cannot lose the presence of the Lord.
> One arm, Humility, takes hold upon
> His dear humanity ; the other, Love,
> Clasps His divinity.   So where I go
> He goes ; and better fire-walled hell with Him
> Than golden-gated Paradise without.

Said Tauler,

> My prayer is answered.   God hath sent the man,
> Long sought, to teach me, by his simple trust,
> Wisdom the weary Schoolmen never knew.

§ 31.   *Henry Suso.*

Henry Suso, 1295 ?–1366, a man of highly emotional
nature, has on the one hand been treated as a hysterical

[1] *The Inner Way*, p. 57 sqq., 77 sqq.

visionary, and on the other as the author of the most finished
product of German mysticism. Born on the Lake of Constance, and perhaps in Constance itself, he was of noble
parentage, but on the death of his mother, abandoned his
father's name, Berg, and adopted his mother's maiden name,
Seuse, Suso being the Latin form.[1] At thirteen, he entered
the Dominican convent at Constance, and from his eighteenth
year on gave himself up to the most exaggerated and painful
asceticisms. At twenty-eight, he was studying at Cologne,
and later at Strassburg.

For supporting the pope against Lewis the Bavarian, the
Dominicans in Constance came into disfavor, and were banished from the city. Suso retired to Diessehoven, where he
remained, 1339–1346, serving as prior. During this period,
he began to devote himself to preaching. The last eighteen
years of his life were spent in the Dominican convent at
Ulm, where he died, Jan. 25, 1366. He was beatified by
Gregory XVI., 1831.

Suso's constitution, which was never strong, was undermined by the rigorous penitential discipline to which he
subjected himself for twenty-two years. An account of it
is given in his *Autobiography*. Its severity, so utterly
contrary to the spirit of our time, was so excessive that
Suso's statements seem at points to be almost incredible.
The only justification for repeating some of the details is to
show the lengths to which the penitential system of the
Mediæval Church was carried by devotees. Desiring to
carry the marks of the Lord Jesus, Suso pricked into his bare
chest, with a sharp instrument, the monogram of Christ,
IHS. The three letters remained engraven there till his
dying day and, " Whenever my heart moved," as he said, " the
name moved also." At one time he saw in a dream rays of
glory illuminating the scar.

He wore a hair shirt and an iron chain. The loss of blood
forced him to put the chain aside, but for the hair shirt he
substituted an undergarment, studded with 150 sharp tacks.

---

[1] Bihlmeyer, p. 65, decides for 1295 as the probable date of Suso's birth.
Other writers put it forward to 1300.

This he wore day and night, its points turned inwards towards his body.   Often, he said, it made the impression on him as if he were lying in a nest of wasps.   When he saw his body covered with vermin, and yet he did not die, he exclaimed that the murderer puts to death at one stroke, "but alas, O tender God, — *zarter Gott*, — what a dying is this of mine!" Yet this was not enough.   Suso adopted the plan of tying around his neck a part of his girdle.   To this he attached two leather pockets, into which he thrust his hands.   These he made fast with lock and key till the next morning.   This kind of torture he continued to practise for sixteen years, when he abandoned it in obedience to a heavenly vision. How little had the piety of the Middle Ages succeeded in correcting the perverted views of the old hermits of the Nitrian desert, whose stories this Swiss monk was in the habit of reading, and whose austerities he emulated!

God, however, had not given any intimation of disapproval of ascetic discipline, and so Suso, in order further to impress upon his body marks of godliness, bound against his back a wooden cross, to which, in memory of the 30 wounds of Christ, he affixed 30 spikes.   On this instrument of torture he stretched himself at night for 8 years.   The last year he affixed to it 7 sharp needles.   For a long time he went through 2 penitential drills a day, beating with his fist upon the cross as it hung against his back, while the needles and nails penetrated into his flesh, and the blood flowed down to his feet. As if this were not a sufficient imitation of the flagellation inflicted upon Christ, he rubbed vinegar and salt into his wounds to increase his agony.   His feet became full of sores, his legs swelled as if he had had the dropsy, his flesh became dry and his hands trembled as if palsied.   And all this, as he says, he endured out of the great inner love which he had for God, and our Lord Jesus Christ, whose agonizing pains he wanted to imitate.   For 25 years, cold as the winter might be, he entered no room where there was a fire, and for the same period he abstained from all bathing, water baths or sweat baths — *Wasserbad und Schweissbad*.   But even with this list of self-mortifications, Suso said, the whole of the story was not told.

In his fortieth year, when his physical organization had been reduced to a wreck, so that nothing remained but to die or to desist from the discipline, God revealed to him that his long-practised austerity was only a good beginning, a breaking up of his untamed humanity, — *Ein Durchbrechen seines ungebrochenen Menschen*, — and that thereafter he would have to try another way in order to " get right." And so he proceeded to macerations of the inner man, and learned the lessons which asceticisms of the soul can impart.

Suso nowhere has words of condemnation for such barbarous self-imposed torture, a method of pleasing God which the Reformation put aside in favor of saner rules of piety.

Other sufferings came upon Suso, but not of his own infliction. These he bore with Christian submission, and the evils involved he sought to rectify by services rendered to others. His sister, a nun, gave way to temptation. Overcoming his first feelings of indignation, Suso went far and near in search of her, and had the joy of seeing her rescued to a worthy life, and adorned with all religious virtues. Another cross he had to bear was the charge that he was the father of an unborn child, a charge which for a time alienated Henry of Nördlingen and other close friends. He bore the insinuation without resentment, and even helped to maintain the child after it was born.

Suso's chief writings, which abound in imagery and comparisons drawn from nature, are an *Autobiography*,[1] and works on The Eternal Wisdom — *Büchlein von der ewigen Weisheit* — and the Truth — *Büchlein von der Wahrheit*. To these are to be added his sermons and letters.

The *Autobiography* came to be preserved by chance. At the request of Elsbet Staglin, Suso told her a number of his experiences. This woman, the daughter of one of the leading men of Zürich, was an inmate of the convent of Tosse, near Winterthur. When Suso discovered that she had committed his conversations to writing, he treated her act as " a

[1] It contains 53 chapters. Diepenbrock's ed., pp. 137–306 ; Bihlmeyer's ed., pp. 1–195. Diepenbrock's edition has the advantage for the modern reader of being transmuted into modern German.

spiritual theft," and burnt a part of the manuscript. The remainder he preserved, in obedience to a supernatural communication, and revised. Suso appears in the book as "The Servant of the Eternal Wisdom."

The *Autobiography* is a spiritual self-revelation in which the author does not pretend to follow the outward stages of his career. In addition to the facts of his religious experience, he sets forth a number of devotional rules containing much wisdom, and closes with judicious and edifying remarks on the being of God, which he gave to Elsbet in answer to her questions.[1]

The *Book of the Eternal Wisdom*, which is in the form of a dialogue between Christ, the Eternal Wisdom, and the writer, has been called by Denifle, who bore Suso's name, the consummate fruit of German mysticism. It records, in German,[2] meditations in which use is made of the Scriptures. Here we have a body of experimental theology such as ruled among the more pious spirits in the German convents of the fourteenth century.

Suso declares that one who is without love is as unable to understand a tongue that is quick with love as one speaking in German is unable to understand a Fleming, or as one who hears a report of the music of a harp is unable to understand the feelings of one who has heard the music with his own ears. The Saviour is represented as saying that it would be easier to bring back the years of the past, revive the withered flowers or collect all the droplets of rain than to measure the love — *Minne* — he has for men.

The Servant, after lamenting the hardness of heart which refuses to be moved by the spectacle of the cross and the love of God, seeks to discover how it is that God can at once be so loving and so severe. As for the pains of hell, the lost are represented as exclaiming, "Oh, how we desire that

---

[1] A translation of these definitions is given by Inge, in *Light, Life and Love*, pp. 66–82.

[2] Suso made a revision of his work in Latin under the title *Horologium eternæ sapientiæ*, a copy of which Tauler seems to have had in his possession. Preger, II. 324.

there might be a millstone as wide as the earth and reaching to all parts of heaven, and that a little bird might alight every ten thousand years and peck away a piece of stone as big as the tenth part of a millet seed and continue to peck away every ten thousandth year until it had pecked away a piece as big as a millet seed, and then go on pecking at the same rate until the whole stone were pecked away, so only our torture might come to an end; but that cannot be."

Having dwelt upon the agony of the cross and God's immeasurable love, the bliss of heaven and the woes of hell, Suso proceeds to set forth the dignity of suffering.   He had said in his *Autobiography* that " every lover is a martyr," [1] and here the Eternal Wisdom declares that if all hearts were become one heart, that heart could not bear the least reward he has chosen to give in eternity as a compensation for the least suffering endured out of love for himself. . . .   This is an eternal law of nature that what is true and good must be harvested with sorrow.   There is nothing more joyous than to have endured suffering.   Suffering is short pain and prolonged joy.   Suffering gives pain here and blessedness hereafter.   Suffering destroys suffering — *Leiden tödtet Leiden.* Suffering exists that the sufferer may not suffer.   He who could weigh time and eternity in even balances would rather lie in a glowing oven for a hundred years than to miss in eternity the least reward given for the least suffering, for the suffering in the oven would have an end, but the reward is forever.

After dwelling upon the advantages of contemplation as the way of attaining to the heavenly life, the Eternal Wisdom tells Suso how to die both the death of the body and the soul; namely, by penance and by self-detachment from all the things of the earth — *Entbrechen von allen Dingen.*   An unconverted man is introduced in the agonies of dying.   His hands grow cold, his face pales, his eyes begin to lose their sight.   The prince of terrors wrestles with his heart and deals it hard blows. The chill sweat of death creeps over his body and starts haggard fears.   " O angry countenance of the severe Judge, how sharp are thy judgments! " he exclaims.   In imagination,

---

[1] Bihlmeyer's ed., p. 13.

or with real sight, he beholds the host of black Moors approaching to see whether he belongs to them, and then the beasts of
hell surrounding him.   He sees the hot flames rising up above
the denizens of purgatory, and hears them cry out that the
least of their tortures is greater than the keenest suffering
endured by martyr on the earth.   And that a day there is as
a hundred years.   They exclaim, "Now we roast, now we
simmer and now we cry out in vain for help."   The dying
man then passes into the other world, calling out for help to
the friends whom he had treated well on the earth, but in vain.

The treatise, which closes with excellent admonitions on the
duty of praising God continually, makes a profound spiritual
impression, but it presents only one side of the spiritual life,
and needs to be supplemented and expurgated in order to present a proper picture.   Christ came into the world that we
might have everlasting life now, and that we might have
abundance of life, and that his joy might remain in us and our
joy might be full.   The patient endurance of suffering puri-
fies the soul and the countenance, but suffering is not to be
counted as always having a sanctifying power, much less is it
to be courted.   Macerations have no virtue of themselves, and
patience in enduring pain is only one of the Christian virtues,
and not their crown.   Love, which is the bond of perfectness,
finds in a cheerful spirit, in hearty human fellowships and in
well-doing also, its ministries.   The mediæval type of piety
turned the earth into a vale of tears.   It was cloistral.   For
nearly 30 years, as Suso tells us, he never once broke through
the rule of silence at table.[1]   Innocent III. could write, just
before becoming world-ruler, a treatise on the contempt of the
world.   The piety of the modern Church is of a cheerful type,
and sees good everywhere in this world which God created.
Suso's piety was what the Germans have called the mysticism
of suffering — *die Mystik des Leidens*.   His way of self-in-
flicted torture was the wrong way.   In going, however, with
Suso we will not fail to reach some of the heights of religious
experience and to find nearness to God.

Suso kept company with the Friends of God, and acknowl-

----

[1] *Autobiog.*, ch. XIV, Bihlmeyer's ed., p. 38.

edged his debt to Eckart, " the high teacher," " his high and holy master," from whose " sweet teachings he had taken deep draughts." As he says in his *Autobiography*, he went to Eckart in a time of spiritual trial, and was helped by him out of the hell of distress into which he had fallen.   He uses some of Eckart's distinctive vocabulary, and after the Cologne mystic's death, Suso saw him " in exceeding glory " and was admonished by him to submission.   This quality forms the subject of Suso's *Book on the Truth*, which in part was meant to be a defence of his spiritual teacher.

A passage bearing on the soul's union with Christ will serve as a specimen of Suso's tropical style, and may fitly close this chapter.   The soul, so the Swiss mystic represents Christ as saying —

" the soul that would find me in the inner closet of a consecrated and self-detached life, — *abgeschiedenes Leben*, — and would partake of my sweetness, must first be purified from evil and adorned with virtues, be decked with the red roses of passionate love, with the beautiful violets of meek submission, and must be strewn with the white lilies of purity.   It shall embrace me with its arms, excluding all other loves, for these I shun and flee as the bird does the cage.   This soul shall sing to me the song of Zion, which means passionate love combined with boundless praise. Then I will embrace it and it shall lean upon my heart."[1]

§ 32.   *The Friends of God.*

The Friends of God attract our interest both by the suggestion of religious fervor involved in their name and the respect with which the prominent mystics speak of them.   They are frequently met within the writings of Eckart, Tauler, Suso, and Ruysbroeck, as well as in the pages of other writers of the fourteenth century.   Much mystery surrounds them, and efforts have failed to define with precision their teachings, numbers and influence.   The name had been applied to the Waldenses,[2] but in the fourteenth century it came to be a designation for coteries of pietists scattered along the Rhine, from Basel to Strassburg and to the Netherlands, laymen and priests who felt spiritual longings the usual church services did not satisfy.   They did not constitute an organized sect.

[1] *Von der ewigen Weisheit*, Bihlmeyer's ed., p. 296 sq.
[2] Preger, III. 370 ; Strauch, p. 205.

They were addicted to the study of the Scriptures, and sought close personal fellowship with God. They laid stress upon a godly life and were bent on the propagation of holiness. Their name was derived from John 16·: 15, "Henceforth I call you not servants, but I have called you friends." Their practices did not involve a breach with the Church and its ordinances. They had no sympathy with heresy, and antagonized the Brethren of the Free Spirit. The little treatise, called the *German Theology*, at the outset marks the difference between the Friends of God and the false, free spirits, especially the Beghards.[1]

A letter written by a Friend to another Friend[2] represents as succinctly as any statement their aim when it says, "The soul that loves God must get away from the world, from the flesh and all sensual desires and away from itself, that is, away from its own self-will, and thus does it make ready to hear the message of the work and ministry of love accomplished by our Lord Jesus Christ." The house which Rulman Merswin founded in Strassburg was declared to be a house of refuge for honorable persons, priests and laymen who, with trust in God, choose to flee the world and seek to improve their lives. The Friends of God regarded themselves as holding the secret of the Christian life and as being the salt of the earth, the instructors of other men.[3]

Among the leading Friends of God were Henry of Nördlingen, Nicolas of Löwen, Rulman Merswin and "the great Friend of God from the Oberland." The personality of the Friend of God from the Oberland is one of the most evasive in the religious history of the Middle Ages. He is presented as a leader of great personal power and influence, as the man who determined Tauler's conversion and wrote a number of tracts, and yet it is doubtful whether such a personage ever lived. Rulman Merswin affirms that he had been widely active between Basel and Strassburg and in the region of Switzerland, from which he got his name, the Oberland. In

---

[1] See Rulman Merswin's condemnation of the Beguines and Beghards in the *Nine Rocks*, chs. XIII., XIV.   [2] As printed by Preger, III. 417 sq.
[3] See the last chapter of R. Merswin's *Nine Rocks*.

1377, according to the same authority, he visited Gregory XI.
in Rome and, like Catherine of Siena, petitioned the pontiff
to set his face against the abuses of Christendom.   Rulman
was in correspondence with him for a long period, and held
his writings secret until within four years of his (Rulman's)
death, when he published them.   They were 17 in number,
all of them bearing on the nature and necessity of a true
conversion of heart.[1]

This mystic from the Oberland, as Rulman's account goes,
led a life of prayer and devotion, and found peace, performed
miracles and had visions.   He is placed by Preger at the
side of Peter Waldo as one of the most influential laymen of
the Middle Ages, a priest, though unordained, of the Church.
After Rulman's death, we hear no more of him.

Rulman Merswin, the editor of the Oberland prophet's
writings, was born in Strassburg, 1307, and died there, 1382.
He gave up merchandise and devoted himself wholly to a
religious life.   He had undergone the change of conversion
— *Kehr*.   For four years he had a hard struggle against
temptations, and subjected himself to severe asceticisms, but
was advised by his confessor, Tauler, to desist, at least for a
time.   It was towards the end of this period that he met the
man from the Oberland.   After his conversion, he purchased
and fitted up an old cloister, located on an island near Strassburg, called *das grüne Wört*, to serve as a refuge for clerics and
laymen who wished to follow the principles of the Friends of
God and live together for the purpose of spiritual culture.   In
1370, after the death of his wife, Rulman himself became an
inmate of the house, which was put under the care of the
Knights of St. John a year later.   Here he continued to ex-
hort by pen and word till his death.   He lies buried at the
side of his wife in Strassburg.

Merswin's two chief writings are entitled *Das Bannerbüch-*

---

[1] The two leading writings are *Das Buch von den zwei Mannen*, an account
of the first five years immediately succeeding the author's conversion, and given
in Schmidt's *Nic. von Basel*, pp. 205–277, and *Das Buch von den fünf Mannen*,
in which the Oberlander gives an account of his own life and the lives of his
friends.   For the full list of the writings, see Preger, III. 270 sqq., and
Strauch, p. 209 sqq.

lein, the Banner-book, and *Das Buch von den neun Felsen*, the
Nine Rocks.   The former is an exhortation to flee from the
banner of Lucifer and to gather under the blood-red banner
of Christ.[1]   The *Nine Rocks*, written in the form of a dialogue, 1352, opens with a parable, describing innumerable
fishes swimming down from the lakes among the hills through
the streams in the valleys into the deep sea.   The author
then sees them attempting to find their way back to the hills.
These processes illustrate the career of human souls departing from God into the world and seeking to return to Him.
The author also sees a " fearfully high mountain," on which
are nine rocks.   The souls that succeed in getting back to
the mountain are so few that it seemed as if only one out of
every thousand reached it.   He then proceeds to set forth
the condition of the eminent of the earth, popes and kings,
cardinals and princes; and also priests, monks and nuns, Beguines and Beghards, and people of all sorts and classes.
He finds the conditions very bad, and is specially severe on
women who, by their show of dress and by their manners, are
responsible for men going morally astray and falling into sin.
Many of these women commit a hundred mortal sins a day.

Rulman then returns to the nine rocks, which represent the
nine stages of progress towards the source of our being, God.
Those who are on the rocks have escaped the devil's net, and
by climbing on up to the last rock, they reach perfection.
Those on the fifth rock have gained the point where they
have completely given up their own self-will.   The sixth
rock represents full submission to God.   On the ninth the
number is so small that there seemed to be only three persons
on it.   These have no desire whatever except to honor God,
fear not hell nor purgatory, nor enemy nor death nor life.

The Friends of God, who are bent on something more than
their own salvation, are depicted in the valley below, striving to rescue souls from the net in which they have been
ensnared.   The Brethren of the Free Spirit resist this merciful procedure.

[1] See Preger, III. 349 sqq.   C. Schmidt gives the text, as does also Diepenbrock, *H. Suso*, pp. 505–572.

The presentation is crude, and Scripture is not directly quoted. The biblical imagery, however, abounds, and, as in the case of the ancient allegory of Hermas, the principles of the Gospel are set forth in a way adapted, no doubt, to reach a certain class of minds, even as in these modern days the methods of the Salvation Army appeal to many for whom the discourses of Bernard or Gerson might have little meaning.[1]

Rulman Merswin is regarded by Denifle, Strauch and other critics as the author of the works ascribed to the Friend of God from the Oberland, and the inventor of this fictitious personage.[2] The reason for this view is that no one else knows of the Oberlander and that, after Rulman's death, attempts on the part of the Strassburg brotherhood to find him, or to find out something about him, resulted in failure. On the other hand, it is difficult to understand why Rulman did not continue to keep his writings secret till after his own death, if the Oberlander was a fictitious character.[3]

Whatever may be the outcome of the discussion over the historic personality of the man from the Oberland, we have in the writings of these two men a witness to the part laymen were taking in the affairs of the Church.

§ 33.   *John of Ruysbroeck.*

Independent of the Friends of God, and yet closely allied with them in spirit, was Jan von Ruysbroeck, 1293–1381. In 1350, he sent to the Friends in Strassburg his Adornment of the Spiritual Marriage — *Chierheit der gheesteleker*

---

[1] Strauch, p. 208, and others regard Merswin's works as in large part compilations from Tauler and other writers. Strauch pronounces their contents garrulous — *geschwätzig.* The *Nine Rocks* used to be printed with Suso's works. Merswin's authorship was established by Schmidt.

[2] *Rulman hat den Gottesfreund einfach erfunden.* Strauch, p. 217.

[3] Preger and Schmidt are the chief spokesmen for the historic personality of the man from the Oberland. Rieder has recently relieved Rulman from the stain of forgery, and placed the responsibility upon Nicolas of Löwen, who entered *das grüne Wört* in 1366. The palaeographic consideration is emphasized, that is, the resemblance between Nicolas' handwriting and the script of the reputed Oberlander.

Brulocht. He forms a connecting link between them and the Brothers of the Common Life. The founder of the latter brotherhood, de Groote, and also Tauler, visited him. He was probably acquainted with Eckart's writings, which were current in the Lowlands.[1]

The Flemish mystic was born in a village of the same name near Brussels, and became vicar of St. Gudula in that city. At sixty he abandoned the secular priesthood and put on the monastic habit, identifying himself with the recently established Augustinian convent Groenendal, — Green Valley, — located near Waterloo. Here he was made prior. Ruysbroeck spent most of his time in contemplation, though he was not indifferent to practical duties. On his walks through the woods of Soignes, he believed he saw visions and he was otherwise the subject of revelations. He was not a man of the schools. Soon after his death, a fellow-Augustinian wrote his biography, which abounds in the miraculous element. The very trees under which he sat were illuminated with an aureole. At his passing away, the bells of the convent rang without hands touching them, and perfume proceeded from his dead body.

The title, *doctor ecstaticus*, which at an early period was associated with Ruysbroeck, well names his characteristic trait. He did not speculate upon the remote theological themes of God's being as did Eckart, nor was he a popular preacher of every-day Christian living, like Tauler. He was a master of the contemplative habit, and mused upon the soul's experiences in its states of partial or complete union with God. His writings, composed in his mother-tongue, were translated into Latin by his pupils, Groote and

---

[1] The extent to which Eckart influenced the mystics of the Lowlands is a matter of dispute. The clergy strove to keep his works from circulation. Langenberg, p. 181, quotes Gerherd Zerbold von Zütphen's, d. 1398, tract, *De libris Teutonicalibus*, which takes the position that, while wholesome books might be read in the vulgar tongue, Eckart's works and sermons were exceedingly pernicious, and not to be read by the laity. Langenberg, pp. 184–204, gives descriptions and excerpts from four MSS. of Eckart's writings in Low German, copied in the convent of Nazareth, near Bredevoorde, and now preserved in the royal library of Berlin, but they do not give Eckart as the author.

William Jordaens. The chief products of his pen are the
Adornment of the Spiritual Marriage, the *Mirror of Blessedness* and *Samuel*, which is a defence of the habit of contemplation, and the *Glistening Stone*, an allegorical meditation
on the white stone of Rev. 2 : 17, which is interpreted to
mean Christ.

Ruysbroeck laid stress upon ascetic exercises, but more
upon love. In its highest stages of spiritual life, the soul
comes to God "without an intermediary." The name and
work of Christ are dwelt upon on every page. He is our
canon, our breviary, our every-day book, and belongs to
laity and clergy alike. He was concerned to have it understood that he has no sympathy with pantheism, and opposed
the heretical views of the Brethren of the Free Spirit and
the Beghards. He speaks of four sorts of heretics, the marks
of one of them being that they despise the ordinances and
sacraments of the Catholic Church, the Scriptures and the
sufferings of Christ, and set themselves above God himself.
He, however, did not escape the charge of heresy. Gerson,
who received a copy of the *Spiritual Marriage* from a Carthusian monk of Bruges, found the third book teaching
pantheism, and wrote a tract in which he complained that
the author, whom he pronounced an unlearned man, followed
his feelings in setting forth the secrets of the religious life.
Gerson was, however, persuaded that he had made a mistake
by the defence written by John of Schoenhofen, one of the
brethren of Groenendal. However, in his reply written 1408,
he again emphasized that Ruysbroeck was a man without
learning, and complained that he had not made his meaning
sufficiently clear.[1]

The *Spiritual Marriage*, Ruysbroeck's chief contribution
to mystical literature, is a meditation upon the words of the
parable, " Behold, the bridegroom cometh, go ye out to meet
him." It sets forth three stages of Christian experience, the

---

[1] Engelhardt, pp. 265–297, gives a full statement of the controversy. For
Gerson's letters to Bartholomew and Schoenhofen and Schoenhofen's letter,
see Du Pin, *Works of Gerson*, pp. 29–82. Maeterlinck, p. 4, refers to the
difficulty certain passages in Ruysbroeck's writings offer to the interpreter.

active, the inner and the contemplative.   In the active stage
the soul adopts the Christian virtues and practises them, fighting against sin, and thus it goes out "to meet the bridegroom."
We must believe the articles of the Creed, but not seek to fully
understand them.   And the more subtle doctrines of the Scripture we should accept and explain as they are interpreted by
the life of Christ and the lives of his saints.   Man should study
nature, the Scriptures and all created things, and draw from
them profit.   To understand Christ he must, like Zaccheus,
run ahead of all the manifestations of the creature world, and
climb up the tree of faith, which has twelve branches, the
twelve articles of the Creed.

As for the *inner* life, it is distinguished from the active by
devotion to the original Cause and to truth itself as against
devotion to exercises and forms, to the celebration of the
sacrament and to good works.   Here the soul separates itself
from outward relations and created forms, and contemplates
the eternal love of God.   Asceticism may still be useful, but
it is not essential.

The contemplative stage few reach.   Here the soul is transferred into a purity and brightness which is above all natural
intelligence.   It is a peculiar adornment and a heavenly
crown.   No one can reach it by learning and intellectual
subtlety nor by disciplinary exercises.   In order to attain to
it, three things are essential.   A man must live virtuously;
he must, like a fire that never goes out, love God constantly,
and he must lose himself in the darkness in which men of the
contemplative habit no longer find their way by the methods
known to the creature.   In the abyss of this darkness a light
incomprehensible is begotten, the Son of God, in whom we
"see eternal life."

At last the soul comes into essential unity with God, and,
in the fathomless ocean of this unity, all things are seized
with bliss.   It is the dark quiet in which all who love God
lose themselves.   Here they swim in the wild waves of the
ocean of God's being.[1]

[1] I have followed the German text given by Lambert, pp. 3-160.   Selections, well translated into English, are given in *Light, Life and Love.*

He who would follow the Flemish mystic in these utterances must have his spirit.   They seem far removed from the
calm faith which leaves even the description of such ecstatic
states to the future, and is content with doing the will of God
in the daily avocations of this earthly life.   Expressions he
uses, such as "spiritual intoxication,"[1] are not safe, and the
experiences he describes are, as he declares, not intended for
the body of Christian people to reach here below.   In most
men they would take the forms of spiritual hysteria and the
hallucinations of hazy self-consciousness.   It is well that Ruysbroeck's greatest pupil, de Groote, did not follow along this
line of meditation, but devoted himself to practical questions
of every-day living and works of philanthropy.   The ecstatic
mood is characteristic of this mystic in the secluded home in
Brabant, but it is not the essential element in his religious
thought.   His descriptions of Christ and his work leave little
to be desired.   He does not dwell upon Mary, or even mention her in his chief work.   He insists upon the works which
proceed from genuine love to God.   The chapter may be
closed with two quotations : —

" Even devotion must give way to a work of love to the spiritual and
to the physical man.   For even should one rise in prayer higher than
Peter or Paul, and hear that a poor man needed a drink of water, he
would have to cease from the devotional exercise, sweet though it were,
and do the deed of love.   It is well pleasing to God that we leave Him
in order to help His members.   In this sense the Apostle was willing to
be banished from Christ for his brethren's sake."

"Always before thou retire at night, read three books, which thou
oughtest always to have with thee.   The first is an old, gray, ugly volume,
written over with black ink.   The second is white and beautifully written
in red, and the third in glittering gold letters.   First read the old volume.
That means, consider thine own past life, which is full of sins and errors,
as are the lives of all men.   Retire within thyself and read the book of
conscience, which will be thrown open at the last judgment of Christ.
Think over how badly thou hast lived, how negligent thou hast been in
thy words, deeds, wishes and thoughts.   Cast down thy eyes and cry,
' God be merciful to me a sinner.'   Then God will drive away fear and
anxious concern and will give thee hope and faith.   Then lay the old
book aside and go and fetch from memory the white book.   This is the

[1] See Lambert, pp. 62, 63, etc.

guileless life of Christ, whose soul was pure and whose guileless body was bruised with stripes and marked with rose-red, precious blood. These are the letters which show his real love to us. Look at them with deep emotion and thank him that, by his death, he has opened to thee the gate of heaven. And finally lift up thine eyes on high and read the third book, written in golden script; that is, consider the glory of the life eternal, in comparison with which the earthly vanishes away as the light of the candle before the splendor of the sun at midday."[1]

§ 34. *Gerrit de Groote and the Brothers of the Common Life.*

It was fortunate for the progress of religion, that mysticism in Holland and Northwestern Germany did not confine itself to the channel into which it had run at Groenendal. In the latter part of the fourteenth century, and before Ruysbroeck's death, it associated with itself practical philanthropic activities under the leadership of Gerrit Groote, 1340–1384, and Florentius Radewyn, 1350–1400, who had finished his studies in Prag. They were the founders of the Windesheim Congregation and the genial company known as the Brothers of the Common Life, called also the Brothers of the New Devotion. To the effort to attain to union with God they gave a new impulse by insisting that men imitate the conduct of Christ.[2] Originating in Holland, they spread along the Rhine and into Central Germany.

Groote was born at Deventer, where his father had been burgomaster. After studying at Paris, he taught at Cologne, and received the appointment of canon, enjoying at least two church livings, one at Utrecht and one at Aachen. He lived the life of a man of the world until he experienced a sudden conversion through the influence of a friend, Henry of Kolcar, a Carthusian prior. He renounced his ecclesiastical livings and visited Ruysbroeck, being much influenced by him. Thomas à Kempis remarks that Groote could say, after his

---

[1] Quoted by Galle, pp. 184–224.

[2] See Grube, *Gerh. Groot*, p. 9 ; Langenberg, p. ix ; Pastor, I. 150. The Latin titles of the brotherhood were *fratres vitæ communis, fratres modernæ devotionis, fratres bonæ voluntatis*, with reference to Luke 11: 14, and *fratres collationarii* with reference to their habit of preaching. Groote's name is spelled Geert de Groote, Gherd de Groet (Langenberg, p. 3), Gerhard Groot (Grube), etc.

visits to Ruysbroeck, "Thy wisdom and knowledge are greater than the report which I heard in my own country."

At forty he began preaching. Throngs gathered to hear him in the churches and churchyards of Deventer, Zwolle, Leyden and other chief towns of the Lowlands.[1] Often he preached three times a day. His success stirred up the Franciscans, who secured from the bishop of Utrecht an inhibition of preaching by laymen. Groote came under this restriction, as he was not ordained. An appeal was made to Urban VI., but the pope put himself on the side of the bishop. Groote died in 1384, before the decision was known.

Groote strongly denounced the low morals of the clergy, but seems not to have opposed any of the doctrines of the Church. He fasted, attended mass, laid stress upon prayer and alms, and enforced these lessons by his own life. To quote an old writer, he taught by living righteously — *docuit sancte vivendo*. In 1374, he gave the house he had inherited from his father at Deventer as a home for widows and unmarried women. Without taking vows, the inmates were afforded an opportunity of retirement and a life of religious devotion and good works. They were to support themselves by weaving, spinning, sewing, nursing and caring for the sick. They were at liberty to leave the community whenever they chose. John Brinkerinck further developed the idea of the female community.

The origin of the Brothers of the Common Life was on this wise. After the inhibition of lay preaching, Groote settled down at Deventer, spending much time in the house of Florentius Radewyn. He had employed young priests to copy manuscripts. At Radewyn's suggestion they were united into a community, and agreed to throw their earnings into a com-

---

[1] The title, hammer of the heretics, — *malleus hereticorum*, — was applied to him for his defence of the orthodox teaching. For the application of this expression, see Hansen, *Gesch. des Hexenwahns*, p. 361. On Groote's fame as a preacher, see Grube, p. 14 sqq., 23. Thomas à Kempis vouches for Groote's popularity as a preacher. See Kettlewell, I. 130–134. Among his published sermons is one against the concubinage of the clergy — *de focaristis*. For a list of his printed discourses, see Herzog, VII., 692 sqq., and Langenberg, p. 35 sqq.

mon fund.   After Groote's death, the community received a
more distinct organization through Radewyn.   Other societies
were established after the model of the Deventer house, which
was called " the rich brother house," — *het rijke fraterhuis*, —
as at Zwolle, Delft, Liége, Ghent, Cologne, Münster, Marburg
and Rostock, many of them continuing strong till the Reformation.[1]

A second branch from the same stock, the canons Regular
of St. Augustine, established by the influence of Radewyn
and other friends and pupils of Groote, had as their chief
houses Windesheim, dedicated 1387, and Mt. St. Agnes,
near Zwolle.   These labored more within the convent, the
Brothers of the Common Life outside of it.

The Brotherhood of the Common Life never reached the
position of an order sanctioned by Church authority.   Its
members, including laymen as well as clerics, took no irrevo-
cable vow, and were at liberty to withdraw when they pleased.
They were opposed to the Brethren of the Free Spirit, and were
free from charges of looseness in morals and doctrine.   Like
their founder, they renounced worldly goods and remained
unmarried.   They supported the houses by their own toil.[2]

To gardening, making clothes and other occupations pertaining to the daily life, they added preaching, conducting
schools and copying manuscripts.   Groote was an ardent
lover of books, and had many manuscripts copied for his
library.   Among these master copyists was Thomas à Kempis.
Classical authors as well as writings of the Fathers and books
of Scripture were transcribed.   Selections were also made
from these authors in distinct volumes, called *ripiaria* — little
river banks.   At Liége they were so diligent as copyists as
to receive the name *Broeders van de penne*, Brothers of the
Quill.   Of Groote, Thomas à Kempis reports that he had a

---

[1] See Grube, p. 88, and Schulze, p. 492 sqq., who gives a succinct history
of 18 German houses and 20 houses in the Lowlands.   The last to be established was at Cambray, 1505.

[2] Writing of Radewyn, Thomas à Kempis, *Vita Florentii*, ch. XIV., says
that work was most profitable to spiritual advancement, and adapted to hold
in check the lusts of the flesh.   One brother who was found after his death
to be in possession of some money, was denied prayer at his burial.

chest filled with the best books standing near his dining table, so that, if a course did not please him, he might reach over to them and give his friends a cup for their souls. He carried books about with him on his preaching tours. Objection was here and there made to the possession of so many books, where they might have been sold and the proceeds given to the poor.[1] Translations also were made of the books of Scripture and other works. Groote translated the Seven Penitential Psalms, the Office for the Dead and certain Devotions to Mary. The houses were not slow in adopting type, and printing establishments are mentioned in connection with Maryvale, near Geissenheim, Windesheim, Herzogenbusch, Rostock, Louvaine and other houses.

The schools conducted by the Brothers of the Common Life, intended primarily for clerics, have a distinguished place in the history of education. Seldom, if ever before, had so much attention been paid to the intellectual and moral training of youth. Not only did the Brothers have their own schools. They labored also in schools already established. Long lists of the teachers are still extant. Their school at Herzogenbusch had at one time 1200 scholars, and put Greek into its course at its very start, 1424. The school at Liége in 1524 had 1600 scholars.[2] The school at Deventer acquired a place among the notable grammar schools of history, and trained Nicolas of Cusa, Thomas à Kempis, John Wessel and Erasmus, who became an inmate of the institution, 1474, and learned Greek from one of its teachers, Synthis. Making the mother-tongue the chief vehicle of education, these schools sent out the men who are the fathers of the modern literature of Northwestern Germany and the Lowlands, and prepared the soil for the coming Reformation.

Scarcely less influential was the public preaching of the Brethren in the vernacular, and the *collations*, or expositions

---

[1] Uhlhorn, p. 373, gives the case of such an objector, a certain man by the name of Ketel of Deventer. Also Langenberg, p. x.

[2] See Schmid, *Gesch. d. Erziehung vom Anfang bis auf unsere Zeit*, Stuttgart, 1892, II. 164–167; Hirsche in Herzog, II. 759; Pastor's high tribute, I. 152; and Langenberg, p. ix.

of Scripture, given to private circles in their own houses. Groote went to the Scriptures, so Thomas à Kempis says, as to a well of life. Of John Celle, d. 1417, the zealous rector of the Zwolle school, the same biographer writes : " He frequently expounded to the pupils the Holy Scriptures, impressing upon them their authority and stirring them up to diligence in writing out the sayings of the saints. He also taught them to sing accurately, and sedulously to attend church, to honor God's ministers and to pray often." [1] Celle himself played on the organ.

The central theme of their study was the person and life of Christ. "Let the root of thy study," said Groote, "and the mirror of thy life be primarily the Gospel, for therein is the life of Christ portrayed." [2] A period of each day was set apart for reflection on some special religious subject, — Sunday on heaven, Monday on death, Tuesday on the mercies of God, Wednesday on the last judgment, Thursday on the pains of hell, Friday on the Lord's passion and Saturday on sins. They laid more stress upon inward purity and rectitude than upon outward conformities to ritual. [3]

The excellent people joined the other mystics of the fourteenth century in loosening the hold of scholasticism and sacerdotalism, those two master forces of the Middle Ages. [4] They gave emphasis to the ideas brought out strongly from other quarters, — the heretical sects and such writers as Marsiglius of Padua, — the idea of the dignity of the layman, and that monastic vows are not the condition of pure religious devotion. They were the chief contributors to the vigorous religious current which was flowing through the Lowlands. Popular religious literature was in circulation. Manuals of devotion were current, cordials and præcordials for the soul's needs. Written codes of rules for laymen were passed from hand to

---

[1] Kettlewell, I. 111.

[2] Thos. à Kempis, *Vita Gerard.* XVIII. 11 ; Kettlewell, I. 166. A life of a cleric he declared to be the people's Gospel — *vita clerici evangelium populi.*   [3] See Langenberg, p. 51.

[4] See Ullman, II. 82, 115 sq. Schulze, p. 190, is not so clear on this point. Kettlewell, II. 440, says that the Brothers were " the chief agents in pioneering the way for the Reformation."

hand, giving directions for their conduct at home and abroad.
Religious poems in the vernacular, such as the poem on the
wise and foolish virgins, carried biblical truth.

> *Van viff juncfrou wen de wis weren*
> *Unde van vif dwasen wilt nu hir leren.*

Some of these were translations from Bernard's *Jesu dulcis
memoria*, and some condemned festivities like the Maypole
and the dance.[1]

Eugene IV., Pius II., and Sixtus IV. gave the Brothers marks
of their approval, and the great teachers, Cardinal Cusa, D'Ailly
and John Gerson spoke in their praise.   There were, however,
detractors, such as Grabon, a Saxon Dominican who presented,
in the last days of the Council of Constance, 1418, no less
than twenty-five charges against them.   The substance of
the charges was that the highest religious life may not be
lived apart from the orders officially sanctioned by the
Church.   A commission appointed by Martin V., to which
Gerson and D'Ailly belonged, reported adversely, and Grabon was obliged to retract.   The commission adduced the
fact that there was no monastic body in Jerusalem when the
primitive Church practised community of goods, and that conventual walls and vows are not essential to the highest religious life.   Otherwise the pope, the cardinals and the prelates
themselves would not be able to attain to the highest reach
of religious experience.[2]

With the Reformation, the distinct mission of the Brotherhood was at an end, and many of the communities fell in with

---

[1] See Langenberg.   The poem he gives on the dance, 68 sqq., begins —

> *Hyr na volget eyn lere schone*
> *Teghen dantzen unde van den meybome.*

Here follows a nice teaching against dancing and the May tree.   One reason
given against dancing was that the dancers stretched out their arms, and so
showed disrespect to Christ, who stretched out his arms on the cross.   One
of the documents is a letter in which a monk warns his niece, who had gone
astray, against displays of dress and bold gestures, intended to attract the
attention of young men, especially on the Cathedral Square.   With the letter
he sent his niece a book of devotional literature.

[2] Van der Hardt, *Conc. Const.*, III. 107–121, gives Grabon's charges, the
judgments of D'Ailly and Gerson and the text of Grabon's retraction.

the new movement.   As for the houses which maintained
their old rules, Luther felt a warm interest in them.   When,
in 1532, the Council of Hervord in Westphalia was proposing
to abolish the local sister and brother houses, the Reformer
wrote strongly against the proposal as follows: "Inasmuch as
the Brothers and Sisters, who were the first to start the Gospel among you, lead a creditable life, and have a decent and
well-behaved community, and faithfully teach and hold the
pure Word, such monasteries and brother-houses please me
beyond measure."   On two other occasions, he openly showed
his interest in the brotherhood of which Groote was the
founder.[1]

§ 35.   *The Imitation of Christ.   Thomas à Kempis.*

> . . . mild saint
> À Kempis overmild.
>   — LANIER.

The pearl of all the mystical writings of the German-Dutch
school is the *Imitation of Christ*, the work of Thomas à Kempis.
With the *Confessions of St. Augustine* and Bunyan's *Pilgrim's
Progress* it occupies a place in the very front rank of manuals
of devotion, and, if the influence of books is to be judged by
their circulation, this little volume, starting from a convent
in the Netherlands, has, next to the Sacred Scriptures, been
the most influential of all the religious writings of Christendom.   Protestants and Catholics alike have joined in giving
it praise.   The Jesuits introduced it into their Exercises.
Dr. Samuel Johnson, once, when ill, taught himself Dutch by
reading it in that language, and said of its author that the
world had opened its arms to receive his book.[2]   It was
translated by John Wesley, was partly instrumental in the
conversion of John Newton, was edited by Thomas Chalmers,
was read by Mr. Gladstone "as a golden book for all times"
and was the companion of General Gordon.   Dr. Charles

---

[1] De Wette, *Luther's Letters*, Nos. 1448, 1449, vol. IV., pp. 358 sqq.
[2] Art. The *Worldly Wisdom of Thos. à Kempis*, in *Dublin Review*, 1908,
pp. 262-287.

Hodge, the Presbyterian divine, said it has diffused itself like incense through the aisles and alcoves of the Universal Church.[1]

The number of counted editions exceeds 2000. The British Museum has more than 1000 editions on its shelves.[2]

Originally written in the Latin, a French translation was made as early as 1447, which still remains in manuscript. The first printed French copies appeared in Toulouse, 1488. The earliest German translation was made in 1434 and is preserved in Cologne, and printed editions in German begin with the Augsburg edition of 1486. Men eminent in the annals of German piety, such as Arndt, 1621, Gossner, 1824, and Tersteegen, 1844, have issued editions with prefaces. The work first appeared in print in English, 1502, the translation being partly by the hand of Margaret, the mother of Henry VII. Translations appeared in Italian in Venice and Milan, 1488, in Spanish at Seville, 1536, in Arabic at Rome, 1663, in Arminian at Rome, 1674, and in other languages.[3]

The *Imitation of Christ* consists of four books, and derives its title from the heading of the first book, *De imitatione Christi et contemptu omnium vanitatum mundi*, the imitation of Christ and the contempt of all the vanities of the world. It seems to have been written in metre.[4] The four books are not found in all the manuscripts nor invariably arranged in the same order, facts which have led some to suppose that

[1] *System. Theol.*, I. 79. For Gladstone's judgment, see Morley, II. 186. Butler, p. 191, gives a list of 33 English translations from 1502–1900. De Quincey said : " The book came forward in answer to the sighing of Christian Europe for light from heaven. Excepting the Bible in Protestant lands, no book known to man has had the same distinction. It is the most marvellous biblical fact on record." Quoted by Kettlewell, I.

[2] Backer, in his *Essai bibliogr.*, enumerates 545 Latin editions, and about 900 editions in French. There are more than 50 editions belonging to the fifteenth century. See Funk, p. 426. The Bullingen collection, donated to the city library of Cologne, 1838, contained at the time of the gift 400 different edd. Montmorenci, p. xxii sq., gives the dates of 29 edd., 1471–1503, with places of issue.

[3] Corneille produced a poetical translation in French, 1651. A polyglot edition appeared at Sulzbach, 1837, comprising the Latin text and translations in Italian, French, German, Greek and English.

[4] Hirsche discovered the rhythm and made it known, 1874.

they were not all written at the same time.   The work is a manual of devotion intended to help the soul in its communion with God.   Its sententious statements are pitched in the highest key of Christian experience.   Within and through all its reflections runs the word, self-renunciation.   Its opening words, "whoso followeth me, shall not walk in darkness but shall have the light of life," John 8 : 12, are a fitting announcement of the contents.   The life of Christ is represented as the highest study it is possible for a mortal to take up.   He who has his spirit has found the hidden manna.   What can the world confer without Jesus?   To be without him is the direst hell; to be with him, the sweetest paradise.

Here are counsels to read the Scriptures, statements about the uses of adversity and advice for submission to authority, warnings against temptations, reflections upon death, the judgment and paradise.   Here are meditations on Christ's oblation on the cross and the advantages of the communion, and also admonitions to flee the vanities and emptiness of the world and to love God, for he that loveth, knoweth God.   Christ is more than all the wisdom of the schools.   He lifts up the mind in a moment of time to perceive more reasons for eternal truth than a student might learn over books in ten years.   He teaches without confusion of words, without the clashing of opinions, without the pride of reputation, — *sine fastu honoris*, — the contention of arguments.   The concluding words are : "My eyes are unto Thee.   My God, in Thee do I put my trust, O Thou Father of mercies.   Accompany thy servant with Thy grace and direct him by the path of peace to the land of unending light — *patriam perpetuæ claritatis*."

The plaintive minor key, the gently persuasive tone of the work are adapted to attract serious souls seeking the inner chamber of religious peace and purity of thought, but especially those who are under the shadow of pain and sorrow.   The praise of Christ is so unstinted, and the dependence upon him so unaffected, that one cannot help but feel, in reading this book, that he is partaking of the essence of the Gospel.   The work, however, presents only one side of the Christian life.   It commends humility, submission, gentleness and the passive virtues. It does not emphasize the manly virtues of courage and loyalty to the truth, nor elaborate upon Christian activities to be done to our fellow-men. To fall in completely with the spirit of Thomas à Kempis, and to abide there, would mean to follow the best cloistral ideal of the Middle Ages, or rather of the fourteenth century. Its counsels and reflections were meant primarily for those who had made the convent their home, not for the busy traffickers in the marts of the world, and in association with men of all classes. It leans to quietism, and is calculated to promote personal piety for those who dwell much alone rather than to fit men for engaging in the public battles which fall to men's usual lot. Its admonitions are adapted to help men to bear with patience rather than to rectify the evils in the world, to be silent rather than to speak to the throng, to live well in seclusion rather than set an example of manly and womanly endeavor in the shop, on the street and in the family. The charge has been made, and not without some ground, that the *Imitation of Christ* sets forth a selfish type of religion.[1] Its soft words are fitted to quiet the soul and bring it to meek contentment rather than to stir up the combatant virtues of courage and of assistance to others. Its message corresponds to the soft glow of the summer evening, and not to the fresh hours filled with the rays of the morning sun. This plaintive note runs through Thomas' hymns, as may be seen from a verse taken from " The Misery of this Life ": —

> Most wonderful would it be
> If one did not feel and lament
> That in this world to live
> Is toil, affliction, pain.[2]

---

[1] This is Milman's judgment. *Hist. of Lat. Christ.*, Bk. XIV., 3, Milman said, "The book's sole, single, exclusive object is the purification, the elevation of the individual soul, of the man absolutely isolated from his kind, of the man dwelling alone in the heritage of his thoughts."

> [2] *Mirum est, si non lugeat*
> *Experimento qui probat*
> *Quod vivere in sæculo*
> *Labor, dolor, afflictio.*

Blume and Dreves: *Analecta hymnica*, XLVIII. 503. Thomas à Kempis' hymns are given Blume and Dreves, XLVIII. 475–514.

Over the pages of the book is written the word Christ.   It is for this reason that Protestants cherish it as well as Catholics.   The references to mediæval errors of doctrine or practice are so rare that it requires diligent search to find them.   Such as they are, they are usually erased from English editions, so that the English reader misses them entirely. Thomas introduces the merit of good works, transubstantiation, IV. 2, the doctrine of purgatory, IV. 9, and the worship of saints, I. 13, II. 9, II. 6, 59.   But these statements, however, are like the flecks on the marbles of the Parthenon.

The author, Thomas à Kempis, 1380–1471, was born in Kempen, a town 40 miles northwest of Cologne, and died at Zwolle, in the Netherlands.   His paternal name was Hemerken or Hämmerlein, Little Hammer.   He was a follower of Groote.   In 1395, he was sent to the school of Deventer, under the charge of Florentius Radewyn and the Brothers of the Common Life.   He became skilful as a copyist, and was thus enabled to support himself.   Later he was admitted to the Augustinian convent of Mt. St. Agnes, near Zwolle, received priest's orders, 1413, and was made subprior, 1429.   His brother John, a man of rectitude of life, had been there before him, and was prior.   Thomas' life seems to have been a quiet one, devoted to meditation, composition and copying.   He copied the Bible no less than four times, one of the copies being preserved at Darmstadt.   His works abound in quotations of the New Testament.   Under an old picture, which is represented as his portrait, are the words, " In all things I sought quiet, and found it not save in retirement and in books."[1]   They fit well the author of the famous *Imitation of Christ*, as the world thinks of him.   He reached the high age of fourscore years and ten.   A monument was dedicated to his memory in the presence of the archbishop of Utrecht in St Michael's Church, Zwolle, Nov. 11, 1897. The writings of à Kempis, which are all of a devotional

---

[1] *In omnibus requiem quœsivi et non inveni nisi in een huechsken met een buexken.*   Franciscus Tolensis is the first to ascribe the portrait to à Kempis. Kettlewell's statements about à Kempis' active religious services are imaginary, I. 31, 322, etc.   See Lindsay's statement, *Enc. Brit.*, XIV. 32.

character, include tracts and meditations, letters, sermons, a Life of St. Lydewigis, a steadfast Christian woman who endured a great fight of afflictions, and the biographies of Groote, Florentius and nine of their companions.   Works similar to the *Imitation of Christ* are his prolonged meditation upon the Incarnation, and a meditation on the Life and Blessings of the Saviour,[1] both of which overflow with admiration for Christ.

In these writings the traces of mediæval theology, though they are found, are not obtrusive.   The writer followed his mediæval predecessors in the worship of Mary, of whom he says, she is to be invoked by all Christians, especially by monastics.[2]   He prays to her as the "most merciful," the "most glorious" mother of God, and calls her the queen of heaven, the efficient mediatrix of the whole world, the joy and delight of all the saints, yea, the golden couch for all the saints.   She is the chamber of God, the gate of heaven, the paradise of delights, the well of graces, the glory of the angels, the joy of men, the model of manners, the brightness of virtues, the lamp of life, the hope of the needy, the salvation of the weak, the mother of the orphaned.   To her all should flee as sons to a mother's bosom.[3]

From these tender praises of Mary it is pleasant to turn away to the code of twenty-three precepts which the Dutch mystic laid down under the title, *A Small Alphabet for a Monk in the School of God*.[4]   Here are some of them. Love to be unknown and to be reputed as nothing.   Love solitude and silence, and thou wilt find great quiet and a good conscience.   Where the crowd is, there is usually confusion and distraction of heart.   Choose poverty and simplicity.   Humble thyself in all things and under all things, and thou wilt merit kindness from all.   Let Christ be thy life, thy reading, thy meditation, thy conversation, thy desire, thy gain, thy hope and thy reward.   Zaccheus, brother, descend

---

[1] Pohl's ed., II. 1–59 ; V. 1–363.

[2] *De disciplina claustralium,* Pohl's ed., II. 313.   For prayers to Mary III. 355–368 and sermons on Mary, VI. 218–238.

[3] Pohl, III. 357; VI. 219, 235 sq.   [4] III. 317–322.

from the height of thy secular wisdom.   Come and learn in God's school the way of humility, long-suffering and patience, and Christ teaching thee, thou shalt come at last safely to the glory of eternal beatitude.

NOTE. — THE AUTHORSHIP OF THE IMITATION OF CHRIST. This question has been one of the most hotly contested questions in the history of pure literature.   National sentiments have entered into the discussion, France and Italy contending for the honor of authorship with the Lowlands.   The work is now quite generally ascribed to Thomas à Kempis, but among those who dissent from this opinion are scholars of rank.

Among the more recent treatments of the subject not given in the Literature, § 27, are V. BECKER : *L'auteur de l'Imitat. et les documents néerlandais*, Hague, 1882.   Also *Les derniers travaux sur l'auteur de l'Imitat.*, Brussels, 1889. — DENIFLE : *Krit. Bemerk. zur Gersen-Kempis Frage, Zeitung für kath. Theol.*, 1882 sq. — A. O. SPITZEN : *Th. à K. als schrijver der navolging*, Utrecht, 1880.   Also *Nouvelle défense en réponse du Denifle*, Utrecht, 1884. — L. SANTINI : *I diritti di Tommaso da Kemp.*, 2 vols., Rome, 1879–1881. — F. X. FUNK : *Gerson und Gersen* and *Der Verfasser der Nachfolge Christi* in his *Abhandlungen*, Paderborn, 1899, II. 373–444. — P. E. PUYOL : *Descript. bibliogr. des MSS. et des princip. edd. du livre de imitat.*, Paris, 1898.   Also *Paléographie, classement, généalogie du livre de imitat.*, Paris, 1898.   Also *L'auteur du livre de imitat.*, 2 vols., Paris, 1899. — SCHULZE'S art. in HERZOG. — G. KENTENICH : *Die Handschriften der Imitat. und die Autorschaft des Thomas*, in *Brieger's Zeitschrift*, 1902, 18 sqq., 1903, 594 sqq.

Pohl gives a list of no less than 35 persons to whom with more or less confidence the authorship has been ascribed.   The list includes the names of John Gerson, chancellor of the University of Paris ; John Gersen, the reputed abbot of Vercelli, Italy, who lived about 1230 ; Walter Hylton, St. Bernard, Bonaventura, David of Augsburg, Tauler, Suso and even Innocent III.   The only claimants worthy of consideration are Gerson, Gersen, and Thomas à Kempis, although Montmorency is inclined to advance the claim of Walter Hylton.   The uncertainty arises from the facts (1) that a number of the MSS. and printed editions of the fifteenth century have no note of authorship ; (2) the rest are divided between these, Gerson, Gersen, à Kempis, Hylton, and St. Bernard ; (3) the MSS. copies show important divergencies. The matter has been made more difficult by the forgery of names and dates in MSS. since the controversy began, these forgeries being almost entirely in the interest of a French or Italian authorship.   A reason for the absence of the author's name in so many MSS. is found in the desire of à Kempis, if he indeed be the author, to remain incognito, in accordance with his own motto, *ama nesciri*, "love to be unknown."

Of the Latin editions belonging to the fifteenth century, Pohl gives 28 as accredited to Gerson, 12 to Thomas, 2 to St. Bernard, and 6 as anonymous. Or, to follow Funk, p. 426, 40 editions of that century were ascribed to Gerson, 11 to à Kempis, 2 to Bernard, 1 to Gersen, and 2 are anonymous.   Spitzen gives 15 as ascribed to à Kempis.   Most of the editions ascribing the work to Gerson were printed in France, the remaining editions being printed in Italy or Spain. The editions of the sixteenth century show a change, 37 Latin editions ascribing the authorship to à Kempis, and 25 to Gerson. As for the MSS. dated before 1450, and whose dates may be said to be reasonably above suspicion, all were written in Germany and the Lowlands. The oldest, included in a codex preserved since 1826 in the royal library of Brussels, probably belongs before 1420. The codex contains 9 other writings of à Kempis besides the *Imitation*, and contains the note, *Finitus et completus MCCCCXLI per manus fratris Th. Kempensis in Monte S. Agnetis prope Zwollis* (finished and completed, 1441, by the hands of brother Thomas à Kempis of Mount St. Agnes, near Zwolle). See Pohl, II. 461 sqq. So this is an autographic copy. The text of the *Imitation*, however, is written on older paper than the other documents, and has corrections which are found in a Dutch translation of the first book, dating from 1420. For these reasons, Funk, p. 424, and others, puts the MS. back to 1416–1420.

The literary controversy over the authorship began in 1604, when Dom Pedro Manriquez, in a work on the Lord's Supper issued at Milan, and on the alleged basis of a quotation by Bonaventura, declared the *Imitation* to be older than that Schoolman. In 1606, Bellarmin, in his *Descript. eccles.*, was more precise, and stated it was already in existence in 1260. About the same time, the Jesuit, Rossignoli, found in a convent at Arona, near Milan, a MS. without date, but bearing the name of an abbot, John Gersen, as its author; the house had belonged to the Benedictines once. In 1614 the Benedictine, Constantius Cajetan, secretary of Paul V., issued his *Gersen restitutus* at Rome, and later his *Apparatus ad Gersenem restitutum*, in which he defended the Italian's claim. This individual was said to have been a Benedictine abbot of Vercelli, in Piedmont, in the first half of the thirteenth century. On the other hand, the Augustinian, Rosweyde, in his *vindiciæ Kempenses*, Antwerp, 1617, so cogently defended the claims of à Kempis that Bellarmin withdrew his statement. In the nineteenth century the claims of Gersen were again urged by a Piedmontese nobleman, Gregory, in his *Istoria della Vercellese letteratura*, Turin, 1819, and subsequent publications, and by Wolfsgruber of Vienna in a scholarly work, 1880. But Hirsche and Funk are, no doubt, right in pronouncing the name Gersen a mistake for Gerson, and Funk, after careful criticism, declares the Italian abbot a fictitious personage. The most recent Engl. writer on the subject, Montmorenciy, p. xiii, says, "there is no evidence that there was ever an abbot of Vercelli by the name of Gersen."

The claims of John Gerson are of a substantial character, and France was not slow in coming to the chancellor's defence. An examination of old MSS., made in Paris, had an uncertain issue, so that, in 1640, Richelieu's splendid edition of the *Imitation* was sent forth without an author's name. The French parliament, however, in 1652, ordered the book printed under the name of à Kempis. The matter was not settled and, at three gatherings, 1671, 1674, 1687, instituted by Mabillon, a fresh examination of MSS. was made, with the result that the case went against à Kempis. Later, Du Pin, after a comparison of Gerson's writings with the *Imitation*, concluded that it was impossible to decide with certainty between these two writers and Gersen. (See his 2d ed. of Gerson's Works, 1728, I. lix–lxxxiv); but in a special work, Amsterdam, 1706, he had decided in favor of the Dutchman. French editions of the *Imitation* continued to be issued under the name of Gerson, as, for example, those of Erhard-Mezler, 1724, and Vollardt, 1758. On the other hand, the Augustinian, Amort, defended the à Kempis authorship in his *Informatio de statu controversiæ*, Augsburg, 1728, and especially in his *Scutum Kempense*, Cologne, 1728.   After the unfavorable statement of Schwab, *Life of Gerson*, 1858, pp. 782-786, declaring that the *Imitation* is in an altogether different style from Gerson's works, the theory of the Gerson authorship seemed to be finally abandoned.   The first collected edition of Gerson's Works, 1483, knows nothing about the *Imitation*.   Nor did Gerson's brother, prior of Lyons, mention it in the list he gave of the chancellor's works, 1423.   The author of the *Imitation* was, by his own statements, a monk, IV. 5, 11 ; III., 56.   Gerson would have been obliged to change his usual habit of presentation to have written in the monastic tone.

After the question of authorship seemed to be pretty well settled in favor of à Kempis, another stage in the controversy was opened by the publications of Puyol in 1898, 1899.   Puyol gives a description of 348 manuscripts, and makes a sharp distinction between those of Italian origin and other manuscripts.   He also annotates the variations in 57, with the conclusion that the Italian text is the more simple, and consequently the older and original text. He himself based his edition on the text of Arona.   Puyol is followed by Kentenich, and has been answered by Pohl and others.

Walter Hylton's reputed authorship of the *Imitation* is based upon three books of that work, having gone under the name *De musica ecclesiastica* in MSS. in England and the persistent English tradition that Hylton was the author.   Montmorency, pp. xiv, 138-170, while he pronounces the Hylton theory of authorship untenable, confesses his inability to explain it.

The arguments in favor of the à Kempis authorship, briefly stated, are as follows : —

1. External testimony.   John Busch, in his *Chronicon Windesemense*, written 1464, seven years before à Kempis' death, expressly states that à Kempis wrote the *Imitation*.   To this testimony are to be added the testimonies of Caspar of Pforzheim, who made a German translation of the work, 1448 ; Hermann Rheyd, who met Thomas, 1454, and John Wessel, who was attracted to Windesheim by the book's fame.   For other testimonies, see Hirsche and Funk, pp. 432-436.

2. Manuscripts and editions.   The number of extant MSS. is about 500. See Kentenich, p. 294.   Funk, p. 420, gives 13 MSS. dated before 1500, ascribing the *Imitation* to à Kempis.   The autograph copy, contained in the Brussels codex of 1441, has already been mentioned.   It must be said, however, the conclusion reached by Hirsche, Pohl, Funk, Schulze and others that this text is autographic has been denied by Puyol and Kentenich, on the basis of its divergences from other copies, which they claim the author could not have made.   A second autograph, in Louvaine (see Schulze, p. 730), seems to be nearly as old, 1420, and has the note *scriptus manibus et characteribus Thomæ qui est autor horum devotorum libellorum*, "written by the hand of Thomas," etc. (Pohl, VI. 456 sq.).   A third MS., stating that Thomas is the author, and preserved in Brussels, is dated 1425. — As for the

printed editions of the fifteenth century, at least 13 present Thomas as the author, from the edition of Augsburg, 1472, to the editions of Paris, 1493, 1500.

3. Style and contents.   These agree closely with à Kempis' other writings, and the flow of thought is altogether similar to that of his *Meditation on Christ's Incarnation*.   Spitzen seems to have made it at least very probable that the author was acquainted with the writings of Ruysbroeck, John of Schoenhoven, and other mystics and monks of the Lowlands.   Funk has brought out references to ecclesiastical customs which fit the book into the time between the fourteenth and fifteenth centuries.   Hirsche laid stress on Germanisms in the style.

Among recent German scholars, Denifle sets aside à Kempis' claims and ascribes the work to some unknown canon regular of the Lowlands.   Karl Müller, in a brief note, *Kirchengesch.*, II. 122, and Loof's *Dogmengesch.*, 4th ed., p. 633, pronounce the à Kempis authorship more than doubtful. On the other hand, Schwab, Hirsche, Schulze and Funk agree that the claims of Thomas are almost beyond dispute.   It is almost impossible to give a reason why the *Imitation* should have been ascribed to the Dutch mystic, if he were not indeed its author.   The explanation given by Kentenich, p. 603, seems to be utterly insufficient.

§ 36. *The German Theology.*

The evangelical teachings of the little book, known as *The German Theology*, led Ullmann to place its author in the list of the Reformers before the Reformation.[1]   The author was one of the Friends of God, and no writing issuing from that circle has had a more honorable and useful career.   Together with the *Imitation of Christ*, it has been the most profitable of the writings of the German mystics.   Its fame is derived from Luther's high praise as much as from its own excellent contents.   The Reformer issued two editions of it, 1516, with a partial text, and 1518, in the second edition giving it the name which remains with it to this day, *Ein Deutsch Theologia* — A German treatise of Theology.[2]   Luther desig-

---

[1] The best German ed., Stuttgart, 1858.   The text is taken from Pfeiffer's ed., Strassburg, 1851, 3d ed. unchanged ; Gütersloh, 1875, containing Luther's Preface of 1518 and the Preface of Joh. Arndt, 1632.   Pfeiffer used the MS. dated 1497, the oldest in existence.   The best Engl. trans., by Susannah Winkworth, from Pfeiffer's text, London, 1854, Andover, 1856.   The Andover ed. contains an Introd. by Miss Winkworth, a Letter from Chevalier Bunsen and Prefaces by Canon Kingsley and Prof. Calvin E. Stowe.

[2] Luther's full title in the ed. of 1518 is *Ein Deutsch Theologia, das ist ein edles Büchlein vom rechten Verstande was Adam und Christus sei und wie*

nated as its author a Frankfurt priest, a Teutonic knight, but
for a time it was ascribed to Tauler. The Preface of the
oldest MS., dated 1497, and found in 1850, made this view
impossible, for Tauler is himself quoted in ch. XIII. Here
the author is called a Frankfurt priest and a true Friend of
God.

Luther announced his high obligation to the teachings of
the manual of the way of salvation when he said that next
to the Bible and St. Augustine, no book had come into his
hands from which he had learnt more of what God and man
and all things are and would wish to learn more. The author,
he affirmed, was a pure Israelite who did not take the foam
from the surface, but drew from the bed of the Jordan. Here,
he continued, the teachings of the Scriptures are set forth as
plain as day which have been lying under the desk of the
universities, nay, have almost been left to rot in dust and
muck. With his usual patriotism, he declared that in the
book he had found Christ in the German tongue as he and the
other German theologians had never found him in Greek,
Latin or Hebrew.

The German Theology sets forth man's sinful and helpless
condition, Christ's perfection and mediatorial work and calls
upon men to have access to God through him as the door.
In all its fifty-four chapters no reference is made to Mary or
to the justifying nature of good works or the merit of sacramental observances.[1] It abounds as no other writing of the
German mystics did in quotations from the New Testament.
In its pages the wayfaring man may find the path of salvation
marked out without mystification.

The book, starting out with the words of St. Paul, " when
that which is perfect is come, then that which is in part shall be

Adam in uns sterben und Christus in uns erstehen soll. A German the-
ology, that is, a right noble little book about the right comprehension of what
Adam and Christ are, and how Adam is to die in us and Christ is to arise.
Cohrs in Herzog, XIX. 626, mentions 28 editions as having appeared in High
German previous to 1742. Luther's Prefaces are given in the Weimar ed. of
his Works, pp. 153, 376–378.

[1] Dr. Calvin E. Stowe said " the book sets forth the essential principle of
the Gospel in its naked simplicity," Winkworth's ed., p. v.

done away," declares that that which is imperfect has only
a relative existence and that, whenever the Perfect becomes
known by the creature, then "the I, the Self and the like
must all be given up and done away." Christ shows us
the way by having taken on him human nature. In chs.
XV.–LIV., it shows that all men are dead in Adam, and that
to come to the perfect life, the old man must die and the new
man be born. He must become possessed with God and de-
possessed of the devil. Obedience is the prime requisite of
the new manhood. Sin is disobedience, and the more " of
Self and Me, the more of sin and wickedness and the more
the Self, the I, the Me, the Mine, that is, self-seeking and selfishness, abate in a man, the more doth God's I, that is, God
Himself, increase." By obedience we become free. The life
of Christ is the perfect model, and we follow him by heark-
ening unto his words to forsake all. This is nothing else than
saying that we must be in union with the divine will and be
ready either to do or to suffer. Such a man, a man who is a
partaker of the divine nature, will in sincerity love all men
and things, do them good and take pleasure in their welfare.
Knowledge and light profit nothing without love. Love
maketh a man one with God. The last word is that no man
can come unto the Father but by Christ.

In 1621 the Catholic Church placed the *Theologia Germanica* on the Index. If all the volumes listed in that catalogue
of forbidden books were like this one, making the way of
salvation plain, its pages would be illuminated with ineffable
light.[1]

§ 37. *English Mystics.*

England, in the fourteenth century, produced devotional
writings which have been classed in the literature of mysticism. They are wanting in the transcendental flights of
the German mystics, and are, for the most part, marked by
a decided practical tendency.

---

[1] Stöckl and other Catholics, though not all, are bitter against the *Theologia*
and charge it with pantheism. Bunsen ranked it next to the Bible. Winkworth's ed., p. liv.

The *Ancren Riwle* was written for three sisters who lived as anchoresses at Tarrant Kaines, Dorsetshire.[1] It was the custom in their day in England for women living a recluse life to build a room against the wall of some church or a small structure in a churchyard and in such a way that it had windows, but no doors of egress. This little book of religious counsels was written at the request of the sisters, and is usually ascribed to Simon of Ghent, bishop of Salisbury, d. 1315. The author gives two general directions, namely, to keep the heart "smooth and without any scar of evil," and to practise bodily discipline, which "serveth the first end, and of which Paul said that it profiteth little." The first is the lady, the second the handmaid. If asked to what order they belonged, the sisters were instructed to say to the Order of St. James, for James said, " Pure religion and undefiled before our God and Father is this : to visit the fatherless and widows in their affliction and to keep one's self unspotted from the world." It is interesting to note that they are bidden to have warm clothes for bed and back, and to wash "as often as they please." They were forbidden to lash themselves with a leathern thong, or one loaded with lead except at the advice of their confessor. Richard Rolle, d. 1349, the author of a number of devotional treatises, and also translations or paraphrases of the Psalms, Job, the Canticles and Jeremiah, suddenly left Oxford, where he was pursuing his studies, discontented with the scholastic method in vogue at the university, and finally settled down as a hermit at Hampole, near Doncaster. Here he attained a high fame for piety and as a worker of miracles. He wrote in Latin and English, his chief works being the Latin treatises, *The Emendation of Life* and *The Fervor of Love*. They were translated in 1434, 1435, by Rich Misyn. His works are extant in many manuscript copies. Rolle exalted the contemplative life, indulged in much dreamy religious speculation, but also denounced the vice and worldliness of his time. In the last state of the contemplative

---

[1] *The Ancren Riwle*, ed. by J. Morton, Camden series, London, 1853. See W. R. Inge, *Studies in Engl. Mystics*, London, 1906, p. 38 sqq.

life he represents man as "seeing into heaven with his ghostly eye."[1]

Juliana of Norwich, who died 1443, as it is said, at the age of 100, was also an anchoress, having her cell in the churchyard of St. Julian's church, Norwich. She received 16 revelations, the first in 1373, when she was 30 years old. At that time, she saw "God in a point." She laid stress upon love, and presented the joyful aspect of religion. God revealed Himself to her in three properties, life, light and love. Her account of her revelations is pronounced by Inge "a fragrant little book."[2]

The Ladder of Perfection, written by Walter Hylton, an Augustinian canon of Thurgarton, Nottinghamshire, who died 1396,[3] depicts the different stages of spiritual attainment from the simple knowledge of the facts of religion, which is likened to the water of Cana which must be turned into wine, to the last stages of contemplation and divine union. There is no great excellency, Hylton says, "in watching and fasting till thy head aches, nor in running to Rome or Jerusalem with bare feet, nor in building churches and hospitals." But it is a sign of excellency if a man can love a sinner, while hating the sin. Those who are not content with merely saving their souls, but go on to the higher degrees of contemplation, are overcome by "a good darkness," a state in which the soul is free and not distracted by anything earthly. The light then arises little by little. Flashes come through the chinks in the walls of Jerusalem, but Jerusalem is not reached by a bound. There must be transformation, and the power that transforms is the love of God shed

---

[1] C. Horstman, *Richard Rolle of Hampole,* 2 vols. The Early Engl. Text Soc. publ. the Engl. versions of Misyn, 1896. G. G. Perry edited his liturgy in the vol. giving the York Breviary, Surtees Soc. The poem, *Pricke of Conscience,* was issued by H. R. Bramley, Oxford, 1884. See Stephen, *Dict. Natl. Biog.* XLIX. 164–165.

[2] *The Revelations of Divine Love* has been ed. by R. F. S. Cressy, London, 1670, reprinted 1843; by H. Collins, London, 1817, and by Grace Warrack. 3d ed. Lond., 1909. See Inge and *Dict. of Natl. Biog.*

[3] Written in English, the *Ladder* was translated by the Carmelite friar, Thomas Fyslawe, into Latin. Hylton's death is also put in 1433.

abroad in the soul.   Love proceeds from knowledge, and the
more God is known, the more is He loved.   Hylton's wide
reputation is proved by the ascription of Thomas à Kempis' *Imitation* to him and its identification in manuscripts with
his *De musica ecclesiastica*.[1]

These writings, if we except Rolle, betray much of that
sobriety of temper which characterizes the English religious
thought.   They contain no flights of hazy mystification and
no rapturous outbursts of passionate feeling.   They emphasize features common to all the mystics of the later Middle Ages, the gradual transformation through the power of
love into the image of God, and ascent through inward contemplation to full fellowship with Him.   They show that the
principles of the imitation of Christ were understood on the
English side of the channel as well as by the mystics of the
Lowlands, and that true godliness is to be reached in another
way than by the mere practice of sacramental rites.

These English pietists are to be regarded, however, as isolated figures who, so far as we know, had no influence in
preparing the soil for the seed of the Reformation that was
to come, as had the pietists who lived along the Rhine.[2]

[1] *The Ladder of Perfection* was printed 1494, 1506, and has been recently
ed. by R. E. Guy, London, 1869, and J. B. Dalgairns, London, 1870.   See Inge,
pp. 81–124 ; Montmorency, *Thomas à Kempis*, etc., pp. 138–174 ; and *Dict. of
Natl. Biog.*, XXVI. 435 sqq.

[2] Montmorency, p. 69, makes a remark for which, so far as I know, there
is no corroborative testimony in the writings of the English Reformers, that
" in this English mystical movement — of which a vast unprinted literature
survives — is to be found the origin of Lollardism and of the Reformation in
England."

CHAPTER V.

REFORMERS BEFORE THE REFORMATION.

§ 38. *Sources and Literature.*

For § 39. CHURCH AND SOCIETY IN ENGLAND, ETC. — THOMAS WALSINGHAM: *Hist. Anglicana,* ed. by RILEY, Rolls Ser., London, 1869. — WALTER DE HEIMBURGH: *Chronicon,* ed. by HAMILTON, 2 vols., 1848 sq. — ADAM MERIMUTH: *Chronicon,* and ROBT. DE AVESBURY: *De gestis mirabilibus Edwardi III.,* ed. by THOMPSON with Introd., Rolls Ser., 1889. — *Chron. Angliæ* (1326–1388), ed. by THOMPSON, Rolls Ser., 1874. — HENRY KNIGHTON: *Chronicon,* ed. by LUMBY, Rolls Ser., 2 vols., 1895. — RANULPH HIGDEN, d. bef. 1400: *Polychronicon,* with trans. by TREVISA, Rolls Ser., 9 vols., 1865–1886. — THOS. RYMER, d. 1713: *Fœdera, Conventiones et Litera,* London, 1704–1715. — WILKINS: *Concilia.* — W. C. BLISS: *Calendar of Entries in the Papal Registers relating to G. Britain and Ireland,* vols. II.–IV., London, 1897–1902. Vol. II. extends from 1305–1342; vol. III., 1342–1362; vol. IV., 1362–1404. A work of great value. — GEE and HARDY: *Documents,* etc. — HADDAN and STUBBS: *Councils and Eccles. Doc'ts.* — STUBBS: *Constit. Hist. of Engl.,* III. 294–387. — The *Histt. of Engl.,* by LINGARD, bks. III., IV., and GREEN, bk. IV. — CAPES: *The Engl. Ch. in the 14th and 15th Centt.,* London, 1900. — HALLER: *Papsttum und Kirchenreform,* pp. 375–465. — JESSOPP: *The Coming of the Friars.* — CREIGHTON: *Hist. of Epidemics in England.* — GASQUET: *The Great Pestilence,* 1893. — RASHDALL and others: *Histt. of Oxford and Cambridge.* — The *Dict. of Nat. Biog.* — Also THOS. FULLER's *Hist. of Gr. Brit.,* for its general judgments and quaint statements. — LOSERTH: *Studien zur Kirchenpolitik Englands im 14 Jahrh.* in *Sitzungsberichte d. kaiserl. Akademie d. Wissenschaften in Wien,* Vienna, 1897. — G. KRIEHN: *Studies in the Sources of the Social Revol. of 1381,* Am. Hist. Rev., Jan.–Oct., 1902. — C. OMAN: *The Great Revolt in 1381,* Oxford, 1906. — TRAILL: *Social Engl.,* vol. II., London, 1894. — ROGERS: *Six Centt. of Work and Wages.* — CUNNINGHAM: *Growth of Engl. Industry.*

For §§ 40–42. JOHN WYCLIF. — I. The publication of Wyclif's works belongs almost wholly to the last twenty-five years, and began with the creation of the Wyclif Society, 1882, which was due to a summons from German scholars. In 1858, Shirley, *Fasc.,* p. xlvi, could write, "Of Wyc's Engl. writings nothing but two short tracts have seen the light," and in 1883, Loserth spoke of his tráctates "mouldering in the dust." The MSS. are found for the most part in the libraries of Oxford, Prag and Vienna. The *Trialogus* was publ. Basel, 1525, and *Wycliffe's Wycket,* in Engl., Nürnberg, 1546. Reprinted at Oxford, 1828. — Latin Works, ed. by the Wyclif Soc., organized, 1882, in answer to Buddensieg's appeal in the *Academy,* Sept. 17,

1881, 31 vols., London, 1884–1907. — *De officio pastorali*, ed. by LECHLER, Leipzig, 1863. — *Trialogus*, ed. by LECHLER, Oxford, 1869. — *De veritate sac. Scripturæ*, ed. by RUDOLF BUDDENSIEG, 3 vols., Leipzig, 1904. — *De potestate papae*, ed. by LOSERTH, London, 1907. — Engl. Works : *Three Treatises*, by J. WYCLIFFE, ed. by J. H. TODD, Dublin, 1851. — * *Select Engl. Works*, ed. by THOS. ARNOLD, 3 vols., Oxford, 1869–1871. — * *Engl. Works Hitherto Unprinted*, ed. by F. D. MATTHEW, London, 1880, with valuable Introd. — * WYCLIF's trans. of the Bible, ed. by FORSHALL and MADDEN, 4 vols., Oxford, 1850. — His New Test. with *Introd. and Glossary*, by W. W. SKEAT, Cambridge, 1879. — The trans. of Job, Pss., Prov., Eccles. and Canticles, Cambridge, 1881. — For list of Wyclif's works, see CANON W. W. SHIRLEY : *Cat. of the Works of J. W.*, Oxford, 1865. He lists 96 Latin and 65 Engl. writings. — Also LECHLER in his *Life of Wiclif*, II. 559–573, Engl. trans., pp. 483–498. — Also Rashdall's list in *Dict. of Nat. Biog.* — II. Biographical. — THOMAS NETTER of Walden, a Carmelite, d. 1430 : *Fasciculi zizaniorum Magistri Joh. Wyclif cum tritico* (Bundles of tares of J. Wyc. with the wheat), a collection of indispensable documents and narrations, ed. by SHIRLEY, with valuable Introd., Rolls Ser., London, 1858. — Also *Doctrinale fidei christianæ adv. Wicleffitas et Hussitas* in his *Opera*, Paris, 1532, best ed., 3 vols., Venice, 1757. Walden could discern no defects in the friars, and represented the opposite extreme from Wyclif. He sat in the Council of Pisa, was provincial of his order in England, and confessor to Henry V. — The contemporary works given above, *Chron. Angliæ, Walsingham, Knighton,* etc. — *England in the Time of Wycliffe* in trans. and reprints, Dept. of Hist. Univ. of Pa., 1895. — JOHN FOXE : *Book of Martyrs*, London, 1632, etc. — JOHN LEWIS : *Hist. of the Life and Sufferings of J. W.*, Oxford, 1720, etc., and 1820. — R. VAUGHAN : *Life and Opinions of J. de Wycliffe*, 2 vols., London, 1828, 2d ed., 1831. — V. LECHLER : *J. von Wiclif und die Vorgesch. der Reformation*, 2 vols., Leipzig, 1873. — * Engl. trans., *J. W. and his Engl. Precursors*, with valuable Notes by PETER LORIMER, 2 vols., London, 1878, new edd., 1 vol., 1881, 1884. — * R. BUDDENSIEG : *J. Wiclif und seine Zeit*, Gotha, 1883. Also *J. W. as Patriot and Reformer*, London, 1884. — E. S. HOLT : *J. de W., the First Reformer, and what he did for England*, London, 1884. — V. VATTIER : *J. W., sa vie, ses œuvres et sa doctrine*, Paris, 1886. — * J. LOSERTH : *Hus und Wiclif*, Prag and Leipzig, 1883, Engl. trans., London, 1884. Also *W.'s Lehre v. wahrem u. falschem Papsttum*, in *Hist. Zeitschrift*, 1907, p. 237 sqq. — L. SERGEANT : *John Wyclif*, New York, 1893. — H. B. WORKMAN : *The Age of Wyclif*, London, 1901. — GEO. S. INNES : *J. W.*, Cin'ti. — J. C. CARRICK : *Wyc. and the Lollards*, London, 1908. — C. BIGG, in *Wayside Sketches in Eccles. Hist.*, London, 1906. — For other *Biogg.*, see SHIRLEY : *Fasciculus*, p. 531 sqq. — III. J. L. POOLE : *W. and Movements for Reform*, London, 1889, and *W.'s Doctr. of Lordship in Illustr. of Med. Thought*, 1884. — WIEGAND : *De eccles. notione quid Wiclif docuerit*, Leipzig, 1891. — * G. M. TREVELYAN : *Engl. in the Age of W.*, London, 2d ed., 1899. — POWELL and TREVELYAN : *The Peasants' Rising and the Lollards*, London, 1899. — H. FÜRSTENAU : *J. von W.'s Lehren v. d. Stellung d. weltl. Gewalt*, Berlin, 1900. — HADDAN and STUBBS : *Councils and Eccles. Docts.* — GEE and HARDY. — STUBBS : *Constit. Hist.*, III. 314–374. — The Histt. of CAPES, GREEN and

LINGARD, vol. IV.—The *Histt. of the Engl. Bible*, by EADIE, WESTCOTT, MOULTON, STOUGHTON, MOMBERT, etc. — MATTHEW : *Authorship of the Wycliffite Bible*, Engl. Hist. Rev., January, 1895. — GASQUET : *The Eve of the Reformation*, new ed., London, 1905 ; *The Old Engl. Bible and Other Essays*, London, 1908. — R. S. STORRS : *J. Wyc. and the First Engl. Bible* in *Sermons and Addresses*, Boston, 1902. An eloquent address delivered in New York on the 500th anniversary of the appearance of Wyclif's New Test. — RASHDALL in *Dict. of Natl. Biog.*, LXIII. 202–223. — G. S. INNIS: *Wycliffe* Cin[ti].

For § 43. LOLLARDS. — The works noted above of KNIGHTON, WALSINGHAM, RYMER'S *Fœdera*, the *Chron. Angliœ*, WALDEN'S *Fasc. ziz.*, FOXE's *Book of Martyrs*. Also ADAM USK : *Chronicle.* — THOS. WRIGHT : *Polit. Poems and Songs*, Rolls Ser., 2 vols., London, 1859. — FREDERICQ : *Corp. inquis. Neerl.*, vols. I.–III. — REGINALD PECOCK : *The Repressor of overmuch Blaming of the Clergy*, ed. by BABINGTON, Rolls Ser., 2 vols., London, 1860. — *The Histt. of Engl. and the Church of Engl.* — A. M. BROWN : *Leaders of the Lollards*, London, 1848. — W. H. SUMMERS : *Our Lollard Ancestors*, London, 1904. — *JAMES GAIRDNER : *Lollardy and the Reform. in Engl.*, 2 vols., London, 1908. — E. P. CHEYNEY : *The Recantations of the Early Lollards*, Am. Hist. Rev., April, 1899. — H. S. CRONIN : *The Twelve Conclusions of the Lollards*, Engl. Hist. Rev., April, 1907. — Art. *Lollarden*, by BUDDENSIEG in HERZOG, XI. 615–626. — The works of TREVELYAN and FORSHALL and MADDEN, cited above, and *Oldcastle*, vol. XLII. 86–93, and other artt. in *Dict. of Nat. Biog.*

For §§ 44–46. JOHN HUSS. — *Hist. et monumenta J. Hus atque Hieronymi Pragensis, confessorum Christi*, 2 vols., Nürnberg, 1558, Frankfurt, 1715. I have used the Frankfurt ed. — W. FLAJSHANS : *Mag. J. Hus Expositio Decalogi*, Prag, 1903 ; *De corpore Christi : De sanguine Christi*, Prag, 1904 ; *Sermones de sanctis*, Prag, 1908 ; *Super quatuor sententiarum*, etc. — *FRANCIS PALACKY : *Documenta Mag. J. Hus, vitam, doctrinam, causam in Constantiensi actam consilio illustrantia, 1403–1418*, pp. 768, Prag, 1869. Largely from unpublished sources. Contains the account of Peter of Mladenowitz, who was with Huss at Constance. — K. J. ERBEN (archivarius of Prag) : *Mistra Jana Husi sebrané spisy Czeske.* A collection of Huss' Bohemian writings, 3 vols., Prag, 1865–1868. — Trans. of Huss' *Letters*, first by LUTHER, Wittenberg, 1536 (four of them, together with an account by Luther of Huss' trial and death), republ. by C. VON KÜGELGEN, Leipzig, 1902. — MACKENZIE : *Huss' Letters*, Edinburgh, 1846. — * H. B. WORKMAN and R. M. POPE : *Letters of J. Hus with Notes.* — For works on the Council of Constance, see MANSI, vol. XXVIII., VAN DER HARDT, FINKE, RICHENTAL, etc., see § 12. — C. VON HÖFLER: *Geschichtsschreiber der hussitischen Bewegung*, 3 vols., Vienna, 1856–1866. Contains Mladenowitz and other contemporary documents. — * PALACKY, a descendant of the Bohemian Brethren, d. 1876 : *Geschichte von Böhmen*, Prag, 1836 sqq., 3d ed., 5 vols., 1864 sqq. Vol. III. of the first ed. was mutilated at Vienna by the censor of the press (the office not being abolished till 1848), on account of the true light in which Huss was placed. Nevertheless, it made such an impression that Baron Helfert was commissioned to write a reply, which appeared, Prag, 1857, pp. 287. In 1870, Palacky publ. a second ed. of vol. III., containing all the excerpted parts.

—Palacky : *Die Vorläufer des Hussitenthums in Böhmen*, Prag, 1869. — L. Köhler : *J. Hus u. s. Zeit*, 3 vols., Leipzig, 1846. — E. H. Gillett, Prof. in New York Univ., d. New York, 1875 : *Life and Times of J. Huss*, 2 vols., Boston, 1863, 3d ed., 1871. — W. Berger : *J. Hus u. König Sigismund*, Augsburg, 1871. — Bonnechose : *J. Hus u. das Concil zu Kostnitz*, Germ. trans., 3d ed., Leipzig, 1870. — F. v. Bezold : *Zur Gesch. d. Husitenthums*, Munich, 1874. — E. Denis : *Huss et la guerre des Hussites*, Paris, 1878. — A. H. Wratislaw : *J. Hus*, London, 1882. — *J. Loserth : *Wiclif and Hus*, also *Beiträge zur Gesch. der Hussit. Bewegung*, 5 small vols., 1877-1895, reprinted from magazines. Also Introd. to his ed. of Wiclif's *De ecclesia.* Also art. *J. Huss* in Herzog, Encyc., VIII. 473-489. — Lechler : *J. Hus*, Leipzig, 1890. — *J. H. Wylie : *The Counc. of Constance to the Death of J. Hus*, London, 1900. — * H. B. Workman : *The Dawn of the Reformation, The Age of Hus*, London, 1902. — Lea : *Hist. of the Inquis.*, II. 431-566. — Hefele, vol. VII. — * J. B. Schwab : *J. Gerson*, pp. 527-609. — Tschackert : *Von Ailli*, pp. 218-235. — W. Faber and J. Kurth : *Wie sah Hus aus?* Berlin, 1907. — Also *J. Huss* by Lützow, N.Y., 1909, and Kuhr, Cin[ti].

For § 47. The Hussites. — Mansi, XXVII, XXIX. — Haller : *Concil. Basiliense.* — Bezold : *König Sigismund und d. Reichskriege gegen d. Husiten*, 3 vols, Munich, 1872-1877. — *Jaroslav Goll : *Quellen und Untersuchungen zur Gesch. der Böhmischen Brüder*, 2 vols., Prag, 1878-1882. — * L. Keller : *Die Reformation und die älteren Reformparteien*, Leipzig, 1885. — W. Preger : *Ueber das Verhältniss der Taboriten zu den Waldesiern des 14ten Jahrh.*, 1887. — Haupt : *Waldenserthum und Inquisition im südöstlichen Deutschland*, Freiburg i. Br., 1890. — H. Herre : *Die Husitenverhandlungen, 1429*, in *Quellen u. Forschungen d. Hist. Inst. von Rom*, 1899. — *K. Müller : *Böhm. Brüder*, Herzog, III. 445-467. — E. De Schweinitz : *The Hist. of the Church known as the Unitas Fratrum*, Bethlehem, 1885. — Also Hergenröther-Kirsch : *Kirchengesch.*, II. 886-903.

§ 39. *The Church in England in the Fourteenth Century.*

The 14th century witnessed greater social changes in England than any other century xcept the 19th. These changes were in large part a result of the hundred years' war with France, which began in 1337, and the terrible ravages of the Black Death. The century was marked by the legal adoption of the English tongue as the language of the country and the increased respect for parliament, in whose counsels the rich burgher class demanded a voice, and its definite division into two houses, 1341. The social unrest of the land found expression in popular harangues, poems, and tracts, affirming the rights of the villein and serf class, and in the uprising known as the Peasants' Revolt.

The distinctly religious life of England, in this period, was marked by obstinate resistance to the papal claims of jurisdiction, culminating in the Acts of Provisors, and by the appearance of John Wyclif, one of the most original and vigorous personalities the English Church has produced.

An industrial revolution was precipitated on the island by the Great Pestilence of 1348.   The necessities of life rose enormously in value.   Large tracts of land passed back from the smaller tenants into the hands of the landowners of the gentry class.   The sheep and the cattle, as a contemporary wrote, "strayed through the fields and grain, and there was no one who could drive them."   The serfs and villeins found in the disorder of society an opportunity to escape from the yoke of servitude, and discovered in roving or in independent engagements the joys of a new-found freedom.   These unsettled conditions called forth the famous statutes of Edward III.'s reign, 1327–1377, regulating wages and the prices of commodities.

The popular discontent arising from these regulations, and from the increased taxation necessitated by the wars with France, took the form of organized rebellion.   The age of feudalism was coming to an end.   The old ideas of labor and the tiller of the soil were beginning to give way before more just modes of thought.   Among the agitators were John Ball, whom Froissart, with characteristic aristocratic indifference, called "the mad priest of Kent," the poet Longland and the insurgent leader, Watt Tyler.   In his harangues, Ball fired popular feeling by appeals to the original rights of man.   By what right, he exclaimed, "are they, who are called lords, greater folk than we?   On what grounds do they hold us in vassalage?   Do not we all come from the same father and mother, Adam and Eve?"   The spirit of individual freedom breathed itself out in the effective rhyme, which ran like wildfire, —

> When Adam delved and Eve span
> Who was then the gentleman?

The rhymes, which Will Longland sent forth in his *Complaint of Piers Ploughman*, ventilated the sufferings and demands of the day laborer and called for fair treatment such as brother has a right to expect from brother. Gentleman and villein faced the same eternal destinies. "Though he be thine underling," the poet wrote, "mayhap in heaven, he will be worthier set and with more bliss than thou." The rising sense of national importance and individual dignity was fed by the victory of Crécy, 1346, where the little iron balls, used for the first time, frightened the horses ; by the battle of Poictiers ten years later ; by the treaty of Brétigny, 1360, whereby Edward was confirmed in the possession of large portions of France, and by the exploits of the Black Prince. The spectacle of the French king, John, a captive on the streets of London, made a deep impression. These events and the legalization of the English tongue, 1362,[1] contributed to develop a national and patriotic sentiment before unknown in England.

The uprising, which broke out in 1381, was a vigorous assertion of the popular demand for a redress of the social inequalities between classes in England. The insurgent bands, which marched to London, were pacified by the fair promises of Richard II., but the Kentish band led by Watt Tyler, before dispersing, took the Tower and put the primate, Sudbury, to death. He had refused to favor the repeal of the hated decapitation tax. The abbeys of St. Albans and Edmondsbury were plundered and the monks ill treated, but these acts of violence were a small affair compared with the perpetual import of the uprising for the social and industrial well-being of the English people. The demands of the insurgents, as they bore on the clergy, insisted that Church lands and goods, after sufficient allowance had been made for the reasonable wants of the clergy, should be distributed among the parishioners, and that there should be a single bishop for England. This involved a rupture with Rome.[2]

It was inevitable that the Church should feel the effects of these changes. Its wealth, which is computed to have cov-

---

[1] Mandeville composed his travels in 1356 in French, and then translated out of French into English, that every man of his nation might understand. Trevisa, writing in 1387, said that all grammar schools and English children "leaveth French and construeth and learneth English."

[2] See Kriehn, *Am. Hist. Rev.*, pp. 480, 483.

ered one-third of the landed property of the realm, and the idleness and mendicancy of the friars, awakened widespread murmur and discontent.   The ravages made among the clergy by the Black Death rendered necessary extraordinary measures to recruit its ranks.   The bishop of Norwich was authorized to replace the dead by ordaining 60 young men before the canonical age.   With the rise of the staples of living, the stipends of the vast body of the priestly class was rendered still more inadequate.   Archbishop Islip of Canterbury and other prelates, while recognizing in their pastorals the prevalent unrest, instead of showing proper sympathy, condemned the covetousness of the clergy.   On the other hand, Longland wrote of the shifts to which they were put to eke out a living by accepting secular and often menial employment in the royal palace and the halls of the gentry class.

> Parson and parish priest pleyned to the bishop,
> That their parishes were pore sith the pestilence tym,
> To have a license and a leve at London to dwelle
> And syngen there for symonye, for silver is swete.

There was a movement from within the English people to limit the power of the bishops and to call forth spirituality and efficiency in the clergy.   The bishops, powerful as they remained, were divested of some of their prestige by the parliamentary decision of 1370, restricting high offices of state to laymen.   The first lay chancellor was appointed in 1340.   The bishop, however, was a great personage, and woe to the parish that did not make fitting preparations for his entertainment and have the bells rung on his arrival.   Archbishop Arundel, Foxe quaintly says, " took great snuff and did suspend all such as did not receive him with the noise of bells."   Each diocese had its own prison, into which the bishop thrust refractory clerics for penance or severer punishment.

The mass of the clergy had little learning.   The stalls and canonries, with attractive incomes, where they did not go to foreigners, were regarded as the proper prizes of the younger sons of noblemen.   On the other hand, the prelates lived in abundance.   The famous bishop of Winchester, William of Wykeham, counted fifty manors of his own.   In the larger ones, official residences were maintained, including hall and chapel. This prelate travelled from one to the other, taking reckonings of his stewards, receiving applications for the tonsure and ordination and attending to other official business. Many of the lower clergy were taken from the villein class, whose sons required special exemption to attend school. The day they received orders they were manumitted.

The benefit of clergy, so called, continued to be a source of injustice to the people at large. By the middle of the 13th century, the Church's claim to tithes was extended not only to the products of the field, but the poultry of the yard and the cattle of the stall, to the catch of fish and the game of the forests. Wills almost invariably gave to the priest " the best animal" or the "best quick good." The Church received and gave not back, and, in spite of the statute of Mortmain, bequests continued to be made to her. It came, however, to be regarded as a settled principle that the property of Church and clergy was amenable to civil taxation, and bishops, willingly or by compulsion, loaned money to the king. The demands of the French campaigns made such taxation imperative.

Indulgences were freely announced to procure aid for the building of churches, as in the case of York Cathedral, 1396, the erection of bridges, the filling up of muddy roads and for other public improvements. The clergy, though denied the right of participating in bowling and even in the pastime of checkers, took part in village festivities such as the Churchale, a sort of mediæval donation party, in which there was general merrymaking, ale was brewed, and the people drank freely to the health of the priest and for the benefit of the Church. As for the morals of the clergy, care must always be had not to base sweeping statements upon delinquencies which are apt to be emphasized out of proportion to their extent. It is certain, however, that celibacy was by no means universally enforced, and frequent notices occur of dispensations given to clergymen of illegitimate birth. Bishop Quevil of Exeter complained that priests with families invested their savings for the benefit of their marital partners and their children. In the next period, in 1452, De la Bere, bishop of St. David's, by his

own statement, drew 400 marks yearly from priests for the privilege of having concubines, a noble, equal in value to a mark,
from each one.[1]   Gower, in his *Vox clamantis*, gave a dark
picture of clerical habits, and charges the clergy with coarse
vices such as now are scarcely dreamed of.   The Church historian, Capes, concludes that "immorality and negligence were
widely spread among the clergy."[2]   The decline of discipline
among the friars, and their rude manners, a prominent feature
of the times, came in for the strictures of Fitzralph of Armagh,
severe condemnation at the hands of Wyclif and playful sarcasm from the pen of Chaucer.   The zeal for learning which
had characterized them on their first arrival in England, early
in the 13th century, had given way to self-satisfied idleness.
Fitzralph, who was fellow of Balliol, and probably chancellor
of the University of Oxford, before being raised to the episcopate, incurred the hostility of the friars by a series of sermons
against the Franciscan theory of evangelical poverty.   He
claimed it was not scriptural nor derived from the customs of
the primitive Church.   For his temerity he was compelled to
answer at Avignon, where he seems to have died about the
year 1360.[3]   Of the four orders of mendicants, the Franciscans,
Dominicans, Carmelites and Augustinians, Longland sang that
they

> Preached the people for profit and themselve
> Glosed the Gospel as them good lyked,
> For covetis of copis construed it as they would.

Of the ecclesiastics of the century, if we except Wyclif, probably the most noted are Thomas Bradwardine and William of
Wykeham, the one the representative of scholarly study, the
other of ecclesiastical power.   Bradwardine, theologian, phi-

---

[1] Gascoigne, as quoted by Gairdner: *Lollardy and the Reform.*, I. 262.
[2] I. p. 253.
[3] His *Defensio curatorum contra eos qui privilegatos se dicunt* is printed in
Goldast, II. 466 sqq.   See art. Fitzralph, by R. L. Poole, *Dict. of Nat. Biog.*,
XIX. 194–198.   Four books of Fitzralph's *De pauperie salvatoris* were printed
for the first time by Poole in his ed. of Wyclif's *De dominio*, pp. 257–477.
As for libraries, Fitzralph says that in every English convent there was a grand
library.   On the other hand, the author of the *Philobiblion*, Rich. de Bury,
charges the friars with losing their interest in books.

losopher, mathematician and astronomer, was a student at Merton College, Oxford, 1325.   At Avignon, whither he went to receive consecration to the see of Canterbury, 1349, he had a strange experience.   During the banquet given by Clement VI. the doors were thrown open and a clown entered, seated on a jackass, and humbly petitioned the pontiff to be made archbishop of Canterbury.   This insult, gotten up by Clement's nephew Hugo, cardinal of Tudela, and other members of the sacred college, was in allusion to the remark made by the pope that, if the king of England would ask him to appoint a jackass to a bishopric, he would not dare to refuse.   The sport throws an unpleasant light upon the ideals of the curia, but at the same time bears witness to the attempt which was being made in England to control the appointment of ecclesiastics.   Bradwardine enjoyed such an enviable reputation that Wyclif and other English contemporaries gave him the title, the Profound Doctor — *doctor profundus*.[1]   In his chief work on grace and freewill, delivered as a series of lectures at Merton, he declared that the Church was running after Pelagius.[2]   In the philosophical schools he had rarely heard anything about grace, but all day long the assertions that we are *masters of our own wills*. He was a determinist.   All things, he affirmed, which occur, occur by the necessity of the first cause.   In his Nun's Tale, speaking of God's predestination, Chaucer says: —

> But he cannot boult it to the bren
> As can the holie doctour, S. Austin,
> Or Boece (Boethius), or the Bishop Bradwardine.

Wykeham, 1324–1404, the pattern of a worldly and aristocratic prelate, was an unblushing pluralist, and his see of Winchester is said to have brought him in £60,000 of our money annually.   In 1361 alone, he received prebends in St. Paul's, Hereford, Salisbury, St. David's, Beverley, Bromyard, Wherwell Abergwili, and Llanddewi Brewi, and in the following

---

[1] Wyclif: *De verit. scr.*, I. 30, 109, etc.

[2] *De causa Dei contra Pelagium et de virtute causarum ad suos Mertinenses*, ed. by Sir Henry Saville, London, 1618.   For other works, see Seeberg's art. in Herzog, III. 350, and Stephens in *Dict. of Nat. Biog.*, VI. 188 sq.   Also S. Hahn, *Thos. Bradwardinus, und seine Lehre von d. menschl. Willensfreiheit*, Münster, 1905.

year Lincoln, York, Wells and Hastings.　He occupied for a time the chief office of chancellor, but fell into disrepute.　His memory is preserved in Winchester School and in New College, Oxford, which he founded.　The princely endowment of New College, the first stones of which were laid in 1387, embraced 100 scholarships.　These gifts place Wykeham in the first rank of English patrons of learning at the side of Cardinal Wolsey.　He also has a place in the manuals of the courtesies of life by his famous words, "Manners makyth man."[1]

The struggles of previous centuries against the encroachment of Rome upon the temporalities of the English Church was maintained in this period.　The complaint made by Matthew Paris[2] that the English Church was kept between two millstones, the king and the pope, remained true, with this difference, however, the king's influence came to preponderate. Acts of parliament emphasized his right to dictate or veto ecclesiastical appointments and recognized his sovereign prerogative to tax Church property.　The evident support which the pope gave to France in her wars with England and the scandals of the Avignon residence were favorable to the crown's assertion of authority in these respects.　Wyclif frequently complained that the pope and cardinals were "in league with the enemies of the English kingdom"[3] and the papal registers of the Avignon period, which record the appeals sent to the English king to conclude peace with France, almost always mention terms that would have made France the gainer.　At the outbreak of the war, 1339, Edward III. proudly complained that it broke his heart to see that the French troops were paid in part with papal funds.[4]

The three most important religious acts of England between John's surrender of his crown to Innocent III. and the Act of Supremacy, 1534, were the parliamentary statutes of Mort-

[1] See art. by Tait in *Dict. of Nat. Biog.*, LXIII. 225–231.
[2] Rolls Series, IV. 559.　　　　　　　　　[3] *De eccles.*, p. 332.
[4] Walsingham, *Hist. Angl.*, I. 200 sqq., and the pope's reply, p. 208 sqq. Benedict showed his complete devotion to the French king when he wrote that, if he had two souls, one of them should be given for him.　Quoted by Loserth, *Stud. zur Kirchenpol.*, p. 20.

main, 1279, of Provisors, 1351, and for the burning of heretics, 1401. The statute of Mortmain or Dead-hand forbade the alienation of lands so as to remove them from the obligation of service or taxation to the secular power.   The statute of Provisors, renewed and enlarged in the acts of Præmunire, 1353, 1390 and 1393, concerned the subject of the papal rights over appointments and the temporalities of the English Church. This old bone of contention was taken up early in the 14th century in the statute of Carlyle, 1307,[1] which forbade aliens, appointed to visit religious houses in England, taking moneys with them out of the land and also the payment of tallages and impositions laid upon religious establishments from abroad. In 1343, parliament called upon the pope to recall all " reservations, provisions and collations " which, as it affirmed, checked Church improvements and the flow of alms.   It further protested against the appointment of aliens to English livings, " some of them our enemies who know not our language." Clement VI., replying to the briefs of the king and parliament, declared that, when he made provisions and reservations, it was for the good of the Church, and exhorted Edward to act as a Catholic prince should and to permit nothing to be done in his realm inimical to the Roman Church and ecclesiastical liberty.   Such liberty the pope said he would " defend as having to give account at the last judgment."   Liberty in this case meant the free and unhampered exercise of the lordly claims made by his predecessors from Hildebrand down.[2] Thomas Fuller was close to the truth, when, defining papal provisions and reservations, he wrote, " When any bishopric, abbot's place, dignity or good living (*aquila non capit muscas* — the eagle does not take note of flies) was like to be void, the pope, by a profitable prolepsis to himself, predisposed such places to such successors as he pleased.   By this device he defeated, when he so pleased, the legal election of all convents and rightful presentation of all patrons."

[1] Gee and Hardy, pp. 92–94.
[2] For the text of the parliamentary brief and the king's letter, which was written in French, see Merimuth, p. 138 sqq., 153 sqq., and for Clement's reply, Bliss, III., 9 sqq.

The memorable statute of Provisors forbade all papal provisions and reservations and all taxation of Church property contrary to the customs of England. The act of 1353 sought more effectually to clip the pope's power by forbidding the carrying of any suit against an English patron before a foreign tribunal.[1]

To these laws the pope paid only so much heed as expediency required. This claim, made by one of his predecessors in the bull *Cupientes*, to the right to fill all the benefices of Christendom, he had no idea of abandoning, and, whenever it was possible, he provided for his hungry family of cardinals and other ecclesiastics out of the proverbially fat appointments of England. Indeed, the cases of such appointments given by Merimuth, and especially in the papal books as printed by Bliss, are so recurrent that one might easily get the impression that the pontiff's only concern for the English Church was to see that its livings were put into the hands of foreigners. I have counted the numbers in several places as given by Bliss. On one page, 4 out of 9 entries were papal appointments. A section of 2½ pages announces " provisions of a canonry, with expectation of a prebend " in the following churches : 7 in Lincoln, 5 in Salisbury, 2 in Chichester, and 1 each in Wells, York, Exeter, St. Patrick's, Dublin, Moray, Southwell, Howden, Ross, Aberdeen, Wilton.[2] From 1342–1385 the deanery of York was held successively by three Roman cardinals. In 1374, the incomes of the treasurer, dean and two archdeaneries of Salisbury went the same way. At the close of Edward III.'s reign, foreign cardinals held the deaneries of York, Salisbury and Lichfield, the archdeanery of Canterbury, reputed to be the richest of English preferments, and innumerable prebends. Bishops and abbots-elect had to travel to Avignon and often spend months and much money in securing confirmation to their appointments, and, in cases, the prelate-

---

[1] See the texts of these statutes in Gee and Hardy, 103 sqq., 112–123. With reference to the renewal of the act in 1390, Fuller quaintly says : " It mauled the papal power in the land. Some former laws had pared the pope's nails to the quick, but this cut off his fingers."

[2] II. 345 ; III. 54 sq. Prebend has reference to the stipend, canonry to the office.

elect was set aside on the ground that provision had already
been made for his office.   As for sees reserved by the pope,
Stubbs gives the following list, extending over a brief term
of years : Worcester, Hereford, Durham and Rochester, 1317 ;
Lincoln and Winchester, 1320 ; Lichfield, 1322 ; Winchester,
1323 ; Carlisle and Norwich, 1325 ; Worcester, Exeter and
Hereford, 1327 ; Bath, 1329 ; Durham, Canterbury, Winchester and Worcester, 1334.   Provisions were made in full
recognition of the plural system.   Thus, Walter of London,
the king's confessor, was appointed by the pope to the deanery
of Wells, though, as stated in the papal brief, he already held
a considerable list of "canonries and prebends," Lincoln, Salisbury, St. Paul, St. Martin Le Grand, London, Bridgenorth,
Hastings and Hareswell in the diocese of Salisbury.[1]   By the
practice of promoting bishops from one see to another, the
pope accomplished for his favorites what he could not have
done in any other way.   Thus, by the promotion of Sudbury
in 1374 to Canterbury, the pope was able to translate Courtenay from Hereford to London, and Gilbert from Bangor to
Hereford, and thus by a single stroke he was enriched by the
first-fruits of four sees.

In spite of legislation, the papal collectors continued to ply
their trade in England, but less publicly and confidently than
in the two preceding centuries.   In 1379, Urban VI. sent Cos-
matus Gentilis as his nuncio and collector-in-chief, with instructions that he and his subcollectors make speedy returns to Rome,
especially of Peter's pence.[2]   In 1375, Gregory XI. had called
upon the archbishops of Canterbury and York to collect a tax
of 60,000 florins for the defence of the lands of the Apostolic

---

[1] Bliss, II. 521.   Cases of the payment of large sums for appointments to
the pope and of the disappointed ecclesiastics-elect are given in Merimuth,
pp. 31, 57, 59, 60, 61, 71, 120, 124, 172, etc., Bliss and others.   Merimuth,
p. 67, etc., refers constantly to the bribery used by such expressions as *causa
pecunialiter cognita*, and *non sine magna pecuniæ quantitate*.   In cases, the
pope renounced the right of provision, as Clement V., in 1308, the livings held
in commendam by the cardinal of St. Sabina, and valued at 1000 marks.   See
Bliss, II. 48.   For the cases of agents sent by two cardinals to England to
collect the incomes of their livings, and their imprisonment, see Walsingham,
I. 259.   [2] Bliss, IV. 257.

see, the English benefices, however, held by cardinals being exempted.   The chronicler Merimuth, in a noteworthy paragraph summing up the curial practice of foraging upon the English sees and churches, emphasizes the persistence and shrewdness with which the Apostolic chair from the time of Clement V. had extorted gold and riches as though the English might be treated as barbarians.   John XXII. he represents as having reserved all the good livings of England.   Under Benedict XII., things were not so bad.   Benedict's successor, Clement VI., was of all the offenders the most unscrupulous, reserving for himself or distributing to members of the curia the fattest places in England.   England's very enemies, as Merimuth continues, were thus put into possession of English revenues, and the proverb became current at Avignon that the English were like docile asses bearing all the burdens heaped upon them.[1] This prodigal Frenchman threatened Edward III. with excommunication and the land with interdict, if resistance to his appointments did not cease and if their revenues continued to be withheld.   The pope died in 1353, before the date set for the execution of his wrathful threat.   While France was being made English by English arms, the Italian and French ecclesiastics were making conquest of England's resources.

The great name of Wyclif, which appears distinctly in 1366, represents the patriotic element in all its strength.   In his discussions of lordship, presented in two extensive treatises, he set forth the theory of the headship of the sovereign over the temporal affairs of the Church in his own dominions, even to the seizure of its temporalities.   In him, the Church witnessed an ecclesiastic of equal metal with Thomas à Becket, a man, however, who did not stoop, in his love for his order, to humiliate the state under the hand of the Church.   He represented the popular will, the common sense of mankind in regard to

---

[1] *Inter curiales vertitur in proverbium quod Anglici sunt boni asini, omnia onera eis imposita et intolerabilia supportantes.*   Merimuth, p. 175.   To these burdens imposed upon England by the papal see were added, as in Matthew Paris' times, severe calamities from rain and cold.   Merimuth tells of a great flood in 1339, when the rain fell from October to the first of December, so that the country looked like a continuous sea.   Then bitter cold setting in, the country looked like one field of ice.

the province of the Church, the New Testament theory of the spiritual sphere.   Had he not been practically alone, he would have anticipated by more than two centuries the limitation of the pope's power in England.

§ 40. *John Wyclif.*

" A good man was there of religioun
That was a pore Persone of a town ;
But rich he was of holy thought and werk ;
He was also a lerned man, a clerk,
That Christes gospel trewly wolde preche.

*   *   *   *   *   *

This noble ensample to his shepe he gaf,
That first he wrought and after that he taught.

*   *   *   *   *   *

A better priest I trow that nowhere non is,
He waited after no pompe ne reverence ;
Ne maked him no spiced conscience,
But Christes lore and his apostles twelve
He taught, but first he folwed it himselve." [1]

—CHAUCER.

The title, Reformers before the Reformation, has been aptly given to a group of men of the 14th and 15th centuries who anticipated many of the teachings of Luther and the Protestant Reformers.   They stand, each by himself, in solitary prominence, Wyclif in England, John Huss in Bohemia, Savonarola in Florence, and Wessel, Goch and Wesel in Northern Germany. To these men the sculptor has given a place on the pedestal of his famous group at Worms representing the Reformation of the 16th century.   They differ, if we except the moral reformer, Savonarola, from the group of the German mystics, who sought a purification of life in quiet ways, in having expressed open dissent from the Church's ritual and doctrinal teachings.   They also differ from the group of ecclesiastical reformers, D'Ailly, Gerson, Nicolas of Clamanges, who concerned themselves with the fabric of the canon law and did not go beyond the correction of abuses in the administration and morals of the Church. Wyclif and his successors were doctrinal reformers.   In some

[1] Often supposed to be a description of Wyclif.

views they had been anticipated by Marsiglius of Padua and the other assailants of the papacy of the early half of the 14th century.

John Wyclif, called the Morning Star of the Reformation, and, at the time of his death, in England and in Bohemia the Evangelical doctor,[1] was born about 1324 near the village of Wyclif, Yorkshire, in the diocese of Durham.[2] His own writings give scarcely a clew to the events of his career, and little can be gathered from his immediate contemporaries. He was of Saxon blood. His studies were pursued at Oxford, which had six colleges. He was a student at Balliol and master of that hall in 1361. He was also connected with Merton and Queen's, and was probably master of Canterbury Hall, founded by Archbishop Islip.[3] He was appointed in succession to the livings of Fillingham, 1363, Ludgershall, 1368, and by the king's appointment, to Lutterworth, 1374. The living of Lutterworth was valued at £ 26 a year.

Wyclif occupies a distinguished place as an Oxford schoolman, a patriot, a champion of theological and practical reforms

[1] *Fasciculi*, p. 362.

[2] Leland's *Itinerary* placed Wyclif's birth in 1324. Buddensieg and Rashdall prefer 1330. Leland, our first authority for the place of birth, mentions Spresswell (Hipswell) and Wyclif-on-Tees, places a half a mile apart. Wyclif's name is spelled in more than twenty different ways, as Wiclif, accepted by Lechler, Loserth, Buddensieg and German scholars generally; Wiclef, Wicliffe, Wicleff, Wycleff, Wycliffe, adopted by Foxe, Milman, Poole, Stubbs, Rashdall, Bigg; Wyclif preferred by Shirley, Matthew, Sergeant, the Wyclif Society, the Early English Text Society, etc. The form Wyclif is found in a diocesan register of 1361, when the Reformer was warden of Balliol College. The earliest mention in an official state document, July 26, 1374, gives it Wiclif. On Wyclif's birthplace, see Shirley, *Fasciculi*, p. x sqq.

[3] A Wyclif is mentioned in connection with all of these colleges. The question is whether there were not two John Wyclifs. A John de Whyteclyve was rector of Mayfield, 1361, and later of Horsted Kaynes, where he died, 1383. In 1365 Islip, writing from Mayfield, appointed a John Wyclyve warden of Canterbury Hall. Shirley, *Note on the two Wiclifs*, in the *Fasciculi*, p. 513 sqq., advocated the view that this Wyclif was a different person from our John Wyclif, and he is followed by Poole, Rashdall and Sergeant. Principal Wilkinson of Marlborough College, *Ch. Quart. Rev.*, October, 1877, makes a strong statement against this view; Lechler and Buddensieg, the two leading German authorities on Wyclif's career, also admit only a single Wyclif as connected with the Oxford Halls.

and the translator of the Scriptures into English.   The papal schism, occurring in the midst of his public career, had an important bearing on his views of papal authority.

So far as is known, he confined himself, until 1366, to his duties in Oxford and his parish work.   In that year he appears as one of the king's chaplains and as opposed to the papal supremacy in the ecclesiastial affairs of the realm.   The parliament of the same year refused Urban V.'s demand for the payment of the tribute, promised by King John, which was back 33 years.   John, it declared, had no right to obligate the kingdom to a foreign ruler without the nation's consent.   Wyclif, if not a member of this body, was certainly an adviser to it.[1]

In the summer of 1374, Wyclif went to Bruges as a member of the commission appointed by the king to negotiate peace with France and to treat with the pope's agents on the filling of ecclesiastical appointments in England.   His name was second in the list of commissioners, following the name of the bishop of Bangor.   At Bruges we find him for the first time in close association with John of Gaunt, Edward's favorite son, an association which continued for several years, and for a time inured to his protection from ecclesiastical violence.[2]

On his return to England, he began to speak as a religious reformer.   He preached in Oxford and London against the pope's secular sovereignty, running about, as the old chronicler has it, from place to place, and barking against the Church.[3]   It was soon after this that, in one of his tracts, he styled the bishop of Rome " the anti-Christ, the proud, worldly priest of Rome, and the most cursed of clippers and cut-purses."   He maintained that he " has no more power in binding and loos-

---

[1] So Lechler, who advances strong arguments in favor of this view.   Loserth, who is followed by Rashdall, brings considerations against it, and places Wyclif's first appearance as a political reformer in 1376.   *Studien zur Kirchenpol.*, etc., pp. 1, 32, 35, 44, 60.   A serious difficulty with this view is that it crowds almost all the Reformer's writings into 7 years.

[2] John of Gaunt, duke of Lancaster, was the younger brother of the Black Prince.   The prince had returned from his victories in France to die of an incurable disease.   [3] *Chron. Angl.*, p. 115 sq.

ing than any priest, and that the temporal lords may seize the possessions of the clergy if pressed by necessity." The duke of Lancaster, the clergy's open foe, headed a movement to confiscate ecclesiastical property. Piers Ploughman had an extensive public opinion behind him when he exclaimed, "Take her lands, ye Lords, and let her live by dimes (tithes)." The Good Parliament of 1376, to whose deliberation Wyclif contributed by voice and pen, gave emphatic expression to the public complaints against the hierarchy.

The Oxford professor's attitude had become too flagrant to be suffered to go unrebuked. In 1377, he was summoned before the tribunal of William Courtenay, bishop of London, at St. Paul's, where the proceedings opened with a violent altercation between the bishop and the duke. The question was as to whether Wyclif should take a seat or continue standing in the court. Percy, lord marshal of England, ordered him to sit down, a proposal the bishop pronounced an unheard-of indignity to the court. At this, Lancaster, who was present, swore he would bring down Courtenay's pride and the pride of all the prelates in England. "Do your best, Sir," was the spirited retort of the bishop, who was a son of the duke of Devonshire. A popular tumult ensued, Wyclif being protected by Lancaster.

Pope Gregory XI. himself now took notice of the offender in a document condemning 19 sentences from his writings as erroneous and dangerous to Church and state. In fact, he issued a batch of at least five bulls, addressed to the archbishop of Canterbury, the bishop of London, the University of Oxford and the king, Edward III. The communication to Archbishop Sudbury opened with an unctuous panegyric of England's past most glorious piety and the renown of its Church leaders, champions of the orthodox faith and instructors not only of their own but of other peoples in the path of the Lord's commandments. But it had come to his ears that the Lutterworth rector had broken forth into such detestable madness as not to shrink from publicly proclaiming false propositions which threatened the stability of the entire Church. His Holiness, therefore, called upon the archbishop to have

John sent to prison and kept in bonds till final sentence should be passed by the papal court.[1] It seems that the vice-chancellor of Oxford at least made a show of complying with the pope's command and remanded the heretical doctor to Black Hall, but the imprisonment was only nominal.

Fortunately, the pope might send forth his fulminations to bind and imprison but it was not wholly in his power to hold the truth in bonds and to check the progress of thought. In his letter to the chancellor of Oxford, Gregory alleged that Wyclif was vomiting out of the filthy dungeon of his heart most wicked and damnable heresies, whereby he hoped to pollute the faithful and bring them to the precipice of perdition, overthrow the Church and subvert the secular estate. The disturber was put into the same category with those princes among errorists, Marsiglius of Padua and John of Jandun.[2]

The archbishop's court at Lambeth, before which the offender was now cited, was met by a message from the widow of the Black Prince to stay the proceedings, and the sitting was effectually broken up by London citizens who burst into the hall. At Oxford, the masters of theology pronounced the nineteen condemned propositions true, though they sounded badly to the ear. A few weeks later, March, 1378, Gregory died, and the papal schism broke out. No further notice was taken of Gregory's ferocious bulls. Among other things, the nineteen propositions affirmed that Christ's followers have no right to exact temporal goods by ecclesiastical censures, that the excommunications of pope and priest are of no avail if not according to the law of Christ, that for adequate reasons the king may strip the Church of temporalities and that even a pope may be lawfully impeached by laymen.

With the year 1378 Wyclif's distinctive career as a doctrinal reformer opens. He had defended English rights against foreign encroachment. He now assailed, at a number of points, the theological structure the Schoolmen and mediæval popes had laboriously reared, and the abuses that had crept into the Church. The spectacle of Christendom divided by two papal courts, each fulminating anathemas against the other, was

[1] Gee and Hardy, p. 105 sqq.   [2] *Fasc.*, pp. 242–244.

enough to shake confidence in the divine origin of the papacy. In sermons, tracts and larger writings, Wyclif brought Scripture and common sense to bear. His pen was as keen as a Damascus blade. Irony and invective, of which he was the master, he did not hesitate to use. The directness and pertinency of his appeals brought them easily within the comprehension of the popular mind. He wrote not only in Latin but in English. His conviction was as deep and his passion as fiery as Luther's, but on the one hand, Wyclif's style betrays less of the vivid illustrative power of the great German and little of his sympathetic warmth, while on the other, less of his unfortunate coarseness. As Luther is the most vigorous tract writer that Germany has produced, so Wyclif is the foremost religious pamphleteer that has arisen in England; and the impression made by his clear and stinging thrusts may be contrasted in contents and audience with the scholarly and finished tracts of the Oxford movement led by Pusey, Keble and Newman, the one reaching the conscience, the other appealing to the æsthetic tastes; the one adapted to break down priestly pretension, the other to foster it.

But the Reformer of the 14th century was more than a scholar and publicist. Like John Wesley, he had a practical bent of mind, and like him he attempted to provide England with a new proclamation of the pure Gospel. To counteract the influence of the friars, whom he had begun to attack after his return from Bruges, he conceived the idea of developing and sending forth a body of itinerant evangelists. These "pore priests," as they were called, were taken from the list of Oxford graduates, and seem also to have included laymen. Of their number and the rules governing them, we are in the dark. The movement was begun about 1380, and on the one side it associates Wyclif with Gerrit de Groote, and on the other with Wesley and with his more recent fellow-countryman, General Booth, of the Salvation Army.

Although this evangelistic idea took not the form of a permanent organization, the appearance of the pore preachers made a sensation. According to the old chronicler, the disciples who gathered around him in Oxford were many and, clad in long russet gowns of one pattern, they went on foot, ventilating their master's errors among the people and publicly setting them forth in sermons.[1] They had the distinction of being arraigned by no less a personage than Bishop Courtenay "as itinerant, unauthorized preachers who teach erroneous, yea, heretical assertions publicly, not only in churches but also in public squares and other profane places, and who do this under the guise of great holiness, but without having obtained any episcopal or papal authorization."

It was in 1381, the year before Courtenay said his memorable words, that Walden reports that Wyclif "began to determine matters upon the sacrament of the altar."[2] To attempt an innovation at this crucial point required courage of the highest order. In 12 theses he declared the Church's doctrine unscriptural and misleading. For the first time since the promulgation of the dogma of transubstantiation by the Fourth Lateran was it seriously called in question by a theological expert. It was a case of Athanasius standing alone. The mendicants waxed violent. Oxford authorities, at the instance of the archbishop and bishops, instituted a trial, the court consisting of Chancellor Berton and 12 doctors. Without mentioning Wyclif by name, the judges condemned as pestiferous the assertions that the bread and wine remain after consecration, and that Christ's body is present only figuratively or tropically in the eucharist. Declaring that the judges had not been able to break down his arguments, Wyclif went on preaching and lecturing at the university. But in the king's council, to which he made appeal, the duke of Lancaster took sides against him and forbade him to speak any more on the subject at Oxford. This prohibition Wyclif met with a still more positive avowal of his views in his *Confession*, which closes with the noble words, "I believe that in the end the truth will conquer."

The same year, the Peasants' Revolt broke out, but there is no evidence that Wyclif had any more sympathy with the movement than Luther had with the Peasants' Rising of 1525. After the revolt was over, he proposed that Church

---

[1] *Chron. Angl.*, p. 395; also Knighton, II. 184 sq.   [2] *Fasc.*, p. 104.

property be given to the upper classes, not to the poor.[1] The principles, however, which he enunciated were germs which might easily spring up into open rebellion against oppression. Had he not written, " There is no moral obligation to pay tax or tithe to bad rulers either in Church or state. It is permitted to punish or depose them and to reclaim the wealth which the clergy have diverted from the poor " ? One hundred and fifty years after this time, Tyndale said, " They said it in Wyclif's day, and the hypocrites say now, that God's Word arouseth insurrection." [2]

Courtenay's elevation to the see of Canterbury boded no good to the Reformer. In 1382, he convoked the synod which is known in English history as the Earthquake synod, from the shock felt during its meetings. The primate was supported by 9 bishops, and when the earth began to tremble, he showed admirable courage by interpreting it as a favorable omen. The earth, in trying to rid itself of its winds and humors, was manifesting its sympathy with the body ecclesiastic.[3] Wyclif, who was not present, made another use of the occurrence, and declared that the Lord sent the earthquake " because the friars had put heresy upon Christ in the matter of the sacrament, and the earth trembled as it did when Christ was damned to bodily death." [4]

The council condemned 24 articles, ascribed to the Reformer, 10 of which were pronounced heretical, and the remainder to be against the decisions of the Church.[5] The 4 main subjects condemned as heresy were that Christ is not corporally present in the sacrament, that oral confession is not necessary for a soul prepared to die, that after Urban VI.'s death the English Church should acknowledge no pope but, like the Greeks, govern itself, and that it is contrary to Scripture for ecclesiastics to hold temporal possessions. Courtenay followed up the synod's decisions by summoning Rygge, then chancellor

---

[1] See Trevelyan, p. 199 ; Kriehn, pp. 254–286, 458–485.

[2] Pref. to *Expos. of St. John*, p. 225, Parker Soc. ed.

[3] *Sicut in terræ visceribus includuntur aër et spiritus infecti et ingrediuntur in terræ motum, Fasc.*, p. 272.

[4] *Select Engl. Works*, III. 503.   [5] Gee and Hardy, pp. 108–110.

of Oxford, to suppress the heretical teachings and teachers.
Ignoring the summons, Rygge appointed Repyngdon, another
of Wyclif's supporters, to preach, and when Peter Stokys,
"a professor of the sacred page," armed with a letter from the
archbishop, attempted to silence him, the students and tutors
at Oxford threatened the Carmelite with their drawn swords.

But Courtenay would permit no trifling and, summoning
Rygge and the proctors to Lambeth, made them promise on
their knees to take the action indicated.   Parliament supported the primate.   The new preaching was suppressed, but
Wyclif stood undaunted.   He sent a Complaint of 4 articles to
the king and parliament, in which he pleaded for the supremacy
of English law in matters of ecclesiastical property, for the
liberty for the friars to abandon the rules of their orders and
follow the rule of Christ, and for the view that on the Lord's
table the real bread and wine are present, and not merely the
accidents.[1]

The court was no longer ready to support the Reformer,
and Richard II. sent peremptory orders to Rygge to suppress
the new teachings.   Courtenay himself went to Oxford, and
there is some authority for the view that Wyclif again met
the prelate face to face at St. Frideswides.   Rigid inquisition was made for copies of the condemned teacher's writings
and those of Hereford.   Wyclif was inhibited from preaching,
and retired to his rectory at Lutterworth.   Hereford, Repyngdon, Aston and Bedeman, his supporters, recanted.   The whole
party received a staggering blow and with it liberty of teaching
at Oxford.[2]

Confined to Lutterworth, Wyclif continued his labors on the
translation of the Bible, and sent forth polemic tracts, including the *Cruciata*,[3] a vigorous condemnation of the crusade which
the bishop of Norwich, Henry de Spenser, was preparing in
support of Urban VI. against the Avignon pope, Clement VII.
The warlike prelate had already shown his military gifts during the Peasants' Uprising.   Urban had promised plenary

---

[1] *Select Engl. Writings*, III. 507-523.
[2] *Fasc.*, pp. 272-333.   See Shirley, p. xliv.
[3] *Latin Works*, II. 577 sqq.

indulgence for a year to all joining the army. Mass was said and sermons preached in the churches of England, and large sums collected for the enterprise. The indulgence extended to the dead as well as to the living. Wyclif declared the crusade an expedition for worldly mastery, and pronounced the indulgence " an abomination of desolation in the holy place." Spenser's army reached the Continent, but the expedition was a failure. The most important of Wyclif's theological treatises, the Trialogus, was written in this period. It lays down the principle that, where the Bible and the Church do not agree, we must obey the Bible, and, where conscience and human authority are in conflict, we must follow conscience.[1]

Two years before his death, Wyclif received a paralytic stroke which maimed but did not completely disable him. It is possible that he received a citation to appear before the pope. With unabated rigor of conviction, he replied to the supreme pontiff that of all men he was most under obligation to obey the law of Christ, that Christ was of all men the most poor, and subject to mundane authority. No Christian man has a right to follow Peter, Paul or any of the saints except as they imitated Christ. The pope should renounce all worldly authority and compel his clergy to do the same. He then asserted that, if in these views he was found to err, he was willing to be corrected, even by death. If it were in his power to do anything to advance these views by his presence in Rome, he would willingly go thither. But God had put an obstacle in his way, and had taught him to obey Him rather than man. He closed with the prayer that God might incline Urban to imitate Christ in his life and teach his clergy to do the same.

While saying mass in his church, he was struck again with paralysis, and passed away two or three days after, Dec. 29, 1384, "having lit a fire which shall never be put out."[2]

---

[1] *Fasc.*, p. 341 sq.; Lechler-Lorimer, p. 417, deny the citation. The reply is hardly what we might have expected from Wyclif, confining itself, as it does, rather curtly to the question of the pope's authority and manner of life. Luther's last treatment of the pope, *Der Papst der Ende-Christ und Wider Christ*, is not a full parallel. Wyclif was independent, not coarse.

[2] The most credible narrative preserved of Wyclif's death comes from John Horn, the Reformer's assistant for two years, and was written down by Dr.

Fuller, writing of his death, exclaims, "Admirable that a hare, so often hunted with so many packs of dogs, should die quietly sitting in his form."

Wyclif was spare, and probably never of robust health, but he was not an ascetic.   He was fond of a good meal.   In temper he was quick, in mind clear, in moral character unblemished. Towards his enemies he was sharp, but never coarse or ribald. William Thorpe, a young contemporary standing in the court of Archbishop Arundel, bore testimony that "he was emaciated in body and well-nigh destitute of strength, and in conduct most innocent.   Very many of the chief men of England conferred with him, loved him dearly, wrote down his sayings and followed his manner of life." [1]

The prevailing sentiment of the hierarchy was given by Walsingham, chronicler of St. Albans, who characterized the Reformer in these words : "On the feast of the passion of St. Thomas of Canterbury, John de Wyclif, that instrument of the devil, that enemy of the Church, that author of confusion to the common people, that image of hypocrites, that idol of heretics, that author of schism, that sower of hatred, that coiner of lies, being struck with the horrible judgment of God, was smitten with palsy and continued to live till St. Sylvester's Day, on which he breathed out his malicious spirit into the abodes of darkness."

The dead was not left in peace.   By the decree of Arundel, Wyclif's writings were suppressed, and it was so effective that Caxton and the first English printers issued no one of them from the press.   The Lateran decree of February, 1413, ordered his books burnt, and the Council of Constance, from whose

Thomas Gascoigne upon Horn's sworn statement.   Walden twice makes the charge that disappointment at not being appointed bishop of Worcester started Wyclif on the path of heresy, but there is no other authority for the story, which is inherently improbable.   Lies were also invented against the memories of Luther, Calvin and Knox, which the respectable Catholic historians set aside.

[1] Bale, in his account of the Examination of Thorpe, Parker Soc. ed., I. 80–81.   The biographies of Lewis, Vaughan, Lorimer and Sergeant give portraits of Wyclif.   The oldest, according to Sergeant, pp. 16–21, is taken from Bale's Summary, 1548.   There is a resemblance in all the portraits, which represent the Reformer clothed in Oxford gown and cap, with long beard, open face, clear, large eye, prominent nose and cheek bones and pale complexion.

members, such as Gerson and D'Ailly, we might have expected
tolerant treatment, formally condemned his memory and ordered his bones exhumed from their resting-place and "cast
at a distance from the sepulchre of the church."   The holy
synod, so ran the decree, "declares said John Wyclif to have
been a notorious heretic, and excommunicates him and condemns
his memory as one who died an obstinate heretic."[1]   In 1429,
at the summons of Martin IV., the decree was carried out by
Flemmyng, bishop of Lincoln.

The words of Fuller, describing the execution of the decree
of Constance, have engraven themselves on the page of English
history.   " They burnt his bones to ashes and cast them into
Swift, a neighboring brook running hard by.   Thus this brook
hath conveyed his ashes into Avon, Avon into Severn, Severn
into the narrow seas, they into the main ocean.   And thus the
ashes of Wicliffe are the emblem of his doctrine, which now is
dispersed the world over."

In the popular judgment of the English people, John Wyclif,
in company with John Latimer and John Wesley, probably represents more fully than any other English religious leader, independence of thought, devotion to conscience, solid religious
common sense, and the sound exposition of the Gospel.   In the
history of the intellectual and moral progress of his people, he
was the leading Englishman of the Middle Ages.[2]

§ 41. *Wyclif's Teachings.*

Wyclif's teachings lie plainly upon the surface of his many
writings.   In each one of the eminent rôles he played, as school-

---

[1] A part of the sentence runs, *Sancta synodus declarat diffinit et sententiat
eumdem J. Wicleff fuisse notorium hæreticum pertinacem et in hæresi de-
cessisse . . . ordinat corpus et ejus ossa, si ab aliis fidelibus corporibus discerni
possint, exhumari et procul ab ecclesiae sepultura jactari.* Mansi, XXVII. 635.

[2] Green, in his *Hist. of the Engl. People*, passes a notable encomium on the
"first Reformer," and the late Prof. Bigg, *Wayside Sketches*, p. 131, asserts
"that his beliefs are in the main those of the great majority of Englishmen
to-day, and this is a high proof of the justice, the clearness and the sincerity
of his thoughts."   The Catholic historian of England, Lingard, IV. 192, after
speaking of Wyclif's intellectual perversion, refers to him, " as that extraordinary man who, exemplary in his morals, declaimed against vice with the
freedom and severity of an Apostle."

man, political reformer, preacher, innovator in theology and translator of the Bible, he wrote extensively. His views show progress in the direction of opposition to the mediæval errors and abuses. Driven by attacks, he detected errors which, at the outset, he did not clearly discern. But, above all, his study of the Scriptures forced upon him a system which was in contradiction to the distinctively mediæval system of theology. His language in controversy was so vigorous that it requires an unusual effort to suppress the impulse to quote at great length.

Clear as Wyclif's statements always are, some of his works are drawn out by much repetition. Nor does he always move in a straight line, but digresses to this side and to that, taking occasion to discuss at length subjects cognate to the main matter he has in hand. This habit often makes the reading of his larger works a wearisome task. Nevertheless, the author always brings the reader back from his digression or, to use a modern expression, never leaves him sidetracked.

I. As a SCHOOLMAN. — Wyclif was beyond dispute the most eminent scholar who taught for any length of time at Oxford since Grosseteste, whom he often quotes.[1] He was read in Chrysostom, Augustine, Jerome and other Latin Fathers, as well as in the mediæval theologians from Anselm to Duns Scotus, Bradwardine, Fitzralph and Henry of Ghent. His quotations are many, but with increasing emphasis, as the years went on, he made his final appeal to the Scriptures. He was a moderate realist and ascribed to nominalism all theological error. He seems to have endeavored to shun the determinism of Bradwardine, and declared that the doctrine of necessity does not do away with the freedom of the will, which is so free that it cannot be compelled. Necessity compels the creature to will, that is, to exercise his freedom, but at that point he is left free to choose.[2]

---

[1] *Op. evang.*, p. 17, etc., *De dom. div.*, p. 215, etc., *De dom. civ.*, 384 sqq., where the case of Frederick of Lavagna is related at length.

[2] Hergenröther, II. 881, speaks of Wyclif's system as pantheistic realism and fatalism, *D. Lehrsystem des Wiclif ist krasser, pantheistischer Realismus, Fatalismus u. Predestianismus.*

II. As a Patriot. — In this rôle the Oxford teacher took
an attitude the very reverse of the attitude assumed by Anselm and Thomas à Becket, who made the English Church a
servant to the pope's will in all things.   For loyalty to the
Hildebrandian theocracy, Anselm was willing to suffer banishment and à Becket suffered death.   In Wyclif, the mutter-
ings of the nation, which had been heard against the foreign
régime from the days of William the Conqueror, and especially
since King John's reign, found a stanch and uncompromising
mouthpiece.   Against the whole system of foreign jurisdiction
he raised his voice, as also against the Church's claim to hold
lands, except as it acknowledged the rights of the state.   He
also opposed the tenure of secular offices by the clergy and,
when Archbishop Sudbury was murdered, declared that he
died in sin because he was holding the office of chancellor.

Wyclif's views on government in Church and state are chiefly
set forth in the works on Civil and Divine Lordship — *De dominio divino*, and *De dominio civili* — and in his *Dialogus*.[1]   The
Divine Lordship discusses the title by which men hold property and exercise government, and sets forth the distinction between sovereignty and stewardship.   Lordship is not properly
proprietary.   It is stewardship.   Christ did not desire to rule
as a tenant with absolute rights, but in the way of communicat-
ing to others.[2]   As to his manhood, he was the most perfect of
servants.

The *Civil Lordship* opens by declaring that no one in mortal
sin has a right to lordship, and that every one in the state of
grace has a real lordship over the whole universe.   All Christians are reciprocally lords and servants.   The pope, or an ecclesiastical body abusing the property committed to them, may
be deprived of it by the state.   Proprietary right is limited by
proper use.   Tithes are an expedient to enable the priesthood

---

[1] The *De dom. civ.* and the *De dom. div.*, ed. for the Wyclif Soc. by R. L.
Poole, London, 1885, 1890.   See Poole's Prefaces and his essay on Wyclif's
Doctrine of Lordship in his *Illustrations*, etc., pp. 282–311.   The *Dialogus, sive
speculum ecclesiæ militantis*, ed. by A. W. Pollard, 1886.

[2] *Salvator noster noluit esse proprietarie dominans, sed communicative*,
p. 204.

to perform its mission.   The New Testament does not make
them a rule.

From the last portion of the first book of the *Civil Lordship*,
Gregory XI. drew most of the articles for which Wyclif had
to stand trial.   Here is found the basis for the charge ascribing to him the famous statement that God ought to obey the
devil.   By this was meant nothing more than that the jurisdiction of every lawful proprietor should be recognized.

III.   As a Preacher. — Whether we regard Wyclif's constant activity in the pulpit, or the impression his sermons made,
he must be pronounced by far the most notable of English
preachers prior to the Reformation.[1]   294 of his English sermons and 224 of his Latin sermons have been preserved.   To
these discourses must be added his English expositions of the
Lord's prayer, the songs of the Bible, the seven deadly sins
and other subjects.   With rare exceptions, the sermons are
based upon passages of the New Testament.

The style of the English discourses is simple and direct.
No more plainly did Luther preach against ecclesiastical
abuses than did the English Reformer.   On every page are
joined with practical religious exposition stirring passages rebuking the pope and worldly prelates.   They are denounced as
anti-christ and the servants of the devil — the fiend — as they
turn away from the true work of pasturing Christ's flock for
worldly gain and enjoyment.   The preacher condemns the
false teachings which are nowhere taught in the Scriptures,
such as pilgrimages and indulgences.   Sometimes Wyclif
seems to be inconsistent with himself, now making light of
fasting, now asserting that the Apostles commended it ; now
disparaging prayers for the dead, now affirming purgatory.
With special severity do his sermons strike at the friars who
preach out of avarice and neglect to expose the sins of their
hearers.   No one is more idle than the rich friars, who have
nothing but contempt for the poor.   Again and again in these
sermons, as in his other works, he urges that the goods of the

---

[1] Loserth, Introd. to *Lat. sermones*, II., p. xx, pronounces their effect extraordinary.   The Engl. sermons have been ed. by Arnold, *Select Engl. Works*,
vols. I, II, and the Lat. sermons by Loserth, in 4 vols.

friars be seized and given to the needy classes. Wyclif, the
preacher, was always the bold champion of the layman's rights.

His work, *The Pastoral Office*, which is devoted to the duties of the faithful minister, and his sermons lay stress upon
preaching as the minister's proper duty. Preaching he declared the "highest service," even as Christ occupied himself
most in that work. And if bishops, on whom the obligation
to preach more especially rests, preach not, but are content to
have true priests preach in their stead, they are as those that
murder Jesus. The same authority which gave to priests
the privilege of celebrating the sacrament of the altar binds
them to preach. Yea, the preaching of the Word is a more
precious occupation than the ministration of the sacraments.[1]

When the Gospel was preached, as in Apostolic times, the
Church grew. Above all things, close attention should be
given to Christ's words, whose authority is superior to all the
rites and commandments of pope and friars. Again and again
Wyclif sets forth the ideal minister, as in the following description: —

" A priest should live holily, in prayer, in desires and thought, in godly
conversation and honest teaching, having God's commandments and His
Gospel ever on his lips. And let his deeds be so righteous that no man
may be able with cause to find fault with them, and so open his acts that
he may be a true book to all sinful and wicked men to serve God. For
the example of a good life stirreth men more than true preaching with
only the naked word."

The priest's chief work is to render a substitute for Christ's
miracles by converting himself and his neighbor to God's
law.[2] The Sermon on the Mount, Wyclif pronounced sufficient
for the guidance of human life apart from any of the require-
ments and traditions of men.

IV. As a Doctrinal Reformer. —Wyclif's later writings
teem with denials of the doctrinal tenets of his age and indict-

---

[1] *Evangelizatio verbi est preciosior quam ministratio alicujus ecclesiastici
sacramenti, Op. evang.*, I. 375. *Predicatio verbi Dei est solemnior quam
confectio sacramenti, De sac. scr.*, II. 156. See also Arnold, *Engl. Works*, III.
153 sq., 464 ; *Serm. Lat.*, II. 115 ; *De scr. sac.*, II. 138.

[2] *Debemus loco miraculorum Christi nos et proximos ad legem Dei conver-
tere. De ver.*, I. 90 ; *Op. evang.*, I. 368.

ments against ecclesiastical abuses.   There could be no doubt
of his meaning.   Beginning with the 19 errors Gregory XI.
was able to discern, the list grew as the years went on.   The
Council of Constance gave 45, Netter of Walden, fourscore,
and the Bohemian John Lücke, an Oxford doctor of divinity,
266.   Cochlæus, in writing against the Hussites, went beyond
all former computations and ascribed to Wyclif the plump sum
of 303 heresies, surely enough to have forever covered the Reformer's memory with obloquy.   Fuller suggests as the reason
for these variations that some lists included only the Reformer's
primitive tenets or breeders, and others reckoned all the younger
fry of consequence derived from them.

The first three articles adduced by the Council of Constance [1]
had respect to the Lord's Supper, and charged Wyclif with
holding that the substance of the bread remains unchanged
after the consecration, that Christ is not in the sacrament of
the altar in a real sense, and the accidents of a thing cannot
remain after its substance is changed.   The 4th article ac-
cuses him with declaring that the acts of bishop or priest in
baptizing, ordaining and consecrating are void if the celebrant
be in a state of mortal sin.   Then follow charges of other alleged heresies, such as that after Urban VI. the papacy should
be abolished, the clergy should hold no temporal possessions,
the friars should gain their living by manual toil and not
by begging, Sylvester and Constantine erred in endowing the
Church, the papal elections by the cardinals were an invention
of the devil, it is not necessary to salvation that one believe
the Roman church to be supreme amongst the churches and
that all the religious orders were introduced by the devil.

The most of the 45 propositions represent Wyclif's views
with precision.   They lie on the surface of his later writings,
but they do not exhaust his dissent from the teachings and
practice of his time.   His assault may be summarized under
five heads : the nature of the Church, the papacy, the priesthood, the doctrine of transubstantiation and the use of the
Scriptures.

The Church was defined in the *Civil Lordship* to be the

[1] See Mansi, XXVII., 632–636, and Mirbt, p. 157 sq.

body of the elect,—living, dead and not yet born,— whose head is Christ.   Scarcely a writing has come down to us from Wyclif's pen in which he does not treat the subject, and in his special treatise on the Church, written probably in 1378, it is defined more briefly as the body of all the elect — *congregatio omnium predestinatorum.*   Of this body, Christ alone is the head.   The pope is the head of a local church.   Stress is laid upon the divine decree as determining who are the predestinate and who the reprobate.[1]

Some persons, he said, in speaking of "Holy Church, understand thereby prelates and priests, monks and canons and friars and all that have the tonsure,—alle men that han crownes, —though they live ever so accursedly in defiance of God's law."   But so far from this being true, all popes, cardinals and priests are not among the saved.   On the contrary, not even a pope can tell assuredly that he is predestinate.   This knows no one on earth.   The pope may be a *prescitus,* a reprobate.   Such popes there have been, and it is blasphemy for cardinals and pontiffs to think that their election to office of itself constitutes a title to the primacy of the Church.   The curia is a nest of heretics if its members do not follow Christ, a fountain of poison, the abomination of desolation spoken of in the sacred page. Gregory XI. Wyclif called a terrible devil—*horrendus diabolus.* God in His mercy had put him to death and dispersed his confederates, whose crimes Urban VI. had revealed.[2]

Though the English Reformer never used the terms visible and invisible Church, he made the distinction.   The Church militant, he said, commenting on John 10 : 26, is a mixed body. The Apostles took two kinds of fishes, some of which remained in the net and some broke away.   So in the Church some are ordained to bliss and some to pain, even though they live godly for a while.[3]   It is significant that in his English writings Wyclif uses the term Christen men — Christian men — instead of the term the faithful.

---

[1] *De dom. civ.*, I. 358.   *Ecclesia cath. sive apost. est universitas predestinatorum.   De eccles.*, ed. by Loserth, pp. 2, 5, 31, 94, *Engl. Works*, III. 339, 447, etc.   [2] *De eccles.*, 5, 28 sq., 63, 88, 89, 355, 358, 360.

[3] *Engl. Works.*, I. 50.

As for the papacy, no one has used more stinging words against individual popes as well as against the papacy as an institution than did Wyclif. In the treatises of his last years and in his sermons, the pope is stigmatized as anti-christ. His very last work, on which he was engaged when death overtook him, bore the title, *Anti-christ*, meaning the pope. He went so far as to call him the head-vicar of the fiend.[1] He saw in the papacy the revelation of the man of sin. The office is wholly poisonous — *totum papale officium venenosum*. He heaped ridicule upon the address "most holie fadir." The pope is neither necessary to the Church nor is he infallible. If both popes and all their cardinals were cast into hell, believers could be saved as well without them. They were created not by Christ but by the devil. The pope has no exclusive right to declare what the Scriptures teach, or proclaim what is the supreme law. His absolutions are of no avail unless Christ has absolved before. Popes have no more right to excommunicate than devils have to curse. Many of them are damned — *multi papæ sunt dampnati*. Strong as such assertions are, it is probable that Wyclif did not mean to cast aside the papacy altogether. But again and again the principle is stated that the Apostolic see is to be obeyed only so far as it follows Christ's law.[2]

As for the interpretation of Matthew 16 : 18, Wyclif took the view that "the rock" stands for Peter and every true Christian. The keys of the kingdom of heaven are not metal keys, as popularly supposed, but spiritual power, and they were committed not only to Peter, but to all the saints, "for alle men

---

[1] The condemnatory epithets and characterizations are found in the *Engl. Works*, ed. by Matthew, *De papa*, pp. 458–487, and *The Church and her Members*, and *The Schism of the Rom. Pontiffs*, Arnold's ed., III. 262 sqq., 340 sqq., the *Trialogus, Dialogus*, the Latin Sermons, vol. II., and especially the *Opus evangelicum*, parts of which went under the name *Christ and his Adversary, Antichrist*. See Loserth's introductions to Lat. Serm., II. p. iv sq., and *Op. evang.*, vol. II.; also his art. *Wiclif's Lehre, vom wahren, und falschen Papsttum, Hist. Ztschrift*, 1907, and his ed. of the *De potestate papæ*. In these last works Loserth presents the somewhat modified view that when Wyclif inveighed against the papacy it was only as it was abused. The *De potestate* was written perhaps in 1379. His later works show an increased severity.

[2] *Lat. Serm.*, IV. 95 ; *De dom. civ.*, 366–394 ; *De ver. scr.*, II. 56 sqq.; *Dial.*, p. 25 ; *Op. evang.*, I. 38, 92, 98, 382, 414, II. 132, III. 187 ; *Engl. Works*, II. 229 sq., etc.

that comen to hevene have these keies of God."[1] Towards the pope's pretension to political functions, Wyclif was, if possible, more unsparing. Christ paid tribute to Cæsar. So should the pope. His deposition of kings is the tyranny of the devil. By disregarding Peter's injunction not to lord it over God's heritage, but to feed the flock, he and all his sect — *tota secta* — prove themselves hardened heretics.

Constantine's donation, the Reformer pronounced the beginning of all evils in the Church. The emperor was put up to it by the devil. It was his new trick to have the Church endowed.[2] Chapter after chapter of the treatise on the Church calls upon the pope, prelates and priests to return to the exercise of spiritual functions. They had become the prelates and priests of Cæsar. As the Church left Christ to follow Cæsar, so now it should abandon Cæsar for Christ. As for kissing the pope's toe, there is no foundation for it in Scripture or reason.

The pope's practice of getting money by tribute and taxation calls forth biting invective. It was the custom, Wyclif said, to solemnly curse in the parish churches all who clipped the king's coins and cut men's purses. From this it would seem, he continued,

that the proud and worldly priest of Rome and all his advisers were the most cursed of clippers and cut-purses, — cursed of clipperis and purse-ker-veris, — for they drew out of England poor men's livelihoods and many thousands of marks of the king's money, and this they did for spiritual favors. If the realm had a huge hill of gold, it would soon all be spent by this proud and worldly priest-collector. Of all men, Christ was the most poor, both in spirit and in goods, and put from him all manner of worldly lordship. The pope should leave his authority to worldly lords, and speedily advise his clergy to do the same. I take it, as a matter of faith, that no man should follow the pope, nor even any of the saints in heaven, except as they follow Christ.[3]

The priests and friars formed another subject of Wyclif's vigorous attack. Clerics who follow Christ are true priests and

---

[1] *Op. evang.*, II. 105 sq. ; *Engl. Works*, I. 350 sq.

[2] *De ver.*, I. 267 ; *Engl. Works*, III. 341 sq.; *De Eccles.*, 189, 365 sqq. ; *Op. Evang.*, III. 188.

[3] *Engl. Works*, III. 320. Letter to Urban VI., *Fasc. ziz.*, p. 341 ; *Engl. Works*, III. 504–506.

none other.   The efficacy of their acts of absolution of sins
depends upon their own previous absolution by Christ.   The
priest's function is to show forgiveness, already pronounced by
God, not to impart it.   It was, he affirmed, a strange and marvellous thing that prelates and curates should "curse so faste,"
when Christ said we should bless rather than reprove.   A sentence of excommunication is worse than murder.

The rule of auricular confession Wyclif also disparaged.
True contrition of heart is sufficient for the removal of sins.
In Christ's time confession of man to man was not required.
In his own day, he said, " shrift to God is put behind; but privy
(private) shrift, a new-found thing, is authorized as needful for
the soul's health."   He set forth the dangers of the confessional, such as the unchastity of priests.   He also spoke of the
evils of pilgrimages when women and men going together
promiscuously were in temptation of great "lecherie." [1]   Clerical celibacy, a subject the Reformer seldom touched upon, he
declared, when enforced, is against Scripture, and as under the
old law priests were allowed to marry, so under the new the
practice is never forbidden, but rather approved.

Straight truth-telling never had a warmer champion than
Wyclif.   Addressing the clergy, he devotes nearly a hundred
pages of his *Truth of Scripture* to an elaboration of this principle.   Not even the most trifling sin is permissible as a means
of averting a greater evil, either for oneself or one's neighbor.
Under no circumstances does a good intention justify a falsehood.   The pope himself has no right to tolerate or practice
misrepresentation to advance a good cause.   To accomplish a
good end, the priest dare not even make a false appeal to fear.
All lying is of itself sin, and no dispensation can change its
character. [2]

The friars called forth the Reformer's keenest thrusts, and
these increased in sharpness as he neared the end of his life.

---

[1] His *De eucharistia et pœnitentia sive de confessione* elaborates this subject.   See also *Engl. Works*, I. 80, III. 141, 348, 461.

[2] *De eccles.*, p. 162 ; *De ver. scr.*, II. 1–99.   *Omne mendacium est per se peccatum sed nulla circumstantia potest rectificare, ut peccatum sit non peccatum, De ver.*, II. 61.

Quotations, bearing on their vices, would fill a large volume. Entire treatises against their heresies and practices issued from his pen. They were slavish agents of the pope's will; they spread false views of the eucharist; they made merchandise of indulgences and letters of fraternity which pretended to give the purchasers a share in their own good deeds here and at the final accounting. Their lips were full of lies and their hands of blood. They entered houses and led women astray; they lived in idleness; they devoured England.[1]

The Reformer had also a strong word to say on the delusion of the contemplative life as usually practised. It was the guile of Satan that led men to imagine their fancies and dreamings were religious contemplation and to make them an excuse for sloth. John the Baptist and Christ both left the desert to live among men. He also went so far as to demand that monks be granted the privilege of renouncing the monkish rule for some other condition where they might be useful.[2]

The four mendicant orders, the Carmelites, Augustinians, Jacobites or Dominicans, and Minorites or Franciscans gave their first letters to the word Caim, showing their descent from the first murderer. Their convents, Wyclif called Cain's castles. His relentless indignation denounced them as the tail of the dragon, ravening wolves, the sons of Satan, the emissaries of anti-christ and Luciferians and pronounced them worse than Herod, Saul and Judas. The friars repeat that Christ begged water at the well. It were to their praise if they begged water and nothing else.[3]

With the lighter hand of ridicule, Chaucer also held up the mendicants for indictment. In the Prologue to his *Canterbury Tales* he represents the friar as an —

> . . . easy man to yeve penaunce,
> Ther as he wiste to have a good pitaunce
> For unto a powre order for to give
> Is signe that a man is well y-shrive.
> *   *   *   *   *   *

---

[1] *Engl. Works*, III. 420 sqq.; *Op. evang.*, II. 40; *Lat. serm.*, IV. 62, 121, etc.

[2] See the tract *Of Feigned Contemplative Life* in Matthew, pp. 187, 196; *De eccles.*, p. 380; *Lat. Serm.*, II. 112.

[3] *Lat. serm.*, II. 84; *Trial.*, IV. 33; *Engl. Works*, III. 348; *Dial.*, pp. 13, 65, etc.

His wallet lay biforn him in his lappe
Bretful of pardoun come from Rome all hoot,
A voys he hadde as smal as hath a goot
Ne was ther swich another pardonour
For in his male he hadde a pilwe-beer [pillow]
Which that, he seyde, was our Lady's veyl:
And in a glas he hadde a pigges bones.
— Skeat's ed., 4 : 7, 21.

If it required boldness to attack the powerful body of the monks, it required equal boldness to attack the mediæval dogma of transubstantiation.   Wyclif himself called it a doctrine of the moderns and of the recent Church — *novella ecclesia*. In his treatise on the eucharist, he praised God that he had been delivered from its laughable and scandalous errors.[1] The dogma of the transmutation of the elements he pronounced idolatry, a lying fable.   His own view is that of the spiritual presence. Christ's body, so far as its dimensions are concerned, is in heaven.   It is efficaciously or virtually in the host as in a symbol.[2] This symbol "represents" — *vicarius est* — the body.

Neither by way of impanation nor of identification, much less by way of transmutation, is the body in the host.   Christ is in the bread as a king is in all parts of his dominions and as the soul is in the body.   In the breaking of the bread, the body is no more broken than the sunbeam is broken when a piece of glass is shattered : Christ is there sacramentally, spiritually, efficiently — *sacramentaliter, spiritualiter et virtualiter*. Transubstantiation is the greatest of all heresies and subversive of logic, grammar and all natural science.[3]

The famous controversy as to whether a mouse, partaking of the sacramental elements, really partakes of Christ's body is discussed in the first pages of the treatise on the eucharist. Wyclif pronounces the primary assumption false, for Christ is not there in a corporal manner.   An animal, in eating a man,

[1] *Ab isto scandaloso et derisibili errore de quidditate hujus sacramenti*, pp. 52, 199.

[2] *Corpus Chr. est dimensionaliter in cælo et virtualiter in hostia ut in signo.* De euchar., pp. 271, 303. Walden, *Fasc. ziz.*, rightly represents Wyclif as holding that " the host is neither Christ nor any part of Christ, but the effectual sign of him."   [3] *De euchar.*, p. 11; *Trial.*, pp. 248, 261.

does not eat his soul. The opinion that the priest actually breaks Christ's body and so breaks his neck, arms and other members, is a shocking error.   What could be more shocking, — *horribilius*, — he says, than that the priest should daily make and consecrate the Lord's body, and what more shocking than to be obliged to eat Christ's very flesh and drink his very blood. Yea, what could be thought of more shocking than that Christ's body may be burned or eructated, or that the priest carries God in bodily form on the tips of his fingers.   The words of institution are to be taken in a figurative sense.   In a similar manner, the Lord spoke of himself as the seed and of the world as the field, and called John, Elijah, not meaning that the two were one person.   In saying, I am the vine, he meant that the vine is a symbol of himself.

The impossibility of the miracle of elemental transmutation, Wyclif based on the philosophical principle that the substance of a thing cannot be separated from its accidents.   If accidents can exist by themselves, then it is impossible to tell what a thing is or whether it exists at all.   Transubstantiation would logically demand transaccidentation, an expression the English Reformer used before Luther.   The theory that the accidents remain while the substance is changed, he pronounced " grounded neither in holy writt ne reson ne wit but only taughte by newe hypocritis and cursed heretikis that magnyfyen there own fantasies and dremes." [1]

Another proof of Wyclif's freedom of mind was his assertion that the Roman Church, in celebrating the sacrament, has no right to make a precise form of words obligatory, as the words of institution differ in the different accounts of the New Testament.   As for the profitable partaking of the elements, he declared that the physical eating profits nothing except the soul be fed with love.   Announcing it as his expectation that he would be set upon for his views, he closed his notable treatise on the eucharist with the words, The truth of reason will prevail over all things.

Super omnia vincit veritas rationis.

---

[1] *De euch.*, pp. 78, 81, 132; *Engl. Works*, III. 520.

In these denials of the erroneous system of the mediæval Church at its vital points, Wyclif was far in advance of his own age and anticipated the views of the Protestant Reformers.

§ 42. *Wyclif and the Scriptures.*

Wyclif's chief service for his people, next to the legacy of his own personality, was his assertion of the supreme authority of the Bible for clergy and laymen alike and his gift to them of the Bible in their own tongue. His statements, setting forth the Scriptures as the clear and sufficient manual of salvation and insisting that the literal sense gives their plain meaning, were as positive and unmistakable as any made by Luther. In his treatise on the value and authority of the Scriptures, with 1000 printed pages,[1] more is said about the Bible as the Church's appointed guide-book than was said by all the mediæval theologians together. And none of the Schoolmen, from Anselm and Abælard to Thomas Aquinas and Duns Scotus, exalted it to such a position of preëminence as did he. With one accord they limited its authority by coördinating with its contents tradition, that is, the teachings of the Church. This man, with unexcelled precision and cogency, affirmed its final jurisdiction, as the law of God, above all authorities, papal, decretist or patristic. What Wyclif asserts in this special treatise, he said over again in almost every one of his works, English and Latin. If possible, he grew more emphatic as his last years went on, and his *Opus evangelicum*, probably his very last writing, abounds in the most positive statements language is capable of.

To give the briefest outline of the *Truth of Scripture* will be to state in advance the positions of the Protestant Reformers in regard to the Bible as the rule of faith and morals. To Wyclif the Scriptures are the authority for every Catholic tenet.

---

[1] *De veritate Scripturæ*, ed. by Buddensieg, with Introd., 3 vols., Leip., 1904. The editor, I. p. xci, gives the date as 1387, 1388. Wyclif starts out by quoting Augustine at length, I. 6–16. The treatise contains extensive digressions, as on the two natures of Christ, I. 179 sqq., the salutation of Mary, I. 282 sqq., lying, II. 1–99, Mohammedanism, II. 248–266, the functions of prelates and priests, III. 1–104, etc.

They are the Law of Christ, the Law of God, the Word of God, the Book of Life — *liber vitæ*. They are the immaculate law of the Lord, most true, most complete and most wholesome.[1] All things necessary to belief for salvation are found in them. They are the Catholic faith, the Christian faith, — *fides chris-tiana*, — the primal rule of human perfection, the primal foundation of the Christian proclamation.

This book is the whole truth which every Christian should study.[2] It is the measure and standard of all logic. Logic, as in Oxford, changes very frequently, yea, every twenty years, but the Scriptures are yea, yea and nay, nay. They never change. They stand to eternity.[3] All logic, all law, all philosophy and all ethic are in them. As for the philosophy of the pagan world, whatever it offers that is in accord with the Scriptures is true. The religious philosophy which the Christian learns from Aristotle he learns because it was taught by the authors of Scripture.[4] The Greek thinker made mistakes, as when he asserted that creation is eternal. In several places Wyclif confesses that he himself had at one time been led astray by logic and the desire to win fame, but was thankful to God that he had converted to the full acceptance of the Scriptures as they are and to find in them all logic.

All through this treatise, and in other works, Wyclif contends against those who pronounced the sacred writings irrational or blasphemous or abounding in errors and plain falsehoods. Such detractors he labelled modern or recent doctors — *moderni, novelli doctores*. Charges such as these would seem well-nigh incredible, if Wyclif did not repeat them over and over again. They remind us of the words of the priest who told Tyndale, 150 years later, " It were better to be without

---

[1] *lex domini immaculata . . . verissima, completissima et saluberrima*, I. 156.

[2] *Illum librum debet omnis christianus adiscere cum sit omnis veritas*, I. 109, 138.

[3] I. 54. *Aliæ logicæ sæpissime variantur . . . logica scripturæ in eternum stat.*

[4] I. 22, 29, 138. *Christianus philosophiam non discit quia Aristotelis sed quia autorum scripturæ sac. et per consequens tamquam suam scientiam quæ in libris theologiæ rectius est edocta.*

God's laws than to be without the pope's." What could be more shocking,—*horribilius*,—exclaimed Wyclif, than to assert that God's words are false.[1]

The supreme authority of the Scriptures appears from their contents, the beneficent aim they have in view, and from the witness borne to them by Christ. God speaks in all the books. They are one great Word of God. Every syllable of the two Testaments is true, and the authors were nothing more than scribes or heralds.[2] If any error seem to be found in them, the error is due to human ignorance and perverseness. Nothing is to be believed that is not founded upon this book, and to its teachings nothing is to be added.[3]

Wyclif devotes much time to the principles of biblical exposition and brushes away the false principles of the Fathers and Schoolmen by pronouncing the "literal verbal sense" the true one. On occasion, in his sermons, he himself used the other senses, but his sound judgment led him again and again to lay emphasis upon the etymological meaning of words as final. The tropological, anagogical and allegorical meanings, if drawn at all, must be based upon the literal meaning. Wyclif confessed his former mistake of striving to distinguish them with strict precision. There is, in fact, only one sense of Scripture, the one God himself has placed in it as the book of life for the wayfaring man.[4] Heresy is the contradiction of Scripture. As for himself, Wyclif said, he was ready to follow its teachings, even unto martyrdom, if necessary.[5]

---

[1] I. 151, 200, 394, 408; *Lat. serm.*, 179; *De eccles.*, 173, 318, etc.

[2] *Tota scrip. est unum magnum Verbum Dei.*, I. 269. *Autores nisi scribæ vel precones ad scrib. Dei legem.* I. 392. Also I. 86, 156, 198, 220 sqq., III. 106 sqq., 143.

[3] *Falsitas in proposito est in false intelligente et non in Scrip. sac.*, p. 193. *Nulli alii in quoquam credere nisi de quanto se fundaverit ex script.* I. 383. *De civ. dom.*, p. 394.

[4] *De ver.*, 114, 119, 123. *Sensus literalis script. est utrobique verus*, p. 73. *Solum ille est sensus script. quem deus et beati legunt in libro vitæ qui est uni talis et alteri viatoribus, semper verus*, etc., p. 126.

[5] *Oportet conclusiones carnis et seculi me deserere et sequi Christum in pauperie si debeam coronari*, I. 357. Also II. 129–131. In view of the above statement, it is seen how utterly against the truth Kropatschek's statement is, *Man wird den Begriff Vorreformatoren getrost in die historische Rumpel-*

For hundreds of years no eminent teacher had emphasized the right of the laity to the Word of God. It was regarded as a book for the clergy, and the interpretation of its meaning was assumed to rest largely with the decretists and the pope. The Council of Toulouse, 1229, had forbidden the use of the Bible to laymen. The condemned sects of the 12th and 13th centuries, especially the Waldenses, had adopted another rule, but their assailants, such as Alanus ab Insulis, had shown how dangerous their principle was. Wyclif stood forth as the champion of an open Bible. It was a book to be studied by all Christians, for " it is the whole truth." Because it was given to the Church, its teachings are free to every one, even as is Christ himself.[1]

To withhold the Scriptures from the laity is a fundamental sin. To make them known in the mother-tongue is the first duty of the priest. For this reason priests ought always to be familiar with the language of the people. Wyclif held up the friars for declaring it heresy to translate God's law into English and make it known to laymen. He argued against their position by referring to the gift of tongues at Pentecost and to Jerome's translation, to the practice of Christ and the Apostles who taught peoples in their native languages and to the existence in his own day of a French translation made in spite of all hindrances. Why, he exclaims, " should not Englishmen do the same, for as the lords of England have the Bible in French, it would not be against reason if they had the same material in English." Through an English Bible Englishmen would be enabled best "to follow Christ and come to heaven."[2] What could be more positive than the following words?

Christen men and women, olde and young, shulden study fast in the New Testament, and no simple man of wit shulde be aferde unmeasurably

---

kammer werfen können, we may without further thought cast the idea of Reformers before the Reformation into the historical rag bag. The remark he makes after stating how little the expression sola scriptura meant in the mouths of mediæval reformers. See Walter in Litzg., 1905, p. 447.

[1] Illum librum debet omnis Christianus adiscere cum sit omnis veritas. De ver., I. 109. Fideles cujuscunque generis, fuerint clerici vel laici, viri vel feminæ, inveniunt in ea virtutem operandi, etc., pp. 117, 136. Op. evang., II. 36.   [2] Matthew, Sel. Works, p. 429 sq.

to study in the text of holy Writ. Pride and covetise of clerks is cause of their blyndness and heresie and priveth them fro verie understonding of holy Writ. The New Testament is of ful autorite and open to understonding of simple men, as to the pynts that ben most needful to salvation.

Wyclif was the first to give the Bible to his people in their own tongue. He knew no Hebrew and probably no Greek. His version, which was made from the Latin Vulgate, was the outgrowth of his burning desire to make his English countrymen more religious and more Christian. The paraphrastic translation of books which proceeded from the pen of Richard Rolle and perhaps a verse of the New Testament of Kentish origin and apparently made for a nunnery,[1] must be considered as in no wise in conflict with the claim of priority made for the English Reformer. In his task he had the aid of Nicolas Hereford, who translated the Old Testament and the Apocryphal books as far as Baruch 3: 20. A revision was made of Wyclif's Bible soon after his death, by Purvey. In his *prologue*, Purvey makes express mention of the " English Bible late translated," and affirms that the Latin copies had more need of being corrected than it. One hundred and seventy copies of these two English bibles are extant, and it seems strange that, until the edition issued by Forshall and Madden in 1850, they remained unprinted.[2] The reason for their not being struck off on the presses of Caxton and other early English printers, who issued the *Golden Legend*, with its fantastic and often grewsome religious tales, was that Wyclif had been pronounced a heretic and his version of the Scriptures placed under the ban by the religious authorities in England.

[1] The text pub. Cambr., 1902 and 1905, by Anna C. Paues : *A Fourteenth Cent. Engl. Bible Vs.*

[2] *The Holy Bible, containing the Old and New Testaments with the Apocryphal Books, in the earliest English Versions made from the Vulgate by John Wycliffe and his Followers.* 4 vols., Oxford, 1850. The work cost 22 years of labor. It contains Purvey's Prologue and an exhaustive Preface by the editors. Purvey's New Test. had been printed by John Lewis, London, 1731, and reprinted by Henry Baber, Lond., 1810, and in the Bagster English *Hexapla*, Lond., 1841. Adam Clarke had published Wyclif's version of the Canticles in his *Commentary*, 3rd vol., 1823, and Lea Wilson, Wyclif's New Test., Lond., 1848.

A manuscript preserved in the Bodleian, Forshall and Madden affirm to be without question the original copy of Hereford himself. These editors place the dates of the versions in 1382 and 1388. Purvey was a Lollard, who boarded under Wyclif's roof and, according to the contemporary chronicler, Knighton, drank plentifully of his instructions. He was imprisoned, but in 1400 recanted, and was promoted to the vicarage of Hythe. This preferment he resigned three years later. He was imprisoned a second time by Archbishop Chichele, 1421, was alive in 1427, and perhaps died in prison.

To follow the description given by Knighton in his Chronicle, the gift of the English Bible was regarded by Wyclif's contemporaries as both a novel act and an act of desecration. The irreverence and profanation of offering such a translation was likened to the casting of pearls before swine. The passage in Knighton, who wrote 20 years after Wyclif's death, runs thus : —

The Gospel, which Christ bequeathed to the clergy and doctors of the Church, — as they in turn give it to lay and weaker persons, — this Master John Wyclif translated out of the Latin into the Anglican tongue, not the Angelic tongue, so that by him it is become common, — *vulgare*, — and more open to the lay folk and to women, knowing how to read, than it used to be to clerics of a fair amount of learning and of good minds. Thus, the Gospel pearl is cast forth and trodden under foot of swine, and what was dear to both clergy and laity is now made a subject of common jest to both, and the jewel of the clergy is turned into the sport of the laity, so that what was before to the clergy and doctors of the Church a divine gift, has been turned into a mock Gospel [or common thing].[1]

The plain meaning of this statement seems to be that Wyclif translated at least some of the Scriptures, that the translation was a novelty, and that the English was not a proper language for the embodiment of the sacred Word. It was a cleric's book, and profane temerity, by putting it within the reach of the laity, had vulgarized it.

The work speedily received reprobation at the hands of the

---

[1] *Commune æternum.* It is hard to give the exact rendering of these words. Knighton goes on to refer to William of St. Amour, who said of some that they changed the pure Gospel into another Gospel, the *evangelium æternum* or *evangelium Spiritus sancti.* Knighton, *Chronicle*, II. 151 sq.

Church authorities.　A bill presented in the English parliament, 1391, to condemn English versions, was rejected through the influence of the duke of Lancaster, but an Oxford synod, of 1408, passed the ominous act, that upon pain of greater excommunication, no man, by his own authority, should translate into English or any other tongue, until such translation were approved by the bishop, or, if necessary, by the provincial council.　It distinctly mentions the translation "set forth in the time of John Wyclif."　Writing to John XXIII., 1412, Archbishop Arundel took occasion to denounce "that pestilent wretch of damnable memory, yea, the forerunner and disciple of anti-christ who, as the complement of his wickedness, invented a new translation of the Scriptures into his mother-tongue." [1]

In 1414, the reading of the English Scriptures was forbidden upon pain of forfeiture " of land, cattle, life and goods from their heirs forever."　Such denunciations of a common English version were what Wyclif's own criticisms might have led us to expect, and quite in consonance with the decree of the Synod of Toulouse, 1229, and Arundel's reprobation has been frequently matched by prelatical condemnation of vernacular translations of the Bible and their circulation down to the papal fulminations of the 19th century against Bible societies, as by Pius VII., 1816, who declared them "fiendish institutions for the undermining of the foundation of religion." The position, taken by Catholic apologists, that the Catholic hierarchy has never set itself against the circulation of the Scriptures in the vernacular, but only against unauthorized translations, would be adapted to modify Protestantism's notion of the matter, if there were some evidence of only a limited attempt to encourage Bible study among the laity of the Catholic Church with the pages of Scripture open before them.　If we go to the Catholic countries of Southern Europe and to South America, where her sway has been unobstructed, the very opposite is true.

In the clearest language, Wyclif charged the priestly author-

---

[1] *Novæ ad suæ malitiæ complementum Scripturarum in linguam maternam translationis practica adinventa.*　Wilkins, III. 350.

ities of his time with withholding the Word of God from the
laity, and denying it to them in the language the people could
understand.   And the fact remains that, from his day until
the reign of Elizabeth, Catholic England did not produce any
translations of the Bible, and the English Reformers were of
the opinion that the Catholic hierarchy was irrevocably set
against English versions.   Tyndale had to flee from England
to translate his New Testament, and all the copies of the first
edition that could be collected were burnt on English soil.
And though it is alleged that Tyndale's New Testament was
burnt because it was an " unauthorized " translation, it still
remains true that the hierarchy made no attempt to give the
Bible to England until long after the Protestant Reformation
had begun and Protestantism was well established.

The copies of Wyclif's and Purvey's versions seem to have
been circulated in considerable numbers in England, and were
in the possession of low and high.   The Lollards cherished
them.   A splendid copy was given to the Carthusians of London by Henry VI., and another copy was in the possession of
Henry VII.   Sir Thomas More states distinctly that there was
found in the possession of John Hunne, who was afterwards
burnt, a Bible " written after Wyclif's copy and by him translated into our tongue." [1]   While for a century and a half these
volumes helped to keep alive the spirit of Wyclif in England,
it is impossible to say how far Wyclif's version influenced the
Protestant Reformers.   In fact, it is unknown whether they
used it at all.   Some of its words, such as mote and beam and
strait gate, which are found in the version of the 16th century,
seem to indicate, to say the least, that these terms had become
common property through the medium of Wyclif's version.[2]
The priceless heirloom which English-speaking peoples possess
in the English version and in an open Bible free to all who will
read, learned and unlearned, lay and cleric, will continue to be
associated with the Reformer of the 14th century.   As has been
said by one of the ablest of recent Wyclif students, Buddensieg, the call to honor the Scriptures as the Word of God and

---

[1] More's *Works*, p. 240, quoted by Gairdner, I. 112.
[2] See Forshall and Madden, p. xxxii, and Eadie, pp. 90-94.

to study and diligently obey them, runs through Wyclif's writings like a scarlet thread.[1]   Without knowing it, he departed diametrically from Augustine when he declared that the Scriptures do not depend for their authority upon the judgment of the Church, but upon Christ.

In looking over the career and opinions of John Wyclif, it becomes evident that in almost every doctrinal particular did this man anticipate the Reformers.   The more his utterances are studied, the stronger becomes this conviction.   He exalted preaching; he insisted upon the circulation of the Scriptures among the laity; he demanded purity and fidelity of the clergy; he denied infallibility to the papal utterances, and went so far as to declare that the papacy is not essential to the being of the Church.   He defined the Church as the congregation of the elect ; he showed the unscriptural and unreasonable character of the doctrine of transubstantiation ; he pronounced priestly absolution a declarative act.   He dissented from the common notion about pilgrimages ; he justified marriage on biblical grounds as honorable among all men ; he appealed for liberty for the monk to renounce his vow, and to betake himself to some useful work.

The doctrine of justification by faith Wyclif did not state. However, he constantly uses such expressions as, that to believe in Christ is life.   The doctrine of merit is denied, and Christ's mediation is made all-sufficient.   He approached close to the Reformers when he pronounced " faith the supreme theology," — *fides est summa theologia*, — and that only by the study of the Scriptures is it possible to become a Christian.[2]

Behind all Wyclif's other teaching is his devotion to Christ and his appeal to men to follow Him and obey His law.   It is

---

[1] Buddensieg, Introd. to *De ver.*, pp. xxxii, xxxviii.

[2] See *De ver. scr.*, I. 209, 212, 214, 260, II. 234.   He made a distinction between the material and formal principles when he spoke of the words of Christ as something *materiale*, and the inner meaning as something *formale*. Buddensieg, p. xlv, says Wyclif had a dawning presentiment of justifying faith.   According to Poole, he stated the doctrine in other terms in his treatment of lordship.   Rashdall, *Dict. Natl. Biog.*, LXIII. 221, says that, apart from the doctrine of justification by faith, there is little in the teachings of the 16th cent. which Wyclif did not anticipate.

scarcely an exaggeration to say that the name of Christ appears on every page of his writings. To him, Christ was the supreme philosopher, yea, the content of all philosophy.[1]

In reaching his views Wyclif was, so far as we know, as independent as any teacher can well be. There is no indication that he drew from any of the mediæval sects, as has been charged, nor from Marsiglius and Ockam. He distinctly states that his peculiar views were drawn not from Ockam but from the Scriptures.[2]

The Continental Reformers did not give to Wyclif the honor they gave to Huss. Had they known more about him, they might have said more.[3] Had Luther had access to the splendid shelf of volumes issued by the Wyclif Society, he might have said of the English Reformer what he said of Wessel's *Works* when they were put into his hands. The reason why no organized reformation followed Wyclif's labors is best given when we say, the time was not yet ripe. And, after all the parallelisms are stated between his opinions and the doctrines of the Reformers, it will remain true that, evangelical as he was in speech and patriotic as he was in spirit, the Englishman never ceased to be a Schoolman. Luther was fully a man of the new age.

NOTE. — THE AUTHORSHIP OF THE FIRST ENGLISH BIBLE. Recently the priority of Wyclif's translation has been denied by Abbot Gasquet in two elaborate essays, *The Old English Bible*, pp. 87–155. He also pronounces it to be very doubtful if Wyclif ever translated any part of the Bible. All that can be attempted here is a brief statement of the case. In addition to Knighton's testimony, which seems to be as plain as language could put it, we have the testimony of John Huss in his *Reply* to the Carmelite Stokes, 1411, that Wyclif translated the whole Bible into English.

---

[1] *Summus philos., immo summa philosophia est Christus, deus noster, quem sequendo et discendo sumus philosophi. De ver. scr.,* I. 32.

[2] *De ver. scr.,* I. 346 sqq. See Loserth, *Kirchenpolitik,* pp. 2, 112 sq. Buddensieg, *De ver. scr.,* p. viii, says, *Was er war wissen wir, nicht wie er es geworden.* We know what he was, but not how he came to be what he was. See, for a Rom. Cath. judgment, Hergenröther-Kirsch, II. 878, who finds concentrated in Wyclif the false philosophy of the Waldenses and the Apocalyptics, of Marsiglius and Ockam.

[3] Melanchthon, in a letter to Myconius, declared that Wyclif was wholly ignorant of the doctrine of justification, and at another time he said he had foolishly mixed up the Gospel and politics.

No one contends that Wyclif did as much as this, and Huss was no doubt speaking in general terms, having in mind the originator of the work and the man's name connected with it.   The doubt cast upon the first proposition, the priority of Wyclif's version, is due to Sir Thomas More's statement in his *Dialogue*, 1530, *Works*, p. 233.   In controverting the positions of Tyndale and the Reformers, he said, "The whole Bible was before Wyclif's days, by virtuous and well-learned men, translated into English and by good and godly people, with devotion and soberness, well and reverently read." He also says that he saw such copies.   In considering this statement it seems very possible that More made a mistake (1) because the statement is contrary to Knighton's words, taken in their natural sense and Huss' testimony.   (2) Because Wyclif's own statements exclude the existence of any English version before his own.   (3) Because the Lollards associated their Bible with Wyclif's name.   (4) Because before the era of the Reformation no English writer refers to any translating except in connection with Wyclif's name and time.   Sir Thomas More was engaged in controversy and attempting to justify the position that the Catholic hierarchy had not been opposed to translations of the Scriptures nor to their circulation among proper classes of the laity.   But Abbot Gasquet, after proposing a number of conjectural doubts and setting aside the natural sense of Knighton's and Arundel's statements, denies altogether the Wycliffite authorship of the Bible ascribed to him and edited by Forshall and Madden, and performs the feat of declaring this Bible one of the old translations mentioned by More.   It must be stated here, a statement that will be recalled later, that Abbot Gasquet is the representative in England of the school of Janssen, which has endeavored to show that the Catholic Church was in an orderly process of development before Luther arose, and that Luther and the Reformers checked that development and also wilfully misrepresented the condition of the Church of their day.   Dr. Gasquet, with fewer plausible facts and less literature at command than Janssen, seeks to present the English Church's condition in the later Middle Ages as a healthy one.   And this he does (1) by referring to the existence of an English mediæval literature, still in MSS., which he pronounces vast in its bulk; (2) by absolutely ignoring the statements of Wyclif; (3) by setting aside the testimonies of the English Reformers; (4) by disparaging the Lollards as a wholly humble and illiterate folk.   Against all these witnesses he sets up the single witness, Sir Thomas More.

The second proposition advocated by Dr. Gasquet that it is doubtful, and perhaps very improbable, that Wyclif did nothing in the way of translating the Bible, is based chiefly upon the fact that Wyclif does not refer to such a translation anywhere in his writings.   If we take the abbot's own high priest among authorities, Sir Thomas More, the doubt is found to be unjustifiable, if not criminal.   More, speaking of John Hunne, who was burnt, said that he possessed a copy of the Bible which was "after a Wycliffite copy." Eadie, I. 60 sqq.; Westcott, *Hist. of the Eng. Bible.* Gairdner, who discusses the subject fairly in his *Lollardy*, I. 101–117, Capes, pp. 125–128, F. D. Matthew, in *Eng. Hist. Rev.*, 1895, and Bigg, Wayside Sketches, p. 127 sq., take substantially the position taken by the author. Gasquet was preceded by Lingard, *Hist. of Eng.*, IV. 196, who laid stress upon More's testimony to offset and disparage the honor given from time immemorial to Wyclif in connection with the English Bible.

How can a controversialist be deemed fair who, in a discussion of this kind, does not even once refer to Wyclif's well-known views about the value of a popular knowledge of the Scriptures, and his urgency that they be given to all the people through plain preaching and in translation? Dr. Gasquet's attitude to "the strange personality of Wyclif" may be gotten from these words, *Old Eng. Bible*, p. 88: "Whatever we may hold as Catholics as to his unsound theological opinions, about which there can be no doubt, or, as peace-loving citizens, about his wild revolutionary social theories, on which, if possible, there can be less," etc.

The following are two specimens of Wyclif's versions: —

MATT. VIII. 23–27. And Jhesu steyinge vp in to a litel ship, his disciplis sueden him. And loo! a grete steryng was made in the see, so that the litil ship was hilid with wawis; but he slepte. And his disciplis camen nigh to hym, and raysiden hym, sayinge, Lord, saue vs: we perishen. And Jhesus seith to hem, What ben yhee of litil feith agast? Thanne he rysynge comaundide to the wyndis and the see, and a grete pesiblenesse is maad. Forsothe men wondreden, sayinge: What manere *man* is *he* this, for the wyndis and the see obeishen to hym.

ROM. VIII. 5–8. For thei that ben aftir the fleisch saueren tho thingis that ben of the fleisch, but thei that ben aftir the spirit felen tho thingis that ben of the spirit. For the prudence of fleisch: is deeth, but the prudence of spirit: is liif and pees. For the wisdom of fleische is enemye to God, for it is not suget to the lawe of God: for nether it may. And thei that ben in fleisch: moun not please to God.

§ 43. *The Lollards.*

Although the impulse which Wyclif started in England did not issue there in a compact or permanent organization, it was felt for more than a century. Those who adopted his views were known as Wycliffites or Lollards, the Lollards being associated with the Reformer's name by the contemporary chroniclers, Knighton and Walsingham, and by Walden.[1] The for-

[1] In 1382 Repyngdon was called *Lollardus de secta Wyclif*, and Peter Stokes was referred to as having opposed the "Lollards and the sect of Wyclif," *Fasc.*, 296. Knighton, II. 182, 260, expressly calls the Wycliffians Lollards, *Wycliviani qui et Lollardi dicti sunt.*

mer term gradually gave way to the latter, which was used to embrace all heretics in England.

The term Lollards was transplanted to England from Holland and the region around Cologne.   As early as 1300 Lollard heretics were classed by the authorities with the Beghards, Beguines, Fratricelli, Swestriones and even the Flagellants, as under the Church's ban.   The origin of the word, like the term Huguenots, is a matter of dispute.   The derivation from the Hollander, " Walter Lollard," who was burnt in Cologne, 1322, is now abandoned.[1]   Contemporaries derived it from *lolium*, — tares, — and referred it to the false doctrine these sectarists were sowing, as does Knighton, and probably also Chaucer, or, with reference to their habit of song, from the Latin word *laudare*, to praise.[2]   The most natural derivation is from the Low German, *lullen* or *einlullen*, to sing to sleep, whence our English lullaby.   None of the Lollard songs have come down to us. Scarcely a decade after Wyclif's death a bull was issued by Boniface IX., 1396, against the " Lullards or Beghards " of the Low Countries.

The Wycliffite movement was suppressed by a rigid inquisition, set on foot by the bishops and sanctioned by parliament. Of the first generation of these heretics down to 1401, so far as they were brought to trial, the most, if not all, of them recanted.   The 15th century furnished a great number of Lollard trials and a number of Lollard martyrs, and their number was added to in the early years of the 16th century.   Active measures were taken by Archbishop Courtenay ; and under his successor, Thomas, earl of Arundel, the full force of persecution was let loose.   The warlike bishop of Norwich, Henry

---

[1] Fredericq, I. 172.   A certain Matthew, whose bones were exhumed and burnt, is called Mattæus Lollært.   Fred., I. 250.   For documents associating the Lollards with other sectarists, see Fred., I. 228, II. 132, 133, III. 46, etc.

[2] So Jan Hocsem of Liége, d. 1348, who in his *Gesta pontiff. Leodiensium* says, *eodem anno* (1309) *quidam hypocritæ gyrovagi qui Lollardi sive Deum laudantes vocabuntur*, etc.   Fred., I. 154.   Chaucer, in his Prologue to the *Shipman's Tale*, says : —

> This loller here wol prechen us somewhat
> He wolde sowen some difficulte
> Or sprenge cokkle in our clene corn.

Spenser, joined heartily in the repressive crusade, swearing to put to death by the flames or by decapitation any of the dissenters who might presume to preach in his diocese. The reason for the general recantations of the first generation of Wyclif's followers has been found in the novelty of heresy trials in England and the appalling effect upon the accused, when for the first time they felt themselves confronted with the whole power of the hierarchy.[1]

In 1394, they were strong enough to present a petition in full parliament, containing twelve Conclusions.[2] These propositions called the Roman Church the stepmother of the Church in England, declared that many who had priestly ordination were not ordained of God, took up the evils growing out of enforced celibacy, denied Christ's material presence in the eucharist, condemned pilgrimages and image-worship, and pronounced priestly confession and indulgences measures invented for the profit of the clergy. The use of mitres, crosses, oil and incense was condemned and also war, on the ground that warriors, after the first blood is let, lose all charity, and so " go straight to hell." In addition to the Bible, the document quotes Wyclif's *Trialogus* by name.

From about 1390 to 1425, we hear of the Lollards in all directions, so that the contemporary chronicler was able to say that of every two men found on the roads, one was sure to be a Lollard.[3] With the accession of Henry IV. of Lancaster (1399–1413), a severe policy was adopted. The culminating point of legislation was reached in 1401, when parliament passed the act for the burning of heretics, the first act of the kind in England.[4] The statute referred to the Lollards as a new sect, damnably thinking of the faith of the Church in respect to the sacraments and, against the law of God and the Church, usurping the office of preaching. It forbade this people to preach, hold schools and conventicles and issue books. The violators were to be tried in the diocesan courts and, if

---

[1] Cheyney, p. 436 sqq.

[2] Gee and Hardy, pp. 126–132. *Fasc.*, pp. 360–369. See Gairdner, I. 44–46.

[3] Knighton, II. 191.

[4] *De comburendo hæretico*, Gee and Hardy, pp. 133–137.

found guilty and refusing to abjure, were to be turned over
to the civil officer and burnt.   The burning, so it was stipulated, was to be on a high place where the punishment might be
witnessed and the onlookers be struck with fear.

The most prominent personages connected with the earliest
period of Wycliffism, Philip Repyngdon, John Ashton, Nicolas Hereford and John Purvey, all recanted.   The last three
and Wyclif are associated by Knighton as the four arch-heretics.

Repyngdon, who had boldly declared himself at Oxford for
Wyclif and his view of the sacrament, made a full recantation,
1382.   Subsequently he was in high favor, became chancellor
of Oxford, bishop of Lincoln and a cardinal, 1408.   He showed
the ardor of his zeal by treating with severity the sect whose
views he had once espoused.

John Ashton had been one of the most active of Wyclif's
preachers.   In setting forth his heretical zeal, Knighton describes him as "leaping up from his bed and, like a dog, ready to
bark at the slightest sound."   He finally submitted in Courtenay's court, professing that he "believed as our modur, holy
kirke, believes," and that in the sacrament the priest has in
his hand Christ's very body.   He was restored to his privileges as lecturer in Oxford, but afterwards fell again into heretical company.[1]

Hereford, Wyclif's fellow-translator, appealed to Rome, was
condemned there and cast into prison.   After two years of confinement, he escaped to England and, after being again imprisoned, made his peace with the Church and died a Carthusian.

In 1389, nine Lollards recanted before Courtenay, at Leicester.   The popular preacher, William Swynderby, to whose
sermons in Leicester the people flocked from every quarter,
made an abject recantation, but later returned to his old ways,

---

[1] Knighton, II. 171 sqq., gives the recantation in English, the *Fasc.*, p. 329,
in Latin.   John Foxe's accounts of the Lollard martyrs are always quaintly
related.   Gairdner is the fullest and best of the recent treatments.   For his
judgment of Foxe, see I. 159, 336 sqq.   He ascribes to him accuracy in tran-
scribing documents.   The articles in the *Dict. of Natl. Biog.* are always to be
consulted.

and was tried in 1391 and convicted.   Whether he was burnt
or died in prison, Foxe says, he could not ascertain.

The number suffering death by the law of 1401 was not
large in the aggregate.   The victims were distributed through
the 125 years down to the middle of Henry VIII.'s reign.   There
were among them no clergymen of high renown like Ridley and
Latimer.   The Lollards were an humble folk, but by their
persistence showed the deep impression Wyclif's teachings
had made.   The first martyr, the poor chaplain of St. Osythe,
William Sawtré, died March 2, 1401, before the statute for
burning heretics was passed.   He abjured and then returned
again to his heretical views.   After trying him, the spiritual
court ordered the mayor or sheriff of London to "commit him
to the fire that he be actually burnt." [1]   The charges were that
he denied the material presence, condemned the adoration of
the cross and taught that preaching was the priesthood's most
important duty.

Among other cases of burnings were John Badby, a tailor
of Evesham, 1410, who met his awful fate chained inside of a
cask ; two London merchants, Richard Turming and John
Claydon at Smithfield, 1415 ; William Taylor, a priest, in 1423
at Smithfield ; William White at Norwich, 1428 ; Richard Hove-
den, a London citizen, 1430 ; Thomas Bagley, a priest, in the
following year; and in 1440, Richard Wyche, who had corresponded with Huss.   Peter Payne, the principal of St. Edmund's
College, Oxford, took refuge in flight, 1417, and became a
leader among the Hussites, taking a prominent part as their
representative at the Council of Basel.   According to Foxe
there were, 1424–1430, 100 prosecutions for heresy in Norwich
alone.   The menace was considered so great that, in 1427,
Richard Flemmyng, bishop of Lincoln, founded Lincoln College, Oxford, to counteract heresy.   It was of this college that
John Wesley was a fellow, the man who made a great breach
in the Church in England.

[1] Gee and Hardy give the sentence and the *Fasc.* the proceedings of the trial.
It is a matter of dispute under what law Sawtré was condemned to the flames.
Prof. Maitland, in his *Canon Law*, holds that it was under the old canon
practice as expressed in papal bulls.   The statute *De comburendo* was before
parliament at the time of Sawtre's death.

The case of William Thorpe, who was tried in 1397 and again before Arundel, 1407, is of interest not only in itself, but for the statements that were made in the second trial about Wyclif. The archbishop, after accusing Thorpe of having travelled about in Northern England for 20 years, spreading the infection of heresy, declared that he was called of God to destroy the false sect to which the prisoner belonged, and pledged himself to "punish it so narrowly as not to leave a slip of you in this land."[1]   Thorpe's assertion that Wyclif was the greatest clerk of his time evoked from Arundel the acknowledgment that he was indeed a great clerk and, by the consent of many, "a perfect liver," but that many of the conclusions of his learning were damned, as they ought to be.

Up to the close of the 14th century, a number of laymen in high position at court had favored Wycliffism, including Sir Lewis Clifford, Sir Richard Stury and Sir John Clanvowe, all of the king's council, Sir John Cheyne, speaker of the lower house, the Lord Chancellor, Sir Thomas Erpingham and also the earl of Salisbury.[2]   This support was for the most part withdrawn when persecution took an active form.   With Sir John Oldcastle, otherwise known as Lord Cobham from his marriage with the heiress of the Cobham estate, it was different.   He held firm to the end, encouraged the new preachers on his estates in Kent, and condemned the mass, auricular confession and the worship of images.   Arundel's court, before which he appeared after repeated citations, turned him over to the secular arm " to do him to death."   Oldcastle was imprisoned in the Tower, but made his escape and was at large for four years.   In 1414, he was charged with being a party to an uprising of 20,000 Lollards against the king.   Declared an outlaw, he fled to Wales, where he was seized three years later and taken to London to be hanged and burnt as a traitor and heretic, Dec. 15, 1417.[3]   John Foxe saw in him "the blessed martyr of Christ, the good Lord Cobham."

---

[1] The proceedings are given at great length by Foxe and by Bale, who copied Tyndale's account. *Sel. Works* of Bp. Bale, pp. 62–133.

[2] Walsingham, II. 244 ; Knighton, II. 181 ; *Chron. Angl.*, p. 377.

[3] Walsingham, II. 328, says he was hung as a traitor and burnt as a heretic. Usk, p. 317, reports he " was hung on the gallows in a chain of iron after

It is a pleasant relief from these trials and puttings-to-death to find the University of Oxford in 1406 bearing good testimony to the memory of its maligned yet distinguished dead, placing on record its high sense of his purity of life, power in preaching and diligence in studies.   But fragrant as his memory was held in Oxford, at least secretly, parliament was fixed in its purpose to support the ecclesiastical authorities in stamping out his doctrine.   In 1414, it ordered the civil officer to take the initiative in ferreting out heresy, and magistrates, from the Lord chancellor down, were called upon to use their power in extirpating "all manner of heresies, errors and lollardies." This oath continued to be administered for two centuries, until Sir Edward Coke, Lord High Sheriff of Buckinghamshire, refused to take it, with the name Lollard included, insisting that the principles of Lollardy had been adopted by the Church of England.[1]

Archbishop Chichele seemed as much bent as his predecessor, Arundel, on clearing the realm of all stain of heresy.   In 1416 he enjoined his suffragans to inquire diligently twice a year for persons under suspicion and, where they did not turn them over to the secular court, to commit them to perpetual or temporary imprisonment, as the nature of the case might require. It was about the same time that an Englishman, at the trial of Huss in Constance, after a parallel had been drawn between Wyclif's views and those of the Bohemian, said, "By my soul, if I were in your place I would abjure, for in England all the masters, one after another, albeit very good men, when suspected of Wicliffism, abjured at the command of the archbishop."[2]

Heresy also penetrated into Scotland, James Resby, one of Wyclif's poor priests, being burnt at Perth, 1407, and another at Glasgow, 1422.   In 1433, a Bohemian student at St. Andrews,

that he had been drawn.   He was once and for all burnt up with fierce fire, paying justly the penalty of both swords."   The *Fasciculi* give a protracted account of Sir John's opinions and trial.   Judgments have been much divided about him.   Fuller speaks of him " as a boon companion, jovial roysterer and yet a coward to boot."   Shakespeare presents him in the character of Falstaff.   See Gairdner, I. 97 sq.

[1] Summers, p. 67.   [2] Loserth, *Wiclif and Hus*, p. 175.

Paul Craw, suffered the same penalty for heresy.[1] The Scotch parliament of 1425 enjoined bishops to make search for heretics and Lollards, and in 1416 every master of arts at St. Andrews was obliged to take an oath to defend the Church against them.

Between 1450–1517, Lollardy was almost wholly restricted to the rural districts, and little mention is made of it in contemporary records. At Amersham, one of its centres, four were tried in 1462, and some suffered death, as William Barlowe in 1466, and John Goose a few years later. In 1507, three were burnt there, including William Tylsworth, the leading man of the congregation. At the crucial moment he was deserted by the members, and sixty of them joined in carrying fagots for his burning. This time of recantation continued to be known in the district as the Great Abjuration. The first woman to suffer martyrdom in England, Joan Broughton, was burnt at Smithfield, 1494, as was also her daughter, Lady Young. Nine Lollards made public penance at Coventry, 1486, but, as late as 1519, six men and one woman suffered death there. Foxe also mentions William Sweeting and John Brewster as being burnt at Smithfield, 1511, and John Brown at Ashford the same year. How extensively Wyclif's views continued to be secretly held and his writings read is a matter of conjecture. Not till 1559 was the legislation directed against Lollardy repealed.

Our knowledge of the tenets and practices of the Lollards is derived from their Twelve Conclusions and other Lollard documents, the records of their trials and from the *Repressor for over-much Blaming of the Clergy*, an English treatise written by Dr. Pecock, bishop of Chichester, and finished 1455. Inclined to liberal thought, Bishop Pecock assumed a different attitude from Courtenay, Arundel and other prelates, and sought by calm reasoning to win the Lollards from their mistakes. He mentioned the designation of Known Men — 1 Cor. 14: 38, 2 Tim. 2:19 — as being one of old standing for them, and he also calls them " the lay party " or " the Bible Men." He proposed to consider their objections against 11 customs and institutions, such as the worship of images, pilgrimages,

---

[1] Mitchell: *Scottish Reformation*, p. 15.

landed endowments for the church, degrees of rank among the
clergy, the religious orders, the mass, oaths and war.   Their
tenet that no statute is valid which is not found in the Scriptures he also attempted to confute.   In advance of his age,
the bishop declared that fire, the sword and hanging should
not be resorted to till the effort had been made " by clene wit
to draw the Lollards into the consent of the true faith."   His
sensible counsel brought him into trouble, and in 1457 he was
tried by Archbishop Bouchier and offered the alternative of
burning or public recantation.   Pecock chose the latter, and
made abjuration at St. Paul's Cross before the archbishop and
thousands of spectators.   He was clothed in full episcopal
robes, and delivered up 14 of his writings to be burnt.[1]   He
was forced to resign his see, and in 1459 was, at the pope's
instance, remanded to close confinement in Thorney Abbey.
His *Repressor* had been twice burnt in Oxford.

There seems to have been agreement among the Lollards
in denying the material presence of Christ in the eucharistic
bread and in condemning pilgrimages, the worship of images and
auricular confession.   They also held to the right of the people
to read the Scriptures in their own tongue.[2]   The expression,
God's law, was widely current among them, and was opposed
to the canon law and the decisions of the Church courts.   Some
denied purgatory, and even based their salvation on faith,[3] the
words, "Thy faith hath saved thee," being quoted for this view.
Some denied that the marriage bond was dependent upon the
priest's act, and more the scriptural warrant and expediency
of priestly celibacy.[4]

Lollardy was an anticipation of the Reformation of the

[1] Among these works was the *Provoker*, in which Pecock denied that the
Apostles had compiled the Apostles' Creed.   See Introd. to Babington's Ed. of
the *Repressor* in Rolls Series, and art. Pecock in *Dict. Natl. Biog.*, XLIV.
198–202.

[2] Knighton, II. 155, complains of the Lollards having the Scriptures in the
vulgar tongue.   Such a translation he said the laity regarded as *melior et
dignior quam lingua latina.*   [3] So Walsingham, II. 253.

[4] Summers, p. 60, speaks of an unpublished Lollard MS. of 37 articles which
deal with clerical abuses, such as simony, quarrelling, holding secular offices,
oaths, the worship of images, the eucharist and papal authority.

sixteenth century, and did something in the way of preparing the mind of the English people for that change.   Professed by many clerics, it was emphatically a movement of laymen.   In the early Reformation period, English Lutherans were at times represented as the immediate followers of Wyclif.   Writing in 1523 to Erasmus, Tonstall, bishop of London, said of Lutheranism that "it was not a question of some pernicious novelty, but only that new arms were being added to the great band of Wycliffite heretics." [1]

§ 44. *John Huss of Bohemia.*

Across the seas in Bohemia, where the views of Wyclif were transplanted, they took deeper root than in England, and assumed an organized form.   There, the English Reformer was called the fifth evangelist and, in its earlier stages, the movement went by the name of Wycliffism.   It was only in the later periods that the names Hussites and Hussitism were substituted for Wycliffites and Wycliffism.   Its chief spokesmen were John Huss and Jerome of Prag, who died at the stake at Constance for their avowed allegiance to Wyclif.

Through Huss, Prag became identified with a distinct stage in the history of religious progress.   Distinguished among its own people as the city of St. John of Nepomuk, d. 1383, and in the history of armies as the residence of Wallenstein, the Catholic leader in the Thirty Years' War, Prag is known in the Western world pre-eminently as the home of Huss.   Through his noble advocacy, the principles enunciated by Wyclif became the subject of discussion in oecumenical councils, called forth armed crusades and furnished an imposing spectacle of steadfast resistance against religious oppression.   Wycliffism passed out of view in England; but Hussitism, in spite of the most bitter persecution by the Jesuits, has trickled down in pure though small streamlets into the religious history of modern times, notably through the Moravians of Herrnhut.

During the reign of Charles IV., king of Bohemia and emperor, 1346-1378, the Bohemian kingdom entered upon the

---

[1] Trevelyan, p. 349.

JOHN HUSS OF BOHEMIA

golden era of its literary and religious history.   In 1344, the
archbishopric of Prag was created, and the year 1347 witnessed
an event of far more than local importance in the founding of
the University of Prag.   The first of the German universities,
it was forthwith to enter upon the era of its brightest fame.
The Czech and German languages were spoken side by side
in the city, which was divided, at the close of the 14th century into five quarters.   The Old Town, inhabited chiefly by
Germans, included the Teyn church, the Carolinum, the Bethlehem chapel and the ancient churches of St. Michael and St.
Gallus.   Under the first archbishop of Prag, Arnest of Par-
dubitz, and his successor Ocko of Wlaschim, a brave effort was
made to correct ecclesiastical abuses.   In 1355, the demand for
popular instruction was recognized by a law requiring parish
priests to preach in the Czech.   The popular preachers, Konrad of Waldhausen, d. 1369, Militz of Kremsier, d. 1374, and
Matthias of Janow, d. 1394, made a deep impression.   They
quoted at length from the Scriptures, urged the habit of frequent communion, and Janow, as reported by Rokyzana at the
Council of Basel, 1433, seems to have administered the cup to
the laity.[1]   When John Huss entered upon his career in the
university, he was breathing the atmosphere generated by these
fervent evangelists, although in his writings he nowhere quotes
them.

Close communication between England and Bohemia had
been established with the marriage of the Bohemian king Wenzel's sister, Anne of Luxemburg, to Richard II., 1382.   She was
a princess of cultivated tastes, and had in her possession copies
of the Scriptures in Latin, Czech and German.   Before this
nuptial event, the philosophical faculty of the University of
Prag, in 1367, ordered its bachelors to add to the instructions
of its own professors the notebooks of Paris and Oxford doctors.   Here and there a student sought out the English university, or even went so far as the Scotch St. Andrews.   Among
those who studied in Oxford was Jerome of Prag.   Thus a

---

[1] The truth of Rokyzana's statement is denied by Loserth, in Herzog, VIII.
588 sq.   On other Bohemian preachers of Huss' day, see Flajshans, *Serm. de
Sanctis*, p. iv.

bridge for the transmission of intellectual products was laid from Wyclif's lecture hall to the capital on the Moldau.[1] Wyclif's views and writings were known in Bohemia at an early date. In 1381 a learned Bohemian theologian, Nicolas Biceps, was acquainted with his leading principles and made them a subject of attack. Huss, in his reply to the English Carmelite, John Stokes, 1411, declared that he and the members of the university had had Wyclif's writings in their hands and been reading them for 20 years and more.[2] Five copies are extant of these writings, made in Huss' own hand, 1398. They were carried away in the Thirty Years' War and are preserved in the Royal Library of Stockholm.

John Huss was born of Czech parents, 1369, at Husinec in Southern Bohemia. The word Hus means goose, and its distinguished bearer often applied the literal meaning to himself. For example, he wrote from Constance expressing the hope that the Goose might be delivered from prison, and he bade the Bohemians, "if they loved the Goose," to secure the king's aid in having him released. Friends also referred to him in the same way.[3] His parents were poor and, during his studies in the University of Prag, he supported himself by singing and manual services. He took the degree of bachelor of arts in 1393 and of divinity a year later. In 1396 he incepted as master of arts, and in 1398 began delivering lectures in the university. In 1402 he was chosen rector, filling the office for six months.

With his academic duties Huss combined the activity of a preacher, and in 1402 was appointed to the rectorship of the

---

[1] See Loserth, *Wiclif and Hus*, p. 70. Wenzel or Wenceslaus IV., surnamed the Lazy, was the son of Charles IV. His second wife was Sophia of Bavaria. His half-brother, Sigismund, succeeded him on the throne.

[2] Flajshans : *Serm. de Sanctis*, p. xxi. Nürnb. ed., I. 135.

[3] Workman : *Hus' Letters*, pp. 94, 118, 163, 189, 192, 198, 201. The spelling, Hus, almost universally adopted in recent years by German and English writers, has been exchanged by Loserth in his art. in Herzog for Huss, as a form more congenial to the German mode of spelling. For the same reason this volume has adopted the form Huss as more agreeable to the English reader's eye and more consonant with our mode of spelling. Karl Müller adopts this spelling in his *Kirchengeschichte*. The exact date of Huss' birth is usually given as July 6th, 1369, but with insufficient authority. Loserth, *Wiclif and Hus*, p. 65 sq.

Chapel of the Holy Innocents of Bethlehem. This church, usually known as the Bethlehem church, was founded in 1391 by two wealthy laymen, with the stipulation that the incumbent should preach every Sunday and on festival days in Czech. It was made famous by its new rector as the little church, Anastasia, in Constantinople, was made famous in the fourth century by Gregory of Nazianzus, and by his discourses against the Arian heresy.

As early as 1402, Huss was regarded as the chief exponent and defender of Wycliffian views at the university. Protests, made by the clergy against their spread, took definite form in 1403, when the university authorities condemned the 24 articles placed under the ban by the London council of 1382. At the same time 21 other articles were condemned, which one of the university masters, John Hübner, a Pole, professed to have extracted from the Englishman's writings. The decision forbade the preaching and teaching of these 45 articles. Among Wyclif's warm defenders were Stanislaus of Znaim and Stephen Paletz. The subject which gave the most offence was his doctrine of the Lord's Supper.

A distinct stage in the religious controversies agitating Bohemia was introduced by the election of Sbinko of Hasenburg to the see of Prag, 1403. In the earlier years of his administration Huss had the prelate's confidence, held the post of synodal preacher and was encouraged to bring to the archbishop's notice abuses that might be reformed. He was also appointed one of a commission of three to investigate the alleged miracles performed by the relic of Christ's blood at Wylsnak and attracting great throngs. The report condemned the miracles as a fraud. The matter, however, became subject of discussion at the university and as far away as Vienna and Erfurt, the question assuming the form whether Christ left any of his blood on the earth. In a tract entitled the *Glorification of all Christ's Blood*,[1] Huss took the negative side. In spite of him and of the commission's report, the miracles at Wylsnak went on, until, in 1552, a zealous Lutheran broke the pyx which held the relic and burnt it.

[1] *De omni Christi sanguine glorificato*, ed. by Flajshans, p. 42.

So extensive was the spread of Wycliffism that Innocent VII., in 1405, called upon Sbinko to employ severe measures to stamp it out and to seize Wyclif's writings. The same year a Prag synod forbade the propaganda of Wyclif's views and renewed the condemnation of the 45 articles. Three years later Huss — whose activity in denouncing clerical abuses and advocating Wyclif's theology knew no abatement — was deposed from the position of synodal preacher. The same year the university authorities, at the archbishop's instance, ordered that no public lectures should be delivered on Wyclif's *Trialogus* and *Dialogus* and his doctrine of the Supper, and that no public disputation should concern itself with any of the condemned 45 articles.

The year following, 1409, occurred the emigration from the university of the three nations, the Bavarians, Saxons and Poles, the Czechs alone being left. The bitter feeling of the Bohemians had expressed itself in the demand for three votes, while the other nations were to be restricted to one each. When Wenzel consented to this demand, 2000 masters and scholars withdrew, the Germans going to Leipzig and founding the university of that city. The University of Prag was at once reduced to a provincial school of 500 students, and has never since regained its prestige.[1]

Huss, a vigorous advocate of the use of the Czech, was the recognized head of the national movement at the university, and chosen first rector under the new régime. If possible, his advocacy of Wyclif and his views was more bold than before. From this time forth, his Latin writings were filled with excerpts from the English teacher and teem with his ideas. Wyclif's writings were sown broadcast in Bohemia. Huss himself had translated the *Trialogus* into Czech. Throngs were attracted by preaching. Wherever, wrote Huss in 1410, in city or town, in village or castle, the preacher of the holy truth made his

---

[1] See Rashdall : *Universities of Europe*, I. 211–242. The number of departing students is variously given. The number given above has the authority of Procopius, a chronicler of the 15th century. Only 602 were matriculated at Leipzig the first year, and this figure seems to point to a smaller number than 2000 leaving Prag. Kügelgen, *Die Gefängnissbriefe*, p. ix, adopts the unreasonable number, 5000.

John Rokyzana of the Utraquist party and the Taborite, Procopius. Rokyzana was the pastor of the Teyn Church in Prag.

The council recognized the austere principles of the Hussites
by calling upon the Basel authorities to prohibit all dancing
and gambling and the appearance of loose women on the streets.
On their arrival, Jan. 4, 1433, the Bohemians were assigned to
four public taverns, and a large supply of wine and provisions
placed at their disposal. Delegations from the council and from
the city bade them formal welcome. They followed their own
rituals, the Taborites arousing most curiosity by the omission
of all Latin from the services and discarding altar and priestly
vestments.

On the floor of the council, the Bohemians coupled praise with
the names of Wyclif and Huss, and would tolerate no references
to themselves as heretics. The discussions were prolonged to
a wearisome length, some of their number occupying as much
as two or three days in their addresses. Among the chief
speakers was the Englishman, Peter Payne, whose address consumed three days. The final agreement of four articles, known
as the *Campactata*, was ratified by deputies of the council and
of the three Bohemian parties giving one another the hand.
The main article granted the use of the cup to the laity, where
it was asked, but on condition that the doctrine be inculcated
that the whole Christ is contained in each of the elements.
The use of the cup was affirmed to be wholesome to those partaking worthily.[1] The Compacts were ratified by the Bohemian diet of Iglau, July 5, 1436. All ecclesiastical censures
were lifted from Bohemia and its people. The abbot of Bon-
nival, addressing the king of Castile upon the progress of the
Council of Basel, declared that the Bohemians at the start were
like ferocious lions and greedy wolves, but through the mercy
of Christ and after much discussion had been turned into the
meekest lambs and accepted the four articles.[2]

Although technically the question was settled, the Taborites
were not satisfied. The Utraquists approached closer to the
Catholics. Hostilities broke out between them, and after a
wholesale massacre in Prag, involving, it is said, 22,000 victims,

[1] See Mansi, XXXI. 273 sqq.   [2] Haller, *Concil. Basil.*, I. 291 sqq.

the two parties joined in open war. The Taborites were defeated in the battle at Lipan, May 30, 1434, and Procopius slain. This distinguished man had travelled extensively, going as far as Jerusalem before receiving priestly orders. He was a brilliant leader, and won many successes in Austria, Moravia and Hungary. The power of the Taborites was gone, and in 1452 they lost Mt. Tabor, their chief stronghold.

The emperor now entered upon possession of his Bohemian kingdom and granted full recognition to the Utraquist priests, promising to give his sanction to the elections of bishops made by the popular will and to secure their ratification by the pope. Rokyzana was elected archbishop of Prag by the Bohemian diet of 1435. Sigismund died soon after, 1437, and the archbishop never received papal recognition, although he administered the affairs of the diocese until his death, 1471.

Albert of Austria, son-in-law of Sigismund and an uncompromising Catholic, succeeded to the throne. In 1457 George Podiebrad, a powerful noble, was crowned by Catholic bishops, and remained king of Bohemia till 1471. He was a consistent supporter of the national party which held to the Compactata. The papal authorities, refusing to recognize Rokyzana, despatched emissaries to subdue the heretics by the measures of preaching and miracles. The most noted among them were Fra Giacomo and John of Capistrano. John, whose miraculous agency equalled his eloquence, succumbed to a fever after the battle of Belgrade.

In 1462 the Compacts were declared void by Pius II., who threatened with excommunication all priests administering the cup to the laity. George Podiebrad resisted the papal bull. Four years later, a papal decree sought to deprive that " son of perdition " of his royal dignity, and summoned the Hungarian king, Matthias Corvinus, to take his crown.[1] Matthias

[1] Pius had received at Mt. Tabor hospitable treatment from the Hussites, whom he was afterwards to treat with wonted papal arrogance. Travelling through Bohemia on a mission from Frederick III., and benighted, he preferred to trust himself to the Taborites rather than to their enemies. Although he had found refuge with them, he used ridicule in describing their poverty and peasant condition. Some he found almost naked, some wore only a sheepskin over their bodies, some had no saddle, some no reins for their horses. And

accepted the responsibility, took the cross and invaded Moravia. The war was still in progress when Podiebrad died. By the peace of Kuttenberg 1485 and an agreement made in 1512, the Utraquists preserved their right to exist at the side of their Catholic neighbors. Thus they continued till 1629, when the right of communion in both kinds was withdrawn by Ferdinand II. of Austria, whose hard and bloody hand put an end to all open dissent in Bohemia.[1]

The third outgrowth from the Hussite stock, the *Unitas Fratrum*, commonly called the Bohemian Brethren, has had an honorable and a longer history than the Taborites and Calixtines. This body still has existence in the Moravians, whose missionary labors, with Herrnhut as a centre, have stirred all Protestant Christendom. Its beginnings are uncertain. It appears distinctly for the first time in 1457, and continued to grow till the time of the Reformation. Its synod of 1467 was attended by 60 Brethren. The members in Prag were subjected to persecution, and George Podiebrad gave them permission to settle on the estate, Lititz, in the village corporation of Kunwald.[2] Martin, priest at Königgraetz, with a part of his flock affiliated himself with them, and other congregations were soon formed. They were a distinct type, worshipping by themselves, and did not take the sacraments from the Catholic priests. They rejected oaths, war and military service and resorted, apparently from the beginning, to the lot. They also rejected the doctrine of purgatory and all services of priests of unworthy life.

The exact relation which this Hussite body bore to the Taborites and to the Austrian Waldenses is a matter which has

yet he was obliged to say that, though they were bound by no compulsory system of tithes, they filled their priests' houses with corn, wood, vegetables and meat. See Lea, II. 561.

[1] The Utraquists came into contact with Luther as early as 1519. At the time of the Leipzig Colloquy, two of their preachers in Prag, John Poduschka and Wenzel Rosdalowsky, wrote him letters. The first also sent Luther a gift of knives, and the second, Huss' work *On the Church*, which was reprinted in Wittenberg, 1520. Luther replied by sending them some of his smaller writings. Köstlin, *M. Luther*, I. 290.

[2] The old Moravian school for girls near Lancaster, Pa., gets its name from this colony. The wife of President Benjamin Harrison studied there.

called forth much learned discussion, and is still involved in uncertainty. But there seems to be no doubt that the Bohemian Brethren were moved by the spirit of Huss, and also that in their earliest period they came into contact with the Waldenses. Pressing up from Italy, the followers of Peter Valdez had penetrated into Bohemia in the later part of the 14th century, and had Frederick Reiser as their leader.[1] This Apostolic man was present at the Council of Basel, 1435, and styled himself " the bishop of the faithful in the Romish church, who reject the donation of Constantine." With Anna Weiler, he suffered at the stake in Strassburg, 1458. One of the earliest names associated with the Bohemian Brethren is the name of Peter Chelcicky, a marked religious personage in his day in Bohemia. We know he was a man of authority among them, but little more.[2]

Believing that the papal priesthood had been corrupt since Constantine's donation to Sylvester, the Brethren, at the synod of 1467, chose Michael, pastor of Senftenburg, " presbyter and bishop," and sent him to the Waldensian bishop Stephen for sanction or consecration.[3] It seems probable that Stephen had received orders at Basel from bishops in the regular succession. On his return, Michael consecrated Matthias of Kunwald, while he himself, for a time and for a reason not known, was not officially recognized. The synod had resorted to the lot and placed the words "he is" on 3 out of 12 ballots, 9 being left

[1] For the earlier history of the Austrian Waldensians, see vol. V., part I., p. 500 sq.

[2] Goll, *Untersuchungen*, is a strong advocate of the dependence of the Bohemian Brethren upon the Waldenses for their peculiar views, although he denies that the two sects had any organic connection. Karl Müller, Herzog Enc., III. 448, comes to the same conclusion. He is, however, in doubt whether Chelcicky was associated with the Waldenses. Goll is of the opinion that he was strongly influenced by them. Preger, *Ueber d. Verhältniss der Taboriten zu den Waldesiern des 14ten Jahrh.*, Munich, 1887, occupies an isolated position when he represents the Taborites as a continuation of the Bohemian Waldenses, with some modification. These two bodies were separate when the Bohemian Brethren began to appear on the scene.

[3] So Lucas of Prag. See his writings in Goll, pp. 107, 112. De Schweinitz, *Hist. of the Un. Fratrum*, p. 141 sqq., accepts the ordination of Stephen as regular. Müller questions it, Herzog, III. 452.

blank.　Matthias chose one of the printed ballots.[1]　Matthias, in turn, ordained Thomas and Elias bishops, men who had drawn the other two printed ballots.

By 1500, the Bohemian Brethren numbered 200,000 scattered in 300 or 400 congregations in Bohemia and Moravia.　They had their own confession, catechism and hymnology.[2]　Of the 60 Bohemian books printed 1500–1510, 50 are said to have been by members of the sect.　A new period in their history was introduced by Lucas of Prag, d. 1528, a voluminous writer.　He gave explanations of the Brethren's doctrine of the Lord's Supper to Luther.　Brethren, including Michael Weiss, the hymn-writer, visited the German Reformer, and in 1521 he had in his possession their catechism.

The merciless persecutions of the Brethren and the other remaining Hussite sectarists were opened under the Austrian rule of Ferdinand I. in 1549, and continued, with interruptions, till the Thirty Years' War when, under inspiration of the Jesuits, the government resorted to measures memorable for their heartlessness to blot out heresy from Bohemia and Moravia.

The Church of the Brethren had a remarkable resurrection in the Moravians, starting with the settlement of Christian David and other Hussite families in 1722 on land given by Count Zinzendorf at Herrnhut.　They preserve the venerable name of their spiritual ancestry, *Unitas Fratrum*, and they have made good their heritage by their missionary labors which have carried the Gospel to the remotest ends of the earth, from Greenland to the West Indies and Guiana, and from the leper colony of Jerusalem to Thibet and Australia.　In our own land, David Zeisberger and other Moravian missionaries have shown in their labors among the Indian tribes the godly devotion of John Huss, whose body the flames at Constance were able to destroy, but not his sacred memory and influence.

---

[1] See Goll, p. 87, and the letter to Rokyzana, whose nephew Gregory belonged to the Lititz colony, p. 92.　Of the consecration of Michael by Stephen there is no doubt.　There is some uncertainty about the details.

[2] See Müller's art. on Bohemian Hymnody in Julian's *Dicty.*

CHAPTER VI.

THE LAST POPES OF THE MIDDLE AGES. 1447-1521

§ 48. *Literature and General Survey.*

WORKS ON THE ENTIRE CHAPTER. — *Bullarium*, ed. by TOMASETTI, 5 vols., Turin, 1859 sq. — MANSI : *Councils*, XXXI., XXXII. — MURATORI : *Rerum ital. scriptores.* Gives *Lives* of the popes. — STEFANO INFESSURA : *Diario della città di Roma*, ed. by O. TOMMASINI, Rome, 1890. Extends to 1494, and is the journal of an eye-witness. Also in MURATORI. — JOH. BURCHARD : *Diarium sive rerum urbanarum commentarii, 1483-1506*, ed. by L. THUASNE, 3 vols., Paris, 1883-1885. Also in MURATORI. — B. PLATINA, b. 1421 in Cremona, d. as superintendent of the Vatican libr., 1481 : *Lives of the Popes to the Death of Paul II.*, 1st Lat. ed., Venice, 1479, Engl. trans. by W. BENHAM in *Anc. and Mod. Libr. of Theol.* No date. — SIGISMONDO DEI CONTI DA FOLIGNO : *Le storie de suoi tempi 1475-1510*, 2 vols., Rome, 1883. Lat. and Ital. texts in parallel columns. — PASTOR : *Ungedruckte Akten zur Gesch. der Päpste*, vol. I., 1376-1464, Freiburg, 1904. — RANKE : *Hist. of the Popes.* — A. VON REUMONT : *Gesch. d. Stadt Rom.*, vol. III., Berlin, 1870. — * MANDELL CREIGHTON, bp. of London : *Hist. of the Papacy during the Period of the Reformation*, II. 235-IV., London, 1887. — * GREGOROVIUS : *Hist. of the City of Rome*, Engl. trans., VII., VIII. — * L. PASTOR, R. Cath. Prof. at Innsbruck: *Gesch. der Päpste im Zeitalter der Renaissance*, 4 vols., Freiburg, 1886-1906, 4th ed., 1901-1906, Engl. trans. F. I. Ambrosius, etc., 8 vols., 1908. — WATTENBACH : *Gesch. des röm. Papstthums*, 2d ed., Berlin, 1876, pp. 284-300. — HEFELE-HERGENRÖTHER : *Conciliengeschichte*, VIII. Hergenröther's continuation of Hefele's work falls far below the previous vols. by Hefele's own hand as rev. by KNÖPFLER. — The *Ch. Histt.* of HERGENRÖTHER-KIRSCH, HEFELE, FUNK, KARL MÜLLER. — H. THURSTON : *The Holy Year of Jubilee.* An Account of the Hist. and Ceremonial of the Rom. Jubilee, London, 1900. — Pertinent artt. in WETZER-WELTE and HERZOG. — The Histt. of the Renaissance of BURCKHARDT and SYMONDS. — For fuller lit., see the extensive lists prefixed to Pastor's first three vols. and for a judicious estimate of the contemporary writers, see Creighton at the close of his vols.

NOTE. — The works of Creighton, Gregorovius and Pastor are very full. It is doubtful whether any period of history has been treated so thoroughly and satisfactorily by three contemporary historians. Pastor and Gregorovius have used new documents discovered by themselves in the archives of Mantua, Milan, Modena, Florence, the Vatican, etc. Pastor's notes are vols. of erudite investigation. Creighton is judicial but inclined to be too moderate in his estimate of the vices of the popes, and in details not always reliable. Gregorovius' narration is searching and brilliant. He is unsparing in his reprobation of the dissoluteness of Roman society and backs his statements with authorities. Pastor's masterly and graphic treatment is the most extensive work on the period. Although written with ultramontane prepossessions, it is often unsparing when it deals with the corruption of popes and cardinals, especially Alexander VI., who has never been set forth in darker colors since the 16th century than on its pages.

For § 49. NICOLAS V. — *Lives* by PLATINA and in MURATORI, especially MANETTI. — INFESSURA : pp. 46-59. — GIBBON : *Hist. of Rome*, ch. LXVIII. *For the Fall of Constantinople.* — GREGOROVIUS : VII. 101-160. — CREIGHTON : II. 273-365. — PASTOR : I. 351-774. — GEO. FINDLAY : *Hist. of Greece to 1864*, 7 vols., Oxford, 1877, vols. IV., V. — EDW. PEARS : *The Destruction of the German Empire and the Story of the Capture of Constantinople by the Turks*, London, 1903, pp. 476.

For § 50. PIUS II. — *Opera omnia*, Basel, 1551, 1571, 1589. — *Opera inedita*, by I. CUGNONI, Rome, 1883. — His Commentaries, *Pii pontif. max. commentarii rerum memorabilium quæ temporibus suis contigerunt*, with the continuation of Cardinal Ammanati, Frankfurt, 1614. Last ed. Rome, 1894. — *Epistolæ*, Cologne, 1478, and often. Also in *opera*, Basel, 1551. — A.WEISS : *Æneas Sylvius als Papst Pius II. Rede mit 149 bisher ungedruckten Briefen*, Graz, 1897. — *Eine Rede d. Enea Silvio vor d. C. zu Basel*, ed. J. HALLER in *Quellen u. Forschungen aus ital. Archiven*, etc., Rome, 1900, III. 82-102. — PASTOR : II. 714-747 gives a number of Pius' letters before unpubl. — *Orationes polit. et eccles.* by MANSI, 3 vols., Lucæ, 1755-1759. — *Historia Frid. III.* Best ed. by KOLLAR, Vienna, 1762, Germ. trans. by ILGEN, 2 vols., in *Geschichtschreiber der deutschen Vorzeit.*, Leipzig, 1889 sq. — Addresses at the Congress of Mantua and the bulls *Execrabilis* and *In minoribus* in MANSI : *Concil.*, XXXII., 191-267. — For full list of edd. of Pius' *Works*, see Potthast, I. 19-25. — PLATINA : *Lives of the Popes.* — ANTONIUS CAMPANUS : *Vita Pii II.*, in MURATORI, *Scripp.*, III. 2, pp. 969-992. — G. VOIGT : *Enea Silvio de' Piccolomini als Papst Pius II. und sein Zeitalter*, 3 vols., Berlin, 1856-1863. — K. HASE : *Æn. Syl. Piccolomini*, in *Rosenvorlesungen*, pp. 56-88, Leipzig, 1880. — A. BROCKHAUS : *Gregor von Heimburg*, Leipzig, 1861. — K. MENZEL : *Diether von Isenberg, als Bischof von Mainz, 1459-1463*, Erlangen, 1868. — GREGOROVIUS : VII. 160-218. — BURCKHARDT. — CREIGHTON : II. 365-500. — PASTOR : II. 1-293. Art. *Pius II.* by BENRATH in HERZOG, XV. 422-435.

For § 51. PAUL II. — *Lives* by PLATINA, GASPAR VERONENSIS, and M. CANENSIUS of Viterbo, both in MURATORI, new ed., 1904, III., XVI., p. 3 sqq., with Preface, pp. i-xlvi. — A. PATRITIUS : *Descriptio adventus Friderici III. ad Paulum II.*, MURATORI, XXIII. 205-215. — AMMANATI's Continuation of Pius II.'s *Commentaries*, Frankfurt ed., 1614. Gaspar Veronensis gives a panegyric of the cardinals and Paul's relatives, and stops before really taking up Paul's biography. Platina, from personal pique, disparaged Paul II. Canensius' *Life* is in answer to Platina, and the most important biography. — GREGOROVIUS : VII. — CREIGHTON : III. — PASTOR : II.

For §§ 52, 53. SIXTUS IV., INNOCENT VIII. — INFESSURA, pp. 75-283. —

2 D

402   THE MIDDLE AGES. A.D. 1294-1517.

BURCHARD, in Thuasne's ed., vol. I. — J. GHERARDI DA VOLTERRA : *Diario Romano, 1479-1484*, in MURATORI, *Scripp.*, XXIII. 3, also the ed. of 1904. — PLATINA in MURATORI, III., p. 1053, etc. (accepted by Pastor as genuine and with some question by Creighton). — SIGISMONDO DEI CONTI DA FOLIGNO : vol. I. Infessura is severe on Sixtus IV. and Innocent VIII. Volterra, who received an office from Sixtus, does not pronounce a formal judgment. Sigismondo, who was advanced by Sixtus, is partial to him. — A. THUASNE : *Djem, Sultan, fils de Mohammed II. d'après les documents originaux en grande partie inédits*, Paris, 1892. — GREGOROVIUS : VII. 241-340. — PASTOR : II. 451-III. 284. — CREIGHTON : III. 56-156. — W. ROSCOE : *Life of Lorenzo the Magnificent*, 2 vols., Liverpool, 1795, 6th ed., London, 1825, etc.

§ 54. ALEXANDER VI. — Bulls in *Bullarium Rom.* — The *Regesta* of Alex., filling 113 vols., in the Vatican, Nos. 772-884. After being hidden from view for three centuries, they were opened, 1888, by Leo XIII. to the inspection and use of Pastor. — See Pastor's Preface in his *Gesch. der Päpste.* — INFESSURA. Stops at Feb. 26, 1494. — BURCHARD: vols. II., III. — SIGISMONDO DE' CONTI : *Le storie*, etc. — GORDON : *Life of Alex. VI.*, London, 1728. — ABBÉ OLLIVIER : *Le pape Alex. VI. et les Borgia*, Paris, 1870. — V. NEMEC : *Papst Alex. VI., eine Rechtfertigung*, Klagenfurt, 1879. Both attempts to rescue this pope from infamy. — LEONETTI : *Papa Aless. VI.*, 3 vols., Bologna, 1880. — M. BROSCH : *Alex. VI. u. seine Söhne*, Vienna, 1889. — C. VON HÖFLER : *Don Rodrigo de Borgia und seine Söhne, Don Pedro Luis u. Don Juan*, Vienna, 1889. — HÖFLER : *D. Katastrophe des herzöglichen Hauses des Borgias von Gandia*, Vienna, 1892. — SCHUBERT-SOLDEM : *D. Borgias u. ihre Zeit*, 1907. — REUMONT : *Gesch. der Stadt Rom.* Also art. *Alex. VI.* in WETZER-WELTE, I. 483-491. — H. F. DELABORDE : *L'expédition de Chas. VIII. en Italie*, Paris, 1888. — RANKE : *Hist. of the Popes.* — ROSCOE : *Life of Lorenzo.* — GREGOROVIUS : *Hist. of City of Rome*, vol. VII. Also *Lucrezia Borgia*, 3d ed., Stuttgart, 1875. Engl. trans. by J. L. GARNER, 2 vols., New York, 1903. — CREIGHTON : III. — PASTOR : III. — HERGENRÖTHER-KIRSCH : III. 982-988. — *P. VILLARI : *Machiavelli and his Times*, Engl. trans., 4 vols., London, 1878-1883. — BURCKHARDT and SYMONDS on the Renaissance. — E. G. BOURNE : *Demarcation Line of Alex. VI.* in *Essays in Hist. Criticism.* — LORD ACTON : *The Borgias and their Latest Historian*, in *North Brit. Rev.*, 1871, pp. 351-367.

For § 55. JULIUS II. BULLARIUM IV. — BURCHARD : *Diarium* to May, 1506. — SIGISMONDO : vol. II. — PARIS DE GRASSIS, master of ceremonies at the Vatican, 1504 sqq.: *Diarium* from May 12, 1504, ed. by L. FRATI, Bologna, 1886, and DÖLLINGER in *Beiträge zur pol. kirchl. u. Culturgesch. d. letzen 6 Jahrh.*, 3 vols., Vienna, 1863-1882, III. 363-433. — A. GIUSTINIAN, Venetian ambassador : *Dispacci*, Despatches, 1502-1505, ed. by VILLARI, 3 vols., Florence, 1876, and by RAWDON BROWNING in *Calendar of State Papers*, London, 1864 sq. — FR. VETTORI : *Sommario della storia d'Italia 1511-1527*, ed. by REUMONT in *Arch. Stor. Ital.*, Append. B., pp. 261-387. — DUSMENIL : *Hist. de Jules II.*, Paris, 1873. — *M. BROSCH : *Papst Julius II. und die Gründung des Kirchenstaats*, Gotha, 1878. — P. LEHMANN : *D. pisaner Konzil vom Jahre, 1511*, Breslau, 1874. — HEFELE-HERGENRÖTHER : VIII.

392–592. — BENRATH : Art. *Julius II.*, in HERZOG, IX. 621–625. — VILLARI : *Machiavelli.* — RANKE : I. 36–59. — REUMONT : III., Pt. 2, pp. 1–49. — GREGOROVIUS : VIII. — CREIGHTON : IV. 54–176. — PASTOR : III.

For § 56. LEO X. — *Regesta* to Oct. 16, 1515, ed. by HERGENRÖTHER, 8 vols., Rome, 1884–1891. — MANSI : XXXII. 649–1001. — PARIS DE GRASSIS, as above, and ed. by ARMELLINI : *Il diario de Leone X.*, Rome, 1884. — VETTORI : *Sommario.* — M. SANUTO, Venetian ambassador : *Diarii*, I.-XV., Venice, 1879 sqq. — *PAULUS JOVIUS, b. 1483, acquainted with Leo : *De Vita Leonis*, Florence, 1549. The only biog. till FABRONI'S *Life*, 1797. — *L. LAN- DUCCI : *Diario Fiorentino 1450–1516*, continued to 1542, ed. by BADIA, Florence, 1883. — *W. ROSCOE : *Life and Pontificate of Leo X.*, 4 vols., Liverpool, 1805, 6th ed. rev. by his son, London, 1853. The book took high rank, and its value continues. Apologetic for Leo, whom the author considers the greatest pope of modern times. Put on the Index by Leo XII., d. 1829. A Germ. trans. by GLASER and HENKE, with valuable notes, 3 vols., Leipzig, 1806–1808. Ital. trans. by COUNT L. BOSSI, Milan, 1816 sq. — E. MUNTZ : *Raphael, His Life, Work, and Times*, Engl. trans., W. ARMSTRONG, Lon- don, 1896. — E. ARMSTRONG : *Lor. de' Medici*, New York, 1896. — H. M. VAUGHAN : *The Medici Popes (Leo X. and Clement VII.)*, London, 1908. — HEFELE-HERGENRÖTHER : VIII. 592–855. — REUMONT : III. Pt. 2, pp. 49–146. — VILLARI : *Machiavelli.* — CREIGHTON : IV. — GREGOROVIUS : VIII. — PAS- TOR : IV. — KÖSTLIN : *Life of Luther*, I. 204–525. — *A. SCHULTE : *Die Fugger in Rom. 1495–1523*, 2 vols., Leipzig, 1904. — BURCKHARDT.— SYMONDS.

POPES.— NICOLAS V., 1447–1455 ; CALIXTUS III., 1455–1458 ; PIUS II., 1458– 1464 ; PAUL II., 1464–1471 ; SIXTUS IV., 1471–1484 ; INNOCENT VIII., 1484– 1492 ; ALEXANDER VI., 1492–1503 ; PIUS III., 1503 ; JULIUS II., 1503–1513 ; LEO X., 1513–1521.

The period of the Reformatory councils, closing with the Basel-Ferrara synod, was followed by a period notable in the history of the papacy, the period of the Renaissance popes. These pontiffs of the last years of the Middle Ages were men famous alike for their intellectual endowments, the prostitu- tion of their office to personal aggrandizement and pleasure and the lustre they gave to Rome by their patronage of letters and the fine arts. The decree of the Council of Constance, as- serting the supreme authority of œcumenical councils, treated as a dead letter by Eugenius IV., was definitely set aside by Pius II. in a bull forbidding appeals from papal decisions and affirming finality for the pope's authority. For 70 years no general assembly of the Church was called.

The ten pontiffs who sat on the pontifical throne, 1450–1517, represented in their origin the extremes of fortune, from the occupation of the fisherman, as in the case of Sixtus IV., to the refinement of the most splendid aristocracy of the age, as in the case of Leo X. of the family of the Medici.   In proportion as they embellished Rome and the Vatican with the treasures of art, did they seem to withhold themselves from that sincere religious devotion which would naturally be regarded as a prime characteristic of one claiming to be the chief pastor of the Christian Church on earth.   No great principle of administration occupied their minds.   No conspicuous movement of pious activity received their sanction, unless the proposed crusade to reconquer Constantinople be accounted such, but into that purpose papal ambition entered more freely than devotion to the interests of religion.

This period was the flourishing age of nepotism in the Vatican.   The bestowment of papal favors by the pontiffs upon their nephews and other relatives dates as a recognized practice from Boniface VIII.   In vain did papal conclaves, following the decree of Constance, adopt protocols, making the age of 30 the lowest limit for appointment to the sacred college, and putting a check on papal favoritism.   Ignoring the instincts of modesty and the impulse of religion, the popes bestowed the red hat upon their young nephews and grandnephews and upon the sons of princes, in spite of their utter disqualification both on the ground of intelligence and of morals.   The Vatican was beset by relatives of the pontiffs, hungry for the honors and the emoluments of office.   Here are some of those who were made cardinals before they were 30: Calixtus III. appointed his nephews, Juan and Rodrigo Borgia (Alexander VI.), the latter 25, and the little son of the king of Portugal; Pius II., his nephew at 23, and Francis Gonzaga at 17; Sixtus IV., John of Aragon at 14, his nephews, Peter and Julian Rovere, at 25 and 28, and his grandnephew, Rafaelle Riario, at 17; Innocent VIII., John Sclafenatus at 23, Giovanni de' Medici at 13; Alexander VI., in 1493, Hippolito of Este at 15, whom Sixtus had made archbishop of Strigonia at 8, his son, Cæsar Borgia, at 18, Alexander Farnese (Paul III.), brother of the pope's mistress, at 25, and Frederick Casimir, son of the king of Poland, at 19; Leo X., in 1513, his nephew, Innocent Cibo, at 21, and his cousin, the illegitimate Julius de' Medici, afterwards Clement VII., and in 1517 three more nephews, one of them the bastard son of his brother, also Alfonzo of Portugal at 7, and John of Loraine, son of the duke of Sicily, at 20. This is an imperfect list.[1] Bishoprics, abbacies and other ecclesiastical appointments were heaped upon the papal children, nephews and other favorites. The cases in which the red hat was conferred for piety or learning were rare, while the houses of Mantua, Ferrara and Modena, the Medici of Florence, the Sforza of Milan, the Colonna and the Orsini had easy access to the Apostolic camera.

The cardinals vied with kings in wealth and luxury, and their palaces were enriched with the most gorgeous furnishings and precious plate, and filled with servants. They set an example of profligacy which they carried into the Vatican itself. The illegitimate offspring of pontiffs were acknowledged without a blush, and the sons and daughters of the highest houses in Italy, France and Spain were sought in marriage for them by their indulgent fathers. The Vatican was given up to nuptial and other entertainments, even women of ill-repute being invited to banquets and obscene comedies performed in its chambers.

The prodigal expenditures of the papal household were maintained in part by the great sums, running into tens of thousands of ducats, which rich men were willing to pay for the cardinalate. When the funds of the Vatican ran low, loans were secured from the Fuggers and other banking houses and the sacred things of the Vatican put in pawn, even to the tiara itself. The amounts required by Alexander VI. for marriage

---

[1] Among other youthful appointments to the dignity of cardinal are Jacinto Bobo, afterwards Cœlestine III., at 18, by Honorius III., 1126 ; Peter Roger, afterwards Gregory XI., at 17, Hercules Gonzaga, by Clement VII., at 22 ; Alexander Farnese, by his uncle, Paul III., at 14, who also appointed his grandsons, Guida Sforza at 16 and Ranucio Farnese at 15 ; two nephews, at the ages of 14 and 21, by Julius III., d. 1555, and also Innocent del Monte at 17 ; Ferdinand de' Medici at 14, by Pius IV., d. 1565 ; Andrew and Albert of Austria, sons of Maximilian II., at 18, by Gregory XIII., and Charles of Loraine at 16 ; Alexander Peretti at 14, by his uncle, Sixtus V., d. 1590 ; two nephews at 18, by Innocent IX., d. 1591 ; Maurice of Savoy at 14, and Ferdinand, son of the king of Spain, at 10, by Paul V., d. 1621 ; a nephew at 17, by Innocent X., d. 1655 ; a son of the king of Spain, by Clement XII., d. 1740.

dowries for his children, and by Leo X. for nephews, were enormous.

Popes, like Sixtus IV. and Alexander VI., had no scruple about involving Italy in internecine wars in order to compass the papal schemes either in the enlargement of papal domain or the enrichment of papal sons and nephews.   Julius II. was a warrior and went to the battle-field in armor.   No sovereign of his age was more unscrupulous in resorting to double dealing in his diplomacy than was Leo X.   To reach the objects of its ambition, the holy see was ready even to form alliances with the sultan.   The popes, so Döllinger says, from Paul II. to Leo X., did the most it was possible to do to cover the papacy with shame and disgrace and to involve Italy in the horrors of endless wars.[1] The Judas-like betrayal of Christ in the highest seat of Christendom, the gayeties, scandals and crimes of popes as they pass before the reader in the diaries of Infessura, Burchard and de Grassis and the despatches of the ambassadors of Venice, Mantua and other Italian states, and as repeated by Creighton, Pastor and Gregorovius, make this period one of the most dramatic in human annals.   The personal element furnished scene after scene of consuming interest.   It seems to the student as if history were approaching some great climax.

Three events of permanent importance for the general history of mankind also occurred in this age, the overthrow of the Byzantine empire, 1453, the discovery of the Western world, 1492, and the invention of printing.   It closed with a general council, the Fifth Lateran, which adjourned only a few months before the Reformer in the North shook the papal fabric to its base and opened the door of the modern age.

§ 49.   *Nicolas V.*   1447–1455.

Nicolas V., 1447–1455, the successor of Eugenius IV., was ruled by the spirit of the new literary culture, the Renaissance, and was the first Mæcenas in a line of popes like-minded.   Following his example, his successors were for a century among the foremost patrons of art and letters in Europe.   What Greg-

---

[1] *Papstthum*, p. 192.

ory VII. was to the system of the papal theocracy, that Nicolas was to the artistic revival in Rome. Under his rule, the eternal city witnessed the substantial beginnings of that transformation, in which it passed from a spectacle of ruins and desertion to a capital adorned with works of art and architectural construction. He himself repaired and beautified the Vatican and St. Peter's, laid the foundation of the Vatican library and called scholars and artists to his court.[1]

Thomas Parentucelli, born 1397, the son of a physician of Sarzana, owed nothing of his distinction to the position of his family. His father was poor, and the son was little of stature, with disproportionately short legs. What he lacked, however, in bodily parts, he made up in intellectual endowments, tact and courtesies of manner. His education at Bologna being completed, his ecclesiastical preferment was rapid. In 1444, he was made archbishop of Bologna and, on his return from Germany as papal legate, 1446, he was honored with the red hat. Four months later he was elevated to the papal throne, and according to Æneas Sylvius, whose words about the eminent men of his day always have a diplomatic flavor, Thomas was so popular that there was no one who did not approve his election.

To Nicolas was given the notable distinction of witnessing the complete reunion of Western Christendom. By the abdication of Felix V., whom he treated with discreet and liberal generosity, and by Germany's abandonment of its attitude of neutrality, he could look back upon papal schism and divided obediences as matters of the past.

The Jubilee Year, celebrated in 1450, was adapted to bind the European nations closely to Rome, and to stir up anew the fires of devotion which had languished during the ecclesiastical disputes of nearly a century.[2] So vast were the throngs of pilgrims that the contemporary, Platina, felt justified in asserting that such multitudes had never been seen in the holy city before. According to Æneas, 40,000 went daily from church to church. The handkerchief of St. Veronica, — lo sudario, — bearing the

---

[1] Pastor heads his chapter on Nicolas with the caption Nicolas V., der Begründer des päpstlichen Maecenats.

[2] Pastor, I. 417 sq., emphasizes these consequences of the Jubilee Year.

outline of the Lord's face, was exhibited every Sabbath, and the heads of St. Peter and St. Paul every Saturday. The large sums of money which the pilgrims left, Nicolas knew well how to use in carrying out his plans for beautifying the churches and streets of the city.

The calamity, which occurred on the bridge of St. Angelo, and cast a temporary gloom over the festivities of the holy year, is noticed by all the contemporary writers. The mule belonging to Peter Barbus, cardinal of St. Mark's, was crushed to death, so dense were the crowds, and in the excitement two hundred persons or more were trodden down or drowned by being pushed or throwing themselves into the Tiber. To prevent a repetition of the disaster, the pope had several buildings obstructing the passage to the bridge pulled down.[1]

In the administration of the properties of the holy see, Nicolas was discreet and successful. He confirmed the papal rule over the State of the Church, regained Bolsena and the castle of Spoleto, and secured the submission of Bologna, to which he sent Bessarion as papal legate. The conspiracy of Stephen Porcaro, who emulated the ambitions of Rienzo, was put down in 1453 and left the pope undisputed master of Rome. In his selection of cardinals he was wise, Nicolas of Cusa being included in the number. The appointment of his younger brother, Philip Calandrini, to the sacred college, aroused no unfavorable criticism.

Nicolas' reign witnessed, in 1452, the last coronation in Rome of a German emperor, Frederick III. This monarch, who found in his councillor, Æneas Sylvius, an enthusiastic biographer, but who, by the testimony of others, was weak and destitute of martial spirit and generous qualities, was the first of the Hapsburgs to receive the crown in the holy city, and held the imperial office longer than any other of the emperors before or after him. With his coronation the emperor combined the celebration of his nuptials to Leonora of Portugal.

Frederick's journey to Italy and his sojourn in Rome offered to the pen of Æneas a rare opportunity for graphic description, of which he was a consummate master. The meeting with the

---

[1] Infessura, p. 48 ; Platina, II. 242 ; Æneas: *Hist. Frid.* 172 ; Ilgen's trans., I. 214.

future empress, the welcome extended to his majesty, the festivities of the marriage and the coronation, the trappings of
the soldiery, the blowing of the horns, the elegance of the vestments worn by the emperor and his visit to the artistic wonders
of St. Peter's, — these and other scenes the shrewd and facile
Æneas depicted. The Portuguese princess, whose journey
from Lisbon occupied 104 days, disembarked at Leghorn, February, 1452, where she was met by Frederick, attended by
a brilliant company of knights. After joining in gay entertainments at Siena, lasting four days, the party proceeded to
Rome. Leonora, who was only sixteen, was praised by those
who saw her for her rare beauty and charms of person. She
was to become the mother of Maximilian and the ancestress of
Charles V.[1]

On reaching the gates of the papal capital, Frederick was
met by the cardinals, who offered him the felicitations of the
head of Christendom, but also demanded from him the oath
of allegiance, which was reluctantly promised. The ceremonies, which followed the emperor's arrival, were such as to
flatter his pride and at the same time to confirm the papal
tenure of power in the city. Frederick was received by Nicolas on the steps of St. Peter's, seated in an ivory chair, and
surrounded by his cardinals, standing. The imperial visitor
knelt and kissed the pontiff's foot. On March 16, Nicolas
crowned him with the iron crown of Lombardy and united
the imperial pair in marriage. Leonora then went to her
own palace, and Frederick to the Vatican as its guest. The
reason for his lodging near the pope was that Nicolas might
have opportunity for frequent communication with him or, as
rumor went, to prevent the Romans approaching him under
cover of darkness with petitions for the restoration of their
liberties.[2] Three days later, March 19, the crown of the em-

---

[1] Infessura, p. 52, says that language could not exaggerate Leonora's beauty,
bella quanto si potesse dire. Æneas, *Hist. Frid.*, 265, speaks of her dark
complexion, jet-black and lustrous eyes, her soft red cheeks, her intelligent
expression, and her snow-white neck, "in every particular a charming person."

[2] *Hist. Frid.*, 294; Ilgen, II. 84 sq. Æneas gives the alternate reason for
the hospitality shown to his master.

pire was placed upon Frederick's head.[1]   With his consort he
then received the elements from the pope's hand.   The following week Frederick proceeded to Naples.[2]

Scarcely in any pontificate has so notable and long-forecasted
an event occurred as the fall of Constantinople into the hands
of the Turks, which took place May 29, 1453.   The last of the
Constantines perished in the siege, fighting bravely at the gate
of St. Romanos.   The church of Justinian, St. Sophia, was
turned into a mosque, and a cross, surmounted with a janis-
sary's cap, was carried through the streets, while the soldiers
shouted, " This is the Christian's God."   This historic catastrophe would have been regarded in Western Europe as appalling, if it had not been expected.   The steady advance of the
Turks and their unspeakable atrocities had kept the Greek
empire in alarm for centuries.   Three hundred years before,
Latin Christendom had been taught to expect defeats at the
hands of the Mohammedans in the taking of Edessa, 1145, and
the fatal battle of Hattin and the loss of Jerusalem, 1187.

In answer to the appeals of the Greeks, Nicolas despatched
Isidore as legate to Constantinople with a guard of 200 troops,
but, as a condition of helping the Eastern emperor, he insisted
that the Ferrara articles of union be ratified in Constantinople.
In a long communication, dated Oct. 11, 1451, the Roman
pontiff declared that schisms had always been punished more
severely than other evils.   Korah, Dathan and Abiram, who
attempted to divide the people of God, received a more bitter
punishment than those who introduced idolatry.   There could
not be two heads to an empire or the Church.   There is no
salvation outside of the one Church.   He was lost in the flood

[1] The crown used on the occasion was reputed to be the one used by
Charlemagne which Sigismund had removed to Nürnberg.   Æneas, with his
usual journalistic love of detail, noticed the Bohemian lion of Charles IV.
engraven on the sword, which also was brought from Nürnberg.

[2] Æneas, p. 303, who is scrupulous in stating from time to time that Frederick and Leonora lodged in different palaces or tents, now gives a detailed
account of the circumstances attending their first lodging together as man and
wife in Naples.   The account is such as we might expect from Boccaccio and
not from a prelate of the Church, but Æneas' own record fitted him for entering with pruriency into realistic details.   They are characteristic of the times
and of Spanish customs.

who was not housed in Noah's ark. Whatever opinion it may
have entertained of these claims, the Byzantine court was in too
imminent danger to reject the papal condition, and in December, 1452, Isidore, surrounded by 300 priests, announced, in the
church of St. Sophia, the union of the Greek and Latin communions. But even now the Greek people violently resented
the union, and the most powerful man of the empire, Lucas
Notaras, announced his preference for the turban to the tiara.
The aid offered by Nicolas was at best small. The last week
of April, 1453, ten papal galleys set sail with some ships from
Naples, Venice and Genoa, but they were too late to render
any assistance.[1]

The termination of the venerable and once imposing fabric
on the Bosphorus by the Asiatic invader was the only fate possible for an empire whose rulers, boasting themselves the successors of Constantine, Theodosius and Justinian, Christian in
name and most Christian by the standard of orthodox professions, had heaped their palaces full of pagan luxury and excess.
The government, planted in the most imperial spot on the earth,
had forfeited the right to exist by an insipid and nerveless reliance upon the traditions of the past. No elements of revival
manifested themselves from within. Religious formulas had
been substituted for devotion. Much as the Christian student
may regret the loss of this last bulwark of Christianity in the
East, he will be inclined to find in the disaster the judgment
realized with which the seven churches of the Apocalypse were
threatened which were not worthy. The problem which was
forced upon Europe by the arrival of the Grand Turk, as contemporaries called Mohammed II., still awaits solution from
wise diplomacy or force of arms or through the slow and silent
movement of modern ideas of government and popular rights.

The disaster which overtook the Eastern empire, Nicolas
V. felt would be regarded by after generations as a blot upon
his pontificate, and others, like Æneas Sylvius, shared this view.[2]

---

[1] Pastor, I. 588 sqq., devotes much space to an attempt to show that Nicolas made an effort to help the Greeks. Infessura blames him for making none.

[2] Æneas wrote, July 12, 1453, to the pope: " Historians of the Roman pontiffs,
when they reach your time, will write, ' Nicolas V., a Tuscan, was pope for

He issued a bull summoning the Christian nations to a crusade for the recovery of Constantinople, and stigmatized Mohammed II. as the dragon described in the Book of Revelation. Absolution was offered to those who would spend six months in the holy enterprise or maintain a representative for that length of time. Christendom was called upon to contribute a tenth. The cardinals were enjoined to do the same, and all the papal revenues accruing from larger and smaller benefices, from bishoprics, archbishoprics and convents, were promised for the undertaking.

Feeble was the response which Europe gave. The time of crusading enthusiasm was passed. The Turk was daring and to be dreaded. An assembly called by Frederick III., at Regensburg in the Spring of 1454, at which the emperor himself did not put in an appearance, listened to an eloquent appeal by Æneas, but adjourned the subject to the diet to meet in Frankfurt in October. Again the emperor was not present, and the diet did nothing. Down to the era of the Reformation the crusade against the Turk remained one of the chief official concerns of the papacy.

If Nicolas died disappointed over his failure to influence the princes to undertake a campaign against the Turks, his fame abides as the intelligent and genial patron of letters and the arts. In this rôle he laid after generations under obligation to him as Innocent III., by his crusading armies, did not. He lies buried in St. Peter's at the side of his predecessor, Eugenius IV.[1]

The next pontiff, the Spaniard, Calixtus III., 1455-1458, had two chief concerns, the dislodgment of the Turks from Con-

so many years. He recovered the patrimony of the Church from the hands of tyrants, he gave union to the divided Church, he canonized Bernardino, he built the Vatican and splendidly restored St. Peter's, he celebrated the Jubilee and crowned Frederick III.' All this will be obscured by the doleful addition, ' In his time Constantinople was taken and plundered by the Turks.' Your holiness did what you could. No blame can be justly attached to you. But the ignorance of posterity will blame you when it hears that in your time Constantinople was lost." Gibbon makes the observation that " The pontificate of Nicolas V., however powerful and prosperous, was dishonored by the fall of the Eastern Empire," ch. LXVIII. It was not within Nicolas' power to avert the disaster.   [1] His epitaph is given by Mirbt, p. 169.

stantinople and the advancement of the fortunes of the Borgia family, to which he belonged. Made cardinal by Eugenius IV., he was 77 years old when he was elected pope. From his day, the Borgias played a prominent part in Rome, their career culminating in the ambitions and scandals of Rodrigo Borgia, for 30 years cardinal and then pope under the name of Alexander VI.

Calixtus opened his pontificate by vowing "to Almighty God and the Holy Trinity, by wars, maledictions, interdicts, excommunications and in all other ways to punish the Turks." [1] Legates were despatched to kindle the zeal of princes throughout Europe. Papal jewels were sold, and gold and silver clasps were torn from the books of the Vatican and turned into money. At a given hour daily the bells were rung in Rome that all might give themselves to prayer for the sacred war. But to the indifference of most of the princes was added active resistance on the part of France. Venice, always looking out for her own interests, made a treaty with the Turks. Frederick III. was incompetent. The weak fleet the pope was able to muster sailed forth from Ostia under Cardinal Serampo to empty victories. The gallant Hungarian, Hunyady, brought some hope by his brilliant feat in relieving Belgrade, July 14, 1456, but the rejoicing was reduced by the news of the gallant leader's death. Scanderbeg, the Albanian, who a year later was appointed papal captain-general, was indeed a brave hero, but, unsupported by Western Europe, he was next to powerless.

Calixtus' unblushing nepotism surpassed anything of the kind which had been known in the papal household before. Catalan adventurers pressed into Rome and stormed their papal fellow-countrymen with demands for office. Upon the three sons of two of his sisters, Juan of Milan, son of Catherine Borgia, and Pedro Luis and Rodrigo, sons of Isabella, he heaped favor after favor. Adopted by their uncle, Pedro and Rodrigo were the objects of his sleepless solicitude. Gregorovius has compared the members of the Borgia family to the Roman Claudii. By the endowment of nature they were vigorous and handsome, and by nature and practice, sensual, am-

[1] Mansi, XXXII. 159 sq.

bitious, and high-handed, — their coat of arms a bull.   Under protest from the curia, Rodrigo and Juan of Milan were made cardinals, 1457, both the young men still in their twenties.

Their unsavory habits were already a byword in Rome. Rodrigo was soon promoted over the heads of the other members of the sacred college to the place of vice-chancellor, the most lucrative position within the papal gift.   At the same time, the little son — *figliolo* — of the king of Portugal, as Infessura calls him, was given the red hat.

With astounding rapidity Pedro Luis, who remained a layman, was advanced to the highest positions in the state, and made governor of St. Angelo and duke of Spoleto, and put in possession of Terni, Narni, Todi and other papal fiefs.[1]   It was supposed that it was the fond uncle's intention, at the death of Alfonso of Naples, to invest this nephew with the Neapolitan crown by setting aside Alfonso's illegitimate son, Don Ferrante.

Calixtus' death was the signal for the flight of the Spanish lobbyists, whose houses were looted by the indignant Romans. Discerning the coming storm, Pedro made the best bargain he could by selling S. Angelo to the cardinals for 20,000 ducats, and then took a hasty departure.

Like Honorius III., Calixtus might have died of a broken heart over his failure to arouse Europe to the effort of a crusade, if it had not been for this consuming concern for the fortunes and schemes of his relatives.   From this time on, for more than half a century, the gift of dignities and revenues under papal control for personal considerations and to unworthy persons for money was an outstanding feature in the history of the popes.

§ 50.   Æneas Sylvius de' Piccolomini, Pius II.

The next pontiff, Pius II., has a place among the successful men of history.   Lacking high enthusiasms and lofty aims, he was constantly seeking his own interests and, through diplo-

---

[1] Pastor, I. 747, says *ein solches Verfahren war unerhört*, it was an unheard-of procedure.

matic shrewdness, came to be the most conspicuous figure of
his time.   He was ruled by expediency rather than principle.
He never swam against the stream.[1]   When he found himself
on the losing side, he was prompt in changing to the other.

Æneas Sylvius de' Piccolomini was born in 1405 at Cor-
signano, a village located on a bold spur of the hills near Siena.
He was one of 18 children, and his family, which had been
banished from Siena, was poor but of noble rank.   At 18, the
son began studying in the neighboring city, where he heard
Bernardino preach.   Later he learned Greek in Florence.   It
was a great opportunity when Cardinal Capranica took this
young man with him as his secretary to Basel, 1431.   Gregorovius has remarked that it was the golden age of secretaries,
most of the Humanists serving in that capacity.   Later, Æneas
went into the service of the bishop of Novaro, whom he accompanied to Rome.   The bishop was imprisoned for the part
he had taken in a conspiracy against Eugenius IV.   The
secretary escaped a like treatment by flight.   He then served
Cardinal Albergati, with whom he travelled to France.   He
also visited England and Scotland.[2]

Returning to Basel, Æneas became one of the conspicuous
personages in the council, was a member, and often acted as
chairman of one of the four committees, the committee on faith,
and was sent again and again on embassies to Strassburg,
Frankfurt, Trent and other cities.   The council also appointed
him its chief abbreviator.   In 1440 he decided in favor of the
rump-synod, which continued to meet in Basel, and espoused
the cause of Felix V., who made him his secretary.   The same
year he wrote the tract on general councils.[3]   Finding the
cause of the anti-pope waning, he secured a place under Frederick III., and succeeded to the full in ingratiating himself in that
monarch's favor.   His Latin epigrams and verses won for him
the appointment of poet-laureate, and his diplomatic cleverness

---

[1] *Enea ist seiner Tage nie gegen den Strom geschwommen.*   Haller in *Quellen*, etc., IV. 83.

[2] London he found the most populous and wealthy city he had seen.
Scotland he described as a cold, barren, and treeless country.

[3] *Libellus dialogorum de generalis concilii auctoritate.*

and versatility the highest place in the royal council.   At first he joined with Schlick, the chancellor, in holding Frederick to a neutral attitude between Eugenius and the anti-pope, but then, turning apostate to the cause of neutrality, gracefully and unreservedly gave in his submission to the Roman pontiff. While on an embassy to Rome, 1445, he excused himself before Eugenius for his errors at Basel on the plea of lack of experience.   He at once became useful to the pope, and a year later received the appointment of papal secretary.   By his persuasion, Frederick transferred his obedience to Eugenius, which Æneas was able to announce in person to the pope a few days before his death.   From Nicolas V. he received the sees of Trieste, 1447, and Siena, 1450, and in 1456 promotion to the college of cardinals.

At the time of his election as pope, Æneas was 53 years old.   He had risen by tact and an accurate knowledge of men and European affairs.   He was a thorough man of the world, and capable of grasping a situation in a glance.   He had been profligate, and his love affairs were many.   A son was born to him in Scotland, and another, by an Englishwoman, in Strassburg.   In a letter to his father, asking him to adopt the second child, he described, without concealment and apparently without shame, the measures he took to seduce the mother.   He spoke of wantonness as an old vice.   He himself was no eunuch nor without passion.   He could not claim to be wiser than Solomon nor holier than David.   Æneas also used his pen in writing tales of love adventures.   His *History of Frederick III.* contains prurient details that would not be tolerated in a respectable author to-day.   He was even ready to instruct youth in methods of self-indulgence, and wrote to Sigismund, the young duke of the Tyrol, neither to neglect literature nor to deny himself the blandishments of Venus.[1]   This advice

---

[1] Æneas aided Chancellor Schlick in some of his love adventures, and described one of them in the much-read novel, *Eurialus et Lucretia.*   His letters from 1444 on, show a desire to give up the world.   He declared he had had enough of Venus, but he also wrote that Venus evaded him more than he shrank from her.   He seems to have passed into a condition of physical infirmity, and to have been forced to abandon his immoral courses.   He, however, also indicates he had begun to be actuated by feelings of penitence,

was recalled to his face by the canonist George von Heim-burg at the Congress of Mantua. The famous remark belongs to Æneas that the celibacy of the clergy was at one time with good reason made subject of positive legislation, but the time had come when there was better reason for allowing priests to marry. He himself did not join the clerical order till 1446, when he was consecrated subdeacon. Before Pius' election,[1] the conclave bound the coming pope to prosecute the war against the Turk, to observe the rules of the Council of Constance about the sacred college and to consult its members before making new appointments to bishoprics and the greater abbeys. Nominations of cardinals were to be made to the camera, and their ratification to depend upon a majority of its votes. Each cardinal whose income did not amount to 4,000 florins was to receive 100 florins a month till the sum of 4,000 was reached. This solemn compact formed a precedent which the cardinals for more than half a century followed.

Æneas' constitution was already shattered. He was a great sufferer from the stone, the gout and a cough, and spent many months of his pontificate at Viterbo and other baths. His rule was not distinguished by any enduring measures. He conducted himself well, had the respect of the Romans, received the praise of contemporary biographers, and did all he could to further the measures for the expulsion of the Turks from Europe. He appointed the son of his sister, Laodamia, cardinal at the age of 23, and in 1461 he bestowed the same dignity on Francis Gonzaga, a youth of only 17. These appointments seem to have awakened no resentment.

To advance the interest of the crusade against the Turks, Pius called a congress of princes to meet in Mantua, 1460. On his way thither, accompanied by Bessarion, Borgia and other cardinals, he visited his birthplace, Corsignana, and raised it

whether from motives of policy or religion cannot be made out. Gregorovius, VII. 165, combines the inconsistent passages from Pius' letters when he says that, after long striving to renounce the pleasures of the world, exhaustion and incipient disease facilitated the task.

[1] The election was by the *accessus*, that is, after the written ballot was found to be indecisive, the cardinals changed their votes by word of mouth. See Hergenröther, *Kath. Kirchenrecht*, p. 273.

to a bishopric, changing its name to Pienza. He also began
the construction of a palace and cathedral which still endure.
Siena he honored by conferring the Golden Rose on its signiory, and promoting the city to the dignity of a metropolitan
see.   He also enriched it with one of John the Baptist's arms.
Florence arranged for the pope's welcome brilliant amusements,
— theatrical plays, contests of wild beasts, races between lions
and horses, and dances, — worldly rather than religious spectacles, as Pastor remarks.

The princes were slow in arriving in Mantua, and the attendance was not such as to justify the opening of the congress till
Sept. 26.   Envoys from Thomas Palæologus of the Morea,
brother of the last Byzantine emperor, from Lesbos, Cyprus,
Rhodes and other parts of the East were on hand to pour out
their laments.   In his opening address, lasting three hours, Pius
called upon the princes to emulate Stephen, Peter, Andrew, Sebastian, St. Lawrence and other martyrs in readiness to lay
down their lives in the holy war.   The aggression of the Turks
had robbed Christendom of some of its fairest seats,— Antioch,
where the followers of Christ for the first time received the
name Christians, Solomon's temple, where Christ so often
preached, Bethlehem, where he was born, the Jordan, in which
he was baptized, Tabor, on which he was transfigured, Calvary,
where he was crucified.   If they wanted to retain their own
possessions, their wives, their children, their liberty, the very
faith in which they were baptized, they must believe in war
and carry on war.   Joshua continued to have victory over his
enemies till the sun went down; Gideon, with 300, scattered
the Midianites; Jephthah, with a small army, put to flight the
swarms of the Ammonites; Samson had brought the proud
Philistines to shame ; Godfrey, with a handful of men, had destroyed an innumerable number of the enemy and slaughtered
the Turks like cattle.   Passionately the papal orator exclaimed,
O! that Godfrey were once more present, and Baldwin and Eu-
stache and Bohemund and Tancred, and the other mighty men
who broke through the ranks of the Turks and regained Jerusalem by their arms.[1]

[1] Mansi, XXXII. 207–222.

appearance, the people flocked together in crowds and in spite of the clergy.[1]

Following a bull issued by Alexander V., Sbinko, in 1410, ordered Wyclif's writings seized and burnt, and forbade all preaching in unauthorized places. The papal document called forth the protest of Huss and others, who appealed to John XXIII. by showing the absurdity of burning books on philosophy, logic and other non-theological subjects, a course that would condemn the writings of Aristotle and Origen to the flames. The protest was in vain and 200 manuscript copies of the Reformer's writings were cast into the flames in the courtyard of the archiepiscopal palace amidst the tolling of the church bells.[2]

Two days after this grewsome act, the sentence of excommunication was launched against Huss and all who might persist in refusing to deliver up Wyclif's writings. Defying the archbishop and the papal bull, Huss continued preaching in the Bethlehem chapel. The excitement among all classes was intense and men were cudgelled on the streets for speaking against the Englishman. Satirical ballads were sung, declaring that the archbishop did not know what was in the books he had set fire to. Huss' sermons, far from allaying the commotion, were adapted to increase it.

Huss had no thought of submission and, through handbills, announced a defence of Wyclif's treatise on the Trinity before the university, July 27. But his case had now passed from the archbishop's jurisdiction to the court of the curia, which demanded the offender's appearance in person, but in vain. In spite of the appeals of Wenzel and many Bohemian nobles who pledged their honor that he was no heretic, John XXIII. put the case into the hands of Cardinal Colonna, afterwards Martin V., who launched the ban against Huss for his refusal to comply with the canonical citation.

Colonna's sentence was read from all the pulpits of Prag except two. But the offensive preaching continued, and Sbinko

---

[1] Workman: *Hus' Letters*, p. 36.

[2] Among the condemned writings, 17 in all, were the *Dialogus, Trialogus, De incarnatione Verbi* and the *De dominio civili*.

laid the city under the interdict, which, however, was withdrawn on the king's promise to root out heresy from his realm. Wenzel gave orders that " Master Huss, our beloved and faithful chaplain, be allowed to preach the Word of God in peace." According to the agreement, Sbinko was also to write to the pope assuring him that diligent inquisition had been made, and no traces of heresy were to be found in Bohemia. This letter is still extant, but was never sent.

Early in September, 1411, Huss wrote to John XXIII. protesting his full agreement with the Church and asking that the citation to appear before the curia be revoked. In this communication and in a special letter to the cardinals [1] Huss spoke of the punishment for heresy and insubordination. He, however, wrote to John that he was bound to speak the truth, and that he was ready to suffer a dreadful death rather than to declare what would be contrary to the will of Christ and his Church. He had been defamed, and it was false that he had expressed himself in favor of the remanence of the material substance of the bread after the words of institution, and that a priest in mortal sin might not celebrate the eucharist. Sbinko died Sept. 28, 1411. At this juncture the excitement was increased by the arrival in Prag of John Stokes, a Cambridge man, and well known in England as an uncompromising foe of Wycliffism. He had come with a delegation, sent by the English king, to arrange an alliance with Sigismund. Stokes' presence aroused the expectation of a notable clash, but the Englishman, although he ventilated his views privately, declined Huss' challenge to a public disputation on the ground that he was a political representative of a friendly nation. [1]

The same year, 1411, John XXIII. called Europe to a crusade against Ladislaus of Naples, the defender of Gregory XII., and promised indulgence to all participating in it, whether by personal enlistment or by gifts. Tiem, dean of Passau, appointed preacher of the holy war, made his way to Prag and opened the sale of indulgences. Chests were placed in the great churches,

[1] These letters are given by Workman, pp. 51–54.
[2] Huss' reply, *Replica*, and Stokes' statement, which called it forth, are given in the Nürnb. ed., I. 135–139.

and the traffic was soon in full sway. As Wyclif, thirty years before, in his *Cruciata*, had lifted up his voice against the crusade in Flanders, so now Huss denounced the religious war and denied the pope's right to couple indulgences with it. He filled the Bethlehem chapel with denunciations of the sale and, in a public disputation, took the ground that remission of sins comes through repentance alone and that the pope has no authority to seize the secular sword. Many of his paragraphs were taken bodily from Wyclif's works on the Church and on the Absolution from guilt and punishment.[1] Huss was supported by Jerome of Prag.

Popular opinion was on the side of these leaders, but from this time Huss' old friends, Stanislaus of Znaim and Stephen Paletz, walked no more with him. Under the direction of Wok of Waldstein, John's two bulls, bearing on the crusade and offering indulgence, were publicly burnt, after being hung at the necks of two students, dressed as harlots, and drawn through the streets in a cart.[2] Huss was still writing that he abhorred the errors ascribed to him, but the king could not countenance the flagrant indignity shown to the papal bulls, and had three men of humble position executed, Martin, John and Stanislaus. They had cried out in open church that the bulls were lies, as Huss had proved. They were treated as martyrs, and their bodies taken to the Bethlehem chapel, where the mass for martyrs was said over them.

To reaffirm its orthodoxy, the theological faculty renewed its condemnation of the 45 articles and added 6 more, taken from Huss' public utterances. Two of the latter bore upon preaching.[3] The clergy of Prag appealed to be protected "from the ravages of the wolf, the Wycliffist Hus, the despiser of the keys," and the curia pronounced the greater excommunication. The heretic was ordered seized, delivered over to the archbishop, and the Bethlehem chapel razed to the ground.

---

[1] Huss' tract is entitled *De indulgentiis sive de cruciatu papæ Joh. XXIII. fulminata contra Ladislaum Apuliæ regem.* Nürnb. ed., 213–235.

[2] Workman : *Hus' Letters.*

[3] See Huss' reply, *Defensio quorundam articulorum J. Wicleff*, and the rejoinder of the theol. faculty, Nürnb. ed., I. 139–146.

Three stones were to be hurled against Huss' dwelling, as a sign of perpetual curse. Thus the Reformer had against him the archbishop, the university, the clergy and the curia, but popular feeling remained in his favor and prevented the papal sentence from being carried out. The city was again placed under the interdict. Huss appealed from the pope and, because a general council's action is always uncertain and at best tardy, looked at once to the tribunal of Christ. He publicly asserted that the pope was exercising prerogatives received from the devil.

To allay the excitement, Wenzel induced Huss to withdraw from the city. This was in 1412. In later years Huss expressed doubts as to whether he had acted wisely in complying. He was moved not only by regard for the authority of his royal protector but by sympathy for the people whom the interdict was depriving of spiritual privileges. Had he defied the sentence and refused compliance with the king's request, it is probable he would have lost the day and been silenced in prison or in the flames in his native city. In this case, the interest of his career would have been restricted to the annals of his native land, and no place would have been found for him in the general history of Europe. So Huss went into exile, but there was still some division among the ecclesiastical authorities of the kingdom over the merits of Wycliffism, and a national synod, convoked February 13, 1413, to take measures to secure peace, adjourned without coming to a decision.

Removed from Prag, Huss was indefatigable in preaching and writing. Audiences gathered to hear him on the marketplaces and in the fields and woods. Lords in their strong castles protected him. Following Wyclif, he insisted upon preaching as the indefeasible right of the priest, and wrote that to cease from preaching, in obedience to the mandate of pope or archbishop, would be to disobey God and imperil his own salvation.[1] He also kept in communication with the city by visiting it several times and by writing to the Bethlehem chapel, the university and the municipal synod. This correspondence abounds in quotations from the Scriptures, and Huss reminds

---

[1] Workman: *Hus' Letters*, pp. 60, 66.

his friends that Christ himself was excommunicated as a male-factor and crucified.   No help was to be derived from the saints. Christ's example and his salvation are the sufficient sources of consolation and courage.   The high priests, scribes, Phari-sees, Herod and Pilate condemned the Truth and gave him over to death, but he rose from the tomb and gave in his stead twelve other preachers.   So he would do again.   What fear, he wrote, "shall part us from God, or what death?   What shall we lose if for His sake we forfeit wealth, friends, the world's honors and our poor life? . . .   It is better to die well than to live badly.   We dare not sin to avoid the punishment of death. To end in grace the present life is to be banished from misery. Truth is the last conqueror.   He wins who is slain, for no adver-sity "hurts him if no iniquity has dominion over him."   In this strain he wrote again and again.   The "bolts of anti-christ," he said, could not terrify him, and should not terrify the "elect of Prag."[1]

Of the extent of Huss' influence during this period he bore witness at Constance when, in answer to D'Ailly, he said: —

I have stated that I came here of my own free will.   If I had been un-willing to come, neither that king [referring to Wenzel] nor this king here [referring to Sigismund] would have been able to force me to come, so nu-merous and so powerful are the Bohemian nobles who love me, and within whose castles I should have been able to lie concealed.

And when D'Ailly rebuked the statement as effrontery, John of Chlum replied that it was even as the prisoner said, "There are numbers of great nobles who love him and have strong castles where they could keep him as long as they wished, even against both those kings."

The chief product of this period of exile was Huss' work on the Church, *De ecclesia*, the most noted of all his writings.   It was written in view of the national synod held in 1413, and was sent to Prag and read in the Bethlehem chapel, July 8.   Of this tractate Cardinal D'Ailly said at the Council of Constance that, by an infinite number of arguments, it combated the pope's

[1] Workman, p. 107–120.   Workman translates seventeen letters written from this exile, pp. 83–138.

plenary authority as much as the Koran, the book of the damned Mohammed, combated the Catholic faith.[1]

In this volume, next to Wyclif's, the most famous treatment on the Church since Cyprian's work, *De ecclesia*, and Augustine's writings against the Donatists, Huss defined the Church and the power of the keys, and then proceeds to defend himself against the fulminations of Alexander V. and John XXIII. and to answer the Prag theologians, Stephen Paletz and Stanislaus of Znaim, who had deserted him. The following are some of its leading positions.

The Holy Catholic Church is the body or congregation of all the predestinate, the dead, the living and those yet to be.[2] The term 'catholic' means universal. The unity of the Church is a unity of predestination and of blessedness, a unity of faith, charity and grace. The Roman pontiff and the cardinals are not the Church. The Church can exist without cardinals and a pope, and in fact for hundreds of years there were no cardinals.[3] As for the position Christ assigned to Peter, Huss affirmed that Christ called himself the Rock, and the Church is founded on him by virtue of predestination. In view of Peter's clear and positive confession, " the Rock — *Petra* — said to Peter — *Petro* — ' I say unto thee, Thou art Peter, that is, a confessor of the true Rock which Rock I am.' And upon the Rock, that is, myself, I will build this Church." Thus Huss placed himself firmly on the ground taken by Augustine in his *Retractations*. Peter never was the head of the Holy Catholic Church.[4]

---

[1] Du Pin, *Opp. Gerson.*, II. 901. The *De ecclesia* is given in the Nürnb. ed., I. 243–319.

[2] *Eccl. est omnium prædestinatorum universitas; quæ est omnes prædestinati, præsentes, præteriti et futuri.* Nürnb. ed. I., 244.

[3] Writing to Christian Prachatitz, in 1413, Huss said, " If the pope is the head of the Roman Church and the cardinals are the body, then they in themselves form the entire Holy Roman Church, as the entire body of a man with the head is the man. The satellites of anti-christ use interchangeably the expressions ' Holy Roman Church ' and 'pope and cardinals' etc." Workman : *Hus' Letters*, p. 121.

[4] *Propter confessionem tam claram et firmam, dixit Petra Petro, et ego dico tibi quia tu es Petrus, id est confessor Petræ veræ qui est Christus et super hanc Petram quam confessus es, id est, super me,* etc., Nürnb. ed., I. 257. *Petrus non fuit nec est caput s. eccles. cathol.*, p. 263. See also the same interpretation in Huss' *Serm. de Sanctis*, p. 84.

He thus set himself clearly against the whole ultramontane theory of the Church and its head. The Roman bishop, he said, was on an equality with other bishops until Constantine made him pope. It was then that he began to usurp authority. Through ignorance and the love of money the pope may err, and has erred, and to rebel against an erring pope is to obey Christ.[1] There have been depraved and heretical popes. Such was Joan, whose case Huss dwelt upon at length and refers to at least three times. Such was also the case of Liberius, who is also treated at length. Joan had a son and Liberius was an Arian.[2]

In the second part of the *De ecclesia*, Huss pronounced the bulls of Alexander and John XXIII. anti-christian, and therefore not to be obeyed. Alexander's bull, prohibiting preaching in Bohemia except in the cathedral, parish and monastic churches was against the Gospel, for Christ preached in houses, on the seaside, and in synagogues, and bade his disciples to go into all the world and preach. No papal excommunication may be an impediment to doing what Christ did and taught to be done.[3]

Turning to the pope's right to issue indulgences, the Reformer went over the ground he had already traversed in his replies to John's two bulls calling for a crusade against Ladislaus. He denied the pope's right to go to war or to make appeal to the secular sword. If John was minded to follow Christ, he should pray for his enemies and say, " My kingdom is not of this world." Then the promised wisdom would be given which no enemies would be able to gainsay. The power to forgive sins belongs to no mortal man any more than it belonged to the priest to whom Christ sent the lepers. The lepers were cleansed before they reached the priest. Indeed, many popes who conceded the most ample indulgences were themselves damned.[4]

---

[1] Nürnb. ed., I. 260, 284, 294, etc.

[2] Huss also in his Letters repeatedly refers to Joan and Liberius, *e.g.* he writes, " I should like to know if pope Liberius the heretic, Leo the heretic and the pope Joan, who was delivered of a boy, were the heads of the Roman Church." Workman : *Hus' Letters*, p. 125.   [3] Nürnb. ed., I. 302.

[4] *De indulgentiis*, Nürnb. ed., pp. 220–228.

Confession of the heart alone is sufficient for the soul's salvation where the applicant is truly penitent.

In denying the infallibility of the pope and of the Church visible, and in setting aside the sacerdotal power of the priesthood to open and shut the kingdom of heaven, Huss broke with the accepted theory of Western Christendom; he committed the unpardonable sin of the Middle Ages. These fundamental ideas, however, were not original with the Bohemian Reformer. He took them out of Wyclif's writings, and he also incorporated whole paragraphs of those writings in his pages. Teacher never had a more devoted pupil than the English Reformer had in Huss. The first three chapters of *De ecclesia* are little more than a series of extracts from Wyclif's treatise on the Church. What is true of this work is also true of most of Huss' other Latin writings.[1] Huss, however, was not a mere copyist. The ideas he got from Wyclif he made thoroughly his own. When he quoted Augustine, Bernard, Jerome and other writers, he mentioned them by name. If he did not mention Wyclif, when he took from him arguments and entire paragraphs, a good reason can be assigned for his silence. It was well known that it was Wyclif's cause which he was representing and Wycliffian views that he was defending, and Wyclif's writings were wide open to the eye of members of the university faculties. He made no secret of following Wyclif, and being willing to die for the views Wyclif taught. As he wrote to

---

[1] Loserth wrote his *Wicliff and Hus* to show the dependence of Huss upon his English predecessor, and the latter half of this work gives proof of it by printing in parallel columns portions of the two authors' compositions. He says, p. 111, that the *De ecclesia* is only "a meagre abridgement of Wyclif's work on the same subject. This author affirms that in his Latin tractates Huss "has drawn all his arguments from Wyclif," and that "the most weighty parts are taken word for word from his English predecessor," pp. xiv, 139, 141, 156, etc. Neander made a mistake in rating the influence of Matthias of Janow upon Huss higher than the influence of Wyclif. He wrote before the Wyclif Society began its publications. Even Palacky, in his *Church History of Bohemia*, III. 190–197, pronounced it uncertain how far Huss was influenced by Wyclif's writings, and questions whether he had attached himself closely to the English Reformer. The publications of the Wyclif Society, which make a comparison possible, show that one writer could scarcely be more dependent upon another than Huss was upon Wyclif.

Richard Wyche, he was thankful that "under the power of Jesus Christ, Bohemia had received so much good from the blessed land of England."[1]

The Bohemian theologian was fully imbued with Wyclif's heretical spirit.   The great Council of Constance was about to meet.   Before that tribunal Huss was now to be judged.

§ 45.   *Huss at Constance.*

> Thou wast their Rock, their fortress and their might;
> Thou, Lord, their captain in the well-fought fight;
> Thou, in the darkness drear, their light of light.   Alleluia.

The great expectations aroused by the assembling of the Council of Constance included the settlement of the disturbance which was rending the kingdom of Bohemia.   It was well understood that measures were to be taken against the heresy which had invaded Western Christendom.   In two letters addressed to Conrad, archbishop of Prag, Gerson bore witness that, in learned centres outside of Bohemia, the names of Wyclif and Huss were indissolubly joined.   Of all Huss' errors, wrote the chancellor, " the proposition is the most perilous that a man who is living in deadly sin may not have authority and dominion over Christian men.   And this proposition, as is well known, has passed down to Huss from Wyclif."[2]

To Constance Sigismund, king of the Romans and heir of the Bohemian crown, turned for relief from the embarrassment of Hussitism; and from Lombardy he sent a deputation to summon Huss to attend the council, at the same time promising him safe conduct.   The Reformer expressed his readiness to go, and had handbills posted in Prag announcing his decision. Writing to Wenzel and his queen, he reaffirmed his readiness, and stated he was willing to suffer the penalty appointed for heretics, should he be condemned.[3]

Under date of Sept. 1, 1414, Huss wrote to Sigismund that he was ready to go to Constance " under safe-conduct of your

[1] Workman : *Hus' Letters*, p. 36.

[2] Van der Hardt, I. 18; Palacky, *Docum.*, pp. 523–528.

[3] For these letters and copies of the handbill, see Workman, *Hus' Letters*, p. 140 sqq.

protection, the Lord Most High being my defender." A week later, the king replied, expressing confidence that, by his appearance, all imputation of heresy would be removed from the kingdom of Bohemia.

Huss set out on the journey Oct. 11, 1414, and reached Constance Nov. 3. He was accompanied by the Bohemian nobles, John of Chlum, Wenzel of Duba and Henry Lacembok. With John of Chlum was Mladenowitz, who did an important service by preserving Huss' letters and afterwards editing them with notes. Huss' correspondence, from this time on, deserves a place in the choice autobiographical literature of the Christian centuries. For pathos, simplicity of expression and devotion to Christ, the writings of the Middle Ages do not furnish anything superior.

In a letter written to friends in Bohemia on the eve of his departure, Huss expressed his expectation of being confronted at Constance by bishops, doctors, princes and canons regular, yea, by more foes than the Redeemer himself had to face. He prayed that, if his death would contribute aught to God's glory, he might be enabled to meet it without sinful fear. A second letter was not to be opened, except in case of his death. It was written to Martin, a disciple whom the writer says he had known from childhood. He binds Martin to fear God, to be careful how he listened to the confessions of women, and not to follow him in any frivolity he had been guilty of in other days, such as chess-playing. Persecution was about to do its worst because he had attacked the greed and incontinence of the clergy. He willed to Martin his gray cloak and bade him, in case of his death, give to the rector his white gown and to his faithful servant, George, a guinea.

The route was through Nürnberg. Along the way Huss was met by throngs of curious people. He sat down in the inns with the local priests, talking over his case with them. At Nürnberg the magistrates and burghers invited him to meet them at an inn. Deeming it unnecessary to go out of its way to meet Sigismund, who was at Spires, the party turned its face directly to the lake of Constance. Arrived on its upper shore, they sent back most of their horses for sale, a wise measure, as it proved, in view of the thousands of animals that had to be cared for at Constance.[1]

Arrived at Constance, Huss took lodgings with a "second widow of Sarepta," who had kept the bakery to the White Pigeon. The house is still shown. His coming was a great sensation, and he entered the town, riding through a large crowd. The day after, John of Chlum and Baron Lacembok called upon pope John XXIII., who promised that no violence should be done their friend, nay, even though he had killed the pope's own brother. He granted him leave to go about the city, but forbade him to attend high mass. Although he was under sentence of excommunication, Huss celebrated mass daily in his own lodgings. The cardinals were incensed that a man charged openly with heresy should have freedom, and whatever misgivings Huss had had of unfair dealing were to be quickly justified. Individual liberty had no rights before the bar of an ecclesiastical court in the 15th century when a heretic was under accusation. Before the month had passed, Huss' imprisonment began, a pretext being found in an alleged attempt to escape from the city concealed in a hay-wagon.[2] On November 28, the two bishops of Trent and Augsburg entered his lodgings with a requisition for him to appear before the cardinals. The house was surrounded by soldiers. Huss, after some hesitation, yielded and left, with the hostess standing at the stairs in tears. It was the beginning of the end.

After a short audience with the cardinals, the prisoner was taken away by a guard of soldiers, and within a week he was securely immured in the dungeon of the Dominican convent. Preparations had been going on for several days to provide the place with locks, bolts and other strong furnishings.

---

[1] Huss kept one for himself, thinking it might be necessary for him to ride and see Sigismund.   Writing from Constance, Nov. 4th, he said that horses were cheap there.   One, bought in Bohemia for 6 guineas, was given away for 7 florins, or one-third the original price. Workman: *Letters*, p. 158.

[2] The charge is reported by Richental, p. 76 sq. His story is invalidated by the false date he gives and also by the testimony of Mladenowitz, who declared it wholly untrue. If there had been any attempt at escape, it would hardly have been allowed to go unnoticed in the trial. See Wylie, p. 139.

In this prison, Huss languished for three months. His cell was hard by the latrines. Fever and vomiting set in, and it seemed likely they would quickly do their dismal work. John XXIII. deserves some credit for having sent his physician, who applied clysters, as Huss himself wrote. To sickness was added the deprivation of books, including the Bible. For two months we have no letters from him. They begin again, with January, 1415, and give us a clear insight into the indignities to which he was exposed and the misery he suffered. These letters were sent by the gaoler.

What was Sigismund doing? He had issued the letter of safe-conduct, Oct. 18. On the day before his arrival in Constance, Dec. 24th, John of Chlum posted up a notice on the cathedral, protesting that the king's agreement had been treated with defiance by the cardinals. Sigismund professed to be greatly incensed, and blustered, but this was the end of it. He was a time-serving prince who was easily persuaded to yield to the arguments of such ecclesiastical figures as D'Ailly, who insisted that little matters like Huss' heresy should not impede the reformation of the church, the council's first concern, and that error unreproved was error countenanced.[1] All good churchmen prayed his Majesty might not give way to the lies and subtleties of the Wycliffists. The king of Aragon wrote that Huss should be killed off at once, without having the formality of a hearing.

During his imprisonment in the Black Friars' convent, Huss wrote for his gaoler, Robert, tracts on the Ten Commandments, the Lord's Prayer, Mortal Sin and Marriage. Of the 13 letters preserved from this time, the larger part were addressed to John of Chlum, his trusty friend. Some of the letters were written at midnight, and some on tattered scraps of paper.[2] In this

[1] In an audience with Sigismund, D'Ailly protested that *factum J. Hus et alia minora non debebant reformationem eccles. et Rom. imperii impedire quod erat principale pro quo fuerat concilium congregatum.* Fillastre, in Finke, p. 253.

[2] On reading a letter in the Bethlehem chapel, Hawlik exclaimed, "Alas, alas, Hus is running out of paper." And John of Chlum spoke of one of Huss' letters as being written "on a tattered, three-cornered bit of paper." Workman : *Hus' Letters*, p. 196.

correspondence four things are prominent: Huss' reliance upon the king and his word of honor, his consuming desire to be heard in open council, the expectation of possible death and his trust in God. He feared sentence would be passed before opportunity was given him to speak with the king. "If this is his honor, it is his own lookout," he wrote.[1]

In the meantime the council had committed the matter of heresy to a commission, with D'Ailly at its head. It plied Huss with questions, and presented heretical articles taken from his writings. Stephen Paletz, his apostate friend, badgered him more than all the rest. His request for a "proctor and advocate" was denied. The thought of death was continually before him. But, as the Lord had delivered Jonah from the whale's belly, and Daniel from the lions, so, he believed, God would deliver him, if it were expedient.

Upon John XXIII.'s flight, fears were felt that Huss might be delivered by his friends, and the keys of the prison were put into the hands of Sigismund. On March 24th the bishop of Constance had the prisoner chained and transferred by boat to his castle, Gottlieben. There he had freedom to walk about in his chains by day, but he was handcuffed and bound to the wall at night. The imprisonment at Gottlieben lasted seventy-three days, from March 24th–June 5th. If Huss wrote any letters during that time none have survived. It was a strange freak of history that the runaway pontiff, on being seized and brought back to Constance, was sent to Gottlieben to be fellow-prisoner with Huss, the one, the former head of Christendom, condemned for almost every known misdemeanor; the other, the preacher whose life was, by the testimony of all contemporaries, almost without a blemish. The criminal pope was to be released after a brief confinement and elevated to an exalted dignity; the other was to be contemned as a religious felon and burnt as an expiation to orthodox theology.

At Gottlieben, Huss suffered from hemorrhage, headache and other infirmities, and at times was on the brink of starvation. A new commission, appointed April 6, with D'Ailly at its head, now took up seriously the heresy of Huss and Wyclif,

---

[1] Workman: *Letters*, p. 174, 182, 184, 190.

whom the council coupled together.[1]   Huss' friends had not
forgotten him, and 250 Moravian and Bohemian nobles signed
a remonstrance at Prag, May 13, which they sent to Sigismund, protesting against the treatment "the beloved master
and Christian preacher" was receiving, and asked that he might
be granted a public hearing and allowed to return home.   Upon
a public hearing Huss staked everything, and with such a hearing in view he had gone to Constance.

In order to bring the prisoner within more convenient reach
of the commission, he was transferred in the beginning of June
to a third prison, — the Franciscan friary.   From June 5–8 public hearings were had in the refectory, the room being crowded
with cardinals, archbishops, bishops, theologians and persons of
lesser degree.   Cardinal D'Ailly was present, and took the leading part as head of the commission.   The action taken May 4th
condemning 260 errors and heresies extracted from Wyclif's
works was adapted to rob Huss of whatever hope of release he
still indulged.   Charges were made against him of holding that
Christ is in the consecrated bread only as the soul is in the body,
that Wyclif was a good Christian, that salvation was not dependent upon the pope and that no one could be excommunicated except by God Himself.   He also had expressed the hope his soul
might be where Wyclif's was.[2]   When a copy of his book on
the Church was shown, they shouted, "Burn it."   Whenever
Huss attempted to explain his positions, he was met with shouts,
"Away with your sophistries.   Say, Yes or No."   The Englishman, John Stokes, who was present, declared that it seemed to
him as if he saw Wyclif himself in bodily form sitting before
him.

On the morning of June 7th, Huss exclaimed that God and
his conscience were on his side.   But, said D'Ailly, "we cannot go by your conscience when we have other evidence, and the
evidence of Gerson himself against you, the most renowned doctor in Christendom."[3]   D'Ailly and an Englishman attempted

---

[1] See Card. Fillastre's *Diary* in Finke's *Forschungen*, pp. 164, 179.

[2] *Utinam anima esset ibi, ubi est anima Joh. Wicleff.*   Mansi, XXVII. 756.

[3] *Nos non possumus secundum tuam conscientiam judicare*, etc., Palacky,
Doc. 278.   Tschackert, pp. 225, 235, says D'Ailly would have been obliged to

to show the logical connection of the doctrine of remanence with realism.   When Huss replied that such reasoning was the logic of schoolboys, another Englishman had the courage to add, Huss is quite right: what have these quibbles to do with matters of faith?   Sigismund advised Huss to submit, saying that he had told the commission he would not defend any heretic who was determined to stick to his heresy.   He also declared that, so long as a single heretic remained, he was ready to light the fire himself with his own hand to burn him.   He, however, promised that Huss should have a written list of charges the following day.

That night, as Huss wrote, he suffered from toothache, vomiting, headache and the stone.   On June 8th, 39 distinct articles were handed to him, 26 of which were drawn from his work on the Church.   When he demurred at some of the statements, D'Ailly had the pertinent sections from the original writings read.   When they came to the passage that no heretic should be put to death, the audience shouted in mockery.   Huss went on to argue from the case of Saul, after his disobedience towards Agag, that kings in mortal sin have no right to authority.   Sigismund happened to be at the moment at the window, talking to Frederick of Bavaria.   The prelates, taking advantage of the avowal, cried out, "Tell the king Huss is now attacking him."   The emperor turned and said, "John Huss, no one lives without sin."   D'Ailly suggested that the prisoner, not satisfied with pulling down the spiritual fabric, was attempting to hurl down the monarchy likewise.   In an attempt to break the force of his statement, Huss asked why they had deposed pope John.   Sigismund replied that Baldassarre was real pope, but was deposed for his notorious crimes.

The 39 articles included the heretical assertions that the Church is the totality of the elect, that a priest must continue preaching, even though he be under sentence of excommunication, and that whoso is in mortal sin cannot exercise authority.

lay aside his purple if he had not resisted Huss' views.   Huss had said of Gerson, *O si deus daret tempus scribendi contra mendacia Parisiensis cancellarii*, Palacky, *Doc.* 97.   Gerson went so far as to say that Huss was condemned for his realism.   See Schwab, pp. 298, 586.

Huss expressed himself ready to revoke statements that might be proved untrue by Scripture and good arguments, but that he would not revoke any which were not so proved. When Sigismund remonstrated, Huss appealed to the judgment bar of God. At the close of the proceedings, D'Ailly declared that a compromise was out of the question. Huss must abjure.[1]

As Huss passed out in the charge of the archbishop of Riga, John of Chlum had the courage to reach out his hand to him. The act reminds us of the friendly words Georg of Frundsberg spoke to Luther at Worms. Huss was most thankful, and a day or two afterward wrote how delightful it had been to see Lord John, who was not ashamed to hold out his hand to a poor, abject heretic, a prisoner in irons and the butt of all men's tongues. In addressing the assembly after Huss' departure, Sigismund argued against accepting submission from the prisoner who, if released, would go back to Bohemia and sow his errors broadcast. "When I was a boy," he said, "I remember the first sprouting of this sect, and see what it is to-day. We should make an end of the master one day, and when I return from my journey we will deal with his pupil. What's his name?" The reply was, Jerome. Yes, said the king, I mean Jerome.

Huss, as he himself states, was pestered in prison by emissaries who sought to entrap him, or to "hold out baskets" for him to escape in. Some of the charges made against him he ascribes to false witnesses. But many of the charges were not false, and it is difficult to understand how he could expect to free himself by a public statement, in view of the solemn condemnation passed upon the doctrines of Wyclif. He was convinced that none of the articles brought against him were contrary to the Gospel of Christ, but canon law ruled at councils, not Scripture. A doctor told him that, if the council should affirm he had only one eye, he ought to accept the verdict. Huss replied if the whole world were to tell him so, he would not say so and offend his conscience, and he appealed to the

---

[1] See Tschackert, p. 230. D'Ailly persisted in this position after he left Constance. Wyclif and Huss remained to him the dangerous heretics, — *pernitiosi heretici.* Van der Hardt, VI. 16.

case of Eleazar in the Book of the Maccabees, who would not make a lying confession.[1] But he was setting his house in order. He wrote affecting messages to his people in Bohemia and to John of Chlum. He urged the Bohemians to hear only priests of good report, and especially those who were earnest students of Holy Writ. Martin he adjured to read the Bible diligently, especially the New Testament.

On June 15th, the council took the far-reaching action forbidding the giving of the cup to laymen. This action Huss condemned as wickedness and madness, on the ground that it was a virtual condemnation of Christ's example and command. To Hawlik, who had charge of the Bethlehem chapel, he wrote, urging him not to withhold the cup from the laity.[2] He saw indisputable proof that the council was fallible. One day it kissed the feet of John, as a paragon of virtue, and called him "most holy," and the next it condemned him as "a shameful homicide, a sodomite, a simoniac and a heretic." He quoted the proverb, common among the Swiss, that a generation would not suffice to cleanse Constance from the sins the body had committed in that city.

The darkness deepened around the prisoner. On June 24th, by the council's orders, his writings were to be burnt, even those written in Czech which, almost in a tone of irony, as he wrote, the councillors had not seen and could not read. He bade his friends not be terrified, for Jeremiah's books, which the prophet had written at the Lord's direction, were burnt.

His affectionate interest in the people of "his glorious country" and in the university on the Moldau, and his feeling of gratitude to the friends who had supported him continued unabated. A dreadful death was awaiting him, but he recalled the sufferings of Apostles and the martyrs, and especially the agonies endured by Christ, and he believed he would be purged of his sins through the flames. D'Ailly had replied to him on one occasion by peremptorily saying he should obey the decision of 50 doctors of the Church and retract without asking any questions. "A wonderful piece of information," he

[1] Workman : *Hus' Letters*, pp. 226, 239–241.
[2] See Workman, pp. 185, 245, 248.

wrote, "As if the virgin, St. Catherine, ought to have re-nounced the truth and her faith in the Lord because 50 phi-losophers opposed her."[1]   In one of his last letters, written to his alma mater of Prag, he declared he had not recanted a single article.

On the first day of July, he was approached by the arch-bishops of Riga and Ragusa and 6 other prelates, who still had a hope of drawing from him a recantation.   A written declara-tion made by Huss in reply showed the hope vain.[2]   Another effort was made July 5th, Cardinals D'Ailly and Zabarella and bishop Hallum of Salisbury being of the party of visiting prel-ates.   Huss closed the discussion by declaring that he would rather be burnt a thousand times than abjure, for by abjuring he said he would offend those whom he had taught.[3]

Still another deputation approached him, his three friends John of Chlum, Wenzel of Duba and Lacembok, and four bishops.   They were sent by Sigismund.   As a layman, John of Chlum did not venture to give Huss advice, but bade him, if he felt sure of his cause, rather than to lie against God, to stand fast, even to death.   One of the bishops asked whether he presumed to be wiser than the whole council.   No, was the reply, but to retract he must be persuaded of his errors out of the Scriptures.   "An obstinate heretic!" exclaimed the bishops.   This was the final interview in private.   The much-desired opportunity was at hand for him to stand before the council as a body, and it was his last day on earth.

After seven months of dismal imprisonment and deepening disappointment, on Saturday, July 6th, Huss was conducted to the cathedral.   It was 6 A.M., and he was kept waiting out-side the doors until the celebration of mass was completed. He was then admitted to the sacred edifice, but not to make a defence, as he had come to Constance hoping to do.   He was to listen to sentence pronounced upon him as an ecclesiastical out-cast and criminal.   He was placed in the middle of the church on a high stool, set there specially for him.[4]   The bishop of Lodi

---

[1] Workman, p. 264.   [2] *Ibid.*, p. 276.

[3] *Non vellet abjurare sed millisies comburi,* Mansi, XXVII. 764.

[4] *Ad medium concilii ubi erat levatus in altum scamnum pro eo.*   Mansi, XXVII. 747.

preached from Rom. 6 : 6, "that the body of sin may be destroyed." The extermination of heretics was represented as one of the works most pleasing to God, and the preacher used the time-worn illustrations from the rotten piece of flesh, the little spark which is in danger of turning into a great flame and the creeping cancer. The more virulent the poison the swifter should be the application of the cauterizing iron. In the style of Bossuet in a later age, before Louis XIV., he pronounced upon Sigismund the eulogy that his name would be coupled with song and triumph for all time for his efforts to uproot schism and destroy heresy.

The commission, which included Patrick, bishop of Cork, appointed to pronounce the sentence, then ascended the pulpit. All expressions of feeling with foot or hand, all vociferation or attempt to start disputation were solemnly forbidden on pain of excommunication. 30 articles were then read, which were pronounced as heretical, seditious and offensive to pious ears. The sentence coupled in closest relation Wyclif and Huss.[1] The first of the articles charged the prisoner with holding that the Church is the totality of the predestinate, and the last that no civil lord or prelate may exercise authority who is in mortal sin. Huss begged leave to speak, but was hushed up.

The sentence ran that "the holy council, having God only before its eye, condemns John Huss to have been and to be a true, real and open heretic, the disciple not of Christ but of John Wyclif, one who in the University of Prag and before the clergy and people declared Wyclif to be a Catholic and an evangelical doctor — *vir catholicus et doctor evangelicus.*" It ordered him degraded from the sacerdotal order, and, not wishing to exceed the powers committed unto the Church, it relinquished him to the secular authority.

Not a dissenting voice was lifted against the sentence. Even John Gerson voted for it. One incident has left its impress upon history, although it is not vouched for by a contemporary. It is said that, when Huss began to speak, he looked at Sigismund, reminding him of the safe-conduct. The king, who sat in state and crowned, turned red, but did not speak.

---

[1] The articles are given in Mansi, pp. 754 sq., 1209–1211, and Hardt, IV. 408–12.

The order of degradation was carried out by six bishops, who disrobed the condemned man of his vestments and destroyed his tonsure.   They then put on his head a cap covered over with pictures of the devil and inscribed with the word, heresiarch, and committed his soul to the devil. With upturned eyes, Huss exclaimed, "and I commit myself to the most gracious Lord Jesus."

The old motto that the Church does not want blood — *ecclesia non sitit sanguinem* — was in appearance observed, but the authorities knew perfectly well what was to be the last scene when they turned Huss over to Sigismund. "Go, take him and do to him as a heretic" were the words with which the king remanded the prisoner to the charge of Louis, the Count Palatine.   A guard of a thousand armed men was at hand.   The streets were thronged with people.   As Huss passed on, he saw the flames on the public square which were consuming his books. For fear of the bridge's breaking down, the greater part of the crowd was not allowed to cross over to the place of execution, called the Devil's Place.   Huss' step had been firm, but now, with tears in his eyes, he knelt down and prayed.   The paper cap falling from his head, the crowd shouted that it should be put on, wrong side front.

It was midday.   The prisoner's hands were fastened behind his back, and his neck bound to the stake by a chain.   On the same spot some time before, so the chronicler notes, a cardinal's worn-out mule had been buried.   The straw and wood were heaped up around Huss' body to the chin, and rosin sprinkled upon them.   The offer of life was renewed if he would recant. He refused and said, "I shall die with joy to-day in the faith of the Gospel which I have preached."   When Richental, who was standing by, suggested a confessor, he replied, "There is no need of one. I have no mortal sin."   At the call of bystanders, they turned his face away from the East, and as the flames arose, he sang twice, Christ, thou Son of the living God, have mercy upon me.   The wind blew the fire into the martyr's face, and his voice was hushed.   He died, praying and singing. To remove, if possible, all chance of preserving relics from the scene, Huss' clothes and shoes were thrown into the merciless flames.   The ashes were gathered up and cast into the Rhine.

While this scene was being enacted, the council was going on with the transaction of business as if the burning without the gates were only a common event.   Three weeks later, it announced that it had done nothing more pleasing to God than to punish the Bohemian heretic.   For this act it has been chiefly remembered by after generations.

Not one of the members of the Council of Constance, after its adjournment, so far as we know, uttered a word of protest against the sentence.   No pope or œcumenical synod since has made any apology for it.   Nor has any modern Catholic historian gone further than to indicate that in essential theological doctrines Huss was no heretic, though his sentence was strictly in accord with the principles of the canon law.   So long as the dogmas of an infallible Church organization and an infallible pope continue to be strictly held, no apology can be expected.   It is of the nature of Protestant Christianity to confess wrongs and, as far as is possible, make reparation for them.   When the Massachusetts court discovered that it had erred in the case of the Salem witchcraft in 1692, it made full confession, and offered reparation to the surviving descendants ; and Judge Sewall, one of the leaders in the prosecution, made a moving public apology for the mistake he had committed.   The same court recalled the action against Roger Williams.   In 1903, the Protestants of France reared a monument at Geneva in expiation of Calvin's part in passing sentence upon Servetus.   Luther, in his *Address to the German Nobility*, called upon the Roman Church to confess it had done wrong in burning Huss.   That innocent man's blood still cries from the ground.

Huss died for his advocacy of Wycliffism.   The sentence passed by the council coupled the two names together.[1]   The

[1] Buddenseig, *Hus, Patriot and Reformer*, p. 11, says, " The whole Hussite movement is mere Wycliffism."   Loserth, *Wiclif and Hus*, p. xvi, says, It was Wyclif's doctrine principally for which Hus yielded up his life.   Invectives flying about in Constance joined their names together.   The *Missa Wiclefistarum* ran, *Credo in Wykleph ducem inferni patronum Boemiæ et in Hus filium ejus unicum nequam nostrum, qui conceptus est ex spiritu Luciferi, natus matre ejus et factus incarnatus equalis Wikleph, secundum malam voluntatem*

25th of the 30 Articles condemned him for taking offence at the reprobation of the 45 articles, ascribed to Wyclif. How much this article was intended to cover cannot be said. It is certain that Huss did not formally deny the doctrine of transubstantiation, although he was charged with that heresy. Nor was he distinctly condemned for urging the distribution of the cup to the laity, which he advocated after the council had positively forbidden it. His only offence was his definition of the Church and his denial of the infallibility of the papacy and its necessity for the being of the Church. These charges constitute the content of all the 30 articles except the 25th. Luther said brusquely but truly, that Huss committed no more atrocious sin than to declare that a Roman pontiff of impious life is not the head of the Church catholic.[1]

John Huss struck at the foundations of the hierarchical system. He interpreted our Lord's words to Peter in a way that was fatal to the papal theory of Leo, Hildebrand and Innocent III.[2] His conception of the Church, which he drew from Wyclif, contains the kernel of an entirely new system of religious authority. He made the Scriptures the final source of appeal, and exalted the authority of the conscience above pope, council and canon law as an interpreter of truth. He carried out these

et major secundum ejus persecutionem, regnans tempore desolationis studii Pragensis, tempore quo Boemia a fide apostotavit. Qui propter nos hereticos descendit ad inferna et non resurget a mortuis nec habebit vitam eternam. Amen.

[1] Note appended to Huss' writings, ed. 1537. See Huss' *Opp.*, Prelim. Statement, I. 4. It did not require the study of the modern historian to affirm the view taken above. John Foxe, in his *Book of Martyrs*, presented it clearly when he said, " By the life, acts and letters of Huss, it is plain that he was condemned not for any error of doctrine, for he neither denied their popish transubstantiation, neither spake against the authority of the church of Rome, if it were well governed, nor yet against the seven sacraments, but said mass himself and in almost all their popish opinions was a papist with them, but only through evil will was he accused because he spoke against the pomp, pride and avarice and other wicked enormities of the pope, cardinals and prelates of the church, etc.

[2] Gerson declared that among the causes for which Huss was condemned was that he had affirmed that the Church could be ruled by priests dispersed throughout the world in the absence of one head as well as with one head. Schwab, p. 588.

views in practice by continuing to preach in spite of repeated sentences of excommunication, and attacking the pope's right to call a crusade. If the Church be the company of the elect, as Huss maintained, then God rules in His people and they are sovereign. With such assertions, the teachings of Thomas Aquinas were set aside.

The enlightened group of men who shared the spirit of Gerson and D'Ailly did not comprehend Wycliffism, for Wycliffism was a revolt against an alleged divine institution, the visible Church. Gerson denied that the appeal to conscience was an excuse for refusing to submit to ecclesiastical authority. Faith, with him, was agreement with the Church's system. The chancellor not only voted for Huss' condemnation, but declared he had busily worked to bring the sentence about. Nineteen articles he drew from Huss' work on the Church, he pronounced "notoriously heretical." However, at a later time, in a huff over the leniency shown to Jean Petit, he stated that if Huss had been given an advocate, he would never have been convicted.[1]

In starting out for Constance, Huss knew well the punishment appointed for heretics. The amazing thing is that he should ever have thought it possible to clear himself by a public address before the council. In view of the procedure of the Inquisition, the council showed him unheard-of consideration in allowing him to appear in the cathedral. This was done out of regard for Sigismund, who was on the eve of his journey to Spain to induce Benedict of Luna to abdicate.[2]

As for the safe-conduct — *salvo-conductus* — issued by Sigismund, all that can be said is that a king did not keep his word. He was more concerned to be regarded as the patron of a great council than to protect a Bohemian preacher, his future subject. Writing with reference to the solemn pledge, Huss said, "Christ deceives no man by a safe-conduct. What he pledges he fulfils. Sigismund has acted deceitfully throughout."[3] The plea,

---

[1] Schwab, pp. 588–599, 600. On the whole subject of Huss' views Schwab has excellent remarks, p. 596 sqq.

[2] See Workman : *Age of Hus*, pp. 284, 293, 364, and Wylie, p. 175 sqq.

[3] Workman : *Hus' Letters*, p. 269 sq.

often made, that the king had no intention of giving Huss an
unconditional pledge of protection, is in the face of the documentary evidence.   In September, 1415, the Council of Constance took formal notice of the criticisms floating about that
in Huss' execution a solemn promise had been broken, and announced that no brief of safe-conduct in the case of a heretic is
binding.   No pledge is to be observed which is prejudicial to
the Catholic faith and ecclesiastical jurisdiction.[1]

The safe-conduct was in the ordinary form, addressed to all
the princes and subjects of the empire, ecclesiastical and secular,
and informing them that Huss should be allowed to pass, remain and return without impediment.   Jerome, according to
the sentence passed upon him by the council, declared that the
safe-conduct had been grossly violated, and when, in 1433, the
legates of the Council of Basel attempted to throw the responsibility for Huss' condemnation on false witnesses, so called,
Rokyzana asked how the Council of Constance could have been
moved by the Holy Ghost if it were controlled by perjurers,
and showed that the violation of the safe-conduct had not been
forgotten.   When the Bohemian deputies a year earlier had
come to Basel, they demanded the most carefully prepared briefs
of safe-conduct from the Council of Basel, the cities of Eger
and Basel and from Sigismund and others.   Frederick of Brandenburg and John of Bavaria agreed to furnish troops to protect the Hussites on their way to Basel, at Basel, and on their
journey home.   A hundred and six years later, Luther profited by Huss' misfortune when he recalled Sigismund's perfidy, perfidy which the papal system of the 16th century
would have repeated, had Charles V. given his consent.[2]

In a real sense, Huss was the precursor of the Reformation.
It is true, the prophecy was wrongly ascribed to him, "To-day
you roast a goose — Huss — but a hundred years from now
a swan will arise out of my ashes which you shall not roast."
Unknown to contemporary writers, it probably originated after

[1] Mansi, XXVII. 791, 799. Also Mirbt, p. 156. Lea, *Inquisition*, II. p. 462
sqq., has an excellent statement of the whole question of Huss' safe-conduct.
[2] Luther declared that a safe-conduct promised to the devil must be kept.
See Köstlin, *M. Luther*, I. 352.

Luther had fairly entered upon his work.   But he struck a
hard blow at hierarchical assumption before Luther raised his
stronger arm.   Luther was moved by Huss' case, and at Leipzig, forced to the wall by Eck's thrusts, the Wittenberg monk
made the open avowal that œcumenical councils also may err,
as was done in putting Huss to death at Constance.   Years
before, at Erfurt, he had taken up a volume of the Bohemian
sermons, and was amazed that a man who preached so evangel-
ically should have been condemned to the stake.   But for fear
of the taint of heresy, he quickly put it down. [1]   The accredited view in Luther's time was given by Dobneck in answer to
Luther's good opinion, when he said that Huss was worse than
a Turk, Jew, Tartar and Sodomite.   In his edition of Huss'
letters, printed 1537, Luther praised Huss' patience and humility under every indignity and his courage before an imposing
assembly as a lamb in the midst of wolves and lions.   If such
a man, he wrote, " is to be regarded as a heretic, then no person under the sun can be looked upon as a true Christian."

A cantionale, dating from 1572, and preserved in the Prag
library, contains a hymn to Huss' memory and three medal-
lions which well set forth the relation in which Wyclif and
Huss stand to the Reformation.   The first represents Wyclif
striking sparks from a stone.   Below it is Huss, kindling a
fire from the sparks.   In the third medallion, Luther is holding aloft the flaming torch.   This is the historic succession,
although it is true Luther began his career as a Reformer before he was influenced by Huss, and continued his work, knowing little of Wyclif.

To the cause of religious toleration, and without intending
it, John Huss made a more effectual contribution by his death
than could have been made by many philosophical treatises,
even as the deaths of Blandina and other martyrs of the early
Church, who were slaves, did more towards the reduction of the
evils of slavery than all the sentences of Pagan philosophers.
Quite like his English teacher, he affirmed the sovereign rights

[1] John Zacharias, one of the professors of the university at Erfurt, had taken
a prominent part in the debates at Constance against Huss, and received as his
reward the red rose from the pope. Köstlin, *M. Luther*, I. 53, 87.

of the truth.   It was his habit, so he stated, to conform his
views to the truth, whatever the truth might be.   If any one,
he said, "can instruct me by the sacred Scriptures or by good
reasoning, I am willing to follow him.   From the outset of my
studies, I have made it a rule to joyfully and humbly recede
from a former opinion when in any matter I perceive a more
rational opinion."[1]

§ 46.   *Jerome of Prag.*

A year after Huss' martyrdom, on May 30, 1416, his friend
Jerome of Prag was condemned by the council and also suffered at the stake.   He shared Huss' enthusiasm for Wyclif,
was perhaps his equal in scholarship, but not in steadfast con-
stancy.   Huss' life was spent in Prag and its vicinity.   Jerome travelled in Western Europe and was in Prag only occasionally.   Huss left quite a body of writings, Jerome, none.

Born of a good family at Prag, Jerome studied in his native
city, and later at Oxford and Paris.   At Oxford he became a
student and admirer of Wyclif's writings, two of which, the
Trialogus and the *Dialogus*, he carried with him back to Bohemia not later than 1402.   In Prag, he defended the English
doctor as a holy man "whose doctrines were more worthy of
acceptance than Augustine himself," stood with Huss in the
contest over the rights of the Bohemian nation, and joined
him in attacking the papal indulgences, 1412.

Soon after arriving in Constance, Huss wrote to John of
Chlum not to allow Jerome on any account to go to join him.
In spite of this warning, Jerome set out and reached Constance
April 4th, 1415, but urged by friends he quit the city.   He was
seized at Hirschau, April 15, and taken back in chains.   There
is every reason for supposing he and Huss did not see one another, although Huss mentions him in a letter within a week

---

[1] *Si aliqua persona ecclesiæ me scrip. s. vel ratione valida, docuerit, para-
tissime consentire.   Nam a primo studii mei tempore hoc mihi statui pro regula,
ut quotiescunque saniorem sententiam in quacunque materia perciperem, a
priori sententia gaudenter et humiliter declinarem.* Wyclif had expressed the
same sentiment in his *De universalibus*, which Huss translated, 1398.   See
Loserth, p. 253.

before his death,[1] expressing the hope that he would die holy
and blameless and be of a braver spirit in meeting pain than he
was.   Huss had misjudged himself.   In the hour of grave
crisis he proved constant and heroic, while his friend gave way.

On Sept. 11, 1415, Jerome solemnly renounced his admiration for Wyclif and professed accord with the Roman church
and the Apostolic see and, twelve days later, solemnly repeated
his abjuration in a formula prepared by the council.[2]

Release from prison did not follow.   It was the council's intention that Jerome should sound forth his abjuration as loudly
as possible in Bohemia, and write to Wenzel, the university and
the Bohemian nobles ; but he disappointed his judges.   Following Gerson's lead, the council again put the recusant heretic
on trial.   The sittings took place in the cathedral, May 23 and
26, 1416.   The charge of denying transubstantiation Jerome
repudiated, but he confessed to having done ill in pledging
himself to abandon the writings and teachings of that good
man John Wyclif, and Huss.   Great injury had been done to
Huss, who had come to the council with assurance of safe-conduct.   Even Judas or a Saracen ought under such circumstances
to be free to come and go and to speak his mind freely.

On May 30, Jerome was again led into the cathedral.   The
bishop of Lodi ascended the pulpit and preached a sermon, calling upon the council to punish the prisoner, and counselling that
against other such heretics, if there should be any, any witnesses whatever should be allowed to testify, — ruffians, thieves
and harlots.   The sermon being over, Jerome mounted a bench
— *bancum ascendens* — and made a defence whose eloquence
is attested by Poggio and others who were present.   Thereupon,
the " holy synod " pronounced him a follower of Wyclif and
Huss, and adjudged him to be cast off as a rotten and withered
branch — *palmitem putridum et aridum*.[3]

Jerome went out from the cathedral wearing a cheerful
countenance.   A paper cap was put on his head, painted over

---

[1] Workman : *Letters*, p. 266.   [2] Mansi, XXVII. 794 sqq., 842–864.
[3] For the sentence, see Mansi, XXVII. 887–897.   Foxe, in his *Book of
Martyrs*, gives a translation and an excellent account of the proceedings
against Jerome and his martyrdom.

with red devils.   No sentence of deposition was necessary or
ceremony of disrobing, for the condemned man was merely a
laic.[1] He died on the spot where Huss suffered.   As the wood
was being piled around him, he sang the Easter hymn, *salva
festa dies*, Hail, festal day.   The flames were slow in putting
an end to his miseries as compared with Huss.   His ashes were
thrown into the Rhine.   And many learned people wept, the
chronicler Richental says, that he had to die, for he was almost
more learned than Huss.   After his death, the council joined
his name with the names of Wyclif and Huss as leaders of
heresy.

Poggio Bracciolini's description of Jerome's address in the
cathedral runs thus : —

It was wonderful to see with what words, with what eloquence, with
what arguments, with what countenance and with what composure, Jerome
replied to his adversaries, and how fairly he put his case. . . .   He advanced
nothing unworthy of a good man, as though he felt confident — as he also
publicly asserted — that no just reason could be found for his death. . . .
Many persons he touched with humor, many with satire, many very often
he caused to laugh in spite of the sad affair, jesting at their reproaches.
. . .   He took them back to Socrates, unjustly condemned by his fellow-
citizens.   Then he mentioned the captivity of Plato, the flight of Anaxag-
oras, the torture of Zeno and the unjust condemnation of many other
Pagans. . . .   Thence he passed to the Hebrew examples, first instancing
Moses, the liberator of his people, Joseph, sold by his brethren, Isaiah,
Daniel, Susannah. . . .   Afterwards, coming down to John the Baptist and
then to the Saviour, he showed how, in each case, they were condemned by
false witnesses and false judges. . . .   Then proceeding to praise John
Huss, who had been condemned to be burnt, he called him a good man, just
and holy, unworthy of such a death, saying that he himself was prepared
to go to any punishment whatsoever. . . .   He said that Huss had never
held opinions hostile to the Church of God, but only against the abuses of
the clergy, against the pride, the arrogance and the pomp of prelates. . . .
He displayed the greatest cleverness, — for, when his speech was often interrupted with various disturbances, he left no one unscathed but turned
trenchantly upon his accusers and forced them to blush, or be still. . . .
For 340 days he lay in the bottom of a foul, dark tower.   He himself did
not complain at the harshness of this treatment, but expressed his wonder
that such inhumanity could be shown him.   In the dungeon, he said, he
had not only no facilities for reading, but none for seeing. . . .   He stood
there fearless and unterrified, not alone despising death but seeking it, so

---

[1] *Laicus*, Mansi, XXVII. 894.

that you would have said he was another Cato. O man, worthy of the ever-lasting memory of men! I praise not that which he advanced, if anything contrary to the institutions of the Church; but I admire his learning, his eloquence, his persuasiveness of speech, his adroitness in reply. . . . Per-severing in his errors, he went to his fate with joyful and willing counte-nance, for he feared not the fire nor any kind of torture or death. . . . When the executioners wished to start the fire behind his back that he might not see it, he said, ' Come here and light the fire in front of me. If I had been afraid of it, I should never have come to this place.' In this way a man worthy, except in respect of faith, was burnt. . . . Not Mutius himself suffered his arm to burn with such high courage as did this man his whole body. Nor did Socrates drink the poison so willingly as he accepted the flames.[1]

Æneas Sylvius, afterwards Pius II., bore similar testimony to the cheerfulness which Huss and Jerome displayed in the face of death, and said that they went to the stake as to a feast and suffered death with more courage than any philosopher.[2]

§ 47. *The Hussites.*

The news of Huss' execution stirred the Bohemian nation to its depths. Huss was looked upon as a national hero and a martyr. The revolt, which followed, threatened the very existence of the papal rule in Bohemia. No other dissenting movement of the Middle Ages assumed such formidable pro-portions. The Hussites, the name given to the adherents of the new body, soon divided into two organized parties, the Taborites and the Calixtines or Utraquists. They agreed in demanding the distribution of the cup to the laity. A third body, the *Unitas Fratrum*, or Bohemian Brethren, originated in the middle of the 15th century, forty years after Huss' death. When it became known that Huss had perished in the flames, the populace of Prag stoned the houses of the priests unfriendly to the martyr; and the archbishop himself was attacked in his palace, and with difficulty eluded the popular rage by flight. King Wenzel at first seemed about to favor the popular party.

The Council of Constance, true to itself, addressed a docu-ment to the bishop and clergy of Prag, designating Wyclif, Huss

---

[1] Huss, *Opera*, II. 532–534. Palacky, *Mon.* 624–699. A full translation is given by Whitcomb in *Lit. Source-Book of the Italian Renaissance*, pp. 40–47.

[2] *Hist. Boh.*, c. 36.

and Jerome as most unrighteous, dangerous and shameful men,[1] and calling upon the Prag officials to put down those who were sowing their doctrines.

The high regard in which Huss was held found splendid expression at the Bohemian diet, Sept. 2, 1415, when 452 nobles signed an indignant remonstrance to the council for its treatment of their "most beloved brother," whom they pronounced to be a righteous and catholic man, known in Bohemia for many years by his exemplary life and honest preaching of the law of the Gospel.   They concluded the document by announcing their intention to defend, even to the effusion of blood, the law of Christ and his devoted preachers.[2]   Three days later, the nobles formed a league which was to remain in force for six years, in which they bound themselves to defend the free preaching of the Gospel on their estates, and to recognize the authority of prelates only so far as they acted according to the Scriptures.

To this manifesto the council, Feb. 20, 1416, replied by citing the signers to appear before it within 50 days, on pain of being declared contumacious.

Huss' memory also had honor at the hands of the university, which, on May 23, 1416, sent forth a communication addressed to all lands, eulogizing him as in all things a master whose life was without an equal.[3]   *In omnibus Magister vitae sine pari.*

Upon the dissolution of the council, Martin V., who, as a member of the curia, had excommunicated Huss, did not allow the measures to root out Hussitism drag.   In his bull *Inter cunctos*,[4] Feb. 22, 1418, he ordered all of both sexes punished as heretics who maintained "the pestilential doctrine of the heresiarchs, John Wyclif, John Huss and Jerome of Prag." Wenzel announced his purpose to obey the council, but many of his councillors left the court, including the statesman, Nicolas of Pistna, and the military leader, the one-eyed John Zizka.   The popular excitement ran so high that, during a

---

[1] *Improbissimos, et periculosissimos, teterrimosque viros*, Mansi, XXVII. 781–783.   [2] Mansi, pp. 789–91.

[3] Palacky, *Monum.*, I. 80–82.

[4] Mansi, XXVII. 1204–15.   Also Mirbt, p. 157 sqq.

Hussite procession, the crowd rushed into the council-house and threw out of the window seven of the councillors who had dared to insult the procession.

Affairs entered a new stage with Wenzel's death, 1419. With considerable unanimity the Bohemian nobles acceded to his successor Sigismund's demand that the cup be withheld from the laity, but the nation at large did not acquiesce, and civil war followed. Convents and churches were sacked. Sigismund could not make himself master of his kingdom, and an event occurred during his visit in Breslau which deepened the feeling against him. A merchant, John Krasa, asserting on the street the innocence of Huss, was dragged at a horse's tail to the stake and burnt. Hussite preachers inveighed against Sigismund, calling him the dragon of the Apocalypse.

Martin V. now summoned Europe to a crusade against Bohemia, offering the usual indulgences, as Innocent III. had done two centuries before, when he summoned a crusade against the Cathari in Southern France. In obedience to the papal mandate, 150,000 men gathered from all parts of Europe. All the horrors of war were perpetrated, and whole provinces desolated. Five times the holy crusaders entered the land of Huss, and five times they were beaten back. In 1424 the Hussites lost their bravest military leader, John Zizka, but in 1427, under his successor, Procopius Rasa, called the Great, the most influential priest of Prag, they took the offensive and invaded Germany.

While they were winning victories over the foreign intruders, the Hussites were divided among themselves in regard to the extent to which the religious reformation should be carried. The radical party, called the Taborites, from the steep hill Tabor, 60 miles south of Prag, on which they built a city, rejected transubstantiation, the worship of saints, prayers for the dead, indulgences and priestly confession and renounced oaths, dances and other amusements. They admitted laymen, including women, to the office of preaching, and used the national tongue in all parts of the public service. Zizka, their first leader, held the sword in the spirit of one of the Judges. After his death, the stricter wing of the Taborites received the name of the Orphans.

The moderate party was called now Pragers, from the chief
seat of their influence, now Calixtines, — from the word *calix*
or cup, — or Utraquists from the expression *sub utraque specie*,
"under both forms," from their insisting upon the administration of the cup to the laity.   The University of Prag took
sides with the Calixtines and, in 1420, the four so-called Prag
articles were adopted.   This compact demanded the free preaching of the Gospel, the distribution of the cup to the laity, the
execution of punishment for mortal sins by the civil court, and
the return of the clergy to the practice of Apostolic poverty.
The Calixtines confined the use of Czech at the church service to the Scripture readings.[1]

After the disastrous rout of the Catholic army, led by Cardinal Cesarini at Tauss, Aug. 14, 1431, the history of the Bohemian
movement passed into a third stage, marked by the negotiations
begun by the Council of Basel and the almost complete annihilation of the Taborite party.   It was a new spectacle for an œcumenical council to treat with heretics as with a party having rights.
Unqualified submission was the demand which the Church had
heretofore made.   On Oct. 15, 1431, the council invited the
Bohemians to a conference and promised delegates safe-conduct.   This promise assured them that neither guile nor deceit
would be resorted to on any ground whatsoever, whether it be
of authority or the privileges of canon law or of the decisions
of the Councils of Constance and Siena or any other council.[2]
Three hundred delegates appointed by the Bohemian diet appeared in Basel.   On the way, at Eger, and in the presence of
the landgrave of Brandenburg and John, duke of Bavaria, they
laid down their own terms, which were sent ahead and accepted
by the council.[3]   These terms, embodied in thirteen articles,
dealt with the method of carrying on the negotiations, the
cessation of the interdict during the sojourn of the delegates
in the Swiss city and the privilege of practising their own religious rites.   The leaders of the Bohemian delegation were

[1] As early as 1423, dissenters with the name of Hussites appeared in Northern
Germany and Holland.   Fredericq, *Corpus Inq.*, III. 65, 142, etc.

[2] *Sine fraude et quolibet dolo, occulte vel manifeste*, etc.   Mansi, XXIX. 27.

[3] See Hefele, VII. 476 sq.

The assembly was stirred to a great heat, but, so a contemporary says, the ardor soon cooled.   Cardinal Bessarion followed Pius with an address which also lasted three hours.   Of eloquence there was enough, but the crusading age was over.   The conquerors of Jerusalem had been asleep for nearly 400 years. Splendid orations could not revive that famous outburst of enthusiasm which followed Urban's address at Clermont.   In this case the element of romance was wanting which the conquest of the Holy Sepulchre had furnished.   The prowess of the conquering Turks was a hard fact.

During the Congress of Mantua the controversy broke out between the German lawyer, Gregor of Heimburg, and Pius. They had met before at Basel.   Heimburg, representing the duke of the Tyrol, who had imprisoned Nicolas of Cusa, spoke against the proposed crusade.   He openly insulted the pope by keeping on his hat in his presence, an indignity he jokingly explained as a precaution against the catarrh.   From the sentence of excommunication, pronounced against his ducal master, he appealed to a general council, August 13, 1460.   He himself was punished with excommunication, and Pius called upon the city of Nürnberg to expel him as the child of the devil and born of the artifice of lies.   Heimburg became a wanderer until the removal of the ban, 1472.   He was the strongest literary advocate in Germany of the Basel decrees and the superiority of councils, and has been called a predecessor of Luther and precursor of the Reformation.[1]   Diether, archbishop of Mainz, another advocate of the conciliar system, who entered into compacts with the German princes to uphold the Basel decrees and to work for a general council on German soil, was deposed, 1461, as Hermann, archbishop of Cologne, was deposed a hundred years later for undertaking measures of reform in his diocese.

Pius left Mantua the last of January, 1461, stopping on the return journey a second time at his beloved Siena, and canon-

---

[1] Gregorovius, VII. 184.   His tract *Admonitio de injustis usurpationibus paparum rom. ad imperatorem . . . sive confutatio primatus papæ*, and other tracts by Heimburg, are given in Goldast, *Monarchia.* See art. *Gregor v. Heimburg,* by Tschackert in Herzog, VII. 133–135, and for quotations, Gieseler.

izing its distinguished daughter, Catherine.[1]   Here Rodrigo
Borgia's gayeties were so notorious as to call forth papal rebuke.
The cardinal gave banquets to which women were invited without their husbands.   In a severe letter to the future supreme
pontiff, Pius spoke of the dancing at the entertainments as being
performed, so he understood, with "all licentiousness."

The ease with which Pius, when it was to his interest, renounced theories which he once advocated is shown in two
bulls.   The first, the famous bull, *Execrabilis*, declared it an
accursed and unheard-of abuse to make appeal to a council
from the decisions of the Roman pontiff, Christ's vicar, to
whom it was given to feed his sheep and to bind and loose on
earth and in heaven.   To rid the Church of this pestiferous
venom, — *pestiferum virus*, — it announced the papal purpose
to damn such appeals and to lay upon the appellants a curse
from which there could be no absolution except by the Roman
pontiff himself and in the article of death.[2]   Thus the solemn
principle which had bloomed so promisingly in the fair days of
the councils of Constance and Basel, and for which Gerson and
D'Ailly had so zealously contended, was set aside by one stroke
of the pen.   Thenceforward, the decree announced, papal decisions were to be treated as final.

Three years later, April 26, 1463, the theory of the supremacy of general councils was set aside in still more precise language.[3]   In an elaborate letter addressed to the rector and
scholars of the University of Cologne, Pius pronounced for the
monarchical form of government in the church — *monarchicum
regimen* — as being of divine origin, and the one given to Peter.
As storks follow one leader, and as the bees have one king, so
the militant church has in the vicar of Christ one who is moderator and arbiter of all.   He receives his authority directly
from Christ without mediation.   He is the prince — *præsul* —
of all the bishops, the heir of the Apostles, of the line of Abel

---

[1] A full translation of the letter is given by Gregorovius in *Lucrez. Borgia*,
p. 7 sq.   [2] Mansi, XXXII. 259 sq. ; Mirbt, p. 169 sq.
[3] Mansi, XXXII. 195-203.   Gieseler quotes at length.   Æneas had written
a letter to the rector of the Univ. of Cologne with the same import, Oct. 13,
1447.

and Melchisedek.   As for the Council of Constance, Pius expressed his regard for its decrees so far as they were approved by his predecessors, but the definitions of general councils, he affirmed, are subject to the sanction of the supreme pontiff, Peter's successor.   With reference to his former utterances at Basel, he expressly revoked anything he had said in conflict with the positions taken in the bull, and ascribed those statements to immaturity of mind, the imprudence of youth and the circumstances of his early training.   *Quis non errat mortalis* — what mortal does not make mistakes, he exclaimed. Reject Æneas and follow Pius — *Æneam rejicite, Pium recipite* — he said.   The first was a Gentile name given by parents at the birth of their son; the second, the name he had adopted on his elevation to the Apostolic see.[1]

It would not be ingenuous to deny to Pius II., in making retractation, the virtue of sincerity.   A strain of deep feeling runs through its long paragraphs which read like the last testament of a man speaking from the heart.   Inspired by the dignity of his office, the pope wanted to be in accord with the long line of his predecessors, some of whom he mentioned by name, from Peter and Clement to the Innocents and Boniface.   In issuing the decree of papal infallibility four centuries later, Pius IX. did not excel his predecessor in the art of composition; but he had this advantage over him that his announcement was stamped with the previous ratification of a general council.   The two documents of the two popes of the name Pius reach the summit of papal assumption and consigned to burial the theories of the final authority of general councils and the infallibility of their decrees.

Scarcely could any two things be thought of more incongruous than Pius II.'s culture and the glorious reception he gave in 1462 to the reputed head of the Apostle Andrew.   This highly prized treasure was brought to Italy by Thomas Palæologus, who, in recognition of his pious benevolence toward the holy see, was given the Golden Rose, a palace in Rome and an annual al-

---

[1] The same time that Pius issued his bull of retractation, Gabriel Biel, called the last of the Schoolmen, issued his tract on *Obedience to the Apostolic see*, taking the same ground that Pius took.

lowance of 6,000 ducats.   The relic was received with ostentatious signs of devotion.   Bessarion and two other members of
the sacred college received it at Narni and conveyed it to Rome.
The pope, accompanied by the remaining cardinals and the Roman clergy, went out to the Ponte Molle to give it welcome.
After falling prostrate before the Apostle's skull, Pius delivered
an appropriate address in which he congratulated the dumb
fragment upon coming safely out of the hands of the Turks to
find at last, as a fugitive, a place beside the remains of its brother
Apostles.   The address being concluded, the procession reformed and, with Pius borne in the Golden Chair, conducted the
skull to its last resting-place.   The streets were decked in holi-
day attire, and no one showed greater zeal in draping his palace
than Rodrigo Borgia.   The skull was deposited in St. Peter's,
after, as Platina says, " the sepulchres of some of the popes and
cardinals, which took up too much room, had been removed."
The ceremonies were closed by Bessarion in an address in which
he expressed the conviction that St. Andrew would join with
the other Apostles as a protector of Rome and in inducing the
princes to combine for the expulsion of the Turks.[1]

In his closing days, Pius II. continued to be occupied with
the crusade.   He had written a memorable letter to Mohammed
II. urging him to follow his mother's religion and turn Christian,
and assuring him that, as Clovis and Charlemagne had been
renowned Christian sovereigns, so he might become Christian
emperor over the Bosphorus, Greece and Western Asia.   No
reply is extant.   In 1458, the year before the Mantuan congress
assembled, the crescent had been planted on the Acropolis of
Athens.   All Southern Greece suffered the indignity and horrors of Turkish oppression.   Servia fell into the hands of the
invaders, 1459, and Bosnia followed, 1462.

Pius' bull of 1463, summoning to a crusade, was put aside
by the princes, but the pontiff, although he was afflicted with
serious bodily infirmities, the stone and the gout, was determined to set an example in the right direction.   Like Moses,
he wanted, at least, to watch from some promontory or ship

---

[1] Pastor, II. 233-236, and Creighton, II. 436-438, give elaborate accounts
of this curious piece of superstition.

the battle against the enemies of the cross.   Financial aid was furnished by the discovery of the alum mines of Tolfa, near Civita Vecchia, in 1462, the revenue from which passed into the papal treasury and was specially devoted by the conclave of 1464 to the crusade.   But it availed little.   Pius proceeded to Ancona on a litter, stopping on the way at Loreto to dedicate a golden cup to the Virgin.   Philip of Burgundy, upon whom he had placed chief reliance, failed to appear.   From Frederick III. nothing was to be expected.   Venice and Hungary alone promised substantial help.   The supreme pontiff lodged on the promontory in the bishop's palace.   But only two vessels lay at anchor in the harbor, ready for the expedition.   To these were added in a few days 14 galleys sent by the doge.   Pius saw them as they appeared in sight.   The display of further heroism was denied him by his death two days later.   A comparison has been drawn by the historian between the pope, with his eye fixed upon the East, and another, a born navigator, who perhaps was even then turning his eyes towards the West, and before many years was to set sail in equally frail vessels to make his momentous discovery.

On his death-bed, Pius had an argument whether extreme unction, which had been administered to him at Basel during an outbreak of the plague, might be administered a second time.   Among his last words, spoken to Cardinal Ammanati, whom he had adopted, were, " pray for me, my son, for I am a sinner.   Bid my brethren continue this holy expedition."   The body was carried to Rome and laid away in St. Peter's.

The disappointment of this restless and remarkable man, in the closing undertaking of his busy career, cannot fail to awaken human sympathy.   Pius, whose aims and methods had been the most practical, was carried away at last by a romantic idea, without having the ability to marshal the forces for its realization.   He misjudged the times.   His purpose was the purpose of a man whose career had taught him never to tolerate the thought of failure.   In forming a general estimate, we cannot withhold the judgment that, if he had made culture and literary effort prominent in the Vatican, his pontificate would have stood out in the history of the papacy

with singular lustre.   It will always seem strange that he did
not surround himself with literati, as did Nicolas V., and that
his interest in the improvement of Rome showed itself only
in a few minor constructions.   His biographer, Campanus, declares that he incurred great odium by his neglect of the Humanists, and Filelfo, his former teacher of Greek, launched
against his memory a biting philippic for this neglect.   The
great literary pope proved to be but a poor patron.[1]   Platina's
praise must not be forgotten, when he says, " The pope's delight, when he had leisure, was in writing and reading, because
he valued books more than precious stones, for in them there
were plenty of gems."   What he delighted in as a pastime himself, he seems not to have been concerned to use his high position to promote in others.   He was satisfied with the diplomatic mission of the papacy and deceived by the *ignis fatuus*
of a crusade to deliver Constantinople.

Platina describes Pius at the opening of his pontificate as
short, gray-haired and wrinkled of face.   He rose at daybreak,
and was temperate at table.   His industry was noteworthy.
His manner made him accessible to all, and he struck the Romans of his age as a man without hypocrisy.   Looked at as a
man of culture, Æneas was grammarian, geographer, historian,
novelist and orator.   Everywhere he was the keen observer of
men and events.   The plan of his cosmography was laid out
on a large scale, but was left unfinished.[2]   His *Commentaries*,
extending from his birth to the time of his death, are a racy
example of autobiographic literature.   His strong hold upon
the ecclesiastics who surrounded him can only be explained
by his unassumed intellectual superiority and a certain moral
ingenuousness.   He is one of the most. interesting figures of
his century.[3]

[1] Creighton, II. 491.   Pastor, II. 28-31, makes a belabored effort to remove in part this stigma, and excuses Pius II. by the lack of funds from
which he suffered and his engrossment in the affairs of the papacy.   Pius
chartered the universities of Nantes, Ingolstadt and Basel.

[2] *Hist. rerum ubique gestarum cum locorum descriptione non finita*, Venice,
1477, in the *Opera*, Basel, 1551, etc.

[3] Voigt and Benrath are severe upon Pius II., and regard the religious attitude of his later years as insincere and the crusade as dictated by a love of

§ 51.   *Paul II.*   1464–1471.

The next occupant of the papal throne possessed none of the intellectual attractiveness of his predecessor, and displayed no interest in promoting the war against the Turks.   He was as difficult to reach as Pius had been accessible, and was slow in attending to official business.   The night he turned into day, holding his audiences after dark, and legates were often obliged to wait far into the night or even as late as three in the morning before getting a hearing.

Pietro Barbo, the son of a sister of Eugenius IV., was born in Venice, 1418.   He was about to set sail for the East on a mercantile project, when the news reached Venice of his uncle's election to the papacy.   Following his elder brother's advice, he gave up the quest of worldly gain and devoted himself to the Church.   Eugenius' favor assured him rapid promotion, and he was successively appointed archdeacon of Bologna, bishop of Cervia, bishop of Vicenza, papal pronotary and cardinal.   On being elected to the papal chair, the Venetian chose the name of Formosus and then Mark, but, at the advice of the conclave, both were given up, as the former seemed to carry with it a reference to the pontiff's fine presence, and the latter was the battle-cry of Venice, and might give political offence. So he took the name, Paul.

Before entering upon the election, the conclave again adopted a pact which required the prosecution of the crusade and the assembling of a general council within three years.   The number of cardinals was not to exceed 24, the age of appointment being not less than 30 years, and the introduction of more than one of the pope's relatives to that body was forbidden.[1]

This solemn agreement, Paul proceeded at once summarily

---

fame.   Gregorovius' characterization is one of the least satisfactory of that impartial historian's pen.   He says, "There was nothing great in him.   Endowed with fascinating gifts, this man of brilliant parts possessed no enthusiasms," etc., VII. 164.   Pastor passes by the failings of Æneas' earlier life with a single sentence, but gives, upon the whole, the most discriminating estimate.   He sees only moral force in his advocacy of the crusade, and pronounces him, with Nicolas V., the most notable of the popes of the 15th century.

[1] The document is given by Raynaldus and Gieseler.

to set aside.   The cardinals were obliged to attach their names
to another document, whose contents the pope kept concealed
by holding his hand over the paper as they wrote.   The vet-
eran Carvajal was the only member of the curia who refused
to sign.   From the standpoint of papal absolutism, Paul was
fully justified.   What right has any conclave to dictate to the
supreme pontiff of Christendom, the successor of St. Peter!
The pact was treason to the high papal theory, and meant nothing less than the substitution of an oligarchy for the papal monarchy.   Paul called no council, not even a congress, to discuss
the crusade against the Turks, and appointed three of his nephews cardinals, Marco Barbo, his brother's son, and Battista Zeno
and Giovanni Michïel, sons of two sisters.[1]   His ordinances for
the city included sumptuary regulations, limiting the prices to
be paid for wearing apparel, banquets and entertainments at
weddings and funerals, and restricting the dowries of daughters to 800 gold florins.

A noteworthy occurrence of Paul's pontificate was the storm
raised in Rome, 1466, by his dismissal of the 70 abbreviators,
the number to which Pius II. had limited the members of that
body.   This was one of those incidents which give variety to
the history of the papal court and help to make it, upon the whole,
the most interesting of all histories.   The scribes of the papal
household were roughly divided into two classes, the secretaries
and the abbreviators.   The business of the former was to take
charge of the papal correspondence of a more private nature,
while the latter prepared briefs of bulls and other more solemn
public documents.[2]   The dismissal of the abbreviators got permanent notoriety by the complaints of one of their number, Platina, and the sufferings he was called upon to endure.   This
invaluable biographer of the popes states that the dispossessed
officials, on the plea that their appointment had been for life,
besieged the Vatican 20 nights before getting a hearing.   Then
Platina, as their spokesman, threatened to appeal to the princes
of Europe to have a general council called and see that justice

[1] Pastor, II. 307, fully justifies Paul for setting aside the pact on the ground
that every pope gets plenary authority directly from God.

[2] Hergenröther : *Kath. Kirchenrecht*, p. 299

was done. The pope's curt answer was that he would rescind or ratify the acts of his predecessors as he pleased.

The unfortunate abbreviator, who was more of a scholar than a politician, was thrown into prison and held there during the four months of Winter without fire and bound in chains. Unhappily for him, he was imprisoned a second time, accused of conspiracy and heretical doctrine. In these charges the Roman Academy was also involved, an institution which cultivated Greek thought and was charged with having engaged in a propaganda of Paganism. There was some ground for the charge, for its leader, Pomponius Læto, who combined the care of his vineyard with ramblings through the old Roman ruins and the perusal of the ancient classics, had deblaterated against the clergy. This antiquary was also thrown into prison. Platina relates how he and a number of others were put to the torture, while Vienesius, his Holiness' vice-chancellor, looked on for several days as the ordeal was proceeding, " sitting like another Minos upon a tapestried seat as if he had been at a wedding, a man in holy orders whom the canons of the Church forbade to put torture upon laymen, lest death should follow, as it sometimes does." On his release he received a promise from Paul of reappointment to office, but waited in vain till the accession of Sixtus IV., who put him in charge of the Vatican library.[1]

Paul pursued an energetic policy against Podiebrad and the Utraquists of Bohemia and, after ordering all the compacts with the king ignored, deposed him and called upon Matthias of Hungary to take his throne. Paul had rejected Podiebrad's offer to dispossess the Turk on condition of being recognized as Byzantine emperor.[2]

In 1468, Frederick III. repeated his visit to Rome, accompanied by 600 knights, but the occasion aroused none of the high expectation of the former visit, when the emperor brought with

[1] Jacob Volaterra in Muratori, new ed., XXIII. 3, p. 98.

[2] Pastor, II. 358 sqq., makes a heroic effort to exempt Paul from the guilt of neglecting the crusade against the Turks. In a letter written by Cardinal Gonzaga, which he prints for the first time (II. 773), the statement is made that Paul was quietly laying aside one-fourth of his income to be used against the Turks. There is no mention of any sum of this kind among the pope's assets.

him the Portuguese infanta.   There was no glittering pageant,
no august papal reception.   On receiving the communion in the
basilica of St. Peter's, he received from the pontiff's hand the
bread, but not the "holy blood," which, as the contemporary relates, Paul reserved to himself as an object-lesson against the
Bohemians, though it was customary on such occasions to give
both the elements.   The successor of Charlemagne and Barbarossa was then given a seat at the pope's side, which was no
higher than the pope's feet.[1]   Patritius, who describes the
scene, remarks that, while the respect paid to the papal dignity
had increased, the imperium of the Roman empire had fallen
into such decadence that nothing remained of it but its name.
Without manifesting any reluctance, the Hapsburg held the
pope's stirrup.

Paul was not without artistic tastes, although he condemned
the study of the classics in the Roman schools,[2] and was pronounced by Platina a great enemy and despiser of learning.
He was an ardent collector of precious stones, coins, vases
and other curios, and took delight in showing his jewels to
Frederick III.   Sixtus IV. is said to have found 54 silver
chests filled with pearls collected by this pontiff, estimated to
be worth 300,000 ducats.   The two tiaras, made at his order,
contained gems said to have been worth a like amount.   At
a later time, Cardinal Barbo found in a secret drawer of one
of Paul's chests sapphires valued at 12,000 ducats.[3]   Platina
was probably repeating only a common rumor, when he reports
that in the daytime Paul slept and at night kept awake, looking over his jewels.

To this diversion the pontiff added sensual pleasures and
public amusements.[4]   He humored the popular taste by restoring heathen elements to the carnival, figures of Bacchus
and the fauns, Diana and her nymphs.   In the long list of the

---

[1] Patritius in Muratori, XXIII. 205–215.

[2] Pastor, II. 347, tries to show that Paul had some mind for humanistic
studies. During his pontificate, 1467, the German printers, Schweinheim and
Pannarts, set up the first printing-presses in Rome, but not under Paul's patronage.   [3] Infessura, p. 167.

[4] A quotation given by Gregorovius, VII. 226, probably exaggerates when
it states he filled his house with concubines — *ex concubina domum replevit.*

gayeties of carnival week are mentioned races for young men, for old men and for Jews, as well as races between horses, donkeys and buffaloes. Paul looked down from St. Mark's and delighted the crowds by furnishing a feast in the square below and throwing down amongst them handfuls of coins. In things of this kind, says Infessura, the pope had his delight.[1] He was elaborate in his vestments and, when he appeared in public, was accustomed to paint his face.

The pope's death was ascribed to his indiscretion in eating two large melons. Asked by a cardinal why, in spite of the honors of the papacy, he was not contented, Paul replied that a little wormwood can pollute a whole hive of honey. The words belong in the same category as the words spoken 300 years before by the English pope, Adrian, when he announced the failure of the highest office in Christendom to satisfy all the ambitions of man.

§ 52. *Sixtus IV.* 1471-1484.

The last three popes of the 15th century, Sixtus IV., Innocent VIII. and Alexander VI., completely subordinated the interests of the papacy to the advancement of their own pleasure and the enrichment and promotion of their kindred.[2] The avenues of the Vatican were filled with upstarts whose only claim to recognition was that they were the children or the nephews of its occupant, the supreme pontiff.

The chief features of the reign of Sixtus IV., a man of great decision and ability, were the insolent rule of his numerous nephews and the wars with the states of Italy in which their intrigues and ambitions involved their uncle. At the time of his election, Francesco Rovere was general of the order of the Franciscans. Born 1414, he had risen from the lowest obscurity, his father being a fisherman near Savona. He took the doctor's degree in theology at Padua, and taught

---

[1] *Et di queste cose lui·si pigliava piacere,* p. 69.

[2] *Den nächst-folgenden Trägern der Tiara schien dieselbe in erster Linie ein Mittel zur Bereicherung und Erhöhung ihrer Familien zu sein. Diesem Zwecke wurde die ganze päpstliche Macht in rücksichtslosester Weise dienstbar gemacht,* Hefele-Knöpfler, *Kirchengesch.*, p. 483.

successively in Bologna, Pavia, Siena, Florence and Perugia. Paul II. appointed him cardinal. In the conclave strong support is said to have come to him through his notorious nephew, Peter Riario, who was active in conducting his canvas and making substantial promises for votes.

The effort to interest the princes in the Turkish crusade was renewed, but soon abandoned. Cardinals were despatched to the various courts of Europe, Bessarion to France, Marco Barbo to Germany, and Borgia to Spain, but only to find these governments preoccupied with other concerns or ill-disposed to the enterprise. In 1472, a papal fleet of 18 galleys actually set sail, with banners blessed by the pope in St. Peter's, and under the command of Cardinal Caraffa. It was met at Rhodes by 30 ships from Naples and 36 from Venice and, after some plundering exploits, returned with 25 Turkish prisoners of war and 12 camels,—trophies enough to arouse the curiosity of the Romans. Moneys realized from some of Paul II.'s gems had been employed to meet the expenditure.

Sixtus' relatives became the leading figures in Rome, and in wealth and pomp they soon rivalled or eclipsed the old Roman families and the older members of the sacred college. Sixtus was blessed or burdened with 16 nephews and grandnephews. All that was in his power to do, he did, to give them a good time and to establish them in affluence and honor all their days. The Sienese had their day under Pius II., and now it was the turn of the Ligurians. The pontiff's two brothers and three, if not four, sisters, as well as all their progeny, had to be taken care of. The excuse made for Calixtus III. cannot be made for this indulgent uncle, that he was approaching his dotage. Sixtus was only 56 when he reached the tiara. And desperate is the suggestion that the unfitness or unwillingness of the Roman nobility to give the pope proper support made it necessary for him to raise up another and a complacent aristocracy.[1]

Sixtus deemed no less than five of his nephews and a grandnephew deserving of the red hat, and sooner or later eight

[1] Hergenröther-Kirsch, II. 979. These most reputable Catholic historians intimate rather than emphasize this consideration.

of them were introduced into the college of cardinals. Two
nephews in succession were appointed prefects of Rome. The
nephews who achieved the rank of cardinals were Pietro Riario
at 25, and Julian della Rovere at 28, in 1471, both Franciscan
monks; Jerome Basso and Christopher Rovere, in 1477; Dominico Rovere, Christopher's brother, in 1478; and the pope's
grandnephew, Raphael Sansoni, at the age of 17, in 1477. The
two nephews made prefects of Rome were Julian's brother
Lionardo, who died in 1475, and his brother Giovanni, d. 1501.
Lionardo was married by his uncle to the illegitimate daughter
of Ferrante, king of Naples.[1]

Upon Peter Riario and Julian Rovere he heaped benefice
after benefice. Julian, a man of rare ability, afterwards made
pope under the name of Julius II., was appointed archbishop of
Avignon and then of Bologna, bishop of Lausanne, Constance,
Viviers, Ostia and Velletri, and placed at the head of several
abbeys. Riario, who, according to popular hearsay, was the
pope's own child, was bishop of Spoleto, Seville and Valencia,
Patriarch of Constantinople, and recipient of other rich places,
until his income amounted to 60,000 florins or about 2,500,000
francs. He went about with a retinue of 100 horsemen. His
expenditures were lavish and his estate royal. His mistresses,
whom he did not attempt to conceal, were dressed in elegant
fabrics, and one of them wore slippers embroidered with pearls.
Dominico received one after the other the bishoprics of Corneto, Tarentaise, Geneva and Turin.

The visit of Leonora, the daughter of Ferrante, in Rome in
1473, while on her way to Ferrara to meet her husband, Hercules of Este, was perhaps the most splendid occasion the city
had witnessed since the first visit of Frederick III. It furnished Riario an opportunity for the display of a magnificent
hospitality. On Whitsunday, the Neapolitan princess was conducted by two cardinals to St. Peter's, where she heard mass
said by the pope and then at high-noon witnessed the miracle

---

[1] A useful genealogical tree of the Rovere is given by Creighton, III. 100.
Pastor takes no pains to hide his righteous indignation at Sixtus' exhaustive
provision for his relatives, — *seine zahlreiche und unwürdige Verwandten*, as
he calls them.

play of Susanna and the Elders, acted by Florentine players. The next evening she sat down to a banquet which lasted 3 hours and combined all the skill which decorators and cooks could apply. The soft divans and costly curtainings, the silk costumes of the servants and the rich courses are described in detail by contemporary writers. In anticipation of modern electrical fans, 3 bellows were used to cool and freshen the atmosphere. In such things, remarks Infessura, the treasures of the Church were squandered.[1]

In 1474, on the death of Peter Riario, a victim of his excesses and aged only 28,[2] his brother Jerome, a layman, came into supreme favor. Sixtus was ready to put all the possessions of the papal see at his disposal and, on his account, he became involved in feuds with Florence and Venice. He purchased for this favorite Imola, at a cost of 40,000 ducats, and married him to the illegitimate daughter of the duke of Milan, Catherine Sforza. The purchase of Imola was resented by Florence, but Sixtus did not hesitate to further antagonize the republic and the Medici. The Medici had established a branch banking-house in Rome and become the papal bankers. Sixtus chose to affront the family by patronizing the Pazzi, a rival banking-firm. At the death of Philip de' Medici, archbishop of Pisa, in 1474, Salviati was appointed his successor against the protest of the Medici. Finally, Julian de' Medici was denied the cardinalship. These events marked the stages in the progress of the rupture between the papacy and Florence. Lorenzo, called the Magnificent, and his brother Julian represented the family which the fiscal talents of Cosmo de' Medici had founded. In his readiness to support the ambitions of his nephew, Jerome Riario, the pope seemed willing to go to any length of violence. A conspiracy was directed against Lorenzo's life, in

[1] *Diario*, p. 77. At the chief banquet, the menu comprised wild boars roasted whole, bucks, goats, hares, pheasants, fish, peacocks with their feathers, storks, cranes, and countless fruits and sweetmeats. An artificial mountain of sugar was brought into the dining-chamber, from which a man stepped forth with gestures of surprise at finding himself amid such gorgeous surroundings.

[2] Sixtus reared to him a splendid monument in the Church of the Apostles. Peter and his brother Jerome are represented as kneeling and praying to the Madonna. See Pastor, II. 294 sq.

which Jerome was the chief actor, — one of the most cold-
blooded conspiracies of history.   The pope was conversant
with the plot and talked it over with its chief agent, Montesecco and, though he may not have consented to murder, which
Jerome and the Pazzi had included in their plan, he fully approved of the plot to seize Lorenzo's person and overthrow
the republic.[1]

The terrible tragedy was enacted in the cathedral of Florence.
When Montesecco, a captain of the papal mercenaries, hired to
carry out the plot, shrank from committing sacrilege by shedding blood in the church of God, its execution was intrusted to
two priests, Antonio Maffei da Volterra and Stefano of Bagno-
rea, the former a papal secretary.   While the host was being
elevated, Julian de' Medici, who was inside the choir, was struck
with one dagger after another and fell dead.   Lorenzo barely
escaped.   As he was entering the sanctuary, he was struck by
Maffei and slightly wounded, and made a shield of his arm by
winding his mantle around it, and escaped with friends to the
sacristy, which was barred against the assassins.   The bloody
deed took place April 26, 1478.

The city proved true to the family which had shed so much
lustre upon it, and quick revenge was taken upon the agents of
the conspiracy.   Archbishop Salviati, his brother, Francesco de'
Pazzi and others were hung from the signoria windows.[2]   The
two priests were executed after having their ears and noses cut
off.   Montesecco was beheaded.   Among those who witnessed
the scene in the cathedral was the young cardinal, Raphael, the
pope's grandnephew, and without having any previous knowledge of the plot.   His face, it was said, turned to an ashen
pallor, which in after years he never completely threw off.

With intrepid resolution, Sixtus resented the death of his
archbishop and the indignity done a cardinal in the imprison-

[1] So Pastor, II. 535, Gregorovius, VII. 239, Karl Müller, II. 130 and Creighton, III. 75.   They all agree that Sixtus knew the details of the plot, and approved them, except in the matter of the murder, which, however, he did not
peremptorily forbid.

[2] See the account of the legate of Milan, publ. by Pastor, II. 785 sq.   Of Sixtus'
connivance at the plot against the Medici, Pastor, II. 541, says, "It calls for
deep lament that a pope should play a part in the history of this conspiracy."

ment of Raphael as an accomplice.   He hurled the interdict at
the city, branding Lorenzo as the son of iniquity and the ward
of perdition, — *iniquitatis filius et perditionis alumnus*, — and
entered into an alliance with Naples against it.   Louis XI. of
France and Venice and other Italian states espoused the cause
of Florence.   Pushed to desperation, Lorenzo went to Naples
and made such an impression on Ferrante that he changed his
attitude and joined an alliance with Florence.   The pope was
checkmated.   The seizure of Otranto on Italian soil by the Turks,
in 1480, called attention away from the feud to the imminent
danger threatening all Italy.   In December of that year, Sixtus
absolved Florence, and the legates of the city were received in
front of St. Peter's and touched with the rod in token of forgiveness.   Six months later, May 26, 1481, Rome received the news
of the death of Mohammed II., which Sixtus celebrated by special services in the church, Maria del Popolo,[1] and the Turks
abandoned the Italian coast.

Again, in the interest of his nephew, Jerome, Sixtus took
Forli, thereby giving offence to Ferrara.   He joined Venice in a
war against that city, and all Italy became involved.   Later, the
warlike pontiff again saw his league broken up and Venice and
Ferrara making peace, irrespective of his counsels.   He vented
his mortification by putting the queen of the Adriatic under the
interdict.

In Rome, the bloody pope fanned the feud between the
Colonna and the Orsini, and almost succeeded in blotting out the
name of the Colonna by assassination and judicial murder.

Sixtus has the distinction of having extended the efficacy of
indulgences to souls in purgatory.   He was most zealous in distributing briefs of indulgence.[2]   The Spanish Inquisition received his solemn sanction in 1478.   Himself a Franciscan, he
augmented the privileges of the Franciscan order in a bull which
that order calls its great ocean — *mare magnum*.   He canonized
the official biographer of Francis d'Assisi, Bonaventura.

He issued two bulls with reference to the worship of Mary and

---

[1] Infessura, p. 86.

[2] Pastor, II. 610 sqq., is very cautious in his remarks on the subject of Sixtus' indulgences, almost to reticence.

the doctrine of the immaculate conception, but he declared her sinlessness from the instant of conception a matter undecided by the Roman Church and the Apostolic see — *nondum ab ecclesia romana et apostolica sede decisum.*[1]   In all matters of ritual and outward religion, he was of all men most punctilious.   The chronicler, Volterra, abounds in notices of his acts of devotion.   As a patron of art, his name has a high place.   He supported Platina with four assistants in cataloguing the archives of the Vatican in three volumes.

Such was Sixtus IV., the unblushing promoter of the interests of his relatives, many of them as worthless as they were insolent, the disturber of the peace of Italy, revengeful, and yet the liberal patron of the arts.   The enlightened diarist of Rome, Infessura,[2] calls the day of the pontiff's decease that most happy day, the day on which God liberated Christendom from the hand of an impious and iniquitous ruler, who had before him no fear of God nor love of the Christian world nor any charity whatsoever, but was actuated by avarice, the love of vain show and pomp, most cruel and given to sodomy.[3]

During his reign, were born in obscure places in Saxony and Switzerland two men who were to strike a mighty blow at the papal rule, themselves also of peasant lineage and the coming leaders of the new spiritual movement.

§ 53.   *Innocent VIII.*   1484–1492.

Under Innocent VIII. matters in Rome were, if anything, worse than under his predecessor, Sixtus IV.   Innocent was an easy-going man without ideals, incapable of conceiving or

[1] Mansi, XXXII. 374 sqq., gives the bull on the immaculate conception dated Sept. 5, 1483 ; also Mirbt, p. 170.

[2] *In quo felicissimo die*, etc., pp. 155–158.

[3] This charge, which Infessura elaborates, Creighton, III. 115, 285, dismisses as unproved ; Pastor, II. 640, also, but less confidently.   Infessura was a friend of the Colonna, to whom Sixtus was bitterly hostile.   Burchard, I. 10 sqq., gives a very detailed account of Sixtus' obsequies.   He spoke from observation as one of the masters of ceremonies.   Pastor makes a bold effort to rescue Sixtus from most of the charges made against his character by Infessura.

carrying out high plans. He was chiefly notable for his open avowal of an illegitimate family and his bull against witchcraft.

At Sixtus' death, wild confusion reigned in Rome. Nobles and cardinals barricaded their residences. Houses were pillaged. The mob held carnival on the streets. The palace of Jerome Riario was sacked. Relief was had by an agreement between the rival families of the Orsini and Colonna to withdraw from the city for a month and Jerome's renunciation of the castle of S. Angelo, which his wife had defended, for 4,000 ducats. Not till then did the cardinals feel themselves justified in meeting for the election of a new pontiff.

The conclaves of 1484 and 1492 have been pronounced by high catholic authority among the " saddest in the history of the papacy." [1] Into the conclave of 1484, 25 cardinals entered, 21 of them Italians. Our chief account is from the hand of the diarist, Burchard, who was present as one of the officials. His description goes into the smallest details. A protocol was again adopted, which every cardinal promised in a solemn formula to observe, if elected pope. Its first stipulation was that 100 ducats should be paid monthly to members of the sacred college, whose yearly income from benefices might not reach the sum of 4,000 ducats (about 200,000 francs in our present money). Then followed provisions for the continuance of the crusade against the Turks, the reform of the Roman curia in head and members, the appointment of no cardinal under 30 for any cause whatever, the advancement of not more than a single relative of the reigning pontiff to the sacred college and the restriction of its membership to 24.[2]

Rodrigo Borgia fully counted upon being elected and, in expectation of that event, had barricaded his palace against being looted. Large bribes, even to the gift of his palace, were offered by him for the coveted prize of the papacy. Cardinal Barbo had 10 votes and, when it seemed likely that he would be the successful candidate, Julian Rovere and Borgia, renouncing their aspirations, combined their forces, and, during the night, went from cell to cell, securing by promises of benefices and money the votes of all but six of

<hr>

[1] Pastor, III. 178. [2] Burchard, I. 33-55

the cardinals.   According to Burchard, the pope about to be elected sat up all night signing promises.   The next morning the two cardinals aroused the six whom they had not disturbed, exclaiming, " Come, let us make a pope."   " Who ? " they said.   " Cardinal Cibo."   " How is that ? " they asked.   " While you were drowsy with sleep, we gathered all the votes except yours," was the reply.

The new pope, Lorenzo Cibo, born in Genoa, 1432, had been made cardinal by Sixtus IV., 1473.   During his rule, peace was maintained with the courts of Italy, but in Rome clerical dissipation, curial venality and general lawlessness were rampant. " In darkness Innocent was elected, in darkness he lives, and in darkness he will die," said the general of the Augustinians.[1] Women were carried off in the night.   The murdered were found in the streets in the morning.   Crimes, before their commission, were compounded for money.   Even the churches were pilfered.   A piece of the true cross was stolen from S. Maria in Trastavere.   The wood was reported found in a vineyard, but without its silver frame.   When the vice-chancellor, Borgia, was asked why the laws were not enforced, he replied, " God desires not the death of a sinner, but rather that he should pay and live."[2]   The favorite of Sixtus IV., Jerome Riario, was murdered in 1488.   His widow, the brave and masculine Catherine Sforza, who was pregnant at the time, defended his castle at Forli and defied the papal forces besieging it, declaring that, if they put her children to death who were with her, she yet had one left at Imola and the unborn child in her womb.   The duke of Milan, her relative, rescued her and put the besiegers to flight.

All ecclesiastical offices were set for sale.   How could it be

---

[1] Infessura, p. 177. The Augustinian was thrown into prison for making the remark. Infessura returns again and again, pp. 237 sq., 243, 256 sq., to the reign of crime going on in the city.

[2] Infessura gives the case of a father who, after committing incest with his two daughters, murdered them and was set free upon the payment of 800 ducats. Gregorovius, VII. 297, says of the Italian character of the last 30 years of the 15th century that " it displays a trait of diabolical passion. Tyrannicide, conspiracies and deeds of treachery are universal, and criminal selfishness reigns supreme."

otherwise, when the papal tiara itself was within the reach of the highest bidder?[1]   The appointment of 18 new papal secretaries brought 62,400 ducats into the papal treasury.   The bulls creating the offices expressly declared the aim to be to secure funds.   52 persons were appointed to seal the papal bulls, called *plumbatores*, from the leaden ball or seal they used, and the price of the position was fixed at 2,500 ducats.   Even the office of librarian in the Vatican was sold, and the papal tiara was put in pawn.   In a time of universal traffic in ecclesiastical offices, it is not surprising that the fabrication of papal documents was turned into a business.   Two papal notaries confessed to having issued 50 such documents in two years, and in spite of the pleas of their friends were hung and burnt, 1489.[2]

Innocent's children were not persons of marked traits, or given to ambitious intrigues.   Common rumor gave their number as 16, all of them children by married women.[3]   Franceschetto and Theorina seem to have been born before the father entered the priesthood.   Franceschetto's marriage to Maddalena, a daughter of Lorenzo the Magnificent, was celebrated in the Vatican, Jan. 20, 1488.   Ten months later, the pope's granddaughter, Peretta, child of Theorina, was also married in the Vatican to the marquis of Finale.   The pontiff sat with the ladies at the table, a thing contrary to all the accepted proprieties.   In 1492, another grandchild, also a daughter of Theorina, Battistana, was married to duke Louis of Aragon.[4]

The statement of Infessura is difficult to believe, although it is made at length, that Innocent issued a decree permitting

---

[1] Funk, *Kirchengesch.*, 373, says, *In Rom. schien alles käuflich zu sein.*

[2] For the details, see Burchard, I. 365–368.

[3] So Marullus in his epigram —

> *Octo nocens pueros genuit totidemque puellas,*
> *Hunc merito poterit dicere Roma patrem.*

> Illegitimately he begat 8 boys and girls as many.
> Hence Rome deservedly may call him father.

Burchard, I. 321, calls Franceschetto *bastardus.*

[4] Burchard, I. 323, 488.   In 1883, the Berlin Museum came into possession of a bust of Theorina bearing the inscription, " *Teorina Cibo Inn. VIII. P. M. f. singuli exempli matrona formæque dignitate conjuaria.*"

concubinage in Rome both to clergy and laity.   The prohibition of concubinage was declared prejudicial to the divine law and the honor of the clergy, as almost all the clergy, from the highest to the lowest, had concubines, or mistresses.   According to the Roman diarist, there were 6,800 listed public courtezans in Rome besides those whose names were not recorded.[1]   To say the least, the statement points to the low condition of clerical morals in the holy city and the slight regard paid to the legislation of Gregory VII.   Infessura was in position to know what was transpiring in Rome.

What could be expected where the morals of the supreme pontiff and the sacred senate were so loose?   The lives of many of the cardinals were notoriously scandalous.   Their palaces were furnished with princely splendor and filled with scores of servants.   Their example led the fashions in extravagance in dress and sumptuous banquetings.   They had their stables, kennels and falcons.   Cardinal Sforza, whose yearly income is reported to have been 30,000 ducats, or 1,500,000 francs, present money, excelled in the chase.   Cardinal Julian made sport of celibacy, and had three daughters.   Cardinal Borgia, the acknowledged leader in all gayeties, was known far and wide by his children, who were prominent on every occasion of display and conviviality.   The passion for gaming ran high in the princely establishments.   Cardinal Raphael won 8,000 ducats at play from Cardinal Balue who, however, in spite of such losses, left a fortune of 100,000 ducats.   This grandnephew of Sixtus IV. was a famous player, and in a single night won from Innocent's son, Franceschetto, 14,000 ducats.   The son complained to his father, who ordered the fortunate winner to restore the night's gains.   But the gay prince of the church excused himself by stating that the money had already been paid out upon the new palace he was engaged in erecting.

The only relative whom Innocent promoted to the sacred college was his illegitimate brother's son, Lorenzo Cibo.   The

[1] Infessura, p. 259 sq.   Pastor, III. 269, pronounces Infessura's statement altogether incredible, — *gänzlich unglaubwürdig*, — and blames Infessura's editor, Tommasini, for allowing the statement to pass in his edition without note or comment.   Pastor, in his 1st ed., III. 252, had pronounced the statement of the Roman diarist *eine ungeheuerliche Behauptung*.

appointment best known to posterity was that of Giovanni de' Medici, son of Lorenzo the Magnificent, afterwards Leo X.

Another appointment, that of D'Aubusson, was associated with the case of the Mohammedan prince, Djem. This incident in the annals of the papacy would seem incredible, if it were not true. A writer of romance could hardly have invented an episode more grotesque. At the death of Mohammed II., his son, Djem, was defeated in his struggle for the succession by his brother Bajazet, and fled to Rhodes for protection. The Knights of St. John were willing to hold the distinguished fugitive as prisoner, upon the promise of 45,000 ducats a year from the sultan. For safety's sake, Djem was removed to one of the Hospitaller houses in France. Hungary, Naples, Venice, France and the pope, — all put in a claim for him. Such competition to pay honor to an infidel prince had never before been heard of in Christendom. The pope won by making valuable ecclesiastical concessions to the French king, among them the bestowal of the red hat on D'Aubusson.

The matter being thus amicably adjusted, Djem was conducted to Rome, where he was received with impressive ceremonies by the cardinals and city officials. His person was regarded as of more value than the knowledge of the East brought by Marco Polo had been in its day, and the reception of the Mohammedan prince created more interest than the return of Columbus from his first journey to the West. Djem was escorted through the streets by the pope's son, and rode a white horse sent him by the pope. The ambassador of the sultan of Egypt, then in Rome, had gone out to meet him, and shed tears as he kissed his feet and the feet of his horse. The popes had not shrunk from entering into alliances with Oriental powers to secure the overthrow of Mohammed II. and his dynasty. Djem, or the Grand Turk, as he was called, was welcomed by the pope surrounded by his cardinals. The proud descendant of Eastern monarchs, however, refused to kiss the supreme pontiff's foot, but made some concession by kissing his shoulder. He was represented as short and stout, with an aquiline nose, and a single good eye, given at times inordinately to drink, though a man of some intellectual culture. He was reported

to have put four men to death with his own hand.   But Djem
was a dignitary who signified too much to be cast aside for such
offences.   Innocent assigned him to elegantly furnished apartments in the Vatican, and thus the strange spectacle was afforded of the earthly head of Christendom acting as the host of
one of the chief living representatives of the faith of Islam,
which had almost crushed out the Christian churches of the East
and usurped the throne on the Bosphorus.

Bajazet was willing to pay the pope 40,000 ducats for the
hospitality extended to his rival brother, and delegations came
from him to Rome to arrange the details of the bargain.   The
report ran that attempts were made by the sultan to poison
both his brother and the pope by contaminating the wells of
the Vatican.   When the ambassador brought from Constantinople the delayed payment of three years, 120,000 ducats,
Djem insisted that the Turk's clothes should be removed and
his skin be rubbed down with a towel, and that he should lick
the letter " on every side," as proof that he did not also carry
poison.[1]   Djem survived his first papal entertainer, Innocent
VIII., three years, and figured prominently in public functions
in the reign of Alexander VI.   He died 1495, still a captive.

Another curious instance was given in Innocent's reign of
the hold open-mouthed superstition had in the reception given
to the holy lance.   This pretended instrument, with which
Longinus pierced the Saviour's side and which was found during
the Crusades by the monk Barthélemy at Antioch, was already
claimed by two cities, Nürnberg and Paris.   The relic made
a greater draft upon the credulity of the age than St. Andrew's
head.   The latter was the gift of a Christian prince, howbeit
an adherent of the schismatic Greek Church; the lance came
from a Turk, Sultan Bajazet.

Some question arose among the cardinals whether it would
not be judicious to stay the acceptance of the gift till the

---

[1] *Totam ab omnibus ejus lateribus lingua sua lambivit.*   Infessura, p. 263.
For the letter of the painter Mantegna to the duke of Mantua and its curious
details, June 15, 1489, see Pastor, 1st ed., III. 218.   The picture of the
Disputation of St. Catherine in the *sala dei santi* in the Vatican contains a
picture of Djem riding a white palfrey.   Infessura and Burchard enter with
journalistic relish into the details of Djem's appearance and treatment in Rome.

claims of the lance in Nürnberg had been investigated.   But
the pope's piety, such as it was, would not allow a question of
that sort to interfere.   An archbishop and a bishop were despatched to Ancona to receive the iron fragment, for only the
head of the lance was extant.   It was conducted from the city
gates by the cardinals to St. Peter's, and after mass the pope
gave his blessing.   The day of the reception happened to be
a fast, but, at the suggestion of one of the cardinals, some of
the fountains along the streets, where the procession was appointed to go, were made to throw out wine to slake the thirst
of the populace.   After a solemn service in S. Maria del Popolo, on Ascension Day, 1492, the Turkish present, encased
in a receptacle of crystal and gold, was placed near the handkerchief of St. Veronica in St. Peter's.[1]

The two great stains upon the pontificate of Innocent VIII.,
the crusade he called to exterminate the Waldenses, 1487, and
his bull directed against the witches of Germany, 1484, which
inaugurated two horrible dramas of cruelty, have treatment in
another place.

Innocent was happy in being permitted to join with Europe in
rejoicings over the expulsion of the last of the Moors from Granada, 1492.   Masses were said in Rome, and a sermon preached
in the pontiff's presence in celebration of the memorable event.[2]
With characteristic national gallantry, Cardinal Borgia showed
his appreciation by instituting a bull-fight in which five bulls
were killed, the first but not the last spectacle of the kind seen
in the papal city.   In his last sickness, Innocent was fed by a
woman's milk.[3]   Several years before, when he was thought to

---

[1] Infessura, p. 224, and especially Burchard, I. 482–486, and Sigismondo, II.
25–29, 69, give extended accounts of the honors paid to the piece of iron, the
sacratissimum ferreum lanceæ.   The sultan's representative, Chamisbuerch,
who was also present, was reported to have handed the pope a package containing 40,000 ducats.   Sigismondo uses the word *spicula*, little point, for the lance.

[2] Burchard, I. 444 sqq.

[3] The harrowing story was told that, at the suggestion of a Jewish physician,
the blood of three boys was infused into the dying pontiff's veins.   They were
ten years old, and had been promised a ducat each.   All three died.   The Jewish physician fled.   The story is told by Infessura and repeated by Raynaldus.
It is pleasant to have Gregorovius, VII. 338, as well as Pastor, III. 275 sq.,
give it no credence.

be dying, the cardinals found 1,200,000 ducats in his drawers and chests.   They now granted his request that 48,000 ducats should be taken from his fortune and distributed among his relatives.

§ 54.   *Pope Alexander VI — Borgia.*   1492-1503.

The pontificate of Alexander VI., which coincides with the closing years of the 15th century and the opening of the 16th, may be compared with the pontificate of Boniface VIII., which witnessed the passage from the 13th to the 14th centuries.   Boniface marked the opening act in the decline of the papal power introduced by the king of France.   Under Alexander, when the French again entered actively into the affairs of Italy, even to seizing Rome, the papacy passed into its deepest moral humiliation since the days of the pornocracy in the 10th century.

Alexander VI., whom we have before known as Cardinal Rodrigo Borgia, has the notorious distinction of being the most corrupt of the popes of the Renaissance period.   Even in the judgment of Catholic historians, his dissoluteness knew no restraint and his readiness to abase the papacy for his own personal ends, no bounds.[1]   His intellectual force, if used aright, might have made his pontificate one of the most brilliant in the annals of the Apostolic see.   The time was ripe.   The conditions offered the opportunity if ever period did.   But moral principle was wanting.   Had Dante lived again, he would have written that Alexander VI. made a greater refusal than the hermit pope, Cœlestine V., and deserved a darker doom than the simoniac pope, Boniface VIII.

At Innocent VIII.'s death, 23 cardinals entered into the conclave which met in the Sistine chapel.   Borgia and Julian Rovere were the leading candidates.   They were rivals, and had

---

[1] Pastor, III. 278, says that, " from the moment he received priestly consecration to the end of his life, he was a slave to the demon of sensuality." Hefele-Knöpfler, *Kirchengesch.*, p. 485, speaks of his career before he reached the papal office as having been " very dissolute " — *sehr dissolut.*   Prof. Villari, *Machiavelli*, I. 279, calls Alexander the worst of the popes, whose "crimes were sufficient to upset any human society."   Gregorovius and Pastor have carried on the most notable researches in this period, and rivalled one another in the brilliant description of Alexander's reign and domestic relations.

been candidates for the papal chair before.   Everything was
to be staked on success in the pending election.   Openly and
without a blush, ecclesiastical offices and money were offered
as the price of the spiritual crown of Christendom.   Julian was
supported by the king of France, who deposited 200,000 ducats
in a Roman bank and 100,000 more in Genoa to secure his election.   If Borgia could not outbid him he was, at least, the more
shrewd in his manipulations.   There were only five cardinals,
including Julian, who took nothing.   The other members of
the sacred college had their price.   Monticelli and Soriano were
given to Cardinal Orsini and also the see of Cartagena, and the
legation to the March; the abbey of Subiaco and its fortresses
to Colonna; Civita Castellana and the see of Majorca to Savelli; Nepi to Sclafetanus; the see of Porto to Michïel; and
rich benefices to other cardinals.   Four mules laden with gold
were conducted to the palace of Ascanio Sforza, who also received Rodrigo's splendid palace and the vice-chancellorship.
Even the patriarch of Venice, whose high age — for he had
reached 95 — might have been expected to lift him above the
seduction of filthy lucre, accepted 5,000 ducats.   Infessura caus-
tically remarks that Borgia distributed all his goods among the
poor.[1]

The ceremonies of coronation were on a scale which appeared
to the contemporaries unparalleled in the history of such occasions.   A figure of a bull, the emblem of the Borgias, was
erected near the Palazzo di S. Marco on the line of the procession, from whose eyes, nostrils and mouth poured forth water,
and from the forehead wine.   Rodrigo was 61 years of age,
had been cardinal for 37 years, having received that dignity
when he was 25.   His fond uncle, Calixtus III., had made him
archbishop of Valencia, heaped upon him ecclesiastical offices,
including the vice-chancellorship, and made him the heir of his

[1] P. 281. In his despatch to the duchess of Este, published by Pastor, 1st ed.,
III. 879, Giovanni Boccaccio, bishop of Modena, gives an estimate of Borgia's
ability to pay for the tiara, the vice-chancellorship worth 8,000 ducats, the cities
of Nepi and Civita Castellana, abbeys in Aquila and Albano, each worth 1,000
ducats a year, two large abbeys in the kingdom of Naples, the abbey of Subiaco,
worth 2,000 a year, abbeys in Spain, 16 bishoprics in Spain, the see of Porto,
worth 1,200 ducats, and numerous other ecclesiastical places.

personal possessions. His palace was noted for the splendor
of its tapestries and carpets and its vessels of gold and silver.[1]
The new pope possessed conspicuous personal attractions. He
was tall and well-formed, and his manners so taking that a contemporary, Gasparino of Verona, speaks of his drawing women
to himself more potently than the magnet attracts iron.[2] The
reproof which his gallantries of other days called forth from
Pius II. at Siena has already been referred to.

The pre-eminent features of Alexander's career, as the supreme pontiff of Christendom, were his dissolute habits and his
extravagant passion to exalt the worldly fortunes of his children. In these two respects he seemed to be destitute at once
of all regard for the solemnity of his office and of common conscience. A third feature was the entry of Charles VIII. and the
French into Italy and Rome. During his pontificate two events
occurred whose world-wide significance was independent of the
occupant of the papal throne, — the one geographical, the other
religious, — the discovery of America and the execution of the
Florentine preacher, Savonarola. As in the reign of Calixtus
III., so now Spaniards flocked to Rome, and the Milanese ambassador wrote that ten papacies would not have been able to satisfy their greed for official recognition. In spite of a protocol
adopted in the conclave, a month did not pass before Alexander
appointed his nephew, Juan of Borgia, cardinal, and in the next
years he admitted four more members of the Borgia family to
the sacred college, including his infamous son, Cæsar Borgia, at
the age of 18.[3]

Alexander's household and progeny call for treatment first.
It soon became evident that the supreme passion of his pontificate was to advance the fortunes of his children.[4] His parental relations were not merely the subject of rumor; they are
vouched for by irresistible documentary proof.

Alexander was the acknowledged father of five children by

[1] The letter of Cardinal Sforza to his brother, dated 1484, and publ. by Pastor, III. 876, gives a description of his associate's palace.

[2] Sigismondo, II. 53, ascribes to Alexander *majestas formæ*.

[3] Burchard, I. 577.

[4] *Seine Kinder zu erhöhen war sein vorzüglichstes Ziel* is the statement of
the calm Catholic historian, Funk, p. 373.

Vanozza de Cataneis: Pedro Luis, Juan, Cæsar, Lucretia, Joffré
and, perhaps, Pedro Ludovico. The briefs issued by Sixtus
IV. legitimating Cæsar and Ludovico are still extant.[1] Two
bulls were issued by Alexander himself in 1493, bearing on
Cæsar's parentage. The first, declaring him to be the son of
Vanozza by a former husband, was intended to remove the
objections the sacred college naturally felt in admitting to its
number one of uncertain birth. In the second, Alexander announced him to be his own son.[2] Tiring of Vanozza, who was
11 years his junior, Alexander put her aside and saw that she
was married successively to three husbands, himself arranging
for the first relationship and making provision for the second
and the third.[3] In her later correspondence with Lucretia she
signed herself, thy happy and unhappy mother — *la felice ed
infelice matre.*

These were not the only children Alexander acknowledged.
His daughters Girolama and Isabella were married 1482 and
1483.[4] Another daughter, Laura, by Julia Farnese, born in
1492, he acknowledged as his own child, and in 1501 the pope
formally legitimated, as his own son, Juan, by a Roman woman.
In a first bull he called the boy Cæsar's, but in a second he
recognized him as his own offspring.[5]

[1] They are given in Burchard, Supplement to vol. III, and dated Oct. 1, 1480,
and Nov. 4, 1481.

[2] See W. H. Woodward, *Two Bulls of Alex. VI.*, Sept., 1493, in *Engl. Hist.
Rev.*, 1908, pp. 730-734.

[3] Vanozza outlived Alexander 15 years, dying 1518. Her epitaph formerly
in S. Maria del Popolo reads, *Vanotiæ Cathanæ, Cæsare Valentiæ, Joane
Candiæ, Jufredo Scylatii et Lucretiæ Ferrariæ, ducibus filiis*, etc. See
Creighton, III. 163, Pastor, III. 279. Pastor says that to deny the authenticity
of this inscription as Ollivier does is nothing less than ridiculous — *geradezu
lächerlich.* On Ollivier's attempt to rehabilitate Alexander, see Pastor's caustic
words in 1st ed., I. 589. Burchard constantly calls Lucretia *papæ filia*, II. 278,
386, 493, etc., and Joffré and the other boys his sons. So also Sigismondo II.
249, 270, etc. The nativity of Pedro Ludovico is not absolutely certain, but it
is highly probable that Vanozza was his mother.

[4] Gregorovius, *Lucrezia Borgia*, p. 19, and Appendix, Germ. ed., where the
marriage contract of Girolama is given.

[5] These two bulls, extant at Mantua and first published by Gregorovius,
Lucr. Borgia, Appendix, 76-85, were issued the same day. Burchard, III.
170, calls the child's mother *quædam Romana.* Following Burchard, Grego-

Among Alexander's mistresses, after he became pope, the most famous was cardinal Farnese's sister, Julia Farnese, called for her beauty, La Bella. Infessura repeatedly refers to her as Alexander's concubine. Her legal husband was appeased by the gift of castles.

The gayeties, escapades, marriages, worldly distinctions and crimes of these children would have furnished daily material for paragraphs of a nature to satisfy the most sensational modern taste. Don Pedro Luis, Alexander's eldest son, and his three older brothers began their public careers in the service of the Spanish king, Ferdinand, who admitted them to the ranks of the higher nobility and sold Gandia, with the title of duke, to Don Pedro. This gallant young Borgia died in 1491 at the age of 30, on the eve of his journey from Rome to Spain to marry Ferdinand's cousin. His brother, Don Juan, fell heir to the estate and title of Gandia and was married with princely splendor in Barcelona to the princess to whom Don Pedro had been betrothed.

Alexander's son, Cæsar Borgia, was as bad as his ambition was insolent. The annals of Rome and of the Vatican for more than a decade are filled with his impiety, his intrigues and his crimes. At the age of six, he was declared eligible for ordination. He was made protonotary and bishop of Pampeluna by Innocent VIII. At his father's election he hurried from Pisa, where he was studying, and on the day of his father's coronation was appointed archbishop of Valencia. He was then sixteen.

Don Joffré was married, at 13, to a daughter of Alfonso of Naples and was made prince of Squillace.

The personal fortunes of Alexander's daughter, Lucretia, constitute one of the notorious and tragic episodes of the 15th century.

The most serious foreign issue in Alexander's reign was the in-

rovius and Pastor have no doubt that it was Alexander's own child. Pastor, III. 475, says that the bull is unquestionably genuine. A satire of the year 1500 ascribes to Alexander 3 or 4 children by Julia Farnese. According to Villari, *Life of Savonarola*, p. 376, note, the *Civilta cattolica*, the papal organ at Rome, March 15, 1873, acknowledged the existence of Giovanni, as Alexander's sixth or seventh child.

vasion of Charles VIII., king of France. The introductory act
in what seemed likely to be the complete transformation of Italy
was the sale of Cervetri and Anguillara to Virginius Orsini for
40,000 ducats by Franceschetto, the son of Innocent VIII. This
papal scion was contented with a life of ease and retired to Florence. The transfer of these two estates was treated by the
Sforza as disturbing the balance of power in the peninsula, and
Ludovico and Ascanio Sforza pressed Alexander to check the influence of Ferrante, king of Naples, who was the supporter of the
Orsini. Ferrante, a shrewd politician, by ministering to Alexander's passion to advance his children's fortunes, won him from
the alliance with the Sforza. He promised to the pope's son,
Joffré, Donna Sancia, a mere child, in marriage. Ludovico
Sforza, ready to resort to any measure likely to promote his own
personal ambition, invited Charles VIII. to enter Italy and make
good his claim to the crown of Naples on the ground of the former
Angevin possession. He also applauded the French king's announced purpose to reduce Constantinople once more to Christian dominion.

On Ferrante's death, 1494, Alfonso II. was crowned king of
Naples by Alexander's nephew, Cardinal Juan Borgia. Charles,
then only 22, was short, deformed, with an aquiline nose and an
inordinately big head. He set out for Italy at the head of a
splendid army of 40,000 men, equipped with the latest inventions in artillery. Julian Rovere, who had resisted Alexander's
policy and fled to Avignon, joined with other disaffected cardinals in supporting the French and accompanying the French
army. Charles' march through Northern Italy was a series of
easy and almost bloodless triumphs. Milan threw open its gates
to Charles. So did Pisa. Before entering Florence, the king
was met by Savonarola, who regarded him as the messenger
appointed by God to rescue Italy from her godless condition.
Rome was helpless. Alexander's ambassadors, sent to treat
with the invader, were either denied audience or denied satisfaction. In his desperation, the pope resorted to the Turkish
sultan, Bajazet, for aid. The correspondence that passed between the supreme ruler of Christendom and the leading sovereign of the Mohammedan world was rescued from oblivion by

the capture of its bearer, George Busardo.[1] 40,000 ducats were found on Busardo's person, a payment sent by Bajazet to Alexander for Djem's safe-keeping. Alexander had indicated to the sultan that it was Charles' aim to carry Djem off to France and then use him as the admiral of a fleet for the capture of Constantinople. In reply, Bajazet suggested that such an issue would result in even greater damage to the pope than to himself. His papal friend, whom he addressed as his Gloriosity —*gloriositas*,— might be pleased to lift the said prisoner, Djem, out of the troubles of this present world and transfer his soul into another, where he would enjoy more quiet.[2] For performing such a service, he stood ready to give him the sum of 300,000 ducats, which, as he suggested, the pope might use in purchasing princedoms for his children.

On the last day of 1494, the French army entered the holy city, dragging with it 36 bronze cannon. Such military discipline and equipment the Romans had not seen, and they looked on with awe and admiration. To the king's demand that the castle of S. Angelo be surrendered, Alexander sent a refusal declaring that, if the fortress were attacked, he would take his position on the walls, surrounded with the most sacred relics in Rome. Cardinals Julian Rovere, Sforza, Savelli and Colonna, who had ridden into the city with the French troops, urged the king to call a council and depose Alexander for simony. But when it came to the manipulation of men, Alexander was more than a match for his enemies. Charles had no desire to humiliate the pope, except so far as it might be necessary for the accomplishment of his designs upon Naples. A pact was arranged, which included the delivery of Djem to the French and the promise that Cæsar Borgia should accompany the French troops to Naples as papal legate. In the meantime the French soldiery had sacked the city, even to Vanozza's house. Henceforth the

---

[1] These letters are given in full by Burchard, II. 202 sqq. Alexander's letters Gregorovius pronounces to be genuine beyond a doubt. The sultan's are matter of dispute. Ranke discredited them, but Gregorovius regards their contents as genuine, though the form may be spurious. Creighton, III. 300 sqq., gives reasons for accepting them.

[2] *Dictum Gem levare facere ex angustiis istius mundi et transferre ejus animan in aliud seculum ubi meliorem habebit quietem*, Burchard, II. 209.

king occupied quarters in the Vatican, and the disaffected cardinals, with the exception of Julian, were reconciled to the pope.

On his march to Naples, which began Jan. 25, 1495, Charles took Djem with him.   That individual passed out of the gates of Rome, riding at the side of Cæsar.   These two personages, the Turkish pretender and the pontiff's son, had been on terms of familiarity, and often rode on horseback together.   Within a month after leaving Rome, and before reaching Naples, the Oriental died.   The capital of Southern Italy was an easy prize for the invaders.   Cæsar had been able to make his escape from the French camp.   His son's shrewdness and good luck afforded Alexander as much pleasure as did the opportunity of joining the king of Spain and the cities of Northern Italy in an alliance against Charles.   In 1496, the alliance was strengthened by the accession of Henry VII. of England.   After abandoning himself for several months to the pleasures of the Neapolitan capital, the French king retraced his course and, after the battle of Fornuovo, July 6, 1495, evacuated Italy. Alexander had evaded him by retiring from Rome, and sent after the retreating king a message to return to his proper dominions on pain of excommunication.   The summons neither hastened the departure of the French nor prevented them from returning to the peninsula again in a few years.[1]

The misfortunes and scandals of the papal household were not interrupted by the French invasion, and continued after it. In the summer of 1497, occurred the mysterious murder of Alexander's son, the duke of Gandia, then 24 years old.   It was only a sample of the crimes being perpetrated in Rome. The duke had supped with Cæsar, his brother, and Cardinal Juan Borgia at the residence of Vanozza.   The supper being over, the two brothers rode together as far as the palace of Cardinal Sforza.   There they separated, the duke going, as he said, on some private business, and accompanied by a masked man who had been much with him for a month past.   The next day, Alexander waited for his son in vain.   In the evening, un-

---

[1] The French left behind them a terrible legacy in the disease which they are said to have carrried during the Crusades and again a century ago, under Napoleon, to Syria, and known as the French disease.   See Pastor, III. 7.

able to bear the suspense longer, he instituted an investigation.
The man in the mask had been found mortally wounded. A
charcoal-dealer deposed that, after midnight, he had seen several men coming to the brink of the river, one of them on a
white horse, over the back of which was thrown a dead man.
They backed the horse and pitched the body into the water.
The pope was inconsolable with grief, and remained without
food from Thursday to Sunday.   He had recently made his son
lord of the papal patrimony and of Viterbo, standard-bearer
of the church and duke of Benevento.   In reporting the loss
to the consistory of cardinals, the father declared that he loved
Don Juan more than anything in the world, and that if he had
seven papacies he would give them all to restore his son's life.

The origin of the murder was a mystery.   Different persons
were picked out as the perpetrators.   It was surmised that the
deed was committed by some lover who had been abused by
the gay duke.   Suspicion also fastened on Ascanio Sforza, the
only cardinal who did not attend the consistory.   But gradually the conviction prevailed that the murderer was no other
than Cæsar Borgia himself, and the Italian historian, Guicciardini, three years later adopted the explanation of fratricide.
Cæsar, it was rumored, was jealous of the place the duke of
Gandia held in his father's affections, and hankered after the
worldly honors which had been heaped upon him.

When the charcoal-dealer was asked why he did not at once
report the dark scene, he replied that such deeds were a common occurrence and he had witnessed a hundred like it.[1]

In the first outburst of his grief, Alexander, moved by feelings akin to repentance, appointed a commission of six cardinals
to bring in proposals for the reformation of the curia and the

---

[1] Burchard's account of the tragedy, II. 387-390. Gregorovius, VIII. 424,
confidently advocates the theory of fratricide.   This explains why Alexander
dropped the investigation two weeks after it was begun, and why he and Cæsar
in the first meetings after the event were silent in each other's presence.   However, it is almost too much to believe that Alexander would at once begin to
heap honors upon Cæsar, as he did, if the father believed him to be the murderer.   Roscoe, I. 153 sq., and Pastor discredit the theory of fratricide, to which
Creighton, III. 388, also inclines.   Don Juan was the only one of the Borgias
that founded a family.

Church.   His reforming ardor was, however, soon spent, and the proposals, when offered, were set aside as derogatory to the papal prerogative.   For the next two years, the marriages and careers of his children, Cæsar and Lucretia, were treated as if they were the chief concern of Christendom.

Lucretia, born in 1480, had already been twice betrothed to Spaniards, when the father was elected pope and sought for her a higher alliance.   In 1493, she was married to John Sforza, lord of Pesaro, a man of illegitimate birth.   The young princess was assigned a palace of her own near the Vatican, where Julia Farnese ruled as her father's mistress.   It was a gay life she lived, as the centre of the young matrons of Rome.   Accompanied by a hundred of them at a time, she rode to church. She was pronounced by the master of ceremonies of the papal chapel most fair, of a bright disposition, and given to fun and laughter.[1]   The charges of incest with her own father and brother Cæsar made against her on the streets of the papal city, in the messages of ambassadors and by the historian, Guicciardini, seem too shocking to be believed, and have been set aside by Gregorovius, the most brilliant modern authority for her life.   The distinguished character of her last marriage and the domestic peace and happiness by which it was marked seem to be sufficient to discredit the damaging accusations.

The marriage with the lord of Pesaro was celebrated in the Vatican, after a sermon had been preached by the bishop of Concordia.   Among the guests were 11 cardinals and 150 Roman ladies.   The entertainment lasted till 5 in the morning. There was dancing, and obscene comedies were performed, with Alexander and the cardinals looking on.   And all this, exclaims a contemporary, " to the honor and praise of Almighty God and the Roman church!"[2]

After spending some time with her husband on his estate, Lucretia was divorced from him on the charge of his impotency, the divorce being passed upon by a commission of cardinals.

---

[1] Burchard, II. 280, 493, *filia clarissima, filia jocosa et risoria.*

[2] Infessura, p. 286 sq., closes his account by saying he would not tell all, lest it might seem incredible.   The account of Boccaccio, ambassador of Ferrara, who was present, is given by Gregorov., *Lucr. Borgia,* pp. 59–61.

After spending a short time in a convent, the princess was married to Don Alfonso, duke of Besiglia, the bastard son of Alfonso II. of Naples.   The Vatican again witnessed the nuptial ceremony, but the marriage was, before many months, to be brought to a close by the duke's murder.

In the meantime Donna Sancia, the wife of Joffré, had come to the city, May, 1496, and been received at the gates by cardinals, Lucretia and other important personages.   The pope, surrounded by 11 cardinals, and with Lucretia on his right hand, welcomed his son and daughter-in-law in the Vatican. According to Burchard, the two princesses boldly occupied the priests' benches in St. Peter's.   Later, it was said, Sancia's two brothers-in-law, the duke of Gandia and Cæsar, quarrelled over her and possessed her in turn.   Alexander sent her back to Naples, whether for this reason or not is not known.   She was afterwards received again in Rome.

Cæsar, in spite of his yearly revenues amounting to 35,000 ducats, had long since grown tired of an ecclesiastical career. Bishop and cardinal-deacon though he was, he deposed before his fellow-cardinals that from the first he had been averse to orders, and received them in obedience to his father's wish. These words Gregorovius has pronounced to be perhaps the only true words the prince ever spoke.   Cæsar's request was granted by the unanimous voice of the sacred college.   Alexander, whose policy it now was to form a lasting bond between France and the papacy, looked to Louis XII., successor of Charles VIII., for a proper introduction of his son upon a worldly career.[1]   Louis was anxious to be divorced from his deformed and childless wife, Joanna of Valois, and to be united to Charles' young widow, Anne, who carried the dowry of Brittany with her.   There were advantages to be gained on both sides.   Dispensation was given to the king, and Cæsar was made duke of Valentinois and promised a wife of royal line.

The arrangements for Cæsar's departure from Rome were on a grand scale.   The richest textures were added to gold and silver vessels and coin, so that, when the young man de-

---

[1] Alexander had courteously attended a mass for the repose of the soul of his old enemy, Charles, in the Sistine chapel, Burchard, II. 461.

parted from the city, he was preceded by a line of mules carrying goods worth 200,000 ducats on their backs.   The duke's horses were shod with silver.   The contemporary writer gives a picture of Alexander standing at the window, watching the cortege, in which were four cardinals, as it passed towards the West.   The party went by way of Avignon.   After some disappointment in not securing the princess whom Cæsar had picked out, Charlotte d'Albret, then a young lady of sixteen, and a sister of the king of Navarre, was chosen.   When the news of the marriage, which was celebrated in May, 1499, reached Rome, Alexander and the Spaniards illuminated their houses and the streets in honor of the proud event.   The advancement of this abandoned man, from this time forth, engaged Alexander VI.'s supreme energies.   The career of Cæsar Borgia passes, if possible, into stages of deeper darkness, and the mind shrinks back from the awful sensuality, treachery and cruelty for which no crime was too revolting.   Everything had to give way that stood in the hard path of his vulgar ambition and profligate greed.   And at last his father, ready to sacrifice all that is sacred in religion and human life to secure his son's promotion, became his slave, and in fear dared not to offer resistance to his plans.

The duke was soon back in Italy, accompanying the French army led by Louis XII.   The reduction of Milan and Naples followed.   The taking of Milan reduced Alexander's former ally and brought captivity to Ascanio Sforza, the cardinal, but it was welcome news in the Vatican.   Alexander was bent, with the help of Louis, upon creating a great dukedom in central Italy for his son, with a kingly dominion over all the peninsula as the ultimate act of the drama.   The fall of Naples was due in part to the pope's perfidy in making an alliance with Louis and deposing the Neapolitan king, Frederick.

Endowed by his father with the proud title of duke of the Romagna and made captain-general of the church, Cæsar, with the help of 8,000 mercenaries, made good his rights to Imola, Forli, Rimini and other towns, some of the victories being celebrated by services in St. Peter's.   At the same time, Lucretia was made regent of Nepi and Spoleto.   As a part of the family program, the indulgent father proceeded to declare war against the Gaetani house and to despoil the Colonna, Savelli and Orsini.   No obstacle should be allowed to remain in the ambitious path of the unscrupulous son.   Upon him was also conferred that emblem of purity of character or of high service to the Church, the Golden Rose.

The celebration of the Jubilee in the opening year of the new century, which was to be so eventful, brought hundreds of thousands of pilgrims to the holy city, and the great sums which were collected were reserved for the Turkish crusade, or employed for the advancement of the Borgias.   The bull announcing the festival offered to those visiting Rome free indulgence for the most grievous sins.[1]   On Christmas eve, 1499, Alexander struck the Golden Gate with a silver mallet, repeating the words of Revelation, " He openeth and no man shutteth."

In glaring contrast to the religious ends with which the Jubilee was associated in the minds of the pilgrims, Cæsar entered Rome, in February, surrounded with all the trappings of military conquest.   Among the festivities provided to relieve the tedium of religious occupations was a Spanish bull-fight.   The square of St. Peter's was enclosed with a railing and the spectators looked on while the pope's son, Cæsar, killed five bulls. The head of the last he severed with a single stroke of his sword.

Another of the fearful tragedies of the Borgia family filled the atmosphere of this holy year with its smothering fumes, the murder of Lucretia's husband, the duke of Besiglia, to whom she had borne a son.[2]   On returning home at night he was fallen upon at the steps of St. Peter's and stabbed.   Carried to his palace, he was recovering, when Cæsar, who had visited him several times, at last had him strangled, August 18, 1500.   The pope's son openly declared his responsibility,

---

[1] Burchard, II. 591–593.

[2] Rodrigo, who was baptized in St. Peter's, Nov. 1, 1499, the 16 cardinals then in Rome, many ambassadors and other dignitaries being present.   In 1501 he was invested with the duchy of Sermoneta.   Burchard, II. 575, 578; III. 170.

and gave as an explanation that he himself was in danger from the prince.

With such scenes the new century was introduced in the papal city. But the end was not yet. The appointment of cardinals had been prostituted into a convenient device for filling the papal coffers and advancing the schemes of the papal family. In 1493 Alexander added 12 to the sacred college, including Alexander Farnese, afterwards Paul III., and brother to the pope's mistress. From these creations more than 100,000 ducats are said to have been realized.[1] In 1496 four more were added, all Spaniards, including the pope's nephew, Giovanni Borgia, and making 9 Spaniards in Alexander's cabinet. When 12 cardinals were appointed, Sept. 28, 1500, Cæsar reaped 120,000 ducats as his reward. He had openly explained that he needed the money for his designs in the Romagna. In 1503, just before his father's death, the duke received 130,000 more for 9 red hats. He raised 64,000 by the appointment of new abbreviators. Nor were the dead to go free. At the death of Cardinal Ferrari, 50,000 ducats were seized from his effects, and when Cardinal Michïel died, nephew of Paul II., 150,000 ducats were transferred to the duke's account.

One iniquity only led to another. Cardinal Orsini, while on a visit to the pope, was taken prisoner. His palace was dismantled, and other members of the family seized and their castles confiscated. The cardinal's mother, aged fourscore, secured from Alexander, upon the payment of 2,000 ducats and a costly pearl which Orsini's mistress had in her possession and, dressed as a man, took to Alexander,[2] the privilege of supplying her son with a daily dole of bread. But the unfortunate man's doom was sealed. He came to his death, as it was believed, by poison prepared by Alexander.[3]

The last of Alexander's notable achievements for his family was the marriage of Lucretia to Alfonso, son of Hercules, duke of Ferrara, 1502. The young duke was 24, and a widower.

---

[1] Infessura, p. 293.   [2] Burchard, III. 236.
[3] So Pastor, though with some hesitation, III. 491. Even Creighton, IV. 40, is unwilling to dismiss the charge as groundless. But in another place, p. 265, he seems to contradict himself.

The prejudices of his father were removed through the good offices of the king of France and a reduction of the tribute due from Ferrara, as a papal fief, from 400 ducats to 100 florins, the college of cardinals giving their assent.   While the negotiations were going on, Alexander, during an absence of three months from Rome, confided his correspondence and the transaction of his business to the hands of his daughter.   This appointment made the college of cardinals subject to her.

Lucretia entered with zest into the settlement of the preliminaries leading up to the betrothal and into the preparations for the nuptials.   When the news of the signing of the marriage contract reached Rome, early in September, 1501, she went to S. Maria del Popolo, accompanied by 300 knights and four bishops, and gave public thanks.   On the way she took off her cloak, said to be worth 300 ducats, and gave it to her buffoon.   Putting it on, he rode through the streets crying out, "Hurrah for the most illustrious duchess of Ferrara.   Hurrah for Alexander VI."[1]   For three hours the great bell on the capitol was kept ringing, and bonfires were lit through the city to "incite everybody to joy."   The pope's daughter, although she had been four times betrothed and twice married, was only 21 at the time of her last engagement.   According to the Ferrarese ambassador, her face was most beautiful and her manners engaging.[2]   In the brilliant escort sent by Hercules to conduct his future daughter-in-law to her new home, were the duke's two younger sons, who were entertained at the Vatican.   Cæsar and 19 cardinals, including Cardinal Hippolytus of Este, met the escort at the Porto del Popolo.   Night after night, the Vatican was filled with the merriment of dancing and theatrical plays.   At her father's request, Lucretia performed special dances.   The formal ceremony of marriage was performed, December 30th, in St. Peter's, Don Ferdinand acting as proxy for his brother.   Preceded by 50 maids of honor, a duke on each side of her, the bride proceeded to the basilica.   Her approach was announced by musicians playing in the portico. Within on his throne sat the pontiff, surrounded by 13 cardi-

---

[1] Burchard, III. 161 sq.

[2] The letter is given in Gregor., *Lucr. Borgia*, p. 212.

nals.   After a sermon, which Alexander ordered made short,
a ring was put on Lucretia's finger by Duke Ferdinand.   Then
the Cardinal d'Este approached, laying on a table 4 other rings,
a diamond, an emerald, a turquoise and a ruby, and, at his
order, a casket was opened which contained many jewels, including a head-dress of 16 diamonds and 150 large pearls.
But with exquisite courtesy, the prelate begged the princess not
to spurn the gift, as more gems were awaiting her in Ferrara.

The rest of the night was spent in a banquet in the Vatican,
when comedies were rendered, in which Cæsar was one of the
leading figures.   To their credit be it said, that some of the
cardinals and other dignitaries preferred to retire early.   The
week which followed was filled with entertainments, including
a bull-fight on St. Peter's square, in which Cæsar again was
entered as a matador.

The festivities were brought to a close Jan. 6th, 1502.
150 mules carried the bride's trousseau and other baggage.
The lavish father had told her to take what she would.   Her
dowry in money was 100,000 ducats.   A brilliant cavalcade,
in which all the cardinals and ambassadors and the magistrates of the municipality took part, accompanied the party to
the city gates and beyond, while Cardinal Francesco Borgia
accompanied the party the whole journey.   In this whole affair, in spite of ourselves, sympathy for a father supplants our
indignation at his perfidy in violating the sacred vows of a
Catholic priest and the pledge of the supreme pontiff.   Alexander followed the cavalcade as far as he could with his eye,
changing his position from window to window.   But no mention is made by any of the writers of the bride's mother.
Was she also a witness of the gayeties from some concealed or
open standing-place ?

Lucretia never returned to Rome.   And so this famous
woman, whose fortunes awaken the deepest interest and also
the deepest sympathy, passes out from the realm of this history and she takes her place in the family annals of the noble
house of Este.   She gained the respect of the court and the
admiration of the city, living a quiet, domestic life till her
death in 1519.   Few mortals have seen transpire before their

own eyes and in so short a time so much of dissemblance and crime as she. She was not forty when she died. The old representation, which made her the heroine of the dagger and the poisoned cup and guilty of incest, has given way to the milder judgment of Reumont and Gregorovius, with whom Pastor agrees. While they do not exonerate her from all profligacy, they rescue her from being an abandoned Magdalen, and make appeal to our considerate judgment by showing that she was made by her father an instrument of his ambitions for his family and that at last she exhibited the devotion of a wife and of a mother. Her son, Hercules, who reigned till 1559, was the husband of Renée, the princess who welcomed Calvin and Clement Marot to her court.

Death finally put an end to the scandals of Alexander's reign. After an entertainment given by Cardinal Hadrian, the pope and his son Cæsar were attacked with fever. It was reported that the poison which they had prepared for a cardinal was by mistake or intentionally put into the cups they themselves used.[1] The pontiff's sickness lasted less than a week. The third day he was bled. On his death-bed he played cards with some of his cardinals. At the last, he received the eucharist and extreme unction and died in the presence of five members of the sacred college. It is especially noted by that well-informed diarist, Burchard, that during

---

[1] The question of whether or no poison was the cause of the pope's death must be regarded as an open one. This is the view taken by Gregorovius, Roscoe, I. 193 sq., Reumont, Pastor, III. 499. Creighton, IV. 43, and Hergenröther, III. 987, are against the theory of poisoning. Neither Burchard nor the ambassador of Venice speak of poison. The ambassador of Mantua, writing on the 19th, denies the charge, which was freely made on the streets. Ranke, *D. röm. Päpste*, p. 35, distinctly decides for poisoning. So also Hase, *Kirchengesch.*, III. 353. Many contemporary writers pronounced for poisoning, Guicciardini, Cardinal Bembo, Jovius, Cardinal Ægidius, etc. Alexander's physician gave as the immediate cause of death apoplexy. Against the theory of poisoning is the fact that Cardinal Hadrian was also taken sick. On the other hand is the evidence that Alexander's body immediately after death was bloated and disfigured and his mouth was filled with foam, and that Cæsar was taken sick at the same time with the same symptoms, a fact which Gregorovius, VII. 521, pronounces the strongest evidence for the theory of poisoning.

his sickness Alexander never spoke a single word about Lucretia or his son, the duke.   Cæsar was too ill to go to his father's sick-bed but, on hearing of his death, he sent Micheletto to demand of the chamberlain the keys to the papal exchequer, threatening to strangle the cardinal, Casanova, and throw him out of the window in case he refused.   Terrified out of his wits, — *perterritus*, — the cardinal yielded, and 100,000 ducats of gold and silver were carried away to the bereaved son.

In passing an estimate upon Alexander VI., it must be remembered that the popular and also the carefully expressed judgments of contemporaries are against him.[1]   The rumor was current that the devil himself was present at the death-scene and that, paying the price he had promised him for the gift of the papacy 12 years before, Alexander replied to the devil's beckonings that he well understood the time had come for the final stage of the transaction.[2]

Alexander's intellectual abilities have abundant proof in the results of his diplomacy by which he was enabled to plot for the political advancement of Cæsar Borgia, with the support of France, at whose feet he had at one time been humbled, by his winning back the support of the disaffected cardinals, and by his immunity from personal hurt through violence, unless it be through poison at last.   That which marks him out for unmitigated condemnation is his lack of principle.   Mental ability, which is ascribed to the devil himself, is no substitute for moral qualities.   Perfidy, treachery, greed, lust and murder were stored up in Alexander's heart.[3]   While he shrank from the commission of no crime to reach the objects of his ambition, he was wont to engage in the solemn exercises of devotion, and

---

[1] There is one exception, the address made in the conclave after Alexander's death by the bishop of Gallipolis.   See Garnett's art. *Engl. Hist. Rev.*, 1892, p. 311 sq., giving the text of the British Museum, the only copy in existence.

[2] The duke of Mantua, whose camp was near Rome, wrote to his duchess that seven devils appeared in the pope's room at the moment of his death, that the body swelled and was dragged from the bed with a cord.   Gregorovius, *Lucr. Borgia*, p. 288.

[3] Bishop Creighton, IV. 44, lays stress on the fact that hypocrisy was not added to Alexander's other vices.

even to say the mass with his own lips. To measure his iniquity,
as has been said, one need only compare his actions with the
simple statement of the precepts, " Thou shalt not kill, thou
shalt not commit adultery, thou shalt not steal." Elevation
to a position of responsibility usually has the effect of sobering
a man's spirit, but Rodrigo Borgia degraded the highest office
in the gift of Christendom for his own carnal designs. The
moral qualities and aims of Gregory VII. and Innocent III.,
however much we may dissent from those aims, command respect. Alexander VI. was sensual, and his ability to govern
men, no matter how great it was, should not moderate the
abhorrence which his depraved aims arouse. The man with
brute force can hold others in terror, but he is a brute,
nevertheless. The standards, it must be confessed, of life
in Rome were low when Rodrigo was made cardinal, and a
Roman chronicler could say that every priest had his mistress and almost all the Roman monasteries had been turned
into *lupinaria* — brothels.[1] But holy traditions still lingered
around the sacred places of the city ; the solemn rites of the
Christian ritual were still performed ; the dissoluteness of the
Roman emperors still seemed hellish when compared with the
sacrifice of the cross. And yet, two years before Alexander's
death, October 31, 1501, an orgy took place in the Vatican by
Cæsar's appointment whose obscenity the worst of the imperial
revels could hardly have surpassed. 50 courtezans spent the
night dancing, with the servants and others present, first with
their clothes on and then nude, the pope and Lucretia looking on. The women, still naked, and going on their hands and
feet, picked up chestnuts thrown on the ground, and then received prizes of cloaks, shoes, caps and other articles.[2]

[1] Infessura, p. 287.

[2] Burchard, III. 167, who reports the wild scene, was reticent about many
of the evil happenings in the papal palace. The other authorities for the orgy
may be seen in Thuasne's ed. of Burchard. See also Villari, *Machiavelli*,
I. 538. When we are taken to the square of St. Peter's, where the pope and
the cardinals watched a feat of tight-rope walking, an expert walking with a
child in his arms, we may easily applaud or tolerate the recreation, Burchard,
III. 210 ; but the dark furies of evil seem at will to have had mastery over
Alexander's soul.

To Alexander nothing was sacred,—office, virtue, marriage, or life.   As cardinal he was present at the nuptials of the young Julia Farnese, and probably at that very moment conceived the purpose of corrupting her, and in a few months she was his acknowledged mistress.   The cardinal of Gurk said to the Florentine envoy, " When I think of the pope's life and the lives of some of his cardinals, I shudder at the thought of remaining in the curia, and I will have nothing to do with it unless God reforms His Church."   It was a biting thrust when certain German knights, summoned to Rome, wrote to the pontiff that they were good Christians and served the Count Palatine, who worshipped God, loved justice, hated vice and was never accused of adultery.   " We believe," they went on, "in a just God who will punish with eternal flames robbery, sacrilege, violence, abuse of the patrimony of Christ, concubinage, simony and other enormities by which the Christian Church is being scandalized." [1]

It is pleasant to turn to the few acts of this last pontificate of the 15th century which have another aspect than pure selfishness or depravity.   In 1494, Alexander canonized Anselm without, however, referring to the Schoolman's great treatise on the atonement, or his argument for the existence of God.[2] He promoted the cult of St. Anna, the Virgin Mary's reputed mother, to whom Luther was afterwards devoted.[3] He almost blasphemously professed himself under the special protection of the Virgin, to whom he ascribed his deliverance from death on several occasions, by sea and in the papal palace.

In accord with the later practice of the Roman Catholic Church, Alexander restricted the freedom of the press, ordering that no volume should be published without episcopal sanction.[4] His name meets the student of Western discovery in its earliest period, but his treatment of America shows that he was not informed of the purposes of Providence.   In two bulls,

[1] Burchard, III. 110.   [2] Mansi, XXXII. 533 sq.
[3] Calvin spoke of having been taken as a child by his mother to the abbey of Ourscamp, near Noyon, where a part of St. Anna's body was preserved, and of having kissed the relic.
[4] *Decretum de libris non sine censura imprimendis*, 1501. Reusch, *Index*, p. 54.

issued May 4th and 5th, 1493, he divided the Western world
between Portugal and Spain by a line 100 leagues west of the
Azores, running north and south. These documents mention
Christopher Columbus as a worthy man, much to be praised,
who, apt as a sailor, and after great perils, labors and expenditures, had discovered islands and continents — *terras firmas* —
never before known. The possession of the lands in the West,
discovered and yet to be discovered, was assigned to Spain and
Portugal to be held and governed in perpetuity, — *in per-
petuum*, — and the pope solemnly declared that he made the
gift out of pure liberality, and by the authority of the omnipotent God, conceded to him in St. Peter, and by reason of the
vicarship of Jesus Christ, which he administered on earth.[1]
Nothing could be more distinctly stated. As Peter's successor, Alexander claimed the right to give away the Western
Continent, and his gift involved an unending right of tenure.
This prerogative of disposing of the lands in the West was in
accordance with Constantine's invented gift to Sylvester,
recorded in the spurious Isidorian decretals.[2]

If any papal bull might be expected to have the quality of
inerrancy, it is the bull bearing so closely on the destinies of
the great American continent, and through it on the world's
history. But the terms of the bull of May 4th were set aside
a year after its issue by the political treaty of Tordesillas, June
7, 1494, which shifted the line to a distance 370 leagues west
of the Cape Verde Islands. And the centuries have rudely
overturned the supreme pontiff's solemn bequest until not a
foot of land on this Western continent remains in the pos-

---

[1] *De nostra mera liberalitate . . . auctoritate omnip. Dei, nobis in beato
Petro concessa, ac vicariatus J. Christi, qua fungimur in terris.* For the
bull, see Mirbt, pp. 174–176. Also Fiske, *Disc. of Am.*, I. 454–458 ; II. 581–593.

[2] Pastor, III. 520, seeks to break the force of the charge that Alexander's
gift was a short-sighted piece of work by putting the unnatural interpretation
upon *donamus et assignamus*, that it referred only to what Portugal and Spain
had already acquired. But the very wording of the bull makes this impossible,
for it is distinctly said that all islands and continents were given to Spain and
Portugal which were to be discovered in the future, as well as those which
were already discovered — *omnes insulas et terras firmas inventas et inveni-
endas, detectas et detegendas.* For the bull of Sept. 26, 1493, giving India to
Spain, see Davenport in *Am. Hist. Rev.*, 1909, p. 764 sqq.

session of the kingdoms to which it was given.   Putting aside the distinctions between doctrinal and disciplinary decisions, which are made by many Catholic exponents of the dogma of papal infallibility, Alexander's bull conferring the Americas, as Innocent III.'s bull pronouncing the stipulations of the Magna Charta forever null, should afford a sufficient refutation of the dogma.

The character and career of Alexander VI. afford an argument against the theory of the divine institution and vicarial prerogatives of the papacy which the doubtful exegesis of our Lord's words to Peter ought not to be allowed to counteract.   If we leave out all the wicked popes of the 9th and 10th centuries, forget for a moment the cases of Honorius and other popes charged with heresy, and put aside the offending popes of the Renaissance period and all the bulls which sin against common reason, such as Innocent VIII.'s bull against witchcraft, Alexander is enough to forbid that theory.   Could God commit his Church for 12 years to such a monster?   It is fair to recognize that Catholic historians feel the difficulty, although they find a way to explain it away.   Cardinal Hergenröther says that "Christendom was delivered from a great offence by Alexander's death, but even in his case, unworthy as this pope was, his teachings are to be obeyed, and in him the promise made to the chair of St. Peter was fulfilled (Matt. 23 : 2, 3).   In no instance did Alexander VI. prescribe to the Church anything contrary to morals or the faith, and never did he lead her astray in disciplinary decrees which, for the most part, were excellent." [1]

In like strain, Pastor writes: [2]   "In spite of Alexander, the purity of the Church's teaching continued unharmed.   It was as if Providence wanted to show that men may injure the Church, but that it is not in their power to destroy it.   As a bad setting does not diminish the value of the precious stone, so the sinfulness of a priest cannot do any essential detriment either to his dispensation of her sacraments or to the doctrines committed to her.   Gold remains gold, whether dispensed by clean hands or unclean.   The papal office is exalted far above

---

[1] Hergenröther-Kirsch, II. 987.   [2] III. 503.

the personality of its occupants, and cannot lose its dignity or gain essential worth by the worthiness or unworthiness of its occupants. Peter sinned deeply, and yet the supreme pastoral office was committed to him. It was from this standpoint that Pope Leo the Great declared that the dignity of St. Peter is not lost, even in an unworthy successor. *Petri dignitas etiam in indigno hæredo non deficit.*" Leo's words Pastor adopts as the motto of his history.

In such reasoning, the illustrations beg the question. No matter how clean or unclean the hands may be which handle it, lead remains lead, and no matter whether the setting be gold or tin, an opaque stone remains opaque which is held by them. The personal opinion of Leo the Great will not be able to stand against the growing judgment of mankind, that the Head of the Church does not commit the keeping of sacred truth to wicked hands or confide the pastorate over the Church to a man of unholy and lewd lips. The papal theory of the succession of Peter, even if there were no other hostile historic testimony, would founder on the personality of Alexander VI., who set an example of all depravity. Certainly the true successors of Peter will give in their conduct some evidence of the fulfilment of Christ's words "the kingdom of heaven is within you." Who looks for an illustration of obedience to the mandates of the Most High to the last pontiff of the 15th century! [1]

[1] Pastor, in the course of prolonged estimates, *Gesch. der Päpste*, III. pp. vi, 501 sq., etc., says: "The life of this voluptuary — *Genussmenschen* — a man of untamed sensuality, contradicted at every point the demands of him he was called upon to represent. With unrestrained abandon, he gave himself up to a vicious life until his end." Ranke thus expresses himself, *Hist. of the Popes*, Germ. ed., I. 32. "All his life through, Alexander was bent on nothing else than to enjoy the world, to live pleasurably, to satisfy his passions and ambitions." The estimate of Gregorovius, *City of Rome*, VII. 525, is this: "No one can ever discover in Alexander's history any other guiding principle than the contemptible one of aggrandizing his children at any cost. To the despicable objects of nepotism and self-preservation he sacrificed his own conscience, the happiness of nations, the existence of Italy and the good of the Church." Bishop Creighton, IV. 43–49, lays such elaborate emphasis upon Alexander's knowledge of politics, firmness of purpose and affability of manners that one loses the impression of the baseness of his morals and the sacrilege to which he subjected his office and himself. He seems to have been influenced by Roscoe's presentation of Alexander's "many great qualities," I. 195.

§ 55. *Julius II., the Warrior-Pope.* 1503–1513.

Alexander's successor, Pius III., a nephew of Pius II., and a man of large family, succumbed, within a month after his election, to the gout and other infirmities. He was followed by Julian Rovere, Alexander's old rival, who, as cardinal, had played a conspicuous part for more than 30 years. He proved to be the ablest and most energetic pontiff the Church had had since the days of Innocent III. and Gregory IX. in the 13th century.

At Alexander's death, Cæsar Borgia attempted to control the situation. He afterwards told Machiavelli that he had made provision for every exigency except the undreamed-of conjunction of his own and his father's sickness.[1] Consternation ruled in Rome, but with the aid of the ambassadors of France, Germany, Venice and Spain, Cæsar was prevailed upon to withdraw from the city, while the Orsini and the Colonna families, upon which Alexander had heaped high insult, entered it again.

The election of Julian Rovere, who assumed the name of Julius II., was accomplished with despatch October 31, 1503, after bribery had been freely resorted to.   The Spanish cardinals, 11 in number and still in a measure under Cæsar's control, gave their votes to the successful candidate on condition that Cæsar should be recognized as gonfalonier of the church.   The faithful papal master-of-ceremonies, whose *Diary* we have had occasion to draw on so largely, was appointed bishop of Orta, but died two years later.   Born in Savona of humble parentage and appointed to the sacred college by his uncle, Sixtus IV., Julius had recently returned to Rome after an exile of nearly 10 years. The income from his numerous bishoprics and other dignities made him the richest of the cardinals.   Though piety was not one of the new pontiff's notable traits, his pontificate furnished an agreeable relief from the coarse crimes and domestic scandals of Alexander's reign.   It is true, he had a family of three daughters, one of whom, Felice, was married into the Orsini family in 1506, carrying with her a splendid dowry of 15,000 ducats. But the marriage festivities were not appointed for the Vatican, nor

[1] *The Prince*, ch. VII.

did the children give offence by their ostentatious presence in
the pontifical palace. Julius also took care of his nephews.
Two of them were appointed to the sacred college, Nov. 29, 1503,
and later two more were honored with the same dignity. For
making the Spanish scholar, Ximenes, cardinal, Julius deserved
well of other ages as well as his own. He was a born ruler. He
had a dignified and imposing presence and a bright, penetrating
eye. Under his white hair glowed the intellectual fire of youth.
He was rapid in his movements even to impetuosity, and brave
even to daring. Defeats that would have disheartened even the
bravest, seemed only to intensify Julius' resolution. If his language was often violent, the excuse is offered that violence of
speech was common at that time. As a cardinal he had shown
himself a diplomat rather than a saint, and as pope he showed
himself a warrior rather than a priest. When Michael Angelo,
who was ordered to execute the pope's statue in bronze, was
representing Julius with his right hand raised, the pope asked,
"What are you going to put into the left?" "It may be a
book," answered the artist. "Nay, give me a sword, for I am
no scholar," was the pope's reply. Nothing could be more characteristic.[1]

Julius' administration at once brought repose and confidence
to the sacred college and Rome. If he did not keep his promise
to abide by the protocol adopted in the conclave calling for the
assembling of a council within two years, he may be forgiven on
the ground of the serious task he had before him in strengthening
the political authority of the papal see. This was the chief aim
of his pontificate. He deserves the title of the founder of the
State of the Church, a realm that, with small changes, remained
papal territory till 1870. This end being secured, he devoted
himself to redeeming Italy from its foreign invaders. Three
foes stood in his way, Cæsar and the despots of the Italian cities,
the French who were intrenched in Milan and Genoa, and the
Spaniards who held Naples and Sicily. His effort to rescue Italy

---

[1] The statue was placed in front of St. Petronio in Bologna. The left hand
held neither book nor sword, but the keys. Pastor, III. 569, says, *in einer
derartigen Persönlichkeit lag mehr Stoff zu einem Könige und Feldherrn als zu
einem Priester.*

for the Italians won for him the grateful regard due an Italian patriot.   Like Innocent III., he closed his reign with an œcumenical council.

Cæsar Borgia returned to Rome, was recognized as gonfalonier and given apartments in the Vatican.   Julius had been in amicable relations with the prince in France and advanced his marriage, and Cæsar wrote that in him he had found a second father.   But Cæsar, now that Alexander was dead, was as a galley without a rudder.   He was an upstart; Julius a man of power and far-reaching plans.   Prolonged co-operation between the two was impossible.   The one was sinister, given to duplicity; the other frank and open to brusqueness.   The encroachment of Venice upon the Romagna gave the occasion at once for Cæsar's fall and for the full restoration of papal authority in that region. Supporters Cæsar had none who could be relied upon in the day of ill success.   He no longer had the power which the control of patronage gives.   Julius demanded the keys of the towns of the Romagna as a measure necessary to the dislodgment of Venice. Cæsar yielded, but withdrew to Ostia, meditating revenge.   He was seized, carried back to Rome and placed in the castle of S. Angelo, which had been the scene of his dark crimes.   He was obliged to give up the wealth gotten at his father's death and to sign a release of Forli and other towns.   Liberty was then given him to go where he pleased.   He accepted protection from the Spanish captain, Gonsalvo de Cordova, but on his arrival in Naples the Spaniard, with despicable perfidy, seized the deceived man and sent him to Spain, August, 1504.   For two years he was held a prisoner, when he escaped to the court of his brother-in-law, the king of Navarre.   He was killed at the siege of Viana, 1507, aged 31.   Thus ended the career of the man who had once been the terror of Rome, whom Ranke calls "a virtuoso in crime," and Machiavelli chose as the model of a civil ruler.   This political writer had met Cæsar after Julius' elevation, and in his *Prince*[1]

[1] The *Prince*, written in 1515, was dedicated to Leo X.'s nephew, Lorenzo de' Medici, at a time when it was contemplated giving Lorenzo a large slice of Italian territory to govern.   See Villari : *Machiavelli*, III. 372-424.   Also Louis Dyer : *Machiavelli and the Modern State*, Boston, 1904.   Cæsar Borgia had his laureate, who sung his praises in 12 Latin lyrics, Peter Franciscus Justulus

says, " It seems good to me to propose Cæsar Borgia as an example to be imitated by all those who through fortune and the
arms of others have attained to supreme command.   For, as he
had a great mind and great ambitions, it was not possible for him
to govern otherwise."   Cæsar had said to the theorist, " I rob no
man.   I am here to act the tyrant's part and to do away with tyrants."   Only if to obtain power by darkness and assassination
is worthy of admiration, and if to crush all individual liberty is
a just end of government, can the Machiavellian ideal be regarded with other feelings than those of utter reprobation.
There is something pathetic in the recollection that, to the end,
this inhuman brother retained the affection of his sister, Lucretia.   She pled for his release from imprisonment in Spain, and
Cæsar's letter to her announcing his escape is still extant.[1]
When the rumor came of his death, Lucretia despatched her servant, Tullio, to Navarre to find out the truth, and gave herself up
to protracted prayer on her brother's behalf.   This beautiful example of a sister's love would seem to indicate that Cæsar possessed by nature some excellent qualities.

Julius was also actively engaged in repairing some of the
other evils of Alexander's reign and making amends for its
injustices.   He restored Sermoneta to the dukes of Gaetani.
The document which pronounced severe reprobation upon Alexander ran, " our predecessor, desiring to enrich his own kin,
through no zeal for justice, but by fraud and deceit, sought for
causes to deprive the Gaetani of their possessions."   With decisive firmness, he announced his purpose to assert his lawful
authority over the papal territory and, accompanied by 9 cardinals, he left Rome at the head of 500 men and proceeded to
make good the announcement.   Perugia was quickly brought
to terms ; and, aided by the French, the pope entered Bologna,
against which he had launched the interdict.   Returning to
Rome, he was welcomed as a conqueror.   The victorious troops

of Spoleto. Jupiter, who is represented as about to destroy the world for its
wickedness, perceives that it contains at least one excellent young man,
Cæsar, and sends Mercury to urge him to take up arms for the world's deliverance. *Engl. Hist. Rev.*, Jan., 1902, pp. 15–20.

[1] The letter is given by Gregorovius, *Lucr. Borgia*, p. 319.

passed under triumphal arches, including a reproduction of
Constantine's arch erected on St. Peter's square; and, accompanied by 28 members of the sacred college, Julius gave solemn thanks in St. Peter's.[1]

The next to be brought to terms was Venice.   In vain had
the pope, through letters and legates, called upon the doge to
give up Rimini, Faenza, Forli and other parts of the Romagna
upon which he had laid his hand.   In March, 1508, he joined
the alliance of Cambrai, the other parties being Louis XII.
and the emperor Maximilian, and later, Ferdinand of Spain.
This agreement decided in cold blood upon the division of the
Venetian possessions, and bound the parties to a war against
the Turk.   France was confirmed in the tenure of Milan, and
given Cremona and Brescia.   Maximilian was to have Verona, Padua and Aquileja; Naples, the Venetian territories
in Southern Italy; Hungary, Dalmatia; Savoy, Cyprus; and
the Apostolic see, the lands of which it had been dispossessed.
It was high-handed robbery, even though a pope was party to
it.   Julius, who had promised to add the punishments of the
priestly office to the force of arms, proceeded with merciless
severity, and placed the republic under the interdict, April
27, 1509.   In vain did Venice appeal to God and a general
council.   Past sins enough were written against her to call
for severe treatment.   She was forced to surrender Rimini,
Faenza and Ravenna, and was made to drink the cup of humiliation to its dregs.   The city renounced her claim to nominate
to bishoprics and benefices and tax the clergy without the papal
consent.   The Adriatic she was forced to open to general commerce.   Her envoys, who appeared in Rome to make public
apology for the sins of the proud state, were subjected to
the insult of listening on their knees to a service performed
outside the walls of St. Peter's and lasting an hour; at
every verse of the *Miserere* the pope and 12 cardinals, each
with a golden rod, touched them.   Then, service over, the
doors of the cathedral were thrown open and absolution pro-

[1] The expedition is described by de Grassis, the new master of ceremonies
at the papal palace, who accompanied the expedition, and also by Ægidius of
Viterbo.

nounced.[1] The next time Venice was laid under the papal ban, the measure failed.

Julius' plans were next directed against the French, the impudent invaders of Northern Italy and claimants of sovereignty over it. Times had changed since the pope, as cardinal Julian Rovere, had accompanied the French army under Charles VIII. The absolution of Venice was tantamount to the pope's withdrawal from the alliance of Cambrai. By making Venice his ally, he hoped to bring Ferrara again under the authority of the holy see. The duchy had flourished under the warm support of the French.

Julius now made a far-reaching stroke in securing the help of the Swiss, who had been fighting under the banners of France. The hardy mountaineers, who now find it profitable to entertain tourists from all over the world, then found it profitable to sell their services in war. With the aid of their vigorous countryman, Bishop Schinner of Sitten, afterwards made cardinal, the pope contracted for 6,000 Swiss mercenaries for five years. The localities sending them received 13,000 gulden a year, and each soldier 6 francs a month, and the officers twice that sum. As chaplain of the Swiss troops, Zwingli went to Rome three times, a course of which his patriotism afterwards made him greatly ashamed. The descendants of these Swiss mercenaries defended Louis XVI., and their heroism is commemorated by Thorwaldsen's lion, cut into the rock at Lucerne. Swiss guards, dressed in yellow suits, to this day patrol the approaches and halls of the Vatican.[2]

[1] Pastor, III. 643, contents himself with the simple mention of the absolution of the Venetians, and omits all reference to the humiliating conditions. The Venetian scribblers let loose their pens against Julius and, among other charges, made against him the charge of sodomy. Pastor, III. 644, Note.

[2] Zwingli's friend, Thomas Platter (1499-1582), in speaking in his *Autobiography* of his travels in Germany as a boy to get knowledge and begging his bread, mentions how willing the people were to give him ear, " for they were very fond of the Swiss." At Breslau a family was ready to adopt him, partly on this ground. After the defeat of Marignano, 1515, it was a common saying, so Platter says, " The Swiss have lost their good luck." On one occasion near Dresden, after a good dinner, to which he had been treated, he was taken in to see the mother of the home, who was on her death-bed. She said to Platter and his Swiss companions, " I have heard so many good things about the

The French king, Louis XII. (1498–1515), sought to break Julius' power by adding to the force of arms the weight of a religious assembly and, at his instance, the French bishops met in council at Tours, September, 1510, and declared that the pope had put aside the keys of St. Peter, which his predecessors had employed, and seized the sword of Paul.   They took the ground that princes were justified in opposing him with force, even to withdrawing obedience and invading papal territory.[1]   As in the reign of Philip the Fair, so now, moneys were forbidden transferred from France to Rome, and a call was made by 9 cardinals for a council to meet at Pisa on Sept. 1st, 1511.   This council of Tours denounced Julius as "the new Goliath," and Louis had a coin struck off with the motto, I will destroy the name of Babylon — *perdam Babylonis nomen.*   Calvin, in the year of his death, sent to Renée, duchess of Ferrara, one of these medals which in his letter, dated Jan. 8, 1564, he declared to be the finest present he had it in his power to make her.   Renée was the daughter of Louis XII.   Julius excommunicated Alfonso, duke of Ferrara, as a son of iniquity and a root of perdition.   Thus we have the spectacle of the supreme priest of Christendom and the most Christian king, the First Son of the Church, again engaged in war with one another.

At the opening of the campaign, Julius was in bed with a sickness which was supposed to be mortal; but to the amazement of his court, he suddenly arose and, in the dead of Winter, January, 1511, betook himself to the camp of the papal forces. His promptness of action was in striking contrast to the dilatory policy of Louis, who spent his time writing letters and summoning ecclesiastical assemblies when he ought to have been on the march.   From henceforth till his death, the pope wore a beard, as he is represented in Raphael's famous portrait.[2]   Snow covered the ground, but Julius set an example by enduring all the hardships of the camp.   To accomplish the defeat of the

Swiss that I was very anxious to see one before my death."   See Whitcomb, *Renaissance Source-Book*, p. 108 ; Monroe, *Thos. Platter*, p. 107.

[1] Mansi, XXXII. 555–559.

[2] Creighton, IV. 123, unguardedly says that Julius was the first pope who let his beard grow.   Many of the early bishops of Rome, as depicted in St. Peter's, wore beards.   So did Clement VII. after him, and other popes.

French, he brought about the Holy League, October, 1511, Spain
and Venice being the other parties. Later, these three allies
were joined by Maximilian and Henry VIII. of England. Henry
had been honored with the Golden Rose.[1] Henry's act was England's first positive entrance upon the field of general European
politics.

In the meantime the French were carrying on the Council of
Pisa. The pope prudently counteracted its influence by calling a council to meet in the Lateran. Christendom was rent
by two opposing ecclesiastical councils as well as by two opposing armies. The armies met in decisive conflict under the walls
of the old imperial city of Ravenna. The leader of the French,
Gaston de Foix, nephew of the French king, though only 24,
approved himself, in spite of his youth, one of the foremost captains of his age. Bologna had fallen before his arms, and now
Ravenna yielded to the same necessity after a bloody battle.
The French army numbered 25,000, the army of the League
20,000. In the French camp was the French legate, Cardinal
Sanseverino, mounted and clad in steel armor, his tall form tow-
ering above the rest. Prominent on the side of the allied army
was the papal legate, Cardinal de' Medici, clad in white, and Giulio Medici, afterwards Clement VII. The battle took place on
Easter Day, 1512. Gaston de Foix, thrown to the ground by the
fall of his horse, was put to death by some of the seasoned Spanish soldiers whom Gonsalvo had trained. The victor, whose
battle cry was " Let him that loves me follow me," was borne
into the city in his coffin. Rimini, Forli and other cities of the
Romagna opened their gates to the French. Cardinal Medici
was in their hands.

The papal cause seemed to be hopelessly lost, but the spirit
of Julius rose with the defeat. He is reported to have exclaimed,
" I will stake 100,000 ducats and my crown that I will drive the
French out of Italy," and the victory of Ravenna proved to be
another Cannæ. The hardy Swiss, whose numbers Cardinal
Schinner had increased to 18,000, and the Venetians pushed the
campaign, and the barbarians, as Julius called the French, were
forced to give up what they had gained, to surrender Milan and

[1] See the pope's letter granting it, Mansi, XXXII. 554.

gradually to retire across the Alps.   Parma and Piacenza, by
virtue of the grant of Mathilda, passed into his hands, as did also
Reggio.   The victory was celebrated in Rome on an elaborate
scale.   Cannons boomed from S. Angelo, and thanks were
given in all the churches.   In recognition of their services, the
pope gave to the Swiss two large banners and the permanent
title of Protectors of the Apostolic see — *auxiliatores sedis apostolicæ.*   Such was the end of this remarkable campaign.

Julius purchased Siena from the emperor for 30,000 ducats
and, with the aid of the seasoned Spanish troops, took Florence
and restored the Medici to power.   In December, 1513, Maximilian, who at one time conceived the monstrous idea of combining with his imperial dignity the office of supreme pontiff,
announced his support of the Lateran council, the pope having
agreed to use all the spiritual measures within his reach to secure the complete abasement of Venice.   The further execution of the plans was prevented by the pope's death.   In his
last hours, in a conversation with Cardinal Grimani, he pounded
on the floor with his cane, exclaiming, " If God gives me life, I
will also deliver the Neapolitans from the yoke of the Spaniards
and rid the land of them." [1]

The Pisan council had opened Sept. 1, 1511, with only two
archbishops and 14 bishops present.   First and last 6 cardinals
attended, Carvajal, Briçonnet, Prie, d'Albret, Sanseverino and
Borgia.   The Universities of Paris, Toulouse and Poictiers were
represented by doctors.   After holding three sessions, it moved
to Milan, where the victory of Ravenna gave it a short breath of
life.   When the French were defeated, it again moved to Asti
in Piedmont, where it held a ninth session, and then it adjourned
to Lyons, where it dissolved of itself. [2]   Hergenröther, Pastor and
other Catholic historians take playful delight in calling the council the little council — *conciliabulum* — and a conventicle, terms
which Julius applied to it in his bulls. [3]   Among its acts were a
fulmination against the synod Julius was holding in the Lateran,
and it had the temerity to cite the pope to appear, and even to
declare him deposed from all spiritual and temporal authority.

[1] Pastor, III. 725.   [2] Hefele-Hergenröther, VIII. 520.
[3] See Mansi, XXXII. 570.

The synod also reaffirmed the decrees of the 5th session of the Council of Constance, placing general councils over the pope.

Very different in its constitution and progress was the Fifth Lateran, the last œcumenical council of the Middle Ages, and the 18th in the list of œcumenical councils, as accepted by the Roman Catholic Church. It lasted for nearly five years, and closed on the eve of the nailing of the XCV theses on the church door in Wittenberg. It is chiefly notable for what it failed to do rather than for anything it did. The only one of its declarations which is of more than temporary interest was the deliverance, reaffirming Boniface's theory of the supremacy of the Roman pontiff over all potentates and individuals whatsoever.

In his summons calling the council, Julius deposed the cardinals, who had entered into the Pisan synod, as schismatics and sons of darkness.[1] The attendance did not compare in weight or numbers with the Council of Constance. At the 1st session, held May 3, 1512, there were present 16 cardinals, 12 patriarchs, 10 archbishops, 70 bishops and 3 generals of orders. The opening address by Ægidius of Viterbo, general of the Augustinian order, after dwelling upon the recent glorious victories of Julius, magnified the weapons of light at the council's disposal, piety, prayers, vows and the breastplate of faith. The council should devote itself to placating all Christian princes in order that the arms of the Christian world might be turned against the flagrant enemy of Christ, Mohammed. The council then declared the adherents of the Pisan conventicle schismatics and laid France under the interdict. Julius, who listened to the eloquent address, was present at 4 sessions.

At the 2d session, Cajetan dilated at length on the pet papal theory of the two swords.

In the 4th session, the Venetian, Marcello, pronounced a eulogy upon Julius which it would be hard to find excelled for

---

[1] A pamphlet war was waged over the council. Among the writers on the papal side was Thomas de Vio Gaeta, general of the Dominican order and afterwards famous as Cardinal Cajetan, who had the colloquies with Luther. His tracts were ordered burnt by Louis XII. He took the ground that no council can be œcumenical which has not the pope's support. An account of this literary skirmish is given by Hefele-Hergenröther, VIII. 470–480.

fulsome flattery in the annals of oratory. After having borne intolerable cold, so the eulogist declared, and sleepless nights and endured sickness in the interests of the Church, and having driven the French out of Italy, there remained for the pontiff the greater triumphs of peace. Julius must be pastor, shepherd, physician, ruler, administrator and, in a word, another God on earth.[1]

At the 5th session, held during the pope's last illness, a bull was read, severely condemning simony at papal elections. The remaining sessions of the council were held under Julius' successor.

When Julius came to die, he was not yet 70. No man of his time had been an actor in so many stirring scenes. On his deathbed he called for Paris de Grassis, his master of ceremonies, and reminded him how little respect had been paid to the bodies of deceased popes within his recollection. Some of them had been left indecently nude. He then made him promise to see to it that he should have decent care and burial.[2] The cardinals were summoned. The dying pontiff addressed them first in Latin, and implored them to avoid all simony in the coming election, and reminded them that it was for them and not for the council to choose his successor. He pardoned the schismatic cardinals, but excluded them from the conclave to follow his death. And then, as if to emphasize the tie of birth, he changed to Italian and besought them to confirm his nephew, the duke of Urbino, in the possession of Pesaro, and then he bade them farewell. A last remedy, fluid gold, was administered, but in vain. He died Feb. 20, 1513.[3]

[1] *Tu pastor, tu medicus, tu gubernator, tu cultor, tu denique alter Deus in terris*, Mansi, XXXII. 761. Hefele-Hergenröther, VII. 528-531, pronounce this expression, God on earth, used before by Gregory II., a rhetorical flourish and nothing more. See also Pastor, III. 725.

[2] De Grassis reports the rumors abroad concerning the pope's mortal malady. One of them was the Gallic disease, and another that the pope's stomach had given way under excessive indulgence. He also speaks of the great number who went to look at the pope's corpse and to kiss his feet. Döllinger, III. 432.

[3] A satire, called *Julius exclusus*, which appeared after the pontiff's death, represented him as appearing at the gate of heaven with great din and noise. Peter remarked that, as he was a brave man, had a large army and much gold and was a busy builder, he might build his own paradise. At the same time the Apostle reminded him he would have to build the foundations deep and strong

The scenes which ensued were very different from those which followed upon the death of Alexander VI. A sense of awe and reverence filled the city. The dead pontiff was looked upon as a patriot, and his services to civil order in Rome and its glory counterbalanced his deficiencies as a priest of God.[1]

It was of vast profit that the Vatican had been free from the domestic scandals which had filled it so long. From a worldly standpoint, Julius had exalted the papal throne to the eminence of the national thrones of Europe. In the terrific convulsion which Luther's onslaughts produced, the institution of the papacy might have fallen in ruins had not Julius re-established it by force of arms. But in vain will the student look for signs that Julius II. had any intimation of the new religious reforms which the times called for and Luther began. What measures this pope, strong in will and bold in execution, might have employed if the movement in the North had begun in his day, no one can surmise. The monk of Erfurt walked the streets of Rome during this pontificate for the first and only time. While Luther was ascending the *scala santa* on his knees and running about to the churches, wishing his parents were in purgatory that he might pray them out, Julius was having per-

---

to resist the assaults of the devil. Julius retorted by peremptorily giving Peter three weeks to open heaven to him. In case he refused, he would open siege against him with 60,000 men. This recalls a story Dr. Philip Schaff used to tell of Gregory XVI., with whom, as a young graduate of Berlin, he had an audience. Gregory had a reputation with the Romans for being a connoisseur of wines. At his death, so the Roman wits reported, he appeared at the gate of heaven and, drawing out his keys, tried to unlock the gate. The keys would not fit. Peter, hearing the noise, looked out and, seeing the bunch of keys, told his vicar that he had brought with him by mistake the keys to his wine cellar, and must return to his palace and get the right set.

[1] Guicciardini pronounces Julius a priest only in name. A letter dated Rome, Feb. 24, 1513, and quoted by Brosch, p. 363, has this statement, *hic pontifex nos omnes, omnem Italiam a Barbarorum et Gallorum manibus eripuit*, an expression used by Ægidius and Marcello before the Lateran council. See also Paris de Grassis in Döllinger, p. 432. Pastor, III. 732, and Hergenröther, *Conciliengesch.*, VIII. 535, justify Julius' attention to war on the ground that he was fighting in a righteous cause and for possessions he had held as temporal prince ever since the 8th century. The right of a pope to defend the papal state is inherent in the very existence of a papal state. Even a saint, Leo IX., urges Pastor, p. 741, followed the camp.

fected a magnificently jewelled tiara costing 200,000 ducats, which he put on for the first time on the anniversary of his coronation, 1511.   These two men, both of humble beginnings, would have been more a match for each other than Luther and Julius' successor, the Medici, the man of luxurious culture.[1]

Under Julius II. the papal finances flourished.   Great as were the expenditures of his campaigns, he left plate and coin estimated to be worth 400,000 ducats.   A portion of this fund was the product of the sale of indulgences.   He turned the forgiveness of sins for the present time and in purgatory into a matter of merchandise.[2]

In another place, Julius will be presented from the standpoint of art and culture, whose splendid patron he was.   What man ever had the privilege of bringing together three artists of such consummate genius as Bramante, Michael Angelo and Raphael!   His portrait in the Pitti gallery, Florence, forms a rich study for those who seek in the lines and colors of Raphael's art the secret of the pontiff's power.[3]   The painter has represented Julius as an old man with beard, and with his left hand grasping the arm of the chair in which he sits.   His fingers wear jewelled rings.   The forehead is high, the lips firmly pressed, the eyes betokening weariness, determination and commanding energy.

In the history of the Western Continent, Julius also has some place.   In 1504 he created an archbishopric and two bishoprics of Hispaniola, or Hayti.   The prelates to whom they were assigned never crossed the seas.   Seven years later, 1511, he revoked these creations and established the sees of San Domingo and Concepcion de la Vega on the island of Hayti and the see of San Juan in Porto Rico, all three subject to the metropolitan supervision of the see of Seville.

---

[1] See Ranke : *Hist. of the Popes*, I. 35.

[2] Pastor, III. 575, condemns Julius under this head, *tadelnswerth erscheint dass das Ablassgeschäft vielfach zu einer Finanzoperation wurde.*

[3] An original cartoon of this portrait is preserved in the Corsini palace, Florence.   In 1889 I met Professor Weizsäcker of Tübingen in Florence standing before Julius' portrait and studying it.   I had been with him in his home before he started on his journey, and he told me that one of the chief pleasures which he was anticipating from his Italian trip was the study of that portrait of one of the most vigorous — *thatkräftig* — of the popes.

§ 56. *Leo X.* 1513-1521.

The warlike Julius II. was followed on the pontifical throne by the voluptuary, Leo X., — the prelate whose iron will and candid mind compel admiration by a prince given to the pursuit of pleasure and an adept in duplicity. Leo loved ease and was without high aims. His Epicurean conception of the supreme office of Christendom was expressed in a letter he sent a short time after his election to his brother Julian. In it were these words, " Let us enjoy the papacy, for God has given it to us." [1] The last pontificate of the Middle Ages corresponded to the worldly philosophy of the pontiff. Leo wanted to have a good time. The idea of a spiritual mission never entered his head. No effort was made, emanating from the Vatican, to further the interests of true religion.

Born in Florence, Dec. 11, 1475, Giovanni de' Medici, the second son of Lorenzo the Magnificent, had every opportunity which family distinction, wealth and learned tutors, such as Poliziano, could give. At 7 he received the tonsure, and at once the world of ecclesiastical preferment was opened to the child. Louis XI. of France presented him with the abbey of Fonte Dolce, and at 8 he was nominated to the archbishopric of Aix, the nomination, however, not being confirmed. A canonry in each of the cathedral churches of Tuscany was set apart for him, and his appointments soon reached the number of 27, one of them being the abbacy of Monte Cassino, and another the office of papal pronotary. [2]

The highest dignities of the Church were in store for the lad and, before he had reached the age of 14, he was made cardinal-deacon by Innocent VIII., March 9, 1489. Three

---

[1] These words are upon the testimony of the contemporary ambassador, Marino Giorgi, and cannot be set aside. Similar testimony is given by a biographer of Leo in *Cod. Vat.*, 3920, which Döllinger quotes, *Papstthum*, p. 484, and which runs *volo ut pontificatu isto quam maxime perfruamur.* Pastor, IV. 353, while trying to break the force of the testimony for Leo's words, pronounces the love of pleasure a fundamental and insatiable element of his nature — *eine unersättliche Vergnügungssucht*, etc. Hefele-Knöpfler, *Kirchengesch.*, p. 488, speak in the same vein when they say, *Des neuen Papstes vorzüglichstes Streben galt heiterem Lebensgenuss*, etc.

[2] See Vaughan, p. 13 sq.

years later, March 8, 1492, Giovanni received in Rome formal
investment into the prerogatives of his office. The letter, which
Lorenzo wrote on this latter occasion, is full of the affectionate
counsels of a father and the prudent suggestions of the tried
man of the world, and belongs in a category with the letters
of Lord Chesterfield to his son.   Lorenzo reminded Giovanni
of his remarkable fortune in being made a prince of the church,
all the more remarkable because he was not only the youngest
member of the college of cardinals, but the first cardinal to
receive the dignity at so tender an age.   With pardonable
pride, he spoke of it as the highest honor ever conferred upon
the Medicean house.   He warned his son that Rome was the
sink of all iniquities and exhorted him to lead a virtuous life,
to avoid ostentation, to rise early, an admonition the son never
followed, and to use his opportunities to serve his native city.
Lorenzo died a few months later.[1] Forthwith the young prelate was appointed papal legate to Tuscany, with residence in
his native city.

When Julius died, Giovanni de' Medici was only 37.   In
proceeding to Rome, he was obliged to be carried in a litter,
on account of an ulcer for which an operation was performed
during the meeting of the conclave.   Giovanni, who belonged
to the younger party, had won many friends by his affable
manners and made no enemies, and his election seems to have
been secured without any special effort on his part.   The great-
grandson of the banker, Cosimo, chose the name of Leo X.
He was consecrated to the priesthood March 17, 1513, and to
the episcopate March 19.   The election was received by the
Romans with every sign of popular approval.   On the festivities of the coronation 100,000 ducats, or perhaps as much as
150,000 ducats, were expended, a sum which the frugality of
Julius had stored up.

The procession was participated in by 250 abbots, bishops
and archbishops.   Alfonso of Este, whom Julius II. had excommunicated, led the pope's white horse, the same one he
had ridden the year before at Ravenna.   On the houses and

[1] The famous letter is given by Roscoe, Bohn's ed., pp. 285–288, and
Vaughan, p. 23 sqq.

POPE LEO X

on the arches, spanning the streets, might be seen side by side statues of Cosmas and Damian, the patrons of the Medicean house, and of the Olympian gods and nymphs. On one arch at the Piazza di Parione were depicted Perseus, Apollo, Moses and Mercury, sacred and mythological characters conjoined, as Alexander Severus joined the busts of Abraham and Orpheus in his palace in the third century. A bishop, afterwards Cardinal Andrea della Valle, placed on his arch none but ancient divinities, Apollo, Bacchus, Mercury, Hercules and Venus, together with fauns and Ganymede. Antonio of San Marino, the silversmith, decorated his house with a marble statue of Venus, under which were inscribed the words —

> Mars ruled; then Pallas, but Venus will rule forever.[1]

As a ruler, Leo had none of the daring and strength of his predecessor. He pursued a policy of opportunism and stooped to the practice of duplicity with his allies as well as with his enemies. On all occasions he was ready to shift to the winning side. To counteract the designs of the French upon Northern Italy, he entered with Maximilian, Henry VIII. and Ferdinand of Spain into the treaty of Mechlin, April 5, 1513. He had the pleasure of seeing the French beaten by Henry VIII. at the battle of the Spurs[2] and again driven out of Italy by the bravery of the Swiss at Novara, June 6. Louis easily yielded to the pope's advances for peace and acknowledged the authority of the Lateran council. The deposed cardinals, Carvajal and Sanseverino, who had been active in the Pisan council, signed a humiliating confession and were reinstated. Leo

---

[1] See Schulte, p. 198 sq., and Reumont, III., part II., p. 57. In front of the house of the banker, Agostino Chigi, were seen two persons representing Apollo and Mercury, and two little Moors, together with the inscription —

> *Olim habuit Cypria sua tempora, tempora Mavors*
> *Olim habuit, sua nunc tempora Pallas habet.*

> The goddess of Cyprus had her day and also Mars,
> But now Minerva reigns.

[2] August 16, 1513. The Scotch king, James IV., who had married Henry's sister, Margaret, joined the French. The memorable defeat at Flodden followed, Sept. 9, 1513. James and the flower of the Scotch nobility fell. Leo recognized Henry's victories by conferring upon him the consecrated sword and hat which it was the pope's custom to set aside on Christmas day.

remarked to them that they were like the sheep in the Gospel which was lost and was found. A secret compact, entered into between the pontiff and King Louis, and afterwards joined by Henry VIII., provided for the French king's marriage with Mary Tudor, Henry's younger sister, and the recognition of his claims in Northern Italy. But at the moment these negotiations were going on, Leo was secretly engaged in the attempt to divorce Venice from the French and to defeat the French plans for the reoccupation of Milan. Louis' career was suddenly cut short by death, Jan. 1, 1515, at the age of 52, three months after his nuptials with Mary, who was sixteen at the time of her marriage.

The same month Leo came to an understanding with Maximilian and Spain, whereby Julian de' Medici, the pope's brother, should receive Parma, Piacenza and Reggio. Leo purchased Modena from the emperor for 40,000 ducats, and was sending 60,000 ducats monthly for the support of the troops of his secret allies.

At the very same moment, faithless to his Spanish allies, the pope was carrying on negotiations with Venice to drive them out of Italy.

Louis' son-in-law and successor, Francis I., a warlike and enterprising prince, held the attention of Europe for nearly a quarter of a century with his campaigns against Charles V., whose competitor he was for the imperial crown. Carrying out Louis' plans, and accompanied by an army of 35,000 men with 60 cannon, he marched in the direction of Milan, inflicting at Marignano, Sept., 1515, a disastrous defeat upon the 20,000 Swiss mercenaries.[1] At the first news of the disaster, Leo was thrown into consternation, but soon recovered his composure, exclaiming in the presence of the Venetian ambassador, "We

---

[1] The battle is vividly described by D. J. Dierauer, *Gesch. der schweizer-ischen Eidgenossenschaft*, 2 vols., Gotha, 1892, vol. II. 451 sqq. On the second day of the battle, the arrival of the Venetian troops gave victory to the French. Of the 12,000 left on the field dead, the most were Swiss. Before entering the battle, as was their custom, the mountaineers engaged in prayer, and the leader, Steiner of Zug, after repeating the usual formula of devotion unto death, threw, in the name of the Trinity, a handful of earth over his fellow-soldiers' heads.

shall have to put ourselves into the hands of the king and cry out for mercy." The victory, was the reply, "will not inure to your hurt or the damage of the Apostolic see. The French king is a son of the Church." And so it proved to be. Without a scruple, as it would seem, the pope threw off his alliances with the emperor and Ferdinand and hurried to get the best terms he could from Francis.

They met at Bologna. Conducted by 20 cardinals, Francis entered Leo's presence and, uncovering his head, bowed three times and kissed the pontiff's hand and foot. Leo wore a tiara glittering with gems, and a mantle, heavy with cloth of gold. The French orator set forth how the French kings from time immemorial had been protectors of the Apostolic see, and how Francis had crossed the mountains and rivers to show his submission. For three days pontiff and king dwelt together in the same palace. It was agreed that Leo yield up Parma and Piacenza to the French, and a concordat was worked out which took the place of the Pragmatic Sanction. This document, dating from the Council of Basel, and ratified by the synod of Bourges, placed the nomination to all French bishoprics, abbeys and priories in the hands of the king, and this clause the concordat preserved. On the other hand, the clauses in the Pragmatic Sanction were omitted which made the pope subject to general councils and denied to him the right to collect annates from French benefices higher and lower.

The election of a successor to the emperor Maximilian, who died Jan., 1519, put Leo's diplomacy to the severest test. Ferdinand the Catholic, who had seen the Moorish domination in Spain come to an end and the Americas annexed to his crown, and had been invested by Julius II. in 1510 with the kingdom of Naples, died in 1516, leaving his grandson, Charles, heir to his dominions. Now, by the death of his paternal grandfather Maximilian, Charles was heir of the Netherlands and the lands of the Hapsburgs and natural claimant of the imperial crown. Leo preferréd Francis, but Charles had the right of lineage and the support of the German people. To prevent Charles' election, and to avoid the ill-will of Francis, he agitated through his legate, Cajetan, the election of either Frederick the

Wise, elector of Saxony, or the elector of Brandenburg. Secretly
he entered into the plans of Francis and allowed the archbishops
of Treves and Cologne to be assured of their promotion to the
sacred college, provided they would cast their electoral vote for
the French king.   But to be sure of his ground, no matter who
might be elected, Leo entered also into a secret agreement with
Charles.   Both candidates had equal reason for believing they
had the pope on their side.[1]   Finally, when it became evident
that Francis was out of the race, and after the electors had
already assembled in Frankfurt, Leo wrote to Cajetan that
it was no use beating one's head against the wall and that he
should fall in with the election of Charles.   Leo had stipulated
100,000 ducats as the price of his support of Charles.[2] He
sent a belated letter of congratulation to the emperor-elect,
which was full of tropical phrases, and in 1521, at the Diet of
Worms, the assembly before which Luther appeared, he concluded with Charles an alliance against his former ally, Francis.
The agreement included the reduction of Milan, Parma and
Piacenza. The news of the success of Charles' troops in taking these cities reached Leo only a short time before his death,
Dec. 1. 1521.   For the cause of Protestantism, the papal alliance with the emperor against France proved to be highly
favorable, for it necessitated the emperor's absence from Germany.

In his administration of the papacy, Leo X. was not unmindful of the interests of his family.   Julian, his younger brother,
was made gonfalonier of the Church, and was married to the
sister of Francis I.'s mother.   For a time he was in possession
of Parma, Piacenza and Reggio. Death terminated his career,
1516.   His only child, the illegitimate Hippolytus, d. 1535,
was afterwards made cardinal.

The worldly hopes of the Medicean dynasty now centred in
Lorenzo de' Medici, the son of Leo's older brother.   After the

---

[1] Pastor, IV. 185 sq., strongly condemns Leo's two-tongued diplomacy,
doppelzüngiges Verhalten. Leo's brief, authorizing Francis to make a promise
of red hats to the two archbishops, is dated March 12, 1519.

[2] One-half was to be paid in cash and the other half to be deposited with
the Fuggers, Schulte, p. 196.

deposition of Julius' nephew, he was invested with the duchy of Urbino.   In 1518 he was married to Madeleine de la Tour d'Auvergne, a member of the royal house of France.   Leo's presents to the marital pair were valued at 300,000 ducats, among them being a bedstead of tortoise-shell inlaid with mother-of-pearl and precious stones.   They took up their abode at Florence, but both husband and wife died a year after the marriage, leaving behind them a daughter who, as Catherine de' Medici, became famous in the history of France and the persecution of the Huguenots.   With Lorenzo's death, the last descendant of the male line of the house founded by Cosimo de' Medici became extinct.

In 1513 Leo admitted his nephew, Innocent Cibo, and his cousin, Julius, to the sacred college.   Innocent Cibo, a young man of 21, was the son of Franceschetto Cibo, Innocent VIII.'s son, and Maddelina de' Medici, Leo's sister.   His low morals made him altogether unfit for an ecclesiastical dignity.   Julius de' Medici, afterwards Clement VII., was the bastard son of Leo's uncle, who was killed in the Pazzi conspiracy under Sixtus IV., 1478.   The impediment of the illegitimate birth was removed by a papal decree.[1]   Two nephews, Giovanni Salviati and Nicolas Ridolfi, sons of two of Leo's sisters, were also vested with the red hat, 1517.   On this occasion Leo appointed no less than thirty-one cardinals.   Among them were Cajetan, the learned general of the Dominicans, Ægidius of Viterbo, who had won an enviable fame by his address opening the Lateran council, and Adrian of Utrecht, Leo's successor in the papal chair.   Of the number was Alfonso of Portugal, a child of 7, but it was understood he was not to enter upon the duties of his office till he had reached the age of 14.   Among the other appointees were princes entirely unworthy of any ecclesiastical office.[2]

The Vatican was thrown into a panic in 1517 by a conspiracy

---

[1] The investigation, started by Leo, resulted in making it appear that Julius' mother, Floreta, and his father had agreed to regard themselves as married, though a formal service was wanting.

[2] Silvio Passerini, one of the fortunate candidates, was a prince of benefice-hunters.   Pastor, IV. 139, gives fifty-five notices of benefices bestowed on him from Leo's *Regesta*.   He calls the list of the places he received as *wahrhaft erschreckend*, "something terrifying."

directed by Cardinal Petrucci of Siena, one of the younger set
of cardinals with whom the pope had been intimate. Embittered
by Leo's interference in his brother's administration of Siena and
by the deposition of the duke of Urbino, Petrucci plotted to have
the pope poisoned by a physician, Battesta de Vercelli, a special-
ist on ulcers. The plot was discovered, and Petrucci, who came
to Rome on a safe-conduct procured from the pope by the Spanish ambassador, was cast into the Marroco, the deepest dungeon
of S. Angelo. On being reminded of the safe-conduct, Leo replied to the ambassador that no one was safe who was a poisoner.
Cardinals Sauli and Riario were entrapped and also thrown into
the castle-dungeons. Two other cardinals were suspected of
being in the plot, but escaped. Petrucci and the physician were
strangled to death; Riario and Sauli were pardoned. Riario,
who had witnessed the dastardly assassination in the cathedral
of Florence 40 years before, was the last prominent representative of the family of Sixtus IV. Torture brought forth the
confession that the plotters contemplated making him pope.
Leo set the price of the cardinal's absolution high, — 150,000
ducats to be paid in a year, and another 150,000 to be paid
by his relatives in case Riario left his palace. He finally secured the pope's permission to leave Rome, and died, 1521, at
Naples.

One of the sensational pageants which occurred during Leo's
pontificate was on the arrival of a delegation from Portugal,
1514, to announce to the pope the obedience of its king, Emmanu-
el. The king sent a large number of presents, among them
horses from Persia, a young panther, two leopards and a white
elephant. The popular jubilation over the procession of the
wild beasts reached its height when the elephant, taking water
into his proboscis, spurted it over the onlookers.[1] In recognition of the king's courtesy, the pope vested in Portugal all the
lands west of Capes Bojador and Non to the Indies.

The Fifth Lateran resumed its sessions in April, 1513, a month
after Leo's election. The council ratified the concordat with
France, and at the 8th session, Dec. 19, 1513, solemnly affirmed

---

[1] The elephant became the subject of quite an extensive literature, poets joining others in setting forth his peculiarities. See Pastor, IV. 52, Note.

the doctrine of the soul's immortality.[1]   The affirmation was called forth by the scepticism of the Arabic philosophers and the Italian pantheists.   A single vote recorded against the decree came from the bishop of Bergamo, who took the ground that it is not the business of theologians to spend their time sitting in judgment upon the theories of philosophers.

The invention of printing was recognized by the council as a gift from heaven intended for the glory of God and the propagation of good science, but the legitimate printing of books was restricted to such as might receive the sanction of the master of the palace in Rome or, elsewhere, by the sanction of the bishop or inquisitors who were charged with examining the contents of books.[2]   The condemnation of all books, distasteful to the hierarchy, was already well under way.

The council approved the proposed Turkish crusade and levied a tenth on Christendom.   Its collection was forbidden in England by Henry VIII.   Cajetan presented the cause in an eloquent address at the Diet of Augsburg, 1518.   Altogether the most significant of the council's deliverances was the bull, *Pater æternus*, labelled as approved by its authority and sent out by Leo, 1516.[3]   Here the position is reaffirmed — the position taken definitely by Pius II. and Sixtus IV. — that it is given to the Roman pontiff to have authority over all Church councils and to appoint, transfer and dissolve them at will. This famous deliverance expressly renewed and ratified the constitution of Boniface VIII., the *Unam sanctam*, asserting it

[1] The concordat met with serious resistance in France both from parliament and the University of Paris on the ground that it set aside the decisions of the Councils of Constance and Basel on the question of conciliar authority, and thus overthrew the Gallican liberties.   The rector of the university forbade the university printer issuing the document, but he was brought to time by Leo instructing his legate to pronounce censure against him and the university, who "thinking themselves to be wise, had become fools."

[2] *Perpetuis futuris temporibus, nullus librum aliquem seu aliam quamcunque scripturam tam in urbe nostra quam aliis quibusvis civitatibus et diocesibus imprimere seu imprimi facere præsumat*, Mansi, XXXII. 912 sq.   Also in part in Mirbt, p. 177.

[3] *Sacro concilio approbante.*   Döllinger, *Papstthum*, p. 185, affirms that, in far-reaching significance, no other rule ever passed in a Roman synod equals this bull.

to be altogether necessary to salvation for all Christians to be
subject to the Roman pontiff.[1] To this was added the atrocious declaration that disobedience to the pope is punishable
with death.   Innocent III. had quoted Deut. 17 : 12 in favor
of this view, falsifying the translation of the Vulgate, which he
made to read, "that whoever does not submit himself to the
judgment of the high-priest, him shall the judge put to death."
The council, in separating the quotations, falsely derived it
from the Book of the Kings.[2]

Nor should it be overlooked that in his bull the infallible
Leo X. certified to a falsehood when he expressly declared that
the Fathers, in the ancient councils, in order to secure confirmation for their decrees, "humbly begged the pope's approbation." This he affirmed of the councils of Nice, 325, Ephesus,
Chalcedon, Constantinople, 680, and Nice, 787.   214 years before, when Boniface VIII. issued his bull, Philip the Fair was
at hand to resist it.   The French sovereign now on the throne,
Francis I., made no dissent.   The concordat had just been ratified by the council.

The council adjourned March 16, 1517, a bare majority of
two votes being for adjournment.   Writers of Gallican sympathies have denied its œcumenical character.   On the other
hand, Cardinal Hergenröther regrets that the Church has taken
a position to it of a stepmother to her child.   Pastor says there
was already legislation enough before the Fifth Lateran sat
to secure all the reforms needed.   Not laws but action was required.   Funk expresses the truth when he says, what the
council did for Church reform is hardly worth noting down.[3]

In passing judgment upon Leo X., the chief thing to be said
is that he was a worldling.   Religion was not a serious matter with him.   Pleasure was his daily concern, not piety.   He
gave no earnest thought to the needs of the Church.   It would

---

[1] Mansi, XXXII. 968; Mirbt, p. 178. *Solum Rom. pontificem auctoritatem super omnia concilia habentem et conciliorum indicendorum transferendorum ac dissolvendorum plenum jus et potestatem habere . . . et cum de necessitate salutis existat omnes Christi fideles Romano pontifici subesse*, etc.

[2] *Petri successores . . . quibus ex libri Regum testimonio ita obedire necesse
est, ut qui non obedierit, morte moriatur.*

[3] *Kirchengesch.*, p. 383.

scarcely be possible to lay more stress upon this feature in the life of Louis XIV., or Charles II., than does Pastor in his treatment of Leo's career.   Reumont[1] says it did not enter Leo's head that it was the task and duty of the papacy to regenerate itself, and so to regenerate Christendom.   Leo's personal habits are not a matter of conjecture.   They lie before us in a number of contemporary descriptions.   In his reverend regard for the papal office, Luther did Leo an unintentional injustice when he compared him to Daniel among the lions. The pope led the cardinals in the pursuit of pleasure and in extravagance in the use of money.   To one charge, unchasteness, Leo seems not to have exposed himself.   How far this was a virtue, or how far it was forced upon him by nature, cannot be said.

The qualities, with which nature endowed him, remained with him to the end.   He was good-humored, affable and accessible.   He was often found playing chess or cards with his cardinals.   At the table he was usually temperate, though he spent vast sums in the entertainment of others.   He kept a monk capable of swallowing a pigeon at one mouthful and 40 eggs at a sitting.   To his dress he gave much attention, and delighted to adorn his fingers with gems.

The debt art owes to Leo X. may be described in another place.   Rome became what Paris afterwards was, the centre of luxury, art and architectural improvement.   The city grew with astonishing rapidity.   "New buildings," said an orator, "are planted every day.   Along the Tiber and on the Janicular hill new sections arise."   Luigi Gradenigo, the Venetian ambassador, reports that in the ten years following Leo's election, 10,000 buildings had been put up by persons from Northern Italy.   The palaces of bankers, nobles and cardinals were filled with the richest furniture of the world.   Artists were drawn from France and Spain as well as Italy, and every kind of personality who could afford amusement to others.

The Vatican was the resort of poets, musicians, artists, and also of actors and buffoons.   Leo joined in their conversation and laughed at their wit.   He even vied with the poets in

[1] III., part II., p. 128.

making verses off-hand.   Musical instruments ornamented
with gold and silver he purchased in Germany.   With almost
Oriental abandon he allowed himself to be charmed with entertainments of all sorts.

Among Leo's amusements the chase took a leading place,
though it was forbidden by canonical law to the clergy.   Fortunately for his reputation, he was not bound, as pope, by
canon law.   As Louis XIV. said, "I am the state," so the pope
might have said, "I am the canon law."   Portions of the year
he passed booted and spurred.   He fished in the lake of Bolsena and other waters.   He takes an inordinate pleasure in
the chase, wrote the Venetian ambassador.   He hunted in the
woods of Viterbo and Nepi and in the closer vicinity of Rome,
but with most pleasure at his hunting villa, Magliana.   He
reserved for his own use a special territory.   The hunting
parties were often large.[1]   At a meet, prepared by Alexander Farnese, the pope found himself in the midst of 18 cardinals, besides other prelates, musicians, actors and servants.
A pack of sixty or seventy dogs aided the hunters.   Magliana
was five miles from Rome, on the Tiber.   This favorite pleasure castle is now a desolate farmhouse.   In strange contrast
to his own practice, the pope, at the appeal of the king of
Portugal, forbade the privileges of the chase to the Portuguese clergy.

The theatre was another passion to which Leo devoted himself.   He attended plays in the palaces of the cardinals and
rich bankers and in S. Angelo, and looked on as they were performed in the Vatican itself.   Bibbiena, one of the favorite
members of his cabinet, was a writer of salacious comedies.
One of these, the *Calandria*, Leo witnessed performed in
1514 in his palace.   The ballet was freely danced in some of
these plays, as in the lascivious *Suppositi* by Ariosto, played
before the pope in S. Angelo on Carnival Sunday.   Another
of the plays was the *Mandragola*, by Machiavelli, to modern
performances of which in Florence young people are not ad-

---

[1] Pastor, who gives eight solid pages, IV. 407-415, to an account of Leo's
hunting expeditions, speaks of his passion for the chase as his *leidenschaftliche
Jagdliebhaberei*.

mitted.[1]   An account given of one of these plays by the ambassador of Ferrara, Paolucci, represented a girl pleading with
Venus for a lover.   At once, eight monks appeared on the
scene in their gray mantles.   Venus bade the girl give them
a potion.   Amor then awoke the sleepers with his arrow.
The monks danced round Amor and made love to the girl.
At last they threw aside their monastic garb and all joined
in a moresca.   On the girl's asking what they could do with
their arms, they fell to fighting, and all succumbed except
one, and he received the girl as the prize of his prowess.[2]
And Leo was the high-priest of Christendom, the professed
successor of Peter the Apostle!

Festivities of all sorts attracted the attention of the good-
natured pope.   With 14 cardinals he assisted at the marriage
of the rich Sienese banker, Agostino Chigi, to his mistress.
The entertainment was given at Chigi's beautiful house, the
Farnesina. This man was considered the most fortunate banker
of his day in Rome.   The kings of Spain and France and
princes of Germany sent him presents, and sought from him
loans.   Even the sultan was said to have made advances for
his friendship.   His income was estimated at 70,000 ducats a
year, and he left behind him 800,000 ducats. This Crœsus was
only fifty-five when death separated him from his fortune.   At
one of his banquets, the gold plates were thrown through the
windows into the Tiber after they were used at the table, but
fortunately they were saved from loss by being caught in a
net which had been prepared for them.   On another occasion, when Leo and 13 cardinals were present, each found his
own coat-of-arms on the silver dishes he used.   At Agostino's
marriage festival, Leo held the bride's hand while she received
the ring on one of her fingers.   The pontiff then baptized
one of Chigi's illegitimate children.   Cardinals were not
ashamed to dine with representatives of the *demi-monde,* as
at a banquet given by the banker Lorenzo Strozzi.[3]   But in

---

[1] Vaughan, p. 177.   [2] See Reumont, III, Part II., 134 sq.
[3] Sanuto, as quoted by Pastor, IV. 384. For some of the entertainments
given by Cardinal Riario Cornaro, see Vaughan, p. 186 sqq. At one of the
banquets given by Cardinal Cornaro, sixty-five courses were served, three

scandals of this sort Alexander's pontificate could not well be outdone.

With the easy unconcern of a child of the world, spoiled by fortune, the light-hearted de' Medici went on his way as if the resources of the papal treasury were inexhaustible.   Julius was a careful financier.   Leo's finances were managed by incompetent favorites.[1]   In 1517 his annual income is estimated to have been nearly 600,000 ducats.   Of this royal sum, 420,000 ducats were drawn from state revenues and mines.   The alum deposits at Tolfa yielded 40,000; Ravenna and the salt mines of Cervia, 60,000 ; the river rents in Rome, 60,000 ; and the papal domains of Spoleto, Ancona and the Romagna, 150,000. According to another contemporary, the papal exchequer received 160,000 ducats from ecclesiastical sources.   The vendable offices at the pope's disposal at the time of his death numbered 2,150, yielding the enormous yearly income of 328,000 ducats.[2]

Two years after Leo assumed the pontificate, the financial problem was already a serious one.   All sorts of measures had to be invented to increase the papal revenues and save the treasury from hopeless bankruptcy.   By augmenting the number of the officials of the Tiber—*porzionari di ripa*—from 141 to 612, 286,000 ducats were secured.   The enlargement of the colleges of the *cubiculari* and *scudieri*, officials of the Vatican, brought in respectively 90,000 and 112,000 ducats more.   From the erection of the order of the Knights of St. Peter,— *cavalieri di San Pietro*,—with 401 members, the considerable sum of 400,000 ducats was realized, 1,000 ducats from each knight. The sale of indulgences did not yield what it once did, but the

dishes to each course, and all served on silver.   Such devices as a huge pie, from which blackbirds or nightingales flew forth, or dishes of peacocks' tails, or a construction of pastry from which a child would emerge to say a piece, — these were some of the inventions prepared for the amusement of guests at the tables of members of the sacred college.

[1] Vettori, a contemporary, as quoted by Villari, IV. 4, says, "It was no more possible for his Holiness to keep 1,000 ducats than it is for a stone to fly upwards of itself."   Villari, IV. 45, gives a list of Leo's enormous debts.

[2] These two lists of figures are taken from the Venetian ambassadors, Giorgi and Gradenigo.   Schulte, *Die Fugger*, p. 97 sq., gives many cases of the payment of annates and the servitia through the Fuggers.

revenue from this source was still large.[1]   The highest ecclesiastical offices were for sale, as in the reign of Alexander.
Cardinal Innocent Cibo paid 30,000 ducats or, as another report
went, 40,000, for his hat, and Francesco Armellini bought his
for twice that amount.[2]

The shortages were provided for by resort to the banker and
the usurer and to rich cardinals.   Loan followed loan.   Not
only were the tapestries of the Vatican and the silver plate
given as securities, but ecclesiastical benefices, the gems of the
papal tiara and the rich statues of the saints were put in pawn.
Sometimes the pope paid 20 per cent for sums of 10,000 ducats
and over.[3]   It occasions no surprise that Leo's death was followed by a financial collapse, and a number of cardinals passed
into bankruptcy, including Cardinal Pucci, who had lent the
pope 150,000 ducats.   From the banker, Bernado Bini, Leo had
gotten 200,000 ducats.   His debts were estimated as high as
800,000 ducats.   It was a common joke that Leo squandered
three pontificates, the legacy Julius left and the revenues of
his successor's pontificate, as well as the income of his own.

For the bankers and all sorts of money dealers the Medicean
period was a flourishing time in Rome.   No less than 30 Florentines are said to have opened banking institutions in the city,
and, at the side of the Fuggers and Welsers, did business with
the curia.   The Florentines found it to be a good thing to have
a Medicean pope, and swarmed about the Vatican as the Spaniards had done in the good days of Calixtus III. and Alexander VI., the Sienese, during the reign of Pius II., and the
Ligurians while Sixtus IV. of Savona was pope.   They stormed
the gates of patronage, as if all the benefices of the Church were
intended for them.[4]

[1] Schulte, I. 174, 223 sqq.

[2] Pastor, IV. 368, has said, *Um Geld herbeizuschaffen schreckte man vor
keinem Mittel zurück.*   Döllinger, *Papstthum*, p. 485, quotes a contemporary
as saying *ea tempestate Romæ, sacra omnia venalia erant*, etc.

[3] These figures are given by Schulte, I. 224–227, upon the basis of Sanuto
and other contemporary writers.   The ill odor of usury was avoided by representing the charges of the bankers as gifts.

[4] Pastor, IV. 371, in his striking way says, *Der Zudrang der Florentiner in
der ersten Zeit dieses Pontificats war ein enormer.   Die Begehrlichkeit dieser*

Leo's father, Lorenzo, said of his three sons that Piero was a fool, Giuliano was good and Giovanni shrewd.   The last characterization was true to the facts.   Leo X. was shrewd, the shrewdness being of the kind that succeeds in getting temporary personal gain, even though it be by the sacrifice of high and accessible ends.   His amiability and polish of manners made him friends and secured for him the tiara.   He was not altogether a degenerate personality like Alexander VI., capable of all wickedness.   But his outlook never went beyond his own pleasures.   The Vatican was the most luxurious court in Europe ; it performed no moral service for the world.   The love of art with Leo was the love of color, of outline, of beauty such as a Greek might have had, not a taste controlled by regard for spiritual grace and aims.   In his treatment of the European states and the Italian cities, his diplomacy was marked by dissimulation as despicable as any that was practised by secular courts.   Without a scruple he could solemnly make at the same moment contradictory pledges.   Perfidy seemed to be as natural to him as breath.[1]

At the same time, Leo followed the rubrics of religion.   He fasted, so it is reported, three times a week, abstained from meat on Wednesday and Friday, daily read his Breviary and was accustomed before mass to seek absolution from his confessor.   But he was without sanctity, without deep religious conviction.   The issues of godliness had no appreciable effect upon him in the regulation of his habits.   Even in his patronage of art and culture, he forgot or ignored Ariosto, Machia-

Leute war grenzenlos.   The Fuggers, who carried on the most extensive dealings with the papal treasury and the sacred college, had been firmly established in Rome since the beginning of Alexander VI.'s pontificate.   They came originally from Langen to Augsburg, where they started business as weavers, and then branched off into trading in spices and other commodities reaching Europe through Venice, and in copper and other metals, under the name of Ulrich Fugger and Brothers (George and Jacob), and their capital, estimated by the taxes they paid, increased, between 1480 and 1501, 1,634 per cent. Schulte, p. 3.   After its transfer to Rome, the house became the depository of the papal treasurer and cardinals, and was the intermediary for the payment of annates and *servitia* to the papal and camera treasuries.   The exact amounts, as furnished in the ledger entries, are given by Schulte.

[1] See Pastor's terrific indictment, IV. 359 sq.

velli, Guicciardini and Erasmus. What a noble substitution it would have been, if these men had found welcome in the Vatican, and the jesters and buffoons and gormandizers been relegated to their proper place ! The high-priest of the Christian world is not to be judged in the same terms we would apply to a worldly prince ruling in the closing years of the Middle Ages. The Vatican, Leo turned into a house of revelling and frivolity, the place of all others where the step and the voice of the man of God should have been heard. The Apostle, whom he had been taught to regard as his spiritual ancestor, accomplished his mission by readiness to undergo, if necessary, martyrdom. Leo despoiled his high office of its sacredness and prostituted it into a vehicle of his own carnal propensities. Had he followed the advice of his princely father, man of the world though he was, Leo X. would have escaped some of the reprobation which attaches to his name.

There is no sufficient evidence that Leo ever used the words ascribed to him, "how profitable that fable of Christ has been to us."[1] Such blasphemy we prefer not to associate with the de' Medici.   Nevertheless, no sharper condemnation of one claiming to be Christ's vicar on earth could well be thought of than that which is carried by the words of Sarpi, the Catholic historian of the Council of Trent,[2] who said, " Leo would have been a perfect pope, if he had combined with his other good qualities a moderate knowledge of religion and a greater inclination to piety, for neither of which he shewed much concern."   Before Leo's death, the papacy had lost a part of its European constituency, and that part which, in the centuries since, has represented the furthest progress of civilization.   The bull which this pontiff hurled at Martin Luther, 1520, was consumed into harmless ashes at Wittenberg, ashes which do not speak forth from the earth as do the ashes of John Huss.   To the despised Saxon miner's son, the Protestant world looks back for the assertion of the right to study

---

[1] *Quantum nobis nostrisque ea de Christo fabula profuerit, satis est omnibus sæculis notum.*   The words, said to have been spoken to Cardinal Bembo, were noted down for the first time by Bale in his Pageant of the Popes, ed. 1574, p. 179.   Bale, bishop of Ossory, had been a Carmelite.   [2] I : 1.

the Scriptures, a matter of more importance than all the circumstance and rubrics of papal office and sacerdotal functions. Not seldom has it occurred that the best gifts to mankind have come, not through a long heritage of prerogatives but through the devotion of some agent of God humbly born. It seemed as if Providence allowed the papal office at the close of the mediæval age to be filled by pontiffs spiritually unworthy and morally degenerate, that it might be known for all time that it was not through the papacy the Church was to be reformed and brought out of its mediæval formalism and scholasticism. What popes had refused to attempt, another group of men with no distinction of office accomplished.

CHAPTER VII.

HERESY AND WITCHCRAFT.

§ 57. *Literature.*

For § 58. — For the BRETHREN OF THE FREE SPIRIT, FREDERICQ: *Corpus doc. hær. pravitalis*, etc., vols. I-III.— HAUPT, art. in HERZOG, III. 467–473, *Brüder des Freien Geistes.* See lit., vol. V., I. p. 459. — For the FRATICELLI, F. EHRLE: *Die Spiritualen. Ihr Verhältniss zum Franciskanerorden u. zu d. Fraticellen* in *Archiv f. K. u. Lit. geschichte,* 1885, pp. 1509–1570; 1886, pp. 106–164; 1887, pp. 553–623.— DÖLLINGER: *Sektengesch.,* II. — LEA: *Inquisition,* III. 129 sqq., 164–175. — WETZER-WELTE, IV, 1926–1935. — For the WALDENSES, see lit., vol. V., I. p. 459. — Also, W. PREGER: *Der Traktat des Dav. von Augsburg über die Waldenser,* Munich, 1878. — HANSEN: *Quellen,* etc., Bonn, 1901, 149–181, etc. See full title below. — For the FLAGELLANTS, see lit., vol. V., I. p. 876. Also PAUL RUNGE: *D. Lieder u. Melodien d. Geissler d. Jahres* 1349, *nach. d. Aufzeichnung Hugo's von Reutlingen nebst einer Abhandlung über d. ital. Geisslerlieder von H. Schneegans u. einem Beitrage über d. deutschen u. niederl. Geissler von* H. PFANNENSCHMID, Leipzig, 1900.

For § 59. WITCHCRAFT. — For the treatments of the Schoolmen and other med. writers, see vol. V., I. p. 878. — Among earlier modern writers, see J. BODIN: *Magorum Daemonomania,* 1579.— REG. SCOTT: *Discovery of Witchcraft,* London, 1584. — P. BINSFELD: *De confessionibus maleficarum et sagarum,* Treves, 1596. — M. DELRIO: *Disquisitiones magicae,* Antwerp, 1599, Cologne, 1679. — ERASTUS, of Heidelberg: *Repititio disputationis de lamiis seu strigibus,* Basel, 1578. — J. GLANVILL: *Sadducismus triumphatus,* London, 1681. — R. BAXTER: *Certainty of the World of Spirits,* London, 1691. — Recent writers. — * T. WRIGHT: *Narrative of Sorcery and Magic,* 2 vols., London, 1851. — G. ROSKOFF: *Gesch. des Teufels,* 2 vols., Leipzig, 1869. — W. G. SOLDAN: *Gesch. der Hexenprocesse,* Stuttgart, 1843; new ed., by HEPPE, 2 vols., Stuttgart, 1880. — LEA: *History of the Inquisition,* III. 379–550. — * LECKY: *History of the Rise and Influence of the Spirit of Rationalism in Europe,* ch. I. — DÖLLINGER-FRIEDRICH: *D. Papstthum,* pp. 123–131. — A. D. WHITE, *History of the Warfare of Science and Theology in Christendom,* 2 vols., New York, 1898. — * J. HANSEN: *Zauberwahn, Inquisition und Hexenprocess im Mittelalter und die Entstehung der grossen Hexenverfolgung,* Munich, 1900; * *Quellen und Untersuchungen zur Gesch. des Hexenwahns und der Hexenverfolgung im M.A.,* Leipzig, 1901. — GRAF VON HOENSBROECH: *D. Papstthum in seiner sozialkulturellen Wirksamkeit,* Leipzig, 2 vols., 1900; 4th ed., 1901, I. 380–599. — J.

DIEFENBACH: *Der Hexenwahn, vor u. nach Glaubenspaltung in Deutschland*, Mainz, 1886 (the last chapter — on the *conciones variae* — gives sermons on the weather, storms, winds, dreams, mice, etc.); also, *Besessenheit, Zauberei u. Hexenfabeln*, Frankfurt, 1893; also, *Zauberglaube des 16ten Jahrh. nach d. Katechismen M. Luthers und d. P. Canisius*, Mainz, 1900. — BINZ: *Dr. Joh. Weyer*, Bonn, 1885, 2d ed., Berlin, 1896. A biography of one of the early opponents of witch-persecution, with sketches of some of its advocates. — BAISSAC: *Les grands jours de la sorcellerie*, Paris, 1890. — H. VOGELSTEIN and P. RIEGER, *Gesch. d. Juden in Rom*, 2 vols., Berlin, 1895 sq. — S. RIEZLER: *Gesch. d. Hexenprocesse in Baiern*, Stuttgart, 1896. — C. LEMPENS: *D. grösste Verbrechen aller Zeiten. Pragmatische Gesch. d. Hexenprocesse*, 2d ed., 1904. — JANSSEN-PASTOR: *Gesch. d. deutschen Volkes*, etc., vol. VIII., 531-751. — The Witch-Persecutions, in Un. of Pa. *Transll. and Reprints*, vol. III.

For § 60. THE SPANISH INQUISITION. — See lit., V. I. p. 460 sqq. — HEFELE: *D. Cardinal Ximines und d. kirchl. Zustände in Spanien am Ende d. 15 u. Anfang d. 16. Jahrh.*, Tübingen, 1844, 2d ed., 1851. Also, art. *Ximines* in Wetzer-Welte, vol. XII. — C. V. LANGLOIS: *L'inq., d'après les travaux récents*, Paris, 1902. — H. C. LEA: *Hist. of the Inquisition of Spain*, 4 vols., New York, 1906 sq. Includes Sicily, Sardinia, Mexico and Peru, but omits Holland. — E. VACANDARD: *The Inquisition. A criticism and history. Study of the Coercive Power of the Church*, transl. by B. L. Conway, London, 1908. — C. G. TICKNOR: *Hist. of Spanish Literature*, I. 460 sqq. — PASTOR: *Gesch. d. Päpste*, III. 624-630.

Dr. Lea's elaborate work is the leading modern treatment of the subject and is accepted as an authority in Germany. See Benrath in *Lit-Zeitung*, 1908, pp. 203-210. The author has brought out as never before the prominent part the confiscation of property played in the Spanish tribunal. The work of Abbé Vacandard, the author of the *Life of St. Bernard*, takes up the positions laid down in Dr. Lea's general work on the Inquisition and attempts to break the force of his statements. Vacandard admits the part taken by the papacy in prosecuting heresy by trial torture and even by the death penalty, but reduces the Church's responsibility on the ground of the ideas prevailing in the Middle Ages, and the greater freedom and cruelty practised by the state upon its criminals. He denies that Augustine favored severe measures of compulsion against heretics and sets forth, without modification, the unrelenting treatment of Thomas Aquinas.

§ 58. *Heretical and Unchurchly Movements.*

In the 14th and 15th centuries, the seat of heresy was shifted from Southern France and Northern Italy to Bohemia and Northern Germany, the Netherlands and England. In Northern and Central Europe, the papal Inquisition, which had been so effective in exterminating the Albigenses and in repressing or scattering the Waldenses, entered upon a new period of its history, in seeking to crush out a new enemy of the Church, witchcraft. The rise and progress of the two most powerful and promising forms of popular heresy, Hussitism and Lollardy, have already been traced. Other sectarists who came under the Church's ban were the Beghards and Beguines, who had their origin in the 13th century,[1] the Brethren of the Free Spirit, the Fraticelli, the Flagellants and the Waldenses.

It is not possible to state with exactness the differences between the Beghards, Beguines, the Brethren of the Free Spirit and the Fraticelli as they appeared from 1300 to 1500. The names were often used interchangeably as a designation of foes of the established Church order.[2] The court records and other notices that have come down to us indicate that they were represented in localities widely separated, and excited alarm which neither their numbers nor the station of their adherents justified. The orthodox mind was easily thrown into a panic over the deviations from the Church's system of doctrine and government. The distribution of the dissenters proves that a widespread religious unrest was felt in Western Christendom. They may have imbibed some elements from Joachim of Flore's millenarianism, and in a measure partook of the same spirit as German mysticism. There was a spiritual hunger the Church's aristocratic discipline and its priestly ministrations did not satisfy. The Church authorities had learned no other method of dealing with heresy than the method in vogue in the days of Innocent III. and Innocent IV., and sought, as before, by imprisonments, the sword and fire, to prevent its predatory ravages.

The Brethren of the Free Spirit [3] were infected with pantheistic notions and manifested a tendency now to free thought, now to libertinism of conduct. At times they are identified with the Beghards and Beguines. The pantheistic element suggests a connection with Amaury of Bena or Meister Eckart, but of this the extant records of trials furnish

---

[1] See vol. V., I. 489 sqq.

[2] Haupt, pp. 467, 471. Bezold: *Gesch. d. deutschen Reform.*, p. 120 sqq.

[3] *Secta spiritus libertatis, liberi spiritus*, etc.

no distinct evidence.   To the Beghards and Beguines likewise were ascribed pantheistic tenets.

To the general class of free thinkers belonged such individuals as Margaret of Henegouwen, usually known as
Margaret of Porete, a Beguine, who wrote a book advocating
the annihilation of the soul in God's love, and affirmed that,
when this condition is reached, the individual may, without
qualm of conscience, yield to any indulgence the appetites of
nature call for.   After having several times relapsed from
the faith, she was burnt, together with her books, in the Place
de Grève, Paris, 1310.[1]   Here belong also the Men of Reason,
— homines intelligentiæ, — who appeared at Brussels early in
the 14th century and were charged with teaching the final
restoration of all men and of the devil.[2]

The Fraticelli, also called the Fratricelli, — the Little
Brothers, — represented the opposite tendency and went to an
extravagant excess in insisting upon a rigid observance of the
rule of poverty.   Originally followers of the Franciscan Observants, Peter Olivi, Michael Cesena and Angelo Clareno,
they offered violent resistance to the decrees of John XXII.,
which ascribed to Christ and the Apostles the possession of
property.   Some were given shelter in legitimate Franciscan
convents, while others associated themselves in schismatic
groups of their own.   They were active in Italy and Southern France, and were also represented in Holland and even in
Egypt and Syria, as Gregory XI., 1375, declared; but it would
be an error to regard their number as large.   In his bull,
Sancta romana, issued in 1317, John XXII. spoke of "men of
the profane multitude, popularly called Fràticelli, or brethren
of the poor life, Bizochi or Beguines or known by other names."
This was not the first use of the term in an offensive sense.
Villani called two men Fraticelli, a mechanic of Parma, Sega-

[1] Fredericq, I. 155–160, II. 63 sqq.   Another writer of the same class was
Mary of Valenciennes, whose book was condemned by the Inquisition, about
1400, as a work of "incredible subtlety."   It was mentioned by Gerson in his
tract on false and true visions.   Fredericq, II. 188.

[2] For a list of their errors, see Fredericq, I. 267–279.   A sect of free thinkers
known as the Loists flourished in Antwerp in the 16th century.   Döllinger,
II. 664 sqq., gives one of their documents.

relli and his pupil Dolcino of Novara, both of whom were burnt, Segarelli in 1300 and Dolcino some time later. Friar Bonato, head of a small Spiritual house in Catalonia, after being roasted on one side, proffered repentance and was released, but afterwards, 1335, burnt alive.[1] Wherever the Fraticelli appeared, they were pursued by the Inquisition. A number of bulls of the 14th century attacked them for denying the papal edicts and condemned them to rigorous prosecution. A formula, which they were required to profess, ran as follows: "I swear that I believe in my heart and profess that our Lord Jesus Christ and his Apostles, while in mortal life, held in common the things the Scriptures describe them as having and that they had the right of giving, selling and alienating them."

In localities they seem to have carried their opposition to the Church so far as to set up a hierarchy of their own.[2] The regular priests they denounced as simonists and adulterers. In places they were held in such esteem by the populace that the Inquisition and the civil courts found themselves powerless to bring them to trial. Nine were burnt under Urban V. at Viterbo, and in 1389 Fra Michaele Berti de Calci, who had been successful in making converts, met the same fate at Florence. In France also they yielded victims to the flames, among them, Giovanni da Castiglione and Francese d'Arquata at Montpellier, 1354, and Jean of Narbonne and Maurice at Avignon. These enthusiasts are represented as having met death cheerfully.

Early in the 15th century, we find the Fraticelli again the victims of the Inquisition. In 1424 and 1426, Martin V. ordered proceedings against certain of their number in Florence and in Spain. The vigorous propaganda of the papal preachers, John of Capistrano and James of the Mark, succeeded in securing the return of many of these heretics to the Church, but, as late as the reign of Paul II., 1466, they were represented in Rome, where six of their number were imprisoned and subjected to torture. The charges against them were the denial of the validity of papal decrees of indulgence

[1] Lea: *Span. Inq.*, III. 190.
[2] Wetzer-Welte, IV. 1931, quoting Mansi-*Miscell.* IV. 595–610.

other than the Portiuncula decree.[1] In Northern Europe the
Fraticelli were classified with the Lollards and Beghards or
identified with these heretics. The term, however, occurs
seldom. Walter, the Lollard, was styled "the most wicked
heresiarch of the Fraticelli, a man full of the devil and most
perverse in his errors."[2]

Of far more interest to this age are the Flagellants who attracted attention by the strange outward demonstrations in
which their religious fervor found expression. Theirs was a
militant Christianity. They made an attempt to do something.
They correspond more closely to the Salvation Army of the
19th century than any other organization of the Middle Ages.
There is no record that the beating of drums played any part
in the movement, but they used popular songs, a series of distinctive physical gestures and peculiar vociferations, uniforms
and some of the discipline of the camp. Their campaigns were
penitential crusades in which the self-mortifications of the monastery were transferred to the open field and the public square,
and were adapted to impress the impenitent to make earnest
in the warfare against the passions of the flesh. The Flagellants buffeted the body if they did not always buffet Satan.

An account has already been given of the first outbreak of
the enthusiasm in Italy in 1259, which, starting in Perugia,
spread to Northern Italy and extended across the Alps to
Austria, Prag and Strassburg.[3] Similar outbreaks occurred
in 1296, 1333, 1349, 1399, and again at the time of the Spanish
evangelist, Vincent Ferrer.

From being regarded as harmless fanatics they came to be
treated as disturbers of the ecclesiastical peace, and in Northern Europe were classed with Beghards, Lollards, Hussites
and other unchurchly or heretical sectarists.

[1] Lea: *Inquis.*, III. 178 ; *Aur. Conf.*, III. 377.

[2] Döllinger, II. 381, 407 sq. The first three volumes of Fredericq contain
the term Fraticelli only twice, III. 17, 225.

[3] Vol. V., 1, p. 876 sqq. The Flagellants were also known as Flagellatores,
Cruciferi, Pænitentes, Disciplinati, Battisti, etc., and in German and Dutch as
Geissler, Geeselaars, Cruusbroeders, Kreuzbrüder, etc. The references under
Geeselaars in Fredericq fill four closely printed pages of the Index, III. 297–
300.

The movement of 1333 was led by an eloquent Dominican, Venturino of Bergamo, and is described at length by Villani. Ten thousand followed this leader, wearing head-bands inscribed with the monogram of Christ, IHS, and on their chests a dove with an olive-branch in her mouth. Venturino led his followers as far as Rome and preached on the Capitoline. The penniless enthusiasts soon became a laughing-stock, and Venturino, on going to Avignon, gained absolution and died in Smyrna, 1346.

The earlier exhibitions of Flagellant zeal were as dim candle-lights compared with the outbursts of 1349, during the ravages of the Black Death, which in contemporary chronicles and the Flagellant codes was called the great death — *das grosse Sterben, pestis grandis, mortalitas magna.* Bands of religious campaigners suddenly appeared in nearly all parts of Latin Christendom, Hungary, Bohemia, Italy, France, Germany and the Netherlands. John du Fayt, preaching before Clement VI., represented them as spread through all parts — *per omnes provincias* — and their numbers as countless. The exact numbers of the separate bands are repeatedly given, as they appeared in Ghent, Tournay, Dort, Bruges, Liége and other cities.[1] Even bishops and princes took part in them. There were also bands of women.

Our knowledge of the German and Lowland Flagellants is most extensive. While the accounts of chroniclers differ in details, they agree in the main features. The Flagellants clad themselves in white and wore on their mantles, before and behind, and on their caps, a red cross, from which they got the name, the Brothers of the Cross. They marched from place to place, stopping only a single day and night at one locality, except in case of Sunday, when they often made an exception. In the van of their processions were carried crosses and banners. They sang hymns as they marched. The public squares in front of churches and fields, near-by towns, were chosen for their encampments and disciplinary drill, which was repeated twice a day with bodies bared to the waist. A special feature

[1] Fredericq, II. 120, III. 19, 21, 33, etc. Also Förstemann, pp. 74 sqq. Runge, 99–209.

was the reading of a letter which, so it was asserted, was originally written on a table of stone and laid by an angel on the
altar of St. Peter's in Jerusalem.[1] It represented Christ as
indignant at the world's wickedness, and, more especially, at
the desecration of Sunday and the prevalence of usury and
adultery, but as promising mercy on condition that the Flagellants gather and make pilgrimages of penance lasting $33\frac{1}{2}$ days,
a period corresponding to the years of his earthly life.

The letter being read, the drill began in earnest.   It consisted of their falling on their knees and on the ground three
times, in scourging themselves and in certain significant gestures to indicate to what sin each had been specially addicted.
Every soldier carried a whip, or scourge, which, as writers are
careful to report, was tipped with pieces of iron.   These were
often so sharp as to justify their comparison to needles, and the
blood was frequently seen trickling down the bodies of the
more zealous, even to their loins.[2]   The blows were executed
to the rhythmic music of hymns, and the ruddy militiamen, —
milites rubicundi, — as they were sometimes called, believed
that the blood which they shed was one with Christ's blood or
was mixed with it.   They found a patron in St. Paul, whose
stigmata they thought of, not as scars of conscience but bodily
wounds.[3]   At each genuflection they sang a hymn, four
hymns being sung during the progress of a drill.   The first
calling to the drill began with the words: —

> *Nun tretet herzu wer büsen welle*
> *Fliehen wir die heisse Hölle.*
> *Lucifer ist bös Geselle*
> *Wen er habet mit Pech er ihn labet.*
> *Darum fliehen wir mit ihm zu sein.*
> *Wer unser Busse wolle pflegen*
> *Der soll gelten und wieder geben.*

[1] Fredericq, II. 119, III. 22, etc.   Runge, 152 sqq.

[2] *Pointillons de fer ; aculeis ferreis ; habentes in fine nodos aculeatos ; quasi
acus acuti infixi.*   Fredericq, I. 197, II. 120 sqq., III. 19, 20, 35, etc.   *Le
sang leur couloit parmy les rains*, Fredericq, III. 19.   Hugo of Reutlingen
also speaks of the sharp iron tips.   Runge, p. 25.

[3] *Si sanguis istorum militum est justus, et unitus cum sanguine Christi*, etc.
Fredericq, III. 18.   *Dicebant quod eorum sanguis per flagella effusus cum
Christi sanguine miscebatur*, II. 125.

> Now join us all who will repent
> Let's flee the fiery heat of hell.
> Lucifer is a bad companion
> Whom he clutches, he covers with pitch.
> Let us flee away from him.
> Whoso will through our penance go
> Let him restore what he's taken away.[1]

In falling flat on the ground, they stretched out their arms
to represent the arms of the cross.   The fourth hymn, sung at
the third genuflection, was a lament over the punishment of
hell to which the usurer, the liar, the murderer, the road-
robber, the man who neglected to fast on Friday and to keep
Sunday, were condemned, and with this was coupled a prayer
to Mary.

> *Das Hilf uns Maria Königin,*
> *Dass wir deines Kindes Huld gewin.*
>
> Mary, Queen, help us, pray,
> To win the favor of thy child.[2]

Each penitent indicated his besetting sin.   The hard drinker
put his finger to his lips.   The perjurer held up his two front
fingers as if swearing an oath.   The adulterer fell on his belly.
The gambler moved his hand as if in the act of throwing dice.

During the ravages of the Black Death a contingent of 120
of these penitential warriors crossed the channel from Holland
and marched through London and other English towns, wearing red crosses and having their scourges pointed with pieces
of iron as sharp as needles.[3]   But they failed to secure a
following.

It was inevitable that the Flagellants should incur opposition from the Church authorities.   The mediæval Church as
little tolerated independence in ritual or organization as in
doctrine.   In France, they were opposed from the first.   The
University of Paris issued a deliverance against them, and
Philip VI. forbade their manœuvres on French soil under
pain of death.   A harder blow was struck by the head of
Christendom, Clement VI., who fulminated his sweeping bull

---

[1] Hugo von Reutlingen, p. 36.

[2] Hugo von Reutlingen, in Runge, p. 38.

[3] So Robert of Avesbury, *Rolls Series*, p. 407 sqq.

Oct. 20, 1349. Flagellants starting from Basel appeared in Avignon to the number, according to one document, of 2000. Before issuing his bull, Clement and his cardinals listened to the sermon on the subject preached by the Paris doctor, John du Fayt. The preacher selected 13 of the Flagellant tenets and practices for his reprobation, including the shedding of their own blood, a practice, he declared, fit for the priests of Baal, and the murder of Jews for their supposed crime of poisoning the wells, in which was sought the origin of the Black Plague. Clement pronounced the Flagellant movement a work of the devil and the angelic letter a forgery. He condemned the warriors for repudiating the priesthood and treating their penances as equivalent to the journey to the jubilee in Rome, set for 1350.[1] The bull was sent to the archbishops of England, France, Poland, Germany and Sweden, and it called upon them to invoke, if necessary, the secular arm to put down the new rebellion against the ordinances of the Church.

Against such opposition the Flagellants could not be expected to maintain themselves long. Sharp enactments were directed against them by the Fleming cities and by archbishops, as in Prag and Magdeburg. Strassburg forbade public scourgings on its streets. As late as 1353, the archbishop of Cologne found it necessary to order all priests who had favored them to confess on pain of excommunication.[2]

We are struck with four features of the Flagellant movement during the Black Death, — its organization, the part assumed in it by the laity, the use of music and, in general, its strong religious and ethical character. In Italy, before this time, these people had their organizations. There was scarcely

[1] Clement's bull is given by Fredericq, I. 199-201, and in translation by Förstemann, p. 97 sqq. Du Fayt's sermon is full of interest, and is one of the most important documents given by Fredericq, III. 28-37. Du Fayt ascribed the Black Death to an infection of the air due to the celestial bodies — *infectionem æris creatam a corporibus cœlestibus.* The deliverance of the University of Paris is lost. See *Chartul.* III. 655 sqq.

[2] Fredericq, II. 116, etc. The magistrates, as at Tournay, sometimes found it necessary to repeat their proclamations against the Flagellants as often as three times.

an Italian city which did not have one or more such brotherhoods.   Padua had six, Perugia and Fabiano three, but the
movement does not seem to have developed opposition to
Church authority.   In some of the outbreaks priests were the
leaders, and the permanent organizations seem to have formed
a close association with the Dominicans and Franciscans and
to have devoted themselves to the care of the poor and sick.

On the other hand, in the North, a spirit of independence
of the clergy manifested itself.   This is evident from the
Flagellant codes of the German and Dutch groups, current at
the time of the great pestilence and in after years.   The conditions of membership included reconciliation with enemies,
the consent of husband or wife or, in the case of servants, the
consent of their masters, strict obedience to the leaders, who
were called master or rector, and ability to pay their own expenses.   During the campaigns, which lasted $33\frac{1}{2}$ days, they
were to ask no alms nor to wash their persons or their clothing, nor cut their beards nor speak to women, nor to lie on
feather beds.   They were forbidden to carry arms or to pursue the flagellation to the limit where it might lead to sickness or death.[1]

Five *pater nosters* and *ave Marias* were prescribed to be said
before and after meals, and it was provided that, so long as
they lived, they should flagellate themselves every Friday
three times during the day and once at night.   The associations were called brotherhoods, and the members were bidden
to call each other not chum — *socium* — but brother, "seeing
that all were created out of the same element and bought
with the same price."[2]

The leaders of the fraternities were laymen, and, as just
indicated, the equality of the members before God and the
cross was emphasized.   The movement was essentially a lay
movement, an expression of the spirit of dissatisfaction in

[1] *Usque ad mortem vel infirmitatem.*   See especially the 35 articles of
Bruges, Fredericq, II. 111 sqq. ; 50 articles given by Förstemann, p. 164
sqq. and the several codes given by Runge, 115 sqq.   Hugo of Reutlingen,
in Runge, 27, mentions the strict prohibition against bathing, *balnea fratri
non licet ulli tempore tali.*

[2] Fredericq, III. 15, Runge, pp. 25, 41, 118, etc.

Northern Germany and the Lowlands with the sacerdotal
class.[1] Some of the codes condemn the worship of images,
the doctrine of transubstantiation, indulgences, priestly unction and, in cases, they substituted the baptism of blood for
water baptism. One of these, containing 50 articles, expressly
declared that the body of Christ is not in the sacrament, and
that "indulgences amount to nothing and together with
priests are condemned of God." The 26th article said, "It
is better to die with a skin tanned with dust and sweat than
with one smeared with a whole pound of priestly ointment."[2]

The German hymns as well as the codes of the Flagellants
urge the duty of prayer and the mortification of the flesh and
the preparation for death, the abandonment of sin, the reconciliation of enemies and the restoration of goods unjustly
acquired. These sentiments are further vouched for by the
chroniclers.

To these religionists belongs the merit of having revived the
use of popular religious song. Singing was a feature of the
earliest Flagellant movement, 1259.[3] Their hymns are in
Latin, Italian, French, German and Dutch. In Italian they
went by the name of *laude*, and in German *leisen*. The Italian hymns, like the German, agree that sins have brought
down the judgment of God and in appealing to the Virgin
Mary, and call upon the "brethren" to castigate themselves,
to confess their sins and to live in peace and brotherhood.
They beseech the Virgin to prevail upon her son to stop "the
hard death and pestilence" — *Gesune tolga via l' aspra morte
e pistilentia*.[4] Most of these hymns are filled with the thought
of death and the woes of humanity, but the appeals to Mary
are full of tenderness, and every conceivable allegory is applied to her from the dove to the gate of paradise, from the

[1] Runge, pp. 130, 215.

[2] Förstemann, p. 165 sqq.

[3] Schneerganz speaks of the number of their hymns in manuscript in Italian
libraries as " exceedingly large." He gives a list of such libraries and also a
list of the published *laude*. See Runge, pp. 50–54. It is not, however, to be
supposed that more than a few were in popular use and sung.

[4] See, for example, Runge, p. 68 sqq.

rose to a true medicine for every sickness. The songs of the
Italian and the Northern Flagellants seem to have been independent of each other.[1]

The cohorts in the North agreed in using the same penitential song at their drills, but they had a variety of scores
and songs for their marches.[2] While the most of the words
of their songs have been known, it is only recently that some
of the music has been found to which the Flagellants sang
their hymns. A manuscript of Hugo of Reutlingen, dating
from 1349 and discovered at St. Petersburg, gives 8 such
tunes, together with the words and an account of the movement.[3] The hearers, in describing the impression made upon
them by the melodies, mention their sweetness, their orderly
rhythm, — *ordine miro hymnos cantabant*, — and their pathos
capable of "moving hearts of stone and bringing tears to the
eyes of the most stolid."[4]

Altogether, the Flagellant movement during the Black
Death, 1349, must be regarded as a genuinely popular religious movement.

The next outbreak of Flagellant zeal, which occurred in 1399,
was confined for the most part to Italy. The Flagellants, who
were distinguished by mantles with a red cross, appeared in

[1] Schneerganz, p. 85, emphatically denies all connection.

[2] Fr. Chrysander as quoted by Runge, p. 1. For specimen of the hymns
and accounts of the singing, see Runge, Förstemann, p. 255 sqq., Fredericq,
I. 197 ; II. 108, 123, 127–129, 137–139, 140 ; III. 23–27.

[3] This most interesting document, edited by Runge, gives the original
music. Here are two lines with a translation of the German words : —

Now   let   us   all   lift   up . .   our   hands

And   pray   to   God   this death   to   a - vert.

[4] See Runge, pp. 27, 140, 157.

Genoa, Piacenza, Modena, Rome and other Italian cities.   A
number of accounts have come down to us, now favorable as
the account of the "notary of Pistoja," now unfavorable
as the account of von Nieheim.   According to the Pistojan
writer, the movement had its origin in a vision seen by a
peasant in the Dauphiné, which is of interest as showing the
relative places assigned in the popular worship to Christ and
Mary.   After a midday meal, the peasant saw Christ as a
young man.   Christ asked him for bread.   The peasant told
him there was none left, but Christ bade him look, and behold !
he saw three loaves.   Christ then bade him go and throw the
loaves into a spring a short distance off.   The peasant went,
and was about to obey, when a woman, clad in white and
bathed in tears, appeared, telling him to go back to the young
man and say that his mother had forbidden it.   He went, and
Christ repeated his command, but at the woman's mandate the
peasant again returned to Christ.   Finally he threw in one
of the loaves, when the woman, who was Mary, informed him
that her Son was exceedingly angry at the sinfulness of the
world and had determined to punish it, even to destruction.
Each loaf signified one-third of mankind and the destruction
of one-third was fixed, and if the peasant should cast in the
other two loaves, all mankind would perish.   The man cast
himself on his knees before the weeping Virgin, who then assured him that she had prayed her Son to withhold judgment,
and that it would be withheld, provided he and others went
in processions, flagellating themselves and crying "mercy"
and "peace," and relating the vision he had seen.[1]

The peasant was joined by 17 others, and they became the nu-
cleus of the new movement.   The bands slept in the convents
and church grounds, sang hymns, — *laude*, — from which they
were also called *laudesi*, and scourged themselves with thongs
as their predecessors had done.   Miracles were supposed to
accompany their marches.   Among the miracles was the bleed-
ing of a crucifix, which some of the accounts, as, for example,
von Nieheim's, explain by their pouring blood into a hole in
the crucifix and then soaking the wood in oil and placing it

[1] See Förstemann, p. 111 sqq.

in the sun to sweat. According to this keen observer, the bands traversed almost the whole of the peninsula. Fifteen thousand, accompanied by the bishop of Modena, marched to Bologna, where the population put on white. Not only were the people and clergy of Rome carried away by their demonstrations, but also members of the sacred college and all classes put on sackcloth and white. The pope went so far as to bestow upon them his blessing and showed them the handkerchief of St. Veronica. Nieheim makes special mention of their singing and their new songs — *nova carmina*. But the historian of the papal schism could see only evil and fraud in the movement,[1] and condemns their lying together promiscuously at night, men and women, boys and girls. On their marches they stripped the trees bare of fruit and left the churches and convents, where they encamped, defiled by their uncleanness. An end was put to the movement in Rome by the burning of one of the leading prophets.

The bull of Clement VI. was followed, in 1372, by the fulmination of Gregory XI., who associated the Flagellants with the Beghards, and by the action of the Council of Constance. In a tract presented to the council in 1417, Gerson asserted that the sect made scourging a substitute for the sacrament of penance and confession.[2] He called upon the bishops to put down its cruel and sanguinary members who dared to shed their own blood and regarded themselves as on a par with the old martyrs. The laws of the decalogue were sufficient without the imposition of any new burdens, as Christ himself taught, when he said, "If thou wilt enter into life, keep the commandments." This judgment of the theologians the Flagellants might have survived, but the merciless probe of the Inquisition to which they were exposed in the 15th century took their life. Trials were instituted against them in Thuringia under the Dominican agent, Schönefeld, 1414. At one place, Sangerhausen, near Erfurt, 91 were burnt at one time and, on

---

[1] *Omnem populum mirabiliter deceperunt.* *De schismate*, II. 26. Erler's ed., p. 168 sq.

[2] *Contra sectam flagellantium.* Du Pin's ed., II. 659–664. Van der Hardt, III. 99 sqq.

another occasion, 22 more.   The victims of the second group
died, asserting that all the evils in the Church came from the
corrupt lives of the clergy.

The Flagellant movement grew out of a craving which the
Church life of the age did not fully meet.   Excesses should
not blind the eye to its good features.   Hugo of Reutlingen
concludes his account of the outbreak of 1349 with the words :
"Many good things were associated with the Flagellant brothers, and these account for the attention they excited."

A group of sectaries, sometimes associated by contemporary writers with the Flagellants, was known as the Dancers.
These people appeared at Aachen and other German and
Dutch towns as early as 1374.   In Cologne they numbered
500.   Like the Flagellants, they marched from town to town.
Their dancing and jumping — *dansabant et saltabant* — they
performed half naked, sometimes bound together two and two,
and often in the churches, where they had a preference for the
spaces in front of the images of the Virgin.   Cases occurred
where they fell dead from exhaustion.   In Holland, the Dancers
were also called Frisker or Frilis, from *frisch*, — spry, — the
word with which they encouraged one another in their terp-
sichorean feats.[1]

To another class of religious independents belong the Waldenses, who, in spite of their reputation as heretics, continued
to survive in France, Piedmont and Austria.   They were still
accused of allowing women to preach, denying the real presence and abjuring oaths, extreme unction, infant baptism and
also of rejecting the doctrines of purgatory and prayers for
the dead.[2]

With occasional exceptions, the Waldensians of Italy and
France were left unmolested until the latter part of the 15th
century and the dukes of Savoy were inclined to protect them

[1] The bad effects of the delusion upon morals is given by chroniclers, one of
whom says that during one of the epidemics 100 unmarried women became
pregnant.   See Fredericq, I. 231 sq., III. 41, etc.   Other names given to the
Dancers were Chorizantes and Tripudiantes.

[2] Döllinger, II. 365 sqq.   Here the *barbs*, — uncles, — the religious leaders
of the Waldenses, are represented as making affidavit of the tenets of their
people.

in their Alpine abodes. But the agents of the Inquisition were keeping watch, and the Franciscan Borelli is said to have burned, in 1393, 150 at Grenoble in the Dauphiné in a single day. It remained for Pope Innocent VIII. to set on foot a relentless crusade against this harmless people as his predecessor of the same name, Innocent III., set on foot the crusade against the Albigenses. His notorious bull of May 5, 1487, called upon the king of France, the duke of Savoy and other princes to proceed with armed expeditions against them and to crush them out "as venomous serpents."[1] It opened with the assertion that his Holiness was moved by a concern to extricate from the abyss of error those for whom the sovereign Creator had been pleased to endure sufferings. The striking difference seems not to have occurred to the pontiff that the Saviour, to whose services he appealed, gave his own life, while he himself, without incurring any personal danger, was consigning others to torture and death.

Writing of the crusade which followed, the Waldensian historian, Leger, says that all his people had suffered before was as "flowers and roses" compared to what they were now called upon to endure. Charles VIII. entered heartily into the execution of the decree, and sent his captain, Hugo de la Palu. The crusading armies may have numbered 18,000 men.

The mountaineer heretics fled to the almost inaccessible platform called Pré du Tour, where their assailants could make no headway against their arrows and the stones they hurled. On the French side of the Alps the crusade was successful. In the Val de Louise, 70, or, according to another account, 3000, who had fled to the cave called Balme de Vaudois, were choked to death by smoke from fires lit at the entrance. Many of the Waldenses recanted, and French Waldensianism was well-nigh blotted out. Their property was divided between the bishop of Embrun and the secular princes. As late as 1545, 22 villages inhabited by French Waldenses were pillaged and burnt by order of the parliament of Provence. With the unification of Italy in 1870, this ancient and respectable people was granted toleration and began to descend

[1] The bull is given by Comba: *The Waldenses of Italy*, p. 126 sq.

from its mountain fastnesses, where it had been confined for the half of a millennium.

In Austria, the fortunes of the Waldensians were more or less interwoven with the fortunes of the Hussites and Bohemian Brethren.   In parts of Northern Germany, as in Brandenburg in 1480, members of the sect were subjected to severe persecutions.   In the Lowlands we hear of their imprisonment, banishment and death by fire.[1]

The mediæval horror of heresy appears in the practice of ascribing to heretics nefarious performances of all sorts.   The terms Waldenses and Waldensianism were at times made synonymous with witches and witchcraft.   Just how the terms *Vauderie, Vaudoisie, Vaudois, Waudenses* and *Valdenses* came to be used in this sense has not been satisfactorily explained. But such usage was in vogue from Lyons to Utrecht, and the papal bull of Eugenius IV., 1440, refers to the witches in Savoy as being called Waldenses.[2]   An elaborate tract entitled the Waldensian Idolatry,[3] — *Valdenses ydolatræ,* — written in 1460 and giving a description of its treatment in Arras, accused the Waldenses with having intercourse with demons and riding through the air on sticks, oiled with a secret unguent.

§ 59. *Witchcraft and its Punishment.*

Perhaps no chapter in human history is more revolting than the chapter which records the wild belief in witchcraft and the merciless punishments meted out for it in Western Europe in the century just preceding the Protestant Reformation and

---

[1] Fredericq, I. 26, 50, 351 sqq.; 501 sq., 512; II. 263 sqq.; III. 109.   This author, I. 357 sqq., gives a sermon by a canon of Tournay against Waldensian tenets, which was much praised at the time. A French translation by Hansen, *Quellen,* p. 184 sq.

[2] See the bull in Hansen, *Quellen,* p. 18, and an extended section, pp. 408 sqq., on the use of the term *Vauderie* for witchcraft. In the 14th century it was used to designate the practice of unnatural crimes, just as was the term *Bougerie* in France, which, at the first, was applied to the Catharan heresy.

[3] This document is given in part by Fredericq, III. 94-109, and in full by Hansen, pp. 149-182. Its details are as disgusting as the imagination could well invent.

the succeeding century.[1] In the second half of that century, the Church and society were thrown into a panic over witchcraft, and Christendom seemed to be suddenly infested with a great company of bewitched people, who yielded themselves to the irresistible discipline of Satan.   The mania spread from Rome and Spain to Bremen and Scotland.   Popes, lawyers, physicians and ecclesiastics of every grade yielded their assent, and the only voices lifted up in protest which have come down to us from the Middle Ages were the voices of victims who were subjected to torture and perished in the flames.   No Reformer uttered a word against it.   On the contrary, Luther was a stout believer in the reality of demonic agency, and pronounced its adepts deserving of the flames.   Calvin allowed the laws of Geneva against it to stand.   Bishop Jewel's sermon before Queen Elizabeth in 1562 was perhaps the immediate occasion of a new law on the subject.[2] Baxter proved the reality of witchcraft in his *Certainty of the World of Spirits*.   On the shores of New England the delusion had its victims, at Salem, 1692, and a century later, 1768, John Wesley, referring to occurrences in his own time, declared that "giving up witchcraft was, in effect, giving up the Bible."

In the establishment of the Inquisition, 1215, Innocent III. made no mention of sorcery and witchcraft.   The omission may be explained by two considerations.   Provision was made for the prosecution of sorcerers by the state, and heretical depravity, a comparatively novel phenomenon for the Middle

---

[1] Lempens pronounces the prosecution of witchcraft the greatest crime of all times, *das grösste Verbrechen aller Zeiten*.   Witches were called *fascinarei, strigimagæ, lamiæ, phytonissæ, strigæ, streges, maleficæ, Gazarii*, that is, Cathari, and *Valdenses*, etc.   For the derivation of the German term, *Hexe*, see J. Francke's discussion in Hansen, *Quellen*, pp. 615–670.

[2] In Protestant Scotland the iron collar and gag were used.   The last trial in England occurred in 1712.   A woman was executed for witchcraft in Seville in 1781 and another in Glarus in 1782.   Dr. Diefenbach, in his *Aberglaube*, etc., attempts to prove that the belief in witchcraft was more deepseated in Protestant circles than in the Catholic Church.   Funk, *Kirchengesch.*, p. 419, Hefele, *Kirchengesch.*, p. 522, and other Catholic historians take care to represent the share Protestants had in the persecution of witches as equal to the share of the Catholics.

Ages, was in Innocent's age regarded as the imminent danger
to which the Church was exposed.

Witchcraft was one of the forms of *maleficium*, the general
term adopted by the Middle Ages from Roman usage for
demonology and the dark arts, but it had characteristic features
of its own.[1] These were the transport of the bewitched through
the air, their meetings with devils at the so-called *sabbats* and
indulgence in the lowest forms of carnal vice with them.
Some of these features were mentioned in the *canon episcopi*, —
the bishop's canon, — which appeared first in the 10th century
and was incorporated by Gratian in his collection of canon law,
1150.   But this canon treated as a delusion the belief that
wicked women were accustomed to ride together in troops
through the air at night in the suite of the Pagan goddess,
Diana, into whose service they completely yielded themselves,
and this in spite of the fact that women confessed to this affinity.[2]   The night-riding, John of Salisbury, d. 1182, treated as
an illusion with which Satan vexed the minds of women; but
another Englishman, Walter Map, in the same century, reports
the wild orgies of demons with heretics, to whom the devil
appeared as a tom-cat.[3]

From the middle of the 13th century the distinctive features
of witchcraft began to engage the serious attention of the
Church authorities.   During the reign of Gregory IX., 1227–
1241, it became evident to them that the devil, not satisfied
with inoculating Western Europe with doctrinal heresy, had
determined to vex Christendom with a new exhibition of his
malice in works of sorcery and witchcraft.   Strange cases were
occurring which the inquisitors of heresy were quick to detect.
The Dominican Chantimpré tells of the daughter of a count of

---

[1] Alexander Hales distinguished eight sorts of *maleficium*.   Martin V. and
Eugenius IV. call the workers of the dark arts *sortilegi, divinatores, demonum
invocatores, carminatores, conjuratores, superstitiosi, augures, utentes artibus
nefariis et prohibitis*.   See Hansen, *Quellen*, p. 16 sqq.   Henry IV.'s council
of bishops, met at Worms, 1076, in deposing Gregory VII., accused him of
witchcraft and making covenant with the devil.

[2] *Sceleratæ mulieres . . . credunt se et profitentur nocturnis horis cum Diana
paganorum dea et innumera multitudine mulierum equitare super quasdam
bestias,* etc.   Hansen, *Quellen*, p. 38 sq.

[3] See Vol. V., I. 889–897, and Hansen, *Zauberwahn*, p. 144.

Schwanenburg, who was carried every night through the air, even eluding the strong hold of a Franciscan who one night tried to hold her back. In 1275 a woman of Toulouse, under torture, confessed she had indulged in sexual intercourse with a demon for many years and given birth to a monster, part wolf and part serpent, which for two years she fed on murdered children. She was burnt by the civil tribunal.

But it is not till the 15th century that the era of witchcraft properly begins. From about 1430 it was treated as a distinct cult, carefully defined and made the subject of many treatises. The punishments to be meted out for it were carefully laid down, as also the methods by which witches should be detected and tried. The cases were no longer sporadic and exceptional; they were regarded as being a gild or sect marshalled by Satan to destroy faith from the earth.

It is probable that the responsibility for the spread of the wild witch mania rests chiefly with the popes. Pope after pope countenanced and encouraged the belief. Not a single utterance emanated from a pope to discourage it.[1] Pope after pope called upon the Inquisition to punish witches.

The list of papal deliverances opened in 1233, when Gregory IX., addressing the bishops of Mainz and Hildesheim, accepted the popular demonology in its crudest forms.[2] The devil, so Gregory asserted, was appearing in the shapes of a toad, a pallid ghost and a black cat. In language too obscene to be repeated, he described at length the orgies which took place at the meetings of men and women with demons. Where medicines did not cure, iron and fire were to be used. The rotting flesh was to be cut out. Did not Elijah slay the four hundred priests of Baal and Moses put idolaters to death?

[1] Michelet, p. 9, says: " I unfalteringly declare that the witch appeared in the age of that deep despair which the gentry of the Church engendered. The witch is a crime of their own achieving." Döllinger, *Papstthum*, p. 123, says that witchcraft in its different manifestations, from the 13th to the 17th century, is " a product of the faith in the plenary authority of the pope. This may seem to be a paradox, but it is not hard to prove." Hoensbroech's language, I., 381, is warm but true, when he says, " In all this period the pope was the patron and the prop of the belief in witchcraft, spreading it and confirming it."

[2] A translation of Gregory's bull, *Vox rama*, is given by Hoensbroech, I. 215–218. See Döllinger: *Papstthum*, pp. 125, 144.

Before the close of the 13th century, popes themselves were accused of having familiar spirits and practising sorcery, as John XXI., 1276, and Boniface VIII.   Boniface went so far, 1303, as to order the trial of an English bishop, Walter of Coventry and Lichfield, on the charge of having made a pact with the devil and habitually kissing the devil's posterior parts.   Under his successor, Clement, the gross charges of wantonness with the devil were circulated against the Knights of the Temple.   In his work, *De maleficiis*, Boniface VIII.'s physician, Arnold of Villanova, stated with scientific precision the satanic devices for disturbing and thwarting the marital relation.   Among the popes of the 14th century, John XXII. is distinguished for the credit he gave to all sorts of malefic arts and his instructions to the inquisitors to proceed against persons in league with the devil.[1]

Side by side with the papal utterances went the authoritative statements of the Schoolmen.   Leaning upon Augustine, Thomas Aquinas, d. 1274, accepted as real the cohabitation of human beings with demons, and declared that old women had the power by the glance of their eye of injecting into young people a certain evil essence.   If the horrible beliefs of the Middle Ages on the subject of witchcraft are to be set aside, then the bulls of Leo XIII. and Pius X.[2] pronouncing Thomas the authoritative guide of Catholic theology must be modified.

The definitions of the Schoolmen justified the demand which papal deliverances made, that the Church tribunal has at least equal jurisdiction with the tribunal of the state in ferreting out and prosecuting the adepts of the dark arts.   Manuals of procedure in cases of sorcery used by the Inquisition date back at least to 1270.[3]   The famous Interrogatory of Bernard Guy of 1320 contains formulas on the subject.   The canonists, however, had difficulty in defining the point at which *maleficium* became a capital crime.   Oldradus, professor of canon law in turn at Bologna, Padua and Avignon, sought, about

---

[1] So, in 1326, John inveighed against those who *cum morte fœdus ineunt et pactum faciunt cum inferno*.   For the text of this and other papal documents, see Hansen, *Quellen*, pp. 1–37.

[2] In his bull *Pascendi gregis*, 1907.

[3] Hansen: *Zauberwahn*, pp. 241, 263 sq., 271.

1325, to draw a precise distinction between the two, and gave
the opinion that, only when sorcery savors strongly of heresy,
should it be dealt with as heresy was dealt with, the position
assumed before by Alexander IV., 1258–1260.   The final step
was taken when Eymericus, in his Inquisitorial Directory and
special tracts, 1370–1380, affirmed the close affinity between
maleficium and heresy, and threw the door wide open for the
most rigorous measures against malefics.

To such threefold authorization was added the weight of the
great influence of the University of Paris, which, in 1378, two
years after the issue of Eymericus' work, sent out 28 articles
affirming the reality of *maleficium*.

Proceeding to the second period in the history of our subject, beginning with 1430, it is found to teem with tracts and
papal deliverances on witchcraft.

Gerson, the leading theologian of his age, said it was heresy
and impiety to question the practice of the malefic arts, and
Eugenius IV., in several deliverances, beginning with 1434,
spoke in detail of those who made pacts with demons and sacrificed to them.[1]   Witchcraft was about to take the place in
men's minds which heresy had occupied in the age of Innocent III.   The frightful mania was impending which spread
through Latin Christendom under the Renaissance popes, from
Pius II. to Clement VII., and without a dissenting voice received their sanction.   Of the Humanist, Pius II., better
things might have been expected, but he also, in 1459, fulminated against the malefics of Brittany.   To what length the
Vatican could go in sanctioning the crassest superstition is
seen from Sixtus IV.'s bull, 1471, in which that pontiff reserved
to himself the right to manufacture and consecrate the little
waxen figures of lambs, the touch of which was pronounced to be
sufficient to protect against fire and shipwreck, storm and hail,
lightning and thunder, and to preserve women in the hour of
parturition.[2]

---

[1] *Principis tenebrarum suasus et illusiones cœcitate noxia sectantes demoni-
bus immolant, eos adorant*, etc. . . . . *illis homagium faciunt*, etc.   Hansen,
Quellen, p. 17.

[2] *Cereæ formæ innocentissimi agni*, Hansen, etc. : *Quellen*, p. 21 sq.

Among the documents on witchcraft, emanating from papal or other sources, the place of pre-eminence is occupied by the bull, *Summis desiderantes*, issued by Innocent VIII., 1484. This notorious proclamation, consisting of nearly 1000 words, was sent out in answer to questions proposed to the papal chair by German inquisitors, and recognizes in clearest language the current beliefs about demonic bewitchment as undeniable. It had come to his knowledge, so the pontiff wrote, that the dioceses of Mainz, Cologne, Treves, Salzburg and Bremen teemed with persons who, forsaking the Catholic faith, were consorting with demons. By incantations, conjurations and other iniquities they were thwarting the parturition of women and destroying the seed of animals, the fruits of the earth, the grapes of the vine and the fruit of the orchard. Men and women, flocks and herds, trees and all herbs were being afflicted with pains and torments. Men could no longer beget, women no longer conceive, and wives and husbands were prevented from performing the marital act. In view of these calamities, the pope authorized the Dominicans, Heinrich Institoris and Jacob Sprenger, professors of theology, to continue their activity against these malefics in bringing them to trial and punishment. He called upon the bishop of Salzburg to see to it that they were not impeded in their work and, a few months later, he admonished the archbishop of Mainz to give them active support. In other documents, Innocent commended Sigismund, archbishop of Austria, the count of the Tyrol and other persons for the aid they had rendered to these inquisitors in their effort to crush out witchcraft.

The burning of witches was thus declared the definite policy of the papal see and the inquisitors proceeded to carry out its instructions with untiring and merciless severity.[1]

Innocent's communication, so abhorrent to the intelligent judgment of modern times, would seem of itself to sweep away the dogma of papal infallibility, even if there were no cases of Liberius, the Arian, or Honorius, the Monothelite. The argument is made by Pastor and Cardinal Hergenröther

---

[1] See Hansen, p. 27–29. Döllinger-Friedrich, p. 126, says, " *Mit Inn. VIII. beginnt das regelmässige Verbrennen der Hexen.*"

that Innocent did not officially pronounce on the reality of witchcraft when, proceeding upon the basis of reports, he condemned it and ordered its punishment.[1] However, in case this explanation be not regarded as sufficient, these writers allege that the decision, being of a disciplinary nature, would have no more binding force than any other papal decision on non-dogmatic subjects. This distinction is based upon the well-known contention of Catholic canonists that the pope's inerrancy extends to matters of faith and not to matters of discipline. Leaving these distinctions to the domain of theological casuistry, it remains a historic fact that Innocent's bull deepened the hold of a vicious belief in the mind of Europe and brought thousands of innocent victims to the rack and to the flames. The statement made by Dr. White is certainly not far from the truth when he says that, of all the documents which have issued from Rome, imperial or papal, Innocent's bull first and last cost the greatest suffering.[2] Innocent might have exercised his pontifical infallibility in denying, or at least doubting, the credibility of the witnesses. A simple word from him would have prevented untold horrors. No one of his successors in the papal chair has expressed any regret for his deliverance, much less consigned to the Index of forbidden books the *Malleus maleficarum*, the inquisitors' official text-book on witchcraft, most of the editions of which printed Innocent's bull at length.

Innocent's immediate successors followed his example and persons or states opposing repressive measures against witches were classed with malefactors and, as in the case of Venice, the state was threatened by Leo X. with the fulminations of the Church if it did not render active assistance. At the papal rebuke, Brescia changed its attitude and in a single year sentenced 70 to the flames.

Next to Innocent's bull, the *Witches Hammer*, — *Malleus*

---

[1] *Gesch. der Päpste*, III. 266 sqq., Hergenröther-Kirsch, II. 1040 sq. Vacandard, *Inquisition*, p. 200, takes the same view and says " Innocent assuredly had no intention of committing the Church to a belief in the phenomena he mentions in his bull; but his personal opinion did have an influence upon the canonists and Inquisitors of his day," etc.

[2] *Warfare of Science and Theology*, I. 351.

maleficarum, — already referred to, is the most important and
nefarious legacy the world has received on witchcraft.   Dr.
Lea pronounces it "the most portentous monument of superstition the world has produced." [1]   These two documents were
the official literature which determined the progress and
methods of the new crusade.

The *Witches Hammer,* published in 1486, proceeded from
the hands of the Dominican Inquisitors, Heinrich Institoris,
whose German name was Krämer, and Jacob Sprenger.   The
plea cannot be made that they were uneducated men.   They
occupied high positions in their order and at the University of
Cologne.   Their book is divided into three parts : the first
proves the existence of witchcraft ; the second sets forth the
forms in which it manifested itself; the third describes the
rules for its detection and prosecution.   In the last quarter
of the 15th century the world, so it states, was more given over
to the devil than in any preceding age.   It was flooded with
all kinds of wickedness.   In affirming the antics of witches and
other malefics, appeal is made to the Scriptures and to the teachings of the Church and especially to Augustine and Thomas
Aquinas.   Witches and sorcerers, whose father is the devil,
are at last bound together in an organized body or sect.
They meet at the weekly sabbats and do the devil homage
by kissing his posterior parts.   He appears among them as a
tom-cat, goat, dog, bull or black man, as whim and conven-
ience suggest.   Demons of both sexes swarm at the meetings.
Baptism and the eucharist are subjected to ridicule, the cross
trampled upon.   After an abundant repast the lights are ex-
tinguished and, at the devil's command " Mix, mix," there follow scenes of unutterable lewdness.   The devil, however, is a
strict disciplinarian and applies the whip to refractory members.

The human members of the fraternity are instructed in all
sorts of fell arts.   They are transported through the air.   They
kill unbaptized children, keeping them in this way out of
heaven.   At the sabbats such children are eaten.   Of the
carnal intercourse, implied in the words *succubus* and *incubus,*

[1] *Inquisition,* III. 543.

the authors say, there can be no doubt.   To quote them, "it is common to all sorcerers and witches to practise carnal lust with demons."[1]   To this particular subject are devoted two full chapters, and it is taken up again and again.

In evidence of the reality of their charges, the authors draw upon their own extensive experience and declare that, in 48 cases of witches brought before them and burnt, all the victims confessed to having practised such abominable whoredoms for from 10 to 30 years.

Among the precautions which the book prescribed against being bewitched, are the Lord's Prayer, the cross, holy water and salt and the Church formulas of exorcism.   It also adds that inner grace is a preservative.[2]

The directions for the prosecution of witches, given in the third part of the treatise, are set forth with great explicitness. Public rumor was a sufficient cause for an indictment.   The accused were to be subjected to the indignity of having the hair shaved off from their bodies, especially the more secret parts, lest perchance some imp or charm might be hidden there.   Careful rules were given to the inquisitors for preserving themselves against being bewitched, and Institoris and Sprenger took occasion to congratulate themselves that, in their long experience, they had been able to avoid this calamity.   In case the defender of a witch seemed to show an excess of zeal, this was to be treated as presumptive evidence that he was himself under the same influence.   One of the

---

[1] *Hoc est commune omnium maleficarum spurcitias carnales cum dæmonibus exercere, Malleus,* II. 4.   The author goes into all the details of the demon's procedure, the demon as he approaches men being known as the *succubus,* and women as the *incubus.*   Many of the details are too vile to repeat.   Such passages of Scripture are quoted as Gen. vi. 2 and 1 Cor. xi. 10, which is made to teach that the woman wears a covering on her head to guard herself against the looks of lustful angels.   The demons, in becoming *succubi* and *incubi,* are not actuated by carnal lust, so the author asserts, but by a desire to make their victims susceptible to all sorts of vices.

[2] Many cases are given to show the efficacy of these preservatives.   For example, a man in Ravensburg, who was tempted by the devil in the shape of a woman, became much concerned, and at last, recalling what a priest had said in the pulpit, sprinkled himself with salt and at once escaped the devil's influence.

devices for exposing guilt was a sheet of paper of the length of Christ's body, inscribed with the seven words of the cross. This was to be bound on the witch's body at the time of the mass, and then the ordeal of torture was applied. This measure almost invariably brought forth a confession of guilt. The ordeal of the red-hot iron was also recommended, but it was to be used with caution, as it was the trick of demons to cover the hands of witches with a salve made from a vegetable essence which kept them from being burnt. Such a case happened in Constance, the woman being able to carry the glowing iron six paces and thus going free.

Of all parts of this manual, none is quite so infamous as the author's vile estimate of woman. If there is any one who still imagines that celibacy is a sure highway to purity of thought, let him read the testimonies about woman and marriage given by mediæval writers, priests and monks, themselves celibate and presumably chaste. Their impurities of expression suggest a foul atmosphere of thought and conversation. The very title of the *Malleus maleficarum* — the Hammer of the *Female* Malefics — is in the feminine because, as the authors inform their readers, the overwhelming majority of those who were behagged and had intercourse with demons were women.[1] In flat contrast to our modern experience of the religious fidelity of women, the authors of this book derive the word *femina* — woman — from *fe* and *minus*, that is, *fides minus*, less in faith. Weeping and spinning and deceiving they represent as the very essence of her nature. She deceives, because she was formed from Adam's rib and that was crooked.

A long chapter, I. 6, is devoted to showing woman's inferiority to man and the subject of her alliance with demons is dwelt upon, apparently with delight. The cohabitation with fiends was in earlier ages, the authors affirm, against the will of women, but in their own age it was with their full consent and by their ardent desire. They thank God for being men. Few of their sex, they say, consent to such obscene relations, — one man to ten women. This refusal was due to the male's natu-

---

[1] *Hæresis dicenda est non maleficorum sed maleficarum, ut fiat a potiori denominatio.* See Hansen: *Quellen*, 416–444, and *Zauberwahn*, 481–490.

ral vigor of mind, *vigor rationis*. To show the depravity of woman and her fell agency in history, Institoris and Sprenger quote all the bad things they can heap up from authors, biblical and classic, patristic and scholastic, Cato, Terence, Seneca, Cicero, Jerome. Jesus Sirach's words are frequently quoted, " Woman is more bitter than death." Helen, Jezebel and Cleopatra are held forth as examples of pernicious agency which wrought the destruction of kingdoms, such catastrophes being almost invariably due to woman's machinations.

It was the common representation of the writers of the out-going century of the Mediæval Age that God permits the intervention of Satan's malefic agency through the marriage bed more than through any other medium, and for the reason that the first sin was carried down through the marital act. On this point, Thomas Aquinas is quoted by one author after the other.[1] Preachers, as well as writers on witchcraft, took this disparaging view of woman. Geiler of Strassburg gave as the reason for ten women being burnt to one man on the charge of witchcraft, woman's loquacity and frivolity. He quoted Ambrose that woman is the door to the devil and the way of iniquity — *janua diaboli et via iniquitatis*. Another noted preacher of the 15th century, John Nider, gave ten cases in which the cohabitation of man and woman is a mortal sin and, in a Latin treatise on moral leprosy, included the marriage state.[2] A century earlier, in his *De planctu ecclesiæ*, written from Avignon, Bishop Alvarez of Pelayo enumerated 102 faults common to women, one of these their cohabitation with the denizens of hell. From his own experience, the prelate states, he knew this to be true. It was practised, he

---

[1] *Com. ad Sent.*, IV. 34, qu. I. 3, *quia corruptio peccati prima . . . in nos per actum generantem devenit, ideo maleficii potestas permittitur diabolo adeo in hoc actu magis quam aliis.* See Hansen: *Quellen*, pp. 88–99. In answering the question why more women were given to sorcery than men, Alexander Hales declared that it was because she had less intellectual vigor than man, *minus habet discretionem spiritus.*

[2] See Hansen: *Quellen*, p. 423 sqq. Wyclif does not seem to have had so low an opinion of woman as did the writers of the century after him. And yet he says, *Lat. Serm.* II. 161, *Femina superat in malicia multos viros . . . veritas est quod natura feminea est virtute inferior*, etc.

says, in a convent of nuns and vain was his effort to put a stop to it.

Experts gave it as their opinion that "the new sect of witches" had its beginning about the year 1300.[1] But the writers of the 15th and 16th centuries were careful to prove that their two characteristic performances, the flight through the air and demonic intercourse, were not illusions of the imagination, but palpable realities.[2] To the testimonies of the witches themselves were added the ocular observations of church officials.[3] Other devilish performances dwelt upon, were the murder of children before baptism, the eating of their flesh after it had been consecrated to the devil and the trampling upon the host.[4] One woman, in 1457, confessed she had been guilty of the last practice 30 years.

The more popular places of the weekly sabbats were the Brocken, Benevento, Como and the regions beyond the Jordan.   Here the witches and demons congregated by the thousands and committed their excesses.   The witches went from congregation to congregation as they pleased[5] and, according to Prierias, children as young as eight and ten joined in the orgies.

Sometimes it went hard with the innocent, though prurient, onlookers of these scenes, as was the case with the inquisitor of Como, Bartholomew of Homate, and some of his companions.   Determined to see for themselves, they looked on at a sabbat in Mendrisio from a place of concealment.   As

---

[1] *Ista secta strigiarum.*   So Bernard of Como, who was followed by Nicolas Jacquier, Prierias, etc.   Hansen : *Quellen*, pp. 282, 319.

[2] Turrecremata, the Spanish dogmatician and canonist, dissents from the opinion that the flying women were led by Diana and Herodias, on the rational grounds that Diana never existed and Herodias probably was never permitted to leave hell.

[3] See the realistic language of Jacquier, Prierias, Bartholomew of Spina, etc.   *Quellen*, p. 136, etc.

[4] Jacquier, Widman of Kemnat, Barthol. of Spina, etc., *Quellen*, pp. 141, 234, 327, sq.

[5] *Valdenses ydolatræ*, *Quellen*, pp. 157, 165.   The poet Martin le Franc, secretary to Felix V., in his *Champion des dames*, about 1440, speaks of 10,000 witches celebrating a sabbat in the Valley of Wallis.   Six hundred of them were brought to confess they had cohabited with demons.   *Quellen*, 99–104.

if unaware of their presence, the presiding devil dismissed the assembly, but immediately calling the revellers back, had them drag the intruders forth and the demons belabored them so lustily that they survived only 15 days.[1] The forms the devil usually assumed were those of a large tom-cat or a goat. If the meeting was in a building, he was wont to descend by a ladder, tail foremost. The witches kissed his posterior parts and, after indulging in a feast, the lights were put out and wild revels followed. As early as 1460, pictures were printed representing women riding through the air, straddling stocks and broomsticks, on goats or carried by demons. In Normandy, the obsessed were called broom-riders — *scobaces*.[2] Taught by demons, they made a salve of the ashes of a toad fed on the wafer, the blood of murdered children and other ingredients, which they applied to their riding sticks to facilitate their flights. According to the physician, John Hartlieb, who calls this salve the "unguent of Pharelis" — Herodias — it was made from seven different herbs, each gathered on a different day of the week and mixed with the fat of birds and animals.[3]

The popularity of the witch-delusion as a subject of literary treatment is shown by the extracts Hansen gives from 70 writings, without exhausting the list.[4] Most of the writers were Dominicans. The *Witches Hammer* was printed in many editions, issued 13 times before 1520 and, from 1574–1669, 16 times. The most famous of these writers in the earlier half of

[1] The incident is told by that famous witch-inquisitor, Bernard of Como, in his *De strigiis*. Hansen : *Quellen*, pp. 279–284.

[2] From *scoba*, meaning broom. So in the tract *Errores Gazariorum seu illorum qui scobam vel baculum equitare probantur*, *Quellen*, pp. 118–123.

[3] *Quellen*, p. 131 sq. This medical expert declared that women and men were often turned into toads and cats. When such a cat's paw was cut off, it was found that the foot of the suspected witch was gone. With his own eyes, this mediæval practitioner says he saw such a woman burnt in Rome, and he states that many such cases occurred in the papal metropolis. Hartlieb was medical adviser to Duke Albert III. of Bavaria. His *Buch aller verbotenen Kunst, Unglaubens u. d. Zauberei*, was written 1456.

[4] Hansen devotes 60 pages of his *Quellen* to the title, date and authors of the *Malleus*. An excellent German translation is by J. W. R. Schmidt : *Der Hexenhammer*, Berlin, 3 vols., 1906.

the 15th century was John Nider, d. 1438, in his *Formicarius*
or Ant-Industry. He was a member of the Dominican order,
professor of theology in Vienna and attended the Council of
Basel. Writers like Jacquier were not satisfied with sending
forth a single treatise.[1] Writers like Sylvester Prierias, d.
1523, known in the history of Luther, and Bartholomew Spina,
d. 1546, occupied important positions at the papal court.[2]
These two men expounded Innocent VIII.'s bull, and quote
the *Witches Hammer*. Geiler of Strassburg repeated from
the pulpit the vilest charges against witches. Pico della
Mirandola, the biographer of Savonarola, filled a book with
material of the same sort, and declared that one might as well
call in question the discovery of America as the existence of
witches.[3]

The prosecution of witches assumed large proportions first
in Switzerland and Northern Italy and then in France and
Germany. In Rome, the first reported burning was in 1424.[4]
In the diocese of Como, Northern Italy, 41 were burnt the
year after the promulgation of Innocent VIII.'s bull. Between
1500–1525 the yearly number of women tried in that district
was 1000 and the executions averaged 100. In 1521, Prierias
declared that the Apennine regions were so full of witches that
they were expected soon to outnumber the faithful.

---

[1] *Flagellum hæreticorum fascinariorum, The Heretics' Flail.* Extracts
in Hansen, 133–144. *Tract. de calcinatione dæmonum seu malignorum
spirituum,* still in MS. in Brussels.

[2] *De strigmagarum dæmonumque mirandis,* Rome, 1521, and *De strigibus et
lamiis,* Venice, 1535. Hansen, pp. 317–339.

[3] *Strix sive de ludificatione dæmonum,* 1523. See Burckhardt-Geiger:
Renaissance, Excursus, II. 359–362. The official papal view at the close of the
16th century was set forth by the canonist, Francis Pegna, d. in Rome 1612.
He held an appointment on the papal commission for the revision of Gratian's
Decretals, and asserts that the aerial flights and cohabitation of witches
could be proved beyond all possible doubt. See extracts from his *Com. on
Eymericus Directorium.* Hansen: *Quellen,* p. 358 sq.

[4] Infessura, Tommasini's ed., p. 25. For another burning in Rome, 1442,
Burckhardt-Geiger, II. 359. For witchcraft in Italy, see this author, II. 255–
264. Also the extensive lists of trials, 1245–1540, noted down in Hansen's
Quellen; the ecclesiastical trials, pp. 445–516; the civil, pp. 517–615. In 1623
Gregory XV. renewed the penalty of lifelong imprisonment for making pacts
with the devil.

In France, one of the chief victims, the Carmelite William Adeline, was professor in Paris and had taken part in the Council of Basel.   Arraigned by the Inquisition, 1453, he confessed to being a Vaudois, and having habitually attended their synagogues and done homage to the devil.   In spite of his abjurations, he was kept in prison till he died.[1]   In Briançon, 1428–1447, 110 women and 57 men were executed for witchcraft in the flames or by drowning.

In Germany, Heidelberg, Pforzheim, Nürnberg, Würzburg, Bamberg, Vienna, Cologne, Metz and other cities were centres of the craze and witnessed many executions.   It was during the five years preceding 1486 that Heinrich Institoris and Sprenger sent 48 to the stake.   The Heidelberg court-preacher, Matthias Widman, of Kemnat, pronounced the "Cathari or heretical witches" the most damnable of the sects, one which should be subjected to "abundance of fire and without mercy."   He reports that witches rode on broom-sticks, spoons, cats, goats and other objects, and that he had seen many of them burnt in Heidelberg.   In 1540, six years before Luther's death, four witches and sorcerers were burnt in Protestant Wittenberg.   And in 1545, 34 women were burnt or quartered in Geneva.   In England the law for the burning of heretics, 1401, was applied to these unfortunate people, not a few of whom were committed to the flames.   But the persecution in the mediæval period never took on the proportions on English soil it reached on the Continent; and there, it was not the Church but the state that dealt with the crime of sorcery.

According to the estimate of Louis of Paramo, himself a distinguished inquisitor of Sicily who had condemned many to the flames, there had been during the 150 years before 1597, the date of his treatise on the *Origin and Progress of the Inquisition*, 30,000 executions for witchcraft.[2]

[1] Hansen : *Quellen*, pp. 467–472.   For the notorious case of Gilles de Rais, the reputed original Bluebeard, see Lea : *Inq.*, III. 468–487.

[2] For other figures, see Hansen: *Zauberwahn*, p. 532 sqq., Hoensbroech, I. 500 sqq., and Lecky, I. 29 sqq.   Seven thousand are said to have been burnt at Treves.   In 1670, 70 persons were arraigned in Sweden and a large number of them burnt.

The judgments passed upon witches were whipping, banishment and death by fire, or, as in Cologne, Strassburg and other places, by drowning. The most common forms of torture were the thumb-screw and the strappado. In the latter the prisoner's hands were bound behind his back with a rope which was drawn through a pulley in the ceiling. The body was slowly lifted up, and at times left hanging or allowed to suddenly drop to the floor. In our modern sense, there was no protection of law for the accused. The suspicion of an ecclesiastical or civil court was sufficient to create an almost insurmountable presumption of guilt. Made frantic by the torture, the victims were willing to confess to anything, however untrue and repulsive it might be. Death at times must have seemed, even with the Church's ban, preferable to protracted agonies, for the pains of death at best lasted a few hours and might be reduced to a few minutes. As Lecky has said, these unfortunate people did not have before them the prospect of a martyr's crown and the glory of the heavenly estate. They were not buoyed up by the sympathies and prayers of the Church. Unpitied and unprayed for, they yielded to the cold scrutiny of the inquisitor and were consumed in the flames.

Persons who took the part of the supposed witch, or ventured to lift up their voices against the trials for witchcraft, did so at the risk of their lives. In 1593, the Dutch priest, Cornelius Loos Callidus, was imprisoned at Treves for declaring that women, making confession under torture to witch devices, confessed to what was not true. And four years before, 1589, Dr. Dietrich Flade, a councillor of Treves, was burnt for attacking the prosecution of witchcraft.[1]

The belief in demonology and all manner of malefic arts was a legacy handed down to the Church from the old Roman

[1] Döllinger-Friedrich, pp. 130, 447. For Loos' recantation as given by Delrio, see *Phil. Trsll. and Reprints*, III. In a letter, written in 1629, the chancellor of the bishop of Würzburg states that the week before a beautiful maiden of 19 had been executed as a witch. Children of three and four years, he adds, to the number of 300, were reported to have had intercourse with the devil. He himself had seen children of seven and promising students of 12 and 15 put to death. *Phil. Trsll.*, etc., III.

world and, where the influence of the Northern mythologies was felt, the belief took still deeper roots. But it cannot be denied that cases and passages taken from the Scriptures, especially the Old Testament, were adduced to justify the wild dread of malign spirits in the Middle Ages. Saul's experience with the witch of Endor, the plagues brought by the devil upon Job, the representations in Leviticus and Deuteronomy, incidents from the Apocrypha and the cases of demonic agency in the New Testament were dwelt upon and applied with literal and relentless rigor.

It is a long chapter which begins with the lonely contests the old hermits had with demons, recounts the personal encounters of mediæval monks in chapel and cell and relates the horrors of the inquisitorial process for heresy. Our more rational processes of thought and our better understanding of the Christian law of love happily have brought this chapter to a close in enlightened countries. The treatment here given has been in order to show how greatly a Christian society may err, and to confirm in this generation the feeling of gratitude for the better sentiments which now prevail. It is perhaps also due to those who suffered, that a general description of the injustice done them should be given. The chapter may not unfitly be brought to a close by allowing one of the victims to speak again from his prison-cell, the burgomaster of Bamberg, though he suffered a century after the Middle Ages had closed, 1628. After being confronted by false witnesses he confessed, under torture, to having indulged in the practices ascribed to the bewitched and he thus wrote to his daughter: —

Many hundred good nights, dearly beloved daughter, Veronica. Innocent have I come into prison, innocent must I die. For whoever comes into a witchprison must become a witch or be tortured till he invents something out of his head and — God pity him — bethinks himself of something. I will tell you how it has gone with me. . . . Then came the executioner and put the thumbscrews on me, both hands bound together, so that the blood ran out at the nails and everywhere, so that for four weeks I could not use my hands, as you can see from the writing. . . . Then they stripped me, bound my hands behind my back and drew me up. I thought heaven and earth were at an end. Eight times did they do this and let me drop again so that I suffered terrible agony. . . . [Here follows a rehearsal of the confessions he was induced to make.] . . . Now, dear child, you have all my confessions for which I must

die.   They are sheer lies made up.   All this I was forced to say through fear of
the rack, for they never leave off the torture till one confesses something. . . .
Dear child, keep this letter secret so that people may not find it or else I shall
be tortured most piteously and the jailers be beheaded. . . .   I have taken
several days to write this for my hands are both lame.   Good night, for your
father Johannes Junius will never see you more.[1]

Innocent VIII.'s Bull, Summis desiderantes.   December 5,
1484 : In Part :[2]

Innocentius episcopus, servus servorum dei, ad perpetuam rei memoriam.
Summis desiderantes affectibus, prout pastoralis sollicitudinis cura requirit,
ut fides catholica nostris potissime temporibus ubique augeatur et floreat ac
omnis hæretica pravitas de finibus fidelium procul pellatur, ea libenter declaramus ac etiam de novo concedimus per quæ huiusmodi pium desiderium
nostrum votivum sortiatur effectum ; cunctisque propterea, per nostræ operationis ministerium, quasi per providi operationis sæculum erroribus exstir-
patis, eiusdem fidei zelus et observantia in ipsorum corda fidelium fortius
imprimatur.

Sane nuper ad nostrum non sine ingenti molestia pervenit auditum, quod
in nonnullis partibus Alemaniæ superioris, necnon in Maguntinensi, Coloni-
ensi, Treverensi, Saltzumburgensi, et Bremensi, provinciis, civitatibus, terris,
locis et diœcesibus complures utriusque sexus personæ, propriæ salutis imme-
mores et a fide catholica deviantes, cum dæmonibus, incubis et succubis abuti,
ac suis incantationibus, carminibus et coniurationibus aliisque nefandis super-
stitiosis, et sortilegis excessibus, criminibus et delictis, mulierum partus, ani-
malium fœtus, terræ fruges, vinearum uvas, et arborum fructus ; necnon
homines, mulieres, pecora, pecudes et alia diversorum generum animalia ;
vineas quoque, pomeria, prata, pascua, blada, frumenta et alia terræ legumina
perire, suffocari et extingui facere et procurare ; ipsosque homines, mulieres,
iumenta, pecora, pecudes et animalia diris tam intrinsecis quam extrinsecis
doloribus et tormentis afficere et excruciare ; ac eosdem homines ne gignere,
et mulieres ne concipere, virosque, ne uxoribus, et mulieres, ne viris actus
coniugales reddere valeant, impedire; fidem præterea ipsam, quam in sacri sus-
ceptione baptismi susceperunt, ore sacrilego abnegare, aliaque quam plurima
nefanda, excessus et crimina, instigante humani generis inimico, committere
et perpetrare non verentur in animarum suarum periculum, divinæ maiesta-
tis offensam ac perniciosum exemplum ac scandalum plurimorum.   Quodque
licet dilecti filii Henrici Institoris in prædictis partibus Alemaniæ superioris
. . . necnon Iacobus Sprenger per certas partes lineæ Rheni, ordinis Prædi-
catorum et theologiæ professores, hæreticæ pravitatis inquisitores per literas

---

[1] The translation taken from the *Phila. Trsll. and Reprints*, vol. III.

[2] Reprinted from Hansen : *Quellen*, pp. 25–27.   The Latin text is also found
in Soldan, p. 215, and Mirbt, p. 171 sq.   Germ. trsl. in Schmidt, pp. xxxvi–xli,
and Hoensbroech, I. 384–386.   Engl. trsl. in *Phila. Trsll. and Reprints,*
vol. III.

apostolicas deputati fuerunt, prout adhuc existunt ; tamen nonnulli clerici et laici illarum partium, quærentes plura sapere quam oporteat, pro eo quod in literis deputationis huiusmodi provinciæ, civitates dioeceses, terræ et alia loca prædicta illarumque personæ ac excessus huiusmodi nominatim et specifice expressa non fuerunt, illa sub eisdem partibus minime contineri, et propterea præfatis inquisitoribus in provinciis, civitatibus, dioecesibus, terris et locis prædictis huiusmodi inquisitionis officium exequi non licere ; et ad personanarum earundem super excessibus et criminibus antedictis punitionem, incarcerationem et correctionem admitti non debere, pertinaciter asserere non erubescunt. . . . Huiusmodi inquisitionis officium exequi ipsasque personas, quas in præmissis culpabiles reperierint, iuxta earum demerita corrigere, incarcerare, punire et mulctare. . . . Quotiens opus fuerunt, aggravare et reaggravare auctoritate nostra procuret, invocato ad hoc, si opus fuerit, auxilio brachii sæcularis.

§ 60. *The Spanish Inquisition.*

Torquemada's name, with clouds o'ercast,
Looms in the distant landscape of the past
Like a burnt tower upon a blackened heath,
Lit by the fires of burning woods beneath.

— LONGFELLOW.

The Inquisition of Spain is one of the bywords of history. The horrors it perpetrated have cast a dark shadow over the pages of Spanish annals.   Organized to rid the Spanish kingdoms of the infection of heresy, it extended its methods to the Spanish dependencies in Europe, Sicily and Holland and to the Spanish colonies of the new world.   After the marriage of Philip II. with Mary Tudor it secured a temporary recognition in England.   In its bloody sacrifices, Jews, Moors, Protestants and the practitioners of the dark arts were included. No country in the world was more concerned to maintain the Catholic faith pure than was Spain from the 15th to the 18th century, and to no Church organization was a more unrestricted authority given than to the Spanish Inquisition. Agreeing with the papal Inquisition established by Innocent III. in its ultimate aim, the eradication of heresy, it differed from that earlier institution by being under the direction of a tribunal appointed by the Spanish sovereign, immediately amenable to him and acting independently of the bishops. The papal Inquisition was controlled by the Apostolic see,

which appointed agents to carry its rules into effect and
whose agency was to a certain extent subject to the assent of
the bishops.

Engaged in the wars for the dispossession of the Pagan
Moors, the Spanish kingdoms had shown little disposition to
yield to the intrusion of Catharan and other heresy from the
North.   The menace to its orthodox repose came from the
Jews, Jews who held firmly to their ancestral faith and Jews
who had of their own impulse or through compulsion adopted
the Christian rites.   In no part of Europe was the number of
Jews so large and nowhere had they been more prosperous in
trade and reached such positions of eminence as physicians and
as counsellors at court.   The Jewish literature of mediæval
Spain forms a distinct and notable chapter in Hebrew literary
history.   To rid the land of the Jews who persisted in their
ancestral belief was not within the jurisdiction of the Church.
That belonged to the state, and, according to the canon law,
the Jew was not to be molested in the practice of his religion.
But the moment Jews or Moors submitted to baptism they became amenable to ecclesiastical discipline.   Converted Jews
in Spain were called *conversos*, or *maranos* — the newly converted — and it was with them, in its first period, that the
Spanish Inquisition had chiefly to do.   After Luther's doctrines began to spread it addressed itself to the extirpation
of Protestants, but, until the close of its history, in 1834, the
Jewish Christians constituted most of its victims.

From an early time Spanish legislation was directed to the
humiliation of the Jews and their segregation from the Christian population.   The œcumenical Council of Vienne, 1312,
denounced the liberality of the Spanish law which made a
Jewish witness necessary to the conviction of a Jew.   Spanish
synods, as those of Valladolid and Tarragona, 1322, 1329, gave
strong expression to the spirit of intolerance with which the
Spanish church regarded the Jewish people.   The sacking
and wholesale massacre of their communities, which lived apart
in quarters of their own called Juderias, were matters of frequent occurrence, and their synagogues were often destroyed
or turned into churches.   It is estimated that in 1391, 50,000

Jews were murdered in Castile, and the mania spread to Aragon.[1]

The explanation of this bitter feeling is to be sought in the haughty pride of the descendants of Abraham according to the flesh, their persistent observance of their traditions and the exorbitant rates of usury which they charged.   Not content with the legal rate, which in Aragon was 20% and in Castile $33\frac{1}{3}$%, they often compelled municipalities to pay even higher rates. The prejudice and fears of the Christian population charged them with sacrilege in the use of the wafer and the murder of baptized children, whose blood was used in preparations made for purposes of sorcery.   Legislation was made more exacting. The old rules were enforced enjoining a distinctive dress and forbidding them to shave their beards or to have their hair cut round.   All employment in Christian households, the practice of medicine and the occupation of agriculture were denied them.   Scarcely any trade was left to their hand except the loaning of money, and that by canon law was illegal for Christians.

The joint reign of Ferdinand, 1452–1516, and Isabella, 1451–1504, marked an epoch in the history of the Jews in Spain, both those who remained true to their ancestral faith and the large class which professed conversion to the Christian Church.[2]

In conferring the title "Catholic" upon Ferdinand and Isabella, 1495, Alexander VI. gave as one of the reasons the expulsion of the Jews from Spain, 1492.   The institution of the Spanish Inquisition, which began its work twelve years before, was directed primarily against the *conversos*, people of

---

[1] Lea, I. 100 sqq., 107 sq.

[2] Ferdinand was associated with his father, John of Navarre, in the government of Aragon from the year 1469.   The same year he was married to Isabella, sister of Henry IV., king of Castile.   At Henry's death, Isabella's title to the throne was disputed by Juana who claimed to be a daughter of Henry, but was popularly believed to be the child of Beltram de la Cueva and so called La Beltraneja.   The civil war, which followed, was brought to a close in 1479 by Juana's retirement to a convent, and the undisputed recognition of Isabella. Ferdinand and Isabella's reign is regarded as the most glorious in Spanish annals.   Ferdinand's grandson, through his daughter Juana, Charles V., succeeded to his dominions.

Jewish blood and members of the Church who in heart and secret usage remained Jews.

The papal Inquisition was never organized in Castile, and in Aragon it had a feeble existence. With the council of Tortosa, 1429, complaints began to be made that the *conversos* neglected to have their children baptized, and by attending the synagogues and observing the Jewish feasts were putting contempt upon their Christian faith. That such hypocrisy was practised cannot be doubted in view of the action of the Council of Basel which put its brand upon it. In 1451 Juan II. applied to the papal court to appoint a commission to investigate the situation. At the same time the popular feeling was intensified by the frantic appeals of clerics such as Friar Alfonso de Espina who in his *Fortalicium fidei* — the Fortification of the Faith — brought together a number of alleged cases of children murdered by Jews and argued for the Church's right to baptize Jewish children in the absence of the parents' consent.[1] The story ran that before Isabella's accession her confessor Torquemada, that hammer of heretics, secured from her a vow to leave no measure untried for the extirpation of heresy from her realm. Sometime later, listening to this same ecclesiastic's appeal, Ferdinand and his consort applied to the papal see for the establishment of the Inquisition in Castile.

Sixtus IV., who was then occupying the chair of St. Peter, did not hesitate in a matter so important, and on Nov. 1, 1478, issued the bull sanctioning the fell Spanish tribunal. It authorized the Spanish sovereigns to appoint three bishops or other ecclesiastics to proceed against heretics and at the same time empowered them to remove and replace these officials as they thought fit. After a delay of two years, the commission was constituted, 1480, and consisted of two Dominican theologians, Michael de Morillo and John of St. Martin, and a friar of St. Pablo, Seville. A public reception was given to the commission by the municipal council of Seville. The number of prisoners was soon too large for the capacity of St. Pablo, where the court first established itself, and it was removed to the chief stronghold of the city, the fortress of Triana, whose

[1] Lea, I. 15.

ample spaces and gloomy dungeons were well fitted for the dark work for which it had been chosen.

Once organized, the Inquisition began its work by issuing the so-called Edict of Grace [1] which gave heretics a period of 30 or 40 days in which to announce themselves and, on making confession, assured them of pardon. Humane as this measure was, it was also used as a device for detecting other spiritual criminals, those confessing, called *penitentes*, being placed under a vow to reveal the names of heretics. The humiliations to which the penitents were subjected had exhibition at the first *auto de fe* held in Toledo, 1486, when 750 penitents of both sexes were obliged to march through the city carrying candles and bare-headed; and, on entering the cathedral, were informed that one-fifth of their property had been confiscated, and that they were thenceforth incapacitated to hold public office. The first *auto de fe* was held in Seville, Feb. 6, 1481, six months after the appointment of the tribunal, when six men and women were cremated alive. The ghastly spectacle was introduced with a sermon, preached by Friar Alfonso de Hojeda. A disastrous plague, which broke out in the city, did not interrupt the sittings of the tribunal, which established itself temporarily at Aracena, where the first holocaust included 23 men and women. According to a contemporary, by Nov. 4, 1491, 298 persons had been committed to the flames and 79 condemned to perpetual imprisonment.[2] The tribunal established at Ciudad Real, 1483, burnt 52 heretics within two years, when it was removed, in 1485, to Toledo. In Avila, from 1490–1500, 75 were burnt alive, and 26 dead bodies exhumed and cast into the flames. In cases, the entire *conversos* population was banished, as in Guadalupe, by the order of the inquisitor-general, Deza, in 1500. From Castile, the Inquisition extended its operations to Aragon, where its three chief centres were Valencia, Barcelona and Saragossa, and then to the Balearic Islands, where it was especially active. The first burning in Saragossa took place, 1484, when two men were burnt alive and one woman in effigy, and at Barcelona in 1488, when four persons were consumed alive.

---

[1] Lea, II. 457–463.   [2] Lea, I. 165.

The interest of Sixtus IV. continued to follow the tribunal he had authorized and, in a letter addressed to Isabella,
Feb. 13, 1483, he assured the queen that its work lay close to
his heart.   The same year, to render the tribunal more efficient,
it was raised by Ferdinand to the dignity of the fifth council
of the state with the title, *Concejo de la Suprema y General
Inquisicion*.   Usually called the *suprema*, this body was to
have charge of the Holy Office throughout the realm.   The
same end was promoted by the creation of the office of
inquisitor-general, 1483, to which the power was consigned of
removing and appointing inquisitorial functionaries.   The
first incumbent was Thomas de Torquemada, at that time prior
of Santa Cruz in Segovia.   This fanatical ecclesiastic, whose
name is a synonym of uncompromising religious intolerance
and heartless cruelty, had already been appointed, in 1482, an
inquisitor by the pope.   He brought to his duties a rare
energy and formulated the rules characteristic of the Spanish
Inquisition.

With Torquemada at its head, the Holy Office became, next
to royalty itself, the strongest power in Spain.   Its decisions
fell like the blow of a great iron hammer, and there was no
power beneath the sovereign that dared to offer them resistance.   In 1507, at the death of Deza, third inquisitor-general,
Castile and Aragon were placed under distinct tribunals.
Cardinal Ximenes, 1436–1517, a member of the Franciscan
order and one of the foremost figures in Spanish church history,
was elevated to the office of supreme inquisitor of Castile.   His
distinction as archbishop of Toledo pales before his fame as a
scholar and patron of letters.   He likewise was unyielding in
the prosecution of the work of ridding his country of the taint
of heresy, but he never gave way to the temptation of using
his office for his own advantage and enriching himself from the
sequestrated property of the *conversos*, as Torquemada was
charged with doing.

Under Adrian of Utrecht, at first inquisitor-general of Aragon, the tribunals of the two kingdoms were again united in
1518, and, by the addition of Navarre, which Ferdinand had
conquered, the whole Iberian peninsula, with the exception of

Portugal, came under the jurisdiction of a single supreme official. Adrian had acted as tutor to Charles V., and was to succeed Leo X. on the papal throne. From his administration, the succession of inquisitors-general continued unbroken till 1835, when the last occupant of the office died, Geronimo Castellan y Salas, bishop of Tarazona.[1]

The interesting question has been warmly discussed, whether the Inquisition of Spain was a papal institution or an institution of the state, and the attempt has been made to lift the responsibility for its organization and administration from the supreme pontiff. The answer is, that it was predominantly an ecclesiastical institution, created by the authority of Sixtus IV. and continuously supported by pontifical sanction. On the other hand, its establishment was sought after by Ferdinand and Isabella, and its operations, after the papal authorization had been secured, was under the control of the Spanish sovereign. So far as we know, the popes never uttered a word in protest against the inhuman measures which were practised by the Spanish tribunals. Their only dissent arose from the persistence with which Ferdinand kept the administrative agency in his own hands and refused to allow any interference with his disposition of the sequestrated estates.[2] The hearty

[1] The list is given by Lea, I. 556–559.

[2] Hefele, in his *Life of Cardinal Ximenes*, p. 265 sqq., took the position that the Spanish Inquisition was a state institution, *Staatsanstalt*, pointing out that the inquisitor-general was appointed by the king, and the inquisitors proceeded in his name. Ranke, *Die Osmanen u. d. span. Monarchie* in *Fürsten u. Völker*, 4th ed., 1877, calls it "a royal institution fitted out with spiritual weapons." On the other hand, the Spanish historians, Orti y Lara and Rodrigo take the position that it was a papal institution. Pastor takes substantially this view when he insists upon the dominance of the religious element and the bull of Sixtus IV. authorizing it. *So*, he says, *erscheint d. span. Inquisition als ein gemischtes Institut mit vorwiegend kirchlichem Charakter*, 1st ed., II. 542–546, 4th ed., III. 624–630. Wetzer-Welte, VI. 777, occupies the same ground and quotes Orti y Lara as saying, "The Inquisition fused into one weapon the papal sword and the temporal power of kings." Dr. Lea emphasizes the mixed character of the agency, and says that the chief question is not where it had its origin, but which party derived the most advantage. It is, however, of much importance for the history of the papacy as a divine or human institution to insist upon its responsibility in authorizing and supporting the nefarious Holy Office. Funk says that "the assumption that the Spanish Inquisition was primarily a state institution does not hold good."

approbation of the Apostolic see is vouched for in many documents, and the responsibility for the Spanish tribunal was distinctly assumed by Sixtus V., Jan. 22, 1588, as an institution
established by its authority.   Sixtus IV. and his successors
sought again and again to get its full management into their
own hands, but were foiled by the firmness of Ferdinand.
When, for example, in a bull dated April 18, 1482, the pope
ordered the names of the witnesses and accusers to be communicated to the suspects, that the imprisonments should be
in episcopal gaols, that appeal might be taken to the Apostolic
chair and that confessions to the bishop should stop all prosecution, Ferdinand sharply resented the interference and hinted
that the suggestion had started with the use of *conversos* gold
in the curia.   This papal action was only a stage in the battle
for the control of the Holy Office.[1]   Ferdinand was ready to
proceed to the point of rupture with Rome rather than allow
the principle of appeals which would have reduced the power
of the *suprema* to impotence.   Sixtus wrote a compromising
reply, and a year later, October, 1483, Ferdinand got all he
asked for, and the appointment of Torquemada was confirmed.

The royal management of the Inquisition was also in danger
of being fatally hampered by letters of absolution, issued according to custom by the papal penitentiary, which were valid
not only in the court of conscience but in stopping public
trials.   Ferdinand entered a vigorous protest against their
use in Spain, when Sixtus, 1484, confirmed the penitentiary's
right; but here also Sixtus was obliged to retreat, at least in
part, and Alexander VI. and later Clement VII., 1524, made
such letters invalid when they conflicted with the jurisdiction
of the Spanish tribunal.   Spain was bent on doing things in
its own way and won practical independence of the curia.[2]

The principle, whereby in the old Inquisition the bishops were
co-ordinate in authority with the inquisitors or superior to them,

[1] Lea, I. 235 ; II. 103 sqq.

[2] Lea, II. 116, etc., insists upon the double-dealing of the papacy, from
Sixtus IV. to Julius II., " who with one hand sold letters of absolution and
with the other declared them invalid by revocation." Sixtus' bull of 1484
was confirmed by Paul III., 1549. Its claim, an infallible papacy cannot well
abandon.

had to be abandoned in Spain in spite of the pope's repeated attempts to apply it. Innocent VIII., 1487, completely subjected the bishops to the inquisitorial organization, and when Alexander, 1494, annulled this bull and required the inquisitors to act in conjunction with the bishop, Ferdinand would not brook the change and, under his protection, the *suprema* and its agents asserted their independence to Ferdinand.

Likewise, in the matter of confiscations of property, the sovereign claimed the right to dictate their distribution, now applying them for the payment of salaries to the inquisitors and their agents, now appropriating them for the national exchequer, now for his own use or for gifts to his favorites.

No concern of his reign, except the extension of his dominions, received from Ferdinand more constant and sympathetic attention than the deletion of heresy. With keen delight he witnessed the public burnings as adapted to advance the Catholic faith. He scrutinized the reports sent him by inquisitors and, at times, he expressed his satisfaction with their services by gifts of money. In his will, dated the day before his death, he enjoined his heir, Charles V., to be strenuous in supporting the tribunal. As all other virtues, so this testament ran, " are nothing without faith by which and in which we are saved, we command the illustrious prince, our grandson, to labor with all his strength to destroy and extirpate heresy from our kingdoms and lordships, appointing ministers, God-fearing and of good conscience, who will conduct the Inquisition justly and properly for the service of God and the exaltation of the Catholic faith, and who will also have a great zeal for the destruction of the sect of Mohammed." [1] Without doubt, the primary motive in the establishment of the tribunal was with Ferdinand, and certainly with Isabella, religious.

There seems at no time to have been any widespread revolt against the procedure of the Inquisition. In Aragon, some mitigation of its rigors and rules was proposed by the Cortes

---

[1] Lea, I. 214. For Ferdinand's expressions of satisfaction with the zeal shown in the burning of heretics, as after a holocaust at Valladolid, September, 1509, see Lea, I. 189, 191, etc.

of Barcelona, 1512, such as the withdrawal from the inquisitors of the right to carry weapons and the exemption of women from the seizure of their property, in cases where a husband or father was declared a heretic, but Ferdinand and Bishop Enguera, the Aragonese inquisitor-general, were dispensed by Leo X., 1514, from keeping the oath they had taken to observe the rules.   At Charles V.'s accession, an effort was made to have some of the more offensive evils abolished, such as the keeping of the names of witnesses secret, and in 1520 the Cortes of Valladolid and Corunna made open appeal for the amendment of some of the rules.   Four hundred thousand ducats were offered, presumably by *conversos*, to the young king if he would give his assent, and, as late as 1528, the kingdom of Granada, in the same interest, offered him 50,000 ducats.   But the appeals received no favorable action and, under the influence of Ximines, in 1517, the council of Castile represented to Charles that the very peace of Spain depended upon the maintenance of the Inquisition. The cardinal wrote a personal letter to the king, declaring that interference on his part would cover his name with infamy.[1]

The most serious attempt to check the workings of the Inquisition occurred in Saragossa and resulted in the assassination of the chief inquisitor, Peter Arbues, an act of despair laid at the door of the *conversos*.   Arbues was murdered in the cathedral Jan. 25, 1485, the fatal blow being struck from behind, while the priest was on his knees engaged in prayer.   He knew his life was threatened and not only wore a coat of mail and cap of steel, but carried a lance.   He lingered twenty-four hours.   Miracles wrought at the coffin vouched for the sanctity of the murdered ecclesiastic.   The sacred bell of Villela tolled unmoved by hands.   Arbues' blood liquefied on the cathedral floor two weeks after the deed.   Within two years, the popular veneration showed itself in the erection of a splendid tomb to the martyr's memory and the Catholic Church, by the bull of Pius IX., June 29, 1867, has given him the honors of canonization.   As the

[1] Lea, I. 217.

assassination of the papal delegate, Peter of Castelnau, at the opening of the crusade against the Albigenses, 1208, wrought to strengthen Innocent in his purpose to wipe out heresy, even with the sword, likewise the taking off of Arbues only tightened the grip of the Spanish Inquisition in Aragon. His murderers and all in any way accessory to the crime were hunted down, their hands were cut off at the portal of the cathedral and their bodies dragged to the market-place, where they were beheaded and quartered or burnt alive.[1]

Next to the judicial murders perpetrated by the Inquisition, its chief evil was the confiscation of estates. The property of the *conversos* offered a tempting prize to the cupidity of the inquisitors and to the crown. The tribunal was expected to live from the spoils of the heretics. Torquemada's *Instructions* of 1484 contained specific rules governing the disposition of goods held by heretics. There was no limit put upon their despoilment, except that lands transferred before 1479 were exempted from seizure, a precaution to avoid the disturbance of titles. The property of dead heretics, though they had lain in their graves fifty years, was within the power of the tribunal. The dowries of wives were mercifully exempted whose husbands were adjudged heretical, but wives whose fathers were found to be heretics lost their dowries. The claims of the children of heretic fathers might have been expected to call for merciful consideration, but the righteousness of their dispossession had no more vigorous advocates than the clergy. To such property, as the bishop of Simancas argued, the old Christian population had a valid moral claim. The *Instructions* of 1484 direct that, if the children were under age at the time of the confiscation, they were to be distributed among pious families, and announced it as the king's intention, in case they grew up good Christians, so to endow them with alms, especially the girls, that they might marry or enter religion.[2]

The practice of confiscation extended to the bedding and wearing apparel of the victims. One gracious provision was that the slaves of condemned heretics should receive free-

---

[1] Lea, I. 250 sqq.; Wetzer-Welte, *Petrus Arbues*, vol. IX.
[2] Lea, II. 336.

dom. Lands were sold at auction 30 days after their sequestration, but the low price which they often brought indicates
that purchasers enjoyed special privileges of acquisition. Ferdinand and his successor, Charles, were profuse in their disposition of such property. Had the moneys been used for the
wars against the Moors, as at first proposed by Torquemada, the
plea might be made that the tribunal was moved by unselfish
considerations, but they were not. Not only did Ferdinand
take money for his bankrupt treasury, but he appropriated
hunting horses, pearls and other objects for his own use. The
Flemish favorites of Charles V., in less than ten months, sent
home 1,100,000 ducats largely made up of bequests derived
from the exactions of the sacred court.[1] Dr. Lea, whose merit
it is to have shown the vast extent to which the sequestration
of estates was carried, describes the money transactions of the
Inquisition as " a carnival of plunder." It was even found to
be not incompatible with a purpose to maintain the purity of the
faith to enter into arrangements whereby, for a sufficient consideration, communities received protection from inquisitorial
charges. The first such bargain was made at Valencia, 1482.
The king, however, did not hesitate on occasion to violate his
pact and allow unfortunate *conversos*, who had paid for exemption, to be arraigned and condemned. No law existed requiring faith to be kept with a heretic. It also happened that
condemned *conversos* purchased freedom from serving in the
galleys or wearing the badge of heresy, the *sanbenito*.[2]

As early as 1485, Ferdinand and Isabella were able to erect
a royal palace at Guadalupe, costing 2,732,333 maravedis, with
the proceeds of sequestrated property and, in a memorial address to Charles V., 1524, Tristan de Leon asserted that these
sovereigns had received from the possessions of heretics no less
than 10,000,000 ducats. Torquemada also was able to spend
vast sums upon his enterprises, such as the conventual building of St. Thomas at Avila, which it was supposed were drawn
from the victims whom his religious fervor condemned to the
loss of their goods and often of their lives.[3] When the hereti

---

[1] Peter Martyr, as quoted by Lea, II. 381.
[2] Lea, I. 217 ; II. 353, sq., 400–413.   [3] Lea, II. 363.

cal mine was showing signs of exhaustion in Spain, the Spanish colonies of Mexico and Peru poured in their spoils to enable the Holy Office to maintain the state to which it had been accustomed. At an early period, it began to take care for its own perpetuation by making investments on a large scale.[1]

After Ferdinand's death, the *suprema's* power increased, and it demanded a respect only less than that which was yielded to the crown. Its arrogance and insolence in administration kept pace with the high pretension it made to sacredness of aim and divine authority. The institution was known as the Holy Office, the building it occupied was the holy house, *casa santa*, and the public solemnity at which the tribunal appeared officially before the public and announced its decisions was called the act of faith, *auto de fe*.

The *suprema* acted upon the principle started by Paramo, that the inquisitor was the chief personage in his district. He represented both the pope and king.[2] On the one hand, he claimed the right to arrest at will and without restriction from the civil authority; on the other, he demanded freedom for his officials from all arrest and violence.

In trading and making exports, the Holy Office claimed exemption from the usual duties levied upon the people at large. Immunity from military service and the right to carry deadly weapons by day and night were among other privileges to which it laid claim. A deliverance of the Apostolic see, 1515, confirmed it in its right to arrest the highest noble in the land who dared to attack its prerogatives or agents and, in case of need, to protect itself by resort to bloodshed. Its jurisdiction extended not only to the lower orders of the clergy, but also to members of the orders, a claim which, after a long struggle, was confirmed by the edicts of Pius IV. and V., 1559, 1561. A single class was exempted from the rules of its procedure, the bishops. However, the exemption was rather apparent than real, for the Holy Office exercised the right of arraigning bishops under suspicion before the papal chair.

[1] Lea : *The Inq. in the Span. Dependencies*, p. 219.
[2] Lea heads a chapter on this subject, *Supereminence*, I. 350–375.

The first cases of this kind were prelates of Jewish extraction, Davila of Segovia, 1490, and Aranda of Calahorra, 1498. Both were tried in Rome, the former being exonerated, and Aranda kept in prison in S. Angelo, where he is supposed to have died, 1500. The most famous of the episcopal suspects, the archbishop of Toledo, Bartholomew of Carranza, 1503–1576, was kept in prison for 17 years, partly in Spain and partly in Rome. The case enjoyed a European reputation.

Carranza had the distinction of administering the last rites to Charles V. and was for a time a favorite of Philip II., but that sinister prince turned against him. Partly from jealousy of Carranza's honors, as has been surmised, and chiefly on account of his indiscretions of speech, the inquisitor-general Valdes decided upon the archbishop's prosecution, and when his Commentary on the Catechism appeared in Spanish, he was seized under authorization from the Apostolic see, 1559. For two years the prelate was kept in a secret prison and then brought to trial. After delay, Pius IV., 1564, appointed a distinguished commission to investigate the case and Pius V. forced his transfer in 1567 to Rome, where he was confined in S. Angelo for nine years. Under Pius V.'s successor, Gregory XIII., Carranza was compelled to abjure alleged errors, suspended from his seat for five years and remanded to confinement in a Roman convent, where he afterwards died. The boldness and vast power of the Inquisition could have no better proof than the indignity and punishment placed upon a primate of Spain.

The procedure of the Holy Office followed the rules drawn by Torquemada, 1484, 1485, called the *Instructions of Seville*, and the *Instructions of Valladolid* prepared by the same hand, 1488 and 1498. These early codes were afterwards known as the *Instructiones antiguas*, and remained in force until superseded by the code of 1561 prepared by the inquisitor-general, Valdes.

Torquemada lodged the control of the Inquisition in the *suprema*, to which all district tribunals were subordinated. Permanent tribunals were located at Seville, Toledo, Valladolid, Madrid (Corte), Granada, Cordova, Murcia Llerena,

Cuenca, Santiago, Logroño and the Canaries under the crown
of Castile and at Saragossa, Valencia, Barcelona and Majorca
under the crown of Aragon.[1]

The officials included two inquisitors, an assessor or consulter
on modes of canonical procedure, an alguazil or executive officer,
who executed the sentences of the tribunal, notaries who kept
the records, and censors or *califadores* who pronounced elaborate
opinions on points of dispute.   To these was added an official
who appraised and took charge of confiscated property.   A
large body of subordinates, such as the *familiars* or confidential
agents, complete the list of officials.   Laymen were eligible to
the office of inquisitor, provided they were unmarried, and a
condition made for holding any of these places was purity of
blood, *limpieza*, freedom from all stain of Morisco, Jewish or
heretic parentage and of ancestral illegitimacy.   This peculiar
provision led to endless investigation of genealogical records
before appointments were made.[2]

Each tribunal had a house of its own, containing the audience
chamber, rooms for the inquisitors, a library for the records, —
le secreto de la Inquisicion, — a chamber of torture and secret
prisons.   The *familiars* have a dark fame.   They acted as a
body of spies to detect and report cases of heresy.   Their zeal
made them the terror of the land, and the Cortes of Monzon,
1512, called for the reduction of their number.

In its procedure, the Inquisition went on the presumption
that a person accused was guilty until he had made out his
innocence.   The grounds of arrest were rumor or personal
denunciation.   Informing on suspects was represented to the
people as a meritorious act and inculcated even upon children as a duty.   The instructions of 1484 prescribed a miti-
gated punishment for minors who informed on heretical fathers,
and Bishop Simancas declared it to be the sacred obligation of
a son to bring his father, if guilty, to justice.[3]   The spiritual offender was allowed an advocate.   Secrecy was a prime feature

[1] For list of temporary tribunals, see Lea, I. 541–555.
[2] Lea devotes a whole chapter to the subject, II. 285–314.   In time *limpieza*
was made a condition of holding church offices of any sort in Spain.
[3] Lea, II. 485.

in the procedure.   After his arrest, the prisoner was placed in one of the secret prisons, — *carceres secretas*, — and rigidly deprived of all intercourse with friends.   All papers bearing upon his case were kept from him.   The names of his accusers and of witnesses for his prosecution were withheld.   In the choice of its witnesses the Inquisition allowed itself great liberty, even accepting the testimony of persons under the Church's sentence of excommunication, of Jews who remained in the Hebrew faith and of heretics.   Witnesses for the accused were limited to persons zealous for the orthodox faith, and none of his relatives to the fourth generation were allowed to testify. Heresy was regarded as a desperate disorder and to be removed at all costs.   On the other hand, the age of amenability was fixed at 12 for girls and 14 for boys.   The age of fourscore gave no immunity from the grim rigors of the exacting tribunal.[1]

The charges, on which victims were arraigned, included the slightest deflection in word or act from strict Catholic usage, such as the refusal to eat pork on a single occasion, visiting a house where Moorish notions were taught, as well as saying that the Virgin herself and not her image effected cures, and that Jews and Moors would be saved if they sincerely believed the Jewish and the Moorish doctrines to be true.[2]   Recourse was had to torture, not only to secure evidence of guilt.   Even when the testimony of witnesses was sufficient to establish guilt, resort was had to torture to extract a confession from the accused that thereby his soul might be delivered from the burden of secret guilt, to extract information of accomplices, and that a wholesome influence might be exerted in deterring others from heresy by giving them an example of punishment. The modes of torture most in use were the water ordeal and the garruche.   In the water-cure, the victim, tightly bound, was stretched upon a rack or bed, and with the body in an inclined position, the head downward.   The jaws were distended, a linen cloth was thrust down the victim's throat and water from a quart jar allowed to trickle through it into his

[1] Lea, II. 137, gives cases of accused women, respectively 78, 80 and 86.
[2] Lea, III. 8, 14, etc.

inward parts.[1] On occasion, seven or eight such jars were slowly emptied. The *garrucha*, otherwise known as the *strappade*, has already been described. In its application in Spain it was customary to attach weights to the feet and to suspend the body in such a manner that the toes alone touched the ground, and the Spanish rule required that the body be raised and lowered leisurely so as to increase the pain.

The final penalties for heresy included, in addition to the spiritual impositions of fasting and pilgrimage, confiscation of goods, imprisonment, public scourging, the galleys, exile and death. Confiscation and burning extended to the dead, against whom the charge of heresy could be made out. At Toledo, July 25, 1485, more than 400 dead were burnt in effigy. Frequently at the *autos* no living victims suffered. In cases of the dead their names were effaced from their tombstones, that "no memory of them should remain on the face of the earth except as recorded in our sentence." Their male descendants, including the grandchildren, were incapacitated from occupying benefices and public positions, from riding on horseback, carrying weapons and wearing silk or ornaments.

The penalty of scourging was executed in public on the bodies of the victims, bared to the waist, by the public executioner. Women of 86 to girls of 13 were subjected to such treatment. Galley labor as a mode of punishment was sanctioned by Alexander VI., 1503. The sentence of perpetual imprisonment was often relaxed, either from considerations of mercy or for financial reasons. Up to 1488, there had been 5000 condemnations to lasting imprisonment.[2]

The *saco bendito*, or *sanbenito*, another characteristic feature of the Spanish Inquisition, was a jacket of gray or yellow texture, furnished before and behind with a large cross as prescribed by Torquemada. This galling humiliation was aggravated by the rule that, after they were laid aside, the *sanbenitos* should be hung up in the churches, together with a record of the wearer's

---

[1] In Paris the usual method was to inject water into the mouth, oil and vinegar also being used. The amount of water was from 9 to 18 pints. La Croix: *Manners, Customs and Dress of the M. A.*, N.Y. 1874, chapter on Punishments, pp. 407–433.

[2] Lea, III. 140–159.

name inscribed and his sentence. To avoid the shame of this public display, descendants often sought to change their names, a practice the law soon checked. The precedent for the *sanbenito* was found in the covering our first parents wore to hide their nakedness, or in the sackcloth worn in the early Church as a mark of penance.

The *auto de fe*, the final act in the procedure of the Inquisition, shows the relentlessness of this tribunal, and gave the spectators a foretaste of the solemnities of the day of judgment.   There heretics, after being tried by the inquisitorial court, were exposed to public view, [1] and received the first official notice of their sentence. The ceremonial took place on the public squares, where platforms and staging were erected at municipal expense, and such occasions were treated as public holidays.   On the day appointed, the prisoners marched in procession, led by Dominicans and others bearing green and white crosses, and followed by the officials of the Holy Office.   Arrived at the square, they were assigned seats on benches. A sermon was then preached and an oath taken from the people and also from the king, if present, to support the Inquisition.   The sentences were then announced.   Unrepentant heretics were turned over to the civil officers. Wearing *benitos*, inscribed with their name, they were conducted on asses to the *brasero*, or place of burning, which was usually outside the city limits, and consigned to the flames.   The other heretics were then taken back to the prisons of the Inquisition.   Inquisitorial agents were present at the burnings and made a record of them for the use of the religious tribunal. The solemnities of the *auto de fe* were usually begun at 6 in the morning and often lasted into the afternoon.

Theoretically, the tribunal did not pass the sentence of blood. The ancient custom of the Church and the canon law forbade such a decision. Its authority ceased with the abandonment — or, to use the technical expression, the relaxation — of the offender to the secular arm.   By an old custom in passing sentence of incorrigible heresy, it even prayed the secular officer to avoid the spilling of blood and to exercise

---

[1] For a description of an *auto*, see Lea, III. 214–224.

mercy. The prayer was an empty form. The state well understood its duty, and its failure to punish with death heretics convicted by the spiritual court was punishable with excommunication. It did not presume to review the case, to take new evidence or even to require a statement of the evidence on which the sentence of heresy was reached. The duty of the secular officer was ministerial, not judicial. The sentence of heresy was synonymous with burning at the stake. The Inquisition, however, did not stop with turning heretics over to the state, but, as even Vacandard admits, at times pronounced the sentence of burning.[1]

So honorable to the state and to religion were the *autos de fe* regarded that kings attended them and they were appointed to commemorate the marriage of princes or their recovery from sickness. Ferdinand was in the habit of attending them. On the visit of Charles V. to Valencia, 1528, public exhibition was given at which 13 were relaxed in person and 10 in effigy. Philip II.'s marriage, in 1560, to Isabella of Valois was celebrated by an *auto* in Toledo and, in 1564, when this sovereign was in Barcelona, a public exhibition was arranged in his honor, at which eight were sentenced to death. Such spectacles continued to be witnessed by royal personages till 1701, when Philip V. set an example of better things by refusing to be present at one.

[1] Lea, III. 185 sq., quotes the sentence upon Mencia Alfonso, tried at Guadalupe, 1485, which runs : "As a limb of the devil, she shall be taken to the place of burning so that by the secular officials of this town justice may be executed upon her according to the custom of these kingdoms." Paul III., 1547, and Julius III., 1550, conferred upon clerics the right of condemning to mutilation and death in cases where, as with the Venetian government, delays were interposed in the execution of the ecclesiastical sentence. Vacandard says, p. 180 : " Some inquisitors, realizing the emptiness of the formula, *ecclesia abhorret a sanguine*, dispensed with it altogether and boldly assumed the full responsibility for their sentences. The Inquisition is the real judge, — it lights the fires. . . . It is erroneous to pretend that the Church had absolutely no part in the condemnation of heretics to death. Her participation was not direct and immediate, but, even though indirect, it was none the less real and efficacious." This author, p. 211, misrepresents history when he makes the legislation of Frederick II. responsible for the papal treatment of heresy. Innocent III. had been punishing the Albigenses to death long before the appearance of Frederick's *Constitutions*.

The last case of an execution by the Spanish Inquisition was a schoolmaster, Cayetano Ripoll, July 26, 1826. His trial lasted nearly two years. He was accused of being a deist, and substituting in his school the words "Praise be to God" for "Ave Maria purissima." He died calmly on the gibbet after repeating the words, "I die reconciled to God and to man."[1]

Not satisfied with putting heretical men out of the world, the Inquisition also directed its attention to noxious writings.[2] At Seville, in 1490, Torquemada burnt a large number of Hebrew copies of the Bible, and a little later, at Salamanca, he burnt 6000 copies. Ten years later, 1502, Ferdinand and Isabella promulgated a law forbidding books being printed, imported and sold which did not have the license of a bishop or certain specified royal judges. All Lutheran writings were ordered by Adrian, in 1521, delivered up to the Inquisition. Thenceforth the Spanish tribunal proved itself a vigorous guardian of the purity of the press. The first formal Index, compiled by the University of Louvain, 1546, was approved by the inquisitor-general Valdes and the *suprema*, and ordered printed with a supplement. This was the first *Index Expurgatorius* printed in Spain. All copies of the Scriptures in Spanish were seized and burnt, and the ferocious law of 1558 ordered booksellers keeping or selling prohibited books punished with confiscation of goods or death. Strict inquisitorial supervision was had over all libraries in Spain down into the 19th century. Of the effect of this censorship upon Spanish culture, Dr. Lea says: "The intellectual development which in the 16th century promised to render Spanish literature and learning the most illustrious in Europe was stunted and starved into atrophy, the arts and sciences were neglected,

[1] The Spanish Inquisition was introduced into Sicily in 1487, where it met with vigorous resistance from the parliament, and in Sardinia, 1492. In the New World its victims were Protestants, *conversos*, bigamists and fornicators. The Mexican tribunal was abolished in 1820, and that of Peru, the same year. As late as 1774 a Bogota physician was tried "as the first and only one who in this kingdom and perhaps in all America" had publicly declared himself for the Copernican system.

[2] Lea, chapter on Censorship, III. 481-548; Ticknor: *Span. Lit.*, I. 461 sqq.

and the character which Spain acquired among the nations was tersely expressed in the current saying that Africa began at the Pyrenees."

The " ghastly total " of the victims consigned by the Spanish Inquisition to the flames or other punishments has been differently stated. Precise tables of statistics are of modern creation, but that it was large is beyond question. The historian, Llorente, gives the following figures : From 1480–1498, the date of Torquemada's death, 8800 were burnt alive, 6500 in effigy and 90,004 subjected to other punishments. From 1499–1506, 1664 were burnt alive, 832 in effigy and 32,456 subjected to other punishments. From 1507–1517, during the term of Cardinal Ximines, 2536 were burnt alive, 1368 in effigy and 47,263 subjected to other penalties. This writer gives the grand totals up to 1524 as 14,344 burnt alive, 9372 in effigy and 195,937 condemned to other penalties or released as penitents. In 1524, an inscription was placed on the fortress of Triana, Seville, running : "In the year 1481, under the pontificate of Sixtus IV. and the rule of Ferdinand and Isabella, the Inquisition was begun here. Up to 1524, 20,000 heretics and more abjured their awful crime on this spot and nearly 1000 were burnt." From records still extant, the victims in Toledo before 1501 are found to have numbered 297 burnt alive and 600 in effigy, and 5400 condemned to other punishment or reconciled. The documents, however, are not preserved or, at any rate, not known from which a full estimate could be made. In any case the numbers included thousands of victims burnt alive and tens of thousands subjected to other punishments.[1]

The rise of the Spanish Inquisition was contemporary with Spain's advance to a foremost place among the nations of Europe. After eight centuries, her territory was for the first time

---

[1] See Hoensbroech, I. 139, quoting Llorente. Dr. Lea speaks of the apparent tendency of early writers to exaggerate the achievements of the " Holy Office," and calls in question, though with some hesitation, Llorente's figures and the figures given by an early secretary of the tribunal, Zurita, who records 4000 burnings and 30,000 reconciliations in Seville alone before 1520. See Lea's figures, IV. 513–524. Father Gams, in his *Kirchengesch. Spaniens*, reckons the number of those burnt, up to 1504, at 2000, but he excludes from these figures the burnings for other crimes than heresy. See Lea, IV. 517.

completely free from the government of the Mohammedan. The renown of her regiments was soon to be unequalled. Spanish ships opened the highways of the sea and returned from the New World freighted with its wealth. Spanish diplomacy was in the ascendant in Italy. But the decay of her vital forces her religious zeal did not check. Spain's Catholic orthodoxy was assured, but Spain placed herself outside the current of modern culture and progress. By her policy of religious seclusion and pride, she crushed independence of thought and virility of moral purpose. One by one, she lost her territorial acquisitions, from the Netherlands and Sicily to Cuba and the Philippines in the far Pacific. Heresy she consumed inside of her own precincts, but the paralysis of stagnation settled down upon her national life and institutions, and peoples professing Protestantism, which she still calls heresy, long since have taken her crown in the world of commerce and culture, invention and nautical enterprise. The present map of the world has faint traces of that empire on which it was the boast of the Spaniard of the 16th century that the sun never set. This reduction of territory and resources calls forth no spirit of denunciation. Nay, it attracts a sympathetic consideration which hopes for the renewed greatness of the land of Ferdinand and Isabella, through the introduction of that intellectual and religious freedom which has stirred the energies of other European peoples and kept them in the path of progress and new achievement.

CHAPTER VIII.

THE RENAISSANCE.

§ 61. *Literature of the Renaissance.*

FOR an extended list of literature, see VOIGT: *Wiederbelebung des class. Alterthums*, II. 517–529, bringing it down to 1881, and PASTOR: *Gesch. der Päpste*, I., pp. xxxii–lxiii, III., pp. xlii–lxix. Also this vol., pp. 400 sqq. Geiger adds lit. notices to his *Renaissance und Humanismus*, pp. 564 sqq. The edd. of most of the Humanists are given in the footnotes. — M. WHITCOMB: *A Lit. Source-Book of the Ital. Renaiss.*, Phila., 1898, pp. 118.

GENL. WORKS. — * G. TIRABOSCHI, a Jesuit and librarian of the duke of Modena, d. 1794: *Storia della Letteratura Italiana*, 13 vols., Modena, 1771–1782; 9 vols., Roma, 1782–1785; 16 vols., Milan, 1822–1826. Vol. V. of the Roman ed. treats of Dante, Petrarca and Boccaccio. — HEEREN: *Gesch. d. class. Lit.*, etc., 2 vols., Götting., 1797–1802. — ROSCOE: *Life of Lorenzo de' Medici* and *Life and Pontificate of Leo X.* — J. CH. L. SISMONDI, d. 1842: *Hist. des Républiques Ital.*, Paris, 1807–1818, 5th ed., 10 vols., 1840–1844. Engl. trsl., Lond., 1832, and *Hist. de la renaiss. de la liberté en Italie*, 2 vols., 1832. — J. MICHELET, d. 1874: *Renaissance*, the 7th vol. of his *Hist. de France*, Paris, 1867. — * J. BURCKHARDT, Prof. in Basel, d. 1897: *Die Cultur der Renaissance in Italien*, Basel, 1860; 3rd ed. by L. GEIGER, 1878. 9th ed., 1904. A series of philosophico-historical sketches on the six aspects of the Italian Renaissance, namely, the new conception of the state, the development of the individual, the revival of classic antiquity, the discovery of the world and of man, the new formation of society and the transformation of morals and religion. Engl. trsl. by Middlemore from the 3rd ed., 2 vols., Lond., 1878, 1 vol., 1890. Also his *Cicerone; Anleitung zum Genuss der Kunstwerke Ital.*, 4th ed. by BODE, Leipz., 1879; 9th ed., 2 vols., 1907. — * G. VOIGT: *Wiederbelebung des classischen Alterthums oder das erste Jahrhundert des Humanismus*, 1859; 2 vols., 3rd ed., 1893. — T. D. WOOLSEY, Pres. of Yale Col., d. 1889: *The Revival of Letters in the 14th and 15th Centuries.* A series of valuable articles in the line of Voigt's first ed., in the *New Englander* for 1864 and 1865. — M. MONNIER: *La Renaiss. de Dante à Luther*, Paris, 1884. Crowned by the French Acad. — * P. VILLARI: *Nic. Machiavelli e i suoi tempi*, 3 vols., Flor., 1877–1882; Engl. trsl. by the author's wife, 4 vol., Lond., 1878–1883. An introd. chap. on the Renaiss. New ed., 2 vols. 1891. — J. A. SYMONDS: *Renaissance in Italy*, Lond., 1877 sqq.; 2d, cheaper ed., 7 vols., 1888. Part I., *The Age of the Despots;* Part II., *The Revival of Learning;* Part III., *The Fine Arts;* Part IV., *Ital. Literature*, 2 vols.;

Part V., *The Cath. Reaction*, 2 vols. The most complete Engl. work on the subject and based upon the original sources, but somewhat repetitious. Also his *Life of Michelangelo*, etc. See below.— G. KOERTING : *Gesch. der Lit. Italiens im Zeitalter der Renaiss.*, Leipz., Vol. I., 1878, Petrarca; Vol. II., 1880, Boccaccio; Vol. III., 1884, the forerunners and founders of the Renaissance. — * L. GEIGER, Prof. in Berlin : *Renaissance u. Humanismus in Ital. und Deutschland*, Berlin, 1882, 2nd ed., 1899. Part of Oncken's *Allg. Gesch.* — MRS. OLIPHANT : *The Makers of Florence*, Lond., 1888. Sketches of Dante, Giotto, Savonarola, Michelangelo.— P. SCHAFF : *The Renaissance*, N.Y., 1891, pp. 132.— * GREGOROVIUS : *Hist. of the City of Rome*, vols. vi–viii. — * PASTOR : *Gesch. d. Päpste*, especially vols. I. 3–63 ; III. 3–172. — CREIGHTON : *Hist. of the Papacy.* — P. and H. VAN DYKE : *The Age of the Renascence*, 1377–1527, N.Y., 1897. — K. BRANDI : *D. Renaiss. in Florenz u. Rom*, 2nd ed., Leipz., 1900. — W. S. LILLY : *Renaiss. Types*, Lond., 1901. — E. STEINMANN : *Rom u. d. Renaiss.*, von Nik. V. — Leo X., 2nd ed., Leipz., 1902. — * JOHN OWEN : *The Skeptics of the Ital. Renaiss.*, Lond., 1893. — J. KLACZKO : *Rome and the Renaiss.*, trsl. by Dennie, N.Y., 1903.— P. VAN DYKE : *Aretino, Th. Cromwell and Maximilian I.*, N.Y., 1905. — L. SCHMIDT : *D. Renaiss. in Briefen v. Dichtern, Künstlern, Staatsmännern u. Frauen.* — J. E. SANDYS : *Hist. of Class. Scholarship*, 3 vols. — A. BAUDRILLART : *The Cath. Ch., the Renais. and Protestantism*, Lond., 1908. — IMBART DE LA TOUR : *L'église cathol. : la crise et la renaiss.*, Paris, 1909.

For § 3. — For DANTE. Best Italian text of the *Div. Commedia* is by WITTE. The ed. of Fraticelli, Flor., 1881, is used in this vol. See also Toynbee's text, Lond., 1900. The latest and best Ital. commentaries by SCARTAZZINI, Leipz., 3 vols., 1874–1894, 3rd, small ed., 1899, P. G. CAMPI, Turin, 1890 sqq., and W. W. VERNON, based on Benvenuto da Imola, 2 vols., Lond., 1897.— Engl. trsll. of Dante's *Div. Com. :* In verse by REV. H. F. CARY, 1805, etc., amended ed. by O. KUHNS, N.Y., 1897. — J. C. WRIGHT, Lond., 1843, etc. ; LONGFELLOW, 3 vols., 1867, etc. ; E. H. PLUMPTRE, 2 vols., Lond., 1887 sqq. ; T. W. PARSONS, Bost., 1896. — H. K. HASELFOOT, Lond., 1899. — M. R. VINCENT, N.Y., 1904. — In prose : J. A. CARLYLE, Lond., 1848, etc. ; W. S. DUGDALE, *Purgatorio*, Lond., 1883. — A. J. BUTLER, Lond., 1894. — G. C. NORTON, Boston, 1892, new ed., 1901. — P. H. WICKSTEED, Lond., 1901 sqq. — H. F. TOZER, Lond., 1904. — * G. A. SCARTAZZINI, a native of the Grisons, Reformed minister : *Prolegomeni della Div. Com.*, etc., Leipz., 1890. Engl. trsl. *A Companion to Dante*, by A. J. BUTLER, Lond., 1893 ; *Dante Handbuch*, etc., Engl. trsl. *Hdbook. to Dante*, etc., by T. DAVIDSON, Bost., 1887. — E. A. FAY : *Concordance to the Div. Com.*, Cambr., Mass., 1880. — P. SCHAFF : *Dante and the Div. Com.*, in *Literature and Poetry*, 1890, pp. 279–429, with list of Dante lit., pp. 328–337. — TOZER : *Engl. Concordance on Dante's Div. Com.*, Oxf., 1907. — * E. MOORE : *Studies in Dante*, 3 vols., Lond., 1896–1903. — *Lives* of Dante : *Dante and his Early Biographers*, being a résumé by E. MOORE of five, Lond., 1880. A trsl. of Boccaccio's and Bruni's *Lives*, by WICKSTEED, Hull, 1898. — F. X. KRAUS, Berl., 1897. — P. VILLARI : *The First Two Centt. of Florent. Hist. The Republic, and Parties at the Time of Dante.* Engl. trsl. by L. Villari. — * WITTE : *Essays on Dante*, trsl. by Lawrence and Wicksteed. — Essays on Dante by * R. W. CHURCH, 1888, and

* LOWELL. — M. F. ROSSETTI : *Shadow of Dante*, Edin., 1884. — OWEN : *Skeptics of the Ital. Renaiss.* — J. A. SYMONDS : *Introd. to the Study of Dante*, Lond., 1893. — D. G. C. ROSSETTI : *Dante and Ital. Poets preceding him*, 1100–1300, Boston, 1893. — C. A. DINSMORE : *The Teachings of Dante*, Bost., 1901. — C. E. LAUGHLIN : *Stories of Authors' Loves*, Phila., 1902. — A. H. STRONG : *Dante*, in *Great Poets and their Theol.*, Phila., 1897, pp. 105–155. — Art. *Dante* with lit. in the SCHAFF-HERZOG, III. 353 sqq. by M. R. VINCENT.

For PETRARCA : *Opera omnia*, Venice, 1503 ; Basel, 1554, 1581. — *Epistolæ* ed. in Lat. and Ital. by Fracassetti, Flor., 1859–1870, in several vols. The *Canzoniere* or *Rime in Vita e Morte di Mad. Laura* often separately edited by Marsand, Leopardi, Carducci and others, and in all collections of the Ital. classics. — *Sonnets, Triumphs and other Poems*, with a *Life* by T. CAMPBELL, Lond., 1889–1890. — *Lives* by BLANC, Halle, 1844. — MÉZIÈRES, Paris, 1868, 2d ed., 1873. — GEIGER, Leipz., 1874. — KOERTING, Leipz., 1878, pp. 722. — MARY A. WARD, Bost., 1891. — F. HORRIDGE, 1897. — * J. H. ROBINSON and H. W. ROLFE, N.Y., 1898. — L. O. KUHNS, *Great Poets of Italy*, 1904. — E. J. MILLS : *Secret of Petr.*, 1904. — R. DE NOLHAC : *Petr. and the Art World*, 1907.

For BOCCACCIO : *Opere volgari*, ed. by MOUTIER, 17 vols., Flor., 1827–1834, *Le Lettere edite ed inedite*, trsl. by FR. CORRAGINI, Flor., 1877. — *Lives* of Boccaccio by MANETTI, BALDELLI, LANDAU, KOERTING, Leipz., 1880. — GEIGER : *Renaissance*, pp. 448–474. — * OWEN : *Skeptics*, etc., pp. 128–147. — N. H. DOLE : *Boccaccio and the Novella* in *A Teacher of Dante*, etc., N.Y., 1908.

For § 64. — For *Lives* of the popes, see pp. 401–403. *Lives* of Cosimo de' Medici by FABRONI, Pisa, 1789 ; K. D. EWART, Lond., 1899 ; and of Lorenzo by FABRONI, 2 vols., Pisa, 1784 ; ROSCOE ; VON REUMONT ; B. BUSER, Leipz., 1879 ; CASTELNAU, 2 vols., Paris, 1879. — VAUGHAN : *The Medici Popes*, 1908. — G. F. YOUNG : *The Medici, 1400–1743*, Lond., 1909. — LOR. DE' MEDICI : *Opere*, 4 vols., Flor., 1825, *Poesie*, ed. by Carducci, Flor., 1859. — E. L. S. HORSBURGH : *Lor. the Magnificent*, Lond., 1909.

For § 66. — G. VASARI, pupil of Michelangelo, d. 1574 ; *Lives of the More Celebrated Painters, Sculptors and Architects*, 1550 ; best ed. by Milanesi, 9 vols., Flor., 1878–1885. Small ed., 1889. Engl. trsl., new ed., 1878, 5 vols. in Bohn's Library. Vasari is the basis of most works in this department. — BENVENUTO CELLINI, goldsmith and sculptor at Florence, d. 1570 : *Vita scritta da lui medesimo*. An autobiog. giving a lively picture of the life of an Ital. artist of that period. German trsl. by GOETHE ; Engl. trsll. by ROSCOE and SYMONDS, Lond., 1890. — A. LUIGI LANZA, d. 1810 : *The Hist. of Painting in Italy, from the Period of the Revival of the Fine Arts to 1800*. Trsl. by T. Roscoe, 3 vols., Lond., 1852. — W. LÜBKE : *Hist. of Sculpture*, Engl. trsl. by Bunnett, 2 vols., 1872 ; Outlines of the *Hist. of Art*, ed. by R. STURGIS, 2 vols., N.Y., 1904. — J. A. CROWE and G. B. CAVALCASELLE : *Hist. of Painting in Italy, etc., to the 16th Cent.*, Lond., 1864–1867, ed. by Douglass, Lond., 3 vols., 1903–1908. — MRS. JAMESON and LADY EASTLAKE : *Hist. of our Lord as exemplified in Works of Art.* — MRS. JAMESON : *Legends of the Madonna as repres. in the Fine Arts ; Sacr. and Leg. Art ; Legends of the Monastic Orders as expressed in the Fine Arts.* — H. TAINE : *Lectures on Art,*

Paris, 1865 sq. — 1st series : *The Philos. of Art.* 2nd series : *Art in Italy*, etc. Trsl. by Durand, N.Y., 1875. — A. WOLTMANN and K. WOERMANN : *Hist. of Anc., Early Christian and Med. Painting.* Trsl. by Colvin, Lond., 1880, illus. — E. MÜNTZ : *Hist. de l'Art pendant la Renaiss.*, 5 vols., Paris, 1889–1905. The first 3 vols. are devoted to Italy, the 4th to France, the 5th to other countries. *Les Antiquités de la ville de Rom*, 1300–1600, Paris, 1886. — *Histt. of Archit.* by FERGUSON and R. STURGIS. — C. H. MOORE : *Character of Renaiss. Archit.*, N.Y., 1905. — R. LANCIANI : *Golden Days of the Renaiss. in Rome*, 1906. — A. K. PORTER : *Med. Archit. Its Origin and Development*, 2 vols., N.Y., 1909. — *Lives* of Michelangelo by * H. GRIMM, 2 vols., Berl., 1860, 5th ed., 1879. Engl. trsl. by Bunnett, 12th ed., 2 vols., Bost., 1882 ; A. SPRENGER : *Raffaele u. Michelangelo*, 2nd ed., 1883 ; C. CLEMENT, Lond., 1888 ; J. A. SYMONDS, 2 vols., N.Y., 1892 ; F. HORRIDGE, 1897 ; C. HOLROYD, 1903. — *Lives* of Raphael by RULAND, Lond., 1870 ; LÜBKE, Dresden, 1881 ; MÜNTZ, trsl. by Armstrong, 1888 ; CROWE and CAVALCASELLE, 2 vols., Lond., 1882–1888 ; MINGHETTI, Ger. ed., Breslau, 1887 ;* H. GRIMM, trsl. by S. H. Adams, Bost., 1888 ; KNACKFUSS, trsl. by Dodgson, N.Y., 1899.

For §§ 68, 69. — K. HAGEN : *Deutschland literarische und religiöse Verhältnisse im Reformations-Zeitalter*, Erlang., 1841–1844, 3 vols., 2d ed., Frankf., 1868. — J. JANSSEN-PASTOR : *Gesch. des deutschen Volkes*, 18th ed., I. 77–166, II. Comp. his alphab. list of books, I., pp. xxxi–lv. — GEIGER : *Renaiss. u. Humanismus*, pp. 323–580. — ZARNCKE : *D. deutschen Universitäten im MA.*, Leip., 1857. — PAULSEN : *Germ. Universities*, etc., trsl. by Perry, Lond., 1895. — G. KAUFMANN : *Gesch. d. deutschen Universitäten*, 2 vols., Stuttg., 1888–1896. — For monographs on the universities, see Lit. in Rashdall and Schmid, pp. 51–54.

For REUCHLIN : *Briefwechsel*, ed. L. Geiger, Tübing., 1875. Monographs on Reuchlin by MAYERHOF, Berl., 1830 ; LAMAY, Pforzheim, 1855 ; GEIGER, Leipz., 1871 ; A. HORAWITZ, Vienna, 1877. — On Reuchlin's conflict with the Dominicans of Cologne and Hutten's part in it, see STRAUSS : *U. von Hutten*, pp. 132–164 ; BÖCKING, II. 55–156. — N. PAULUS : *D. deutschen Dominikaner im Kampfe mit Luther*, Freib., 1903, p. 94 sqq., 119 sqq. — JANSSEN, II. 40 sqq.

For ERASMUS : *Opera*, ed. B. Rhenanus, 9 vols., Basel, 1540, by Le Clerc, 10 vols., Leyden, 1703–1706. — *Epistolæ*, ed. ALLEN, Oxf., 1906. In Engl. trsl. by * F. M. NICHOLS, 2 vols., Lond., 1901–1904. In Engl. trsl., *Praise of Folly*, Lond., 1876. *Colloquies*, Lond., 1724, new ed., 2 vols., 1878. *Enchiridion*, Lond., 1905. — *Bibl. Erasmania*, 5 vols., Ghent, 1897–1907 sqq. — *Lives* of Erasmus, by H. DURAND DE LAUR : *Er. précurseur et initiateur de l'esprit mod.*, 2 vols., Paris, 1872. — * R. B. DRUMMOND, 2 vols., Lond., 1873. — * F. SEEBOHM: *The Oxf. Reformers*, Lond., 1887, etc. — AMIEL, Paris, 1889. — J. A. FROUDE, 1896. — * E. EMERTON, N.Y., 1899. — A. B. PENNINGTON, Lond., 1875, 1901. — E. F. H. CAPEY, Lond., 1903. — * J. A. FAULKNER, Cin'ti, 1907. — A. RICHTER : *Erasmienstudien*, Dresden, 1901. — GEIGER, 526 sqq. — JANSSEN, II. 1–24.

For general education : RASHDALL : *Universities*, II., pp. 211–285. — K. A. SCHMID : *Gesch. d. Erziehung*, Stuttg., 1892, II. 51–126. — J. MÜLLER : *Quel-*

lenschriften zur Gesch. d. deutschsprachl. Unterrichts bis zur Mitte d. 16. Jahrh., Gotha, 1882.

For ULRICH VON HUTTEN: E. BÖCKING: *Ulrichi Hutteni opp.*, 7 vols., Leipz., 1859–1870.— S. SZAMATOLSKI: *Huttens deutsche Schriften*, 1891.— D. F. STRAUSS, author of the *Life of Jesus: U. von Hutten*, 3 vols., Leipz., 1858, 1 vol., 1871, Engl. trsl., Lond., 1874. Also *Gespräche von U. von Hut.*, the *Epp. obscurorum virorum* in German, Leipz., 1860.— J. DECKERT: *Ul. v. Hutten's Leben u. Wirken*, Vienna, 1901.

For § 70. IMBART DE LA TOUR, Prof. at Bordeaux: *L'église catholique: la crise et la renaissance*, Paris, 1909, being vol. II. of *Les origines de la réforme*, vol. I., *La France moderne*, 1905. To be completed in 4 vols.— SCHMID: *Gesch. d. Erziehung*, II., 40 sqq.— H. M. BAIRD: *Hist. of the Huguenots*, I. 1–164.— BONET MAURY, art. *Faber* in Herzog, V. 715 sqq. — Works on the Univ. of Paris and French Lit.: H. VAN LAUN: *Hist. of French Lit.*, 3 vols. in one, N.Y., 1895, pp. 259–296.— *The Histt. of France* by MARTIN and GUIZOT.

For § 71.— F. SEEBOHM: *The Oxford Reformers, Colet, Erasmus, More*, Lond., 1887. — Colet's writings ed. with trsl. and notes by LUPTON, 5 vols., Lond., 1867–1876. — *Lives of Colet*, by S. KNIGHT, 1823.— J. H. LUPTON: *Life of Dean Colet*, Lond., 1887, new ed., 1908. — Artt. in *Dict. Natl. Biogr., Colet, Fisher*, etc. — *Histt. of Engl.* by LINGARD and GREEN. — *Histt. of the Engl. Ch.* by GAIRDNER and by CAPES. — WARD-WALLER: *Cambr. Hist. of Engl. Lit.*, vol. III., Cambr., 1909. — H. MORLEY: *Engl. Writers*, vol. VII., 1891.— MULLINGER: *Hist. of Univ. of Cambridge.* — For edd. of Sir Thos. More's Works, see Dict. Natl. Biogr., XXXVIII., 445 sqq. — *Lives of More* by ROPER, written in Mary Tudor's reign, publ. Paris, 1626; STAPLETON, Douay, 1588; E. MORE, a grandson, 1627; T. E. BRIDGETT, Rom. Cath., 2nd ed., 1892: W. H. HUTTON, 1895. — W. S. LILLY: *Renaiss. Types*, 1901, III., Erasmus, IV., More.—L. EINSTEIN: *The Ital. Renaiss. in England.* —A. D. INNES: *Ten Tudor Statesmen*, Lond., 1906. More is treated pp. 76–111.— A. F. LEACH: *Engl. Schools at the Reformation*, Lond., 1896. — Eng. Works of Bp. J. FISHER, ed. MAJOR, Lond., 1876.— *Life of Fisher*, by BRIDGETT, 1888.

§ 62. *The Intellectual Awakening.*

The discussions, which issued in the Reformatory councils and which those councils fostered, were a worthy expression of an awakening freedom of thought in the effort to secure relief from ecclesiastical abuses. The movement, to which the name Renaissance has been given, was a larger and far more successful effort, achieving freedom from the intellectual bondage to which the individual man had been subjected by the theology and hierarchy of the Church. The intelligence of Italy, and indeed of Western Europe as a whole, had grown weary of the monastic ideal of life, and the one-sided purpose of the scholastic systems to exalt heavenly concerns by ignoring or degrading things terrestrial.   The Renaissance insisted upon the rights of the life that now is, and dignified the total sphere for which man's intellect and his æsthetic and social tastes by nature fit him.   It sought to give just recognition to man as the proprietor of the earth.   It substituted the enlightened observer for the monk; the citizen for the contemplative recluse.   It honored human sympathies more than conventual visions and dexterous theological dialectics.   It substituted observation for metaphysics.   It held forth the achievements of history.   It called man to admire his own creations, the masterpieces of classical literature and the monuments of art.   It bade him explore the works of nature and delight himself in their excellency.   How different from the apparent or real indifference to the beauties of the natural world as shown, for example, by the monk, St. Bernard, was the attitude of Leon Battista Alberti, d. 1472, who bore testimony that the sight of a lovely landscape had more than once made him well of sickness.[1]

In the narrower sense, the Renaissance may be confined to the recovery of the culture of Greece and Rome and the revival of polite literature and art, and it is sometimes designated the Revival of Letters.   After having been taught for centuries that the literature of classic antiquity was full of snares and dangers for a Christian public, men opened their eyes and revelled with childlike delight in the discovery of ancient authors and history.   Virgil sang again the Æneid, Homer the Iliad and Odyssey.   Cicero once more delivered his orations and Plato taught his philosophy.   It was indeed an intellectual and artistic new birth that burst forth in Italy, a regeneration, as the word Renaissance means.   But it was more.   It was a revolt against monastic asceticism and scholasticism, the systems which cramped the free flow of bodily enthusiasm and intellectual inquiry.[2]   It called man from

---

[1] Geiger-Burckhardt, I. 152.

[2] Along this line, see the strong remarks of Owen, pp. 72–96.   This vigorous writer traces the roots of the Renaissance back to the liberating influence of the Crusades on the intelligence of Europe.

morbid self-mortifications as the most fitting discipline of
mortal existence here below, and offered him the satisfaction
of all the elements of his nature as his proper pursuit.

Beginning in Italy, this new enthusiasm spread north to
Germany and extended as far as Scotland. North of the
Alps, it was known as Humanism and its representatives
as Humanists, the words being taken from *literæ humanæ*,
or *humaniores*, that is, humane studies, the studies which
develop the man as the proprietor of this visible sphere. In
the wider sense, it comprehends the revival of literature and
art, the development of rational criticism, the transition from
feudalism to a new order of social organization, the elevation
of the modern languages of Europe as vehicles for the highest
thought, the emancipation of intelligence, and the expansion
of human interests, the invention of the printing-press, the
discoveries of navigation and the exploration of America and
the East, and the definition of the solar system by Copernicus
and Galileo, — in one word, all the progressive developments
of the last two centuries of the Middle Ages, developments
which have since been the concern of modern civilization.

The most discriminating characterization of this remarkable movement came from the pen of Michelet, who defined
it as the discovery of the world and man. In this twofold
aspect, Burckhardt, its leading historian for Italy, has treated
the Renaissance with deep philosophical insight.

The period of the Renaissance lasts from the beginning of
the 14th to the middle of the 16th century, from Roger
Bacon, d. 1294, and Dante, d. 1321, to Raphael, d. 1520, and
Michelangelo, d. 1564, Reuchlin, d. 1522, and Erasmus, d.
1536. For more than a century it proceeded in Italy without
the patronage of the Church. Later, from the pontificate
of Nicolas V. to the Medicean popes, Leo X. and Clement
VII., it was fostered by the papal court. For this reason the
last popes of the Middle Ages are known as the Renaissance
popes. The movement in the courts may be divided into
three periods: the age of the great Italian literati, Dante,
Petrarca and Boccaccio, the age from 1400–1460, when the
interest in classic literature predominated, and the age from

1460-1540, when the pursuit of the fine arts was the predominant feature. The first age contributed immortal works to literature. In the second, Plato and the other classics were translated and sedulously studied. In the last, the fine arts and architecture offered their array of genius in Italy.

To some writers it has occurred to go back as far as Frederick II. for the beginnings of the movement. That sovereign embodied in himself a varied culture and a versatility of intellect rare in any age. With authorship and a knowledge of a number of languages, he combined enlightened ideas in regard to government and legislation, the patronage of higher education and the arts. For the varied interests of his mind, he has been called the first modern man.[1] However, the literary activity of his court ceased at his death. Italy was not without its poets in the 13th century, but it is with the imposing figure of Dante that the revival of culture is to be dated. That a Renaissance should have been needed is a startling fact in the history of human development and demands explanation. The ban, which had been placed by the Church upon the study of the classic authors of antiquity and ancient institutions, palsied polite research and reading for a thousand years. Even before Jerome, whose mind had been disciplined in the study of the classics, at last pronounced them unfit for the eye of a Christian, Tertullian's attitude was not favorable. Cassian followed Jerome; and Alcuin, the chief scholar of the 9th century, turned away from Virgil as a collection of lying fables. At the close of the 10th century, a pope reprimanded Arnulf of Orleans by reminding him that Peter was unacquainted with Plato, Virgil and Terence, and that God had been pleased to choose as His agents, not philosophers and rhetoricians, but rustics and unlettered men. In deference to such authorities the dutiful churchman turned from the closed pages of the old Romans and Greeks. Only did a selected author like Terence have here and there in a convent a clandestine though eager reader.

In the 12th century, it seemed as if a new era in literature

[1] Burckhardt, I. 4. See vol. V., Pt. I. 198 of this *History*.

was impending, as if the old learning was about to flourish again.   The works of Aristotle became more fully known through the translations of the Arabs.   Schools were started in which classic authors were read.   Abælard turned to Virgil as a prophet.   The Roman law was discovered and explained at Bologna and other seats of learning.   John of Salisbury, Grosseteste, Peter of Blois and other writers freely quoted from Cicero, Livy, Tacitus, Suetonius, Ovid and other Latin authors.   But the head of Western Christendom discerned in this movement a grave menace to theology and religion, and was quick to blight the new shoot with his curse, and in its early statutes, forced by the pope, the University of Paris excluded the literature of Rome from its curriculum.

But this arbitrary violence could not forever hold the mind of Europe in bonds.   The satisfaction its intelligence was seeking, it did not find in the subtle discussions of the Schoolmen or the dismal pictures of the monastics.   When the new movement burst forth, it burst forth in Italy, that beautiful country, the heir of Roman traditions.   The glories of Italy's past in history and in literature blazed forth again as after a long eclipse, and the cult of the beautiful, for which the Italian is born, came once more into free exercise.   In spite of invasion after invasion the land remained Italian.   Lombards, Goths, Normans had occupied it, but the invaders were romanized much more than the Italians were teutonized.   The feudal system and Gothic architecture found no congenial soil south of the Alps.   In the new era, it seemed natural that the poets and orators of old Italy should speak again in the land which they had witnessed as the mistress of all nations.   The literature and law of Greece and Rome again becamethe educators of the Latin and also of the Teutonic races, preparing them to receive the seeds of modern civilization.

The tap-root of the Renaissance was individualism as opposed to sacerdotal authority.   Its enfranchising process manifested itself in Roger Bacon, whose mind turned away from the rabbinical subtleties of the Schoolmen to the secrets of natural science and the discoveries of the earth reported by Rubruquis or suggested by his own reflection, and more

fully in Dante, Marsiglius of Padua and Wyclif, who resisted
the traditional authority of the papacy.   It was active in the
discussions of the Reformatory councils.   And it received a
strong impetus in the administration of the Lombard cities
which gloried in their independence.   With their authority
the imperial policy of Frederick Barbarossa and Frederick II.
had clashed.   Partly owing to the loose hold of the empire
and partly owing to the papal policy, which found its selfish
interests subserved better by free contending states and republics than by a unified kingdom of Italy under a single
temporal head, these independent municipalities took such
deep root that they withstood for nearly a thousand years
the unifying process which, in the case of France, Great
Britain and Spain, resulted in the consolidation of strong
kingdoms soon after the era of the Crusades closed.   Upon
an oligarchical or a democratic basis, despots and soldiers of
fortune secured control of their Italian states by force of in-
nate ability.   Individualism pushed aside the claims of birth,
and it so happened in the 14th and 15th centuries that the
heads of these states were as frequently men of illegitimate
birth as of legitimate descent.   In our change-loving Italy,
wrote Pius II., " where nothing is permanent and no old dynasty exists, servants easily rise to be kings." [1]

It was in the free republic of Florence, where individualism
found the widest sphere for self-assertion, that the Renaissance took earliest root and brought forth its finest products.
That municipality, which had more of the modern spirit of
change and progress than any other mediæval organism, invited and found satisfaction in novel and brilliant works of
power, whether they were in the domain of government or of
letters or even of religion, as under the spell of Savonarola.
There Dante and Lionardo da Vinci were born, and there
Machiavelli exploited his theories of the state and Michelangelo
wrought.   The Medici gave favor to all forms of enterprise
that might bring glory to the city.   After Nicolas V. ascended
the papal throne, Rome vied with its northern neighbor as a

---

[1] Quoted by Burckhardt, 1. 27.   This author speaks of an *Epidemie für
kleine Dynastien* in Italy.

centre of the arts and culture. The new tastes and pursuits also found a home in Ferrara, Urbino, Naples, Milan and Mantua.

Glorious the achievement of the Renaissance was, but it was the last movement of European significance in which Italy and the popes took the lead. Had the current of æsthetic and intellectual enthusiasm joined itself to a stream of religious regeneration, Italy might have kept in advance of other nations, but she produced no safe prophets. No Reformer arose to lead her away from dead religious forms to living springs of spiritual life, from ceremonies and relics to the New Testament.

In spreading north to Germany, Holland and England, the movement took on a more serious aspect. There it produced no poets or artists of the first rank, but in Reuchlin and Erasmus it had scholars whose erudition not only attracted the attention of their own but benefited succeeding generations and contributed directly to the Reformation. South of the Alps, culture was the concern of a special class and took on the form of a diversion, though it is true all classes must have looked with admiration upon the works of art that were being produced.

It was, then, the mission of the Renaissance to start the spirit of free inquiry, to certify to the mind its dignity, to expand the horizon to the faculties of man as a citizen of the world, to recover from the dust of ages the literary treasures and monuments of ancient Greece and Rome, to inaugurate a style of fresh description, based on observation, in opposition to the dialectic circumlocution of the scholastic philosophy, to call forth the laity and to direct attention to the value of natural morality and the natural relationships of man with man. To the monk beauty was a snare, woman a temptation, pleasure a sin, the world vanity of vanities. The Humanist taught that the present life is worth living. The Renaissance breathed a cosmopolitan spirit and fostered universal sympathies. In the spirit of some of the yearnings of the later Roman authors, Dante exclaimed again, "My home is the world."[1]

[1] Burckhardt, I. 145.

§ 63. *Dante, Petrarca, Boccaccio.*

Dante, Petrarca and Boccaccio represent the birth and glory of Italian literature and ushered in the new literary and artistic age.   Petrarca and Boccaccio belong chiefly to the department of literary culture ; Dante equally to it and the realm of religious thought and composition.   The period covered by their lives extends over more than a hundred years, from Dante's birth in 1265 to Boccaccio's death, 1375.

Dante Alighieri, 1265-1321, the first of Italian and the greatest of mediæval poets, has given us in his *Divina Commedia*, the Divine Comedy, conceived in 1300, a poetic view of the moral universe under the aspect of eternity, — *sub specie æternitatis*.   Born in Florence, he read under his teacher Brunetto Latini, whom in later years he praised, Virgil, Horace, Ovid and other Latin authors.   In the heated conflict of parties, going on in his native city, he at first took the side of the Guelfs as against the Ghibellines, who were in favor of the imperial régime in Italy.   In 1300, he was elected one of the *priori* or chief magistrates, approved the severe measures then employed towards political opponents and, after a brief tenure of office, was exiled.   The decree of exile threatened to burn him alive if he ventured to return to the city.   After wandering about, going to Paris and perhaps further west, he settled down in Ravenna, where he died and where his ashes still lie.   After his death, Florence accorded the highest honors to his memory.   Her request for his body was refused by Ravenna, but she created a chair for the exposition of the *Divine Comedy*, with Boccaccio as its first occupant, and erected to her distinguished son an·imposing monument in the church of Santa Croce and a statue on the square in front.   In 1865, all Italy joined Florence in celebrating the 6th centenary of the poet's birth.   Never has study been given to Dante's great poem as a work of art by wider circles and with more enthusiasm than to-day, and it will continue to serve as a prophetic voice of divine judgment and mercy as long as religious feeling seeks expression.

Dante was a layman, married and had seven children.   An

epoch in his life was his meeting, as a boy of nine years, with
Beatrice, who was a few months younger than himself, at a
festival given in her father's house, where she was tenderly
called, as Boccaccio says, Bice. The vision of Beatrice—for
there is no record that they exchanged words—entered and
filled Dante's soul with an effluence of purity and benignity
which cleared away all evil thoughts.[1] After an interval of
nine years he saw her a second time, and then not again till,
in his poetic dream, he met her in paradise. Beatrice married
and died at 24, 1290.

With this vision, the new life began for Dante, the *vita nuova* which he describes in the book of that name. Beatrice's
features illuminated his path and her pure spirit was his guide.
At the first meeting, so the poet says, " she appeared to me
clothed in a most noble color, a modest and becoming crimson,
garlanded and adorned in such wise as befitted her very youthful age." The love then begotten, says Charles Eliot Norton,
" lasted from Dante's boyhood to his death, keeping his heart
fresh, spite of the scorchings of disappointment, with the
springs of perpetual solace." [2] The last glimpse the poet gives
of her was as he saw her at the side of Rachel in the highest
region of heaven.

> The third in order, underneath her, lo!
> Rachel with Beatrice. — *Par.*, xxxii. 6.

Had Dante written only the tract against the temporal power
of the papacy, the *De monarchia*, his name would have been
restricted to a place in the list of the pamphleteers of the 14th
century. His *Divine Comedy* exalts him to the eminence of the
foremost poetic interpreter of the mediæval world. This immortal poem is a mirror of mediæval Christianity and civilization and, at the same time, a work of universal significance and
perennial interest. It sums up the religious concepts of the
Middle Ages and introduces the free critical spirit of the modern world.[3] It is Dante's autobiography and reflects his own
experiences: —

[1] *Vita Nuova*, 10, 11. See Scartazzini, *Handbuch*, p. 193.
[2] *Vita Nuova*, Norton's trsl., p. 2.
[3] *Die Komödie ist der Schwanengesang des Mittelalters, zugleich aber auch*

All the pains by me depicted, woes and tortures, void of pity,
On this earth I have encountered — found them all in Florence City.[1]

It brings into view the society of mediæval Italy, a long array
of its personages, many of whom had only a local and transient
interest.　At the same time, the *Comedy* is the spiritual biography of man as man wherever he is found, in the three conditions of sin, repentance and salvation.　It describes a
pilgrimage to the world of spirits beyond this life, from the
dark forest of temptation, through the depths of despair in
hell, up the terraces of purification in purgatory, to the realms
of bliss.　Through the first two regions the poet's guide is
Virgil, the representative of natural reason, and through the
heavenly spaces, Beatrice, the type of divine wisdom and love.
The *Inferno* reflects sin and misery; the *Purgatorio*, penitence
and hope; the *Paradiso*, holiness and happiness.　The first
repels by its horrors and laments; the second moves by its
penitential tears and prayers; the third enraptures by its
purity and peace.　Purgatory is an intermediate state, constantly passing away, but heaven and hell will last forever.
Hell is hopeless darkness and despair; heaven culminates in
the beatific vision of the Holy Trinity, beyond which nothing
higher can be conceived by man or angel.　Here are depicted
the extremes of terror and rapture, of darkness and light, of
the judgment and the love of God.　In paradise, the saints
are represented as forming a spotless white rose, whose cup is
a lake of light, surrounded by innocent children praising God.
This sublime conception was probably suggested by the rose-

das begeisterte Lied, welches die Herankunft einer neuen Zeit einleitet. Scar-
tazzini, Dante Alighieri, etc., p. 530. See Geiger, II. 30 sq. Church, p. 2,
calls it " the first Christian poem, the one which opens European literature as
the *Iliad* did that of Greece and Rome." Dante knew scarcely more than a
dozen Greek words, and, on account of its popular language, he called his great
epic and didactic poem a *comedy*, or a village poem, deriving it from κώμη,
villa, without apparently being aware of the more probable derivation from
κῶμος, merry-making.

[1] *Allen Schmerz, den ich gesungen, all die Qualen, Greu'l und Wunden*
　　Hab' ich schon auf dieser Erden, hab' ich in Florenz gefunden.
　　　　　　　　　　　　　　— GEIBEL : *Dante in Verona.*

One of the finest poems on Dante is by Uhland, others by Tennyson,
Longfellow, etc.

windows of Gothic cathedrals, or by the fact that the Virgin Mary was called a rose by St. Bernard and other mediæval divines and poets.

Following the geocentric cosmology of the Ptolemaic system, the poet located hell within the earth, purgatory in the southern hemisphere, and heaven in the starry firmament. Hell is a yawning cavity, widest at the top and consisting of ten circles. Purgatory is a mountain up which souls ascend. The heavenly realm consists of nine circles, culminating in the empyrean where the pure divine essence dwells.

Among these regions of the spiritual and future world, Dante distributes the best-known characters of his and of former generations. He spares neither Guelf nor Ghibelline, neither pope nor emperor, and gives to all their due. He adapts the punishment to the nature of the sin, the reward to the measure of virtue, and shows an amazing ingenuity and fertility of imagination in establishing the correspondence of outward condition to moral character. Thus the cowards and indifferentists in the vestibule of the *Inferno* are driven by a whirling flag and stung by wasps and flies. The licentious are hurried by tempestuous winds in total darkness, with carnal lust still burning, but never gratified.

> The infernal hurricane, that never rests
> Hurtles the spirits onward in its rapine,
> Whirling them round; and smiting, it molests them;
> It hither, thither, downward, upward, drives them.
>
> —*Inferno*, V. 31–43.

The gluttonous lie on the ground, exposed to showers of hail and foul water; blasphemers supine upon a plain of burning sand, while sparks of fire, like flakes of snow in the Alps, slowly and constantly descend upon their bodies. The wrathful are forever tearing one another.

> And I, who stood intent upon beholding,
> Saw people mud-besprent in that lagoon,
> All of them naked and with angry look.
> They smote each other not alone with hands,
> But with the head and with the breast and feet
> Tearing each other piecemeal with their teeth.
>
> —*Inferno*, VII. 100 sqq.

The simonists, who sell religion for money and turn the temple of God into a den of thieves, are thrust into holes, head downwards, with their feet protruding and tormented with flames. The arch-heretics are held in red-hot tombs, and tyrants in a stream of boiling blood, shot at by the centaurs whenever they attempt to rise. The traitors are immersed in a lake of ice with Satan, the arch-traitor and the embodiment of selfishness, malignity and turpitude. Their very tears turn to ice, symbol of utter hardness, and Satan is forever consuming in his three mouths the three arch-traitors, Judas, Brutus and Cassius. Milton represents Satan as the archangel who even in hell exalts himself and in pride exclaims, "Better to reign in hell than serve in heaven," and the poet leaves the mind of the reader disturbed by a feeling of admiration for Lucifer's untamed ambition and superhuman power. Dante's Satan awakens disgust and horror, and the inscription over the entrance to hell makes the reader shudder:—

> Through me ye enter the abode of woe ;
> Through me to endless sorrow are brought ;
> Through me amid the souls accurst ye go.
>
>   *   *   *   *
>
> All hope abandon — ye who enter here !
>
> *Per me si va nella città dolente ;*
> *Per me si va nell' eterno dolore ;*
> *Per me si va tra la perduta gente.*
>
>   *   *   *   *
>
> *Lasciate ogni speranza, voi ch' entrate.*

Passing out from the domain of gloom and dole, Virgil leads the poet to purgatory, where the dawn of day breaks. This realm, as has been said, comes nearer to our common life than hell or paradise.[1] Hope dwells here. Song, not wailing, is heard. A ship appears, moved by an angel and filled with spirits, singing the hymn of redemption. Cato approaches and urges the guide and Dante to wash themselves on the shore from all remainders of hell and to hurry on. In purgatory, they pass through seven stages, which correspond to the seven mortal sins, the two lowest, pride and envy, the highest, wantonness and luxury. All the penitents have stamped on their foreheads seven P's, — the first letter of the word *peccata*, sins,

---

[1] Strong, p. 142.

— which are effaced only one by one, as they pass from stage to stage, "enclasped with scorching fire," until they are delivered through penal fire from all stain. A similar correspondence exists between sin and punishments as in the *Inferno*, but with the opposite effect, for here sins are repented of and forgiven, and the woes are disciplinary until "the wound that healeth last is medicined." Thus the proud, in the first and lowest terrace, are compelled to totter under huge weights, that they may learn humility. The indolent, in the fourth terrace, are exercised by constant and rapid walking. The avaricious and prodigal, with hands and feet tied together, lie with their faces in the dust, weeping and wailing. The gluttons suffer hunger and thirst that they may be taught temperance. The licentious wander about in flames that their sensual passions may be consumed away.

Arriving at paradise, the Roman poet can go no further, and Beatrice takes his place as Dante's guide. The spirits are distributed in glory according to their different grades of perfection. Here are passed in review theologians, martyrs, crusaders, righteous princes and judges, monks and contemplative mystics. In the 9th heaven Beatrice leaves the poet to take her place at the side of Rachel, after having introduced him to St. Bernard. Dante looks again and sees Mary and Eve and Sarah, —

> . . . and the gleaner-maid
> Meek ancestress of him, who sang the songs
> Of sore repentance in his sorrowful mood ;

Gabriel, Adam, Moses, John the Baptist, Peter, St. Augustine and other saints. Then he is led by the devout mystic to Mary, who, in answer to his prayer, shows him the Deity in the empyrean, but what he saw was not for words to utter. Alike are all the saints in enjoying the same reward of the beatific vision.

Dante was in full harmony with the orthodox faith of his age, and followed closely the teachings of Thomas Aquinas' great book of divinity.[1] He accepted all the distinctive tenets

[1] "There is in Dante no trace of doctrinal dissatisfaction. He respects every part of the teaching of the Church in matters of doctrine, authoritatively

of mediæval Catholicism — purgatory, the worship of Mary, the intercession of saints, the efficacy of papal indulgences and the divine institution of the papacy.   He paid deep homage to the monastic life and accords exalted place to Benedict, St. Francis and Dominic.   But he cast aside all traditions in dealing freely with the successors of Peter in the Apostolic see.   Here, too, he was under the direction of the beloved Beatrice.   The evils in the Church he traced to her temporal power and he condemned to everlasting punishment Anastasius II. for heresy, Nicolas III., Boniface VIII. and Clement V. for simony, Cœlestine V. for cowardice in abdicating the pontifical office, and a squad of other popes for avarice.

Following the theology of Augustine and Thomas Aquinas, he put into hell the whole heathen world except two solitary figures, Cato of Utica, who sacrificed life for liberty and keeps watch at the foot of purgatory, and the just emperor, Trajan, who, 500 years after his death, was believed to have been prayed out of hell by Pope Gregory I.   To the region of the *Inferno*, also, though on the outer confines of it, a place is assigned to infants who die in infancy without being baptized, whether the offspring of Christian or heathen parents. Theirs is no conscious pain, but they remain forever without the vision of the blessed.   In the same vicinity the worthies of the old dispensation were detained until Christ descended after his crucifixion and gave them release.   There, John the Baptist had been kept for two years after his pains of martyrdom, *Par.* xxxii. 25.   In the upper regions of the hopeless *Inferno* a tolerably comfortable place is also accorded to the noble heathen poets, philosophers, statesmen and warriors, while unfaithful Christians are punished in the lower circles according to the degrees of their guilt.   The heathen, who followed the light of nature, suffer sorrow without pain. As Virgil says : —

> In the right manner they adored not God.
> For such defects, and not for other guilt,
> Lost are we, and are only so far punished,
> That without hope we live on, in desire.

laid down. . . .   He gives no evidence of free inquiry and private judgment." — Moore, *Studies*, II. 65, 66.

Dante began his poem in Latin and was blamed by Giovanni del Virgilio, a teacher of Latin literature in Bologna,
because he abandoned the language of old Rome for the vulgar dialect of Tuscany. Poggio also lamented this course.
But the poet defended himself in his unfinished book, Eloquence in the Vernacular, *De vulgari eloquio*,[1] and, by writing
the *Commedia*, the *Vita nuova*, the *Convivio* and his sonnets
in his native Florentine tongue, he became the father of
Italian literature and opened the paths of culture to the laity.
Within three years of the poet's death, commentaries began
to be written on the *Divina Commedia*, as by Graziuolo de'
Bambagliolo, 1324, and within 100 years chairs were founded
for its exposition at Florence, Venice, Bologna and Pisa.

A second service which Dante rendered in his poem to the
coming culture was in bringing antiquity once more into the
foreground and treating pagan and Christian elements side by
side, though not as of the same value, and interweaving mythological fables with biblical history, classical with Christian
reminiscences. By this tolerance he showed himself a man
of the new age, while he still held firmly to the mediæval theology.[2]

Dante's abiding merit, however, was his inspiring portrayal
of the holiness and love of God. Sin, the perversion of the
will, is punished with sin continuing in the future world and
pain. Salvation is through the "Lamb of God who takes away
our sins and suffered and died that we might live." This poem,
like a mighty sermon, now depresses, now enraptures the soul,
or, to use the lines of the most poetic of his translators, Longfellow, —

> Thy sacred song is like the trump of doom ;
> Yet in thy heart what human sympathies,
> What soft compassion glows.

Francesco Petrarca, 1304–1374, was the most cultured man
of his time. His Italian sonnets and songs are masterpieces of
Italian poetic diction, but he thought lightly of them and hoped
to be remembered by his Latin writings.[3] He was an enthusi-

[1] Engl. translation by A. G. F. Howell, London, 1890.

[2] See Burckhardt-Geiger, I. 219.

[3] Of his 317 sonnets and 29 *canzoni* all are erotic but 31. For the sake of

ast for the literature of antiquity and gave a great impulse to
its study.   His parents, exiled from Florence, removed to
Avignon, then the seat of the papacy, which remained Francesco's residence till 1333.   He was ordained to the priesthood
but without an inward call.   He enjoyed several ecclesiastical
benefices as prior, canon and archdeacon, which provided for
his support without burdening him with duties.   He courted
and enjoyed the favor of princes, popes and prelates.   He
abused the papal residence on the Rhone as the Babylon of the
West, urged the popes to return to Rome and hailed Cola da
Rienzo as an apostle of national liberty.   His writings contain
outbursts of patriotism but, on the other hand, the author seems
to contradict himself in being quick to accept the hospitality of
the Italian despots of Mantua, Padua, Rimini and Ferrara, and
the viconti of Milan.   In 1350, he formed a friendship with
Boccaccio which remained warm until his death.

In spite of his priestly vows, Petrarca lived with concubines
and had at least two illegitimate children, Giovanni and Fran-
cesca, the stain of whose birth was removed by papal bulls.   In
riper years, and more especially after his pilgrimage to Rome
in the Jubilee year, 1350, he broke away from the slavery of sin.
"I now hate that pestilence," he wrote to Boccaccio, "infinitely
more than I loved it once, so that in turning over the thought
of it in my mind, I feel shame and horror.   Jesus Christ, my
liberator, knows that I say the truth, he to whom I often prayed
with tears, who has given to me his hand in pity and helped me
up to himself."   He took great delight in the *Confessions* of St.
Augustine, a copy of which he carried about with him.

In his *De contemptu mundi*, — the Contempt of the World, —
written in 1343, Petrarca confesses as his greatest fault the love
of glory and the desire for the immortality of his name.   This,
the besetting sin of the ancient Greeks and Romans, the Humanists inherited.   It became with them a ruling passion.   They
found it in Cicero, the most read of all the Latin classics.   Dante
strove after the poet's laurel and often returned to the theme of

euphony, the author changed his patronymic *Petrarco* into *Petrarca*.   In the
English form, *Petrarch*, the accent is changed from the second to the first syllable.

fame as a motive of action — *lo grand disio della eccelenza*.[1]
Petrarca, after much seeking on his own part, was offered
the poet's crown by the University of Paris and the Roman
senate.   He took it from the latter, and was crowned on the
Capitoline Hill at Rome, April 8, 1341, Robert, king of Sicily,
being present on the occasion.   This he regarded as the
proudest moment of his life, the excelling glory of his career.
In ostentatious piety the poet carried his crown to St. Peter's,
where he laid it on the altar of the Apostle.

Petrarca has been called the first modern scholar and man
of letters, the inaugurator of the Italian Renaissance.   Unlike
Dante, he despised scholastic and mystic learning and went
further back to the well of pagan antiquity.   He studied
antiquity, not as a philologist or antiquarian, but as a man of
taste.[2]   He admired the Greek and Roman authors for their
eloquence, grace and finish of style.   Cicero and Virgil were
his idols, the fathers of eloquence, the eyes of the Latin language.   He turned to Plato.   He made a distinction between
the religion of the New Testament as interpreted by Augustine and as interpreted by the Schoolmen.   Petrarca also
opened the period of search and discovery of ancient books
and works of art.   He spared no pains to secure old manuscripts.   In 1345, he found several of Cicero's letters at
Verona, and also a portion of Quintilian which had been
unknown since the 10th century.   A copy of Homer he kept
with care, though he could not read its contents.   All the
Greek he knew was a few rudiments learned from a faithless
Calabrian, Barlaam.   He was the first to collect a private
library and had 200 volumes.   His first thought in passing old
convents was to hunt up books.   He accumulated old coins and
medals and advocated the preservation of ancient monuments.
He seems also to have outlined the first mediæval map of Italy.[3]

---

[1] "The noble desire of fame," *Par.* xi. 85–117.   See, on the subject, Burckhardt-Geiger, I. 154 sq.   Pastor, I. 4 sq., calls special attention to this pursuit
of the phantom, fame, by the Humanists at courts and from the people.

[2] Robinson, *Life*, p. 336, says, " Petrarch's love for Cicero and Virgil springs
from what one may call the fundamental Humanistic impulse, delight in the
free play of mind among ideas that are stimulating and beautiful."

[3] See Burckhardt-Geiger, II., *Excursus* LXI.

Few authors have more fully enjoyed the benefit of their labors than Petrarca. He received daily letters of praise from all parts of Italy, from France, Germany and England. He expressed his satisfaction that the emperor of Byzantium knew him through his writings. Charles IV. invited him three times to Germany that he might listen to his eloquence and learn from him lessons of wisdom ; and Pope Gregory XI. on hearing of his death, ordered good copies of all his books. The next generation honored him, not as the singer of Laura, the wife of another, whose beauty and loveliness he praised in passionate verse,[1] but as the scholar and sage.

The name of Giovanni Boccaccio, 1313–1375, the third of the triumvirate of the Italian luminaries of the 14th century, has also a distinct place in the transition from the Middle Ages to the age of the Renaissance. With his two great predecessors he was closely linked, with Dante as his biographer, with Petrarca as his warm friend. It was given to him to be the founder of easy and elegant Italian prose. The world has had few writers who can equal him in realistic narration.[2] There is ground for the saying that Dante is admired, Petrarca praised, Boccaccio read. He also wrote poetry, but it does not constitute his claim to distinction.

Certaldo, twenty miles from Florence, was probably Boccaccio's birthplace. He was the illegitimate son of a Florentine father and a Parisian mother. After spending six years in business and giving six to the law, — the whole period being looked upon by him later as lost time, — he devoted himself to literature. Several years he spent at the court of Naples, where he fell in love with Maria, the married daughter of King Robert, who yielded her honor to his advances. Later, he represented her passion for him in *L'Amorosa Fiammetta*. Thus the three great Italian literati commemorate the love of women who were bound in matrimony to others, but

---

[1] For Petrarca's attachment to Laura, see Koerting, p. 686 sq., and Symonds, *Ital. Lit.*, I. 92, and *The Dantesque and Platonic Ideals of Love*, in *Contemp. Rev.*, Sept., 1890.

[2] Symonds, *Ital. Lit.*, I. 99, says, " Boccaccio was the first to substitute a literature of the people for the literature of the learned classes and the aristocracy," etc.

there is a wide gulf between the inspiring passion of Dante for Beatrice and Boccaccio's sensual love.[1] Boccaccio was an unmarried layman and freely indulged in irregular love. His three children of unknown mothers died before him.

In his old age he passed, like Petrarca, through a certain conversion, and, with a preacher's fervor, warned others against the vanity, luxury and seductive arts of women. He would fain have blotted out the immoralities of his writings when it was too late. The conversion was brought about by a Carthusian monk who called upon him at Certaldo. Upon the basis of another monk's vision, he threatened Boccaccio with speedy death, if he did not abandon his godless writing. Terrified with the prospect, he determined to renounce the pen and give himself up to penance. Petrarca, on hearing of his state of mind, wrote to him to accept what was good in the monk's advice, but not to abandon studies which he pronounced the nutriment of a healthy mind.

In zeal for the ancient classics, Boccaccio vied with his contemporary. Many of them he copied with his own hand, and bequeathed them to his father-confessor in trust for the Augustinian convent of the Holy Spirit in Florence. He learned the elements of Greek and employed a Greek of Calabria, Leontius Pilatus, to make a literal translation of the *Iliad* and *Odyssey* for learners. An insight into his interest in books is given to us in his account of a visit to Monte Casino. On asking to see the library, a monk took him to a dusty room without a door to it, and with grass growing in its windows. Many of the manuscripts were mutilated. The monks, as his guide told him, were in the habit of tearing out leaves to be used by the children as psalters or to be sold to women for amulets for their arms.

In 1373, the signoria of Florence appointed him to the lectureship on the *Divina Commedia*, with a salary of 100 guldens gold. He had gotten only as far as the 17th canto of the *Inferno* when he was overtaken by death.

Boccaccio's Latin works are mostly compilations from an-

[1] The best edition of his *La Vita di Dante*, with a critical text and introduction of 174 pages, is by Francesco Marci-Leone, Florence, 1888.

cient mythology — *De genealogia deorum* — and biography, and
also treat the subject of geography — *De montium, silvarum,
lacuum et marium nominibus.* In his *De claris mulieribus*, he gave
the biographies of 104 distinguished women, including Eve,
the fictitious popess, Johanna, and Queen Johanna of Naples,
who was still living. His most popular work is the *Decamerone*, the Ten Days' Book — which in later years he would
have destroyed or purged of its immoral and frivolous elements. It is his poetry in prose and may be called a *Commedia
Humana*, as contrasted with Dante's *Commedia Divina*. It
contains 100 stories, told by ten young persons, seven ladies
and three men of Florence, during the pestilence of 1348.
After listening to a description of the horrors of the plague,
the reader is transferred to a beautiful garden, several miles
from the city, where the members of the company, amid laughter and tears, relate the stories which range from moral tales
to indecent love intrigues. One of the well-known stories
is of the Jew, Abraham, who, refusing to comply with the appeals to turn Christian, went to Rome to study the question
for himself. Finding the priestly morals most corrupt, cardinals with concubines and revelling in riches and luxury, he
concluded Christianity must have a divine origin, or it would
not have survived when the centre of Christendom was so
rotten, and he offered himself for baptism. The *Decamerone*
reveals a low state of morals among priests and monks as
well as laymen and women. It derides marriage, the confessional, the hypocrisy of monkery and the worship of relics.
The employment of wit and raillery against ecclesiastical
institutions was a new element in literature, and Boccaccio
wrote in a language the people understood. No wonder that
the Council of Trent condemned the work for its immoralities,
and still more for its anticlerical and antimonastic ridicule;
but it could not prevent its circulation. A curious expurgated edition, authorized by the pope, appeared in Florence in
1573, which retained the indecencies, the impure personages,
but substituted laymen for the priests and monks, thus saving
the honor of the Church.[1]

[1] In an attempt to break the force of the charge that in its beginnings the
Renaissance was wholly an individualistic movement, independent of the

Dante, Petrarca and Boccaccio led the way to a recognition of the worth of man's natural endowment by depicting the passions of his heart. To them also it belonged to have an ardent love for nature and to reproduce it in description. Thus Petrarca described the mountains and the gulfs of the sea as well as Rome, Naples and other Italian places where he loved to be.[1] His description of his delight in ascending a mountain near Vaucluse, it has been suggested, was the first of its kind in literature. In these respects, the appreciation of man and the world, they stood at the opening of the new era.

§ 64. *Progress and Patrons of Classical Studies in the 15th Century.*

The enthusiasm for classical studies and the monuments of antiquity reached its high pitch in Italy in the middle and latter half of the 15th century. Many distinguished classical students appeared, none of whom, however, approached in literary eminence the three Italian literati of the preceding century. Admirable as was their zeal in promoting an acquaintance with the writers of Greece and Rome, they were in danger of becoming mere pedants and imitators of the past. The whole field of ancient literature was searched, poetry and philosophy, letters and works of geography and history. Italy seemed to be bent on setting aside all other studies for the ancient classics. Cicero was taken as the supreme model of style, and his age was referred to as "that immortal and almost heavenly age."[2]

The services of the Italian Humanists in reviving an interest in ancient literature and philosophy were, however, quite enough to give distinction to their era, though their own writings have ceased to be read. One new feature of abiding significance was developed in the 15th century, the science of literary and historical criticism. This was opened by Salutato, d. 1406, who contended that Seneca could not have

Church, Pastor, I. 6 sqq., lays stress upon the gracious treatment Petrarca and Boccaccio received from popes and the repentance of their latter years.

[1] See Burckhardt-Geiger, II. 18 sqq.
[2] Burckhardt-Geiger, I. 277.

been the author of the tragedies ascribed to him, and culminated in Laurentius Valla and the doubts that scholar cast upon the authorship of the Apostles' Creed and the Donation of Constantine. The Fall of Constantinople in 1453, with which the middle of the century was signalized, cannot be regarded as more than an incident in the history of the spread of Greek letters in the West, which would have been accomplished had the city remained under the Greek emperors.

To the discovery and copying of manuscripts, led by such men as Poggio or the monk Nicolas of Treves, who in 1429 brought to Rome 12 hitherto unpublished comedies of Plautus, were added the foundation of princely libraries in Florence, Rome, Urbino and other cities. Numerous were the translations of Greek authors made into Latin, and more numerous the translations from both languages into Italian. By the recovery of a lost or half-forgotten literature, the Italian Renaissance laid the modern world under a heavy debt. But in its restless literary activity, it went still further, imitating the literary forms received from antiquity. Orations became a marked feature of the time, pompous and stately. The envoys of princes were called orators and receptions, given to such envoys, were opened with classical addresses. Orations were also delivered at the reception of relics, at funerals and marriages—the epithalamials—and even at the consecration of bishops. At a betrothal, Filelfo opened his address with the words, "Aristotle, the peripatetic teacher." The orations of this Latinist, most eminent in his day, are pronounced by Geiger a disgusting mixture of classic and biblical quotations.[1] Not seldom these ornate productions were extended to two or three hours. Pius II.'s fame for oratory helped him to the papal throne.

All forms of classic poetry were revived — from the epic to the epigram, from tragedy to satire. Petrarca's *Africa*, an epic on Scipio, and Boccaccio's *Theseid* led the way. Attempts were even made to continue or restore ancient literary works. Maffeo Vegio, under Martin V., composed a 13th book of Virgil, Bruni restored the second decade of Livy.

[1] I. 261 sq.

The poets not only revived the ancient mythologies but peopled Italy with new gods and nymphs.   Especially active were they in celebrating the glories of the powerful men of their age, princes and popes.   A *Borgiad* was dedicated to Alexander VI., a *Borsead* to Borso, duke of Este, a *Sforzias* to one of the viconti of Milan and the *Laurentias* to Lorenzo de' Medici.   The most offensive panegyric of all was the poetical effusion of Ercole Strozzi at the death of Cæsar Borgia. In this laudation, Roma is represented as having placed her hopes in the Borgias, Calixtus III. and Alexander VI., and last of all in Cæsar, whose deeds are then glorified.

In historic composition also, a new chapter was opened. The annals of cities and the careers of individuals were studied and written down.   The histories of Florence, first in Latin by Lionardo Bruni and then down to 1362 by the brothers Villani, who wrote in Italian, and then by Poggio to 1455, were followed by other histories down to the valuable *Diaries* of Rome by Infessura and Burchard, the *History of Venice*, 1487–1513, by Bembo, and the works of Machiavelli and Guicciardini, who wrote in Italian.   In 1463, Flavio Biondo compiled his encyclopædic work in three parts on the history, customs, topography and monuments of Rome and Italy, *Roma instaurata, Roma triumphans* and *Italia illustrata*.   Lionardo Bruni wrote Lives of Cicero and Aristotle in Latin and of Dante and Petrarca in Italian.   The passion for composition was displayed in the despatches of Venetian, Mantuan and other ambassadors at the courts of Rome or Este and by the elaborate letters, which were in reality finished essays, for the most part written in Latin and introducing comments on books and matters of literary interest, by Politian, Bembo and others, a form of writing revived by Petrarca.   The zeal for Latin culture also found exhibition in the habit of giving to children ancient names, such as Agamemnon and Achilles, Atalanta and Pentesilea.   A painter called his daughter Minerva and his son Apelles.   The habit also took root of assuming Latin names.   A Sanseverino, howbeit of illegitimate birth, proudly called himself Julius Pomponius Laetus.   This custom extended to Germany, where Schwarz-

erd gave up his original German patronymic for Melanchthon, Hausschein for Œcolampadius, Reuchlin for Capnio,
Buchmann for Bibliander; Hutten, Luther, Zwingli, who were
more patriotic, adhered to their vernacular names.   Pedants
adopted a more serious change when they paganized sacred
terms and substituted mythological for Christian ideas.   The
saints were called *dii* and *deæ ;* their statues, *simulacra sancta
deorum ;* holy images of the gods, Peter and Paul, *dii titulares
Romæ* or *S. Romulus* and *S. Remus ;* the nuns, *vestales virgines ;*
heaven, *Olympus ;* cardinals, *augurs,* and the College of Cardinals, *Senatus sacer ;* the pope, *pontifex maximus,* and his
thunders, *diræ ;* the tiara, *infula Romulea ;* and God, *Jupiter
optimus maximus !* [1]   Erasmus protested against such absurd
pedantry as characterizing Humanism in its dotage.   Another
sign of the cult of the ancients was the imitation of Roman
burial usages even in the churches.   At Bruni's death in 1443,
the priors of Florence decreed him a public funeral " after
the manner of the ancients."   Before the laying-away of his
body in S. Croce, Manetti pronounced a funeral oration and
placed the crown of laurel on the deceased author's head.

The high veneration of antiquity was also shown in the regard which cities and individuals paid to the relics of classical
writers.   Padua thought she had the genuine bones of Livy,
and Alfonso of Naples considered himself happy in securing
one of the arms of the dead historian.   Naples gloried in the
real or supposed tomb of Virgil.   Parma boasted of the bones
of Cassius.   Como claimed both the Plinies, but Verona proved
that the elder belonged to it.   Alfonso of Naples, as he was
crossing over the Abruzzi, saluted Sulmona, the birthplace of
Ovid.

The larger Italian towns were not without Latin schools.
Among the renowned teachers were Vittorino da Feltre, whom
Gonzaga of Mantua called to his court, and Guarino of Verona.   Children of princes from abroad went to Mantua to sit
at the feet of Feltre, who also gave instruction to as many as
70 poor and talented children at a time.   Latin authors were
committed to memory and translated by the pupils, and math-

[1] Burckhardt-Geiger, I. 274 ; Symonds, II. 396 sqq.

ematics and philosophy were taught. To his literary curriculum Feltre added gymnastic exercises and set his pupils a good example by his chastity and temperance. He was represented as a pelican which nourishes her young with her own blood. Pastor, who calls this teacher the greatest Italian pedagogue of the Renaissance period, is careful to notice that he had mass said every morning before beginning the sessions of the day.

The Humanists were fortunate in securing the encouragement of the rich and powerful. Literature has never had more liberal and intelligent patrons than it had in Italy in the 15th century. The munificence of Mæcenas was equalled and surpassed by Cosimo and Lorenzo de' Medici in Florence and Nicolas V. in Rome. Other cities had their literary benefactors, but some of these were most noted for combining profligacy with their real or affected interest in literary culture. Humanists were in demand. Popes needed secretaries, and princes courted orators and poets who could conduct a polished correspondence, write addresses, compose odes for festive occasions and celebrate their deeds. Lionardo Bruni, Valla, Bembo, Sadoleto and other Humanists were secretaries or annotators at the papal court under Nicolas V. and his successors.

Cosimo de' Medici, d. 1464, the most munificent promoter of arts and letters that Europe had seen for more than a thousand years, was the richest banker of the republic of Florence, scholarly, well-read and, from taste and ambition, deeply interested in literature. We have already met him at Constance during the council. He travelled extensively in France and Germany and ruled Florence, after a temporary exile, as a republican merchant-prince, for 30 years. He encouraged scholars by gifts of money and provided for the purchase of manuscripts, without assuming the air of condescension which spoils the generosity of the gift, but with a feeling of respect for superior merit. His literary minister, Nicolo de' Niccoli, 1364–1437, was a centre of attraction to literary men in Florence and collected and, in great part, copied 800 codices. Under his auspices, Poggio searched some of the South German convents and found at St. Gall the first complete Quintil-

ian.   Niccoli's library, through Cosimo's mediation, was given
to S. Marco, and forms a part of the Medicean library.   With
the same enlightened liberality, Cosimo also encouraged the
fine arts.   He was a great admirer of the saintly painter, Fra
Angelico, whom he ordered to paint the history of the crucifixion on one of the walls of the chapter-house of S. Marco.
Among the scholars protected in Florence under Cosimo's administration were the Platonist Ficino, Lionardo Bruni and
Poggio.   During the last year of his life, Cosimo had read to
him Aristotle's *Ethics* and Ficino's translation of Plato's *The
Highest Good*.   He also contributed to churches and convents,
and by the erection of stately buildings turned Florence into
the Italian Athens.

Cosimo's grandson and worthy successor, Lorenzo de' Medici, d. 1492, was well educated in Latin and Greek by Lan-
dino, Argyropulos and Ficino.   He was a man of polite
culture and himself no mean poet, whose songs were sung on
the streets of Florence.   His family life was reputable.   He
liked to play with his children and was very fond of his son
Giovanni, afterwards Leo X.   Michelangelo and Pico della
Mirandola were among the ornaments of his court.   By his
lavish expenditures he brought himself and the republic to
the brink of bankruptcy in 1490.

Federigo da Montefeltro, duke of Urbino, d. 1482, and
Alfonso of Naples also deserve special mention as patrons of
learning.   Federigo, a pupil of Vittorino da Feltre, was a
scholar and an admirer of patristic as well as classical learning.
He also cultivated a taste for music, painting and architecture,
employed 30 and 40 copyists at a time, and founded, at an expense of 40,000 ducats, a library which, in 1657, was incorporated in the Vatican.

Alfonso was the special patron of the skeptical Laurentius
Valla and the licentious Beccadelli, 1394–1471, and also had at
his court the Greek scholars, George of Trebizond and the
younger Chrysoloras.   He listened with delight to literary,
philosophical and theological lectures and disputes, which were
held in his library.   He paid large sums for literary work, giving Beccadelli 1000 gold guldens for his *Hermaphrodita*, and

Fazio, in addition to his yearly stipend of 500 guldens, 1,500 guldens for his *Historia Alphonsi*. When he took Manetti to be his secretary, he is reported to have said he would be willing to divide his last crust with scholars.

With Nicolas V., 1447–1455, Humanism triumphed at the centre of the Roman Church. He was the first and best pope of the Renaissance and its most liberal supporter. However, Humanism never struck as deep root in Rome as it did in Florence. It was always more or less of an exotic in the papal city.[1] Nicolas caught the spirit of the Renaissance in Florence, where he served as private tutor. For 20 years he acted as the secretary of Cardinal Niccolo Abergati, and travelled in France, England, Burgundy, Germany and Northern Italy. On these journeys he collected rare books, among which were Lactantius, Gregory of Nazianzus, Irenæus, 12 epistles of Ignatius and an epistle of Polycarp. Many manuscripts he copied with his own hand, and he helped to arrange the books Cosimo collected. His pontificate was a golden era for architects and authors. With the enormous sums which the year of Jubilee, 1450, brought to Rome, he was able to carry out his double passion for architecture and literature. In the bank of the Medici alone, 100,000 florins were deposited to the account of the papacy. Nicolas gave worthy scholars employment as transcribers, translators or secretaries, but he made them work night and day. He sent agents to all parts of Italy and to other countries, even to Russia and England, in search of rare books, and had them copied on parchment and luxuriously bound and clasped with silver clasps. He thus collected the works of Homer, Herodotus, Thucydides, Xenophon, Plato, Aristotle, Polybius, Diodorus Siculus, Appian, Philo Judæus, and the Greek Fathers, Eusebius, Basil, Gregory of Nazianzus, Chrysostom, Cyril and Dionysius the Areopagite. He kindled a feverish enthusiasm for the translation of Greek authors, and was determined to enrich the West with versions of all the surviving monuments of Hellenic literature. As Symonds puts it, Rome became a factory of translations from Greek into Latin. Nicolas paid to Valla 500 scudi for a Latin version of Thucy-

---

[1] Gregorovius, VII, 539; Symonds, *Rev. of Learning*, II. 215.

dides and to Guarino 1,500 for his translation of Strabo.   He
presented to Nicolas Perotti for his translation of Polybius a
purse of 500 new papal ducats, — a ducat being the equivalent
of 12 francs, — with the remark that the sum was not equal to
the author's merits.   He offered 5,000 ducats for the discovery
of the Hebrew Matthew and 10,000 gold gulden for a translation
of Homer, but in vain; for Marsuppini and Oratius only furnished fragments of the *Iliad*, and Valla's translation of the first
16 books was a paraphrase in prose.   He gave Manetti, his secretary and biographer, though absent from Rome, a salary of
600 ducats.   No such liberal and enlightened friend of books
ever sat in the chair of St. Peter.

Nicolas found an enduring monument in the Vatican Library,
which, with its later additions, is the most valuable collection
in the world of rare manuscripts in Oriental, Greek, Latin and
ecclesiastical literature.   Among its richest treasures is the
Vatican manuscript of the Greek New Testament.   There had
been older pontifical libraries and collections of archives, first
in the Lateran, afterwards in the Vatican palace, but Nicolas
well deserves to be called the founder of the Vatican Library.
He bought for it about 5,000 volumes of valuable classical and
biblical manuscripts, — an enormous collection for those days,
— and he had besides a private library, consisting chiefly of
Latin classics.   No other library of that age reached 1,000
volumes.   Bessarion had only 600 volumes, Niccoli in Florence
800, Federigo of Urbino 772.   The Vatican now contains
30,000 manuscripts and about 100,000 printed works.   Free
access was offered to its archives for the first time by Leo XIII.

The interest of the later popes of the Renaissance period
was given to art and architecture rather than to letters.   The
Spaniard, Calixtus III., according to the doubtful report of
Vespasiano, regarded the accumulation of books by his predecessor as a waste of the treasures of the Church of God,
gave away several hundred volumes to the old Cardinal Isidore of Kiew and melted the silver ornaments, with which
many manuscripts were bound, into coin for his proposed war
against the Turks.

From the versatile diplomatist and man of letters, Pius II., the Humanists had a right to expect much, but they got little. This, however, was not because Æneas Sylvius had reason to fear rivalry. After being elected pope, he was carried about the city of Rome and to Tusculum, Alba, Ostia and other localities, tracing the old Roman roads and water conduits and examining other monuments. He was a poet, novelist, controversialist, historian, cosmographer. He had a heart for everything, from the boat-race and hunting-party to the wonders of great cities, Florence and Rome. His faculty of observation was as keen as his interests were broad. Nothing seems to have escaped his eye. Everything that was human had an interest for him, and his description of cities and men, as in his *Frederick III.* and *History of Bohemia*, hold the reader's attention by their clever judgments and their appreciation of characteristic and entertaining details.[1] Pius' novels and odes breathe a low moral atmosphere, and his comedy, *Chrisis*, in the style of Terence, deals with women of ill-repute and is equal to the most lascivious of the Humanistic productions. His orations fill three volumes, and over 500 of his letters are still extant.

Under Paul II., the Humanists of the papal household had hard times, as the treatment of Platina shows. Sixtus IV., 1471–1484, has a place in the history of the Vatican library, which he transferred to four new and beautiful halls. He endowed it with a permanent fund, provided for Latin, Greek and Hebrew copyists, appointed as librarians two noted scholars, Bussi and Platina, and separated the books from the archives.[2] The light-hearted Leo X., a normal product of the Renaissance, honored Bembo and other literati, but combined the patronage of frivolous with serious literature. In a letter printed in the first edition of the first six books of the *Annals of Tacitus*, 1515, — discovered in the Westphalian convent of Corbay, 1508, — he wrote that "from his earliest years he had been accustomed to think that, if we except the knowledge and worship of God Himself, nothing more excellent or more

[1] Burckhardt-Geiger, II. 21.
[2] See Pastor, II. 655 sqq., who dwells at length on this pope's service to the library.

useful had been given by the Creator to mankind than classical studies which not only lead to the ornament and guidance
of human life, but are applicable and useful to every particular situation."

As a characteristic development of the Italian Renaissance
must be mentioned the so-called academies of Florence, Rome
and Naples. These institutions corresponded somewhat to
our modern scientific associations. The most noted of them,
the Platonic Academy of Florence, was founded by Cosimo
de' Medici, and embraced among its members the principal
men of Florence and some strangers. It celebrated the birthday of Plato, November 13, with a banquet and a discussion of his writings. It revived and diffused the knowledge
of the sublime truths of Platonism, and then gave way to
other academies in Florence of a more literary and social
character.[1] Its brightest fame was reached under Lorenzo.

The academy at Rome, which had Pomponius Lætus for
its founder, did not confine itself to the study of Plato and
philosophy, but had a more general literary aim. The meetings were devoted to classical discussions and the presentation
of orations and plays. Although Lætus was half a pagan,
Alexander VI. was represented at his funeral, 1498, by members of his court. Cardinal Sadoleto in the 16th century
reckoned the Roman academy among the best teachers of his
youth. The academy at Naples, developed by Jovianus Pon-
tanus, devoted itself chiefly to matters of style. The Florentine academy has been well characterized by Professor Jebb
as predominantly philosophic, the Roman as antiquarian and
the Neapolitan as literary.[2]

§ 65. *Greek Teachers and Italian Humanists.*

The revival of the study of Greek, which had been neglected
for eight centuries or more, was due, not to an interest in the
original text of the New Testament, but to a passion to become
acquainted with Homer, Plato and other classic Greek authors.

---

[1] R. Rocholl, *D. Platonismus d. Renaissancezeit*, in Brieger's *Zeitschr.
für K.-gesch.*, Leipz., 1892, pp. 47–106.

[2] *Cambr. Hist.*, I. 560.

Not even had Gregory the Great any knowledge of the language. The erection of chairs for its study was recommended by the Council of Vienne, but the recommendation came to nothing. The revival of the study of the language was followed by the discovery of Greek manuscripts, the preparation of grammars and dictionaries and the translation of the Greek classics.

If we pass by such itinerating and uncertain teachers as the Calabrians, from whom Petrarca and Boccaccio took lessons, the list of modern teachers of Greek opens with Emanuel Chrysoloras, 1350–1415. He taught in Florence, Milan, Padua, Venice and Rome and, having conformed to the Latin Church, was taken as interpreter to the council at Constance, where he died. He wrote the first Greek grammar, printed in 1484. The first lexicon was prepared by a Carmelite monk, Giovanni Crastone of Piacenza, and appeared in 1497. Provided as we are with a full apparatus for the study of Greek, we have little conception of the difficulty of acquiring a book-knowledge of that language without the elementary helps of grammar and dictionary.

A powerful impetus was given to Greek studies by the Council of Ferrara, 1439, with its large delegation from the Eastern Church and its discussions over the doctrinal differences of Christendom. Its proceedings appeared in the two languages. Among those who attended the council and remained in the West for a period or for life, were Plethon, whose original name was Georgios Gemistos, 1355–1450, and Bessarion, 1403–1472. Cosimo de' Medici heard Plethon often and was led by his lectures on Plato to conceive the idea of the Platonic Academy in Florence.

Bessarion, bishop of Nicæa, became a fixture in the Latin Church and was admitted to the college of cardinals by Eugenius IV. The objection made in conclave to his candidacy for the papal chair by the cardinal of Avignon was that he was a Greek and wore a beard. He died in Ravenna. Like all Greeks, Bessarion was a philosophical theologian, and took more interest in the metaphysical mystery of the eternal procession of the Spirit than the practical work of the Spirit upon

the hearts of men.   He vindicated Plato against the charges
of immorality and alleged hostility to orthodox doctrines,
pointed to that philosopher's belief in the creation and the
immortality of the soul, quoted the favorable opinions of him
given by Basil, Augustine and other Fathers, and represented
him as a bridge from heathenism to Christianity.   Bessarion's
palace in Rome was a meeting-place of scholars.   At an expense of 15,000 ducats or, as Platina says, 30,000, he collected
a valuable library which he gave, in 1468, to the republic of
Venice.[1]

George of Trebizond, 1395–1484, came to Italy about 1420,
conformed to the papal church, taught eloquence and the
Aristotelian philosophy in Venice and Rome, and was appointed an apostolic scribe by Nicolas V.   He was a conceited, disputatious and irascible man and quarrelled with
Valla, Poggio, Theodore of Gaza, Bessarion and Perotti.   The
50 scudi which Sixtus IV. gave him for the translation of
Aristotle's *History of Animals*, he contemptuously threw into
the Tiber.   His chief work was a comparison of Aristotle and
Plato, to the advantage of the former.

Theodore of Gaza, George's rival, was a native of Thessa-
lonica, reached Italy 1430, taught in Ferrara and then passed
into the service of Pope Nicolas.   He was a zealous Platonist, and translated several Greek works into Latin and some
of Cicero's works into Greek and also wrote a Greek grammar.

John Argyropulos, an Aristotelian philosopher and translator, taught 15 years with great success at Florence, and
then at Rome, where Reuchlin heard him lecture on Thucydides.   His death, 1486, was brought about by excess in
eating melons.

The leading Greeks, who emigrated to Italy after the fall
of Constantinople, were Callistus, Constantine Lascaris and
his son John.   John Andronicus Callistus taught Greek at
Bologna and at Rome, 1454–1469, and took part in the disputes between the Platonists and Aristotelians.   Afterwards
he removed to Florence and last to France, in the hope of

[1] *Bessarionis Opera* in Migne's *Patrol. Græca*, vol. CLXI. *Lives* of
Bessarion by Henri Vast, Paris, 1878, and H. Rocholl, Leip., 1904.

better remuneration.   He is said to have read all the Greek
authors and imported six chests of manuscripts from Greece.
Constantine Lascaris, who belonged to a family of high rank
in the Eastern empire, gave instruction in the Greek language to Ippolita, the daughter of Francis Sforza, and later
the wife of Alfonso, son of Ferdinand I. of Naples.   He composed a Greek grammar for her, the first book printed in
Greek, 1476.   In 1470, he moved to Messina, where he established a flourishing school, and died near the close of the
century.   Among his pupils was Cardinal Bembo of Venice.

His son, John Lascaris, 1445–1535, was employed by
Lorenzo de' Medici to collect manuscripts in Greece, and
superintended the printing of Greek books in Florence.   He
accompanied Charles VIII. to France.   In 1513, he was called
by Leo X. to Rome, and opened there a Greek and Latin
school.   In 1518, he returned to France and collected a library
for Francis I. at Fontainebleau.

Among those who did distinguished service in collecting
Greek manuscripts was Giovanni Aurispa, 1369–1459, who
went to Constantinople in his youth to study Greek, and
bought and sold with the shrewdness of an experienced book-
seller.   In 1423, he returned from Constantinople with 238
volumes, including Sophocles, Æschylus, Plato, Xenophon,
Plutarch, Lucian.   Thus these treasures were saved from
ruthless destruction by the Turks, before the catastrophe of
1453 overtook Constantinople.

The study of Greek suffered a serious decline in Italy after
the close of the 15th century, but was taken up and carried to
a more advanced stage by the Humanists north of the Alps.

The study of Hebrew, which had been preserved in Europe
by Jewish scholars, notably in Spain, was also revived in
Italy in the 15th century, but its revival met with opposition.
When Lionardo Bruni heard that Poggio was learning the
language, he wrote contending that the study was not only
unprofitable but positively hurtful.   Manetti, the biographer
of Nicolas V., translated the Psalms out of Hebrew and made
a collection of Hebrew manuscripts for that pontiff.   The
Camalduensian monk, Traversari, learned the language and,

in 1475, began the printing of Hebrew books on Italian presses.   Chairs for the study of Hebrew were founded at Bologna, 1488, and in Rome 1514.

Passing from the list of the Greek teachers to the Italian Humanists, it is possible to select for mention here only a few of the more prominent names, and with special reference to their attitude to the Church.

Lionardo Bruni, 1369–1444, a pupil of Chrysoloras, gives us an idea of the extraordinary sensation caused by the revival of the Greek language.   He left all his other studies for the language of Plato and Demosthenes.   He was papal secretary in Rome and for a time chancellor of Florence, and wrote letters, orations, histories, philosophical essays and translations from the Greek, among them Aristotle's *Ethics, Politics* and *Economics*, and Plato's *Phædo, Crito, Apology, Phædrus* and *Gorgias* and his *Epistles* and six of Plutarch's *Lives.*   Foreigners went to Florence expressly to see his face.   He was a pious Catholic.[1]

Francesco Poggio Bracciolini, 1380–1459, was secretary of Martin V., then of Nicolas V., and lived mostly in Florence and Rome.[2]   He was the most widely known Humanist of his day and had an unbounded passion for classical antiquity and for literary controversy.   He excelled chiefly in Latin, but knew also Greek and a little Hebrew.   He was an enthusiastic book-hunter.   He went to Constance as papal secretary and, besides discovering a complete copy of Quintilian's *Institutes*, made search in the neighboring Benedictine abbeys of Reichenau and Weingarten for old manuscripts.   In Cluny and other French convents he discovered new orations of Cicero.   He also visited "barbarous England."   Although in the service of the curia for nearly 50 years, Poggio detested and ridiculed the monks and undermined respect for the church which supported him.   In his *Dialogue against Hypocrisy*, he gathered a number of scandalous stories of the

---

[1] *Lionardo Bruni Aretini Epistolæ*, ed. Mehus, 2 vols., Flor., 1742.

[2] *Opera Poggii*, Basel, 1513, and other edds.   *Epistolæ Poggii*, ed. Tonelli, 3 vols., Flor., 1832, 1859, 1861.   Shepherd : *Life of Poggio.*   Pastor's castigation of Poggio, I. 33 sqq., is in his most vigorous style.

tricks and frauds practised by monks in the name of religion. His bold description of the martyrdom of the heretic Jerome of Prag has already been cited. When Felix was elected, Poggio exhausted the dictionary for abusive terms and called the anti-pope another Cerberus, a golden calf, a roaring lion, a high-priest of malignity; and he did equally well for the Council of Basel, which had elected Felix. Poggio's self-esteem and quick temper involved him in endless quarrels, and invectives have never had keener edge than those which passed between him and his contestants. To his acrid tongue were added loose habits. He lived with a concubine, who bore him 14 children, and, when reproached for it, he frivo-lously replied that he only imitated the common habit of the clergy. At the age of 54, he abandoned her and married a Florentine maiden of 18, by whom he had 4 children. His *Facetiæ*, or Jest-Book, a collection of obscene stories, acquired immense popularity.

The general of the Camalduensian order, Ambrogio Tra-versari, 1386–1439, combined ascetic piety with interest in heathen literature. He collected 238 manuscripts in Venice and translated from the Greek Fathers. He was, perhaps, the first Italian monk from the time of Jerome to his own day who studied Hebrew.

Carlo Marsuppini, of Arezzo, hence called Carlo Aretino, belonged to the same circle, but was an open heathen, who died without confession and sacrament. He was nevertheless highly esteemed as a teacher and as chancellor of Florence, and honorably buried in the church of S. Croce, 1463, where a monument was erected to his memory.

Francesco Filelfo, 1398–1481, was one of the first Latin and Greek scholars, and much admired and much hated by his con-temporaries. He visited Greece, returned to Italy with a rich supply of manuscripts, and was professor of eloquence and Greek in the University of Florence. He combined the worst and best features of the Renaissance. He was conceited, mean, selfish, avaricious. He thought himself equal if not superior to Virgil and Cicero. In malignity and indecency of satire and invective he rivalled Poggio. His poisonous tongue got him into scandalous literary feuds with Niccolo, Poggio, members of the Medici family and others. He was banished from Florence, but, recalled in his old days by Lorenzo, he died a few weeks after his return, aged 83. He was always begging or levying contributions on princes for his poetry, and he kept several servants and six horses. His 3 wives bore him 24 children. He was ungrateful to his benefactors and treacherous to his friends.[1]

Marsilio Ficino, 1433–1499, one of the circle who made the court of Lorenzo the Magnificent famous, was an ordained priest, rector of two churches and canon of the cathedral of Florence. He eloquently preached the Platonic gospel to his "brethren in Plato," and translated the Orphic hymns, the *Hermes Trismegistos*, and some works of Plato and Plotinus, — a colossal task for that age. He believed that the divine Plotinus had first revealed the theology of the divine Plato and "the mysteries of the ancients," and that these were consistent with Christianity. Yet he was unable to find in Plato's writings the mystery of the Trinity. He wrote a defence of the Christian religion, which he regarded as the only true religion, and a work on the immortality of the soul, which he proved with 15 arguments as against the Aristotelians. He was small and sickly, and kept poor by dishonest servants and avaricious relations.

Politian, to his edition of Justinian's *Pandects*, added translations of Epictetus, Hippocrates, Galen and other authors, and published among lecture-courses those on Ovid, Suetonius, Pliny and Quintilian. His lecture-room extended its influence to England and Germany, and Grocyn, Linacre and Reuchlin were among his hearers.

Three distinguished Italian Humanists whose lives overlap the first period of the Reformation were cardinals, Pietro Bembo, 1470–1547, Giacopo Sadoleto, 1477–1547, and Aleander, 1480–1542. All were masters of an elegant Latin style. For 22 years Bembo lived in concubinage, and had three children. Cardinal Sadoleto is best known for his polite and

[1] His life, Rosmini, 3 vols., Milan, 1808, *Epistolæ Filelfi*, Venet., 1502.

astute letter calling upon the Genevans to abandon the Reformation, to which Calvin replied.[1]

Not without purpose have the two names, Laurentius Valla, 1406–1457, and Pico della Mirandola, 1463–1494, been reserved for the last. These men are to be regarded as having, among the Humanists of the 15th century, the most points of contact with our modern thought,— the one the representative of critical scholarship, the other of broad human sympathies coupled with a warm piety.

Laurentius Valla, the only Humanist of distinction born in Rome, taught at Pavia, was secretary to the king of Naples, and at last served at the court of Nicolas V.[2] He held several benefices and was buried in the Lateran, but was a sceptic and an indirect advocate of Epicurean morality. He combined classical with theological erudition and attained an influence almost equal to that enjoyed by Erasmus several generations later. He was a born critic, and is one of the earliest pioneers of the right of private judgment. He broke loose from the bondage of scholastic tradition and an infallible Church authority, so that in this respect Bellarmin called him a forerunner of Luther. Luther, with an imperfect knowledge of Valla's works, esteemed him highly, declaring that in many centuries neither Italy nor the universal Church could produce another like him.[3] He narrowly escaped the Inquisition. He denied to the monks the monopoly of being " the religious," and attacked their threefold vow. In his *Annotations to the New Testament*, published by Erasmus, 1505, he ventured to correct Jerome's Vulgate. He doubted the genu-

---

[1] *Sadoleti opp.*, Moguntiæ, 1607 ; Verona, 1737, 4 vols. In his *Concilium de emendanda Ecclesia*, 1538, Sadoleto admitted many abuses and proposed a reformation of the Church, which he vainly hoped from the pope.

[2] Valla's *Works*, Basel, 1540, J. Vahlen ; *L. Valla*, Vienna, 1864, 2d ed., 1870 ; Voigt, I. 464 sqq. See Benrath in Herzog, XX. 422 sqq.

[3] *Cui nec Italia nec universa ecclesia multis seculis similem habuit non modo in omni disciplinarum genere sed ex constantia et zelo fide Christianorum non ficto.* See his *Respons. ad Lovan. et Colon theol.* of March, 1520, Weimar ed., VI. 183. In this reply to the Louvain and Cologne theologians who had condemned his writings, Luther also speaks of the injustice of condemning Pico della Mirandola and Reuchlin.

ineness of the writings attributed to Dionysius the Areopagite and rejected as a forgery Christ's letter to King Abgarus
which Eusebius had accepted as genuine.   When he attacked
the Apostolic origin of the Apostles' Creed and, about 1440,
exposed the Donation of Constantine as a fiction, he was calling in question the firm belief of centuries.   In pronouncing
the latter "contradictory, impossible, stupid, barbarous and
ridiculous,"[1] he was wrenching a weapon, long used, out of the
hand of the hierarchy.   His attack was based on the ground
of authentic history, inherent improbability and the mediæval
character of the language.   Not satisfied with refuting its
genuineness, Valla made it an occasion of an assault upon
the whole temporal power of the papacy.   He thus struck at
the very bulwarks of the mediæval theocracy.   In boldness
and violence Valla equalled the anti-papal writings of Luther.
He went, indeed, not so far as to deny the spiritual power
and divine institution of the papacy, but he charged the
bishop of Rome with having turned Peter into Judas and
having accepted the devil's offer of the kingdoms of this
world.   He made him responsible for the political divisions
and miseries of Italy, for rebellions and civil wars, herein
anticipating Machiavelli.   He maintained that the princes
had a right to deprive the pope of his temporal possessions,
which he had long before forfeited by their abuse.   The purity
of Valla's motives are exposed to suspicion.   At the time he
wrote the tract he was in the service of Alfonso, who was engaged in a controversy with Eugenius IV.

Unfortunately, Valla's ethical principles and conduct were
no recommendation to his theology.   His controversy with
Poggio abounds in scandalous personalities.   In the course of
it, Valla was charged with seduction and pederasty.[2]   His

---

[1] *De falso credita et ementita Constantini donatione.* A well-written MS.
copy in the Vatican is dated 1451.   The tract is printed in Valla's *Opera*,
761–795, and in Brown's *Fasciculus rerum*, Rome, 1690, pp. 132–157, French
text, by A. Bonneau, Paris, 1879.   Luther received a copy through a friend,
Feb., 1520, and was strengthened by it in his opposition to popery, which he
attacked unmercifully in the summer of that year in his *Address to the German Nobility*, and his *Babyl. Captivity of the Church.*

[2] The first issues were *Invectivæ in Vallam* and *Antidoti in Poggium.*   The

Ciceronian Dialogues on Lust, written perhaps 1431, are an indirect attack upon Christian morality. Valla defended the Platonic community of wives. What nature demands is good and laudable, and the voice of nature is the voice of God. When he was charged by Poggio with having seduced his brother-in-law's maid, he admitted the charge without shame.

Pico della Mirandola, the most precocious genius that had arisen since Duns Scotus, was cut down when he was scarcely 30 years of age. The Schoolman was far beyond him in dialectic subtlety, but was far inferior to him in independence of thought and, in this quality, Pico anticipated the coming age. He studied canon law, theology, philosophy and the humanities in Ferrara and learned also Hebrew, Chaldee and Arabic.[1] In his twenty-third year, he went to Rome and published 900 theses on miscellaneous topics, in which he anticipated some of the Protestant views ; for example, that no image or cross should be adored and that the words " This is my body " must be understood symbolically, — *significative*, — not materially. He also maintained that the science of magic and the Cabbala confirm the doctrine of the Trinity and the deity of Christ. These opinions aroused suspicion, and 13 of his theses were condemned by Innocent VIII. as heretical ; but, as he submitted his judgment to the Church, he was acquitted of heresy, and Alexander VI. cleared him of all charges.

To his erudition, Pico added sincere faith and ascetic tendencies. In the last years of his short life, he devoted himself to the study of the Bible with the purpose of preaching Christ throughout the world. He was an admirer of Savonarola, who blamed him for not becoming a full monk and thought he went to purgatory. Of all Humanists he had the loftiest conception of man's dignity and destiny. In his *De dignitate hominis*, he

coarse controversial language, common to many of the Humanists, unfortunately Luther and Luther's Catholic assailants shared, and also Calvin.

[1] The *Theses* of Pico, Rome, 1486, and Cologne. His *Opera*, Bologna, 1496, and together with the works of his nephew, JOHN F. PICO, Basel, 1572, and 1601. — G. DREYDORFF : *Das System des Joh. Pico von Mir.*, Marb., 1858. — GEIGER, 204 sqq. — His *Life*, by his nephew, J. Fr. Pico. Trsl. from the Latin by Sir Thos. More, 1510. Ed., with Introd. and Notes, by J. M. Rigg, Lond., 1890.

maintained that God placed man in the midst of the world that he might the more easily study all that therein is, and endowed him with freewill, by which he might degenerate into the condition of the beast or rise to a godlike existence. He found the highest truth in the Christian religion. He is the author of the famous sentence : *Philosophia veritatem quærit, theologia invenit, religio possidet,* — philosophy seeks the truth, theology finds it, religion has it.

Mirandola had a decided influence on John Reuchlin, who saw him in 1490 and was persuaded by him of the immense wisdom hid in the Cabbala. He also was greatly admired by Zwingli. He was the only one, says Burckhardt, " who, in a decided voice, fought for science and the truth of all the ages against the one-sided emphasis of classic antiquity. In him it is possible to see what a noble change Italian philosophy would have undergone, if the counter-Reformation had not come in and put an end to the whole higher intellectual movement."[1] Giordano Bruno, one of the last representatives of the philosophical Renaissance, was condemned as a heretic by the Roman Inquisition and burnt on the Campo de' Fiori in 1600. To the great annoyance of Pope Leo XIII., his admirers erected a statue to his memory on the same spot in 1889.

§ 66. *The Artists.*

Hæc est Italia diis sacra. — PLINY.

Italian Humanism reproduced the past. Italian art was original. The creative productions of Italy in architecture, sculpture and painting continue to render it the world's chief centre of artistic study and delight. Among Italian authors, Dante alone has a place at the side of Michelangelo, Raphael and Lionardo da Vinci. The cultivation of art began in the age of Dante with Cimabue and Giotto, but when Italian Humanism was declining Italian painting and sculpture were celebrating their highest triumphs. Such a combination and succession of men of genius in the fine arts as Italy produced, in a period extending over three centuries, has nowhere else been known.

[1] I. 217. See also II. 73, 306 sq.

They divided their triumphs between Florence and Rome, but imparted their magic touch to many other Italian cities, including Venice, which had remained cold to the literary movement. Here again Rome drew upon Florence for painters such as Giotto and Fra Angelico, and for sculptors such as Ghiberti, Donatello, Brunelleschi and Michelangelo.

While the Italy of the 15th century — or the quattrocento, as the Italians call it — was giving expression to her own artistic conceptions in color and marble and churchly dome, masterpieces of ancient sculpture, restless, in the graves where for centuries they had had rude sepulture, came forth to excite the admiring astonishment of a new generation. What the age of Nicolas V. was for the discovery of manuscripts, the age of Julius II. was for the discovery of classic Greek statuary. The extensive villa of the Emperor Hadrian at Tivoli, which extended over several miles and embraced a theatre, lyceum, temple, basilica, library, and race-course, alone furnished immense treasures of art. Others were found in the bed of the Tiber or brought from Greece or taken from the Roman baths, where their worth had not been discerned. In Alexander VI.'s pontificate the Apollo Belvedere was found ; under Julius II. the torso of Hercules, the Laocoön group [1] and the Vatican Venus. The Greek ideals of human beauty were again revealed and kindled an enthusiasm for similar achievements.

Petrarca's collections were repeated. Paul II. deposited his rich store of antiquities in his palace of San Marco. In Florence, Lorenzo de' Medici was active in securing pieces of ancient art. The museum on the Capitoline Hill in Rome, where Nicolas V. seems to have restored the entire palace of the senate, dates from 1471, one of its earliest treasures being the statue of Marcus Aurelius. The Vatican museum was the creation of Julius II. To these museums and the museums in Florence were added the galleries of private collectors.

In architecture, the Renaissance artists never adopted the stern Gothic of the North. In 1452, Leon Battista Alberti

---

[1] The discovery of the Laocoön in a vineyard in Rome was "like a Jubilee." Michelangelo was one of the first to see it. Sadoleto praised it in Latin verses. See description in Klaczko, W. 93–96.

showed to Nicolas V. a copy of his *De re œdificatoria*, a work
on architecture, based upon his studies of the Roman monuments. Nicolas opened the line of great builders in Rome and
his plans were on a splendid scale.

The art of the Renaissance blends the glorification of mediæval Catholicism with the charms of classical paganism, the
history of the Bible with the mythology of Greece and Rome.
The earlier painters of the 14th and 15th centuries were more
simple, chaste and devout than those of the 16th, who reached
a higher distinction as artists.   The Catholic type of piety is
shown in the preponderance of the pictures of the Madonna
holding the infant Saviour in her arms or on her lap and in
the portraiture of St. Sebastian and other saints.   Heavenly
beauty and earthly sensuality meet side by side, and the
latter often draws attention away from the former.   The
same illustrious painters, says Hawthorne, in the *Marble Faun*,
" seem to take up one task or the other — the disrobed woman
whom they called Venus, or the type of highest and tenderest
womanhood in the mother of their Saviour — with equal readiness, but to achieve the former with far more satisfactory success."   One moment the painter represented Bacchus wedding
Ariadne and another depicted Mary on the hill of Calvary.
Michelangelo now furnished the Pietà for St. Peter's, now
designed the Rape of Ganymede for Vittoria Colonna and the
statue of the drunken Bacchus for the Roman Jacopo Galli.
Titian's Magdalen in the Pitti gallery, Florence, exhibits in
one person the voluptuous woman with exposed breasts and
flowing locks and the penitent saint looking up to heaven.   Of
Sandro Botticelli, Vasari said that "in many homes he painted
of naked women a plenty."   If, however, the Christian religion
furnished only to a single writer, Dante, the subject of his
poem, it furnished to all the painters and sculptors many subjects from both Testaments and also from Church history, for
the highest productions of their genius.

In looking through the long list of distinguished sculptors,
painters and architects who illuminated their native Italy in
the Renaissance period, one is struck with the high age which
many of them reached and, at the same time, with the brief

period in which some of them acquired undying fame. Michelangelo lived to be 89, while Correggio died before he was 44. Titian, had he lived one year longer, would have rounded out a full century, while death took the brush out of Raphael's hand before he was 37, a marvellous example of production in a short period, to be compared with Mozart in the department of music and Blaise Pascal in letters. And again, several of the great artists are remarkable examples of an extraordinary combination of talents. Lionardo da Vinci and Michelangelo excelled alike as architects, sculptors, painters and poets. Lionardo was, besides being these, a chemist, engineer, musician, merchant and profound thinker, yea, "the precocious originator of all modern wonders and ideas, a subtle and universal genius, an isolated and insatiate investigator," and is not unjustly called, on his monument at Milan, "the restorer of the arts and sciences."[1] His mural picture of the Last Supper in Milan, best known by the engraving of Raphael Morghen, in spite of its defaced condition, is a marvellous reproduction of one of the sublimest events, adapted to the monks seated around their refectory table (instead of the reclining posture on couches), and every head a study. As for Michelangelo, he has been classed by Taine with Dante, Shakespeare and Beethoven among the four great intellects in the world of art and literature.

Distinguishing in the years between 1300–1550 two periods, the earlier Renaissance to 1470 and the high Renaissance, from that date forward, we find that Italian art had its first centre in Florence, and its most glorious exhibition under Julius II. and Leo X. in Rome.[2] The earlier period began with Cimabue, who died about 1302, and Giotto, 1276–1336, the

---

[1] Taine, *Lectures on Art*, I. 16. — Lübke, *Hist. of Art*, II. 280 sq. says: "Lionardo was one of those rare beings in whom nature loves to unite all conceivable human perfections, — strikingly handsome, and at the same time of a dignified presence and of an almost incredible degree of bodily strength; while mentally he possessed such various endowments as are rarely united in a single person," etc. See also Symonds, III. 314.

[2] Julius ordered a colossal tomb wrought for himself, but he could not be depended upon as a paymaster, as Michelangelo complained. See Klaczko, p. 62.

friend of Dante. According to the story, Cimabue found Giotto, then ten years old, drawing sheep on a stone with a piece of charcoal and, with his father's consent, took the lad to Florence. These two artists employed their genius in the decoration of the cathedral erected to the memory of St. Francis in Assisi. The visitor to S. Croce and other sacred places in Florence looks upon the frescos of Giotto. His Dante, like Guido Reni's Beatrice Cenci, once seen can never be forgotten. Symonds has remarked that it may be said, without exaggeration, that Giotto and his scholars, within the space of little more than half a century, painted upon the walls of the churches and the public places of Italy every great conception of the Middle Ages.[1] Fra Angelico da Fiesole, 1387-1455, is the most religious of the painters of this period, and his portraiture of saints and angels is so pure as to suggest no other impression than saintliness.

The mind is almost stunned by the combination of brilliant artistic achievement, of which the pontificate of Julius II. may be taken as the centre. There flourished in that age Perugino, 1446-1524, — Raphael's teacher, — Lionardo da Vinci, 1452-1519, Raphael, 1483-1520, Michelangelo, 1475-1564, Correggio, 1493-1534, Andrea del Sarto, 1487-1531, and Titian, 1477-1576, all Italians.

Of Raphael, his German biographer has said his career is comprised in four words, "he lived, he loved, he worked, he died young."[2] He was an attractive and amiable character, free from envy and jealousy, modest, magnanimous, patient of criticism, as anxious to learn as to teach, always ready to assist poor artists. Michelangelo and he labored in close proximity in the Vatican, Michelangelo in the Sistine chapel, Raphael in the stanze and loggie. Their pupils quarrelled among themselves, each depreciating the rival of his master; but the masters rose above the jealousy of small minds. They form a noble pair, like Schiller and Goethe among poets. Raphael seemed almost to have descended from a higher world. Vasari

---

[1] The Renaissance, III. 191.

[2] *Seine Geschichte ist in den vier Begriffen enthalten: leben, lieben. arbeiten und jung sterben.*

says that he combined so many rare gifts that he might be called a mortal god rather than a simple man.   The portraits, which present him as an infant, youth and man, are as characteristic and impressive as Giotto's Dante and Guido Reni's Beatrice Cenci.

Like Goethe, Raphael was singularly favored by fortune and was free from the ordinary trials of artists — poverty, humiliation and neglect.   He held the appointment of papal chamberlain and had the choice between a cardinal's hat and marriage to a niece of Cardinal Bibbiena, with a dowry of three thousand gold crowns.   But he put off the marriage from year to year, and preferred the dangerous freedom of single life.   His contemporary and admirer, Vasari, says, when Raphael felt death approaching, he " as a good Christian dismissed his mistress from his house, making a decent provision for her support, and then made his last confession. "

The painter's best works are devoted to religious characters and events.   On a visit to Florence after the burning of Savonarola, he learned from his friend Fra Bartolomeo to esteem the moral reformer and gave him, as well as Dante, a place among the great teachers of the Church in his fresco of the *Theologia* in the Vatican.   His Madonnas represent the perfection of human loveliness and purity.   In the Madonna di San Sisto at Dresden, so called because Sixtus IV. is introduced into the picture, the eye is divided between the sad yet half-jubilant face of the Virgin Mother, the contemplative gaze of the cherubs and the pensive and sympathetic expression of the divine child.

Grimm says, Raphael's Madonnas are not Italian faces but women who are lifted above national characteristics.   The Madonnas of da Vinci, Correggio, Titian, Murillo and Rubens contain the features of the nationality to which these painters belonged.   Raphael alone has been able to give us feminine beauty which belongs to the European type as such.[1]

The last, the greatest, and the purest of Raphael's works is the Transfiguration in the Vatican.   While engaged on it, he died, on Good Friday, his birthday.   It was suspended over

[1] *Raphael*, p. 428 sqq.

his coffin and carried to the church of the Pantheon, where his remains repose in his chosen spot near those of his betrothed bride, Maria di Bibbiena.   In that picture we behold the divinest figure that ever appeared on earth, soaring high in the air, in garments of transparent light, and with arms outspread, adored by Moses on the right hand and by Elijah on the left, who represent the Old Covenant of law and promise.   The three favorite disciples are lying on the ground, unable to face the dazzling splendor from heaven.   Beneath this celestial scene we see, in striking contrast, the epileptic boy with rolling eyes, distorted features, and spasmodic limbs, held by his agonized father and supported by his sister; while the mother imploringly appeals to the nine disciples who, in their helplessness, twitted by scribes, point up to the mountain where Jesus had gone.   In connecting the two scenes, the painter followed the narrative of the Gospels, Matt. xvii. 1–14; Mark ix. 2–14; Luke ix. 28–37.   The connection is being continually repeated in Christian experience.   Descending from the Mount of Transfiguration, we are confronted with the misery of earth and, helpless in human strength, we look to heaven as the only source of help.

> Earth has no sorrow that heaven cannot heal.

Michelangelo Buonarroti was 10 years older than Raphael, and survived him 44 years.   He drew the inspiration for his sculptures and pictures from the Old Testament, from Dante and from Savonarola.   He praised Dante in two sublime sonnets and heard Savonarola's thrilling sermons against wickedness and vice, and witnessed his martyrdom.   Vasari and Condivi both bear witness to his spotless morality.   He deplored the corruptions of the papal court.

> For Rome still slays and sells Christ at the court,
> Where paths are closed to virtue's fair increase.[1]

The artist's works have colossal proportions, and refuse to be judged by ordinary rules.   They are divided between painting, as the frescos in the Sistine chapel of St. Peter's, architecture as in St. Peter's dome, and works of statuary, as Moses in Rome and David in Florence.   His Pietà in St. Peter's, a

[1] Symonds, III. 516.

marble group representing the Virgin Mary holding the crucified Saviour in her arms, raised him suddenly to the rank of the first sculptor of Italy.[1] His *Last Judgment*, on the altar wall of the Sistine chapel, represents the dominant conception of the Middle Ages of Christ as an angry judge, and is as Dantesque as Dante's *Inferno* itself.[2] The artist's last work in marble was the unfinished Pietà, in the cathedral of Florence; his last design a picture of the crucifixion. In his last poems, he took farewell of the fleeting pleasures of life, turned to God as the only reality and found in the crucified Saviour his only comfort. This is the core of the evangelical doctrine of justification rightly understood.

The day of Michelangelo's death was the day of Galileo Galilei's birth in Florence. The golden age of art had passed: the age of science was at hand.

Among the greater churches of Italy, — the cathedrals of Milan, Venice, Pisa, Siena, Florence and Rome, — St. Peter's stands pre-eminent in dimensions, treasures of art and imposing ecclesiastical associations.[3] This central cathedral of Christendom was not dedicated till 1626 by Urban VIII. Its reconstruction was planned on a colossal scale by Nicolas V., but little was done till Julius II. took up the work. Among the architects who gave to the building their thought, Bramante and Michelangelo did most. On April 18, 1506, Julius II. laid the first stone according to Bramante's design. A mass being said by Cardinal Soderini, the old pope descended by a ladder into the trench which had been dug at the spot where the statue of St. Veronica now stands. There was much fear, says Paris de Grassis, that the ground would fall in and the pope, before consecrating the foundations, cried out to those above not to come too near the edge. Under Leo X., Raphael was appointed sole architect, and was about to deviate from Bramante's plan, when death stayed his hand. Michelangelo, taking up the

[1] See Grimm's description, I. 186 sqq.

[2] Grimm, II. 224, speaks of the expression on Christ's face as indescribably repelling, but says, if a last judgment has to be painted with Christ as the judge, such an aspect must be given him.

[3] Pastor, III. 54-9, following Redtenbacher, gives a list of the more important pieces of ecclesiastical architecture in Italy, 1401-1518.

task in 1535, gave to the structure its crowning triumph in the dome, the noblest in Western Europe, and the rival of the dome of St. Sophia.

> That vast and wondrous dome,
> To which Diana's marvel was a cell, —
> Christ's mighty shrine above his martyr's tomb.[1]

§ 67. *The Revival of Paganism.*

The revival of letters and the cultivation of art brought no purification of morals to Italy nor relief from religious formalism.   The great modern historians of the period, — Voigt, Burckhardt, Gregorovius, Pastor, Creighton and Symonds, — agree in depicting the decline of religion and the degeneracy of morals in dark colors, although Pastor endeavors to rescue the Church from the charge of total neglect of its duty and to clear the mediæval hierarchy and theology from the charge of being responsible for the semi-paganism of the Renaissance.

The mediæval theology had put the priesthood in the place of the individual conscience.   Far from possessing any passion to rescue Italy from a religious formalism which involved the seeds of stagnation of thought and moral disintegration, the priesthood was corrupt at heart and corrupt in practice in the highest seats of Christendom.[2]   Finding the clerical mind of Italy insincere and the moral condition of the Church corrupt, Humanism not only made no serious effort to amend this deplorable state but, on the contrary, it contributed to the further decadence of morals by a revival of paganism, now Epicurean, now Stoical, attested both in the lives and the writings of many of its chief leaders.   Gregorovius has felt justified in pronouncing the terrible sentence that the sole end of the Italian Renaissance was paganism.[3]

The worship of classical forms led to the adoption of classical ideas.   There were not wanting Humanists and artists who combined culture with Christian faith, and devoted their

---

[1] With these lines of Byron may be coupled those of Schiller : —

> *Und ein zweiter Himmel in den Himmel*
> *Steigt Sanct Peter's wundersamer Dom.*

[2] See Burckhardt-Geiger, II. 178 sqq.   [3] VII. 536.

genius to the cause of truth and virtue. Traversari strictly observed the rules of his monastic order; Manetti, Lionardo Bruni, Vittorino da Feltre, Ficino, Sadoleto, Fra Angelico, Fra Bartolomeo, Michelangelo and others were devout Christian believers. Traversari at first hesitated to translate classic authors and, when he did, justified himself on the ground that the more the Pagan writers were understood, the more would the excellence of the Christian system be made manifest. But Poggio, Filelfo, Valla and the majority of the other writers of the Renaissance period, such as Ariosto, Aretino, Machiavelli, were indifferent to religion, or despised it in the form they saw it manifested. Culture was substituted for Christianity, the worship of art and eloquence for reverence for truth and holiness. The Humanists sacrificed in secret and openly to the gods of Greece and Rome rather than to the God of the Bible. Yet, they were not independent enough to run the risk of an open rupture with orthodoxy, which would have subjected them to the Inquisition and death at the stake.[1] Yea, those who were most flagrant in their attacks upon the ecclesiastics of their time often professed repentance for their writings in their last days, as Boccaccio and Bandello, and applied for extreme unction before death. So it was with Machiavelli, who died with the consolations of the Church which he undermined with his pen, with the half-Pagan Pomponius Laetus of Rome and the infamous Sigismondo Malatesta of Rimini, who joined to his patronage of culture the commission of every crime.

Dangerous as it may be to pronounce a final judgment upon the moral purity of a generation, even though, as in the case of the 15th century, it reveals itself clearly in its literature and in the lives of the upper classes, literary men, popes and princes, nevertheless this it is forced upon us to do. The Renaissance in Italy produced no Thomas à Kempis. No devout mystics show signs of a reform movement in her convents and among her clergy, though, it is true, there were earnest preachers who cried out for moral reform, as voices crying in the wilderness. Nor are we unmindful of the ethical disinte-

[1] Voigt, II. 213.

gration of the Church and society at other periods and in other countries, as in France under Louis XIV., when we call attention to the failure of religion in the country of the popes and at a time of great literary and artistic activity to bear fruits in righteousness of life.

The Humanists were the natural enemies of the monks. For this they cannot be blamed. As a class, the monks hated learning, boasted of superior piety, made a display of their proud humility and yet were constantly quarrelling with each other. Boccaccio and the novelists would not have selected monks and nuns as heroes and heroines of their obscene tales if monastic life had not been in a degenerate state. Poggio, Filelfo, Valla, Bandello, Machiavelli, Ariosto, Aretino and Erasmus and the writers of the *Epistolæ virorum obscurorum* chastised with caustic irony and satire the hypocrisy and vices of the monastic class, or turned its members into a butt of ridicule. To the charges of unchastity and general hypocrisy was added the imposition of false miracles upon the ignorant and credulous. It was common rumor that the nuns were the property of the monks.[1] The literature of the 15th century teems with such charges, and Savonarola was never more intense than when he attacked the clergy for their faithlessness and sins. Machiavelli openly declared " we Italians are of all most irreligious and corrupt," and he adds, " we are so because the representatives of the Church have shown us the worst example." Pastor has suggested that Humanists, who were themselves leading corrupt lives, were ill-fitted to sit in judgment upon the priesthood. This in a sense is true, and their representations, taken alone, would do no more than create an unfavorable presumption, but their statements are confirmed by the scandals of the papal court and the social conditions in Rome; and Rome was not worse than Venice, Florence and other Italian towns. The same distinguished historian seeks to parry the attacks of Humanistic writers and to offset the lives of the hierarchy by a long list of 89 saints of the calendar who lived 1400–1520.[2] The number is imposing, but outside of Ber-

[1] Geiger, II. 182–4.

[2] Pastor, I. 44 sqq., III. 66–8. It would be scarcely possible to furnish a

nardino da Siena, Fra Angelico, Jacopo della Marca and John of Capistrano, few of the names are known to general history, and the last two showed traits which the common judgment of mankind is not inclined to regard as saintly. Pastor also adduces the wills of the dying, in which provision was made for ecclesiastical objects, but these may indicate superstitious fear as well as intelligent piety. After all is said, it remains true that the responsibility and the guilt were with the clergy, who were rightly made the targets of the wits, satirists and philosophers of the time.

But while the Humanists were condemning the clerical class, many, yea, the most of them, lived in flagrant violation of the moral code themselves and inclined to scepticism or outright paganism. In their veneration of antiquity, they made the system of Plato of equal authority with the Christian system, or placed its authority above the Christian scheme. They advocated a return to the dictates of nature, which meant the impulses of the natural and sensuous man. The watchword, *sequere naturam*, " follow nature," was launched as a philosophical principle. The hard-fought controversy which raged over the relative merits of the two Greek thinkers, Aristotle and Plato, was opened by Plethon, who accused Aristotle of atheism. The battle was continued for many years, calling forth from contestants the bitterest personal assaults. In defending Plato, Ficino set the philosopher so high as to obscure the superior claims of the Christian religion, and it was seriously proposed to combine with the Scripture readings of the liturgy excerpts from Plato's writings.[1]
The immortality of the soul was formally questioned by

more offensive portrait of a priest than the living person, Don Nicolo de Pelagait di Firarola. He had become the leader of a robber band and, in 1495, was confined in an iron cage in the open air in Ferrara. He had committed murder the day he celebrated his first mass and was absolved in Rome. Afterwards he killed four men and married two women who went about with him, violated women without number and led them captive, and carried on wholesale murder and pillage. But how much worse was this priest than John XXIII., charged by a Christian council with every crime, and Alexander VI., whose papal robes covered monstrous vice ?

[1] See Pastor, III. 117 ; Symonds, II. 208, etc.

Pietro Pomponazzi, a popular teacher of the Aristotelian philosophy in Padua and Bologna.   His tract, published in 1516,
was burnt by the Franciscans at Venice, but was saved from
a like fate in Rome and Florence by the intervention of
Bembo and Julius de' Medici.   So widespread was the philosophy of materialism that the Fifth Lateran three years
before, Dec. 19, 1513, deemed it necessary to reaffirm the
doctrine of the soul's immortality and to instruct professors
at the universities to answer the arguments of the materialists.
In the age of Julius II. and Leo X., scepticism reigned universally in Rome, and the priests laughed among themselves
over their religious functions as the augurs once did in the
ancient city.[1]

The chief indictment against Humanism is, that it lacked
a serious moral sense, which is an essential element of the
Christian system.   Nor did it at any time show a purpose of
morally redeeming itself or seek after a regenerative code of
ethics.   It declined into an intellectual and æsthetic luxury,
a habit of self-indulgence for the few, with no provision for
the betterment of society at large and apparently no concern
for such betterment.   The Humanists were addicted to arrogance, vanity, and lacked principle and manly dignity.   They
were full of envy and jealousy, engaged in disgraceful personal quarrels among themselves and stooped to sycophancy
in the presence of the rich and powerful.   Politian, Filelfo
and Valla agreed in begging for presents and places in terms
of abject flattery.   While they poured contempt upon the
functionaries of religion, they failed to imitate the self-deny-
ing virtues which monasticism enjoined and that regard for
the rights of others which Christian teaching commands.
Under the influence of the Renaissance was developed that
delusive principle, called honor, which has played such an
extensive rôle in parts of Europe and under which a polished
culture may conceal the most refined selfishness.[2]

No pugilistic encounter could be more brutal than the

---

[1] Gregorovius, VIII. 300. For an excellent account of Pomponazzi and his
views, see Owen : *Skeptics*, pp. 184–240.

[2] See Burckhardt-Geiger, II. 155 sqq. and his quotation from Rabelais.

literary feuds between distinguished men of letters. Poggio
and Filelfo fought with poisoned daggers. To sully these
pages, says Symonds, "with Poggio's rank abuse would be
impossible." Poggio, not content with thrusts at Filelfo's
literary abilities, accused him of the worst vices, and poured
out calumnies on Filelfo's wife and mother. In Poggio's contest with George of Trebizond, the two athletes boxed each
other's ears and tore one another's hair. George had accused
Poggio of taking credit for translations of Xenophon and
Diodorus which did not belong to him. Between Valla and
Fazio eight books of invectives were exchanged. Bezold is
forced to say that such feuds revealed perhaps more than the
cynicism of the Italian poetry the complete moral decay.[1]

To the close of the period, the Renaissance literature
abounds in offences against morality and decency. Poggio
was already 70 years of age when he published his filthy
Facetiæ, Jest-book, which appeared 26 times in print before
1500 and in 3 Italian translations. Of Poggio's works, Burckhardt says, "They contain dirt enough to create a prejudice
against the whole class of Humanists." Filelfo's epigrams,
De jocis et seriis, are declared by his biographer, Rosmini, to
contain "horrible obscenities and expressions from the streets
and the brothels." Beccadelli and Aretino openly preached
the emancipation of the flesh, and were not ashamed to em-
bellish and glorify licentiousness in brilliant verses, for which
they received the homage of princes and prelates. Beccadelli's
Hermaphroditus was furiously attacked by the monks in the
pulpit, but applauded by the Humanists. Cosimo allowed the
indecent work to be dedicated to himself, and the author was
crowned by the Emperor Sigismund in Siena, 1433, and died
old and popular at Naples, 1471. The critics of his obscenities, Beccadelli pointed to the ancient writers. Nicolas was
loaned a copy of his notorious production, kept it for nine
days and then returned the work without condemning it.
Pietro Aretino, d. 1557, the most obscene of the Italian poets,
was called *il divino Aretino*, honored by Charles V., Francis I.
and Clement VII., and even dared to aspire to a cardinal's hat,

[1] Bezold, p. 200, *die vollendete sittliche Verkommenheit.*

but found a miserable end.   Bandello, d. 1562, in his *Facetiœ*, paints society in dissolution. Moral badness taints every one's lips.   Debauchery in convents is depicted as though it were a common occurrence.   And he was a bishop![1]

Machiavelli, the Florentine politician and historian, a worshipper of ability and power, and admirer of Cæsar Borgia, built upon the basis of the Renaissance a political system of absolute egotism ; yet he demands of the prince that he shall guard the appearance of five virtues to deceive the ignorant.[2] Under the cover of Stoicism, many Humanists indulged in a refined Epicureanism.

The writers of novels and plays not only portrayed social and domestic immorality without a blush, but purposely depicted it in a dress that would call forth merriment and laughter.   Tragedy was never reached by the Renaissance writers.   The kernel of this group of works was the faithlessness of married women, for the unmarried were kept under such close supervision that they were with difficulty reached. The skill is enlarged upon with which the paramour works out his plans and the outwitted husband is turned into an object of ridicule.   Here we are introduced to courtesans and taken to brothels.[3]

In the *Mandragola* by Machiavelli, Callimaco, who has been in Paris, returns to Florence determined to make Lucrezia, of whose charms he has heard, his mistress.   Assuming the roll of a physician, he persuades her husband, who is anxious for an heir, to allow him to use a potion of mandragora, which will relieve his wife of sterility and at the same time kill the paramour.   Working upon the husband's mind through the mother-in-law and Lucrezia's confessor, who consents to the plot for a bribe, he secures his end.   Vice and adultery are glorified.   And this was one of the plays on which Leo X. looked with pleasure!   In 1513, in face of the age-long pro-

---

[1] He furnished the text to a series of obscene pictures by Giulio Romano. Symonds, *Ital. Lit.*, II. 383 sqq. Reumont, *Hist. of Rome*, III., Part II. 367, calls Aretino " *die Schandsäule der Literatur.*"

[2] The principles of his *Principe* are fully discussed by Villari in his *Machiavelli*, II. 403-473, and by Symonds, *Age of the Despots*, p. 306 sqq.

[3] See Symonds, *Ital. Lit.*, II. 174 sqq.

hibition of the theatre by the Church, this pontiff opened the playhouse on the Capitol. A few years later he witnessed the performance of Ariosto's comedy the *Suppositi*. The scenery had been painted by Raphael. The spectators numbered 2,000, Leo looking on from a box with an eye-glass in his hand. The plot centres around a girl's seduction by her father's servant. One of the first of the cardinals to open his palace to theatrical representations was Raffaele Riario.

Intellectual freedom in Italy assumed the form of unrestrained indulgence of the sensual nature. In condemning the virginity extolled by the Church, Beccadelli pronounced it a sin against nature. Nature is good, and he urged men to break down the law by mixing with nuns.[1] The *hetœrœ* were of greater service to mankind than monastic recluses. Illegitimacy, as has already been said, was no bar to high position in the state or the Church. Æneas Sylvius declared that most of the rulers in Italy had been born out of wedlock,[2] and when, as pope, he arrived in Ferrara, 1459, he was met by eight princes, not a single one of them the child of legitimate marriage. The appearance of the Gallic disease in Italy at the close of the 15th century may have made men cautious; the rumor went that Julius II., who did not cross his legs at public service on a certain festival, was one of its victims.[3] Aretino wrote that the times were so debauched that cousins and kinsfolk of both sexes, brothers and sisters, mingled together without number and without a shadow of conscientious scruple.[4]

What else could be expected than the poisoning of all grades of society when, at the central court of Christendom, the fountain was so corrupt. The revels in the Vatican under Alexander VI. and the levity of the court of Leo X. furnished a spectacle which the most virtuous principles could

[1] *Non est nefas se virginibus sanctimonialibus immiscere.* Pastor, I. 21.

[2] *Frederick III.*, Ilgen's trsl., II. 135 sqq.

[3] Burckhardt-Geiger, II. 161, 343 sqq. Symonds, II. 477. The *mal franzese* is said to have appeared in Naples in 1495. It spread like wildfire. During the Crusades the syphilitic disease, so ran the belief, was spread in the East through the French.

[4] *Cortigiana*, as quoted by Symonds, *Ital. Lit.*, II. 191.

scarcely be expected to resist.   Did not a harlequin monk on one occasion furnish the mirth at Leo's table by his extraordinary voracity in swallowing a pigeon whole, and consuming forty eggs and twenty capons in succession !   Innocent VIII.'s son was married to a daughter of the house of the Medici, and Alexander's son was married into the royal family of France and his daughter Lucrezia into the scarcely less proud family of Este. Sixtus IV. taxed and thereby legalized houses of prostitution for the increase of the revenues of the curia.   The 6,800 public prostitutes in Rome in 1490, if we accept Infessura's figures, were an enormous number in proportion to the population.   This Roman diarist says that scarcely a priest was to be found in Rome who did not keep a concubine "for the glory of God and the Christian religion."   All parts of Italy and Spain contributed to the number of courtesans. They lived in greater splendor in Rome than the hetæræ in Athens, and bore classical names, such as Diana, Lucrezia, Camilla, Giulia, Costanza, Imperia, Beatrice.   They were accompanied on their promenades and walks to church by poets, counts and prelates, but usually concluded their gilded misery in hospitals after their beauty had faded away.[1]

The almost nameless vice of the ancient world also found its way into Italy, and Humanists and sons of popes like the son of Paul III., Pierluigi Farnese, if not popes themselves, were charged with pederasty.   In his 7th satire, Ariosto, d. 1533, went so far as to say it was the vice of almost all the Humanists.   For being addicted to it, a Venetian ambassador lost his position, and the charge was brought against the Venetian annalist, Sanuto.   Politian, Valla and Aretino and the academicians of Rome had the same accusation laid at their door.   The worst cannot be told, so abhorrent to the prime instincts of humanity do the crimes against morality seem. No wonder that Symonds speaks of "an enervation of Italian society in worse than heathen vices."[2]

---

[1] Reumont, III., Pt. II. 461 sqq. ; Gregorovius, viii, 306 sqq. ; Burckhardt-Geiger, II. 331–336.

[2] *Rev. of Learning*, 407 ; Geiger, II. 176 ; *Excursus* II., 348 sqq. ; Pastor, III. 101 sqq. ; Voigt, II. 471 ; Gregorovius, viii, 308, says: " we should inspire

To licentiousness were added luxury, gaming, the *vendetta* or the law of blood-revenge, and murder paid for by third parties. Life was cheap where revenge, a licentious end or the gain of power was a motive. Cardinals added benefice to benefice in order to secure the means of gratifying their luxurious tastes.[1] In the middle of the 16th century, Italy, says Burckhardt, was in a moral crisis, out of which the best men saw no escape. In the opinion of Symonds, who has written seven volumes on the Renaissance, it is "almost impossible to overestimate the moral corruption of Rome at the beginning of the 16th century. And Gregorovius adds that "the richest intellectual life blossomed in a swamp of vices."[2]

Of open heresy and attacks upon the papal prerogatives, popes were intolerant enough, as was quickly proved, when Luther appeared and Savonarola preached, but not of open immorality and secret infidelity. In the hierarchical interest they maintained the laws of sacerdotal celibacy, but allowed them to be broken by prelates in their confidence and employ, and openly flaunted their own bastard children and concubines. And unfortunately, as has been said, not only did the Humanists, with some exceptions, fall in with the prevailing

disgust did we attempt to depict the unbounded vice of Roman society in the corrupt times of Leo X. The moral corruption of an age, one of the best of whose productions has the title of *Syphilis*, is sufficiently known." Bandello, as quoted by Burckhardt, says: "Nowadays we see a woman poison her husband to gratify her lusts, thinking that a widow may do whatever she desires. Another, fearing the discovery of an illicit amour, has her husband murdered by her lover. And though fathers, brothers and husbands arise to extirpate the shame with poison, with the sword, and by every other means, women still continue to follow their passions, careless of their honor and their lives." Another time, in a milder strain, he exclaims : "Would that we were not daily forced to hear that one man has murdered his wife because he suspected her of infidelity ; that another has killed his daughter, on account of a secret marriage ; that a third has caused his sister to be murdered, because she would not marry as he wished ! It is great cruelty that we claim the right to do whatever we list, and will not suffer women to do the same."

[1] Burckhardt-Geiger, II. 172 sqq. ; Pastor, III. 128.

[2] Burckhardt-Geiger, II. 153 ; Symonds, *Rev. of Learning*, p. 406 ; Gregorovius, viii, 282.

licentiousness: there even was nothing in their principles to prevent its practice. As a class, the artists were no better than the scholars and, if possible, even more lax in regard to sexual license. Such statements are made not in the spirit of bitterness toward the Church of the Middle Ages, but in deference to historic fact, which ought at once to furnish food for reflection upon the liability of an ecclesiastical organization to err and even to foster vice as well as superstition by its prelatical constitution and unscriptural canons, and also to afford a warning against the captivating but fallacious theory that literature and art, not permeated by the principles of the Christian faith, have the power to redeem themselves or purify society. They did not do it in the palmy days of Greece and Rome, nor did they accomplish any such end in Italy.

In comparing our present century with the period of the Renaissance, there is at least one ground for grateful acknowledgment.[1] The belief in astrology, due largely to the rise of astronomical science, has been renounced. Thomas Aquinas had decided that astrology was a legitimate art when it is used to forecast natural events, such as drought and rain, but when used to predict human actions and destiny it is a dæmonic cult.[2] At an early period it came to be classed with heresy, and was made amenable to the Inquisition. In 1324, Cecco d'Ascoli, who had shown that the position of *libra* rendered the crucifixion of Christ inevitable, was obliged to abjure, and his astrolabe and other instruments were burnt, 1327, by the tribunal at Florence. In spite of Petrarca's ridicule, the cult continued. The Chancellor D'Ailly gave it credit. Scarcely a pope or Italian prince or republic of the latter part of the Renaissance period who did not have his astrologer or yield to the delusion in a larger or smaller measure, as, for example, Sixtus IV., Julius II. and Leo X., as well as Paul III. at a period a little later. Julius II. delayed his coronation several weeks, to Nov. 26, 1503, the lucky day announced by the as-

---

[1] See Burckhardt-Geiger, II. 235 sqq. ; Art. *Astrologie* in Wetzer-Welte, I. 1526 sqq., by Pastor ; and Lea, *Inquisition*, III. 437 sqq.
[2] *Summa*, II. 2, 95; Migne's ed., III. 729-731.

trologer. Ludovico of Milan waited upon favorable signs in
the heavens before taking an important step.[1]

On the other hand, Savonarola condemned the belief, and
was followed by Pico della Mirandola and Erasmus.[2] To the
freedom of human action astrology opposed a fatalistic view
of the world. This was felt at the time, and Matteo Villani
said more than once that "no constellation is able to compel
the free-will of man or thwart God's decree." Before the
15th century had come to a close, the cult was condemned to
extinction in France, 1494, but in Germany, in spite of the
spread of the Copernican system, it continued to have its followers for more than a century. The great Catholic leader
in the Thirty Years' War, Wallenstein, continued, in the face
of reverses, to follow the supposed indications of the heavenly
bodies, and Schiller puts into his mouth the words:—

> The stars lie not; what's happened
> Has turned out against the course of star and fate;
> Art does not play us false. The false heart
> 'Tis, which drags falsehood into the truth-telling heavens.

The revolt against the ascendancy of mediæval priestcraft
and scholastic dialectic was a great and necessary movement
demanded by the sane intents of mankind. The Italian Renaissance led the revolt. It gave liberty to the individual and
so far its work was wholesome, but it was liberty not bound
by proper restraints. It ran wild in an excess of indulgence,
so that Machiavelli could say, "Italy is the corruption of
the world." When the restraint came, it came from the
North as it had come centuries before, in the days of the Ottos,
in the 10th century. When studies in Italy set aside the ideals
of Christianity, when religion seemed to be in danger of expir-
ing and social virtue of altogether giving way, then the voice

---

[1] Villari, *Machiavelli*, I. 275.

[2] Villari, *Life and Times of Savonarola*, p. 183. Savonarola, in a sermon,
said: " Wouldst thou see how the Church is ruled by the hands of astrologers?
There is no prelate or great lord that hath not intimate dealings with some
astrologer, who fixeth the hour and the moment in which he is to ride out or
undertake some piece of business. For these great lords venture not to stir
a step save at their astrologer's bidding." See the remarks of Baudrillart,
p. 507, on the powerlessness of culture to restrain the delusion of astrology.

was raised in Wittenberg which broke with monastic asceticism and scholasticism and, at the same time, asserted an individualism under the control of conscience and reverence for God.

§ 68. *Humanism in Germany.*

Humanistic studies were late in finding entrance into Germany. They were opposed not so much by priestly ignorance and prejudice, as was the case in Italy, as by the scholastic theology which reigned at the universities. German Humanism may be dated from the invention of the printing-press about 1450. Its flourishing period began at the close of the 15th century and lasted only till about 1520, when it was absorbed by the more popular and powerful religious movement, the Reformation, as Italian Humanism was superseded by the papal counter-Reformation. Marked features distinguished the new culture north of the Alps from the culture of the Italians. The university and school played a much more important part than in the South. The representatives of the new scholarship were teachers, even Erasmus, who taught in Cambridge, and was on intimate terms with the professors at Basel. During the progress of the movement new universities sprang up, from Basel to Rostock. Again, in Germany, there were no princely patrons of arts and learning to be compared in intelligence and munificence to the Renaissance popes and the Medici. Nor was the new culture here exclusive and aristocratic. It sought the general spread of intelligence, and was active in the development of primary and grammar schools. In fact, when the currents of the Italian Renaissance began to set toward the North, a strong, independent, intellectual current was pushing down from the flourishing schools conducted by the Brothers of the Common Life. In the Humanistic movement, the German people was far from being a slavish imitator. It received an impulse from the South, but made its own path. Had Italy been careful to take lessons from the pedagogy of the North, it is probable her people would to-day be advanced far beyond what they are in intelligence and letters.

In the North, Humanism entered into the service of religious progress. German scholars were less brilliant and elegant, but more serious in their purpose and more exact in their scholarship than their Italian predecessors and contemporaries. In the South, the ancient classics absorbed the attention of the literati. It was not so in the North. There was no consuming passion to render the classics into German as there had been in Italy. Nor did Italian literature, with its loose moral teachings, find imitators in the North. Boccaccio's *Decameron* was first translated into German by the physician, Henry Stainhöwel, who died in 1482. North of the Alps, the attention was chiefly centred on the Old and New Testaments. Greek and Hebrew were studied, not with the purpose of ministering to a cult of antiquity, but to more perfectly reach the fountains of the Christian system. In this way, preparation was made for the constructive work of the Protestant Reformation.

And what was true of the scholarship of Germany was also true of its art. The painters, Albrecht Dürer, who was born and died at Nürnberg, 1471–1528, Lukas Kranach, 1472–1553, and for the most part Hans Holbein, 1497–1543, were free from the pagan element and contributed to the spread of the Reformation. Kranach lived in Wittenberg after 1504 and painted portraits of Luther, Melanchthon and other leaders of the German Reformation. Holbein gave illustrations for some of the new writings and painted portraits of Erasmus and Melanchthon. His Madonna, now at Darmstadt, has a German face and wears a crown on her head, while the child in her arms reflects his concern for the world in the sadness of his countenance.

If any one individual more than another may be designated as the connecting link between the learning of Italy and Germany, it is Æneas Sylvius. By his residence at the court of Frederick III. and at Basel, as one of the secretaries of the council, he became a well-known character north of the Alps long before he was chosen pope. The mediation, however, was not effected by any single individual. The fame of the Renaissance was carried over the pathways of trade which led from Northern Italy to Augsburg, Nürnberg, Constance and other German cities. The visits of Frederick III. and the campaigns of Charles VIII. and the ascent of the throne of Naples by the princes of Aragon carried Germans, Frenchmen and Spaniards to the greater centres of the peninsula. A constant stream of pilgrims itinerated to Rome and the Spanish popes drew to the city throngs of Spaniards. As the fame of Italian culture spread, scholars and artists began to travel to Venice, Florence and Rome, and caught the inspiration of the new era.

To the Italians Germany was a land of barbarians. They despised the German people for their ignorance, rudeness and intemperance in eating and drinking. Æneas found that the German princes and nobles cared more for horses and dogs than for poets and scholars and loved their wine-cellars better than the muses. Campanus, a witty poet of the papal court, who was sent as legate to the Diet of Regensburg by Paul II., and afterwards was made a bishop by Pius II., abused Germany for its dirt, cold climate, poverty, sour wine and miserable fare. He lamented his unfortunate nose, which had to smell everything, and praised his ears, which understood nothing. Such impressions were soon offset by the sound scholarship which arose in Germany and Holland. And, if Italy contributed to Germany an intellectual impulse, Germany sent out to the world the printing-press, the most important agent in the history of intellectual culture since the invention of the alphabet.

Before the first swell of the new movement was felt, the older German universities were already established: Prag in 1347, Vienna 1365, Heidelberg 1386, Cologne 1388, Erfurt 1392, Würzburg 1402, Leipzig 1409 and Rostock 1419. During the last half of the 15th century, there were quickly added to this list universities at Greifswald and Freiburg 1456, Treves 1457, Basel 1459, Ingolstadt 1472, Tübingen and Mainz 1477, and Wittenberg 1502. Ingolstadt lost its distinct existence by incorporation in the University of Munich, 1826, and Wittenberg by removal to Halle. Most of these universities had the four faculties, although the popes were slow to give their assent to the sanction of the theological department, as in the case of Vienna and Rostock, where the charter of the secular prince authorized their establishment. Strong as the religious influences of the age were, the social and moral habits of the students were by no means such as to call for praise. Parents, Luther said, in sending their sons to the universities, were sending them to destruction, and an act of the Leipzig university, dating from the close of the 15th century, stated that students came forth from their homes obedient and pious, but "how they returned, God alone knew."[1] In 1510, the student-body at Erfurt were so turbulent that the citizens and the peasant-folk turned cannons upon the collegiate building and, after the students had fled, battered down its walls and did great damage to university archives and library.

The theological teaching was ruled by the Schoolmen, and the dialectic method prevailed in all departments. In clashing with the scholastic method and curricula, the new teaching met with many a repulse, and in no case was it thoroughly triumphant till the era of the Reformation opened. Erfurt may be regarded as having been the first to give the new culture a welcome. In 1466, it received Peter Luder of Kislau, who had visited Greece and Asia Minor, and had been previously appointed to a chair in Heidelberg, 1456. He read on Virgil, Jerome, Ovid and other Latin writers. There Agricola studied and there Greek was taught by Nicolas Marschalck, under whose supervision the first Greek book printed in Germany issued from the press, 1501. There John of Wesel taught. It was Luther's *alma mater* and, among his professors, he singled out Trutvetter for special mention as the one who directed him to the study of the Scriptures.[2]

Heidelberg, chartered by the elector Ruprecht I. and Pope Urban VI., showed scant sympathy with the new movement.

---

[1] Schmid, II. 83.

[2] Köstlin, *Leben Luthers*, I. 45. Rashdall, II., pp. 245, speaks of Erfurt as the first university formed after the model of Paris in which the organization by nations does not appear. It was abolished 1816. The endowments of the German universities came largely through the appropriation of prebends.

However, the elector-palatine, Philip, 1476–1508, gathered at his court some of its representatives, among them Reuchlin. Ingolstadt for a time had Reuchlin as professor and, in 1492, Konrad Celtis was appointed professor of poetry and eloquence.

In 1474, a chair of poetry was established at Basel. Founded by Pius II., it had among its early teachers two Italians, Finariensis and Publicius. Sebastian Brant taught there at the close of the century and among its notable students were Reuchlin and the Reformers, Leo Jud and Zwingli. In 1481, Tübingen had a stipend of *oratoria*. Here Gabriel Biel taught till very near the close of the century. The year after Biel's death, Heinrich Bebel was called to lecture on poetry. One of Bebel's distinguished pupils was Philip Melanchthon, who studied and taught in the university, 1512–1518. Reuchlin was called from Ingolstadt to Tübingen, 1521, to teach Hebrew and Greek, but died a few months later.

Leipzig and Cologne remained inaccessible strongholds of scholasticism, till Luther appeared, when Leipzig changed front. The last German university of the Middle Ages, Wittenberg, founded by Frederick the Wise and placed under the patronage of the Virgin Mary and St. Augustine, acquired a world-wide influence through its professors, Luther and Melanchthon. Not till 1518, did it have instruction in Greek, when Melanchthon, soon to be the chief Greek scholar in Germany, was called to one of its chairs at the age of 21. According to Luther, his lecture-room was at once filled brimful, theologians high and low resorting to it.

As seats of the new culture, Nürnberg and Strassburg occupied, perhaps, even a more prominent place than any of the university towns. These two cities, with Basel and Augsburg, had the most prosperous German printing establishments. At the close of the 15th century, Nürnberg, the fountain of inventions, had four Latin schools and was the home of Albrecht Dürer the painter and Willibald Pirkheimer, a patron of learning.

Popular education, during the century before the Reformation, was far more advanced in Germany than in other nations.

The chief schools, conducted by the Brothers of the Common Life, were located at Zwolle, Deventer, Herzogenbusch and Liége. All the leading towns had schools.[1] The attendance at Deventer ran as high as 2,200. Melanchthon attended the Latin school at Pforzheim, now in Baden. Here Reuchlin found his young grand-nephew and gave him a Greek grammar, promising him a *Vocabulary*, provided Melanchthon would have ready some verses in Latin on his return. It is needless to say that the boy was ready and received the book. The town of Schlettstadt in Alsace was noted as a classical centre. Here Platter found Sapidus teaching, and he regarded it as the best school he had found. In 1494, there were five pedagogues in Wesel, teaching reading, writing, arithmetic and singing. One Christmas the clergy of the place entertained the pupils, giving them each cloth for a new coat and a piece of money.[2] The primary or trivial schools, as they were called from teaching the *trivium*, — grammar, rhetoric and dialectic, — gradually extended their courses and, before the Reformation, such schools as Liége and Schlettstadt had eight classes.[3] Greek was begun with the 4th class.

Among the noted schoolmasters was Alexander Hegius, who taught at Deventer for nearly a quarter of a century, till his death in 1498. At the age of 40 he was not ashamed to sit at the feet of Agricola. He made the classics central in education and banished the old text-books. Trebonius, who taught Luther at Eisenach, belonged to a class of worthy men. The penitential books of the day called upon parents to be diligent in keeping their children off the streets and sending them to school.[4] It remained for Luther to issue a stirring appeal to the magistrates of the Saxon towns to establish schools for both girls and boys and he called for a curriculum, which

---

[1] Bezold, p. 204.   [2] Janssen, I. 27.   [3] Schmid, II. 112.

[4] It seems to have been the custom to apply the rod without mercy. Luther speaks of the number of floggings he got a day. No case is more famous than that of Hans Butzbach. As a little fellow he was accustomed to play truant. When the teacher, an Erfurt B.A., found it out, he took off the child's clothes and, binding him to a post, flogged him till the blood covered his body. His mother, hearing the cries, hurried to the school, and bursting the door open and seeing her child, fell fainting to the floor. Schmid, II. 125.

included not only history and Latin but vocal and instrumental music.

The chief Humanists of Germany were Rudolph Agricola, Reuchlin and Erasmus.   To the last two a separate treatment is given as the pathfinders of biblical learning, the *venerabiles inceptores* of modern biblical research.

Agricola, whose original name was Roelef Huisman, was born near Groningen, 1443, and died 1485.   He enjoyed the highest reputation in his day as a scholar and received unstinted praise from Erasmus and Melanchthon.   He has been regarded as doing for Humanism in Germany what was done for Italy by Petrarca, the first life of whom, in German, Agricola prepared.   He was far in advance of the Italian poet in the purity of his life.   After studying in Erfurt, Louvain and Cologne, Agricola went to Italy, spending some time at the universities in Pavia and Ferrara.   He declined a professor's chair in favor of an appointment at the court of Philip of the Palatinate in Heidelberg.   He made Cicero and Quintilian his models.   In his last years, he turned his attention to theology and studied Hebrew.   Like Pico della Mirandola, he was buried in the cowl of a monastic order.   The inscription on his tomb in Heidelberg stated that he had studied what is taught about God and the true faith of the Saviour in the books of Scripture.

Another Humanist was Jacob Wimpheling, 1450–1528, of Schlettstadt, who taught in Heidelberg.   He was inclined to be severe on clerical abuses but, at the close of his career, wanted to substitute for the study of Virgil and Horace, Sedulius and Prudentius.   The poetic Sebastian Brant, 1457–1521, the author of the *Ship of Fools*, began his career as a teacher of law in Basel.   Mutianus Rufus, d. at Gotha 1526, in his correspondence, went so far as to declare that Christianity is as old as the world and that Jupiter, Apollo, Ceres and Christ are only different names of the one hidden God.[1]

A name which deserves a high place in the German literature of the last years of the Middle Ages is John Trithemius, 1462–1505, abbot of a Benedictine convent at Sponheim, which,

[1] Bezold, p. 226.

under his guidance, gained the reputation of a learned academy. He gathered a library of 2,000 volumes and wrote a patrology, or encyclopædia of the Fathers, and a catalogue of the renowned men of Germany. Prelates and nobles visited him to consult and read the Latin and Greek authors he had collected. These men and others contributed their part to that movement of which Reuchlin and Erasmus were the chief lights and which led on easily to the Protestant Reformation.[1]

§ 69. *Reuchlin and Erasmus.*

In his fresco of the Reformation on the walls of the Berlin museum, Kaulbach has given a place of great prominence to Reuchlin and Erasmus. They are represented in the group of the Humanists, standing side by side, with books under their arms and clad in scholar's cap and gown, their faces not turned toward the central figure on the platform, Martin Luther. The artist has presented the truth of history. These two most noteworthy German scholars prepared the way for the Reformation and the modern study of the Greek and Hebrew Scriptures, but remained and died in the Roman Church in which they were born. Rightly did Ulrich von Hutten call them "the two eyes of Germany." To them, and more especially to Erasmus, did all the greater Reformers owe a debt, Luther, Calvin, Zwingli, Œcolampadius, Melanchthon and Beza.

John Reuchlin, 1455–1522, known also by the Latin name Capnion,[2] was born in Pforzheim and studied at Schlettstadt, Freiburg, Paris, Basel, Orleans, Poictiers, Florence and Rome. He learned Greek from native Greeks, Hebrew from John Wessel and from Jewish rabbis in Germany and Italy. He bought many Hebrew and rabbinical books, and marked down the time and place of purchase to remind him of the happiness

---

[1] Among the other German Humanists were Crotus Rubeanus, 1480–1540, Georg Spalatin, 1484–1545, Beatus Rhenanus, 1485–1547, Eoban Hesse or Hessus, 1488–1540, Vadianus, 1484–1551, Glareanus or Loriti of Glarus, 1488–1563, and Bonifacius Amerbach, 1495–1562, the last three from German Switzerland.

[2] From κάπνιον, *i.e. little smoke*, the Greek equivalent for *Reuchlin*, the diminutive of *Rauch, smoke.*

their first acquaintance gave him.   A lawyer by profession,
he practised law in Stuttgart and always called himself *legum
doctor*.   He was first in the service of Eberhard, count of
Würtemberg, whom he accompanied to Italy in 1482 as he
later accompanied his son, 1490.   He served on diplomatic
missions and received from the Emperor Maximilian the rank
of a count of the Palatinate.   At Eberhard's death he removed
to Heidelberg, 1496, where he was appointed by the elector
Philip chief tutor in his family.   His third visit to Rome,
1498, was made in the elector's interest.   Again he returned
to Stuttgart, from which he was called in 1520 to Ingolstadt
as professor of Greek and Hebrew at a salary of 200 gulden.
In 1521, he was driven from the city by the plague and was
appointed lecturer in Tübingen.   His death occurred the following spring at Liebenzell in the Black Forest.

Reuchlin recommended Melanchthon as professor of Greek
in the University of Wittenberg, and thus unconsciously secured him for the Reformation.   He was at home in almost
all the branches of the learning of his age, but especially in
Greek and Hebrew.   He translated from Greek writings into
Latin, and a part of the *Iliad* and two orations of Demosthenes
into German.   His first important work appeared at Basel when
he was 20, the *Vocabularius breviloquus*, a Latin lexicon which
went through 25 editions, 1475-1504.   He also prepared a
Greek Grammar.   His chief distinction, however, is as the
pioneer of Hebrew learning among Christians in Northern
Europe.   He gave a scientific basis for the study of this language in his Hebrew Grammar and Dictionary, the *De rudi-
mentis hebraicis*, which he published in 1506 at his own cost
at Pforzheim.   Its circulation was slow and, in 1510, 750 copies
of the edition of 1,000 still remained unsold.   The second edition appeared in 1537.   The author proudly concluded this
work with the words of Horace, that he had reared a monument more enduring than brass.[1]   In 1512, he issued the Peni-

---

[1] "*Stat [exegi] monumentum œre perennius.*" Reuchlin also explained the
difficult theory of Hebrew accentuation, in *De accentibus et orthographia
linguœ hebr.*, 1518.   Comp. Geiger, *Das Studium der hebr. Sprache in Deutschland v. Ende des 15ten bis zur Mitte des 16ten Jahrh.*, Breslau, 1870, and his
Reuchlin, 161, etc.

tential Psalms with a close Latin translation and grammatical notes, a work used by Luther. The printing of Hebrew books had begun in Italy in 1475.

Reuchlin pronounced Hebrew the oldest of the tongues — the one in which God and angels communicated with man. In spite of its antiquity it is the richest of the languages and from it other languages drew, as from a primal fountain. He complained of the neglect of the study of the Scriptures for the polite study of eloquence and poetry.[1] Reuchlin studied also the philosophy of the Greeks and the Neo-Platonic and Pythagorean mysticisms. He was profoundly convinced of the value of the Jewish Cabbala, which he found to be a well of hidden wisdom. In this rare branch of learning he acknowledged his debt to Pico della Mirandola, whom he called " the greatest scholar of the age." He published the results of his studies in two works — one, *De verbo mirifico*, which appeared at Basel in 1494, and passed through eight editions; and one, *De arte cabbalistica*, 1517. " The wonder-working word " is the Hebrew tetragrammaton IHVH, the unpronounceable name of God, which is worshipped by the celestials, feared by the infernals and kissed by the soul of the universe. The word *Jesu, Ihsvh*, is only an enlargement of *Ihvh* by the letter *s*. The Jehovah- and Jesus-name is the connecting link between God and man, the infinite and the finite. Thus the mystic tradition of the Jews is a confirmation of the Christian doctrine of the trinity and the divinity of Christ. Reuchlin saw in every name, in every letter, in every number of the old Testament, a profound meaning. In the three letters of the word for create, *bara*, Gen. 1 : 1, he discerned the mystery of the Trinity; in one verse of Exodus, 72 inexpressible names of God; in Prov. 30 : 31, a prophecy that Frederick the Wise, of Saxony, would follow Maximilian as emperor of Germany, a prophecy which was not fulfilled. We may smile at these fantastic vagaries; but they stimulated and deepened the zeal for the hidden wisdom of the Orient, which Reuchlin called forth from the grave.

Through his interest in the Jews and in rabbinical litera-

[1] See quotation in Janssen, II. 40.

ture, Reuchlin became involved in a controversy which spread over all Europe and called forth decrees from Cologne and other universities, the archbishop of Mainz, the inquisitor-general of Germany, Hoogstraten, the emperor, Maximilian, and Pope Leo X.   The monks were his chief opponents, led by John Pfefferkorn, a baptized Jew of Cologne.   The controversy was provoked by a tract on the misery of the Jews, written by Reuchlin, 1505 — *Missive warumb die Juden so lang im Elend sind*.   Here the author made the obstinacy of the Jews in crucifying Christ and their persistence in daily blaspheming him the just cause of their sorrows, but, instead of calling for their persecution, he urged a serious effort for their conversion.   In a series of tracts, Pfefferkorn assaulted this position and demanded that his former coreligionists, as the sworn enemies of Christ, should be compelled to listen to Christian preaching, be forbidden to practise usury and that their false Jewish books should be destroyed.[1]   The flaming anti-Semite prosecuted his case with the vigor with which a few years later Eck prosecuted the papal case against Luther.   Maximilian, whose court he visited three times to present the matter, Hoogstraten and the University of Cologne took Pfefferkorn's side, and the emperor gave him permission to burn all Jewish books except, of course, the Old Testament.   Called upon to explain his position by the archbishop of Mainz, with whom Maximilian left the case, Reuchlin exempted from destruction the Talmud, the Cabbala and all other writings of the Jews except the *Nizahon* and the *Toledoth Jeshu*, which, after due examination and legal decision, might be destroyed, as they contained blasphemies against Christ, his mother and the Apostles.   He advised the emperor to order every university in Germany to establish chairs of Hebrew for ten years.[2]

Pfefferkorn, whom Reuchlin had called a "buffalo or an ass," replied in a violent attack, the Handmirror — *Handspiegel wider und gegen die Juden* — 1511.   Both parties appeared before the emperor, and Reuchlin replied in the Spectacles — *Au-*

---

[1] *Judenspiegel; Judenbeichte; Osternbuch; Judenfeind*, 1507–'09.
[2] " *Rathschlag, ob man den Juden alle ihre Bücher nehmen, abthun und verbrennen soll*," Stuttgart, Nov. 6, 1510.

genspiegel, — which in its turn was answered by his antagonist in the Burning Glass — *Brandspiegel*. The sale of the *Spectacles* was forbidden in Frankfurt. Reuchlin followed in a *Defense against all Calumniators*, 1513, and after the manner of the age cudgelled them with such epithets as goats, biting dogs, raving wolves, foxes, hogs, sows, horses, asses and children of the devil.[1] An appeal he made to Frederick the Wise called forth words of support from Carlstadt and Luther. The future Reformer spoke of Reuchlin as a most innocent and learned man, and condemned the inquisitorial zeal of the Cologne theologians who "might have found worse occasions of offence on all the streets of Jerusalem than in the extraneous Jewish question." The theological faculty of Cologne, which consisted mostly of Dominicans, denounced 43 sentences taken from Reuchlin as heretical, 1514. The Paris university followed suit. Cited before the tribunal of the Inquisition by Hoogstraten, Reuchlin appealed to the pope. Hoogstraten had the satisfaction of seeing the *Augenspiegel* publicly burnt at Cologne, Feb. 10, 1514. The young bishop of Spires, whom Leo X. appointed to adjudicate the case, cleared Reuchlin and condemned Hoogstraten to silence and the payment of the costs, amounting to 111 gulden, April 24, 1514.[2] But the indomitable inquisitor took another appeal, and Leo appointed Cardinal Grimani and then a commission of 24 to settle the dispute. All the members of the commission but Sylvester Prierias favored Reuchlin, who was now supported by the court of Maximilian, by the German "poets" as a body and by Ulrich von Hutten, but opposed by the Dominican order. When a favorable decision was about to be rendered, Leo interposed, June 23, 1520, and condemned Reuchlin's book, the *Spectacles*, as a work friendly to the Jews, and obligated the author to pay the costs of trial and thereafter to keep silence. The monks had won and Pfefferkorn, with papal au-

---

[1] Janssen, II. 51, in justifying the inquisitorial process and the action of the Un. of Cologne against Reuchlin, makes a great deal of these epithets.

[2] For an account of Hoogstraten, d. 1527, who came from Brabant, see Paulus: *Die deutschen Dominikaner*, etc., pp. 86–106. Among other writings, he wrote a book on witchcraft and two books, 1525, 1526, against Luther's tracts, the *Babylonian Captivity* and *Christian Freedom*, Paulus, p. 105.

thority on his side, could celebrate his triumph over scholarship
and toleration in a special tract, 1521.

With the Reformation, which in the meantime had broken
out at Wittenberg, the great Hebrew scholar showed no sympathy. He even turned away from Melanchthon and cancelled
the bequest of his library, which he had made in his favor, and
gave it to his native town, Pforzheim. He prevented, however,
Dr. Eck, during his brief sojourn at Ingolstadt, from burning
Luther's writings. His controversy with Pfefferkorn had
shown how strong in Germany the spirit of obscurantism was,
but it had also called forth a large number of pamphlets and
letters in favor of Reuchlin. The Hebrew pathfinder prepared
a collection of such testimonies from Erasmus, Mutianus, Peu-
tinger, Pirkheimer, Busch, Vadianus, Glareanus, Melanchthon,
Æcolampadius, Hedio and others, — in all, 43 eminent scholars
who were classed as Reuchlinists.

Among the writings of the Reuchlinists against the opponents of the new learning, the Letters of Unfamed Men — *Epistolæ virorum obscurorum* — occupy the most prominent place.
These epistles are a fictitious correspondence of Dominican
monks who expose their own old-fogyism, ignorance and vul-
garity to public ridicule in their barbarous German-Latin
jargon, which is called kitchen-Latin, *Küchenlatein*, and which
admits of no adequate translation. They appeared anonymously, but were chiefly written by Ulrich von Hutten and
Crotus Rubeanus whose German name was Johannes Jäger.
The authors were friends of Luther, but Crotus afterwards
fell out with the Reformation, like Erasmus and other Humanists.

Ulrich von Hutten, 1488–1523, after breaking away from
the convent in which his father had placed him six years before,
pursued desultory studies in the University of Cologne, developed a taste for the Humanistic culture and travelled in
Italy. In 1517, he returned to Germany and had a position
at the court of the pleasure-loving Albrecht, archbishop of
Mainz, a patron of the new learning. He was crowned with
the poet's crown by Maximilian and was hailed as the future
great epic poet of Germany by Erasmus, but later incurred

the hostility of that scholar who, after Hutten's death, directed against his memory the shafts of his satire. He joined Franz von Sickingen in standing ready to protect Luther at Worms. Placed under the ban, he spent most of his time after 1520, till his death, in semi-concealment at Schlettstadt, Basel and at Zürich under the protection of Zwingli.

Hutten's life at Cologne and in Rome gave him opportunity enough to find out the obscurantism of the Dominicans and other foes of progress as well as the conditions prevailing at the papal court. In 1517, he edited Valla's tract on the spurious Donation of Constantine and, with inimitable irony, dedicated it to Leo X. In ridicule and contempt it excelled everything, Janssen says, that had been written in Germany up to that time against the papacy. As early as 1513, Hutten issued epigrams from Italy, calling Julius II. "the corrupter of the earth, the plague of mankind."[1] His Latin poem, the *Triumph of Reuchlin*, 1518, defended the Hebrew scholar, and called for fierce punishment upon Pfefferkorn. It contained a curious woodcut, representing Reuchlin's triumphal procession to his native Pforzheim, and his victory over Hoogstraten and Pfefferkorn with their four idols of superstition, barbarism, ignorance and envy.[2]

The 10 *Epistles of the Unfamed Men*, written first in Latin and then translated by Hutten into German, with genial and not seldom coarse humor, demanded the restriction of the pope's tyranny, the dissolution of the convents, the appropriation of annates and lands of abolished convents and benefices for the creation of a fund for the needy. The amorous propensities of the monks are not spared. The author called the holy coat of Treves a lousy old rag, and declared the relics of the three kings of Cologne to be the bodies of three Westphalian peasants. In the 4th letter, entitled the Roman trinity, things are set forth and commented upon which were found in three's in Rome. Three things were considered ridiculous at Rome: the example of the ancients, the papacy of Peter and

---

[1] Strauss, I. 99 sqq.

[2] Böcking, III. 413–448. Geiger: *Reuchlin*, p. 522, gives a facsimile of the picture.

the last judgment. There were three things of which they had
a superabundance in the holy city: antiquities, poison and
ruins; three articles were kept on sale: Christ, ecclesiastical
places and women; three things which gave the Romelings
pain: the unity among the princes, the growing intelligence
of the people and the revelation of their frauds; three things
which they disliked most to hear about: a general council, a
reformation of the clerical office and the opening of the eyes
of the Germans; three things held as most precious: beautiful
women, proud horses and papal bulls. These were some of
the spectacles which Rome offered. Had not Hutten himself
been in Rome, when the same archbishop's pall was sold twice
in a single day! The so-called "gracious expectations," which
the pope distributed, were a special mark of his favor to the
Germans.[1] Hutten's wit reached the popular heart, drew
laughter from the educated and stirred up the wrath of the
self-satisfied advocates of the old ways. As a knight, he
touched a new chord, the national German pride, a chord on
which Luther played as a master.

What Reuchlin did for Hebrew learning, Erasmus, who was
twelve years his junior, accomplished for Greek learning and
more. He established the Greek pronunciation which goes by
his name; he edited and translated Greek classics and Church
Fathers and made them familiar to northern scholars, and he
furnished the key to the critical study of the Greek Testament,
the *magna charta* of Christianity. He was the contemporary
of the Protestant Reformers and was an invaluable aid to the
movement led by them through his edition of the New Testament, his renunciation of scholastic subtlety in its interpretation and his attacks on the ceremonial religiosity of his age.
But, when the time came for him to take open sides, he protested his aversion to the course which the Reformers had taken
as a course of violence and revolution. He died in isolation,
without a party. The Catholics would not claim him; the
Protestants could not.[2]

[1] Strauss: *Hutten's Gespräche*, pp. 121–3, etc., 143.
[2] Volume VI. of this *History* gives an extended survey of Erasmus' career,
writings and theological opinions. He belongs to the Middle Ages as much

Desiderius Erasmus, 1466–1536, was born at Rotterdam out of wedlock, his father probably a priest at the time.[1] His school life began at Deventer when he was nine years old, Hegius then being in charge. His parents died when he was 13 and, in 1481, he was in the school at Herzogenbusch where he spent three years, a period he speaks of as lost time. His letters of after years refer to his school experiences without enthusiasm or gratitude. After wandering about, he was persuaded against his will to enter a convent at Steyn. This step, in later years, he pronounced the most unfortunate calamity of his life. To his experience in the convent he ascribed the physical infirmity of his manhood. But he certainly went forth with the great advantage of having become acquainted with conventual life on its inside, and wholesome moral influence must have been exerted from some quarter in his early life to account for the moral discrimination of his later years. His ability secured for him the patronage of the bishop of Cambray, who intended taking him as his interpreter to Italy, where he hoped to receive the cardinal's hat. So far as Italy went, the young scholar was disappointed, but the bishop sent him to Paris, without, however, providing him with much financial assistance. He was able to support himself from the proceeds of instruction he gave several young Englishmen and, through their mediation, Erasmus made his first visit to England, 1499. This visit seems to have lasted only two or three months.[2]

At Oxford, the young scholar met Colet and Sir Thomas More and, through the influence of the former, was induced to give more attention to the Greek than he had been giving. The next years he spent in France and Holland writing his book of Proverbs, — *Adagia*, — issued 1500, and his Manual of

as to the modern period if not more, and the salient features of his life and historical position must be given here, even if there be a partial repetition of the treatment of vol. VI.

[1] In the compendium which he wrote of his life, Erasmus distinctly states that he was born out of wedlock and seems to imply that his father was a priest at the time. See Nichols, *Letters*, I. 14. The other view that the father became a priest later is taken by Froude, p. 2, and most writers.

[2] Nichols, I. 224.

the Christian soldier, — *Enchiridion militis Christiani*, — issued in 1502.   In 1505, he was back in England, remaining there for three years.   He then embraced an opportunity to travel in Italy with the two sons of Henry VII.'s Genoese physician, Battista Boerio.   At Turin, he received the doctor's degree, spent a number of months in Venice, turning out work for the Aldine presses, and visited Bologna, Rome and other cities. There is no indication in his correspondence that he was moved by the culture, art or natural scenery of Italy, nor does he make a single reference to the scenery of the Alps which he crossed.

Expecting lucrative appointment from Henry VIII., Erasmus returned to England, 1509, remaining there five years. On his way, he wrote for diversion his Praise of Folly, — *Encomium moriæ*, — a book which received its title from the fact that he was thinking of Sir Thomas More when its conception took form in his mind.   The book was completed in More's house and was illustrated with life-like pictures by Holbein.[1] During part of this sojourn in England, Erasmus was entered as " Lady Margaret's Professor of Divinity " at Cambridge and taught Greek.   The salary was 65 dollars a year, which Emerton calls "a respectable sum."   He was on intimate terms with Colet, now dean of St. Paul's, More, Fisher, bishop of Rochester, Archbishop Warham and other Englishmen. Lord Mountjoy provided him with an annuity and Archbishop Warham with the living of Aldington in 1411, which Erasmus retained for a while and then exchanged for an annuity of £20 from the archbishop.[2]

From 1515–1521, he had his residence in different cities in the Lowlands, and it was at this time he secured complete dispensation from the monastic vow which had been granted in part by Julius II. some years earlier.[3]   Erasmus' fame now exceeded the fame of any other scholar in Europe.   Wherever he went, he was received with great honors.   Princes joined scholars and prelates in doing him homage.   Melanch-

[1] Nichols, II. 2 sqq., 262.
[2] See Emerton's remarks on this matter, p. 184 sqq.
[3] Nichols, II. 148 sq., 462.

thon addressed to him a poem, "Erasmus the best and greatest," *Erasmum optimum, maximum.* His edition of the Greek
New Testament appeared in 1516, and in 1518 his *Colloquies,*
a collection of familiar relations of his experiences with men
and things.

When persecution broke out in the Netherlands after Leo's
issuance of his bull against Luther, Erasmus removed to
Basel, where some of his works had already been printed on
the Froben presses. At first he found the atmosphere of his
new home congenial, and published one edition after the other
of the Fathers, — Hilary 1523, Irenæus 1526, Ambrose 1527,
Augustine 1528, Epiphanius 1529, Chrysostom 1530. But
when the city, under the influence of Œcolampadius, went
Protestant and Erasmus was more closely pushed to take definite sides or was prodded with faithlessness to himself in not
going with the Reformers, he withdrew to the Catholic town
of Freiburg in Breisgau, 1529. The circulation of his *Colloquies* had been forbidden in France and burnt in Spain, and
his writings were charged by the Sorbonne with containing
32 heretical teachings. On the other hand, he was offered
the red hat by Paul III., 1535, but declined it on account of
his age.

After the death of Œcolampadius, he returned to Basel,
1535, broken down with the stone and catarrh. The last
work on which he was engaged was an edition of Origen.
He died calling out, " Oh, Jesus Christ, thou Son of God, have
mercy on me," but without priest or extreme unction, — *sine
lux, sine crux, sine Deus,* as the Dominicans of Cologne in
their joy and bad Latin expressed it. He was buried in the
Protestant cathedral of Basel, carried to the grave, as his
friend and admirer, Beatus Rhenanus, informs us, on the
shoulders of students. The chief magistrate of the city and
all the professors and students were present at the burial.

Erasmus was the prince of Humanists and the most influential and useful scholar of his age. He ruled with undisputed sway as monarch in the realm of letters. He combined
brilliant genius with classical and biblical learning, keen wit
and elegant taste. He rarely wrote a dull line. His exten-

sive travels made him a man of the world, a genuine cosmopolitan, and he stood in correspondence with scholars of all
countries who consulted him as an oracle.   His books had
the popularity and circulation of modern novels.   When the
rumor went abroad that his *Colloquies* were to be condemned
by the Sorbonne, a Paris publisher hurried through the press
an edition of 24,000 copies.   To the income from his writings
and an annuity of 400 gulden which he received as counsellor
of Charles V. — a title given him in 1516 — were added the
constant gifts from patrons and admirers.[1]

Had Erasmus confined himself to scholarly labors, though
he secured eminence as the first classicist of his age, his influence might have been restricted to his time and his name to
a place with the names of Politian of Italy and Budæus of
France, whose works are no longer read.   But it was otherwise.   His labors had a far-reaching bearing on the future.
He was a leading factor in the emancipation of the mind cf
Europe from the bondage of ignorance and superstition, and
he uncovered a lifeless formalism in religion.   He unthawed
the frost-bitten intellectual soil of Germany.   The spirit of
historical criticism which Laurentius Valla had shown in the
South, he represented north of the Alps, and of Valla he
spoke as "unrivalled both in the sharpness of his intelligence
and the tenacity of his memory."[2]   But the sweep of his influence is due to the mediation of his pupils and admirers,
Zwingli, Œcolampadius and Luther.

Erasmus' break with the old mediæval ecclesiasticism was
shown in a fourfold way.   He scourged the monks for their
ignorance, pride and unchastity, and condemned that ceremo-
nialism in religion which is without heart; he practised the
critical method in the treatment of Scripture; he issued the
first Greek New Testament; he advocated the translation of
the Bible into the languages spoken in his day.

In almost every work that he wrote, Erasmus, in a vein of
satire or in serious statement, inveighed against the hypocritical pretension of the monkery of his time and against the use-
lessness of hollow religious rites.   In his edition of the New

[1] See Drummond, II. 268.   [2] Nichols, I. 64.

Testament, he frequently returns to these subjects. For example, in a note on Matt. 19 : 12 he speaks of the priests "who are permitted to fornicate and may freely keep concubines but not have a wife." [1] Nowhere is his satire more keen on the clergy than in the *Praise of Folly*. In this most readable book, Folly represented as a female, delivers an oration to an audience of all classes and conditions and is most explicit and elaborate when she discourses on the priests, monks, theologians and the pope. After declaring with consummate irony that of all classes the theologians were the least dependent upon her, Folly proceeds to exhibit them as able to give the most exquisite solutions for the most perplexing questions, how in the wafer accidents may subsist without a subject, how long a time it required for the Saviour to be conceived in the Virgin's womb, whether God might as easily have become a woman, a devil, a beast, an herb or a stone as a man. In view of such wonderful metaphysics, the Apostles themselves would have needed a new illuminating spirit could they have lived again.

As for the monks, whose name signifies solitude, they were to be found in every street and alley. They were most precise about their girdles and hoods and the cut of their crowns, yet they easily provoked quarrels, and at last they would have to search for a new heaven, for entrance would be barred them to the old heaven prepared for such as are true of heart. As for the pope, Luther's language never pictured more distinctly the world-wide gulf between what the successor of St. Peter should be and really was, than did the biting sentences of Erasmus. Most liberal, he said, were the popes with the weapons of the Spirit,—interdicts, greater and lesser excommunications, roaring bulls and the like,—which they launch forth with unrestrained vehemence when the authority of St. Peter's chair is attacked. These are they who by their lusts and wickedness grieve the Holy Spirit and make their Saviour's wounds to bleed afresh.[2] In the *Enchiridion*, he says, "Apostle, pastor and

---

[1] For a number of quotations, see Froude, 123 sqq.

[2] Compare Erasmus' disparaging remarks on the papacy on the occasion of the pageant of Julius II. at Bologna when an arch bore the inscription, "To Julius II., Conqueror of the Tyrant," Faulkner, p. 82 sqq.

bishop" are names of duties not of government, and *papa*, pope, and *abbas*, abbot, are titles of love.   The sale of indulgences, saint worship and other mediæval abuses came in for Erasmus' poignant thrusts.

In addition to his own Annotations and Paraphrases of the New Testament, he edited the first printed edition of Valla's *Annotations*, which appeared in Paris, 1505.   It was his great merit to call attention to the plain meaning of Scripture and to urge men " to venerate the living and breathing picture of Christ in the sacred books, instead of falling down before statues of wood and stone of him, adorned though they were with gold.   What were Albertus Magnus, Thomas Aquinas and Ockam compared with him, whom the Father in heaven called His beloved Son!"   As for the Schoolmen, he said, " I would rather be a pious divine with Jerome than invincible with Scotus.   Was ever a heretic converted by their subtleties!" [1]

The appearance of Erasmus' edition of the Greek Testament at Basel, 1516, marked an epoch in the study and understanding of the Scriptures.   It was worth more for the cause of religion than all the other literary works of Erasmus put together, yea, than all the translations and original writings of all the Renaissance writers.   The work contained a dedication to Leo X., a man whom Erasmus continued to flatter, as in the epistle dedicating to him his edition of Jerome, but who of all men was destined to oppose the proclamation of the true Gospel.   The volume, 672 pages in all, contained the Greek text in one column and Erasmus' own Latin version in the other, together with his annotations.   It was hurried through the press in order to anticipate the publication of the New Testament of the Complutensian Polyglot, which was actually printed in 1514, but was not given to the public till 1520.   The editor used three manuscripts of the 12th century, which are still preserved in the university library of Basel and retain the marginal notes of Erasmus and the red lines of the printer to indicate the corresponding pages of the printed edition.   Erasmus did not even take the trouble to copy the manuscripts, but sent them, with

---

[1] *Paraclesis ad lectorem*, prefixed to Erasmus' *New Testament.*

numerous marginal corrections, to the printer.[1] The manuscript of the Apocalypse was borrowed from Reuchlin, and disappeared, but was rediscovered, in 1861, by Dr. Delitzsch in the library of Œttingen-Wallerstein at Mayhingen, Bavaria. It was defective on the last leaf and supplemented by Erasmus, who translated the last six verses from the Vulgate into indifferent Greek, for he was a better Latinist than Hellenist.

In all, Erasmus published five editions of the Greek Testament — 1516, 1519, 1522, 1527 and 1535. Besides, more than 30 unauthorized reprints appeared in Venice, Strassburg, Basel, Paris and other cities. He made several improvements, but his entire apparatus never exceeded eight MSS. The 4th and the 5th editions were the basis of the *textus receptus*, which ruled supreme till the time of Lachmann and Tregelles. His notes and paraphrases on the New Testament, the Apocalypse excepted, were translated into English, and a copy given to every parish in 1547. Zwingli copied the Pauline Epistles from the 1st Greek edition with his own hand in the convent at Einsiedeln, 1516. From the 2d edition of 1519, Luther prepared his German translation on the Wartburg, 1522, and Tyndale his English version, 1526.

Thus Erasmus directly contributed to the preparation of the vernacular versions which he so highly commended in his Preface to the 1st edition of his Greek Testament. He there expressed the hope that the Scriptures might be translated into every tongue and put into the hands of every reader, to give strength and comfort to the husbandman at his plough, to the weaver at his shuttle, to the traveller on his journey and to the woman at her distaff. He declared it a miserable thing that thousands of educated Christians had never read the New Testament. In editing the Greek original, it was his purpose, so he says, to enable the theologians to study Christianity at its fountain-head. It was high praise

---

[1] *Praecipitatum fuit verius quam editum*, says Erasmus himself in the Preface. The 2d edition also contains several pages of errors, some of which have affected Luther's version. The 3d edition first inserts the spurious passage of the three heavenly witnesses, 1 John 5 : 7, to remove any occasion of offence, *ne cui foret ansa calumniandi*.

when Œcolampadius confessed he had learned from Erasmus that " in the Sacred Books nothing was to be sought but Christ," *nihil in sacris scripturis præter Christum quærendum*.[1]

It was a common saying, to which Erasmus himself refers, that he laid the egg which Luther hatched. His relations to the Wittenberg Reformer and to the movement of the Reformation is presented in the 6th volume of this series.   Here it is enough to say that Erasmus desired a reformation by gradual education and gentle persuasion within the limits of the old Church system. He disapproved of the violent measures of Luther and Zwingli, and feared that they would do much harm to the cause of learning and refined culture, which he had more at heart than religion.

He and Luther never met, and he emphatically disavowed all responsibility for Luther's course and declared he had had no time to read Luther's books.   And yet, in a letter to Zwingli, he confessed that most of the positions taken by Luther he had himself taken before Luther's appearance.   The truth is that Erasmus was a critical scholar and not a man of action or of deep fervor of conviction.   At best, he was a moralist. He went through no such religious experiences as Luther, and Luther early wrote to Lange that he feared Erasmus knew little of the grace of God.   The early part of the 16th century was a period when the critic needed to be supplemented. Erasmus had no mind for the fray of battle.   His piety was not deep enough to brave a rupture with the old order.   He courted the flattery of the pope, though his pen poured forth ridicule against him.   And nowhere is the difference of the two men shown in clearer light than in their treatment of Leo X., whom, when it was to his advantage, Erasmus lauded as a paragon of culture.[2]   He did not see that something more was needed than literature and satire to work a change.   The times required the readiness for martyrdom, and Erasmus' religious conviction was not sufficient to make him ready to suffer for principle.   On most controverted points, Emerton well says he had one opinion for his friends and another for the world.   He lacked both the candor and the courage to be

---

[1] Nichols, II. 535.   [2] Nichols, II. 198, 314, 522.

a religious hero. "Erasmus is a man for himself" was the apt characterization often repeated in the *Letters of Unfamed Men*. Luther spoke to the German people and fought for them. Erasmus awakened the admiration of the polite by his scholarship and wit. The people knew him not. Luther spoke in German: Erasmus boasted that he knew as little Italian as Indian and that he was little conversant with German, French or English. He prided himself on his pure Latinity.

Erasmus never intended to separate from Rome any more than his English friends, John Colet and Thomas More. He declared he had never departed from the judgment of the Church, nor could he. "Her consent is so important to me that I would agree with the Arians and Pelagians if the Church should approve what they taught." This he wrote in 1526 after the open feud with Luther in the controversy over the freedom of the will. The Catholic Church, however, never forgave him. All his works were placed on the Index by two popes, Paul IV. in 1559 and Sixtus V., 1590, as intentionally heretical. In 1564, by the final action of the Council of Trent, this sweeping judgment was revoked and all the writings removed from the Index except the *Colloquies, Praise of Folly, Christian Marriage* and one or two others, a decision confirmed by Clement VIII., 1596. And there the matter has rested since.[1]

The Catholic historian of the German people, Janssen, in a dark picture of Erasmus, presents him as vain and conceited, ungrateful to his benefactors, always ready to take a neutral attitude on disputed questions and, for the sake of presents, flattering to the great. Janssen calls attention to his delight over the gold and silver vessels and other valuables he had received in gifts. My drawers, Erasmus wrote, "are filled with presents, cups, bottles, spoons, watches, some of them of pure gold, and rings too numerous to count." In only one respect, says Janssen, did he go beyond his Italian predecessors in his attack upon the Church. The Italians sneered and ridiculed, but kept their statements free from hypocritical piety, which Erasmus often resorted to after he had driven his dagger into

[1] See Emerton, pp. 454-5.

his opponent's breast.[1] In England, the old Puritan, Tyndale,
also gave Erasmus no quarter, but spoke of him as one "whose
tongue maketh little gnats great elephants and lifteth up above
the stars whosoever giveth him a little exhibition."[2]   But no
one has ever understood Erasmus and discerned what was his
mission better than Luther.   That Reformer, who had once
called him " our ornament and hope — *decus nostrum et spes*,"
— expressed the whole truth when, in a letter to Œcolampadius, 1523, he said: " Erasmus has done what he was ordained
to do.   He has introduced the ancient languages in place of
the pernicious scholastic studies.   He will probably die like
Moses in the land of Moab. . . . He has done enough to overcome the evil, but to lead to the land of promise is not, in my
judgment, his business."

§ 70. *Humanism in France.*

Humanism in France found its way from Italy, but did not
become a distinct movement until the 16th century was well
on its way.   Budaeus, 1467-1540, was the chief representative
of classical studies; Faber Stapulensis, or, to use his French
name, Lefèvre d'Etaples, of Christian culture, 1469-1536, both
of them living well into the period of the Reformation.[3]   In
France, as in Germany, the pursuit of the classics never went
to the point of intoxication as it did in Italy.   In France, the
Renaissance did not reach its maturity till after the Reformation was well advanced in Germany, the time at which the springs
of the movement in the Italian peninsula were dried up.

On the completion of the 100 years' war between France and
England, the intellectual currents began to start.   In 1464,
Peter Raoul composed for the duke of Bourgogne a history of

---

[1] Janssen, II. 9 sqq. The inventory of his goods contains a list of his furniture, wardrobe, napkins, nightcaps, cushions, goblets, silver vessels, gold
rings and money (722 gold gulden, 900 gold crowns, etc.). See Sieber, *Inven-
tarium über die Hinterlassenschaft des Erasmus vom 22 Juli, 1536*, Basel, 1889.

[2] *Pref. to Pentateuch*, Parker Soc. ed., p. 395.

[3] Imbart, II. 382. In his *Skeptics of the French Renaissance*, Lond., 1893,
Owen treats of Montaigne, Peter Ramus, Pascal and other men who were imbued with the spirit of free inquiry and lived after the period included in this
volume.

Troy.   At that time the French still regarded themselves as
descendants of Hector.   If we except Paris, none of the French
universities took part in the movement.   Individual writers
and printing-presses at Paris, Lyons, Rouen and other cities
became its centres and sources.   William Fichet and Gaguin
are usually looked upon as the first French Humanists.   Fichet
introduced " the eloquence of Rome " at Paris and set up a
press at the Sorbonne.   He corresponded with Bessarion and
had in his library volumes of Petrarca, Guarino of Verona and
other Italians.   Gaguin copied and corrected Suetonius in 1468
and other Latin authors.   Poggio's *Jest-book* and some of Valla's writings were translated into French.   In the reign of
Louis XI., who gloried in the title " the first Christian king,"
French poets celebrated his deeds.   The homage of royalty
took in part the place among the literary men of France that
the cult of antiquity occupied in Italy.[1]

Greek, which had been completely forgotten in France, had
its first teachers in Gregory Tifernas, who reached Paris, 1458,
John Lascaris, who returned with Charles VIII., and Her-
monymus of Sparta, who had Reuchlin and Budaeus among
his scholars.   An impetus was given to the new studies by
the Italian, Aleander, afterwards famous for his association
with Luther at Worms.   He lectured in Paris, 1509, on Plato
and issued a Latino-Greek lexicon.   In 1512 his pupil, Va-
table, published the Greek grammar of Chrysoloras.   William
Budaeus, perhaps the foremost Greek scholar of his day,
founded the Collège de France, 1530, and finally induced
Francis I. to provide for instruction in Hebrew and Greek.
The University of Paris at the close of the 14th century was
sunk into a low condition and Erasmus bitterly complained
of the food, the morals and the intellectual standards of the
college of Montague which he attended.   Budaeus urged the
combination of the study of the Scriptures with the study of
the classics and exclaimed of the Gospel of John, " What is
it, if not the almost perfect sanctuary of the truth ! "[2]   He

---

[1] Imbart, II. 364–372.   Louis XI. was eulogized as being greater than
Achilles, Alexander and Scipio, and the mightiest since Charlemagne.

[2] Imbart, II. 545.

persisted in setting himself against the objection that the study of the languages of Scripture led on to Lutheranism.

Lefèvre studied in Paris, Pavia, Padua and Cologne and, for longer or shorter periods, tarried in the greater Italian cities. He knew Greek and some Hebrew. From 1492–1506 he was engaged in editing the works of Aristotle and Raymundus Lullus and then, under the protection of Briçonnet, bishop of Meaux, he turned his attention to theology. It was his purpose to offset the *Sentences* of Peter the Lombard by a system of theology giving only what the Scriptures teach. In 1509, he published the *Psalterum quintuplex*, a combination of five Latin versions of the Psalms, including a revision and a commentary by his own hand. In 1512, he issued a revised Latin translation of the Pauline Epistles with commentary. In this work, he asserted the authority of the Bible and the doctrine of justification by faith, without appreciating, however, the far-reaching significance of the latter opinion.[1] He also called in question the merit of good works and priestly celibacy. In his Preface to the Psalms Lefèvre said, "For a long time I followed Humanistic studies and I scarcely touched my books with things divine, but then these burnt upon me with such light, that profane studies seemed to be as darkness in comparison."   Three years after the appearance of Luther's New Testament, Lefèvre's French translation appeared, 1523. It was made from the Vulgate, as was his translation of the Old Testament, 1528. In 1522 and 1525, appeared his commentaries on the four Gospels and the Catholic Epistles. The former was put on the Index by the Sorbonne. The opposition to the free spirit of inquiry and to the Reformation, which the Sorbonne stirred up and French royalty adopted, forced him to flee to Strassburg and then to the liberal court of Margaret of Angoulême.

Among those who came into contact with Lefèvre were Farel and Calvin, the Reformers of Geneva. In the mean-

---

[1] Imbart, II. 394, says, *Il va donner un singulier éclat à la doctrine de la justification par la foi, sans, cependant, sacrifier les œuvres.* This author draws a comparison between Lefèvre and Erasmus. See, however, Lefèvre's Preface itself, and Bonet-Maury in Herzog, V. 715.

time Clement Marot, 1495–1544, the first true poet of the French literary revival, was composing his French versification of the Psalms and of Ovid's *Metamorphoses*. The Psalms were sung for pleasure by French princes and later for worship in Geneva and by the Huguenots. When Calvin studied the humanities and law at Bourges, Orleans and Paris, about 1520, he had for teachers Cordier and L'Etoile, the canonists, and Melchior Wolmar, teacher of Greek, whose names the future Reformer records with gratitude and respect. He gave himself passionately to Humanistic studies and sent to Erasmus a copy of his work on Seneca's *Clemency*, in which he quoted frequently from the ancient classics and the Fathers. Had he not adopted the new religious views, it is possible he would now be known as an eminent figure in the history of French Humanism.

§ 71. *Humanism in England.*

Use well temporal things : desire eternal things.
— JOHN COLET.

Humanism reached England directly from Italy, but was greatly advanced by Erasmus during his three sojourns at Oxford and Cambridge and by his close and abiding friendship with the leading English representatives of the movement. Its history carries us at once to the universities where the conflict between the new learning and the old learning was principally fought out and also to St. Paul's school, London, founded by Colet. It was marked with the usual English characteristics of caution and reserve, and never manifested any of the brilliant or paganizing traits of the Italian literary movement, nor did it reach the more profound classical scholarship of the German Humanists. In the departments of the fine arts, if we except printing, it remained unresponsive to the Continental leadership. English Humanism, like the theology of the English Reformation, adopted the work of others. It was not creative. On the other hand, it laid more distinctive emphasis upon the religious and ethical elements than the Humanistic circles of Italy, though not of Germany. Its chief leaders were John Colet and Sir Thomas More, with whom Erasmus is also to be associated. It had patrons in high places in Archbishop Warham of Canterbury, Cardinal Wolsey and John Fisher, bishop of Rochester.[1]

The English revival of letters was a direct precursor of the English Reformation, although its earliest leaders died in the Catholic Church. Its first distinct impetus was received in the last quarter of the 15th century through English students who visited Italy.   It had been the custom for English archdeacons to go to Italy for the study of the canon law.   Richard de Bury and Peter de Blois had shown interest in books and Latin profane authors.   Italians, Poggio and Polidore Virgil[2] among them, tarried and some of them taught in England, but the first to introduce the new movement were William Sellyng, Thomas Linacre and William Grocyn.

Sellyng, of All Souls' College, Oxford, and afterwards prior of Christ Church, Canterbury, 1471–1495, made a visit to Italy in 1464 and at Bologna was a pupil of Politian.   From this tour, or from a later one, he brought back with him some Greek MSS. and he introduced the studying of Greek in Canterbury. Linacre, d. 1524, the most celebrated medical man of his day in England, studied under Sellyng at Christ Church and then in Oxford, where he took Greek under Cornelio Vitelli, the first to publicly teach that language in England in the later Middle Ages.   He then went to Florence, Rome and Padua, where he graduated in medicine.   On returning to England, he was ordained priest and later made physician to Henry VIII. He translated the works of Galen into English.[3]

While Linacre was studying in Florence, Grocyn arrived in that city.   He was teaching Greek in Oxford before 1488 and, on his return from the Continent, he began, 1491, to give Greek lectures in that university.   With this date the historian,

---

[1] Wolsey applied the proceeds of 20 monasteries, which he closed, to the endowment of a school at Ipswich and of Cardinal College, Oxford. In 1516, Fox, bishop of Winchester, founded Corpus Christi College at the same university to teach the new learning.

[2] He wrote a *History of England* and revenged himself by disparaging Wolsey, who had refused to give him his favor.

[3] For his services to medicine, see W. Osler; *Thos. Linacre*, Cambr., 1908, pp. 23–27.

Green, regards the new period as opening. Grocyn lectured on pseudo-Dionysius and, following Laurentius Valla, abandoned the tradition that he was the Areopagite, the pupil of St. Paul. He and Linacre were close friends of Erasmus, and that scholar couples them with Colet and More as four representatives of profound and symmetrical learning.[1]

At the close of the 15th century, the English were still a "barbarous" people in the eyes of the Italians.[2] According to Erasmus, who ought to have known what a good school was, the schoolteachers of England were "shabby and broken down and, in cases, hardly in their senses." At the universities, the study of Duns Scotus ruled and the old method and text-books were in use. The Schoolmen were destined, however, soon to be displaced and the leaves of the Subtle Doctor to be scattered in the quadrangles of Oxford and trodden under foot.

As for the study of Greek, there were those, as Wood says, who preached against it as "dangerous and damnable" and, long after the new century had dawned, Sir Thomas More wrote to the authorities at Oxford condemning them for opposition to Greek.[3] A course of sermons, to which More refers, had been preached in Lent not only against the study of the Greek classics but also the Latin classics. What right, he went on to say, "had a preacher to denounce Latin of which he knew so little and Greek of which he knew nothing? How can he know theology, if he is ignorant of Hebrew, Greek and Latin?" In closing the letter, More threatened the authorities with punishment from Warham, Wolsey and even the king himself, if they persisted in their course. Of the clergy's alarm against the new learning, More took notice again and again. To Lily, the headmaster of St. Paul's school, he wrote, "No wonder your school raises a storm; it is like the wooden horse for the ruin of barbarous Troy." But, if there were those who could see only danger from the new studies, there were also men like

---

[1] Nichols: *Erasmus' Letters*, I. 226. Sir Thomas More, writing to Colet, Nov., 1504, said: "I shall spend my time with Grocyn, Linacre and Lily. The first, as you know, is the director of my life in your absence, the second the master of my studies, the third my most dear companion."

[2] Seebohm, p. 283.   [3] See the letter. Froude: *Erasmus*, 139.

Fisher of Rochester who set about learning Greek when he was 60.   For the venerable *Sentences* of the Lombard, the Scriptures were about to be instituted as the text-book of theology in the English universities.

The man who contributed most to this result was John Colet. Although his name is not even so much as mentioned in the pages of Lingard, he is now recognized, as he was by Tyndale, Latimer and other Reformers of the middle of the 16th century, as the chief pioneer of the new learning in England and as an exemplar of noble purposes in life and pure devotion to culture.

The son of Sir Henry Colet, several times lord mayor of London, the future dean of St. Paul's was one of 22 children. He survived all the members of his family except his mother, to whom he referred, when he felt himself growing old, with admiration for her high spirits and happy old age.   As we think of her, we may be inclined to recall the good mother of John Wesley.   After spending 3 years at Oxford, 1493–1496,[1] young Colet, "like a merchantman seeking goodly wares," as Erasmus put it, went to Italy.   For the places where he studied, we are left to conjecture, but Archbishop Parker two generations later said that he studied "a long time in foreign countries and especially the Sacred Scriptures."   On his return to Oxford, although not yet ordained to the priesthood, he began expounding St. Paul's Greek epistles in public, the lectures being given gratuitously.   At this very moment the Lady Margaret professor of divinity was announcing for his subject the *Quodlibets* of Duns Scotus.   Later, Colet expounded also the First Epistle to the Corinthians.

At this period, he was not wholly freed from the old academic canons and was inclined to reject the reading of classic authors whose writings did not contain a "salutatory flavor of Christ and in which Christ is not set forth. . . .   Books, in which Christ is not found, are but a table of devils."[2]   Of the impression made by his exposition, a proof is given in Colet's own

---

[1] Probably at Magdalen Hall.   See Lupton, 23 sqq., and the same cautious author for Colet's school life in London.   For the facts of Colet's career, our best authority is Erasmus' letter to Justus Jonas.

[2] Quoted by Lupton, p. 76.

description of a visit he had from a priest. The priest, sitting in front of Colet's fire, drew forth from his bosom a small copy of the Epistles, which he had transcribed with his own hand, and then, in answer to his request, his host proceeded to set forth the golden things of the 1st chapter of Romans.[1] His expositions abound in expressions of admiration for Paul.

At Oxford, in 1498, Colet met Erasmus, who was within a few months of being of the same age, and he also came into contact with More, whom he called "a rare genius." The fellowship with these men confirmed him in his modern leanings. He lectured on the Areopagite's *Hierarchies*, but he soon came to adopt Grocyn's view of their late date. The high estimate of Thomas Aquinas which prevailed, he abandoned and pronounced him "arrogant for attempting to define all things" and of "corrupting the whole teaching of Christ with his profane philosophy."[2] Some years later, writing to Erasmus, he disparaged the contemporary theologians as spending their lives in mere logical tricks and dialectic quibbles. Erasmus, replying to him, pronounced the theology which was once venerable become "almost dumb, poor and in rags."

As dean of St. Paul's, an appointment he received in 1504, Colet stands forth as a reformer of clerical abuses, a bold preacher and a liberal patron of education. The statutes he issued for the cathedral clergy laid stress upon the need of reformation "in every respect, both in life and religion." The old code, while it was particular to point out the exact plane the dean should occupy in processions and the choir, did not mention preaching as one of his duties. Colet had public lectures delivered on Paul's Epistles, but it was not long till he was at odds with his chapter. The cathedral school did not meet his standard, and the funds he received on his father's death he used to endow St. Paul's school, 1509.[3] The origi-

---

[1] For the letter to the abbot of Winchcombe, in which Colet describes the priest's visit, see Lupton, p. 90 sqq., and Seebohm, p. 42 sqq.

[2] Seebohm, p. 107.

[3] Seebohm gives 1510. For date and the original name, see correspondence in *London Times*, July 7, 20, 1909, between M. E. J. McDonnell and Gardiner, surmaster and honorable librarian of St. Paul's. The school was some-

nal buildings were burnt down in the London fire, and new buildings reared in 1666. The statutes made the tuition free, and set the number of pupils at 153, since increased threefold. They provided for instruction in "good literature, both Latin and Greek," but especially for Christian authors that "wrote their wisdom with clean and chaste Latin." The founder's high ideal of a teacher's qualifications, moral as well as literary, set forth in his statutes for the old cathedral school, was "that he should be an upright and honorable man and of much and well-attested learning." Along with chaste literature, he was expected "to imbue the tender minds of his pupils with holy morals and be to them a master, not of grammar only, but of virtue." [1]

St. Paul's has the distinction of being the first grammar-school in England where Greek was taught. The list of its masters was opened by William Lily, one of the few Englishmen of his age capable of teaching Greek. After studying at Oxford, he made a journey to Jerusalem, and returned to England by way of Italy. He died in 1522. By his will, Colet left all his books, "imprinted and in paper," to poor students of the school.

As a preacher, the dean of St. Paul's was both bold and Scriptural. Among his hearers were the Lollards. Colet himself seems to have read Wyclif's writings as well as other heretical works.[2] Two of his famous sermons were delivered before convocation, 1511, and on Wolsey's receiving the red hat. The convocation discourse, which has come down to us entire, is a

times called Jesus' School by Colet. The buildings were finished, August, 1510. The present location of the school is Hammersmith.

[1] The statutes are given by Lupton, Appendix A., p. 271 sqq. For the *Accidence* which Colet prepared for the school, see Lupton, Appendix B. In contrasting the recent Latin with the Latin of classic authors, profane and patristic, Colet called the former "blotterature rather than literature." One of the rules required the boys to furnish their own candles, stipulating they should be of wax and not of tallow. For the bishop who preached against St. Paul's school as "a home of idolatry," see Colet's letter to Erasmus, Nichols, II. 63.

[2] The former is an inference from Erasmus' statement in his account of the visit to Walsingham, and the latter Erasmus' plain statement in his letter to Jonas.

vigorous appeal for clerical reform.[1] The text was taken from
Rom. xii : 2. "Be ye not conformed to this world but be ye reformed." The pride and ambition of the clergy were set forth
and their quest of preferment in Church and state condemned.
Some frequented feasts and banquetings and gave themselves
to sports and plays, to hunting and hawking.[2] If priests themselves were good, the people in their turn would be good also.
"Our goodness," exclaimed the preacher, "would urge them
on in the right way far more efficaciously than all your sus-
pensions and excommunications. They should live a good and
holy life, be properly learned in the Scriptures and chiefly and
above all be filled with the fear of God and the love of the
heavenly life."

According to the canons of the age, the preacher went beyond the limits of prudence and Fitz-James, bishop of London,
cited him for trial but the case was set aside by the archbishop.
The charges were that Colet had condemned the worship of
images and declared that Peter was a poor man and enjoyed
no episcopal revenues and that, in condemning the reading of
sermons, Colet had meant to give a thrust to Fitz-James himself, who was addicted to that habit. Latimer, who was at
Cambridge about that time, said in a sermon some years later,
that "in those days Doctor Colet was in trouble and should
have been burned, if God had not turned the king's heart to
the contrary."

When Erasmus' Greek Testament appeared, Colet gave it
a hearty welcome. In a letter to the Dutch scholar acknowledging the receipt of a copy, he expressed his regret at not
having a sufficient knowledge of Greek to read it and his desire to be his disciple in that tongue. It was here he made
the prediction that "the name of Erasmus will never perish."
Erasmus had written to Colet that he had dipped into Hebrew
but gone no further, "frightened by the strangeness of the

---

[1] The text in Lupton, Appendix C.

[2] Lupton, p. 183, says Colet might aptly have referred to the case of the
archdeacon who, in the course of his visitation, went to Bridlington Priory with
97 horses, 21 dogs and 3 hawks. For Colet's description in the *Hierarchies*
of Dionysius of what a priest should be, see Lupton, p. 71; Seebohm, p. 76.

idiom and in view of the insufficiency of the human mind to master a multitude of subjects."[1]   A much younger scholar at Tübingen, Philip Melanchthon, had put his tribute to the *Novum instrumentum* in Greek verse which was transmitted to Erasmus by Beatus Rhenanus. Fox, bishop of Winchester, pronounced the book more instructive to him than 10 commentaries.

Not long before his death, Colet determined to retire to a religious retreat at Shene, a resolution based upon his failing health and the troubles in which his freedom of utterance had involved him. He did not live to carry out his resolution. He was buried in St. Paul's. It is noteworthy that his will contained no benefactions to the Church or provision for masses for his soul. Erasmus paid the high tribute to his friend, while living, that England had not " another more pious or one who more truly knew Christ." And, writing after Colet's death to a correspondent, he exclaimed, " What a man has England and what a friend I have lost!" Colet had often hearkened to Erasmus' appeals in times of stringency.[2] No description in the *Colloquies* has more interest for the Anglo-Saxon people than the description of the journey which the two friends made together to the shrines of Thomas à Becket and of Our Lady of Walsingham. And the best part of the description is the doubting humor with which they passed criticism upon Peter's finger, the Virgin's milk, one of St. Thomas' shoes and other relics which were shown them.

Far as Colet went in demanding a reform of clerical habits, welcoming the revival of letters, condemning the old scholastic disputation and advocating the study of the Scriptures, it is quite probable he would not have fallen in with the Reformation.[3] He was fifty when it broke out. The best word that can be spoken of him is, that he seems to have conformed closely to the demand which he made of Christian men to live good

---

[1] Nichols, I. 376, II. 287.   At a later time, to take More's statement, Colet prosecuted the study, Nichols, II. 393.

[2] Nichols, II. 25, 35 sqq., 72, 258, etc.

[3] Gasquet: *The Eve of the Reformation*, p. 6, insists that the contrary view is " absolutely false and misleading."

and upright lives for, of a surety, he said, "to do mercy and justice is more pleasant to God, than to pray or do sacrifice to Him."[1] What higher tribute could be paid than the one paid by Donald Lupton in his *History of Modern Protestant Divines*, 1637, "This great dean of St. Paul's taught and lived like St. Paul."[2]

Sir Thomas More, 1478–1535, not only died in the Catholic Church, but died a martyr's death, refusing to acknowledge the English king's supremacy so far as to impugn the pope's authority. After studying in Oxford, he practised law in London, rising to be chancellor of the realm. It is not for us here to follow his services in his profession and to the state, but to trace his connection with the revival of learning and the religious movement in England. More was a pattern of a devout and intelligent layman. He wore a hair shirt next to his skin and yet he laughed at the superstition of his age. On taking office, he stipulated that "he should first look to God and after God to the king." At the same time, he entered heartily with his close friends, Erasmus and Colet, into the construction of a new basis for education in the study of the classics, Latin and Greek. He was firmly bound to the Church, with the pope as its head, and yet in his *Utopia* he presented a picture of an ideal society in which religion was to be in large part a matter of the family, and confession was not made to the priest nor absolution given by the priest.

With the exception of the *Utopia*, all of More's genuine works were religious and the most of them were controversial treatises, intended to confute the new doctrines of the Reformation which had found open advocates in England long before More's death. More was beheaded in 1535 and, if we recall that Tyndale's English New Testament was published in 1526, we shall have a standard for measuring the duration of More's contact with the Protestant upheaval. Tyndale himself was strangled and burnt to death a year after More's execution. In answer to

[1] *A Right Fruitful Admonition concerning the Order of a Good Christian Man's Life*. A tract by Colet reprinted in Lupton's *Life*, p. 305 sqq., from an ed. of 1534.

[2] Lupton: *Life of Colet*, p. 143.

Simon Fish's work, *The Supplication of Beggars*, a bitter attack against purgatory, More sent forth the *Supplication of Souls* or *Poor Seely (simple) Souls pewled out of Purgatory*.   Here souls are represented as crying out not to be left in their penal distress by the forgetfulness of the living.   Fish was condemned to death and burnt, 1533.   As the chief controversialist on the old side, More also wrote against John Fryth, who was condemned to the stake 1533, and against Tyndale, pronouncing his translation of the New Testament "a false English translation newly forged by Tyndale."   He also made the strange declaration that "Wyclif, Tyndale and Friar Barnes and such others had been the original cause why the Scripture has been of necessity kept out of lay people's hands." [1]   More said heretical books were imported from the Continent to England "in vats full."   He called Thomas Hylton, a priest of Kent, one of the heretics whom he condemned to the flames, "the devil's stinking pot."   Hylton's crime was the denial of the five sacraments and he was burnt 1530. [2]   As was the custom of the time, More's controversial works abound in scurrilous epithets.   His opponents he distinguishes by such terms as "swine," "hellhounds that the devil hath in his kennel," "apes that dance for the pleasure of Lucifer." [3]   In his works against Tyndale and Fryth, he commended pilgrimages, image-worship and indulgences.   He himself, so the chancellor wrote, had been present at Barking, 1498, when a number of relics were discovered which "must have been hidden since the time when the abbey was burnt by the infidels," and he declared that the main

---

[1] See Gasquet : *Eve of the Reform.*, p. 215 sqq.

[2] What estimate was put upon the life of a heretic in some quarters in England may be gathered from a letter written to Erasmus, 1511, by Ammonius, Latin secretary to Henry VIII.   The writer said, he did "not wonder wood was so scarce and dear, the heretics necessitated so many holocausts."   At the convocation of 1512, an old priest arguing for the burning of heretics repeated the passage louder and louder *hæreticum hominem devita* (avoid) and explained it as if it were *de vita tolli*, to be removed from life, and thus turned the passage into a positive command to execute heretics.   For More's denial of having used cruelty towards heretics, see his *Engl. Works*, p. 901 sqq.   The martyrologist, Foxe, pronounced More "a bitter persecutor of good men and a wretched enemy against the truth of the Gospel."

[3] Dr. Lindsay in *Cambr. Hist. of Engl. Lit.*, III. 19.

thing was that "such relics were the remains of holy men, to be had in reverence, and it was a matter of inferior import whether the right names were attached to them or not."[1]

And yet, More resisted certain superstitions, as of the Franciscan monk of Coventry who publicly preached, that "whoever prayed daily through the Psalter to the Blessed Virgin could not be damned." He denied the Augustinian teaching that infants dying without baptism were consigned to eternal punishment and he could write to Erasmus, that Hutten's *Epistolæ obscurorum virorum* delighted every one in England and that "under a rude scabbard the work concealed a most excellent blade."[2] His intimacy with Colet and Erasmus led to an attempt on the part of the monks, in 1519, to secure his conversion.

More was beatified by Leo XIII., 1886, and with St. Edmund, Bishop Fisher and Thomas à Becket is the chief English martyr whom English Catholics cultivate. He died " unwilling to jeopardize his soul to perpetual damnation " and expressing the hope that, " as St. Paul and St. Stephen met in heaven and were friends, so it might be with him and his judges." Gairdner is led to remark that " no man ever met an unjust doom in a more admirable spirit."[3] We may concur in this judgment and yet we will not overlook the fact that More, gentleman as he was in heart, seems to us to have been unrelenting to the men whom he convicted as heretics and, in his writings, piled upon them epithets as drastic as Luther himself used. Aside from this, he is to be accorded praise for his advocacy of the reform in education and his commendation of Erasmus' Greek Testament. He wrote a special letter to the Louvain professor, Dorpius, up-

---

[1] Gasquet: *The Eve of the Reformation*, p. 378.

[2] Nichols, II. 428. See also Seebohm, pp. 408, 416, 470.

[3] *Hist. of the Engl. Church in the 16th Cent.*, etc., p. 160. Among the affecting scenes in the last experiences recorded of men devoted to martyrdom was the scene which occurred on More's way to the Tower, reported by More's first biographer, Roper (Lumby's ed., p. liii). His favorite daughter, Margaret, longing once more to show her affection, pressed through the files of halberdiers and, embracing her father, kissed him and received his blessing. When she was again outside the ranks of the guards, she forced her way through a second time for a father's embrace.

braiding him for his attack upon the critical studies of Erasmus and upon the revision of the old Latin text as unwarranted.

More's *Utopia*, written in Latin and published in 1516 with a preface by Budæus, took Europe by storm. It was also called *Nusquama* or *Nowhere*. With Plato's *Republic* as a precedent, the author intended to point out wherein European society and especially England was at fault. In More's ideal commonwealth, which was set up on an island, treaties were observed and promises kept, and ploughmen, carpenters, wagoners, colliers and other artisans justly shared in the rewards of labor with noblemen, goldsmiths and usurers, who are called the unproductive classes. " The conspiracy of the rich procuring their own commodities under the name and title of the commonwealth " was not allowed. In *Utopia*, a proper education was given to every child, the hours of physical labor were reduced to six, the streets were 20 feet wide and the houses backed with gardens and supplied with fresh water. The slaughtering was done outside the towns. All punishment was for the purpose of reform and religion, largely a matter of family. The old religions continued to exist on the island, for Christianity had but recently been introduced, but More, apparently belying his later practice as judge, declared that "no man was punished for his religion." Its priests were of both sexes and "overseers and orderers of worship" rather than sacerdotal functionaries. Not to them but to the heads of families was confession made, the wife prostrate on the ground confessing to her husband, and the children to both parents. The priests were married.

Little did More suspect that, within ten years of the publication of his famous book, texts would be drawn from it to support the Peasants' Revolt in Germany.[1] In it are stated some of the sociological hopes and dreams of this present age. The author was voicing the widespread feeling of his own generation

---

[1] *Cambr. Hist. of Engl. Lit.*, p. 20. For an excellent summary of the *Utopia*, see Seebohm, pp. 346–365, and also W. B. Guthrie, in *Socialism before the French Revol.*, pp. 54–132, N.Y., 1907. For the Latin edd. and Engl. transl., see *Dict. of Natl. Biogr.*, p. 444. An excellent ed. of Robynson's trsl., 2d ed., 1556, was furnished by Prof. Lumby, Cambr., 1879. The *Life of More*, by Roper, More's son-in-law and a Protestant, is prefixed. Also Lupton: *The Utopia*, Oxf., 1895. A reprint of the Lat. ed., 1518, and the Engl. ed., 1551.

which was harassed with laws restricting the wages of labor, with the enclosures of the commons by the rich, the conversion of arable lands into sheep farms and with the renewed warfare on the Continent into which England was drawn.[1]

John Fisher, who suffered on the block a few months before More for refusing to take the oath of supremacy, and set aside the succession of Catherine of Aragon's offspring, was 79 years old when he died. Dean Perry has pronounced him "the most learned, the most conscientious and the most devout of the bishops of his day." In 1511, he recommended Erasmus to Cambridge to teach Greek. On the way to the place of beheadal, this good man carried with him the New Testament, repeating again and again the words, "This is life eternal to know Thee and Jesus Christ whom thou hast sent." "That was learning enough for him," he said.

To Grocyn, Colet, More and Fisher the Protestant world gives its reverent regard. It is true, they did not fully apprehend the light which was spreading over Europe. Nevertheless, they went far as pioneers of a more rational system of education than the one built up by the scholastic method and they have a distinct place in the history of the progress of religious thought.[2]

In Scotland, the Protestant Reformation took hold of the nation before the Renaissance had much chance to exercise an independent influence. John Major, who died about 1550, wrote a commentary on the *Sentences* of Peter the Lombard and is called "the last of the Schoolmen." He is, however, a connecting link with the new movement in literature through George Buchanan, his pupil at St. Andrews. Major remained true to the Roman communion. Buchanan, after being held for six months in prison as a heretic in Portugal, returned to Scotland and adopted the Reformation. According to Professor

[1] See Lumby's *Introd.*, p. xiv, and Guthrie, p. 96 sq.

[2] There is, of course, no standing ground except that of generous toleration as between the view taken by the author and the view of Abbot Gasquet, who can find nothing praiseworthy in the Protestant Reformation and closes his chapter on the *Revival of Letters in England*, in *The Eve of the Reform.*, p. 46, with the words, "What put a stop to the Humanist movement in England, as it certainly did in Germany, was the rise of the religious difficulties which were opposed by those most conspicuous for their championship of true learning, scholarship and education," meaning Colet, Erasmus, Fisher and More. For good remarks on the bearing of English Humanism on the Protestant movement, see Seebohm, pp. 494 sqq., 510.

Hume-Brown, his Latin paraphrase of the Psalms in metre " was, until recent years, read in Scotland in every school where Latin was taught." [1] Knox's *History of the Reformation* was the earliest model of prose literature in Scotland.

[1] See chapter *Reformation and Renascence in Scotl.*, by Hume-Brown in *Cambr. Hist. of Eng. Lit.*, III. 156-186.   For the gifted Alesius, who spent the best part of his life as a professor in Germany, see A. F. Mitchell: *The Scottish Reformation*, Edinb., 1900.

CHAPTER IX.

THE PULPIT AND POPULAR PIETY.

§ 72. *Literature.*

FOR §§ 73, 74. — The works of Erasmus, Colet, Tyndale, Geiler of Strassburg and other sources quoted in the notes. — LEA : *Hist. of Cler. Celibacy.* Also *Hist. of Span. Inq.* — *Histt. of the Engl. Ch.* by CAPES and GAIRDNER-TRAILL : *Social Hist. of Engl.,* vol. II. — SEEBOHM : *Oxf. Reformers.* — GASQUET : *The Old Engl. Bible and Other Essays,* Lond., 2d ed., 1907. Also *The Eve of the Reformation,* pp. 245 sqq. — CRUEL : *Gesch. d. deutschen Predigt, im MA,* pp. 431–663, Detmold, 1879. — KOLDE : *D. relig. Leben in Erfurt am Ausgange d. MA,* 1898. — LANDMANN : *D. Predigttum in Westphalen* in *d. letzten Zeiten d. MA,* pp. 256. — SCHÖN : art. *Predigt* in Herzog, XV. 642–656. — JANSSEN-PASTOR : *Hist. of the Ger. People,* vol. I. — PASTOR : *Gesch. d. Päpste,* I. 31 sqq., III. 133 sqq. — HEFELE-HERGENRÖTHER : *Conciliengesch.,* vol. VIII.

For § 75. — ULLMANN : *Reformers before the Reformation,* 2 vols., Hamb., 1841 sq., 2d ed., Gotha, 1866, Engl. trsl., 2 vols., Edinb., 1855 ; Also *J. Wessel, ein Vorgänger Luthers,* Hamb., 1834. — GIESELER, ii., Part IV. 481–503. Copious excerpts from their writings. — HERGENRÖTHER-KIRSCH, II., 1047–1049. — JANSSEN-PASTOR : I. 745–747. — HARNACK : *Dogmengesch.,* III. 518, etc. — LOOFS : *Dogmengesch.,* 4th ed., 655–658. — For GOCH : His *De libertate christ.,* etc., ed. by Corn. Graphaeus, Antw., 1520–1523. — O. CLEMEN : *Joh. Pupper von Goch,* Leip., 1896 and artt. in Herzog, VI. 740–743, and in Wetzer-Welte, VI. 1678–1684. — For WESEL : his *Adv. indulgentias* in Walch's *Monumenta medii aevi* Götting., 1757. — The proceedings of his trial, in ÆNEAS SYLVIUS : *Commentarium de concilio Basileae* and D'ARGENTRÉ : *Col. nov. judiciorum de erroribus novis,* Paris, 1755, and BROWNE : *Fasciculus,* 2d ed., Lond., 1690. — Artt. in Herzog by CLEMEN, xxi, 127–131, and Wetzer-Welte, VI. 1786–1789. — For WESSEL : 1st ed. of his works *Farrago rerum theol.,* a collection of his tracts, appeared in the Netherlands about 1521, 2d ed., Wittenb., 1522, containing Luther's letter, 3d and 4th edd., Basel, 1522, 1523. Complete ed. of his works containing *Life,* by A. HARDENBERG (preacher in Bremen, d. 1574), Groningen, 1614. — MUURLING : *Commentatio historico-theol. de Wesseli cum vita tum meritis,* Trajecti ad Rhenum, 1831 ; also *de Wesseli principiis ac virtutibus,* Amsterd., 1840. — J. FRIEDRICH, Rom. Cath.: *J. Wessel,* Regensb., 1862. — Artt. *Wessel* in Herzog, by VAN VEEN, xxi. 131–147, and Wetzer-Welte, XII. 1339–1343. — P. HOFSTEDE DE GROOT : J. Wessel Ganzevoort, Groningen, 1871.

For § 76. — NICOLAS OF LYRA: *Postillæ sive Commentaria brevia in omnia biblia*, Rome, 1541–1543, 5 vols., *Introd.* — WYCLIF: *De veritate scrip. sac.*, ed. by Buddensieg, 3 vols., Leipzig, 1904. — GERSON: *De sensu litterali scrip: sac.*, Du Pin's ed., 1728, I. 1 sqq. — ERASMUS: Introd. to Gr. Test., 1516. —L. HAIN: *Repertorium bibliographicum*, 4 vols., Stuttg., 1826–1838.— ED. REUSS, d. 1891: *D. Gesch. d. heil. Schriften N.T.*, 6th ed., Braunschweig, 1887, pp. 603 sqq. — F. W. FARRAR: *Hist. of Interpretation*, Lond., 1886, pp. 254–303. — S. BERGER: *La Bible Française au moyen âge*, Paris, 1884.— GASQUET: *The Old Engl. Bible*, etc.; the *Eve of the Reformation*. — F. FALK: *Bibelstudien, Bibelhandschriften und Bibeldrucken*, Mainz, 1901: *Die Bibel am Ausgange des MA, ihre Kenntnis und ihre Verbreitung*, Col., 1905. —W. WALTHER: *D. deutschen Bibelübersetzungen des MA*, Braunschweig, 1889–1892. — A. COPPINGER: *Incunabula bibl. or the First Half Cent. of the Lat. Bible, 1450-1500*, with 54 facsimiles, Lond., 1892. — The *Histt. of the Engl. Bible*, by WESTCOTT, EADIE, MOULTON, KENYON, etc. — JANSSEN-PASTOR: *Gesch. des deutschen Volkes*, I. 9 sqq. — BEZOLD: *Gesch. der Reformation*, pp. 109 sqq. — R. SCHMID: *Nic. of Lyra*, in Herzog XII. 28–30. — Artt. *Bibellesen und Bibelverbot* and *Bibelübersetzungen* in Herzog II. 700 sqq., III. 24 sqq. Other works cited in the notes.

For § 77. — I. SOURCES: Savonarola's Lat. and Ital. writings consist of sermons, tracts, letters and a few poems. The largest collection of MSS. and original edd. is preserved in the National Library of Florence. It contains 15 edd. of the *Triumph of the Cross* issued in the 15th and 16th centt. Epp. *spirituales et asceticae*, ed. QUÉTIF, Paris, 1674. The sermons were collected by a friend, Lorenzo Vivoli, and published as they came fresh from the preacher's lips. Best ed. *Sermoni e Prediche*, Prato, 1846. Also ed. by G. BACCINI, Flor., 1889. A selection, ed. by VILLARI and CASANOVA: *Scelta di prediche e scritti, G. Sav.*, Flor., 1898. — Germ. trsl. of 12 sermons and the poem *de ruina mundi* by H. SCHOTTMÜLLER: Berlin, 1901, pp. 132. — A. GHERARDI: *Nuovi documenti e studii intorno a Savon.*, 1876, 2d ed., Flor., 1887. — *The Triumph of the Cross*, ed. in Lat. and Ital. by L. FERRETTI, O.P., Milan, 1901. Engl. trsl. from this ed. by J. PROCTER, Lond., 1901, pp. 209. — *Exposition of Ps. LI and part of Ps. XXXII*, Lat. text with Engl. trsl. by E. H. PEROWNE, Lond., 1900, pp. 227. — Sav.'s Poetry, ed. by C. GUASTI, Flor., 1862, pp. xxii, 1864. — Rudelbach, Perrens and Villari give specimens in the original. — E. C. BAYONNE: *Œuvres spir. choisies de Sav.*, 3 vols., Paris, 1880. — Oldest biographies by P. BURLAMACCHI, d. 1519, founded on an older Latin Life, the work of an eye-witness, ed. by Mansi, 1761: G. F. PICO DELLA MIRANDOLA (nephew of the celebrated scholar of that name), completed 1520, publ. 1530, ed. by Quétif, 2 vols., Paris, 1674. On these three works, see VILLARI, *Life of Sav.*, pp. xxvii sqq. — Also J. NARDI (a contemporary): *Le storie della città di Firenze, 1494-1531*, Flor., 1584. — LUCA LANDUCCI, a pious Florentine apothecary and an ardent admirer of Sav.: *Diario Fiorentino, 1450-1516*, Florence, 1883. A realistic picture of Florence and the preaching and death of Savonarola.

II. MODERN WORKS. — For extended lit., see POTTHAST: *Bibl. hist. med.*, II. 1564 sqq. — Lives by RUDELBACH, Hamb., 1835. — MEIER, Berl., 1836.— K. HASE in *Neue Propheten*, Leip., 1851. — F. T. PERRENS, 2 vols., Paris,

1853, 3d ed., 1859. — MADDEN, 2 vols., Lond., 1854. — PADRE V. MARCHESE, Flor., 1855. — * PASQUALE VILLARI: *Life and Times of Savon.*, Flor., 1859–1861, 2d ed., 1887, 1st Engl. trsl. by L. Horner, 2d Engl. trsl. by Mrs. Villari, Lond., 2 vols., 1888, 1 vol. ed., 1899. — RANKE in *Hist. biogr. Studien,* Leip., 1877. — BAYONNE: Paris, 1879. — E. WARREN, Lond., 1881. — W. CLARK, Prof. Trinity Col., Toronto, Chicago, 1891. — J. L. O'NEIL, O.P.: *Was Sav. really excommunicated ?* Bost., 1900; * H. LUCAS, St. Louis, 1900. — G. McHARDY, Edinb., 1901. — W. H. CRAWFORD: *Sav. the Prophet* in *Men of the Kingdom* series. — * J. SCHNITZER: *Quellen und Forschungen zur Gesch. Savon.*, 3 vols., Munich, 1902–1904. Vol. II., *Sav. und die Fruerprobe*, pp. 175. — Also *Savon. im Lichte der neuesten Lit.* in *Hist.-pol. Blätter*, 1898–1900. — H. RIESCH: *Savon. u. s. Zeit*, Leip., 1906. — ROSCOE in *Life of Lorenzo the Magnificent.* — E. COMBA: *Storia della riforma in Italia*, Flor., 1881. — P. SCHAFF, art. *Savon.* in Herzog II., 2d ed., XIII. 421–431, and BENRATH in 3d ed., XVII. 502–513. — CREIGHTON: vol. III. — GREGOROVIUS: VII. 432 sqq. — * PASTOR: 4th ed., III. 137–148, 150–162, 396–437: *Zur Beurtheilung Sav.*, pp. 79, Freib. im Br., 1896. This brochure was in answer to sharp attacks upon Pastor's treatment of Savonarola in the 1st ed. of his Hist., especially those of Luotto and Feretti. — P. LUOTTO: *Il vero Savon. ed il Savon. di L. Pastor*, Flor., 1897, p. 620. Luotto also wrote *Dello studio di scrittura sacra secondo G. Savon. e Léon XIII.*, Turin, 1896. — FERETTI: *Per la causa di Fra G. Savon.*, Milan, 1897. — MRS. OLIPHANT: *Makers of Florence.* — GODKIN: *The Monastery of San Marco*, Lond., 1901. — G. BIERMANN: *Krit. Studie zur Gesch. des Fra G. Savon.*, Rostock, 1901. — BRIE: *Savon. und d. deutsche Lit.*, Breslau, 1903. — G. BONET-MAURY: *Les Précurseurs de la Réforme et de la liberté de conscience . . . du XIIᵉ et XIIIᵉ siècle*, Paris, 1904, contains Sketches of Waldo, Bernard of Clairvaux, Peter the Venerable, St. Francis, Dante, Savonarola, etc. — Savonarola has been made the subject of romantic treatment by Lenau in his poem *Savonarola*, 1844, Geo. Eliot in *Romola*, and by Alfred Austin in his tragedy, *Savonarola*, Lond., 1881, with a long preface in which an irreverent, if not blasphemous, parallel is drawn between the Florentine preacher and Christ.

For § 78. — See citations in the Notes.

For § 79. — G. UHLHORN: *Die christl. Liebesthätigkeit im MA*, Stuttg., 1884. — P. A. THIEJM: *Gesch. d. Wohlthätigkeitsanstalten* in Belgien, etc., Freib., 1887. — L. LALLEMAND: *Hist. de la charité*, 3 vols., Paris, 1906. Vol.3 covers the 10th–16th century. — T. KOLDE: Art. *Bruderschaften*, in Herzog, III. 434–441. — A. BLAIZE: *Des monts-de-piété et des banques de prêt sur gage*, Paris, 1856. — H. HOLZAPFEL: *D. Anfänge d. montes pietatis 1462–1515*, Munich, 1903. — TOULMIN SMITH: *Engl. Gilds*, Lond., 1870. — THOROLD ROGERS: *Work and Wages*, ch. XI. sqq. — W. CUNNINGHAM: *Growth of Engl. Industry and Commerce*, Bk. II., ch. III. sqq. — LECKY: *Hist. of Europ. Morals*, II. — STUBBS: *Const. Hist.*, ch. XXI. — W. VON HEYD: *Gesch. d. Levantenhandels im MA*, 2 vols., Stuttg., 1879. — Artt. *Aussatz* and *Zins u. Wucher* in Wetzer-Welte, I. 1706 sqq., XII. 1963–1975. — JANSSEN-PASTOR, I. 451 sqq. — PASTOR: *Gesch. d. Päpste.*, III.

For § 80. — The Sources are THOMAS AQUINAS, the papal bulls of indulgence and treatments by WYCLIF, HUSS, WESSEL, JOHN OF PALTZ, JAMES OF

JÜTERBOCK, etc.   Much material is given by W. KÖHLER : *Dokumente zum Ablassstreit,* Tüb., 1902, and A. SCHULTE: *D. Fugger in Rom,* 2 vols., Leipz., 1904.   Vol. II contains documents. — The authoritative Cath. work is FR. BERINGER : *Die Ablässe, ihr Wesen u. Gebrauch,* pp. 860 and 64, 13th ed., Paderb., 1906. — Also NIC. PAULUS : *J. Tetzel, der Ablassprediger,* Mainz, 1899. — Best Prot. treatments, H. C. LEA: *Hist. of Auric. Conf. and Indulgences in the Lat. Ch.,* 3 vols., Phil., 1896. — T. BRIEGER, art. *Indulgenzen* in Herzog, IX. 76–94, and Schaff-Herzog, V. 485 sqq. and *D. Wesen d. Ablasses am Ausgange d. MA,* a university address.   Brieger has promised an extended treatment in book form. — SCHAFF: *Ch. Hist.,* V., I. p. 729 sqq., VI. 146 sqq.

§ 73. *The Clergy.*

Both in respect of morals and education the clergy, during the period following the year 1450, showed improvement over the age of the Avignon captivity and the papal schism.   Clerical practice in that former age was so low that it was impossible for it to go lower and any appearance of true religion remain.   One of the healthy signs of this latter period was that, in a spirit of genuine religious devotion, Savonarola in Italy and such men in Germany as Busch, Thomas Murner, Geiler of Strassburg, Sebastian Brant and the Benedictine abbot, Trithemius, held up to condemnation, or ridicule, priestly incompetency and worldliness.   The pictures, which they joined Erasmus in drawing, were dark enough.   Nevertheless, the clergy both of the higher and lower grades included in its ranks many men who truly sought the well-being of the people and set an example of purity of conduct.

The first cause of the low condition, for low it continued to be, was the impossible requirement of celibacy.   The infraction of this rule weakened the whole moral fibre of the clerical order.   A second cause is to be looked for in the seizure of the rich ecclesiastical endowments by the aristocracy as its peculiar prize and securing them for the sons of noble parentage without regard to their moral and intellectual fitness. To the evils arising from these two causes must be added the evils arising from the unblushing practice of pluralism.   No help came from Rome.   The episcopal residences of Toledo, Constance, Paris, Mainz, Cologne and Canterbury could not be expected to be models of domestic and religious order when

the tales of Boccaccio were being paralleled in the lives of the
supreme functionaries of Christendom at its centre.

The grave discussions of clerical manners, carried on at the
Councils of Constance and Basel, revealed the disease without
providing a cure. The proposition was even made by Cardinal Zabarella and Gerson, in case further attempts to check
priestly concubinage failed, to concede to the clergy the privilege of marriage.[1] In the programme for a reformation of
the Church, offered by Sigismund at Basel, the concession was
included and Pius II., one of the attendants on that synod,
declared the reasons for restoring the right of matrimony to
priests to be stronger in that day than were the reasons in a
former age for forbidding it. The need of a relaxation of the
rigid rule found recognition in the decrees of Eugenius IV.,
1441, and Alexander VI., 1496, releasing some of the military
orders from the vow of chastity. Here and there, priests like
Lallier of Paris at the close of the 15th century, dared to propose openly, as Wyclif had done a century before, its full abolition. But, for making the proposal, the Sorbonne denied to
Lallier the doctorate.

In Spain, the efforts of synods and prelates to put a check
upon clerical immorality accomplished little. Finally, the
secular power intervened and repeated edicts were issued by
Ferdinand and Isabella against priestly concubinage, 1480,
1491, 1502, 1503. So energetic was the attempt at enforce-
ment that, in districts, clerics complained that the secular
officials made forcible entrance into their houses and carried
off their women companions.[2] In his *History of the Spanish
Inquisition*, Dr. Lea devotes a special chapter to clerical solici-
tation at the confessional. Episcopal deliverances show that
the priests were often illiterate and without even a knowledge
of Latin. The prelates were given to worldliness and the
practice of pluralism. The revenues of the see of Toledo were
estimated at from 80,000 to 100,000 ducats, with patronage at
the disposal of its incumbent amounting to a like sum. A sin-

[1] Lea: *Cler. Celibacy*, II. 25. Gerson: *Dial. naturæ et sophiæ de casti-
tate ecclesiasticorum*. Du Pin's ed., II. 617–636.
[2] Lea: *Inq. of Spain*, I. 15 sqq.

gle instance must suffice to show the extent to which pluralism in Spain was carried.   Gonzalez de Mendoza, while yet a child, held the curacy of Hita, at twelve was archdeacon of Guadalajara, one of the richest benefices of Spain, and retained the bishopric of Seguenza during his successive administrations of the archbishoprics of Seville and Toledo.   Gonzalez was a gallant knight and, in 1484, when he led the army which invaded Granada, he took with him his bastard son, Rodrigo, who was subsequently married in great state in the presence of Ferdinand and Isabella to Ferdinand's niece.   In 1476, when the archbishopric of Saragossa became vacant, king Juan II. applied to Sixtus IV. to appoint his son, Alfonzo, a child of six, to the place.   Sixtus declined, but after a spirited controversy preserved the king's good-will by appointing the boy perpetual administrator of the see.

In France, the bishop of Angers, in an official address to Charles VIII., 1484, declared that the religious orders had fallen below the level of the laity in their morals.[1]   To give a case of extravagant pluralism, John, son of the duke of Lorraine, 1498-1550, was appointed bishop-coadjutor of Metz, 1501, entering into full possession seven years later, and, one after the other, he united with this preferment the bishoprics of Toul, 1517, and Térouanne, 1518, Valence and Die, 1521, Verdun, 1523, Alby, 1536, Macon soon after, Agen, 1541 and Nantes, 1542.   To these were added the archbishoprics of Narbonne, 1524, Rheims, 1533, and Lyons, 1537.   He also held at least nine abbeys, including Cluny.   He resigned the sees of Verdun and Metz to a nephew, but resumed them in 1548 when this nephew married Marguerite d'Egmont.[2]   In 1518, he received the red hat.   During the 15th century one boy of 10 and another of 17 filled the bishopric of Geneva. A loyal Romanist, Sœur Jeanne de Jussie, writing after the beginning of the 16th century, testifies to the dissoluteness of the bishops and clergy of the Swiss city and charged them with living in adultery.[3]

[1] For further testimonies, see Lea : *Cler. Celibacy*, II. 8 sqq.

[2] See Lea in *Cambr. Mod. Hist.*, I. 660.

[3] Quoted by Lindsay : *The Reformation*, II. 90.   Of the Italian convents, Savonarola declared that the nuns had become worse than harlots.

In Germany, although as a result of the labors of the Mystics the ecclesiastical condition was much better, the moral and intellectual unfitness was such that it calls forth severe criticism from Catholic as well as Protestant historians. The Catholic, Janssen, says that "the profligacy of the clergy at German cathedrals, as well as their rudeness and ignorance, was proverbial. The complaints which have come down to us from the 15th century of the bad morals of the German clergy are exceedingly numerous." Ficker, a Protestant, speaks of "the extraordinary immorality to which priests and monks yielded themselves." And Bezold, likewise a Protestant, says that "in the 15th century the worldliness of the clergy reached a height not possible to surpass." [1] The contemporary, Jacob Wimpheling, set forth probably the true state of the case. He was severe upon the clergy and yet spoke of many excellent prelates, canons and vicars, known for their piety and good works. He knew of a German cleric who held at one time 20 livings, including 8 canonries. To the archbishopric of Mainz, Albrecht of Hohenzollern added the see of Halberstadt and the archbishopric of Magdeburg. For his promotion to the see of Mainz he paid 30,000 gulden, money he borrowed from the Fuggers.

The bishops were charged with affecting the latest fashions in dress and wearing the finest textures, keeping horses and huntings dogs, surrounding themselves with servants and pages, allowing their beards and hair to grow long, and going about in green- and red-colored shoes and shoes punctured with holes through which ribbons were drawn. They were often seen in coats of mail, and accoutred with helmets and swords, and the tournament often witnessed them entered in the lists. [2]

The custom of reserving the higher offices of the Church for the aristocracy was widely sanctioned by law. As early as 1281 in Worms and 1294 in Osnabruck, no one could be dean who was not of noble lineage. The office of bishop and preb-

---

[1] Janssen, I. 681, 687, 708; Ficker, p. 27; Bezold, pp. 79, 83.

[2] See Hefele-Hergenröther: *Conciliengesch.*, VIII., under *Kleidung*, and Butzbach: *Satiræ elegiacæ* quoted by Janssen, I. 685 sqq.

end stalls were limited to men of noble birth by Basel, 1474, Augsburg, 1475, Münster and Paderborn, 1480, and Osnabruck, 1517. The same rule prevailed in Mainz, Halberstadt, Meissen, Merseburg and other dioceses. At the beginning of the 16th century, it was the established custom in Germany that no one should be admitted to a cathedral chapter who could not show 16 ancestors who had joined in the tournament and, as early as 1474, the condition of admission to the chapter of Cologne was that the candidate should show 32 members of his family of noble birth. Of the 228 bishops who successively occupied the 32 German sees from 1400–1517, all but 13 were noblemen. The eight occupants of the see of Münster, 1424–1508, were all counts or dukes. So it was with 10 archbishops of Mainz, 1419–1514, the 7 bishops of Halberstadt, 1407–1513, and the 5 archbishops of Cologne, 1414–1515.[1] This custom of keeping the high places for men of noble birth was smartly condemned by Geiler of Strassburg and other contemporaries. Geiler declared that Germany was soaked with the folly that to the bishoprics, not the more pious and learned should be promoted but only those who, " as they say, belong to good families." It remained for the Protestant Reformation to reassert the democratic character of the ministry.

A high standard could not be expected of the lower ranks of the clergy where the incumbents of the high positions held them, not by reason of piety or intellectual attainments but as the prize of birth and favoritism. The wonder is, that there was any genuine devotion left among the lower priesthood. Its ranks were greatly overstocked. Every family with several sons expected to find a clerical position for one of them and often the member of the family, least fitted by physical qualifications to make his way in the world, was set apart for religion. Here again Geiler of Strassburg applied his lash of indignation, declaring that, as people set apart for St. Velten the chicken that had the pox and for St. Anthony the pig that was affected with disease, so they devoted the least likely of their children to the holy office.

[1] Janssen, I. 689–696, gives a full list of these bishops.

The German village clergy of the period were as a rule not university bred. The chronicler, Felix Faber of Ulm, in 1490 declared that out of 1000 priests scarcely one had ever seen a university town and a baccalaureate or master was a rarity seldom met with. With a sigh, people of that age spoke of the well-equipped priest of "the good old times."

From the Alps to Scandinavia, concubinage was widely practised and in parts of Germany, such as Saxony, Bavaria, Austria and the Tirol, it was general. The region, where there was the least of it, was the country along the Rhine. In parts of Switzerland and other localities, parishes, as a measure of self-defence, forced their young pastors to take concubines. Two of the Swiss Reformers, Leo Jud and Bullinger, were sons of priests and Zwingli, a prominent priest, was given to incontinence before starting on his reformatory career. It was a common saying that the Turk of clerical sensualism within was harder to drive out than the Turk from the East.

How far the conscientious effort, made in Germany in the last years of the Middle Ages to reform the convents, was attended with success is a matter of doubt. John Busch labored most energetically in that direction for nearly fifty years in Westphalia, Thuringia and other parts. The things that he records seem almost past belief. Nunneries, here and there, were no better than brothels. In cases, they were habitually visited by noblemen. The experience is told of one nobleman who was travelling with his servant and stopped over night at a convent. After the evening meal, the nuns cleared the main room and, dressed in fine apparel, amused their visitor by exhibitions of dancing.[1] Thomas Murner went so far as to say that convents for women had all been turned into refuges for people of noble birth.[2] The dancing during the sessions of the Diet of Cologne, 1505, was opened by the archbishop and an abbess, and nuns from St. Ursula's

---

[1] Janssen, I. 726. Bezold, p. 83, certainly goes far, when he makes the unmodified statement, that the convents were high schools of the most shameful immorality — *Hochschulen der gräuelichsten Unsittlichkeit.*

[2] *Sind jetzt allgemein Edelleute Spital,* Janssen, I. 724.

and St. Mary's, the king Maximilian looking on.   Preachers,
like Geiler of Strassburg, cried out against the moral dangers
which beset persons taking the monastic vow.[1]   The cloistral
life came to be known as the " the compulsory vocation."   As
the time of the Reformation approached, there was no lessen-
ing of the outcry against the immorality of the clergy and
convents, as appears from the writings of Ulrich von Hutten
and Erasmus.

The practice of priestly concubinage, uncanonical though
it was, bishops were quite ready to turn into a means of gain,
levying a tax upon it.   In the diocese of Bamberg, a toll
of 5 gulden was exacted for every child born to a priest
and, in a single year, the tax is said to have brought in the
considerable sum of 1,500 gulden.   In 1522, a similar tax
of 4 gulden brought into the treasury of the bishop of Constance, 7,500 gulden.   The same year, complaint was made
to the pope by the Diet of Nürnberg of the reckless lawlessness of young priests in corrupting women and of the annual
tax levied in most dioceses upon all the clergy without distinction whether they kept concubines or not.[2]   It is not surprising, in view of these facts, that Luther called upon monks
and nuns unable to avoid incontinence of thought, to come
forth from the monasteries and marry.   On the other hand,
it must not be forgotten that no plausible charge of incontinence was made against the Reformer.

If we turn to England, we are struck with the great dearth
of contemporary religious literature, 1450–1517, as compared
with Germany.[3]   Few writings have come down to us from
which to form a judgment of the condition of the clergy.
Our deductions must be drawn in part from the testimonies

---

[1] *Die jungen Mönchlein*, he said, *und Nönnlein die du machest, die werden
Huren und Buben.*   The young monks and nuns will become harlots and
rascals.   I have not spoken of that custom of mediæval lust, the *jus primæ
noctis* or *droit de marquette* as it was called, whereby the feudal lord had the
privilege of spending the first night with all brides.   Spiritual lords in Southern France, having domains, did not shrink, in cases, from demanding the
same privilege.   Lea : *Celibacy*, I. 441.

[2] Lea, II. 59.

[3] Gee and Hardy: in *Documents*, etc., gives only two ecclesiastical acts between 1402–1532.

of the English Humanists and Reformers and from the records
of the visitations of monasteries and also their suppression
under Henry VIII. In a document, drawn up at the request
of Henry V. by the University of Oxford, 1414, setting forth
the need of a reformation of the Church, one of the articles
pronounced the "undisguised profligacy of the clergy to be
the scandal of the Church." [1] In the middle of the century,
1455, Archbishop Bourchier's Commission for Reforming the
Clergy spoke of the marriage and concubinage of the secular
clergy and the gross ignorance which, in quarters, marked
them. In the latter part of the century, 1489, the investigation of the convents, undertaken by Archbishop Morton,
uncovered an unsavory state of affairs. The old abbey of
St. Albans, for example, had degenerated till it was little better than a house of prostitution for monks. In two priories
under the abbey's jurisdiction, the nuns had been turned out
to give place to avowed courtesans. The Lollards demanded
the privilege of wedlock for priests. When, in 1494, 30
of their number were arraigned by Robert Blacater, archbishop of Glasgow, one of the charges against them was their
assertion that priests had wives in the primitive Church. [2]
Writing at the very close of the 15th century, Colet exclaimed, "Oh, the abominable impiety of those miserable
priests, of whom this age of ours contains a great multitude,
who fear not to rush from the arms of some foul harlot into
the temple of the Church, to the altar of Christ, to the mysteries of God." [3] The famous tract, the *Beggars' Petition*,
written on the eve of the British Reformation, accused the
clergy of having no other serious occupation than the destruction of the peace of family life and the corruption of women. [4]

[1] Wilkins: *Concil.*, III. 360–365.

[2] Capes: *Engl. Ch. in the 14th and 15th Centt.*, p. 259, says that many
of the clergy were actually married.

[3] Seebohm, p. 76. For Hutton's summary of the Norwich visitation, see
Traill: *Social Engl.*, II. 467 sqq. He concludes that "if the religious did
little good, they did no harm." But see same volume, p. 565, for the charge
against the priests of Gloucester.

[4] Froude puts the composition of this tract in 1528. The 16th complaint
runs: "Who is she that will set her hands to work to get 3 pence a day and

As for the practice of plural livings, it was perhaps as much in vogue in England as in Germany. Dr. Sherbourne, Colet's predecessor as dean of St. Paul's, was a notable example of a pluralist, but in this respect was exceeded by Morton and Wolsey. As for the ignorance of the English clergy, it is sufficient to refer to the testimony of Bishop Hooper who, during his visitation in Gloucester, 1551, found 168 of 311 clergymen unable to repeat the Ten Commandments, 40 who could not tell where the Lord's Prayer was to be found and 31 unable to give the author.[1]

In Scotland, the state of the clergy in pre-Reformation times was probably as low as in any other part of Western Europe.[2] John IV.'s bastard son was appointed bishop of St. Andrews at 16 and the illegitimate sons of James V., 1513–1542, held the five abbeys of Holyrood, Kelso, St. Andrews, Melrose and Coldingham. Bishops lived openly in concubinage and married their daughters into the ranks of the nobility. In the marriage document, certifying the nuptials of Cardinal Beaton's eldest daughter to the Earl of Crawford, 1546, the cardinal called her his child. On the night of his murder, he is said to have been with his favorite mistress, Marion Ogilvie.

Side by side with the decline of the monastic institutions, there prevailed among the monks of the 15th century a most exaggerated notion of the sanctifying influence of the monastic vow. According to Luther, the monks of his day recognized two grades of Christians, the perfect and the imperfect. To the former the monastics belonged. Their vow was regarded as a second baptism which cleared those who received it from all stain, restored them to the divine image and put them in a class with the angels. Luther was encouraged by his superiors to feel, after he had taken the vow, that he was as pure as a child. This second regeneration had been taught by St. Bernard and Thomas Aquinas. Thomas said that it may with reason be

---

may have at least 20 pence a day to sleep an hour with a friar, a monk or a priest. Who is she that would labor for a groat a day and may have at least 12 pence a day to be a bawd to a priest, monk or friar?"

[1] See James Gairdner in *Engl. Hist. Rev.*, Jan., 1905.

[2] Dr. Tulloch says in his *Luther and other Leaders of the Reformation*, "Nowhere else had the clergy reached such a pitch of flagrant and disgraceful

affirmed that any one " entering religion," that is, taking the monastic vow, thereby received remission of sins.[1]

§ 74. *Preaching*.

The two leading preachers of Europe during the last 50 years of the Middle Ages were Jerome Savonarola of Florence and John Geiler of Strassburg. Early in the 15th century, Gerson was led by the ignorance of the clergy to recommend a reduction of preaching,[2] but in the period just before the Reformation there was a noticeable revival of the practice of preaching in Germany and a movement in that direction was felt in England. Erasmus, as a cosmopolitan scholar, made an appeal for the function of the pulpit, which went to all portions of Western Europe.

In Germany, the importance of the sermon was emphasized by synodal decrees and homiletic manuals. Such synods were the synods of Eichstädt, 1463, Bamberg, 1491, Basel, 1503, Meissen, 1504. Surgant's noted *Handbook on the Art of Preaching* praised the sermon as the instrument best adapted to lead the people to repentance and inflame Christian love and called it " the way of life, the ladder of virtue and the gate of paradise." [3] It was pronounced as much a sin to let a word from the pulpit fall unheeded as to spill a drop of the sacramental wine. In the penitential books and the devotional manuals of the time, stress was laid upon the duty of attending preaching,

iniquity and the Roman Catholic religion such an utter corruption of all that is good as in Scotland."

[1] Bernard in Migne, 182 : 889, Th. Aq. *Summa*, II. 2, q. 189. Denifle, *Luther und Lutherthum*, I. 208, makes the monstrous charge of deliberate lying and knavery against Luther for his treatment of monkish baptism. Kolde : *Denifle's Beschimpfung M. Luthers*, Leipz., 1904, pp. 33–49, shows the justice of Luther's representations. Their truth is not affected by the statement of Joseph Ries : *Das geistliche Leben nach der Lehre d. hl. Bernard*, p. 36, namely that Bernard and the Church held that outside the convents there may be some who are in the state of perfection while inside cloistral walls there may be those who are in the imperfect state.

[2] *Contra vanam curiositatem*, Du Pin's ed., 1728, I. 106 sqq.

[3] *Manuale curatorum predicandi præbens modum*, 1503, quoted by Janssen, I. 38.

as upon the mass.   Those who left church before the sermon
began were pronounced deserving excommunication.   Wolff's
penitential manual of 1478 made the neglect of the sermon a
violation of the 4th commandment.   The efficacy of sermons
was vouched for in the following story.   A good man met the
devil carrying a bag full of boxes packed with salves.   Holding up a black box, the devil said that he used it to put people
to sleep during the preaching service.   The preachers, he continued, greatly interfered with his work, and often by a single
sermon snatched from him persons he had held in his power
for 30 or 40 years.[1]

By the end of the 15th century, all the German cities and
most of the larger towns had regular preaching.[2]   It was a common thing to endow pulpits, as in Mainz, 1465, Basel, 1469,
Strassburg, 1478, Constance, Augsburg, Stuttgart and other
cities.   The popular preachers drew large audiences.   So it was
with Geiler of Strassburg, whose ministry lasted 30 years.
10,000 are said to have gathered to hear the sermons of the
barefooted monk, Jacob Mene of Cologne, when he held forth
at Frankfurt, the people standing in the windows and crowd-
ing up against the organ to hear him.   It was Mene's practice
to preach a sermon from 7–8 in the morning, and again after
the noon meal.   On a certain Good Friday he prolonged his
effort five hours, from 3–8 P.M.   According to Luther, towns
were glad to give itinerant monks 100 gulden for a series of
Lenten discourses.

Other signs of the increased interest felt in sermons were
the homiletic cyclopædias of the time furnishing materials derived from the Bible, the Fathers, classic authors and from the
realm of tale and story.   To these must be added the *plenaria*,
collections from the Gospels and Epistles with glosses and

---

[1] Wolff's and the Augsburger *Beichtbüchlein*, ed. Falk, pp. 78, 87; *Gute
Vermaninge*, ed. by Bahlmann, p. 73 ; Nicholas Russ of Rostock as quoted by
Janssen, I. 39.   *Der Spiegel des Sünders* about 1470.   See Geffcken, p. 59.
Seelentrost, 1483, etc.

[2] Cruel, pp. 647, 652, closes his treatment of the German pulpit in the M.A.
with the observation that the old view, reducing the amount of preaching in
Germany in the 15th century, must be abandoned.   Cruel's view is now generally accepted by Protestant writers.

comments. The *plenarium* of Guillermus, professor in Paris,
went through 75 editions before 1500. Collections of model
sermons were also issued, some of which had an extensive circulation. The collection of John Nider, d. 1439, passed through
17 editions. His texts were invariably subjected to a threefold
division. The collection of the Franciscan, John of Werden,
who died at Cologne about 1450, passed through 25 editions.
John Herolt's volume of *Sermons of a Disciple — Sermones
discipuli* — went through 41 editions before 1500 and is computed to have had a circulation of no less than 40,000 copies.[1]
One of the most popular of the collections called *Parati sermones — The Ready Man's Sermons* — appeared anonymously.
Its title was taken from 1 Peter 4 : 6, "ready — *paratus* — to
judge the quick and the dead" and Ps. 119 : 60, "I made
haste [ready] and delayed not to observe thy commandments."
In setting forth the words " Be not unwise but understanding
what the will of the Lord is" the author says that such wisdom
is taught by the animals.   1. By the lion who brushes out his
paw-prints with his tail so that the hunter is thrown off the
track. So we should with penance erase the marks of our sins
that the devil may not find us out.   2. The serpent which
closes both ears to the seducer, one ear with his tail and the
other by holding it to the ground.   Against the devil we
should shut our ears by the two thoughts of death and eternity.
3. The ant from which we learn industry in making provision
for the future.   4. A certain kind of fish which sucks itself
fast to the rock in times of storm.   So we should adhere closely
to the rock, Christ Jesus, by thoughts of his passion and thus
save ourselves from the surging of the waves of the world.
Such materials show that the homiletic instinct was alert and
the preachers anxious to catch the attention of the people and
impart biblical truth.

The sermons of the German preachers of the 15th century
were written now in Latin, now in German.   The more famous
of the Latin sermonizers were Gabriel Biel, preacher in Mainz
and then professor in Tübingen, d. 1495, and Jacob Jüterbock,
1383–1465, Carthusian prior in Erfurt and professor in the

[1] Janssen, I : 43.

university in that city.[1]   Among the notable preachers who
preached in German were John Herolt of Basel, already mentioned; the Franciscan John Gritsch whose sermons reached
26 editions before 1500; the Franciscan, John Meder of Basel
whose Lenten discourses on the Prodigal Son of the year 1494
reached 36 editions and Ulrich Krafft, pastor in Ulm, 1500 to
1516, and author of the two volumes, *The Spiritual Battle* and
Noah's Ark.

More famous than all others was Geiler of Strassburg,
usually called from his father's birthplace, Geiler of Kaisersberg, born in Schaffhausen, 1445, died in Strassburg, 1510.
He and his predecessor, Bertholdt of Regensburg, have the
reputation of being the most powerful preachers of mediæval
Germany.   For more than a quarter of a century he stood in
the cathedral pulpit of Strassburg, the monarch of preachers
in the North.   After pursuing his university studies in Freiburg and Basel, Geiler was made professor at Freiburg, 1476.
His pulpit efforts soon made him a marked man.   In accepting the call as preacher in the cathedral at Strassburg, he
entered into a contract to preach every Sunday and on all festival and fast days.   He continued to fill the pulpit till within
two months of his death and lies interred in the cathedral
where he preached.[2]

" The Trumpet of Strassburg," as Geiler was called, gained
his fame as a preacher of moral and social reforms.   He advocated no doctrinal changes.   Called upon, 1500, to explain
his public declaration that the city councillors were "all of
the devil," he issued 21 articles demanding that games of
chance be prohibited, drinking halls closed, the Sabbath and
festival days observed, the hospitals properly cared for and
monkish mendicancy regulated.

---

[1] Ullman : *Reformers*, etc., I. 229 sqq., classes him with the Reformers before the Reformation, and chiefly on the basis of his tract, *De septem ecclesiæ
statibus.*

[2] Lives of Geiler by Abbé L. Dacheux, 1876, and Lindemann, 1877.   For
earlier biographies by Beatus Rhenanus, etc., see Lorenzi, I. 1.   Geiler's
sermons have been issued by Dacheux : *Die ältesten Schriften G.'s*, Freib.,
1882, and by Ph. de Lorenzi, 4 vols., Treves, 1881–1883, with a *Life*.   See also
Cruel, *Deutsche Predigt*, pp. 538–576 ; H. Hering : *Lehrbuch der Homiletik*,
p. 81 sq., and Kawerau, in Herzog VI. 427–432, Janssen, I. 136 sqq.

He was a preacher of the people and now amused, now stung them, by anecdotes, plays on words, descriptions, proverbs, sallies of wit, humor and sarcasm.[1] He attacked popular follies and fashions and struck at the priests " many of whom never said mass," and at the convents in which " neither religion nor virtue was found and the living was lax, lustful, dissolute and full of all levity." [2] Mediæval superstition he served up to his hearers in good doses. He was a firm believer in astrology, ghosts and witches.

Geiler's style may seem rude to the polite age in which we live, but it reached the ear of his own time. The high as well as the low listened. Maximilian went to hear Geiler when he was in Strassburg. No one could be in doubt about the preacher's meaning. In a series of 65 passion sermons, he elaborated a comparison between Christ and a ginger cake — the German *Lebkuchen*. Christ is composed of the bean meal of the deity, the old fruit meal of the body and the wheat meal of the soul. To these elements is added the honey of compassion. He was thrust into the oven of affliction and is divided by preachers into many parts and distributed among the people. In other sermons, he compared perfect Christians to sausages.

In seven most curious discourses on *Der Hase im Pfeffer* — an idiomatic expression for That's the Rub — based on Prov. 30 : 26, " The coney is a weak folk," he made 14 comparisons between the coney and the good Christian. The coney runs better up hill than down, as a good Christian should do. The coney has long ears as also a Christian should have, especially monastics, attending to what God has to say. The coney must be roasted; and so must also the Christian pass through the furnace of trial. The coney being a lank beast must be cooked in lard, so also must the Christian be surrounded with love and devotion lest he be scorched in the furnace. In

---

[1] A remarkable specimen of his power to play on words is given in his use of the word *Affe*, monkey, which he applied to ten different classes of the devil's dupes. See Cruel, p. 543. *Bischof*, bishop, he derived from *Beiss-schaf* — bite-sheep — because prelates bit the sheep instead of taking them to pasture.

[2] Kawerau, VI. 428.

64 discourses, preached two years before his death, Geiler
brought out the spiritual lessons to be derived from ants and
in another series he elaborated the 25 sins of the tongue.   In
a course of 20 sermons to business men, he depicted the six
market days and the devil as a pedler going about selling
his wares.   He preached 17 sermons on the lion in which the
king of beasts was successively treated as the symbol of the
good man, the worldly man, Christ and the devil; 12 of these
sermons were devoted to the ferocious activities of the devil.
A series on the Human Tree comprised no less than 163 discourses running from the beginning of Lent, 1495, to the close
of Lent, 1496.

During the last two years of the 15th century, Geiler
preached 111 homilies on Sebastian Brant's Ship of Fools —
Narren-schiff — all drawn from the text Eccles. 1: 15 as it reads
in the Vulgate, " the fools are without number."   Through
Geiler's intervention Brant had been brought to Strassburg
from Basel, where he was professor.   His famous work, which
is a travesty upon the follies of his time, employed the figure
of a ship for the transport of his fools because it was the
largest engine of transportation the author knew of.   Very
humorously Brant placed himself in the moderator's chair
while all the other fools were gathered in front of him.   He
himself took the rôle of the Book-fool.   Among other follies
which are censured are the doings of the mendicants, the
traffic in relics and indulgences and the multiplication of benefices in single hands.[1]   Geiler's homilies equal Brant's poetry
in humor.   Both were true to life.   No preacher of the Middle Ages held the popular ear so long as Geiler of Strassburg
and no popular poet, not even Will Langland, more effectually wrote for the masses than Sebastian Brant.

In this period, the custom came to be quite general to preach
from the nave of the church instead of from the choir railing.
Preachers limited their discourses by hour-glasses, a custom
later transplanted to New England.[2]   Sermons were at times un-

[1] See Lorenzi, II. 1–321.
[2] Cruel, quoting Surgant, p. 635.   Erasmus, *Praise of Folly*, p. 95, speaks of
the preacher " spending his glass in telling pleasant stories."

duly extended. Gerhard Groote sometimes preached for three hours during Lent and John Gronde extended some of his discourses to six hours, mercifully, however, dividing them into two parts with a brief breathing-spell between, profitable as may well be surmised alike to the preacher and the hearers. Geiler, who at one time had been inclined to preach on without regard to time, limited his discourses to a single hour.

The criticisms which preachers passed upon the customs of the day show that human nature was pretty much the same then as it is now and that the "good old times" are not to be sought for in that age. All sorts of habits were held up to ridicule and scorn. Drunkenness and gluttony, the dance and the street comedy, the dress of women and the idle lounging of rich men's sons, usury and going to church to make a parade were among the subjects dwelt upon. Again and again, Geiler of Strassburg returned to the lazy sons of the rich who spent their time in retailing scandals and doing worse, more silly in their dress than the women, fops who "thought themselves somebody because their fathers were rich." He also took special notice of women and their fripperies. He condemned their belts, sometimes made of silk and adorned with gold, costing as much as 40 or 50 gulden, their padded busts and their extensive wardrobes, enabling them to wear for a week at a time two different garments each day and a third one for a dancing party or the play. He launched out against their long hair, left to fall down over the back and crowned with ribbons or small caps such as the men wore. As examples of warning, Absalom and Holofernes were singled out, the former caught by his hair in the branches of the tree and Holofernes ensnared by the adornments of Judith. Geiler called upon the city authorities to come to the help of society and the preacher and legislate against such evils.[1]

Another preacher, Hollen, condemned the long trails which women wore as "the devil's wagon," for neither men nor angels

---

[1] See Cruel's chapter on pulpit polemics, pp. 617-629 and Janssen, I. 440 sqq. A preacher in Ulm, John Capistran, about 1450, was put by the aldermen in the lock-up for his excessive vehemence in condemning the prevailing luxury in dress and other questionable social customs.

but only the devil has a caudal appendage. As for dancing,
especially the round dances, the devil was the head concert-
master at such entertainments and the higher the dancers
jumped, the deeper their fall into hell and, the more firmly they
held on to each other with their hands, the more closely did the
devil tighten his hold upon them. Dancing was represented
by the preachers as an occasion of much profligacy.

In ridiculing the preaching of his day, Erasmus held forth
the preachers' ignorance, their incongruous introductions,
their use of stories from all departments without any discrimination, their old women's tales and the frivolous topics they
chose — *aniles fabulæ et questiones frivolæ.* A famous passage
in which the great scholar disparages the preaching of the
monks and friars begins with the words: —

All their preaching is mere stage-playing, and their delivery the very transports of ridicule and drollery. Good Lord! how mimical are these gestures!
What heights and falls in their voice! What toning, what bawling, what singing, what squeaking, what grimaces, making of mouths, apes' faces, and dis-
torting of their countenance ; and this art of oratory as a choice mystery, they
convey down by tradition to one another.[1]

Erasmus deserves credit for discerning the need of the times,
and recommending the revival of the practice of preaching and
the mission of preachers to the heathen nations.   His views
were set forth in the *Ecclesiastes* or *Preacher*, a work written
during the Freiburg period and filling 275 pages,[2] each double
the size of the pages of this volume. The chief purpose of
preaching he defined to be instruction. Every preacher is a
herald of Christ, who was himself the great preacher. The
office of preaching is superior in dignity to the office of kings.
" Among the charisms of the Spirit, none is more noble and efficacious than preaching. To be a dispenser of the celestial philosophy and a messenger of the divine will is excelled by no
office in the Church." It is quite in accord with Erasmus' high
regard for the teaching function, that he magnifies the instruc-
tional element of the sermon. Writing to Sapidus, 1516, he
said, " to be a schoolmaster is next to being a king." [3]

[1] *Praise of Folly*, 141 sqq.   [2] Basel, ed. 1540, pp. 643-917.
[3] Nichols: *Erasmus' Letters*, II. 235.

Of the English pulpit, there is little to say. We hear of preaching at St. Paul's Cross and at other places, but there is no evidence that preaching was usual. No volumes of English sermons issued from the printing-press. Colet is the only English preacher of the 15th century of historical importance. The churchly counsel given to priests to impart instruction to the people, issued by the Lambeth synod of 1281, stands almost solitary. In 1466, Archbishop Nevill of York did no more than to repeat this legislation.

In Scotland the history of the pulpit begins with Knox. Dr. Blaikie remarks that, for the three centuries before the Reformation, scarcely a trace of Christian preaching can be found in Scotland worthy the name. The country had no Wyclif, as it had no Anselm.[1] Hamilton and Wishart, Knox's immediate forerunners, were laymen.

The Abbé Dr. Gasquet in a chapter on A Forgotten English Preacher in his *Old Eng. Bible and other Essays* gives extracts from the MS. sermon of Thomas Brunton, Bishop of Rochester, 1372-1389. After saying that we know very little about mediæval preaching in England, Dr. Gasquet, p. 54, remarks that it is perhaps just as well, as the sermons were probably dull and that "the modern sermon" has to be endured as a necessary evil. In his chapter on Teaching and Preaching, pp. 244-284, in his *Eve of the Reformation*, the same author returns to the subject, but the chapter itself gives the strongest evidence of the literary barrenness of the English Church in the closing years of the Middle Ages and the dearth of preaching and public instruction. By far the larger part of the chapter, pp. 254-280, is taken up with quotations from Sir Thomas More, the tract *Dives and Pauper* and other tracts, to show that the doctrine of the worship of images and saints was not taught in its crass form and with a statement of the usefulness of miracle-plays as a means of popular religious instruction. Dr. Gasquet lays stress upon the "simple instruction" given by the English priesthood in the Middle Ages as opposed to formal sermons which he confesses "were probably by no means so frequent as in these times. He makes the astounding assertion, p. 245, that religious instruction as a means of social and moral improvement was not one of the primary aims of the Reformation. The very opposite is proved by the efforts of Luther, Calvin and Knox to secure the establishment of schools in every hamlet and the catechisms which the two former prepared and the numerous catechisms prepared by their fellow Reformers. And what of their habit of constant preaching? Luther preached day after day. One of the first signs of the Reformation in Geneva was that St. Pierre and St. Gervaise were opened for preaching daily. Calvin incorporated into his ecclesiastical polity as one of the orders the ministry, the teaching body.

[1] W. G. Blaikie : *The Preachers of Scotland*, p. 36.

§ 75. *Doctrinal Reformers.*

A group of theologians appeared in Northwestern Germany who, on the one hand, were closely associated by locality and training with the Brothers of the Common Life and, on the other, anticipated the coming age by the doctrinal reforms which they proposed.   On the latter account, John of Goch, John of Wesel and Wessel of Gansfort have been properly classed with Wyclif and Huss as Reformers before the Reformation.[1] Erasmus has no place at their side for, with his satire on ceremonies and church conditions, the question is always raised of his sincerity.   Savonarola suggested no doctrinal changes.   Among the new views emphasized by one or all of these three men were the final authority of the Scriptures, the fallibility of the pope, the sufficiency of divine grace for salvation irrespective of priestly mediation, and the distinction between the visible and the invisible Church.   However, but for the Protestant Reformation, it is not probable their voices would have been heard beyond the century in which they lived.

John Pupper, 1400–1475, usually called John of Goch from his birthplace, a hamlet on the lower Rhine near Cleves, seems to have been trained in one of the schools of the Brothers of the Common Life, and then studied in Cologne and perhaps in Paris.   He founded a house of Augustinians near Mecheln, remaining at its head till his death.   His writings were not published till after the beginning of the Reformation.   He anticipated that movement in asserting the supreme authority of the Bible.   The Fathers are to be accepted only so far as they follow the canonical Scriptures.   In contrast to the works of the philosophers and the Schoolmen, the Bible is a

---

[1] This group of men forms the subject of Ullmann's notable work *The Reformers before the Reformation* published in 1841.   He followed Flacius, Walch and others before him who had treated them as precursors of the Reformation.   Hase: *Kirchengesch.*, II. 551 ; Köstlin: *Leben Luthers*, I. 13 ; Funk, p. 382, and others still hold to this classification.   Loofs: *Dogmengesch.*, p. 658, takes another view and says " they were not Reformers before the Reformation, nevertheless they bear witness that, in the closing years of the Middle Ages, the preparation made for the Reformation was not merely negative." Janssen, I. 745, treats them as followers of Huss.

book of life; theirs, books of death.[1] He also called in question the merit of monastic vows and the validity of the distinction between the higher and lower morality upon which
monasticism laid stress. What is included under the higher
morality is within the reach of all Christians and not the
property of monks only. He renounced the Catholic view of
justification without stating with clearness the evangelical
theory."[2]

John Ruchrath von Wesel, d. 1481, attacked the hierarchy
and indulgences and was charged on his trial with calling in
question almost all the distinctive Roman Catholic tenets.
He was born in Oberwesel on the Rhine between Mainz and
Coblentz. He taught at the University of Erfurt and, in
1458, was chosen its vice-rector. Luther bore testimony to
his influence when he said, "I remember how Master John
Wesalia ruled the University of Erfurt by his writings
through the study of which I also became a master."[3] Leaving Erfurt, he was successively professor in Basel and cathedral preacher in Mainz and Worms.

In 1479, Wesel was arraigned for heresy before the Inquisition at Mainz.[4] Among the charges were that the Scriptures
are alone a trustworthy source of authority; the names of the
predestinate are written in the book of life and cannot be
erased by a priestly ban; indulgences do not profit; Christ is
not pleased with festivals of fasting, pilgrimages or priestly
celibacy; Christ's body can be in the bread without any
change of the bread's substance: pope and councils are not
to be obeyed if they are out of accord with the Scriptures;

---

[1] Goch's words are *Sola scriptura canonica fidem indubiam et irrefragabilem
habet auctoritatem.* The writer in Wetzer-Welte concedes Goch's depreciation of the Schoolmen and of Thomas Aquinas in particular, whom at one
point Goch calls a prince of error — *princeps erroris.*

[2] Ullmann, I. 91, 149 sqq., asserts that Goch stated the doctrine of justification by faith alone. Clemen and the writer in Wetzer-Welte modify this
judgment. Walch, as quoted by Ullmann, p. 150, gives 9 points in which
Goch anticipated the Reformation.

[3] Catholic writers like Funk, p. 390, Wetzer-Welte and Janssen, I. 746,
speak of Wesel as one of the false teachers of the Middle Ages and find many
of the doctrines of the Reformation in his writings.

[4] For detailed account of the trial, Ullman, I. 383–405.

he whom God chooses will be saved irrespective of pope and priests, and all who have faith will enjoy as much blessedness as prelates.   Wesel also made the distinction between the visible and the invisible Church and defined the Church as the aggregation of all the faithful who are bound together by love — *collectio omnium fidelium caritate copulatorum*.   In his trial, he was accused of having had communication with the Hussites.   In matters of historical criticism, he was also in advance of his age, casting doubt upon some of the statements of the Athanasian Creed, abandoning the application of the term Catholic to the Apostles' Creed and pronouncing the addition of the *filioque* clause — and from the Son — unwarranted.   The doctrines of indulgences and the fund of merit he pronounced unscriptural and pious frauds.   The elect are saved wholly through the grace of God — *sola Dei gratia salvantur electi.*

At the request of Diether of Isenburg, archbishop of Mainz, the Universities of Cologne and Heidelberg sent delegates to the trial.   The accused was already an old man, leaning on his staff, when he appeared before the tribunal.   Lacking strength to stand by the heretical articles, he agreed to submit "to mother Church and the teachings of the doctors."   A public recantation in the cathedral followed, and his books were burnt.[1]   These punishments were not sufficient to expiate his offence and he was sentenced to imprisonment for life in the Augustinian convent of Mainz, where he died.

Among Wesel's reported sayings, which must have seemed most blasphemous to the devout churchman of the time, are the following: " The consecrated oil is not better than the oil used for your cakes in the kitchen." " If you are hungry, eat. You may eat a good capon on Friday." "If Peter established fasting, it was in order that he might get more for his fish " on fast days.   To certain monastics, he said, " Not religion " (that is, monastic vows) "but God's grace saves," *religio nullum salvat sed gratia Dei.*

---

[1] During his trial, Wesel acknowledged the following writings as his: 1, *Super modo obligationis legum humanarum ad quemdam Nicolaum de Bohemia.* 2, *De potestate eccles.*   3, *De jejuniis.*   4, *De indulgentiis.*

A still nearer approach to the views of the Reformers was made by Wessel Gansfort, commonly called John Wessel,[1] born in Groningen, 1420, died 1489. In his Preface to Wessel's writings, 1522, Luther said, "If I had read Wessel earlier, my enemies might have said that Luther drew everything from Wessel, so well do our two minds agree." Wessel attended school at Zwolle, where he met Thomas à Kempis of the neighboring convent of Mt. St. Agnes. The story ran that when Thomas pointed him to the Virgin, Wessel replied, "Father, why did you not rather point me to Christ who calls the heavy-laden to himself?" He continued his studies in Cologne, where he took Greek and Hebrew, in Heidelberg and in Paris. He declined a call to Heidelberg. In 1470, we find him in Rome. The story went that, when Sixtus IV. invited him to follow the common custom of visitors to the Vatican and make a request, the German student replied that he would like to have a Hebrew or Greek manuscript of the Bible from the Vatican. The pope, laughing, said, "Why did you not ask for a bishopric, you fool?" Wessel's reply was "Because I do not need it."

Wessel spent some time in Basel, where he met Reuchlin. In 1473, the bishop of Utrecht wrote that many were seeking his life and invited him back to Holland. His last years, from 1474 on, Wessel spent with the Brothers of the Common Life at Mt. St. Agnes, and in the nuns' convent at Groningen. There, in the place of his birth, he lies buried. His last words were, "I know no one save Jesus, the Crucified."

Wessel enjoyed a reputation for great learning. He escaped arraignment at the hands of the Inquisition, but was violently attacked after his death in a tract on indulgences, by Jacob Hoeck, Dean of Naaldwyk. None of Wessel's writings were published till after the outbreak of the Reformation. Although he did not reach the doctrine of justification by faith, he declared that pope and councils may err and he defined the Church to be the communion of the saints. The unity of the Church does not lie in the pope — *unitas ecclesiæ sub uno papa*

[1] The name "*John*" is disputed by Muurling and Wetzer-Welte and shown by Paulus to be a mistake. Gansfort, or Goesevort, was the name of the village from which the family came.

tantum accidentalis est, adeo ut non sit necessaria.   He laid
stress upon the faith of the believer in partaking of the eucharist or, rather, upon his hunger and thirst after the sacrament.
But he did not deny the sacrifice of the mass or the validity
of the communion under one kind.   He gave up the judicial
element in priestly absolution.[1]   There is no such thing as
works of supererogation, for each is under obligation to do all
he can and to do less is to sin.   The prerogative of the keys
belongs to all believers.   Plenary indulgences are a detestable
invention of the papacy to fill its treasury.

In 1522, a Dutch lawyer, von Hoen, joining with other
Netherlanders, sent Luther a copy of some of Wessel's writings.[2]   In the preface which the Reformer wrote for the Wittenberg edition, he said that, as Elijah of old, so he had felt
himself to be the only one left of the prophets of God but he
had found out that God had also had his prophets in secret
like Wessel.

These three German theologians, Goch, Wesel and Wessel,
were quietly searching after the marks of the true Church and
the doctrine of justification by faith in Christ alone.   Without knowing it, they were standing on the threshold of the
Reformation.

§ 76.   *Girolamo Savonarola.*

Ecce gladius Domini super terram cito et velociter.

In the closing decade of the 15th century the city of Florence
seemed to be on the eve of becoming a model municipality, a
pattern of Christian morals, a theocracy in which Christ was
acknowledged as sovereign.   In the movement looking towards
this change, the chief actor was Jerome Savonarola, prior of the

[1] See Ritschl : *The Christian Doctr. of Justification and Reconciliation.*
Edinb. ed., p. 481 sq.

[2] In a letter accompanying the gift, Honius wrote that the words "This is
my body " meant "This represents my body."   For Luther's reply, see Köstlin : *Luthers Leben,* I. 701.   For the 1st edd. of Wessel's works, see Doedes,
pp. 435, 442.   Doedes in *Studien u. Kritiken,* for 1870, p. 409, asks, "Who
in the latter half of the 15th cent. had so much genuine faith and evangelical
knowledge as this man who was always the scholar of the Lord Jesus Christ
and nothing else ? "

SAVONAROLA

Dominican convent of St. Mark's, the most imposing preacher
of the Middle Ages and one of the most noteworthy preachers
of righteousness since St. Paul.   Against the dark moral back-
ground of his generation he appears as a broad sheet of northern
light with its coruscations, mysterious and protentous, but also
quickly disappearing. His message was the prophet's cry, " Who
shall abide the day of His coming and who shall stand when He
appeareth ? "

Savonarola, born in Ferrara Sept. 21, 1452, died in Florence
May 23, 1498, was the third of seven children.   Choosing his
grandfather's profession, he entered upon the study of medicine,
from which he was turned away by a deepening impression of the
corruption of society and disappointment at the refusal of a family
of Strozzi, living at Ferrara, to give him their daughter in marriage.   At the age of 23, he secretly left his father's house and
betook himself to Bologna, where he assumed the Dominican
habit.   Two days after his arrival in Bologna, he wrote thus to
his father explaining the reason of his abrupt departure.

I could not endure any longer the wickedness of the blinded peoples of Italy.
Virtue I saw despised everywhere and vices exalted and held in honor. With
great warmth of heart, I made daily a short prayer to God that He might release me from this vale of tears. 'Make known to me the way,' I cried, ' the
way in which I should walk for I lift up my soul unto Thee,' and God in His
infinite mercy showed me the way, unworthy as I am of such distinguishing
grace.[1]

He begged his father to console his mother and referred him
to a poem by his pen on the contempt of the world, which he
had left among his papers.   In this letter and several letters to
his mother, which are extant, is shown the young monk's warm
affection for his parents and his brothers and sisters.

In the convent, the son studied Augustine and Thomas
Aquinas and became familiar with the Scriptures, sections of
which he committed to memory.   Two copies of the Bible are
extant in Florence, containing copious notes in Savonarola's
own handwriting, made on the margin, between the printed lines

[1] The translation is from Schottmüller, pp. 2, 3.   This writer gives two of
Savonarola's letters to his mother.

and on added leaves.[1]   After his appointment as provincial, he emphasized the study of the Bible in Hebrew and Greek.

In 1481, he was sent to Florence, where he became an inmate of St. Mark's.   The convent had been rebuilt by Cosimo de Medici and its walls illuminated by the brush of Fra Angelico. At the time of Savonarola's arrival, the city was at the height of its fame as a seat of culture and also as the place of light-hearted dissipation under the brilliant patronage of Lorenzo the Magnificent.

The young monk's first efforts in the pulpit in Florence were a failure.   The congregation at San Lorenzo, where he preached during the Lenten season, fell to 25 persons.   Fra Mariano da Gennazzano, an Augustinian, was the popular favorite.   The Dominican won his first fame by his Lenten sermons of 1486, when he preached at Brescia on the Book of Revelation.   He represented one of the 24 elders rising up and pronouncing judgments upon the city for its wickedness.   In 1489, he was invited back to Florence by Lorenzo at the suggestion of Pico della Mirandola, who had listened to Savonarola's eloquence at Reggio. During the remaining nine years of his life, the city on the Arno was filled with Savonarola's personality.   With Catherine of Siena, he shares the fame of being the most religious of the figures that have walked its streets.   During the first part of this short period, he had conflict with Lorenzo and, during the second, with Alexander VI., all the while seeking by his startling warnings and his prophecies to bring about the regeneration of the city and make it a model of civic and social righteousness.   From Aug. 1, 1490, when he appeared in the pulpit of St. Mark's, the people thronged to hear him whether he preached there or in the cathedral.   In 1491, he was made prior of his convent.   To preaching he added writings in the department of philosophy and tracts on humility, prayer and the love of Jesus.   He was of middle height, dark complexion, lustrous eyes dark gray in color, thick lips and aquiline nose.   His features, which of them-

---

[1] The one, the Vulgate printed in Basel, 1491, the other in Venice, 1492.   See Luotto: *Dello Studio*, etc.   This author draws a parallel between Leo XIII.'s commendation of the study of the Bible and Savonarola's emphasis upon it as the seat of authority.

selves would have been called coarse, attracted attention by the
serious contemplative expression which rested upon them, and
the flash of his eye.

Savonarola's sermons were like the flashes of lightning and
the reverberations of thunder. It was his mission to lay the
axe at the root of dissipation and profligacy rather than to
depict the consolations of pardon and communion with God.
He drew more upon the threatenings of the divine wrath than
upon the refreshing springs of the divine compassion. Tender
descriptions of the divine love and mercy were not wanting in
his sermons, but the woes pronounced upon the sinfulness of his
time exceeded the gentle appeals. He was describing his own
method, when he said, "I am like the hail. Cover thyself
lest it come down upon thee, and strike thee. And remember
that I said unto thee, Cover thy head with a helmet, that is
clothe thyself with virtue and no hail stone will touch thee." [1]

In the time of his greatest popularity, the throngs waited
hours at the doors of the cathedral for the preacher's arrival
and it has been estimated by Villari, that audiences of 10,000
or 12,000 hung on his discourses. Like fields of grain under
the wind, the feelings of his audiences were swayed by the
preacher's voice. Now they burned with indignation: now
they were softened to tears. "I was overcome by weeping and
could not go on." So wrote the reporter while taking down
a sermon, and Savonarola himself felt the terrible strain of his
efforts and often sank back into his seat completely exhausted.
His message was directed to the clergy, high and low, as well as
to the people and the flashes of his indignation often fell upon
the palace of Lorenzo. The clergy he arraigned for their greed
of prebends and gold and their devotion to outer ceremonies
rather than to the inner life of the soul. Florence he addressed
in endearing terms as the object of his love. "My Florence,"
he was wont to exclaim. Geneva was no more the city of
Calvin or Edinburgh of Knox than was Florence the city of

---

[1] Sermon, March 14, 1498. Schottmüller, p. 111. Roscoe: *Life of Lorenzo*,
ch. VIII., says: "The divine word from the lips of Savonarola, descended
not amongst his audience like the dews of heaven. It was the piercing hail,
the sweeping whirlwind, the destroying sword."

Savonarola.   Portraying the insincerity of the clergy, he said : —

In these days, prelates and preachers are chained to the earth by the love of earthly things. The care of souls is no longer their concern. They are content with the receipt of revenue. The preachers preach to please princes and to be praised by them. They have done worse. They have not only destroyed the Church of God. They have built up a new Church after their own pattern. Go to Rome and see! In the mansions of the great prelates there is no concern save for poetry and the oratorical art. Go thither and see! Thou shalt find them all with the books of the humanities in their hands and telling one another that they can guide mens' souls by means of Virgil, Horace and Cicero. . . . The prelates of former days had fewer gold mitres and chalices and what few they possessed were broken up and given to relieve the needs of the poor. But our prelates, for the sake of obtaining chalices, will rob the poor of their sole means of support. Dost thou not know what I would tell thee! What doest thou, O Lord! Arise, and come to deliver thy Church from the hands of devils, from the hands of tyrants, from the hands of iniqui-tous prelates.[1]

Dizzy flights of fancy abounded in Savonarola's discourses and took the place of calm and logical exposition.   On the evening before he preached his last sermon in Advent, 1492, Savonarola beheld in the middle of the sky a hand holding a sword with the inscription, Behold the sword of the Lord will descend suddenly and quickly upon the earth — *Ecce gladius Domini super terram cito et velociter*.   Suddenly the sword was turned toward the earth, the sky was darkened, swords, arrows and flames rained down.   The heavens quaked with thunder and the world became a prey to famine and death. The vision was ended by a command to the preacher to make these things known.   Again and again, in after years did he refer to this prophetic vision.[2]   Its memory was also preserved by a medal, representing on one side Savonarola and on the other a sword in the heavens held by a hand and pointing to a city beneath.

The inscription on the heavenly sword well represents the

[1] Villari, I. 183 sqq.
[2] So Nov. 1, 1494, etc. See Schottmüller, p. 28 sqq. The motto, *cito et velociter*, was repeated to Savonarola by the Virgin in his vision of heaven, 1495.

style of Savonarola's preaching. It was impulsive, pictorial, eruptive, startling, not judicial and instructive. And yet it made a profound impression on men of different classes. Pico della Mirandola the elder has described its marvellous effect upon himself. On one occasion, when he announced as his text Gen. 6: 17, " Behold I will bring the flood of waters upon the earth," Pico said he felt a cold shudder course through him, and his hair, as it were, stand on end. One is reminded of some of the impressions made by the sermons of Christmas Evans, the Welsh preacher, and the impression made by Whitefield's oratory upon Lord Chesterfield and Franklin. But the imagery of the sermon, brilliant and weird as it was, is no sufficient explanation of the Florentine preacher's power. The preacher himself was burning with religious passion. He felt deeply and he was a man of deep devotion. He had the eye of the mystic and saw beneath the external and ritual to the inner movements of spiritual power.

The biblical element was also a conspicuous feature of his preaching. Defective as Savonarola's exegesis was, the biblical element was everywhere in control of his thought and descriptions. His famous discourses were upon the ark, Exodus, and the prophets Haggai, Ezekiel, Amos and Hosea, and John's Revelation. He insisted upon the authority of Scripture. " I preach the regeneration of the Church," he said, " taking the Scriptures as my sole guide." [1]

Another element which gave to Savonarola's sermons their virility and power was the prophetic element. Savonarola was not merely the expounder of righteousness. He claimed to be a prophet revealing things which, to use his own words, " are beyond the scope of the knowledge which is natural to any creature." This element would have been a sign of weakness, if it had not been associated with a great personality, bent on noble ends. The severity of his warnings was often so fearful

---

[1] Rudelbach, pp. 333–346, presents an elaborate statement of Savonarola's attitude to the Bible, and quotes from one of his sermons on the Exodus thus: " The theologians of our time have soiled everything by their unseemly disputations as with pitch. They do not know a shred of the Bible, yea, they do not even know the names of its books."

that the preacher himself shrank back from delivering them. On one occasion, he spent the entire night in vigils and prayer that he might be released from the duty of making known a message, but in vain.   The sermon, he then went forth to preach, he called a terrific sermon.

Savonarola's confidence in his divine appointment to be the herald of special communications from above found expression not only from the pulpit but was set forth more calmly in two works, the *Manual of Revelations*, 1495, and a *Dialogue concerning Truth and Prophecy*, 1497.   The latter tract with a number of Savonarola's sermons were placed on the Index.   In the former, the author declared that for a long time he had by divine inspiration foretold future things but, bearing in mind the Saviour's words, "Give not that which is holy unto the dogs," he had practised reserve in such utterances. He expressed his conception of the office committed to him, when he said, "The Lord has put me here and has said to me, ' I have placed thee as a watchman in the centre of Italy . . . that thou mayest hear my words and announce them,' " Ezek. 3 : 17.   If we are inclined to regard Savonarola as having made a mistake in claiming prophetic foresight, we easily condone the mistake on the ground of his impassioned fervor and the pure motives by which he was animated.   To his prophecies he applied Christ's own words, that no jot or tittle should fail till they were fulfilled.

None of his messages was more famous than the one he received on his visit to paradise, March, 1495.   Before starting on his journey, a number of ladies offered to be his companions. Philosophy and Rhetoric he declined. Accepting the company of Faith, Simplicity, Prayer and Patience, he was met on his way by the devil in a monk's garb.[1]   Satan took occasion to present to him objections against the supernatural character of his predictions. Savonarola ought to have stopped with preaching virtue and denouncing vices and left prophecy alone.   A prophet was always accredited by miracles. True prophets were holy men and the devil asked Savonarola whether he felt he had reached a high grade of saintliness.   He then ventured to

---

[1] Lucas, pp. 55–61, gives a translation of the interview. Also Perrens, II. 167–177.

show that Savonarola's prophecies had not always been fulfilled. By this time they had arrived at the gates of paradise where prudently Satan took his leave. The walls of paradise — so Savonarola described them — were of diamonds and other precious stones. Ten banners surmounted them inscribed with the prayers of Florence. Hierarchies and principalities appeared on every side. With the help of angels, the visitor mounted a ladder to the throne of the Virgin who gave him a crown and a precious stone and then, with Jesus in her arms, supplicated the Trinity for Savonarola and the Florentines. Her request was granted and the Florentines promised an era of prosperity preceded by a period of sorrows. In this new time, the city would be more powerful and rich than ever before.

The question arises whether Savonarola was a genuine prophet or whether he was self-deluded, mistaking for the heated imaginations of his own religious fervor, direct communications from God.[1] Alexander VI. made Savonarola's "silly declaration of being a prophet" one of the charges against him.[2] In his *Manual of Revelations*, Savonarola advanced four considerations to prove that he was a true prophet — his own subjective certainty, the fulfilment of his predictions, their result in helping on the cause of moral reform in Florence and their acceptance by good people in the city. His prophecies, he said, could not have come from astrology for he rejected it, nor from a morbid imagination for this was inconsistent with his extensive knowledge of the Scriptures, nor from Satan for Satan hated his sermons and does not know future events.

For us, the only valid test is historical fact. Were Savonarola's prophecies fulfilled? The two prophecies, upon whose fulfilment stress is laid, were the political revolution in Florence, which occurred, and the coming of Charles VIII. from across the Alps. Savonarola saw in Charles a Cyrus whose advent would release Florence from her political bond-

[1] Luotto asserts that the dilemma is presented of the genuineness of Savonarola's predictions or downright imposture and he boldly supports the former view. Pastor, Villari, Lucas and others show that we are not narrowed down to this dilemma.

[2] In his first letter to Savonarola July 21, 1495. See the text in O'Neil, p. 10 sqq. Savonarola's reply, p. 26 sqq.

age and introduce an era of civil freedom.   He also predicted
Charles' subsequent retreat.   Commines, who visited Savonarola
in the convent of St.   Mark's after the trials which followed
Charles' advent in Italy had begun, went away impressed with
the friar's piety and candor, and declared that he predicted
with certainty to him and to the king, "things which no one
believed at the time and which have all been fulfilled since."[1]
On the other hand, such solemn prognostications failed of
fulfilment, as the extension of Florentine dominion even to
the recovery of Pisa, made May 28, 1495, and the speedy conversion of the Turks and Moors, made May 3, 1495.   The
latter purported to be a revelation from the Virgin on his visit
to paradise.   Where a certain number of solemn, prophetic
announcements remained unfulfilled, it is fair to suspect that
the remainder were merely the predictions of a shrewd observer watching the progress of events.   Many people trusted
the friar as a prophet but, as conditions became more and
more involved, they demanded with increasing insistence
that he should substantiate his prophetic claim by a miracle.
Even the predictions which came true in part, such as the
coming of Charles VIII. across the Alps, received no fulfilment in the way of a permanent improvement of conditions, such as Savonarola expected.   The statement of Prof.
Bonet-Maury expresses the case well.   Savonarola's prophetic
gift, so-called, was nothing more than political and religious
intuition.[2]   Some of his predictions were not in the line of
what Christian prophecies might be expected to be, such as
the rehumiliation of Pisa.   The Florentines felt flattered by
the high honor which the prophet paid to their city, and his

[1] Villari I. 355 and Bonet-Maury, p. 232.

[2] This is the view of Lucas, pp. 69 sq., Pastor, Creighton, III. 248, who
pronounces "the prophetic claims a delusion," and Villari.   The last author
says, I. 352 sqq., "Is it not possible that Savonarola was intoxicated by the
feeling that the earlier predictions had been fulfilled, and, as the difficulty of
maintaining his position in Florence in the last years of his life increased, he
felt forced to appeal more and more to this endowment as though it were
real?"   Rudelbach gives a long chapter to Savonarola's prophecies, pp. 281-
333.   Pastor discusses Savonarola's alleged prophetic gift thoroughly in his
Gesch. d. Päpste, III. 145 sqq., and in refutation of Luotto in his *Zur Beurtheilung*.

predictions of her earthly dominion as well as heavenly glory. In his *Manual of Revelations* he exclaims, " Whereas Florence is placed in the midst of Italy, like the heart in the midst of the body, God has chosen to select her, that she may be the centre from which this prophetic announcement should be spread abroad throughout all Italy."

No scene in Savonarola's career excels in moral grandeur and dramatic interest his appearance at the death-bed of Lorenzo the Magnificent, in 1492. History has few such scenes to offer. When it became apparent to the brilliant ruler of the Florentine state that his days were numbered, he felt unwilling to face the mysteries of death and the future without the absolution priestly prerogative pretends to be competent to confer. Savonarola and Lorenzo loved Florence with an equal love, though the one sought its glory through a career of righteousness and the other through a career of worldly dominion and glittering culture. The two leaders found no terms of agreement. Lorenzo had sought to win the preacher by personal attention and blandishments. He attended mass at St. Mark's. Savonarola held himself back as from an elegant worldling and the enemy of the liberties of Florence. " You see," said Lorenzo, "a stranger has come into my house, yet he will not stoop to pay me a visit." " He does not ask for me; let him go or stay at his pleasure," replied the friar to those who told him that Lorenzo was in the convent garden.

Five influential citizens of Florence called and suggested to the friar that he modify his public utterances. Recognizing that they had come at Lorenzo's instance, he bade them tell the prince to do penance for his sins, for the Lord is no respecter of persons and spares not the mighty of the earth. Lorenzo called upon Fra Mariano to publicly take Savonarola to task. This he did from the pulpit on Ascension Day, 1491. Lorenzo himself was present, but the preacher's charges overshot the mark, and Savonarola was more popular than ever. The prior of St. Mark's exclaimed, " Although I am a stranger in the city, and Lorenzo the first man in the state, yet shall I stay here and it is he who will go hence."

When the hour of death approached, Lorenzo was honest

with himself.   In vain did the physician, Lazzaro of Pavia,
resort to the last medical measure, a potion of distilled gems.
Farewell was said to Pico della Mirandola and other literary
friends, and Lorenzo gave his final counsels to his son, Piero.
The solemn rites of absolution and extreme unction were all
that remained for man to receive from man.   Lorenzo's confessor was within reach but the prince looked to St. Mark's.
" I know of no honest friar save this one," he exclaimed.   And
so Savonarola was summoned to the bedside in the villa
Careggi, two miles from the city.   The dying man wanted to
make confession of three misdeeds: the sack of Volterra, the
robbery of Monte delle Fanciulle and the merciless reprisals
after the Pazzi conspiracy.   The spiritual messenger then proceeded to present three conditions on which his absolution
depended.   The first was a strong faith in God's mercy.   The
dying man gave assent.   The second was that he restore his
ill-gotten wealth, or charge his sons to do it.   To this assent
was also given.   The third demand required that he give back
to Florence her liberties.   To this Lorenzo gave no response
and turned his face to the wall.   The priest withdrew and,
in a few hours, April 8, 1492, the ruler of Florence passed into
the presence of the omnipotent Judge who judgeth not according to the appearance but according to the heart and whose
mercy is everlasting.

The surmisal has been made that, if Savonarola had been
less rigid, he might have exercised an incalculable influence
for good upon the dying prince who was still susceptible of
religious impressions.[1]   But who can with probability conjecture the secrets of the divine purpose in such cases ?   Per-

[1] So Pastor, III. 141. The account given of Lorenzo's interview with
Savonarola is based upon Burlamacchi and Mirandola.   Politian, in a letter
to Jacopo Antiquario, gave a different account of the three demands and made
no mention of Savonarola's demand that Florence be restored her liberties.
He also added that Savonarola left the room pronouncing upon the dying man
a blessing.   Politian's version is accepted by Roscoe, ch. X., Creighton, III.
296–299 and Lucas, 83 sq.   The version given above is accepted by Villari,
168 sqq., W. Clark, p. 116, and the rigid critic Hase, p. 20.   Ranke did not see
his way clear to deny its truth and Reumont, II. 443, who denied it in the
1st ed. of his *Lorenzo de' Medici*, hesitates in the 2d ed.   Pastor proceeds upon
the basis of its truth but expresses doubt in a note.

haps, Savonarola's relentless demands awakened in Lorenzo a serious impression showing itself in a cry to God for absolution, while the extreme unction of the priest might have lulled the dying man's conscience to sleep with a false sense of security. At any rate, the influence of the friar of St. Mark's with the people increased.

During the years, beginning with 1494, Savonarola's ascendancy was at its height and so cold a witness as Guicciardini reports his influence as extraordinary. These years included the invasion of Charles VIII., the banishment of the Medici from Florence and the establishment of a theocratic government in the city.

" He will come across the Alps against Italy like Cyrus," Savonarola had prophesied of the French king, Charles VIII. And, when the French army was approaching the confines of Florence, he exclaimed, " Behold, the sword has come upon you. The prophecies are fulfilled, the scourge begun! Behold these hosts are led of the Lord! O Florence, the time of singing and dancing is at an end. Now is the time to shed floods of tears for thy sins."

Florence listened eagerly. Piero de' Medici went to the French camp and yielded to the king's demand for 200,000 florins, and the cession of Pisa, Leghorn and Sarzana. But Savonarola thundered and pled from the pulpit against the Medicean house. The city decreed its banishment and sent commissioners to Charles, with Savonarola among them. In his address, which is preserved, the friar reminded his Majesty that he was an instrument sent by the Lord to relieve Italy of its woes and to reform the Church. Charles entered Florence but, moved by Savonarola's intercession, reduced the tribute to 120,000 florins and restrained the depredations of the French soldiery. The king also seems to have listened to the friar's stern words when he said to him, " Hearken unto the voice of God's servant and pursue thy journey onward without delay."

When Charles, after sacking Rome and occupying Naples, returned to Northern Italy, Savonarola wrote him five letters threatening that, if he did not do for Florence the things about which he had spoken to him, God's wrath would be poured out upon his head.   These things were the recognition of the liberties of Florence and the return of Pisa to her dominion.   In his letter of May 25, 1495, bidding Charles favor the city of Florence, he asserted, " God has chosen this city and determined to magnify her and raise her up and, whoso toucheth her, toucheth the apple of His eye."   Certainly, from the standpoint of the welfare of Italy, the French invasion was not of Providential origin.   Although the banners of his army were inscribed with the words *Voluntas Dei* — the Will of God — and *Missus Dei* — the legate of God — Charles was bent on territorial aggrandizement and not on breaking the bonds of civic despotism.

The time had now come to realize in Florence Savonarola's ideal of government, a theocracy with Christ at its head.   The expulsion of the Medici made possible a reorganization of the state and the new constitution, largely a matter of Savonarola's creation, involved him inextricably in civic policies and the war of civic factions.   However, it should not be forgotten that his municipal constitution secured the commendation of Guicciardini and other Italian political writers.   It was a proof of the friar's remarkable influence that, at his earnest advice, a law was passed which prevented retaliatory measures against the followers of the Medici.   Landucci wrote in his diary that, but for Savonarola, the streets would have been bathed in blood. In his great sermons on Haggai, during the Advent season of 1494, and on the Psalms in 1495, Savonarola definitely embarked as a pilot on the political sea.   " The Lord has driven my bark into the open ocean," he exclaimed from the pulpit. Remonstrating with God for imposing this duty upon him, he declared, ' I will preach, if so I must, but why need I meddle with the government of Florence.'   And the Lord said, ' If thou wouldst make Florence a holy city, thou must establish her on firm foundations and give her a government which cherishes righteousness.'   Thus the preacher was committed. He pronounced from the pulpit in favor of virtue as the foundation of a sound government and democracy as its form. " Among northern nations," he affirmed, where there is great strength and little intellect, and among southern nations where there is great intellect and little strength, the rule of a single despot may sometimes be the best of governments. But in Italy and, above all in Florence, where both strength and intellect abound, — where men have keen wits and restless spirits, — the government of the one can only result in tyranny."

In the scheme, which he proposed, he took for his model the great council of Venice, leaving out its head, the doge, who was elected for life. The great council of Florence was to consist of, at least, 1500 men, who had reached the age of 29, paid their taxes and belonged to the class called *beneficiati*, that is, those who held a civil office themselves or whose father, grandfather, or great-grandfather had held a civil office. A select council of 80 was to be chosen by it, its members to be at least forty years of age. In criminal cases, an appeal from a decision of the signory was allowed to the great council, which was to meet once a week and to be a voting rather than a deliberative body.

The place of the supreme doge or ruler, Savonarola gave to God himself. "God alone," he exclaimed from the pulpit, "God alone will be thy king, O Florence, as He was king of Israel under the old Covenant." "Thy new head shall be Jesus Christ," — this was the ringing cry with which he closed his sermons on Haggai. Savonarola's recent biographer, Villari, emphasizes "the masterly prudence and wisdom shown by him in all the fundamental laws he proposed for the new state." He had no seat in the council and yet he was the soul of the entire people.[1]

In the last chapter of his career, Savonarola was pitted against Alexander VI. as his contestant. The conflict began with the demand made by the pope July 25, 1495, that Savonarola proceed to Rome and answer charges. Then followed papal inhibitions of his preaching and the decree of excommunication, and the conflict closed with the appointment of a papal commission which condemned Savonarola to death as a heretic.

Alexander's order, summoning the friar to Rome, was based

---

[1] One of Savonarola's propositions was to levy taxes on real property alone and, it seems, he was not averse to taxing Church property. Landucci, p. 119; Villari, I. 269, 298; II. 81.

on his announcement that his predictions of future events came by divine revelation.[1]   At the same time, the pope expressed his great joy over the report that of all the workers in the Lord's vineyard, Savonarola was the most zealous, and he promised to welcome him to the eternal city with love and fraternal affection.   Savonarola declined the pontiff's summons on the ground of ill-health and the dangers that would beset him on the way to Rome.   His old rival in the pulpit, Fra Mariano de Gennazzano, and other enemies were in Rome intriguing against him, and the Medici were fast winning the pope's favor.

Alexander's first letter inhibiting him from preaching, Sept. 9, 1495, condemned Savonarola's insane folly in mixing up with Italian political affairs and his announcement that he was a special messenger sent from God.   In his reply Savonarola answered the charges and, at the invitation of the signory, continued to preach.   In his third brief, Oct. 16, 1495, the pontiff forbade him to preach openly or in private.   Pastor remarks, " It was as clear as the sun that Savonarola was guilty of rank disobedience to the papal authority." [2]

For five months, the friar held himself aloof in his convent but, Feb. 17, 1496, at the call of the signory to preach the Lenten sermons, he again ascended the pulpit.   He took the bold position that the pope might err.   " The pope," he said, " may command me to do something that contravenes the law of Christian love or the Gospel.   But, if he did so command, I would say to him, thou art no shepherd.   Not the Roman Church, but thou errest."   From that time on, he lifted his voice against the corruptions of the papal city as he had not done before.   Preaching on Amos 4 : 1, Feb. 28, 1496, he exclaimed, " Who are the fat kine of Bashan on the mountains of Samaria?   I say they are the courtesans of Italy and Rome.   Or, are there none?   A thousand are too few for Rome, 10,000, 12,000, 14,000 are too few for Rome.   Prepare thyself, O Rome, for great will be thy punishments." [3]

---

[1] See the document in Lucas, p. 180, and O'Neil, p. 9 sq.   The original in Rudelbach.

[2] *Zur Beurtheilung,* p. 66.   Pastor is refuting Luotto's position.

[3] The Italian text in Perrens, I. 471 sq.   The sermons of this period were on Amos, Zachariah, Micah and Ruth.   According to Burlamacchi, the sultan had some of them translated into Turkish.   Villari, II. 87.

Finding threats would not stop Savonarola's mouth, Alexander resorted to bribery, an art in which he was well skilled. Through a Dominican sent to Florence, he offered to the friar of St. Mark's the red hat. But Alexander had mistaken his man and, in a sermon delivered August, 1496, Savonarola declared that neither mitres nor a cardinal's hat would he have, but only the gift God confers on His saints — death, a crimson hat, a hat reddened with blood. Lucas, strangely enough, ascribes the offer of the red hat, not to vicious shrewdness but to the alleged good purpose of Alexander to show his appreciation of "an earnest but misguided man."

The carnival season of 1496 and the seasons of the next two years gave remarkable proofs of the hold Savonarola had on the popular mind. The carnival, which had been the scene of wild revelries, was turned into a semi-religious festival. The boys had been accustomed to carry their merriment to rude excesses, forcing their demands for money upon older persons, dancing around bonfires at night and pelting people and houses promiscuously with stones. For this "festival of the stones," which the signory had been unable to abolish Savonarola and his co-helpers substituted a religious celebration. It was called the reform of the boys. Savonarola had established boys' brigades in different wards of the city and arranged tiers of seats for them against the walls of the cathedral. These "boys of Fra Girolamo," as Landucci calls them, marched up and down the streets singing hymns which Savonarola and Benivieni composed and taking their places at stands, erected for the purpose, received collections for the poor.

On the last day of the carnival of 1497, occurred the burning of the vanities, as it was called. The young men, who had been stirred to enthusiasm by Savonarola's sermons, went through the city, knocking from door to door and asking the people to give up their trinkets, obscene books such as Ovid and Boccaccio, dice, games of chance, harps, mirrors, masks, cosmetics and portraits of beautiful women, and other objects of luxury. These were piled up in the public square in a pyramid, 60 feet high and 240 feet in circumference at the base. The morning of that day, throngs listened to the mass said

by Savonarola.   The young men went in procession through
the streets and reaching the pile of vanities, they with others
joined hands and danced around the pile and then set fire to
it amid the singing of religious songs.   The sound of bells
and trumpets added to the effect of the strange spectacle.
Men thought of the books and philters, burnt at Ephesus
under the spell of Paul's preaching.   The scene was repeated
the last year of Savonarola's life, 1498.

Savonarola has been charged with having no sympathy with
the Renaissance and the charge it is not easy to set aside.   As
Burckhardt, the historian of that movement, says, he remained
a monastic.   In one writing, he sets forth the dangers of literature.   Plato and Aristotle are in hell.   And this was the judgment expressed in the city of the Platonic Academy !   Virgil
and Cicero he tolerated, but Catullus, Ovid and Terence he
condemned to banishment.[1]

At one time, under the spell of the prior's preaching, all
Florence seemed to be going to religion.   Wives left their
husbands and betook themselves to convents.   Others married, taking the vow of nuptial abstinence and Savonarola
even dreamed that the city might reach so perfect a condition
that all marrying would cease.   People took the communion
daily and young men attended mass and received the eucharistic emblem.   Fra Bartolomeo threw his studies of naked
figures into the fire and for a time continued to think it
sinful to use the hands in painting which ought to be folded
continually in prayer.   It was impossible that such a tension
should continue.   There was enthusiasm but not regeneration.   A reaction was sure to come and the wonder is that
Savonarola retained so much of the popular confidence, almost
to the end of his life.

Alexander would have none of the Florentine reforms and
was determined to silence Savonarola at any cost.   Within the
city, the air was full of rumors of plots to restore the Medici
and some of the conspirators were executed.   Enemies of the
republic avowed their purpose to kill Savonarola and circulated sheets and poems ridiculing and threatening him.   In-

[1] *Die Kultur d. Renaissance*, II. 200 sq.

sulting placards were posted up against the walls of his convent
and, on one occasion, the pulpit of the cathedral was defiled
with ordure and draped in an ass' skin, while spikes were
driven into the place where the preacher was accustomed to
strike his hand. Landucci speaks of it as a "great scandal."
Assassins even gathered in the cathedral and were only cowed
by guards posted by the signory. The friar of St. Mark's
seemed not to be appalled. It was ominous, however, that the
signory became divided in his support.

If possible, Savonarola became more intense in his arraignment of the evils of the Church. He exclaimed: "O prostrate
Church, thou hast displayed thy foulness to the whole earth.
Thou hast multiplied thy fornications in Italy, in France, in
Spain and all other regions. Thou hast desecrated the sacraments with simony. Of old, priests called their bastards
nephews, now they call them outright sons." Alexander
could not mistake the reference nor tolerate such declama-
tions. The integrity of the supreme seat of Christendom
was at stake. A prophetic function superior to the papacy
Eugenius III. might recognize, when it was administered in
the admonitions of a St. Bernard, but the Florentine prophet
had engaged in denunciation even to personal invective. The
prophet was losing his balance. On May 12, 1497, for "his
failure to obey our Apostolic admonitions and commands" and
as "one suspected of heresy" Alexander declared him excommunicate. All were forbidden to listen to the condemned man
or have converse with him.[1]

In a letter addressed a month later "to all Christians, the
elect of God," Savonarola again affirmed his readiness to yield
to the Church's authority, but denied that he was bound to
submit to the commands of his superiors when these were in
conflict with charity and God's law. "Henceforth," exclaimed
the Puritan contemporary, Landucci, "we were deprived of the
Word of God." The signory wrote to Alexander in support
of Savonarola, affirming his purity of character and soundness
of doctrine, and friends, like Pico della Mirandola the younger,
issued defences of his conduct. The elder Pico della Miran-

---

[1] The bull is given by Villari, II. 189 sq. ; Pastor, III. 411 sq.

dola and Politian, both of whom had died a year or two before, showed their reverence for Savonarola by assuming the Dominican garb on their death-beds.

At this time, Savonarola sent forth his *Triumph of the Cross*, in which were set forth the verity and reasonableness of the Catholic faith.[1] After proving from pure reason God's existence and the soul's immortality, the work proceeds to expound the Trinity, which is above man's reason, and articles of the Apostles' Creed, and to set forth the superior excellency of the lives of Christians, on which much stress is laid. It closes with a confutation of Mohammedanism and other false forms of religion.

Savonarola kept silence in the pulpit and refrained from the celebration of the sacrament until Christmas day of 1497, when he celebrated the mass at St. Mark's three times. On the 11th of February, he stood again in the pulpit of the duomo. To a vast concourse he represented the priest as merely an instrument of the Almighty and, when God withdraws His presence, prelate and pope are but as " a broken iron tool." "And, if a prelate commands what is contrary to godly living and charity, he is not only not to be obeyed but deserves to be anathema." On another occasion, he said that not only may the pope be led into error by false reports but also by his own badness, as was the case with Boniface VIII. who was a wicked pope, beginning his pontificate like a fox and ending it like a dog.[2] Many, through reverence for the Church, kept away from Savonarola's preaching from this time on. Among these was the faithful Landucci, who says, " whether justly or unjustly, I was among those who did not go. I believed in him, but did not wish to incur risk by going to hear him, for he was under sentence of excommunication." Savonarola's enemies had made the words of Gregory the Great their war-cry, *Sententia pastoris sive justa sive unjusta timenda est.* — " The sentence of the shepherd is to be respected, whether it be just or unjust."[3] His denunciations of the cor-

---

[1] Published in 1497, both in Latin and Etruscan, the Etruscan translation being by Savonarola himself.

[2] Pastor: *Beurtheilung*, p. 71 sqq. ; Villari, II. 252.

[3] See Schnitzer: *Feuerprobe*, p. 144.

ruption prevailing in the Church became more bold.   The tonsure, he cried,

is the seat of all iniquity.   It begins in Rome where the clergy make mock of
Christ and the saints ; yea, are worse than Turks and worse than Moors.   They
traffic in the sacraments.   They sell benefices to the highest bidder.   Have not
the priests in Rome courtesans and grooms and horses and dogs ?   Have they
not palaces full of tapestries and silks, of perfumes and lackeys ?   Seemeth it,
that this is the Church of God?

Every Roman priest, he said, had his concubine.   No longer
do they speak of nephews but of their sons and daughters.
Savonarola even sought to prove from the pulpit that the papal
brief of excommunication proceeded from the devil, inasmuch
as it was hostile to godly living.

It was becoming evident that the preacher was fighting a losing battle.   His assaults against the morals of the clergy and
the Vatican stirred up the powers in the Church against him ;
his political attitude, factions in Florence.   His assertions, dealing more and more in exaggerations, were developing an expect-
ant and at the same time a critical state of mind in the people
which no religious teacher could permanently meet except
through the immediate and startling intervention of God.   He
called heaven to witness that he was "ready to die for His God"
and invited God to send him to the fires of hell, if his motives
were not pure and his work inspired.   On another occasion, he
invoked the Lord to strike him dead on the spot, if he was not
sincere.   Landucci reports some of these wild protestations
which he heard with his own ears.

One weapon still remained to the pope to bring Savonarola to
terms, — the interdict.   This he threatened to fulminate over
Florence, unless the signory sent this " son of the evil one " to
Rome or cast him into prison.   In case the first course was pursued, Alexander promised to treat Savonarola as a father would
treat a son, provided he repented, for he " desired not the death
of a sinner but that he might turn from his way and live." [1]
He urged the signory not to allow Savonarola to " be as the fly
in the milk, disturbing its relations with Rome " or " to tolerate that pernicious worm fostered by their warmth."

[1] See Alexander's letters in Perrens, I. 481–485 ; Pastor, III. 418 sq.   O'Neil
finds no room for them.

Through epistolary communications and legates, the signory continued its attempts to remove Alexander's objections and protect Savonarola.   But, while all the members continued to express confidence in the friar's purity of motive, the majority came to take the position that it was more expedient to silence the preacher than to incur the pope's ban.   At the public meeting, called by the signory March 9, 1498, to decide the course of action to be taken, the considerations pressed were those of expediency.   The pope, as the vicar of Christ, has his authority directly from God and ought to be obeyed.   A second consideration was the financial straits of the municipality.   A tenth was needed and this could only be ordered through the pope.   Some proposed to leave the decision of the matter to Savonarola himself.   He was the best man the world had seen for 200 years. Others boldly announced that Alexander's letters were issued through the machinations of enemies of Florence and the censures they contained, being unjust, were not to be heeded.[1]   On March 17, 1498, the signory's decision was communicated to Savonarola that he should thenceforth refrain from preaching and the next day he preached his last sermon.

In his last sermon, Savonarola acknowledged it as his duty to obey the mandate.   A measure had been worked out in his mind which was the last open to a churchman.   Already had he hinted from the pulpit at the convention of a general council as a last resort.   The letters are still extant which he intended to send to the kings of Spain, England, France, Germany and Hungary, calling upon them to summon a council. In them, he solemnly declared that Alexander was no pope. For, aside from purchasing his office and from his daily sale of benefices, his manifest vices proved him to be no Christian. The letters seem never to have been received.   Individuals, however, despatched preliminary communications to friends at the different courts to prepare the way for their appeal.[2] One, addressed to Charles VIII., was intercepted at Milan

---

[1] See Schnitzer : *Feuerprobe*, p. 38 sqq.
[2] For the originals, see Perrens, I. 487–492.   Excerpts are given by Villari, II. 292 sq.   See also Hase, p. 59, Creighton, III. 237.   Of the genuineness of the letters, Villari says there can be no doubt.

and sent to the pope. Alexander now had documentary proof
of the Florentine's rebellion against papal authority. But
suddenly a wholly unexpected turn was given to the course
of events.

Florence was startled by the rumor that resort was to be
had to ordeal by fire to decide the genuineness of Savonarola's
claims.[1] The challenge came from a Franciscan, Francesco
da Puglia, in a sermon at S. Croce in which he arraigned the
Dominican friar as a heretic and false prophet. In case Savonarola was not burnt, it would be a clear sign that Florence
was to follow him. The challenge was accepted by Fra
Domenico da Pescia, a monk of St. Mark's and close friend of
Savonarola's, a man of acknowledged purity of life. He took
his friend's place, holding that Savonarola should be reserved
for higher things. Francesco da Puglia then withdrew and
a Franciscan monk, Julian Rondinelli, reluctantly took his
place. Savonarola himself disapproved the ordeal. It was
an appeal to the miraculous. He had never performed a miracle nor felt the importance of one. His cause, he asserted,
approved itself by the fruits of righteousness. But to the
people, as the author of Romola has said, "the fiery trial
seemed a short and easy argument" and Savonarola could not
resist the popular feeling without forfeiting his popularity.
The history of Florence could show more than one case of
saintly men whose profession had been tested by fire. So it
was, during the investiture controversy, with St. John Gual-
berti, in Settimo close by, and with the monk Peter in 1068,
and so it was, a half century later, with another Peter who
cleared himself of the charge of contemning the cross by
walking unhurt over nine glowing ploughshares.[2]

The ordeal was authorized by the signory and set for April 7.
It was decided that, in case Fra Domenico perished, Savonarola should go into exile within three hours. The two parties, Domenico and Rondinelli, filed their statements with
the signory. The Dominican's included the following points.

---

[1] Landucci's account of the *fuoco*, p. 165 sqq., is most vivid. For Cerretani's account, Schnitzer's ed., 59-71.

[2] See Schnitzer: *Feuerprobe*, p. 49 sq.

The Church stands in need of renovation. It will be chastened. Florence will be chastened. These chastisements will happen in our day. The sentence of excommunication against Savonarola is invalid. No one sins in ignoring it.[1]

The ordeal aroused the enthusiasm of Savonarola's friends. When he announced it in a sermon, many women exclaimed, "I, too, I, too." Other monks of St. Mark's and hundreds of young men announced their readiness to pass through the flames out of regard for their spiritual guide.

Alexander VI. waited with intense interest for the last bulletins from Florence. His exact state of mind it is difficult to determine. He wrote disapproving of the ordeal and yet he could not but feel that it afforded an easy way of getting rid of the enemy to his authority. After the ordeal was over, he praised Francesco and the Franciscans in extravagant terms and declared the Franciscans could not have done anything more agreeable to him.[2]

The coming trial was looked for with the most intense interest. There was scarcely any other topic of conversation in Florence or in Rome. Great preparations were made. Two pyres of thorns and other wood were built on the public square about 60 feet in length, 3 feet wide at the base and 3 or 4 feet high,[3] the wood soaked with pitch and oil. The distance between the pyres was two feet, just wide enough for a man to pass through. All entrances to the square were closed by a company of 300 men under Marcuccio Salviatis and two other companies of 500 each, stationed at different points. The people began to arrive the night before. The windows and roofs of the adjoining houses were crowded with the eager spectators.

[1] Schnitzer, p. 54.

[2] Schnitzer, p. 64 sq., who goes into the matter at length, and Villari, II. 306 sqq., agree in the opinion that Alexander fully sympathized with the ordeal. They also agree that the Arrabbiati were largely, if not wholly, responsible for the suggestion of the ordeal and making it a matter of public appointment. Pastor, III. 429, represents Alexander as wholly disapproving the ordeal.

[3] There is a difference among the contemporary writers about the figures. Landucci, p. 168, gives the length at 50 *braccia*, width 10 and height 4 ; Bartolomeo Cerretani, Schnitzer ed. p. 62, the width as 1 *braccio* and the height 2.

The solemnity was set for eleven o'clock. The Dominicans made a solemn impression as they marched to the appointed place. Fra Domenico, in the van, was clothed in a fiery red velvet cope. Savonarola, clad in white and carrying a monstrance with the host, brought up the rear of the body of monks and these were followed by a great multitude of men, women and children, holding lighted tapers. When the hour arrived for the procession to start, Savonarola was preaching. He had again told the people that his work required no miracle and that he had ever sought to justify himself by the signs of righteousness and declared that, as on Mt. Carmel, miraculous intervention could only be expected in answer to prayer and humility.

Later mediæval history has few spectacles to offer to the eye and the imagination equal in interest to the spectacle offered that day. There, stood the greatest preacher of his time and the most exalted moral figure since the days of John Huss and Gerson. And there, the ancient method of testing innocency was once more to be tried, a novel spectacle, indeed, to that cultured generation of Florentines. The glorious pageants of Medicean times had afforded no entertainment more attractive.

The crowds were waiting. The hour was past. There was a mysterious moving of monks in and out of the signory-palace. The whole story of what occurred was later told by Savonarola himself as well as by other eye-witnesses. The Franciscans refused to allow Fra Domenico to enter the burning pathway wearing his red cope or any of the other garments he had on, on the ground that they might be bewitched. So he was undressed to his skin and put on another suit. On the same ground, they also insisted that he keep at a distance from Savonarola. The impatience of the crowds increased. The Franciscans again passed into the signory-hall and had a long conference. They had discerned a wooden crucifix in Domenico's hands and insisted upon its being put away for fear it might also have been bewitched. Savonarola substituted the host but the Franciscans insisted that the host should not be carried through the flames. The signory was appealed to but Savonarola refused to yield, declaring that the accidents might be burnt like a husk but that the essence of the sacred wafer would remain unconsumed. Suddenly a storm came up and rain fell but it as suddenly stopped. The delay continued. The crowds were growing unruly and threatening. Nightfall was at hand. The signory called the ordeal off.

Savonarola's power was gone. The spell of his name had vanished. The spectacle was felt to be a farce. The popular menace grew more and more threatening and a guard scarcely prevented violence to Savonarola's person, as the procession moved back to St. Mark's.

There is much in favor of the view that on that day Savonarola's political enemies, the Arrabbiati, were in collusion with the Franciscans and that the delay on the square, occasioned by interposing objections, was a trick to postpone the ordeal altogether.[1] It was said daggers were ready to put Savonarola out of the way. The populace, however, did not stop to consider such questions. Savonarola had not stood the test. And, it reasoned, if he was sincere and confident of his cause, why did he not enter the flaming pathway himself and brave its fiery perils. If he had not gone through unharmed, he at any rate, in dying, would have shown his moral heroism. It was Luther's readiness to stand the test at Worms which brought him the confidence of the people. Had he shrunk in 1521 in the presence of Charles V., he would have lost the popular regard as Savonarola did in 1498 on the piazza of Florence. The judgment of modern times agrees with the popular judgment of the Florentines. Savonarola showed himself wanting in the qualities of the hero. Better for him to have died, than to have exposed himself to the charge of cowardice.

Florence felt mad anger at having been imposed upon. The next day St. Mark's was stormed by the mob. The signory voted Savonarola's immediate banishment. Landucci, who wept and continued to pray for him, says "that hell seemed to have opened its doors." Savonarola made an address, bidding farewell to his friends. Resistance of the mob was in vain. The convent was broken into and pillaged. Fra Domenico and the prior were bound and taken before the galfonier amidst insults and confined

[1] Schnitzer, p. 159 sq., who says the signory and the Franciscans joined " in packing the cards."

in separate apartments. A day or two later Fra Silvestro, whose visions had favored the ordeal, was also seized. " As for saying a word in Savonarola's favor," wrote Landucci, "it was impossible. One would have been killed."

The pope, on receiving the official news of the occurrences in Florence, sent word congratulating the signory, gave the city plenary absolution and granted it the coveted tithes for three years. He also demanded that Savonarola be sent to Rome for trial, at the same time, however, authorizing the city to proceed to try the three friars, not neglecting, if necessary, the use of torture.[1] A commission was appointed to examine the prisoners. Torture was resorted to. Savonarola was bound to a rope drawn through a pulley and, with his hands behind his back, was lifted from the floor and then by a sudden jerk allowed to fall. On a single day, he was subjected to 14 turnings of the rope. There were two separate trials conducted by the municipality, April 17 and April 21–23. In the delirious condition, to which his pains reduced him, the unfortunate man made confessions which, later in his sane moments, he recalled as untrue.[2] He even denied that he was a prophet. The impression which this denial made upon such ardent admirers as Landucci, the apothecary, was distressing. Writing April 19, 1498, he says: —

I was present at the reading of the proceedings against Savonarola, whom we all held to be a prophet. But he said he is no prophet and that his prophecies were not from God. When I heard that, I was seized with wonder and amazement. A deep pain took hold of my soul, when I saw such a splendid edifice fall to the ground, because it was built upon the sorry foundation of a falsehood. I looked for Florence to become a new Jerusalem whose laws and example of a good life — *buona vita* — would go out for the renovation of the Church, the conversion of infidels and the comfort of the good and I felt the contrary and took for medicine the words, " In thy will, O Lord, are all things placed " — *in voluntate tua, Domine, omnia sunt posita. Diary*, p. 173.

Alexander despatched a commission of his own to conduct the trial anew, Turriano, the Venetian general of the Domini-

---

[1] *Etiam per torturam.* Alexander's letter in Lucas, p. 372.

[2] The reports of Savonarola's trial and confessions are of uncertain value, as they were garbled by the reporter Ser Ceccone. See Pastor, III. 432 sq. Landucci says that from 9 A.M. till nightfall the cries of Domenico and Sylvestro under the strain of torture could be heard in the city prison.

cans and Francesco Romolino, the bishop of Ilerda, afterwards cardinal.   Letters from Rome stated that the commission had instructions "to put Savonarola to death, even if he were another John the Baptist."   Alexander was quite equal to such a statement.   Soon after his arrival in Florence, Romolino announced that a bonfire was impending and that he carried the sentence with him ready, prepared in advance.

Fra Domenico bore himself most admirably and persisted in speaking naught but praise of his friend and ecclesiastical superior.   Fra Silvestro, yielding to the agonies of the rack, charged his master with all sorts of guilt.   Other monks of St. Mark's wrote to Alexander, making charges against their prior as an impostor.   So it often is with those who praise in times of prosperity.   To save themselves, they deny and calumniate their benefactors.   They received their reward, the papal absolution.

The exact charges, upon which Savonarola was condemned to death, are matter of some uncertainty and also matter of indifference, for they were partly trumped up for the occasion. Though no offender against the law of God, he had given offence enough to man.   He was accused by the papal commissioners with being a heretic and schismatic.   He was no heretic.   The most that can be said is, that he was a rebel against the pope's authority and went in the face of Pius II.'s bull *Execrabilis*, when he decided to appeal to a council.[1]

The intervals between his torture, Savonarola spent in composing his *Meditations* upon the two penitential Psalms, the 32d and the 51st.   Here we see the gloss of his warm religious nature.   The great preacher approaches the throne of grace as a needy sinner and begs that he who asks for bread may not be turned away with a stone.   He appeals to the cases of Zaccheus, Mary Magdalene, the woman of Canaan, Peter and the prodigal son.   Deliver me, he cries, "as Thou hast delivered countless sinners from the grasp of death and the gates of hell and my tongue shall sing aloud of thy righteousness."   Luther, who published the expositions with a notable preface, 1523, declared

[1] See the miserable letters sent by the papal commission to Alexander, Lucas, pp. 434–436.

them "a piece of evangelical teaching and Christian piety. For, in them Savonarola is seen entering in not as a Dominican monk, trusting in his vows, the rules of his order, his cowl and masses and good works but clad in the breastplate of righteousness and armed with the shield of faith and the helmet of salvation, not as a member of the Order of Preachers but as an everyday Christian." [1]

At their own request the three prisoners, after a separation of six weeks, were permitted to meet face to face the night before the appointed execution. The meeting occurred in the hall of the signory. When Savonarola returned to his cell, he fell asleep on the lap of Niccolini of the fraternity of the Battuti, a fraternity whose office it was to minister to prisoners. Niccolini reported that the sleep was as quiet as the sleep of a child. On awaking, the condemned man passed the remaining hours of the night in devotions. The next morning, the friends met again and partook together of the sacrament.

The sentence was death by hanging, after which the bodies were to be burnt that "the soul might be completely separated from the body." The execution took place on the public square where, two months before, the crowds had gathered to witness the ordeal by fire. Savonarola and his friends were led forth stripped of their robes, barefooted and with hands bound. Absolution was pronounced by the bishop of Verona under appointment from the pope. In pronouncing Savonarola's deposition, the prelate said, "I separate thee from the Church militant and the Church triumphant" — *separo te ab ecclesia militante et triumphante.* "Not from the Church triumphant," replied Savonarola, "that is not thine to do" — *militante, non triumphante : hoc enim tuum non est.* In silence he witnessed the deaths of Fra Domenico and Fra Silvestro, whose last words were "Jesus, Jesus," and then ascended the platform of execution. There were still left bystanders to fling insults. The

---

[1] Weimar ed. XII. 248. Twenty-three edd. of Savonarola's exposition appeared within two years of the author's death and, before half a century elapsed, it had been translated into Spanish, German, English and French. In Italy, it was used as a tract and put into the hands of prisoners condemned to death. It was embodied in the Salisbury Primer, 1538, and in Henry VIII.'s Primer, 1543.

bodies were burnt and, that no particle might be left to be used as a relic, the ashes were thrown into the Arno.

Savonarola had been pronounced by Alexander's commission "that iniquitous monster — *omnipedium nequissimum* — call him man or friar we cannot, a mass of the most abominable wickedness." The pious Landucci, in thinking of his death, recalled the crucifixion and, at the scene of the execution, again lamented the disappointment of his hopes for the renovation of the Church and the conversion of the infidel — *la novazione della chiesa e la conversione degli infedeli.*

Savonarola was one of the most noteworthy figures Italy has produced. The modern Christian world, Catholic and Protestant, joins him in close fellowship with the flaming religious luminaries of all countries and all centuries. He was a preacher of righteousness and a patriot. Among the religious personalities of Italy, he occupies a position of grandeur by himself, separate from her imposing popes, like Gregory VII. and Innocent III.; from Dante, Italy's poet and the world's; from St. Francis d'Assisi and from Thomas Aquinas. Italy had other preachers, — Anthony of Padua, Bernardino of Siena, — but their messages were local and ecclesiastical. With Arnold of Brescia, Savonarola had something in common. Both had a stirring message of reform. Both mixed up political ideals with their spiritual activity and both died by judicial sanction of the papal see.

Savonarola's intellectual gifts and attainments were not extraordinary. He was great by reason of moral conviction, his eloquence, his disinterested love of his country, his wholesouled devotion to the cause of righteousness. As an administrator, he failed. He had none of the sagacity or tact of the statesman and it was his misfortune to have undertaken to create a new government, a task for which he was the least qualified of all men.[1] He was a preacher of righteousness and has a place in the "goodly fellowship of the prophets." He belonged to the order of Ezekiel and Isaiah, Nathan and John the Baptist, — the company in which the Protestant world also places John Knox.

---

[1] See the excellent remarks of Burckhardt: *Renaiss.*, II. 200.

Savonarola was a true Catholic. He did not deny a single dogma of the mediæval Church. But he was more deeply rooted in the fundamental teachings of Christ than in ecclesiastical formulas. In the deliverance of his message, he rose above rituals and usages. He demanded regeneration of heart. His revolt against the authority of the pope, in appealing to a council, is a serious stumbling-block to Catholics who are inclined to a favorable judgment of the Friar of St. Mark's. Julius II.'s bull *Cum tanto divino*, 1505, pronounced every election to the papacy secured by simony invalid. If it was meant to be retroactive, then Alexander was not a true pope.[1]

The favorable judgments of contemporaries were numerous. Guicciardini called him the saviour of his country — *salvatore di patria* — and said that " Never was there so much goodness and religion in Florence as in his day and, after his death, it was seen that every good thing that had been done was done at his suggestion and by his advocacy." Machiavelli thus expressed himself : " The people of Florence seemed to be neither illiterate nor rude, yet they were persuaded that God spake through Savonarola. I will not decide, whether it was so or not, for it is due to speak of so great a man with reverence."

The day after Savonarola's death, women were seen praying at the spot where he suffered and for years flowers were strewn there. Pico della Mirandola closed his biography with an elaborate comparison between Savonarola and Christ. Both were sent from God. Both suffered in the cause of righteousness between two others. At the command of Julius II., Raphael, 12 years after Savonarola's death, placed the preacher among the saints in his Disputa. Philip Neri and Catherine de Ricci [2]

---

[1] Pastor, III. 436 says that Savonarola was always true to Catholic dogma in theory. His only departure was disobeying the pope and appealing to a council. Father Proctor, Pref. to *Triumph of the Cross*, p. xvii, calls Savonarola " Of Catholics the most Catholic."

[2] Cardinal Capecelatro in his *Life of St. Ph. Neri*. trsl. by Father Pope, I. 278, says, " Philip often read Savonarola's writings especially the *Triumph of the Cross*, and used them in the instruction of his spiritual children." Quoted by Proctor, Preface, p. 6. For Catherine de Ricci, see her *Life* by F. M. Capes, Lond., 1908, pp. 48, 49, 53, 270 sq. She was devoted in her cult

revered him, and Benedict XIV. seems to have regarded him worthy of canonization.[1]

Within the Dominican order, the feeling toward its greatest preacher has undergone a great change.   Respect for the papal decision led it, for a hundred years after Savonarola's death, to make official effort to retire his name to oblivion.   The Dominican general, Sisto Fabri of Lucca, in 1585, issued an order forbidding every Dominican monk and nun mentioning his name and commanded them to give up any article to their superiors which kept warm admiration for him or aroused it. In the latter half of the 19th century, as the 400th anniversary of his execution approached, Catholics, and especially Dominicans, in all parts of the world defended his memory and efforts were made to prepare the way for his canonization.   In the attempt to remove all objections, elaborate arguments have been presented to prove that Alexander's sentence of excommunication was in fact no excommunication at all.[2] The sound and judicious Catholic historians, Hefele-Knöpfler, do not hesitate to pronounce his death a judicial murder.[3]

By the general consent of Protestants, Jerome Savonarola is numbered among the precursors of the Reformation, — the view taken by Ranke.   He was not an advocate of its distinguish-

of Savonarola and wrote a laud to him.   This was the chief objection to her beatification in 1716, but the arguments for an unfavorable judgment of Savonarola were answered on that occasion.

[1] Villari, II. 417, following Schwab and other Catholic writers.   The interpretation put upon Benedict's words is denied by Pastor: *Beurtheilung*, p. 16 sq., and Lucas.

[2] Father O'Neil, a Dominican, in his work, *Was Savonarola really excommunicated?* takes this position and says, p. 132, "Alexander did not inflict any censure on Savonarola."   The fact, however, is that in his letters to the signory, Alexander proceeded on the basis of his brief of excommunication. He stated distinctly the reasons for his being excommunicated and he called upon the priests of Florence to publicly announce his sentence of May 12, 1497, upon pain of drawing ecclesiastical censure upon themselves.   O'Neil replies that a papal decision, based upon a false charge, is invalid, p. 175 sqq.

[3] *Rechtlos hingemordert, Kirchengesch.*, p. 503.   Ranke's statement that the view making Savonarola a hero is a Dominican legend "worked out after the preacher's death" has been rendered untenable by the latest research by the eminent Savonarola scholar, the Catholic Professor Schnitzer.   See his *Feuerprobe*, p. 152.

ing tenet of justification by faith. The Roman church was for
him the mother of all other churches and the pope its head.
In his *Triumph of the Cross,* he distinctly asserts the seven sacraments as an appointment of Christ and that Christ is " wholly
and essentially present in each of the eucharistic elements."
Nevertheless, he was an innovator and his exaltation of divine
grace accords with the teaching of the Reformation. Here
all Protestants would have fellowship with him as when he
said : [1] —

It is untrue that God's grace is obtained by pre-existing works of merit as
though works and deserts were the cause of predestination. On the contrary,
these are the result of predestination. Tell me, Peter ; tell me, O Magdalene, wherefore are ye in paradise ? Confess that not by your own merits
have ye obtained salvation, but by the goodness of God.

Passages abound in his *Meditations* like this one. "Not by
their own deservings, O Lord, or by their own works have
they been saved, lest any man should be able to boast, but
because it seemed good in Thy sight." Speaking of Savonarola's Exposition of the Psalms, Luther said that, although
some clay still stuck to Savonarola's theology, it is a pure and
beautiful example of what is to be believed, trusted and hoped
from God's mercy and how we come to despair of works. And
the whole-souled German Reformer exclaimed, " Christ canon-
izes Savonarola through us even though popes and papists burst
to pieces over it." [2]

The sculptor has given him a place at the feet of Luther and
at the side of Wyclif and Huss in the monument of the Reformation at Worms. When Catholics, who heard that this
was proposed, wrote to show the impropriety of including the
Florentine Dominican in such company, Rietschel consulted
Hase on the subject. The venerable Church historian replied,
"It makes no difference whether they counted Savonarola a
heretic or a saint, he was in either case a precursor of the
Reformation and so Luther recognized him." [3]

[1] Sermon VIII. in Prato ed. quoted by Rudelbach. Bayonne wrote his work
in 1879 to dispose of this charge and to prepare the way for Savonarola's
canonization.

[2] *Canonizat eum Christus per nos, rumpanter etiam papæ et papistæ
simul.* Weimar ed. XII. 248.

[3] *Kirchengesch.,* II. 566.

The visitor in Florence to-day finds two invisible personalities meeting him everywhere, Dante, whom the city banished, and Savonarola, whom it executed. The spirit of the executioner has vanished and the mention of Savonarola's name strikes in all Florentines a tender chord of admiration and love. In 1882, the signory placed his statue in the Hall of the Five Hundred. There, a few yards from the place of his execution, he stands in his Dominican habit and cowl, with his left hand resting on a lion's head and holding aloft in his right hand a crucifix, while his clear eye is turned upwards. Again, on May 22, 1901, the city honored the friar by setting a circular bronze tablet with portrait on the spot where he suffered death. A great multitude attended the dedication and one of the wreaths of flowers bore the name of the Dominicans.

In Savonarola's cell in St. Mark's has been placed a medallion head of the friar, and still another on the cloistral wall over the spot where he was seized and made prisoner, and the visitor will often find there a fresh wreath of flowers, a proof of the undying memory of the Florentine preacher and patriot.

> This was he,
> Savonarola, — the star-look shooting from the cowl.
> — BROWNING, *Casa Guido Windows.*

§ 77. *The Study and Circulation of the Bible.*

The only biblical commentary of the Middle Ages, conforming in any adequate sense to our modern ideas of exegesis, was produced by Nicolas of Lyra, who died 1340. The exegesis of the Schoolmen was a subversion of Scripture rather than an exposition. In their hands, it was made the slave of dogma. Of grammatical and textual criticism they had no conception and they lacked all equipment for the grammatical study of the original Hebrew and Greek. What commentaries were produced in the flourishing era of Scholasticism, were either collections of quotations from the Fathers, called Chains, — *catenæ*, the most noted of which was the catena on the Gospels by Thomas Aquinas, — or, if original works, they teemed with endless suggestions of the fancy and were like continents of tropical vine-growths through which it is next to impossible to find a clear path to Jesus Christ and the meaning of human life. The bulky expositions of the Psalms, Job and other biblical books by such theologians as Rupert of Deutz, Bonaventura and Albertus Magnus, are to-day intellectual curiosities or, at best, manuals from which piety of the conventual type may be fed. They bring out every other meaning but the historical and plain sense intended by the biblical authors. Especially true is this of the Song of Songs, which the Schoolmen made a hunting-ground for descriptions of the Virgin Mary.[1] It is said, Thomas Aquinas was engaged on the exposition of this book when he died.

The traditional mediæval formula of interpretation reduced Tychonius' seven senses to four, — the literal, allegorical, moral and anagogical. The formula ran: —

Litteralis gesta docet; quid credas, allegoria,
Moralis quid agas; quo tendas anagogia.

Thomas Aquinas, fully in accord with this method, said that "the literal sense of Scripture is manifold, its spiritual sense, threefold, viz., allegorical, moral and anagogical."[2] The literal sense teaches the things which have happened, the allegorical what we are to believe, the moral what we are to do and the anagogical directs to things to be awaited. The last three senses correspond to faith, hope and charity. Hugo of Cher compared them to the four coverings of the tabernacle, the four winds, the four wings of the cherubim, the four rivers of paradise, the four legs of the Lord's table. Here are specimens: Jerusalem, literally, is a city in Palestine; allegorically, it is the Church; morally, the faithful soul; anagogically, the heavenly Jerusalem. The Exodus from Egypt is, historically, a fact; allegorically, the redemption of Christ; morally, the soul's conversion; anagogically, the departure for the heavenly land. In his earliest years, Dean Colet followed this method. From Savonarola we would expect it. The literal heaven, earth and light of Genesis 1 : 1, 2, he expounded

---

[1] So sober a writer as Reuss, p. 607, speaks of the commentaries on the Canticles, as being without number.

[2] *Summa,* I. 1 art. x.

as meaning allegorically, Adam, Eve and the light of grace or the Hebrews, Gentiles and Jesus Christ; morally, the soul, body and active intelligence; anagogically, angels, men and the vision of God.   In his later years, Colet, in answer to a letter from Erasmus, who insisted upon the fecundity of meanings of Scripture texts, abandoned his former position and declared that their fecundity consisted not in their giving birth to many senses but to one only and that the truest.[1]   In his better moods, Erasmus laid stress upon the one historical sense, applying to the interpretation of the Bible the rule that is applied to other books.

After the Reformation was well on its way, the old irrational method continued to be practised and Bishop Longland, in a sermon on Prov. 9 : 1, 2, preached in 1525, explained the words "she hath furnished her table" to mean, that wisdom had set forth in her spiritual banquet the four courses of history, tropology, anagogy and allegory.[2]   Three years later, 1528, Tyndale, the translator of the English Bible, had this to say of the mediæval system of exegesis and the new system which sought out the literal sense of Scripture: —

The papists divide the Scripture into four senses, the literal, tropological, allegorical and anagogical. The literal sense has become nothing at all, for the pope hath taken it clean away and hath made it his possession. He hath partly locked it up with the false and counterfeited keys of his traditions, ceremonies and feigned lies. Thou shalt understand that the Scripture hath but one sense, which is the literal sense, and this literal sense is the root and ground of all and the anchor that never faileth whereunto, if thou cleave, thou canst never err or go out of the way.[3]

A decided step in the direction of the new exegesis movement was made by Nicolas of Lyra in his *Postillæ*, a brief commentary on the entire Bible.[4]   This commentator, called by

[1] See Lupton, p. 104, and Seebohm, pp. 30, 124 sq., 445–447.
[2] Farrar, p. 295.
[3] *The Obedience of a Christian Man*, Parker Soc., p. 303 sq. The author of the *Epp. obscurorum virorum* speaks of having listened to a lecture on poetry, in which Ovid was explained *naturaliter, literaliter, historialiter et spiritualiter*. In his preface to the Pentateuch, p. 394, Tyndale said, "The Scripture hath but one simple, literal sense whose light the owls cannot abide."
[4] Lyra's work was printed 8 times before 1500. The ed. printed at Rome, 1471–1473, is in 5 vols.

Wyclif the elaborate and skilful annotator of Scripture, — *tamen copiosus et ingeniosus postillator Scripturæ*,[1]—was born in Normandy, about 1270, and became professor in Paris where he remained till his death. He knew Greek and learned Hebrew from a rabbi and his knowledge of that tongue gave rise to the false rumor that he had a Jewish mother. Lyra made a new Latin translation, commented directly on the original text and ventured at times to prefer the comments of Jewish commentators to the comments of the Fathers. As he acknowledged in his Introduction, he was much influenced by the writings of Rabbi Raschi.

Lyra's lasting merit lies in the stress he laid upon the literal sense which he insisted should alone be employed in establishing dogma. In practice, however, he allowed a secondary sense, the mystical or typical, but he declared that it had been put to such abuse as to have choked out — *suffocare* — the literal sense. The language of Scripture must be understood in its natural sense as we would expect our words to be understood.[2] His method aided in undermining the fanciful and pernicious exegetical system of the Schoolmen who knew neither Greek nor Hebrew and prepared the way for a new period of biblical exposition. He was used not only by Wyclif and Gerson,[3] but also by Luther, who acknowledged his services in insisting upon the literal sense.

Although Wyclif wrote no commentaries on books of Scripture, he gave expositions of the Lord's Prayer and the Decalogue and of many texts, which are thoroughly practical and popular. In his treatise on the *Truth of Scripture*, he seems at times to pronounce the discovery of the literal sense the only object of a sound exegesis.[4] A generation later, Gerson showed an inclination to lay stress upon the literal sense as fundamental but went no further than to say that it is to be accepted so far

---

[1] *De veritate scr. sac.*, I. 275. Wyclif quotes Lyra, II. 100, etc.

[2] Prol. 2. *Omnes presupponunt sensum lit. tanquam fundamentum, unde sicut ædificium declinans a fundamento disponitur ad ruinam expositio mystica discrepans a sensu lit. reputanda est indecens et inepta.* See Reuss, p. 610.

[3] Du Pin's ed., 1728, I. 3, etc.

[4] *Sensus lit. scripturæ est utrobique verus, De ver.*, I. 73, 122.

as it is found to be in harmony with the teachings of the Church.[1]

Later in the 15th century, the free critical spirit which the Revival of Letters was begetting found pioneers in the realm of exegesis in Laurentius Valla and Erasmus, Colet, Wesel and Wessel. As has already been said, Valla not only called in question the genuineness of Constantine's donation, but criticised Jerome's Vulgate and Augustine. Erasmus went still farther when he left out of his Greek New Testament, 1516, the spurious passage about the three witnesses, 1 John 5: 7, though he restored it in the edition of 1522. He pointed out the discrepancy between a statement in Stephen's speech and the account in Genesis and questioned the authorship of the Epistle to the Hebrews, the Apostolic origin of 2d and 3rd John and the Johannine authorship of the Apocalypse.

In opposition to such views the Sorbonne, in 1526, declared it an error of faith to call in question the authorship of any of the books of the New Testament. Erasmus recommended for the student of the Scriptures a fair knowledge of Latin, Greek and Hebrew and also that he be versed in other studies, especially the knowledge of natural objects such as the animals, trees, precious stones and geography of Scripture.[2]

The nearest approach to the exegetical principles as well as doctrinal positions of the Reformers was made by the Frenchman, Lefèvre d'Etaples, whose translations of the New Testament and the Old Testament carry us into the period introduced by Luther. It remained for Luther and the other Reformers to give to the literal or historical sense its due weight, and especially from the sane grammatical exegesis of John Calvin is a new period in the exposition of the sacred writings to be dated.

The early printing-presses, from Lyons to Paris and from Venice and Nürnberg to Cologne and Lübeck, eagerly turned out editions of the entire Bible or parts of it, the vast majority of which, however, gave the Latin text. The first printed

---

[1] Gerson, *De sensu lit. scr. sac.* Du Pin's ed., 1728, I. 2 sq., says, *sensus lit. semper est verus* and *sensus lit. judicandus est prout ecclesia a Sp. S. inspirata determinat et non ad cujuslibet arbitrium.*

[2] *Paraclesis.*

Latin Bible, which appeared at Mainz without date and in two volumes, belongs before 1455 and bears the name of the Gutenberg Bible from the printer or the Mazarin Bible from the copy which was found in the library of Cardinal Mazarin. Before 1520, no less than 199 printed editions of the entire volume appeared. Of these, 156 were Latin, 17 German, — 3 of the German editions being in Low German, — 11 Italian, 2 Bohemian and one Russian.[1] Spain produced two editions, a Limousin version at Valencia, 1478, and the Complutensian Bible of Cardinal Ximenes, 1514–1517. England was far behind and her first printed English New Testament did not appear till 1526, although Caxton had set up his printing-press at Westminster in 1477.

To the printed copies of the whole Scriptures must be added the parts which appeared in *plenaria* and *psalteria*, — copies of the Gospels and of the Psalms,[2] — and in the *postillæ* which contained the Scripture text with annotations. From 1470–1520 no less than 103 *postillæ* appeared from the press.[3]

The number of copies of the Bible sent off in a single edition is a matter of conjecture as must also be the question whether copies were widely held by laymen.[4]

---

[1] Falk, pp. 24, 91–97, gives a full list with the places of issue. Walther gives a list of 120 MSS. of the Bible in German translation. The Lenox Library in New York has a copy of the Mazarin Bible. The first book bearing date, place and name of printers was the *Psalterium* issued by Fust and Schöffer, Aug. 14, 1457. See Copinger: *Incunabula biblica or the First Half Century of the Latin Bible*, Lond., 1892.

[2] Often only a brief selection of Psalms was given. Such collections were meant as manuals of devotion and perhaps also to be used in memorizing. See Falk, p. 28 sqq.

[3] Falk, p. 32. The word *postilla* comes from *post illa verba sicut textus evangelii* and its use goes back to the 13th century.

[4] Janssen, I. 23, 75 attempts to establish it as a fact that the copies struck off were numerous. He cites in confirmation the edition of the Latin Grammar of Cochlæus, 1511, which included 1,000 copies, and of a work of Bartholomew Arnoldi, 1517, 2,000 copies. Sebastian Brant declared that all lands were full of the Scriptures, and the Humanist, Celti, that the priests could find a copy in every inn if they chose to look. 6,000 copies of Tyndale's New Testament were printed in a single edition. The Koberger firm of Nürnberg has the honor of having produced no less than 25 editions, 1475–1520. Its Vulgate was on sale in London as early as 1580.

The new path which Erasmus struck out in his edition of the New Testament was looked upon in some quarters as a dangerous path.   Dorpius, one of the Louvain professors, in 1515, anticipated the appearance of the book by remonstrating with Erasmus for his bold project and pronounced the received Vulgate text free "from all mixture of falsehood and mistake." This, he alleged, was evident from its acceptance by the Church in all ages and the use the Fathers had made of it.   Another member of the Louvain faculty, Latromus, employed his learning in a pamphlet which maintained that a knowledge of Greek and Hebrew was not necessary for the scholarly study of the Scriptures.   In England, Erasmus' New Testament was attacked on a number of grounds by Lee, archbishop of York; and Standish, bishop of St. Asaph, preached a furious sermon in St. Paul's churchyard on Erasmus' temerity in undertaking the issue of such a work.   The University of Cologne was especially outraged by Erasmus' attempt and Conrad of Hersbach wrote:[1] —

They have found a language called Greek, at which we must be careful to be on our guard. It is the mother of all heresies. In the hands of many persons I see a book, which they call the New Testament. It is a book full of thorns and poison. As for Hebrew, my brethren, it is certain that those who learn it will sooner or later turn Jews.

But among the men who read Erasmus' text was Martin Luther, and he was studying it to settle questions which started in his soul.   About one of these he asked his friend Spalatin to consult Erasmus, namely the final meaning of the righteousness of the law, which he felt the great scholar had misinterpreted in his annotations on the Romans in the *Novum instrumentum*.   He believed, if Erasmus would read Augustine's works, he would change his mind. Luther preferred Augustine, as he said, with the knowledge of one tongue to Jerome with his knowledge of five.

Down to the very end of its history, the mediæval Church gave no official encouragement to the circulation of the Bible among the laity.   On the contrary, it uniformly set itself against it.   In 1199 Innocent III., writing to the diocese of

---

[1] Hase: *Ch. Hist.*, II. 2, p. 493. Faulkner: *Erasmus*, p. 127 sqq. Dorpius' letter is given by Nichols, II. 168 sqq.

Metz where the Scriptures were being used by heretics, declared that as by the old law, the beast touching the holy mount was to be stoned to death, so simple and uneducated men were not to touch the Bible or venture to preach its doctrines.[1] The article of the Synod of Toulouse, 1229, strictly forbidding the Old and New Testaments to the laity either in the original text or in the translation[2] was not recalled or modified by papal or synodal action. Neither after nor before the invention of printing was the Bible a free book. Gerson was quite in line with the utterances of the Church, when he stated, that it was easy to give many reasons why the Scriptures were not to be put into the vulgar tongues except the historical sections and the parts teaching morals.[3] In Spain, Ferdinand and Isabella represented the strict churchly view when, on the eve of the Reformation, they prohibited under severe penalties the translation of the Scriptures and the possession of copies. The positive enactment of the English archbishop, Arundel, at the beginning of the 15th century, forbidding the reading of Wyclif's English version, was followed by the notorious pronouncement of Archbishop Bertholdt of Mainz against the circulation of the German Bible, at the close of the same century, 1485. The position taken by Wyclif that the Scriptures, as the sole source of authority for creed and life, should be freely circulated found full response in the closing years of the Middle Ages only in the utterances of one scholar, Erasmus, but he was under suspicion and always ready to submit himself to the judgment of the Church hierarchic. If Wyclif said, "God's law should be taught in that tongue that is more known, for this wit [wisdom] is God's Word," Erasmus in his *Paraclesis*[4] uttered the equally bold words: —

I utterly dissent from those who are unwilling that the sacred Scriptures should be read by the unlearned translated into their own vulgar tongue, as though the strength of the Christian religion consisted in men's

[1] Migne CCXIV : 695 sq.

[2] *Ne præmissos libros laici habeant in vulgari translatos arctissime inhibemus*, Mansi, XXIII. 194.

[3] *Prohibendam esse vulgarem translationem librorum sac*, etc. *Contra vanam curiositatem*, Du Pin's ed., I. 105.

[4] Basel ed., V. 117 sq.

ignorance of it. The counsels of kings are much better kept hidden but Christ wished his mysteries to be published as openly as possible. I wish that even the weakest woman should read the Gospel and the epistles of Paul. And I wish they were translated into all languages, so that they might be read and understood, not only by Scots and Irishmen but also by Turks and Saracens. I long that the husbandman should sing portions of them to himself as he follows the plow, that the weaver should hum them to the tune of his shuttle, that the traveller should beguile with their stories the tedium of his journey.

The utterances of Erasmus aside, the appeals made 1450–1520 for the circulation of the Scriptures among all classes are very sparse and, in spite of all pains, Catholic controversialists have been able to bring together only a few. And yet, the few that we have show that, at least in Germany and the Netherlands, there was a popular hunger for the Bible in the vernacular. Thus, the Preface to the German Bible, issued at Cologne, 1480, called upon every Christian to read the Bible with devotion and honest purpose. Though the most learned may not exhaust its wisdom, nevertheless its teachings are clear and uncovered. The learned may read Jerome's Vulgate but the unlearned and simple folk could and should use the Cologne edition which was in good German. The devotional manual, *Die Himmelsthür*, — Door of Heaven, — 1513, declared that listening to sermons ought to stir up people to read diligently in the German Bible. In 1505, Jacob Wimpheling spoke of the common people reading both Testaments in their mother-tongue and made this the ground of an appeal to priests not to neglect to read the Word of God themselves.[1]

Such testimonies are more than offset by warnings against the danger attending the popular use of Scriptures. Brant spoke strongly in this vein and so did Geiler of Strassburg, who asserted that putting the Scriptures into the hands of laymen was like putting a knife into the hands of children to cut bread. He added that it "was almost a wicked thing to print the sacred text in German."[2] Archbishop Bertholdt's

---

[1] Falk, p. 18. Janssen, I. 72, is careful to tell that the peasant, Hans Werner, who could read, knew his Bible so well by heart that he was able to give the places where this text and that were found.

[2] *Es ist fast ein bös Ding dass man die Bibel zu deutsch druckt.* Quoted by Frietsche-Nestle in Herzog, II. 704.

fulmination against German versions of the Bible and their
circulation among the people no doubt expressed the general
mind of the hierarchy in Germany and all Europe.[1] In this
celebrated edict, the German primate pronounced the German
language too barbarous a tongue to reproduce the high
thoughts expressed by Greek and Latin writers, writing of
the Christian religion.   The Scriptures are not to be given
to simple and unlearned men and, above all, are not to be put
into the hands of women.[2] He spoke of the fools who were
using the divine gift of printing to send forth things proscribed to the public and declared, that the printers of the
sacred text were moved by the vain love of fame or by greed.
In his zeal, the archbishop went so far as to forbid the translation of all works whatsoever, of Greek and Latin authorship, or
their sale without the sanction of the doctors of the Universities of Mainz or Erfurt.   The punishment for the violation
of the edict was excommunication, confiscation of books and
a fine of 100 gulden.

The decree was so effective that, after 1488, only four editions of the German Bible appeared until 1522, when Luther
issued his New Testament, when the old German translations
seemed to be suddenly laid aside.[3] In England, Arundel's
inhibition so fully expressed the mind of the nation that for a
full century no attempt was made to translate the Bible into
English and it was not till after 1530 that the first copy of
the English Scriptures was published on English soil.[4] Sir
Thomas More, it is true, writing on the threshold of the
English Reformation, interpreted Arundel's decree as directed
against corrupt translations and sought to make it appear

---

[1] The text is given in Mirbt : *Quellen zur Gesch. d. Papsttums*, p. 173.

[2] *Quis enim dabit idiotis et indoctis hominibus et femineo sexui*, etc.

[3] Reuss, p. 534.   The last four editions of the old German Bible were 1490,
Augsburg, 1494, Lübeck, Augsburg, 1508, 1518.

[4] We might have expected some definite utterance in regard to Bible translations from Pecock, in his *Repressor of Overmuch Blaming of the Clergy*,
1450–1460. What he says is in the progress of his refutation of the Lollards'
position that all things necessary to be believed and done are to be found in
the Scriptures. He adds, Rolls Series, I. 119, "And thou shalt not find expressly in Holy Scripture that the New and Old Testaments should be writ
in English tongue to laymen or in Latin tongue to clergy."

that it was on account of errors that Wyclif's version had been condemned. He was striving to parry the charge that the Church had withheld the Bible from popular use, but, whatever the interpretation put upon his words may be (see this volume, p. 348), the fact remains that the English were slow in getting any printed version of their own and that the Catholic party issued none till the close of the 16th century.

Distinct witness is borne by Tyndale to the unwillingness of the old party to have the Bible in English, in these words : " Some of the papists say it is impossible to translate the Scriptures into English, some that it is not lawful for the lay-folk to have it in the mother-tongue, some that it would make them all heretics." [1] After the new views were quite prevalent in England, the English Bible had a hard time in winning the right to be read. Tyndale's version, for the printing of which he found no room in England, was at Wolsey's instance proscribed by Henry VIII. and the famous burning of 1527 in St. Paul's churchyard of all the copies Bishop Tonstall could lay his hands on will always rise up to rebuke those who try to make it appear that the circulation of the Word of God was intended by the Church authorities to be free. Tyndale declared that, " in burning the New Testament, the papists did none other thing than I looked for ; no more shall they do if they burn me also." Any fears he may have had were realized in his execution at Vilvorde, 1536.[2] No doubt, the priest repre-

---

[1] *Pref. to the Pentateuch*, Parker Soc. ed., Tyndale's *Doctr. Works*, p. 392. Arundel did not adduce any errors in Wyclif's version. Abbot Gasquet, in *The Old Engl. Bible*, p. 108, and *Eve of the Reform.*, p. 209 sqq., attempts to show that the Bible was not a proscribed book in England before the Reformation. The testimonies he adduces, commending the Scriptures, are so painfully few as to seem to make his case a hopeless one. Dixon, *Hist. of the Ch. of Engl.*, I. 451, speaks of Arundel's " proclaiming the war of authority against English versions."

[2] Cochlæus informed the English authorities of Tyndale's presence in Wittenberg and his proposed issue of the English N. T., in order to prevent "the importation of the pernicious merchandise." Tonstall professed to have discovered no less than 2000 errors in Tyndale's N. T. See Fulke's *Defence* in Parker Soc. ed., p. 61. Tyndale, *Pref. to the Pent.*, p. 373, says, that " the papists who had found all their Scripture before in their Duns or such like devilish doctrine, now spy out mistakes in my transl., even if it be only the dot of an *i*."

sented a large class when he rebuked Tyndale for proposing to translate the Bible in the words, "We were better without God's laws than the pope's." The martyr Hume's body was hung when an English Bible was found on his person. In 1543, the reading of the Scriptures was forbidden in England except to persons of quality. The Scotch joined the English authorities when the Synod of St. Andrews, 1529, forbade the importation of Bibles into Scotland.

In France, according to the testimony of the famous printer Robert Stephens, who was born in 1503, the doctors of the Sorbonne, in the period when he was a young man, knew about the New Testament only from quotations from Jerome and the Decretals. He declared that he was more than 50 years old before he knew anything about the New Testament. Luther was a man before he saw a copy of the Latin Bible. In 1533, Geneva forbade its citizens to read the Bible in German or French and ordered all translations burnt.[1] The strict inquisition of books would have passed to all countries, if the hierarchy had had its way. In 1535, Francis I. closed the printing-presses and made it a capital offence in France to publish a religious book without authorization from the Sorbonne. The attitude of the Roman Catholic hierarchy, since the Reformation as well as during the Reformation, has been against the free circulation of the Bible. In the 19th century, one pope after another anathematized Bible societies. In Spain, Italy and South America, the punishments visited upon Bible colporteurs and the frequent burning of the Bible itself have been quite in the line of the decrees of Arundel and Bertholdt and the treatment of Bishop Tonstall. Nor will it be forgotten that, at the time Rome was made the capital of Italy in 1870, a papal law required that copies of the Bible found in the possession of visitors to the papal city be confiscated.

On the other hand, through the agency of the Reformers, the book was made known and offered freely to all classes. What use the Reformers hoped to make of printing for the dis-

[1] See Baird: *Hist. of the Huguenots*, I. 57 ; Lindsay: *The Reformation*, II. 80.

semination of religion and intelligence is tersely and quaintly
expressed by the martyrologist, Foxe, in these words : [1] —

Either the pope must abolish printing or he must seek a new world to
reign over, for else, as the world stands, printing will abolish him.   The
pope and all the cardinals must understand this, that through the light of
printing the world begins now to have eyes to see and heads to judge. . . .
God hath opened the press to preach, whose voice the pope is never able to
stop with all the puissance of the triple crown.   By printing as by the
gift of tongues and as by the singular organ of the Holy Ghost, the doctrine
of the Gospel sounds to all nations and countries under heaven and what
God reveals to one man, is dispersed to many and what is known to one nation is opened to all.

NOTE. — Both Janssen and Abbot Gasquet spend much pains in the attempt to show that the mediæval Church was not opposed to the circulation
of the Bible in popular versions or the Latin Vulgate.   The proofs they
bring forward must be regarded as strained and insufficient.   They ignore
entirely the vast mass of testimony on the other side, as, for example, the
testimony involved in the popular reception given to the German and English Scriptures when they appeared from the hands of the Reformers and
the mass of testimony given by the Reformers on the subject.   Gasquet endeavors to break the force of the argument drawn from Arundel's edict, but
he has nothing to say of the demand Wyclif made for the popular dissem-
ination of the Bible, a demand which implied that the Bible was withheld
from the people.   Dr. Barry, who belongs to the same school, in the *Cambr.
Mod. Hist.*, I. 640, speaks of "the enormous extent the Bible was read in
the 15th century" and that it was not "till we come within sight of the
Lutheran troubles that preachers, like Geiler of Kaisersberg, hint their
doubts on the expediency of unrestrained Bible-reading in the vernacular."
What is to be said of such an exaggeration in view of the fact that the vast
majority of Bibles were in Latin, a language which the people could not
read, that Geiler died in 1510, seven years before Luther ceased to be a
pious Augustinian monk, and that he did very much more than hint doubts!
He expressed himself unreservedly against Bible-reading.   Janssen-Pastor,
— I. 23 sqq., 72 sqq., VII. 535 sqq. — have a place for stray testimonies between 1480–1520 in favor of the popular reading of the Scriptures, but, so
far as I can see, do not refer to the warnings of Brant, Geiler and others
against their use by laymen, and the only reference they make to Bertholdt's
notorious decree is to the clause in which the archbishop emphasizes the
divine art of printing, *divina quædam ars imprimendi*, I. 15.

[1] *Book of Martyrs*, V. 355.

§ 78. *Popular Piety.*

During the last century of the Middle Ages, the religious life of the laity was stimulated by some new devices, especially in Germany. There, the effort to instruct the laity in the matters of the Christian faith was far more vital and active than in any other part of Western Christendom.

The popular need found recognition in the illustrations, furnished in many editions of the early Bibles. The Cologne Bible of 1480, the Lübeck Bible of 1494 and the Venice Bible of Malermi, 1497, are the best examples of this class of books. Fifteen of the 17 German Bibles, issued before the Reformation, were illustrated.

A more distinct recognition of this need was given in the so-called *biblia pauperum*, — Bibles for the poor, — first single sheets and then books, containing as many as 40 or 50 pictures of biblical scenes.[1] In the first instance, they seem to have been intended to aid priests in giving instruction. Side by side, they set scenes from the two Testaments, showing the prophetic types and their fulfilments. Thus the circumcisions of Abraham, Jacob and Christ are depicted in three separate pictures, the priest being represented in the very act of circumcising Christ. Explanations in Latin, German or French accompany the pictures.

An extract will give some idea of the kind of information furnished by this class of literature. When Adam was dying, he sent Seth into the garden to get medicine. The cherub gave him a branch from the tree of life. When Seth returned, he found his father dead and buried. He planted the branch

---

[1] Ed. Reuss: *D. deutschen Historienbibeln vor d. Erfindung d. Bücherdrucks*, 1855. — J. T. Berjeau: *Biblia pauperum*, Lond., 1859. — Laib u. Schwarz: *D. Biblia pauperum n. d. Original in d. Lyceumsbibl. zu Constanz*, Zürich, 1867. — Th. Merzdorf: *D. deutschen Historienbibeln nach 40 Hdschriften*, Tüb., 1870, 2 vols. — R. Muther: *D. ältesten deutschen Bilderbibeln*, 1883. — Falk: *D. Bibel am Ausgange d. MA*, p. 77 sqq. — *Biblia pauperum n. d. Wolfenbüttel Exemplare jetzt in d. Bibl. nationale*, ed. P. Heintz, *mit Einleitung über d. Entstehung d. biblia pauperum*, by W. L. Schreiber, Strass., 1903. — Artt. *Bilderbibel*, in Herzog, III. 214 and *Historienbibel*, in Herzog, VIII. 155 sqq. and *Bib. pauperum*, in Wetzer-Welte, II. 776 sq. — Reuss: *Gesch. d. N. T.*, 524 sqq.

and in 4000 years it grew to be the tree on which the Saviour was crucified.

The best executed of these biblical picture-books are those in Constance,[1] St. Florian, Austria and in the libraries of Munich and Vienna. The name, *biblia pauperum*, may have been derived from Bonaventura or the statement of Gregory the Great, that pictures are the people's bible. In 1509, Lukas Kranach issued the passion in a series of pictures at Wittenberg.

A marked and most hopeful novelty in Germany were the numerous manuals of devotion and religious instruction which were issued soon after the invention of printing. This literature bears witness to the intelligent interest taken in religious training, although its primary purpose was not for the young but to furnish a guide-book for the confessional and to serve priest and layman in the hour of approaching death.[2] These books are, for the most part, in German, and probably had a wide circulation. They show common Christians what the laws of God are for daily life and what are the chief articles of the Church's faith. Some of the titles give us an idea of the intent, — The Soul's Guide, *Der Seelenführer;* Path to Heaven, *Die Himmelstrasse;* The Soul's Comfort, *Der Seelentrost;* The Heart's Counsellor, *Der Herzmahner;* The Devotional Bell, *Das andächtige Zeitglöcklein;* The Foot-Path to Eternal Bliss, *Der Fusspfad zur ewigen Seligkeit;* The Soul's Vegetable Garden, *Das Seelenwürzgärtlein;* The Soul's Vineyard, *Der*

---

[1] The Constance copy in the Rosengarten museum contains many pictures, with explanatory notes on each page. I was particularly struck with the execution of Christ's entry into Jerusalem.

[2] Bezold, p. 112, speaks of the number of these manuals as *massenhaft* and Dr. Barry, *Cambr. Hist.*, I. 641, with rhetorical unprecision speaks of them as sold in all book-markets. See J. Geffcken: *D. Bibelcatechismen d. 15 Jahrh.*, Leipz., 1855. — B. Hasak: *D. christl. Glaube d. deutschen Volkes beim Schlusse d. MA*, Regensb., 1868. — P. Bahlmann: *Deutschland's kathol. Katechismen bis zum Ende d. 16 Jahrh.*, Münster, 1894. — F. Falk: *D. deutschen Sterbebüchlein bis 1520*, Col., 1890. Also *Drei Beichtbüchlein nach den 10 Geboten*, Münster, 1907. Also *D. Druckkunst im Dienste d. Kirche bis 1520*, Col., 1879. — F. W. Battenberg: *Joh. Wolff, Beichtbüchlein*, Giessen, 1907. — Janssen-Pastor, I. 32 sqq. — Achelis: *Prak. Theol.*, II. 497 sqq. — Wiegand: *D. apost. Symbol im MA*, p. 50 sqq.

Weingarten der Seele ; The Spiritual Chase, *Die geistliche Jagd.*
Others were known by the general title of *Beichtbüchlein —
libri di penitentia* — or penitential books.

A compendious statement of their intent is given in the title
of the *Seelenführer,*[1] namely " The Soul's Guide, a useful book
for every Christian to practise a pious life and to reach a holy
death." This literature deserves closer attention both because
it represents territory hitherto largely neglected by students
of the later Middle Ages and because it bears witness to the zeal
among the German clergy to spread practical religion among
the people. The *Himmelwagen,* the Heavenly Carriage, represents the horses as faith, love, repentance, patience, peace,
humility and obedience. The Trinity is the driver, the carriage itself God's mercy.

With variations, these little books explain the 10 Commandments, the 14 articles of the Creed — the number into which
it was then divided — the Lord's Prayer, the Beatitudes,
mortal sins, the 5 senses, the works of mercy and other topics.
The Soul's Comfort, which appeared in 16 editions, 1474–1523,[2]
takes up the 10 Commandments, 7 sacraments, 8 Beatitudes,
6 works of mercy, the 7 spiritual gifts, 7 mortal sins and 7 cardinal virtues and "what God further thinks me worthy of
knowing." Most useful as this little book was adapted to be,
it sometimes states truth under strange forms, as when it tells
of a man whose soul after death was found, not in his body
but in his money-chest and of a girl who, while dancing on
Friday, was violently struck by the devil but recovered on
giving her promise to amend her ways.

The *Path to Heaven* contains 52 chapters. The first two
set forth faith and hope, the joys of the elect and the pains of
the lost and it closes with 4 chapters describing a holy death,
the devil's modes of tempting the dying and questions which
are to be put to sick people. Dietrich Kolde's *Mirror of a
Christian Man,* one of the most popular of the manuals, in
the first two of its 46 chapters, took up the Apostles' Creed

[1] Printed at Mainz, by Peter Schöffer, 1498, 47 pp.
[2] See list of the editions in Bahlmann, p. 13 sq. The Cologne ed. of 1474
is in the London museum.

and, in the last, the marks of a good Christian man.   The first edition appeared before 1476; the 23d at Delfft, 1518.[1]

Many of the manuals expressly set forth the value of the family religion and call upon parents to teach their children the Creed, the 10 Commandments, the Lord's Prayer, to have them pray morning and evening and to take them to church to hear the mass and preaching.   *The Soul's Guide* says, "The Christian home should be the first school for young children and their first church."

The Path to Heaven,[2] written by Stephen von Landskron or Lanzkranna, dean of Vienna, d. 1477, presents a very attractive picture of a Christian household.   As a model for imitation, the head of a family is represented as going to church with his wife, children and servants every Sunday and listening to the preaching.   On returning home, he reviews the subject of the sermon and hears them recite the Commandments, Lord's Prayer and Creed and the 7 mortal sins. Then, after he has refreshed himself with a draught, *Trinklein*, they sing a song to God or Mary or to one of the saints.   *The Soul's Comfort* counsels parents to examine their households about the articles of faith and the precepts the children had learned at school and at church.   *The Table of a Christian Life* [3] urges the parents to keep their children off the streets, send them to school, making a selection of their teachers and, above all, to live well themselves and "go before" their children in the practice of all the virtues.

Of the penitential books, designed distinctly as manuals of preparation for the confessional, the work of John Wolff is the most elaborate and noteworthy.   This good man, who was chaplain at St. Peter's, Frankfurt, wrote his book 1478.[4]   He was deeply interested in the impartation of religious instruction.   His tombstone, which was unearthed in 1895, calls him

[1] Bahlmann, pp. 17–19.   The first dated MS. copy is 1470.

[2] Bahlmann, p. 7, gives as the probable date of composition, 1450.   The 1st printed ed., Augsburg, 1484.   See also Geffcken, pp. 107–119.

[3] Bahlmann gives it in full, pp. 63–74.

[4] See Falk : *Drei Beichtbüchlein*.   The text of Wolff's manual fills pp. 17–75.   Falk also gives a penitential book, printed at Nürnberg, 1475, pp. 77–81, and a manual printed at Augsburg, 1504, pp. 82–96.

the "doctor of the 10 Commandments" and gives a representation of the 10 Commandments in 10 pictures, each Commandment being designated by a hand with one or more fingers uplifted. Such tables it was not an uncommon thing, in the last years of the Middle Ages, to hang on the walls of churches.

Wolff's book, which is a guide for daily Christian living, sets forth at length the 10 Commandments and the acts and inward thoughts which are in violation of them, and puts into the mouth of the offender an appropriate confession. Thus, confessing to a violation of the 4th Commandment, the offender says, "I have done on Friday rough work, in farming, dunging the fields, splitting wood, spinning, sewing, buying and selling, dancing, striking people at the dance, playing games and doing other sinful things. I did not hear mass or preaching and was remiss in the service of Almighty God." Upon the exposition of the Decalogue follow lists of the five baser sins,—usury, killing, stealing, sodomy and keeping back wages, — the 6 sins against the Holy Ghost, the 7 works of mercy such as visiting the sick, clothing the naked and burying the dead, the sacraments, the Beatitudes, the 7 gifts of the Holy Ghost and an exposition of repentance. The work closes with a summary of the advantages to be derived from the frequent repetition of the 10 Commandments and mentions 13 excuses, given for not repeating them, such as that the words are hard to remember and the unwillingness to have them as a perpetual monitor.

These manuals, having in view the careful instruction of adults and children, indicate a new era in the history of religious training. No catechisms have come down to us from the ancient Church. The catechumens to whom Augustine and Cyril addressed their catechetical discourses were adults. In the 13th century, synods began to call for the preparation of summaries of religious knowledge for laymen. So a synod at Lambeth, 1281, Prag, 1355, and Lavaur, France, 1368. The Synod of Tortosa, 1429, ordered its prelates to secure the preparation of a brief compendium containing in concise paragraphs all that it was necessary for the people to know and that might be explained to them every Sunday during the

year by their pastors.   Gerson approached the catechetical
method (see this volume, p. 216 sq.) and, after long years of
activity made the statement that the reformation of the church
must begin with children, *a parvulis ecclesiæ reparatio et ejus
cultura incipienda.*[1] In his *Tripartite* work he presents the
Ten Commandments, confession and thoughts for the dying.
The catechetical form of question and answer was not
adopted till after the Lutheran Reformation was well on its
way. The term, catechism, as a designation of such a manual
was first used by Luther, 1525, and the first book to bear the
title was Andreas Althammer's Catechism, which appeared
in 1528.   Luther's two catechisms were issued one year later.
The first Catholic book to bear the title was prepared by
George Wicelius, 1535.

In England, we have something similar to the German penitential books in the *Prymers*,[2] the first copy of which dates
from 1410.   They were circulated in Latin and English, and
were intended for the instruction of the laity.   They contained the calendar, the Hours of our Lady, the litany, the
Lord's Prayer, Creed, Ten Commandments, 7 Penitential
Psalms, the 7 deadly sins, prayers and other matters.   The
book is referred to by Piers Plowman, and frequently in the
15th century, as one well known.[3]   The *Horn-book* also deserves mention.   This device for teaching the alphabet and

---

[1] Gerson's *opp.*, Du Pin's ed., III. 280.   Luther, in the same vein, said in
1516, Weimar ed., I. 450, 494, that, if there was to be a revival in the Church,
it must start with the instruction of the children.   A single book, corresponding to the manuals above described, has come down to us, from an
earlier period, the composition of a monk of Weissenberg of the 9th century.
See two Artt. on Catechisms in the *Presb. Banner*, Dec. 31, 1908, Jan. 7,
1909 by D. S. Schaff.

[2] Maskell : *Monumenta ritualia*, 2d ed., 1882, III., pp. ii–lxvii and a reprint of a Prymer, III. 3–183.   Dr. Edward Barton edited three Primers,
dating from 1535, 1539, 1545, Oxf., 1834.   See also Proctor's *Hist. of the Bk.
of Com. Prayer*, p. 14 sq.   Proctor calls the Primer " the book authorized for
150 years before the Reformation by the Engl. Church, for the private devotion of the people."   A. W. Tuer : *Hist. of the Horn Book*, 2 vols., Lond.,
1896.   Highly illust. and most beautiful vols.

[3] Maskell, III., pp. xxxv–xlix, says the word, Prymer, can be traced to
the beginning of the 14th century.

the Lord's Prayer consisted of a rectangular board with a handle, to be held like a modern hand-mirror. On one or both sides were cut or printed the letters of the alphabet and the Lord's Prayer. Horn-books were probably not in general use till the close of the 16th century, but they date back to the middle of the 15th. They probably got their name from a piece of animal horn with which the face of the written matter was covered as a protection against grubby fingers.[1]

A nearer approach to the catechetical idea was made by Colet in his rudiments of religious knowledge appended to his elementary grammar, and intended for use in St. Paul's School. It contains the Apostles' Creed, the Lord's Prayer, an exposition of the love due God and our fellowmen, 46 special "precepts of living," and two prayers, and is generally known as the *Catecheyzon*.[2]

Religious instruction was also given through the series of pictures known as the Dance of Death, and through the miracle plays.[3] In the Dance of Death, a perpetual *memento mori*, death was represented in the figure of a skeleton appearing to persons in every avocation of life and of every class. None were too holy or too powerful to evade his intrusion and none too humble to be beyond his notice. Death wears now a serious, now a comic aspect, now politely leads his victim, now walks arm in arm with him, now drags him or beats him. An hour-glass is usually found somewhere in the pictures, grimly reminding the onlooker that the time of life is certain to run out. These pictures were painted on bridges,

---

[1] Horn-books, as Mr. Tuer says, were much used in England, Scotland and America, down to the close of the 18th century. So completely had they gone out of use, that even Mr. Gladstone declared he knew "nothing at all about them. Tuer, I., p. 8.

[2] Text in Lupton : *Life of Colet*, pp. 285–292.

[3] G. Peignot : *Recherches sur les Danses des morts*, Paris, 1826. — C. Douce : *The Dance of Death*, London, 1833. — Massmann : *Literatur der Todtentänze*, etc., Leipzig, 1841. — R. Fortoul : *Les Danses des morts*, Paris, 1844. — Smith: *Holbein's Dance of Death*, London, 1849. — G. Kastner, *Les Danses des morts*, Paris, 1852. — W. Bäumker : *Der Todtentanz*, Frankfurt, 1881. — W. Combe : *The Engl. Dance of Death*, new ed., 2 vols., N.Y., 1903. — Valentin Dufour, *Recherches sur la danse macabre, peinte en 1425, au cimetiere des innocents*, Paris, 1873. — Wetzer-Welte : *Todtentanz*, XI., 1834–1841.

houses, church windows and convent walls. Among the oldest specimens are those in Minden, 1383, at Paris in the churchyard of the Franciscans, 1425, Dijon, 1436, Basel, 1441, Croyden, the Tower of London, Salisbury Cathedral, 1460, Lübeck, 1463.[1]

In the fifteenth century, the religious drama was in its bloom in Germany and England.[2] The acting was now turned over to laymen and the public squares and streets were preferred for the performances. The people looked on from the houses as well as from the streets. In 1412, while the play of St. Dorothea was being acted in the market-place at Bautzen, the roof of one of the houses fell and 33 persons were killed. The introduction of buffoonery and farce had become a recognized feature and lightened the impression without impairing the religious usefulness of the plays. The devil was made a subject of perpetual jest and fun. The people found in them an element of instruction which, perhaps, the priest did not impart. The scenes enacted reached from the Creation and the fall of Lucifer to the Last Judgment and from Abel's death and Isaac's sacrifice to the crucifixion and resurrection.

Set forth by living actors, the miracle plays and moralities were to the Middle Ages what the Pilgrim's Progress was to Puritans. They were performed from Rome to London, at the marriage and visits of princes and for the delectation of the people. We find them presented before Sigismund and prelates during the solemn discussions of the Council of Constance, as when the play of the Nativity and the Slaughter of the Innocents was acted at the Bishop of Salisbury's lodgings, 1417, and at St. Peter's, as when the play of Susannah and the Elders was performed in honor of Leonora, daughter of Ferrante of Naples, 1473. At a popular dramatization of the parable of the 10 Virgins in Eisenach, 1324, the margrave,

---

[1] William Dunbar, the Scotch poet, wrote with boisterous humor, *The Dance of the Sevin Deidlie Synnis* (1507 ?), perhaps as a picture of a revel held on Shrove Tuesday at the court. Each of the cardinal sins performed a dance. Ward-Waller : *Cambr. Hist. of Lit.*, II. 289, etc.

[2] In addition to the lit. given in vol. V.: 1, p. 869, see F. E. Schelling : *Hist. of the Drama of Engl., 1558–1642, with a Résumé of the Earlier Drama from the Beginning*, Boston, 1908.

Friedrich, was so moved by the pleas of the 5 foolish maidens and the failure to secure the aid of Mary and the saints, that he cried out, "What is the Christian religion worth, if sinners cannot obtain mercy through the intercession of Mary?" The story went, that he became melancholy and died soon afterwards.

Of the four English cycles of miracle plays, York, Chester, Coventry and Towneley or Wakefield, the York cycle dates back to 1360 and contained from 48 to 57 plays. Chester and Coventry were the traditional centres of the religious drama. The stage or pageant, as it was called, was wheeled through the streets. The playing was often in the hands of the guilds, such as the barbers, tanners, plasterers, butchers, spicers, chandlers.[1] The paying of actors dates from the 14th century.

Chester cycles was Noah's Flood, a subject popular everywhere in mediæval Europe. After God's announcement to the patriarch, his 3 sons and their wives offered to take hand in the building of the ark. Noah's wife alone held out and scolded while the others worked. In spite of Noah's well-known quality of patience, her husband exclaimed: —

> Lord, these women be crabbed, aye
> And none are meke, I dare well saye.

Nothing daunted, however, the patriarch went on with his hammering and hewing and remarked: —

> These bordes heare I pinne togither
> To bear us saffe from the weither,
> That we may rowe both heither and theither
> And saffe be from the fludde.[2]

The ark finished, each party brought his portion of animals and birds. But when they were housed, Noah's help-meet again proved a disturbing element. Noah bade Shem go and fetch her.

> Sem, sonne, loe! thy mother is wrawe (angry).

---

[1] Pollock gives 48 York guilds with plays assigned to each, pp. xxxi–xxxiv. There are records of plays in more than 100 Engl. towns and villages, Pollock, p. xxiii.

[2] Text in Pollock, p. 8 sqq. It was common to represent Noah's consort as a shrew. So Chaucer in the *Miller's Tale.*

Shem told her they were about to set sail, but still she resisted
entreaty and all hands were called to join together and " fetch
her in."

One of the best of the English plays, *Everyman*, has for its
subject the inevitableness of death and the judgment.[1] God
sends Death to Everyman and, in his attempt to withstand
his message, Everyman calls upon his friends Fellowship,
Riches, Strength, Beauty and Good Works for help or, at
least, to accompany him on his pilgrimage.   This with one
consent they refused to do.   He then betook himself to Penance, and has explained to him the powers of the priesthood: —

> God hath to priest more power given
> Than to any angel that is in heaven.
> With five words, he may consecrate
> God's body in flesh and blood to take
> And handleth his Maker between his hands :
> The priest bindeth and unbindeth all bands
> Both in earth and in heaven,
> He ministers all the sacraments seven.

Such plays were impressive sermons, a popular summer-school
of moral and religious instruction, the mediæval Chatauqua.
They continued to be performed in England till the 16th century and even till the reign of James I., when the modern drama
took their place.   The last survival of the religious drama of
the Middle Ages is the Passion Play given at Oberammergau
in the highlands of Bavaria.   In obedience to a vow, made during a severe epidemic in 1634, it has been acted every ten years
since and more often in recent years.   Since 1860, the performances have attracted throngs of spectators from foreign lands, a
performance being set for 1910.   Writers have described it as a
most impressive sermon on the most momentous of scenes, as it
is a solemn act of worship for the simple-hearted, pious Catholics
of that remote mountain village.

Pilgrimages and the worship of relics were as popular in the
15th century as they had been in previous periods of the Middle
Ages.[2]   Guide-books for pilgrims were circulated in Germany

[1] The text in Pollock.   It was revived in New York City in the Winter of
1902–1903 and played in three theatres, creating a momentary interest.

[2] See Erasmus: *Praise of Folly*, *Enchiridion* and *Colloquies.* — Gasquet :
Eve of the Reformation, pp. 365–394. — G. Ficker: *D. ausgehende Mittelalter,*

and England and contained vocabularies as well as items of geography and other details.[1] Jerusalem continued to attract the feet of princes and prelates as well as persons of less exalted estate. Frederick the Wise of Saxony, Luther's cautious but firm friend, was one of these pilgrims in the last days of the Middle Ages. William Wey of England, who in 1458 and 1462, went to the Holy Land, tells us how the pilgrims sang "O city dear Jerusalem," *Urbs beata*, as they landed at Joppa. Sir Richard Torkington and Sir Thomas Tappe, both ecclesiastics, made the journey the same year that Luther nailed up the Theses, 1517. The journeys to Rome during the Jubilee Years of 1450, 1500, drew vast throngs of people, eager to see the holy city and concerned to secure the religious benefits promised by the supreme pontiff. Local shrines also attracted constant streams of pilgrims.

Among the popular shrines in Germany were the holy blood at Sternberg from 1492, the image of Mary at Grimmenthal from 1499, as a cure for the French sickness, the head of St. Anna at Düren from 1500, this relic having been stolen from Mainz. The holy coat of Treves was brought to light in 1512. As in the flourishing days of the Crusades, so again, pilgrimage-epidemics broke out among the children of Germany, as in 1457 when large bands went to St. Michael's in Normandy and in 1475 to Wilsnack, where, in spite of the exposure by Nicolas of Cusa, the blood was still reputed holy.[2] The most noted places of pilgrimage in Germany were Cologne with the bodies of the three Magi-kings and Aachen, where Mary's undergarment, Jesus' swaddling-cloth and the loin-cloth he wore on the cross and other priceless relics are kept. Some idea of the popularity of pilgrimages may be had from the numbers that are given, though it is possible they are exaggerated. In 1466, 130,000 attended the festival of the angels at Einsiedeln, Swit-

---

Leipzig, pp. 69-73. — H. Siebert, Rom. Cath.: *Beiträge zur vorreformatorischen Heiligen-und Reliquienverehrung*, Freib. im Br., 1907. — Bezold, p. 105 sqq., Janssen-Pastor.

[1] Falk: *Druckkunst*, pp. 33-37 ; 44-79 etc. Siebert, p. 55 sq. — Wey: *Itineraries*, ed. by Roxburghe Club, 1857.

[2] We have the account of the latter by an eye-witness, the chronicler priest, Conrad Stolle of Erfurt. See Ficker, p. 69 sq.

zerland, and in 1496 the porter at the gate of Aachen counted 146,000.[1] In the 14 days, when the relics were displayed, 85,000 gulden were left in the money-boxes of St. Mary's, Aachen.

Imposing religious processions were also popular, such as the procession at Erfurt, 1483, in a time of drought. It lasted from 5 in the morning till noon, the ranks passing from church to church. Among those who took part were 948 children from the schools, the entire university-body comprising 2,141 persons, 312 secular priests, the monks of 5 convents and a company of 2,316 maidens with their hair hanging loosely down their backs and carrying tapers in their hands. German synods called attention to the abuses of the pilgrimage-habit and sought to check it.[2]

English pilgrims, not satisfied with going to Rome, Jerusalem and the sacred places on their own island, also turned their footsteps to the tomb of St. James of Compostella, Spain. In 1456, Wey conducted 7 ship-loads of pilgrims to this Spanish locality. Among the popular English shrines were St. Edmund of Bury, St. Ethelred of Ely, the holy hood of Boxley, the holy blood of Hailes and, more popular than all, Thomas à Becket's tomb at Canterbury and our Blessed Lady of Walsingham. So much frequented was the road to Walsingham that it was said, Providence set the milky way in the place it occupies in the heavens that it might shine directly upon it and direct the devout to the sacred spot. These two shrines were visited by unbroken processions of religious itinerants, including kings and queens as well as people less distinguished. Reference has already been made to Erasmus' description, which he gives in his *Colloquies*. At Walsingham, he was shown the Virgin's shrine rich with jewels and ornaments of silver and gold and lit up by burning candles. There, was the wicket at which the pilgrim had to stoop to pass but through which, with the Virgin's aid, an armed

---

[1] Bezold, 105 sq., Janssen, I. 748.   See an art., *Relic Worship in the Heart of Europe*, in the *Presb. Banner*, Sept. 16, 1909, by D. S. Schaff on a visit to Einsiedeln, whither 160,000 pilgrims journeyed in 1908, and to Aachen when the " greater relics," which are displayed once in 7 years, were exposed July 9–21, 1909, and according to the Frankfurt press attracted 600,000 pilgrims.

[2] Janssen, I. 748–750, ascribes the popularity of pilgrimages in Germany to the *currendi libido*, the travelling itch.

knight on horseback had escaped from his pursuer. The Virgin's congealed milk, the cool scholar has described with particular precision. Asking what good reason there was for believing it was genuine, the verger replied by pointing him to an authentic record hung high up on the wall. Walsingham was also fortunate enough to possess the middle joint of one of Peter's fingers.

At Canterbury, Erasmus and Colet looked upon Becket's skull covered with a silver case except at the spot where the fatal dagger pierced it and Colet, remarking that Thomas was good to the poor while on earth, queried whether now being in heaven he would not be glad to have the treasures, stored in his tomb, distributed in alms. When a chest was opened and the monk held up the rags with which the archbishop had blown his nose, Colet held them only a moment in his fingers and let them drop in disgust. It was said by Thomas à Kempis, that rarely are they sanctified who jaunt about much on pilgrimages — *raro sanctificantur, qui multum peregrinantur.*[1] One of the German penitential books exclaimed, " Alas ! how seldom do people go on pilgrimages from right motives." Twenty-five years after the visits of Erasmus and Colet, the canons of Walsingham, convicted of forging relics, were dragged by the king's order to Chelsea and burnt and the tomb of St. Thomas was rifled of its contents and broken up.

Saints continued to be in high favor. Every saint has his distinct office allotted to him, said Erasmus playfully. One is appealed to for the toothache, a second to grant easy delivery in childbirth, a third to lend aid on long journeys, a fourth to protect the farmer's live stock. People prayed to St. Christopher every morning to be kept from death during the day, to St. Roche to be kept from contagion and to St. George and St. Barbara to be kept from falling into the hands of enemies. He suggested that these fabulous saints were more prayed to than Peter and Paul and perhaps than Christ himself.[2] Sir Thomas More, in his defence of the worship of saints, expressed his astonishment at the " madness of the heretics that barked against the custom of Christ's Church."

---

[1] *Imit. of Christ*, 1. 1, ch. 23. See Siebert, p. 55.

[2] *Praise of Folly*, pp. 85, 96, and *Enchiridion*, XII., p. 135.

The encouragement, given at Rome to the worship of relics, had a signal illustration in the distinguished reception accorded the head of St. Andrew by the Renaissance pope, Pius II.   In Germany, princes joined with prelates in making collections of sacred bones and other objects in which miraculous virtue was supposed to reside and whose worship was often rewarded by the almost infinite grace of indulgence.   In Germany, in the 15th century as in Chaucer's day in England, the friars were the indefatigable purveyors of this sort of merchandise, from the bones of Balaam's ass to the straw of the manger and feathers from St. Michael's wings.   The Nürnberger, Nicolas Muffel, regretted that, after the effort of 33 years, he had only been able to bring together 308 specimens.   Unfortunately this did not keep him from the crime of theft and the penalty of the gallows.[1]   In Vienna, were shown such rarities as a piece of the ark, drops of sweat from Gethsemane and some of the incense offered by the Wise Men from the East.   Albrecht, archbishop of Mainz, helped to collect no less than 8,133 sacred fragments and 42 entire bodies of saints.   This collection, which was deposited at Halle, contained the host — that is, Christ's own body — which Christ offered while he was in the tomb, a statue of the Virgin with a full bottle of her milk hanging from her neck, several of the pots which had been used at Cana and a portion of the wine Jesus made, as well as some of the veritable manna which the Hebrews had picked up in the desert, and some of the earth from a field in Damascus from which God made Adam.

A most remarkable collection was made by no less a personage than Frederick the Wise of Saxony.[2]   A rich description of its treasures has been preserved from the hand of Andreas Meinhard, then a new master of arts.   On his way to Wittenberg, 1507, he met a raw student about to enter the university, Reinhard by name.   The elector had made good use of the opportunities his pilgrimages to Jerusalem furnished and succeeded in obtaining the very respectable number of 5,005 sacred

---

[1] Bezold, p. 99; Siebert, p. 59.

[2] *Die Universität Wittenberg nach der Beschreibung des Mag. Andreas Meinhard*, ed. by J. Hausleiter, 2d ed., Leipz., 1903.

like Albrecht Dürer, joined her with Mary on the canvas.[1] She was claimed as a patron saint by women in childbirth and by the copper miners. Luther himself was one of her ardent worshippers. Both Albrecht of Mainz and Frederick the Wise were fortunate enough to have in their collections of relics, each, one of the fingers of the saint.[2]

If sacred poetry is any test of the devotion paid to a saint, then the Virgin Mary was far and away the chief personage to whom worshippers in the last centuries of the Middle Ages looked for help. The splendid collection issued by Blume and Dreves, — *Analecta hymnica*, — filling now nearly 8,000 pages, gives the material from which a judgment can be formed as to the relative amount of attention writers of hymns and sequences paid to the Godhead, to Mary and to the other saints. Number XLII., containing 336 hymns, gives 37 addressed to Christ, 110 to Mary and 189 to other saints. Number XLVI. devotes 102 to Mary. These numbers are taken at random. Here are introductory verses from several of the thousands of hymns which were composed in praise of her virtues and the efficacy of her intercession: —

Pulchra regis regia
Regens regentem omnia[3]

Salve deitatis cella
Virgo virginum
  Maria, nostra consolatrix.[4]

Mater altissimi regis
Tu humani altrix gregis
Advocata potissima
In hora mortis ultima.[5]

Anna also has a large place in the hymns of the later Middle

[1] Janssen, I. 248. See E. Schaumkell : *Der Cultus der hl. Anna am Ausgange des MA*, Freib., 1896. J. Trithemius: *De laudibus S. Annæ*, Mainz, 1494.

[2] St. Anne's day was fixed on July 26 by Gregory XIII., 1584. The Western Continent has a great church dedicated to St. Anne at Beau Pré on the St. Lawrence, near Quebec. It possesses one of its patron's fingers. No other Catholic sanctuary of North America, perhaps, has such a reputation for miraculous cures as this Canadian church.

[3] Beautiful ruler of the king, Ruling him who rules all things. Blume and Dreves, XLII. 115.

[4] Hail, cell of the Deity, Virgin of virgins, Mary, our comforter. XLV. 117.

[5] Mother of the most high King, Thou foster-mother of the flock, Advocate most mighty, In the dread hour of death. XLV. 118.

Ages and the 16th century.[1] Here are the opening verses of
two of them:

Dulcis Jesu matris pater   *Gaude, mater Anna*
Joachim, et Anna mater   *Gaude, mater sancta*
Justi, natu nobiles.[2]   *Cum sis Dei facta*
           Genetrix avia.[3]

In England, singing sacred songs seems to have been little
cultivated before the 16th century.   The singing of Psalms in
the days of Anne Boleyn was a novelty and was greatly enjoyed
at the court as it was later in Elizabeth's reign, on the streets.
The vast numbers of sacred pieces, written in Germany,
France and the Lowlands, were intended for conventual devotions not for popular use.[4]   Singing, however, was practised
extensively in pilgrimages and processions and also in churches,
and the Basel synod at its 21st session complained that the
public services were interrupted by hymns in the vernacular.
Germany took the lead in sacred popular music.   From
1470–1520, nearly 100 hymns were printed from German presses,
many of them with original tunes.   Sometimes the hymns were
in German from beginning to end, sometimes they were a mixture of Latin and German.   As the Middle Ages drew to a
close, religious song increased.   The Reformation established
congregational singing and begat the congregational hymn-
book.[5]

[1] Number XLII. of Blume and Dreves' collection gives 10; Number
XLIII. 9, Number XLIV. 8, Anna hymns.

[2] Father of the dear mother of Jesus, Joachim, and her mother Anna,
Righteous and noble of birth.   XLII. 154.

[3] Rejoice Anna mother, Rejoice holy mother, For thou art made grand-
mother of God.   XLIII. 78.

[4] The Cambridge Role, a MS. in Cambridge, contains 12 carols.   John of
Dunstable founded a school of music early in the 15th century.   Traill: *Social
Engl.*, II. 368 sq.   Maskell, *Mon. rit.*, III. 1 sqq., gives a number of English
hymns printed in the *Prymers* of the first half of the 16th century.

[5] Bäumker gives 71 hymns with original melodies printed before 1520.   On
the subject of mediæval hymns, see Mone: *Lateinische Hymnen d. MA*,
3 vols., Freib., 1855; Ph. Wackernagel: *Das deutsche Kirchenlied von der
ältesten Zeit*, etc., 2 vols, Leipz., 1867.   W. Bäumker: *D. kathol. deutsche
Kirchenlied in seinen Singweisen*, 3 vols., Freib., 1886–1891 and *Ein deutsches
geistliches Liederbuch mit Melodieen aus d. 15ten Jahrh.*, etc., Leipz., 1895,
Janssen, I. 283 sqq.   Also artt. *Kirchenlied* and *Kirchenmusik* in Herzog, X.

These adjuncts and elements of Christian worship and training were added to the usual service of the churches, the celebration of the mass, which was central, the confessional and preaching. The age was religious but doubt was growing. A writer of the 15th century says of England :[1] —

There are many who have various opinions concerning religion . . . but all attend mass every day and say many *pater nosters* in public, the women carrying long rosaries in their hands and any who can read taking the Hours of our Lady with them and reciting them in church verse by verse in a low voice as is the manner of the religious. They always hear mass in their parish church on Sunday and give liberal alms nor do they omit any form incumbent upon good Christians.

The age of a more intelligent piety was still to come, though it was to prove itself less submissive to human authority.

§ 79. *Works of Charity.*

Benevolence and philanthropy, which are of the very essence of the Christian religion, flourished in the later Middle Ages. In the endeavor to provoke his generation to good works, Luther asserted that "in the good old papal times everybody was merciful and kind. Then it snowed endowments and legacies and hospitals."[2] Institutions were established to care for the destitute and sick, colleges and bursaries were endowed and protection given to the dependent against the rapacity of unscrupulous money-lenders.

The modern notion of stamping out sickness by processes of sanitation scarcely occurred to the mediæval municipalities. Although the population of Europe was not $\frac{1}{10}$ of what it is to-day, disease was fearfully prevalent. No epidemics so fatal as the Black Death appeared in Europe but, even in

[1] *Italian Relation of Engl.*, Camden Soc. ed., p. 23.
[2] Quoted by Uhlhorn, p. 439. Janssen, II. 325 sq., takes too seriously Luther's complaint that more liberality had been shown and care given to the needy under the old system than under the new, using it as a proof of the influence of Protestantism. Riezler, *Gesch. Baierns*, as quoted by Janssen, I. 679 says, "The Christian spirit of love to one's neighbor was particularly active in the 15th century in works of benevolence and there is scarcely another age so fruitful in them." So also Bezold, p. 94.

England, the return of plagues was frequent, as in 1406, 1439, 1464, 1477.   The famine of 1438, called the Great Famine, was followed the next year by the Great Pestilence, called also the *pestilence sans merci*.   In 1464, to follow the *Chronicle of Croyland*, thousands " died like slaughtered sheep."   The sweating sickness of 1485 reappeared in 1499 and 1504.   In the first epidemic, 20,000 died in London and, in 1504, the mayor of the city succumbed.   The disease took people suddenly and was marked by a chill, which was followed by a fiery redness of the skin and agonizing thirst that led the victims to drink immoderately.   Drinking was succeeded by sweating from every pore.[1]

Provision was made for the sick and needy through the monasteries, gilds and brotherhoods as well as by individual assistance and state collections.   The care of the poor was in England regarded as one of the primary functions of the Church.   Archbishop Stratford, 1342, ordered that a portion of the tithe should be invariably set apart for their needs.   The neglect of the poor was alleged as one of the crying omissions of the alien clergy.

Doles for the poor, a common form of charity in England, were often provided for on a large scale.   During the 40 days the duke of Gaunt's body was to remain unburied, 50 marks were to be distributed daily until the 40th day, when the amount was to be increased to 500 marks.   Bishop Skirland wanted 200 given away between his death and his interment.   A draper of York gave by will 100 beds with furniture to as many poor folk.   A cloth-maker made a doubtful charity when he left a suit of his own make to 13 poor people, with the condition that they should sit around his coffin for 8 days.   There were houses, says Thorold Rogers, where doles of bread and beer were given to all wayfarers, houses where the sick were treated, clothed and fed, particularly the lepers.   One of the hospitals that survives is St. Cross at Winchester for old and indigent people.[2]   The cook Ketel, a Brother of the Common

[1] See C. Creighton in *Social England*, II. 412, 475, 561.
[2] Rogers : *Work and Wages*, p. 417.   Stubbs: *Const. Hist.*, ch. XXI. Capes : *Engl. Ch. Hist. in the 14th and 15th Cent.*, pp. 276 sq., 366 sq.

Life, whose biography Thomas à Kempis wrote, said it would be better to sell all the books of the house at Deventer and give more to the poor.

Hospitals, in the earlier part of our period, were the special concern of the knights of the Teutonic Order and continued throughout the whole of it to engage the attention of the Beguines. It became the custom also for the Beguines to go as nurses to private houses as in Cologne, Frankfurt, Treves, Ulm and other German cities, receiving pay for their services.[1] The Beguinages in Bruges, Ghent, Antwerp and other cities of Belgium and Holland date back to this period. The 15th century also witnessed the growth of municipal hospitals, a product of the civic spirit which had developed in North-Europe. Cities like Cologne, Lübeck and Augsburg had several hospitals. The *Hotel de Dieu*, Paris, did not come under municipal control till 1505. In cases, admission to hospitals was made by their founders conditional on ability to say the Lord's Prayer, the Creed and the *Ave Maria*, as for example to St. Anthony's, Augsburg. In this case, the founder took care to provide for himself, requiring the inmates on entering to say 100 *Pater nosters* and 100 *Ave Marias* over his grave and every day to join in saying over it 15 of each.[2] Damian of Löwen and his wife, who endowed a hospital at Cologne, 1450, stipulated that " the very poorest and sickest were to be taken care of whether they belonged to Cologne or were strangers."

Rome had more than one hospital endowment. The foundation of Cardinal John Colonna at the Lateran, made 1216, still remains. In his *History of the Popes* (III. 51), Pastor has given a list of the hospitals and other institutions of mercy in the different states of Italy and justly laid stress upon this evidence of the power of Christianity. The English gilds, organized, in the first instance, for economic and industrial purposes, also pledged relief to their own sick and indigent members. The gild of Corpus Christi at York provided 8 beds for poor people and paid a woman by the year 14 shillings and

[1] Uhlhorn, p. 383 sq.

[2] Uhlhorn, p. 333. For the conditions of admission to hospitals and medical treatment, Allemand, III. 192 sqq. is to be consulted.

fourpence to keep them.   The gild of St. Helena at Beverley
cared constantly for 3 or 4 poor folk.[1]

Leprosy decreased during the last years of the Middle Ages,
but hospitals for the reception of lepers are still extensively
found, — the lazarettos, so called after Lazarus, who was reputed to have been afflicted with the disease.   Houses for this
malady had been established in England by Lanfranc, Mathilda,
queen of Henry I. at St. Giles, by King Stephen at Burton,
Leicestershire and by others till the reign of John.   St. Hugh
of Lincoln, as well as St. Francis d'Assissi distinguished themselves by their solicitude for lepers.   But the disease seems to
have died out in England in the 14th century and it was hard
to fill the beds endowed for this class of sufferers.   In 1434,
it was ordered that beds be kept for 2 lepers in the great Durham leper hospital " provided they could be found in these
parts."   Originally the hospital had beds for 60.[2]   Late in the
16th century there were still lepers in Germany.   Thomas
Platter wrote, " When we came to Munich, it was so late that
we could not enter the city, but had to remain in the leper-
house."[3]   •

Begging was one of the curses of England and Germany as
it continues to be of Southern Europe to-day.   It was no disgrace to ask alms.   The mendicant friars by their example
consecrated a nuisance with the sacred authority of religion.
Pilgrims and students also had the right of way as beggars.

---

[1] In 1409 was founded an asylum for lunatics in Valencia, Lecky : *Hist. of
Europ. Morals*, II. 94 sq.   There were pest-houses in Oxford and Cambridge
and Continental universities often had special hospitals of their own.   Writing
of the 16th century, Thomas Platter speaks of such a hospital at Breslau.
The town paid 16 hellers for the care of each patient.   These institutions were,
however, far removed from our present methods of cleanliness.   Of the Breslau
hospital, Platter (Monroe's *Life*, p. 103 sq.) says, " We had good attention,
good beds, but there were many vermin there as big as ripe hemp-seed, so that
I and others preferred to lie on the floor rather than in the beds."

[2] Geo. Pernet : *Leprosy* in *Quart. Rev.*, 1903, p. 384 sqq. C. Creighton, *Soc.
Engl.*, II. 413.   This *Hist.*, Vol. V., I., pp. 395, 825, 894.   For the fearful prevalence of cutaneous diseases and crime in England in the 13th century and
as a cure for those who sigh for the fictitious happy conditions of mediæval
society, see Jessopp, *Coming of the Friars*, p. 101 sqq.

[3] Monroe : *Thos. Platter*, p. 107.

Sebastian Brant gave a list of the different ecclesiastical beggars who went about with sacks, into which they put with indiscriminate greed apples, plums, eggs, fish, chickens, meat, butter and cheese, — sacks which had no bottom.

> *Der Bettler Sack wird nimmer voll;*
> *Wie man ihn füllt, so bleibt er hohl.*

In Germany, towns gave franchises to beg.[1]   The habit of mendicancy, which Brant ridiculed, Geiler of Strassburg called upon the municipality to regulate or forbid altogether.   In England, mendicancy was a profession recognized in law.

With the decay of the monastic endowments and the legal maintenance of wages at a low rate, the destitution and vagrancy increased.   The English statutes of laborers at the close of this period, 1495 and 1504, ordered beggars, not able to work, to return to their own towns where they might follow the habit of begging without hindrance.[2]

At a time when in Germany, the richest country of Europe, church buildings were multiplying with great rapidity, many churches in England, on account of the low economic conditions, were actually left to go to ruin or turned into sheepcotes and stables, a transmutation to which Sir Thomas More as well as others refers.   The rapacity of the nobles and abbots in turning large areas into sheep-runs deprived laborers of employment and brought social distress upon large numbers.   On the other hand, parliament passed frequent statutes of apparel, as in 1463 and 1482, restricting the farmer and laborer in his expenditure on dress.   The different statutes of laborers, enacted during the 15th century, had the effect of depressing and impoverishing the classes dependent upon the daily toil of their hands.[3]

In spite of the strict synodal rules, repeated again and

---

[1] Uhlhorn, pp. 433, 456.   Such a license was issued in Vienna, 1442.   Eberlin of Günzburg went so far as to say that in Germany, 14 out of every 15 people lived a life of idleness.

[2] Stubbs, ch. XXI.; *Social Engl.*, II. 548–550.   Cunningham, p. 478 sq.; Rogers, pp. 416–419.

[3] See Traill: *Soc. Engl.*, II. 388, 392–398.   For the activity in church-building in Germany, see Janssen, I. 180 sq.; Bezold, p. 90; Ficker, p. 65.

again, usury was practised by Christians as well as by Jews.
All the greater Schoolmen of the 13th century had discussed
the subject of usury and pronounced it sin, on the ground of
Luke 6 : 34, and other texts.   They held that charges of interest offended against the law of love to our neighbor and
the law of natural fairness, for money does not increase with
use but rather is reduced in weight and value.   It is a species
of greed which is mortal sin.[1]   It was so treated by mediæval
councils when practised by Christians and the contrary opinion was pronounced heretical by the œcumenical council of
Vienne.   Geiler of Strassburg expounded the official church
view when he pronounced usury always wicked.   It was
wrong for a Christian to take back more than the original
principal.   And the substitution of a pig or some other gift
in place of a money payment he also denounced.

The rates of the Jews were exorbitant.   In Florence, they
were 20 % in 1430 and, in 1488, $32\frac{1}{2}$ %.[2]   In Northern Europe
they were much higher, from $43\frac{1}{3}$ to 80 or even 100 %.   Municipalities borrowed.   Clerics, convents and churches mort-
gaged their sacred vessels.   City after city in Germany and
Switzerland expelled the Jews, — from Spires and Zürich,
1435, to Geneva, 1490, and Nürnberg, Ulm and Nördlingen,
1498–1500.   The careers of the great banking-houses in the
second half of the fifteenth century show the extensive demand for loans by popes and prelates, as well as secular
princes.

To afford relief to the needy, whose necessities forced them
to borrow, a measure of real philanthropy was conceived in
the last century of the Middle Ages, the *montes pietatis*, or
charitable accumulations.[3]   They were benevolent loaning
funds.   The idea found widespread acceptance in Italy, where
the first institutions were founded at Perugia, 1462, and Or-

[1] Thos. Aquinas: *Summa*, II. 2, q. 78.

[2] Pastor: *Gesch. d. Päpste*, III. 83 sq. For Germany, see Janssen, I. 460 sqq.

[3] Other names given to them were *montes Christi*, *monte della carità*, *mare
di pietà*. See Holzapfel, pp. 18, 20, for funds to provide for burial, *montes
mortuorum*, made up from contributions, and funds to which mothers contributed at the birth of children, called *montes dotis*. Holzapfel gives the
primary authorities on the benevolent loaning funds, pp. 3–14.

vieto, 1463. City councils aided such funds by contributions, as at Perugia, when it gave 3,000 gulden. But in this case, finding itself unable to furnish the full amount, it mulcted the Jews for 1,200 gulden, Pius II. giving his sanction to the constraint. In cases, bishops furnished the capital, as at Pistoja, 1473, where Bishop Donato de' Medici gave 3,000 gulden. At Lucca, a merchant, who had grown rich through commercial affiliation with the Jews, donated the princely capital of 40,000 gold gulden. At Gubbio, a law taxed all inheritances one per cent in favor of the local fund, and neglect to pay was punished with an additional tax of one per cent.

The popes showed a warm interest in the new benevolence by granting to particular funds their sanction and offering indulgences to contributors. From 1463 to 1515 we have records of 16 papal authorizations from such popes as Pius II., Sixtus IV., Innocent VIII., Alexander VI., Julius II. and Leo X. The sanction of Innocent VIII., given to the Mantua fund, 1486, called upon the preachers to summon the people to support the fund, promised 10 years full indulgence to donors, and excommunicated all who opposed the project. Sixtus IV., in commending the fund for his native town of Savona, 1479, pronounced its worthy object to be to aid not only the poor but also the rich who had pawned their goods. He offered a plenary indulgence on the collection of every 100 gulden. In 1490, the Savona fund had 22,000 gulden and the limit of loans was raised to 100 ducats.[1]

The administration of these bureaus of relief was in the hands of directors, usually a mixed body of clergymen and laymen, and often appointed by municipal councils. The accounts were balanced each month. In Perugia, the rate, which was 12 % in 1463, was reduced to 8 % a year later. In Milan it was reduced from 10 % to 5 %, in 1488. Five per cent was the appointed rate fixed at Padua, Vicenza and Pisa, and 4 % at Florence. The loans were made upon the basis of property put in pawn. The benevolent efficacy of these funds cannot be questioned and to them, in part, is due the

[1] Holzapfel, pp. 10–12, 44, 64, 70.

reduction of interest from 40 % to 4 and 10 % in Italy, before the close of the 15th century.[1] They met, however, with much opposition and were condemned as contravening the traditional law against usury.

A foremost place in advancing the movement was taken by the Franciscans and in the Franciscan Bernardino da Feltre, 1439–1494, it had its chief apostle. This popular orator canvassed all the greater towns of Northern Italy, — Mantua, Florence, Parma, Padua, Milan, Lucca, Verona, Brescia. Wherever he went, he was opposed from the pulpit and by doctors of the canon law. At Florence, so warmly was the controversy conducted in the pulpits that a public discussion was ordered at which Lorenzo de' Medici, doctors of the law, clerics and many laymen were present, with the result that the archbishop forbade opposition to the *mons* on pain of excommunication. The Deuteronomic injunction, 24 : 12 sq., ordering that, if a man borrow a coat, it should be restored before sundown and the Lord's words, Luke 6, were quoted by the opposition. But it was replied, that the object of loaning to the poor was not to enrich the fund or individuals but to do the borrower good. Savonarola gave the institution his advocacy.[2] The Fifth Lateran commended it and in this it was followed, 50 years later, by the Council of Trent.

The attempt to transplant the Italian institution in Germany was unsuccessful and was met by the establishment of banks by municipal councils, as at Frankfurt.[3] In England also, it gained no foothold. So strong was the feeling against lending out money at interest that, at Chancellor Morton's importunity, parliament proceeded against it with severe measures, and a law of Henry VII.'s reign made all lending of money at interest a criminal offence and the bargain between borrower and lender null and void.

Notable expression was also given to the practice of benev-

---

[1] Holzapfel, p. 134.

[2] Villari, I. 294 sqq.; Holzapfel, pp. 124, 135. According to Holzapfel, there were in Italy in 1896, 556 *monti di pietà* with 78,000,000 lire — $16,000,-000 — out in loans.

[3] Holzapfel, p. 102 sqq.; Janssen, I. 464, 489.

olence by the religious brotherhoods of the age. These organizations developed with amazing rapidity and are not to be confounded with the gilds which were organizations of craftsmen, intended to promote the production of good work and also to protect the master-workers in their monopoly of trade. They were connected with the Church and were, in part, under the direction of the priesthood, although from some of them, as in Lübeck, priests were distinctly excluded. Like the gilds, their organization was based upon the principle of mutual aid[1] but they emphasized the principle of unselfish sympathy for those in distress. Luther once remarked, there was no chapel and no saint without a brotherhood. In fact, nothing was so sure to make a saint popular as to name a brotherhood after him. By 1450, there was not a mendicant convent in Germany which had not at least one fraternity connected with it. Cities often had a number of these organizations. Wittenberg had 21, Lübeck 70, Frankfurt 31, Hamburg 100. Every reputable citizen in German cities belonged to one or more.[2] Luther belonged to 3 at Erfurt, the brotherhoods of St. Augustine, St. Anna and St. Catherine.

The dead, who had belonged to them, had the distinct advantage of being prayed for. Their sick were cared for in hospitals, containing beds endowed by them. Sometimes they incorporated the principle of mutual benefit or assurance societies, and losses sustained by the living they made good. At Paderborn, in case a brother lost his horse, every member contributed one or two shillings or, if he lost his house, his fellow-members contributed three shillings each or a load of lumber.

As there were gilds of apprentices as well as of master-workmen, so there were brotherhoods of the poor and humble as well as of those in comfortable circumstances. Even the lepers had fraternities, and one of these clans had fief rights to a spring at Wiesbaden. So also had the beggars and cripples

---

[1] The constitution of the Gild of St. Mary of Lynn contained the clauses, "If any sister or brother of this gild fall into poverty, they shall have help from every other brother and sister in a penny a day." The Gild of St. Catharine, London, had a similar stipulation. Smith: *Engl. Gilds*, p. 185.

[2] Degenhard Pfaffinger, counsellor to Frederick the Wise, belonged to 35. Kolde, 437 ; Uhlhorn, p. 423.

at Zülpich, founded 1454.   The entrance fee in the last case
was 8 shillings, from which there was a reduction of one-half
for widows. [1]

In the case of the Italian brotherhoods, it is often difficult
to distinguish between a society organized for a benevolent
purpose and a society for the cult of some saint.   The gilds
of Northern Italy, as a rule, laid emphasis upon religious
duties such as attendance upon mass, confession of sins and
refraining from swearing.   The Roman societies had their
patron saints, — the blacksmiths and workers in gold, St.
Eligius, the millers Paulinus of Nola, the barrel-makers St.
James, the inn-keepers St. Blasius and St. Julian, the masons
St. Gregory the Great, the barbers and physicians St. Cosmas
and St. Damian, the painters St. Luke and the apothecaries
St. Lawrence.   The popes encouraged the confraternities and
elevated some of them to the dignity of archfraternities, as St.
Saviour in Rome, the first to win this distinction.   Florence
was also good soil for religious brotherhoods.   At the beginning of the 16th century, there were no less than 73 within its
bounds, some of them societies of children.[2]

Society did not wait for the present age to apply the principle of Christian charity.   The development of organizations
and bureaus in the 15th century was not carried as far as it
is to-day, and for the good reason that the same demand for it
did not exist.   The cities were small and it was possible to
carry out the practice of individual relief with little fear of
deception.

§ 80. *The Sale of Indulgences.*

Nowhere, except in the lives of the popes themselves, did
the humiliation of the Western Church find more conspicuous
exhibition than in the sale of indulgences.   The forgiveness
of sins was bought and sold for money, and this sacred privilege formed the occasion of the rupture of Western Christendom as, later, the Lord's Supper became the occasion of the
chief division between the Protestant churches.

[1] Uhlhorn, p. 422.   [2] Pastor, IV. 30–38.

Originally an indulgence was the remission of a part or all of the works of satisfaction demanded by the priest in the sacrament of penance. This is the definition given by Roman Catholic authorities to-day.[1] In the 13th century, it came to be regarded as a remission of the penalty of sin itself, both here and in purgatory. At a later stage, it was regarded, at least in wide circles, as a release from the guilt of sin as well as from its penalty. The fund of merits at the Church's disposition — *thesaurus meritorum* — as defined by Clement VI., in 1343, is a treasury of spiritual assets, consisting of the infinite merits of Christ, the merits of Mary and the supererogatory merits of the saints, which the Church uses by virtue of the power of the keys. One drop of Christ's blood, so it was argued, was sufficient for the salvation of the world, and yet Christ shed all his blood and Mary was without stain. From the vast surplus accumulation supplied by their merits, the Church had the right to draw in granting remission to sinners from the penalties resulting from the commission of sin. The very term "keys," it was said, implies a treasure which is locked away and to which the keys give access.[2] The authority to grant indulgences was shared by the pope and the bishops. The law of Innocent III., intended to check its abuse, restricted the time for which bishops might grant indulgence to 40 days, the so-called *quarantines*. By the decree of Pius X., issued Aug. 28, 1903, cardinals, even though they are not priests, may issue indulgences in their titular churches for 200 days, archbishops for 100 and bishops for 50 days.

The application of indulgence to the realm of purgatory by Sixtus IV. was a natural development of the doctrine that the prayers and other suffrages of the living inure to the benefit

[1] So Paulus ; *J. Tetzel*, p. 88, and Beringer, p. 2, a member of the Society of Jesus, whose work on indulgences has the sanction of the Congregation of Indulgences of the College of Cardinals. Both writers insist that the indulgence does not confer forgiveness of guilt but only the remission of penalty after guilt is forgiven. See also on the general subject this *Hist.*, V. 1, pp. 735–743, VI. 146 sqq.

[2] John of Paltz: *Coelifodina* in Köhler, p. 57. *Nota in hoc quod dicit, claves, innuit thesauros quia omne carum clauditur et seratur potest tamen clavibus adiri.*

of the souls in that sphere. As Thomas Aquinas clearly taught, such souls belong to the jurisdiction of the Church on earth. And, if indulgences may be granted to the living, certainly the benefit may be extended to the intermediate realm, over which the Church also has control.

Sixtus' first bull granting indulgence for the dead was issued 1476 in favor of the church of Saintes. Here was offered to those who paid a certain sum — *certam pecuniam* — for the benefit of the building, the privilege of securing a relaxation of the sufferings of the purgatorial dead, parents for their children, friend for friend. The papal deliverance aroused criticism and in a second bull, issued the following year, the pontiff states that such relaxations were offered by virtue of the fulness of authority vested in the pope from above — *plenitudo potestatis* — to draw upon the fund of merits.[1]

To the abuse, to which this doctrine opened the door, was added the popular belief that letters of indulgence gave exemption both from the culpability and penalty of sin. The expression, " full remission of sins," *plena* or *plenissima remissio peccatorum,* is found again and again in papal bulls from the famous Portiuncula indulgence, granted by Honorius III. to the Franciscans, to the last hours of the undisputed sway of the pope in the West. It was the merit of the late Dr. Lea to have called attention to this almost overlooked element of the mediæval indulgence. Catholic authorities of to-day, as Paulus and Beringer, without denying the use of the expression, *a poena et culpa*, assert that it was not the intent of any genuine papal message to grant forgiveness from the guilt of sin without contrition of heart.[2] The expression was in

---

[1] For the text of the bulls, see Lea III. 585 sqq. and Köhler, pp. 37–40. A bull ascribed to Calixtus III., 1457, also sanctions indulgences for the dead. It is accepted as genuine by Paulus. For Gabriel Biel's acceptance of Sixtus' assertion of power to grant indulgences to the dead, see Köhler, p. 40.

[2] Paulus, 97 sq., and Beringer, p. 11, either explain the expression to mean the penalty of guilt, as if it read *a poena culpæ delicta*, or refer it to venial sins. See Vol. V. 1, p. 741. The Jubilee bull of Boniface VIII., 1300, was interpreted by a cardinal to include in its benefits guilt as well as penalty — *duplex indulgentia culpæ videlicet et poenæ.* Köhler, p. 18 sq., gives the text of the bull. John XXIII. confessed to have often absolved *a culpa et poena.*

current use in tracts and in common talk.[1] John of Paltz, in his *Coelifodina*, an elaborate defence of indulgences written towards the close of the 15th century, affirmed that an indulgence is given by virtue of the power of the keys whereby guilt is remitted and penalty withdrawn. These keys open the fund of the Church to its sons.[2] Luther was only expressing the popular view when, writing to Albrecht of Mainz, 1517, he complained that men accepted the letters of indulgence as giving them exemption from all penalty and guilt — *homo per istas indulgentias liber sit ab omni poena et culpa*. Not only on the Continent but also in England were such forms of indulgence circulated. For example, Leo X.'s indulgence for the hospital S. Spirito in Rome ran in its English translation, "Holy and great indulgence and pardon of plenary remission *a culpa et poena*."[3] The popular mind did not stop to make the fine distinction between guilt and its punishment and, if it had, it would have been quite satisfied to be made free from the sufferings entailed by sin. If by a papal indulgence a soul in purgatory could be immediately released and given access to heavenly felicity, the question of guilt was of no concern.

Long before the days of Tetzel, Wyclif and Huss had condemned the use of the formula, "from penalty and guilt," as did also John Wessel. In denouncing the bulls of indulgence for those joining in a crusade against Ladislaus, issued 1412, Huss copied Wyclif almost word for word.[4] Wyclif fiercely con-

---

[1] It was used by Piers Plowman (see Lea : *Sacerd. Celibacy*, I. 444), by Landucci, 1513, *l' indulgenza di colpa e pena*, Badia's ed., p. 341, by Oldecop, 1516, who listened to Tetzel (see his letter in Paulus, p. 39), etc. Oldecop said that those who cast their money into the chest and confessed their sins were " absolved from all their sins and from pain and guilt." For other cases and a general treatment of the subject, see Lea, III. 67–80.

[2] Köhler, p. 59.

[3] See Maskell : *Monum. rit.*, etc., III. 372 sqq. These indulgences in England were printed on single sheets perhaps by Wynkyn de Worde. Such an English reprint announced an indulgence of 2560 days granted by Julius II. to all contributing to a crusade against the Saracens and other Christian enemies.

[4] Nürnb. ed., 1715, vol. I. 212–257 ; *Defens. quor. artt. J. Wyclif* and the *Reply* of the Prag. theol. faculty, I. 139–146.

demned the papal assumption in granting full indulgence for the crusade of Henry de Spenser.   Priests, he asserted, have no authority to give absolution without proper works of satisfaction and all papal absolution is of no avail, where the offenders are not of good and worthy life.   If the pope has power to absolve unconditionally, he should exercise his power to excuse the sins of all men.   The English Reformer further declared that, to the Christian priest it was given, to do no more than announce the forgiveness of sins just as the old priests pronounced a man a leper or cured of leprosy, but it was not possible for him to effect a cure.   He spoke of " the fond fantasy of spiritual treasure in heaven, that each pope is made dispenser of the treasure at his own will, a thing dreamed of without ground." [1] Such power would make the pope master of the saints and Christ himself.   He condemned the idea that the pope could " clear men of pain and sin both in this world and the other, so that, when they die, they flee to heaven without pain.   This is for blind men to lead blind men and both to fall into the lake." As for the pardoning of sin for money, that would imply that righteousness may be bought and sold.   Wyclif gave it as a report, that Urban VI. had granted an indulgence for 2,000 years. [2]

Indulgences found an assailant in Erasmus, howbeit a genial assailant.   In his *Praise of Folly*, he spoke of the " cheat of pardons and indulgences."   These lead the priests to compute the time of each soul's residence in purgatory and to assign them a longer or shorter continuance according as the people purchase more or fewer of these salable exemptions.   By this easy way of purchasing pardon any notorious highwayman, any plundering bandit or any bribe-taking judge may for a part of their unjust gains secure atonement for perjuries, lusts, bloodsheds, debaucheries and other gross impieties and, having paid off arrears, begin upon a new score.   The popular idea was no doubt stated by Tyndale in answer to Sir Thomas More when he said, that " men might quench almost the terrible fire of hell for three halfpence." [3]

---

[1] *De schis. pontif.*, *Engl. Works*, ed. by Arnold, III. 1262.

[2] *Engl. Works*, Arnold's ed., I. 210, 354 ; *De eccles.*, p. 561.

[3] See Gasquet, *Eve of the Reformation*, p. 384.

It is fair to say that, while the last popes of the Middle Ages granted a great number of indulgences, the exact expression, "from guilt and penalty," does not occur in any of the extant papal copies [1] although some of their expressions seem fully to imply the exemption from guilt. Likewise, it must be said that they also contain the usual expressions for penitence as a condition of receiving the grace — "being truly penitent and confessing their sins" — *vere poenitentibus et confessis.*

Indulgences in the last century of the Middle Ages were given for all sorts of benevolent purposes, crusades against the Turks, the building of churches and hospitals, in connection with relics, for the rebuilding of a town desolated by fire, as Brüx, for bridges and for the repair of dikes, such an indulgence being asked by Charles V. The benefits were received by the payment of money and a portion of the receipts, from 33 % to 50 %, was expected to go to Rome. The territory chiefly, we may say almost exclusively, worked for such enterprises was confined to the Germanic peoples of the Continent — from Switzerland and Austria to Norway and Sweden. England, France and Spain were hardly touched by the traffic. Cardinal Ximenes set forth the damage done to ecclesiastical discipline by the practice and, as a rule, it was under other pretexts that papal moneys were received from England.[2]

In the transmission of the papal portions of the indulgence-moneys, the house of the Fuggers figures conspicuously. Sometimes it charged 5 %, sometimes it appropriated amounts not reckoned strictly on the basis of a fixed per cent. The powerful banking-firm, also responding cheerfully to any request made to them, often secured the grant of indulgences in Rome. The custodianship of the chests, into which the indulgence-moneys were cast, was also a matter of much importance and here also the Fuggers figured prominently. Keys to such

---

[1] James of Jüterbock in his *Tract. de indulg.* about 1451 says he did not recollect to have seen or read a single papal brief promising indulgence *a poena et culpa.* Köhler, p. 48.

[2] For the details which follow, the treatment by Schulte, in his work on the Fuggers, is the chief authority. This book contains a remarkable array of figures and facts based on studies among the sources.

chests were often distributed to two or three parties, one of whom was apt to be the representative of the bankers.

Among the more famous indulgences for the building of German churches were those for the construction of a tower in Vienna, 1514, for the rebuilding of the Cathedral of Constance, which had suffered great damage from fire, 1511, the building of the Dominican church in Augsburg, 1514, the restoration of the Cathedral of Treves, 1515, and the building of St. Annaberg church, 1517, in which Duke George of Saxony was much interested. One-half of the moneys received for these constructions went to Rome. In most of these cases, the Fuggers acted as agents to hold the keys of the chest and transmit the moneys to the papal exchequer. The sees of Constance, Chur, Augsburg and Strassburg were assigned as the territory in which indulgences might be sold for the cathedral in Constance. No less than four bulls of indulgence were issued in 1515 for the benefit of Treves, including one for those who visited the holy coat which was found 1512 and was to be exhibited every 7 years.[1]

Among the noted hospitals to which indulgences were issued — that is, the right to secure funds by their sale — were hospitals in Nürnberg, 1515, Strassburg, 1518 and S. Spirito, Rome, 1516.

Both of the churches in Wittenberg were granted indulgences and a special indulgence was issued for the reliquary-museum which the elector Frederick had collected. An indulgence of 100 days was attached to each of the 5,005 specimens and another 100 to each of the 8 passages between the cases that held them. With the 8,133 relics at Halle and the 42 entire bodies, millions and billions of days of indulgence were associated, a sort of anticipation of the geologic periods moderns demand. To be more accurate, these relics were good for pardons covering 39,245,120 years and 220 days and the still further period of 6,540,000 quarantines, each of 40 days.

In Rome, the residence of the supreme pontiffs, as we might well have expected, the offer of indulgences was the most copi-

---

[1] Treves also boasted of a nail of the cross, the half part of St. Peter's staff and St. Helena's skull.

ous, almost as copious as the drops on a rainy day. According to the Nürnberger relic-collector, Nicolas Muffel, every time the skulls of the Apostles were shown or the handkerchief of St. Veronica, the Romans who were present received a pardon of 7,000 days, other Italians 10,000 and foreigners 14,000. In fact, the grace of the ecclesiastical authorities was practically boundless. Not only did the living seek indulgences, but even the dying stipulated in their wills that a representative should go to Assisi or Rome or other places to secure for their souls the benefit of the indulgences offered there.

Prayers also had remarkable offers of grace attached to them. According to the penitential book, *The Soul's Joy*, the worshipper offering its prayers to Mary received 11,000 years indulgence and some prayers, if offered, freed 15 souls from purgatory and as many earthly sinners from their sins. It professed to give one of Alexander VI.'s decrees, according to which prayer made three times to St. Anna secured 1,000 years indulgence for mortal sins and 20,000 for venial. *The Soul's Garden* claimed that one of Julius II.'s indulgences granted 80,000 years to those who would pray a prayer to the Virgin which the book gave. No wonder Siebert, a Roman Catholic writer, is forced to say that " the whole atmosphere of the later Middle Ages was soaked with the indulgence-passion." [1]

An indulgence issued by Alexander VI., in 1502, was designed to secure aid for the knights of the Teutonic Order against the Russians. The latter was renewed by Julius II. and Cologne, Treves, Mainz, Bremen, Bamberg and other sees were assigned as the territory. Much money was collected, the papal treasury receiving one-third of the returns. The preaching continued till 1510 and Tetzel took a prominent part in the campaign.[2]

It remains to speak of the most important of all of the indulgences, the indulgence for the construction of St. Peter's in Rome. This interest was pushed by two notable popes, Julius II. and Leo X., and called forth the protest of Luther, which shook the power of the papacy to its foundations. It

[1] *Reliquienverehrung*, pp. 33 sq., 60 sq.
[2] A full account in Paulus, *Tetzel*, pp. 6–23.

seems paradoxical that the chief monument of Christian architecture should have been built in part out of the proceeds of
the scandalous traffic in absolutions.

On April 18, 1506, soon after the laying of the corner-stone
of St. Peter's, Julius II. issued a bull promising indulgence
to those who would contribute to its construction, *fabrica*, as
it was called.   Eighteen months later, Nov. 4, 1507, he commissioned Jerome of Torniello, a Franciscan Observant, to
oversee the preaching of the bull in the so-called 25 Cis-
montane provinces, which included Northern Italy, Austria,
Bohemia and Poland.   By a later decree Switzerland was
added.[1]   Germany was not included and probably for the
reason that a number of indulgence bulls were already in force
in most of its territory.   A special rescript appointed Warham, archbishop of Canterbury, as chief overseer of the business in England.   At Julius' death, the matter was taken
up by Leo X. and pushed.

The preaching of indulgences in Germany for the advantage of St. Peter's began in the pontificate of Leo X. and is
closely associated with the elevation of Albrecht of Hohenzollern to the sees of Mainz, Magdeburg and Halberstadt.
Albrecht, a brother of Joachim, elector of Brandenburg, was
chosen in 1513 to the archbishopric of Magdeburg and the
bishopric of Halberstadt.   The objections on the ground of
his age and the combination of two sees — a thing, however,
which was true of Albrecht's predecessor — were set aside by
Leo X., after listening to the arguments made by the German
embassies.

In 1514, Albrecht was further honored by being elected
archbishop of Mainz.   The last incumbent, Uriel of Gemmin-

---

[1] In a pamphlet entitled *Simia* by Andrea Guarna da Salerno, Milan, 1517,
as quoted by Klaczko, *Rome and the Renaissance*, p. 25, Bramante the architect was refused entrance to heaven by St. Peter for destroying the Apostle's
temple in Rome, whose very antiquity called the least devout to God.   And
when the heavenly porter charged him with a readiness to destroy the very
world itself and ruin the pope, the architect confessed and declared that his
failure was due to the fact that " Julius did not put his hand into his pocket
to build the new church but relied on indulgences and the confessional.   Paris
de Grassis called Bramante " the ruiner," *architectum Bramantem seu potius
Ruinantem.*

gen, died the year before. The archdiocese had been unfortunate with its bishops. Berthold of Henneberg had died 1504 and James of Liebenstein in 1508. These frequent changes necessitated a heavy burden of taxation to enable the prelates to pay their tribute to the Holy See, which amounted to 10,000 ducats in each case, with sundry additions. By the persuasion of the elector Joachim and the Fuggers, Leo sanctioned Albrecht's election to the see of Mainz. He was given episcopal consecration and thus the three sees were joined in the hands of a man who was only 24.

But Albrecht's confirmation as archbishop was not secured without the payment of a high price. The price, 10,000 ducats, was set by the authorities in Rome and did not originate with the German embassy, which had gone to prosecute the case. The proposition came from the Vatican itself and at the very moment the Lateran council was voting measures for the reform of the Church. It carried with it the promise of a papal indulgence for the archbishop's territories. The elector Joachim expressed some scruples of conscience over the purchase, but it went through. Schulte exclaims that, if ever a benefice was sold for gold, this was true in the case of Albrecht.[1]

The bull of indulgences was issued March 31, 1515, and granted the young German prelate the right to dispose of pardons throughout the half part of Germany, the period being fixed at 8 years. The bull offered " complete absolution — *plenissimam indulgentiam* — and remission of all sins," sins both of the living and the dead. A private paper, emanating from Leo and dated two weeks later, April 15, mentions the 10,000 ducats proposed by the Vatican as the price of Albrecht's confirmation as having been already placed in Leo's hands.[2] To enable him to pay the full amount of 30,000 ducats his ecclesiastical dignities had cost, Albrecht borrowed from the Fuggers and, to secure funds, he resorted to a two-years' tax of

[1] See his account of the transaction, I. 115–121.

[2] Schulte, I. 125. Leo's bull of March 31 is given by Köhler, pp. 83–93. Even the Rom. Cath., Paulus, *Tetzel*, p. 31, goes as far as to speak of " the miserable business which for both Leo and Albrecht was first of all a financial transaction."

two-fifths which he levied on the priests, the convents and other religious institutions of his dioceses.   In 1517, "out of regard for his Holiness, the pope, and the salvation and comfort of his people," Joachim opened his domains to the indulgence-hawkers.   It was his preaching in connection with this bull that won for Tetzel an undying notoriety.   Oldecop, writing in 1516, of what he saw, said that people, in their eagerness to secure deliverance from the guilt and penalty of sin and to get their parents and friends out of purgatory, were putting money into the chest all day long.

The description of Tetzel's sale of indulgences and Luther's protest are a part of the history of the Reformation.   It remains, however, yet to be said, as belonging to the mediæval period, that the grace of indulgences was popularly believed to extend to sins, not yet committed.   Such a belief seems to have been encouraged by the pardon-preachers, although there is no documentary proof that any papal authorities made such a promise.   In writing to the archbishop of Mainz, Oct. 31, 1517, Luther had declared that it was announced by the indulgence-hawkers that no sin was too great to be covered by the indulgence, nay, not even the sin of violating the Virgin, if such a thing had been possible.   And late in life, 1541, the Reformer stated that the pardoner "also sold sins to be committed."[1]   The story ran that a Saxon knight went to Tetzel and offered him 10 thaler for a sin he had in mind to commit.   Tetzel replied that he had full power from the pope to grant such an indulgence, but that it was worth 30 thaler. The knight paid the amount, but some time later waylaid Tetzel and took all his indulgence-moneys from him.   To Tetzel's complaints the robber replied, that thereafter he must not be so quick in giving indulgence from sins, not yet committed.[2]

[1] An offer of this sort is referred to by John of Paltz (see quotation in Paulus): *Tetzel*, p. 136, and Paulus' attempt to explain it away.

[2] One of the savory pulpit anecdotes bearing on indulgences ran as follows : Certain pilgrims, on their journey, came to a tree on which 5 souls were hanging.   On their return, they found 4 had vanished.   The one left behind reported that his companions had been released by friends, but that he was without a single friend.   So, for the unfortunate soul's benefit, one of the

The traffic in ecclesiastical places and the forgiveness of sins constitutes the very last scene of mediæval Church history. On the eve of the Reformation, we have the spectacle of the pope solemnly renewing the claim to have rule over both spheres, civil and ecclesiastical, and to hold in his hand the salvation of all mankind, yea, and actually supporting the extravagant luxuries of his worldly court with moneys drawn from the trade in sacred things. How deep-seated the pernicious principle had become was made manifest in the bull which Leo issued, Nov. 9, 1518, a full year after the nailing of the Theses on the church door at Wittenberg, in which all were threatened with excommunication who failed to preach and believe that the pope has the right to grant indulgences.[1]

pilgrims made a pilgrimage to Rome, and the soul at once took its flight to heaven. "So may a soul," the moral went on to say, "be released from purgatorial fire, if only 50 *Pater nosters* be said for it."

[1] The bull in Mirbt, p. 182.

CHAPTER X.

THE CLOSE OF THE MIDDLE AGES.

Lit. — The following treatments may be consulted for this chapter. Haller : *Papstthum u. Kirchenreform.* — Döllinger-Friedrich : *D. Papstthum.* — G. Krüger : *The Papacy*, Engl. trsl., N.Y., 1909. — Lea : *The Eve of the Reformation*, in *Cambr. Hist.*, I : 653–692. — Bezold : *Gesch. d. deutschen Reformation*, pp. 1–244. — Janssen-Pastor : vol. I., II. — Pastor : *Gesch. d. Päpste*, III. 3–150, etc. — Gregorovius : vols. VII., VIII. — G. Ficker : *Das ausgehende MA u. sein Verhältniss zur Reformation*, Leipz., 1903. — A. Schulte : *Kaiser Maximilian als Kandidat für d. päpstlichen Stuhl 1511*, Leipz., 1906. — O. Smeaton : *The Medici and the Ital. Renaissance*, Cin'ti. — The works already cited of Th. Rogers and Cunningham. — W. H. Heyd : *Gesch. d. Levantenhandels*, 2 vols., Stuttg., 1859.

> Many great regions are discovered
> Which to late age were ne'er mentioned,
> Who ever heard of th' Indian Peru
> Or who, in venturous vessel, measured
> The Amazon huge river, now found true ?
> Or fruitfullest Virginia who did ever view ?
>
> Yet all these were when no man did them know,
> Yet have from wisest ages hidden been.
> And later times things more unknown shall show.
> Why then should witless man so much misween,
> That nothing is but that which he hath seen.
> — Spenser, *Faerie Queene.*

No period in the history of the Christian Church has a more clear date set for its close than the Middle Ages. In whatever light the Protestant Reformation is regarded there can be no doubt that a new age began with the nailing of the Theses on the church doors in Wittenberg. All attempts to find another date for the beginning of modern history have failed, whether the date be the reign of Philip the Fair or the Fall of Constantinople, 1453, or the invention of printing. Much as the invention of movable type has done for the spread of intelligence, the personality and conduct of Luther must always be looked upon as the source from which the new currents of human thought and action in Western Europe emanated.[1]

Not so easy, however, is it to fix a satisfactory date for the opening of the Middle Ages. They have been dated from Charlemagne, the founder of the Holy German Empire, the patron of learning, the maker of codes of law. The better starting-point is the pontificate of Gregory the Great, who is well called the last of the Fathers and the first of the mediæval popes. From that date, the rift between the Eastern and the Western Churches, which was already wide as a result of the arrogance of the bishops of Rome, rapidly grew to be unhealable.

The Middle Ages, with their limits, fall easily into 3 periods, but it must be confessed that the first, extending from 600–1050, is a period of warring elements, with no orderly development. Hildebrand properly opens the Middle Ages as a period of great ideas, conscious of its power and begetting movements which have exerted a tremendous influence upon the history of the Church. From the moment that monk entered Rome, the stream of ecclesiastical affairs proceeded on its course between well-defined banks. During the 500 years that followed, the voice of the supreme pontiff was heard above all other voices and controlled every movement emanating from the Church. In this period, the doctrinal system, which is distinctively known as the mediæval, came to its full statement. It was the period of great corporate movements, of the Crusades, the Mendicant orders, of the cathedrals and universities, of the canon law and the sacramental combination and of the Reformatory councils.

The third period of the Middle Ages, which this volume traverses, is at once the product of the former period of Gregory VII. and Innocent III. and, at the same time, the germinative seed-plot of new forces. The sacerdotal keeps its hold and the papacy remains the central tribunal and court of Europe, but protests were heard — vigorous and startling from different quarters, from Prag, Paris, Oxford — which, without overthrowing old

---

[1] Gregorovius, VII. 273, well says that "theoretically and practically the Reformation put an end to the universal power of the papacy and closed the Middle Ages as an epoch in the world's history."

institutions, shook the confidence in their Apostolic appointment and perpetuity. These last two centuries of the mediæval world betray no consuming passion like the Crusades, for all efforts of the pope to stir the dead nerves of that remarkable impulse were futile. And Pius II., looking from the bluffs of Ancona out upon the sea in the hope of discerning ships rigged to undertake the reconquest of the East, furnishes a pathetic spectacle of an attempt to call forth energies to achieve the dreams of the past, when for practical minds the illusion itself has already disappeared.

The Reformatory councils endeavored to undo what Hildebrand and Innocent III. had built up and Thomas Aquinas had sanctioned, the control of the Church and society by the will of the supreme pontiff. The system of the Schoolmen broke down. Wyclif, himself endowed with scholastic acuteness, belonged to that modern class of men who find in practical considerations a sufficient reason to ignore the contentions of dialectic philosophy. And, finally, the Renaissance completely set aside some of the characteristic notions of the Middle Ages, stirring the interest of man in all the works of God, and honoring those who in this earthly sphere of action wrought out the products of intellectual endeavor in literature and art, on the platform and in the department of state.

This last period of the Middle Ages appears to the student of general history as a period of presentiments — and efforts on the part of scattered thinkers, to reach a more free and rational mode of thought and living than the mode they had inherited from the past. The period opening with Hildebrand and extending to Boniface VIII. furnished more imposing personalities, — architects compelling by the force of intellectual assertion, — but fewer useful men. It created a dogmatic unity and triumphed by a policy of force, but the rights of the individual and the principle of liberty of thought and conscience, with which God has chosen to endow mankind, it could not consign to permanent burial.

However, in spite of the efforts put forth in the closing period of the Middle Ages to shake off the fetters of the rigid ecclesiastical compulsion, it failed. The individual reformers and prophets prepared the way for a new time, but were unable to marshal forces enough in their own age to inaugurate the new order. This it was the task of Luther to do.

In a retrospect of the marked features of the closing centuries of the Middle Ages, we are struck first of all with the process by which the nations of Western Europe became consolidated until they substantially won the limits which they now occupy. The conquest of the weary Byzantine empire seemed to open the way for the Turks into all Europe. The acropolis of Athens was occupied in 1458. Otranto on the Italian coast was seized and Vienna itself threatened. All Europe felt as Luther did when he offered the prayer, "from the murderous cruelty of the Turk, Good Lord deliver us." Much as the loss of the city on the Bosphorus was lamented at this time, it cannot but be felt that there was no force in Eastern Christendom which gave any promise of progress, theological or civil.

The papacy, claiming to be invested with plenitude of authority, abated none of its claims, but by its history proved that those very claims are fictitious and have no necessary place in the divine appointment.

Seldom has a more impressive spectacle been furnished than was furnished by the Reformatory councils. Following the Avignon period and the age of the papal schism, they struggled to correct the abuses of the papal system and to define its limitations. The first œcumenical council held on German soil, the Council of Constance, made such an authoritative decision. Its weight was derived from its advocates, the most distinguished theologians and canonists of the time, and the combined voice of the universities and the nations of Latin Christendom. But the decision proved to be no stronger than a spider's web. The contention, which had been made by that long series of pungent tracts which was opened with the tract of Gelnhausen, was easily set aside by the dexterous hand of the papacy itself. Gelnhausen had declared that the way to heal the troubles in the papal household was to convoke a general council.[1] To this mode of state-

---

[1] Gelnhausen in Martène, *Thesaur. nov. anec.*, Paris ed., 1717, II. 1203. *Conclusio principalis ista est quod pro remediando et de medio auferendo schismate moderno expedit, potest et debet concilium generale convocari.*

ment Pius II. opposed his bull, *Execrabilis*, and his successors went on untroubled by the outcry of Latin Christendom for some share in the government of the Church.

But the appeal for a council was an ominous portent. It had been made by Philip the Fair and the French Parliament, 1303. It was made by the Universities of Paris and Oxford and the great churchmen of France. It was made by Wyclif, by Huss and Savonarola. In vain, to be sure, but the body of the Church was thinking and the arena of free discussion was extending.

The most extravagant claims of the papacy still had defenders. Augustus Triumphus and Alvarus Pelayo declared there could be no appeal from the pope to God, because the pope and God were in agreement. He who looks upon the pope with intent and trusting eye, looks upon Christ, and wherever the pope is, there is the Church. Yea, the pope is above canon law. But these men were simply repeating what was current tradition. Dante struck another note, when he put popes in the lowest regions of hell, and Marsiglius of Padua, when he cast doubt upon Peter's ever having been in Rome and insisted that the laity are also a part of the Church.

The scandalous lives of the popes whose names fill the last paragraph of the history of the Middle Ages would have excluded them from decent modern circles and exposed them to sentence as criminals. They were perjurers, adulterers. Avarice, self-indulgence ruled their life. They had no mercy. The charges of murder and vicious disease were laid to their door. They were willing to set the states of Italy one over against the other and to allow them to lacerate each other to extend their own territory or to secure power and titles for their own children and nephews. Luther was not far out of the way when, in his *Appeal to the German Nobility*, he declared "Roman avarice is the greatest of robbers that ever walked the earth. All goes into the Roman sack, which has no bottom, and all in the name of God." In all history, it would be difficult to discover a more glaring inconsistency between profession and practice than is furnished by the careers of the last popes of the Middle Ages.

Upon freedom of thought, the papacy continued to lay the

mortmain of alleged divine appointment. Dante's *De monarchia* was burnt by John XXII. The evangelical text-book, the *Theologia Germanica*, has been put on the Index. Erasmus' writings were put on the Index. Curses were hurled against a German emperor by Clement VI. which it would almost be sacrilege to repeat with the lips. Eckart was declared a heretic. Wyclif's bones were dug up and cast into the flames. Huss was burnt. Savonarola was burnt. And, from nameless graves in Spain and Germany rises the protest against the papacy as a divine institution.

Valla said again and again that the papacy was responsible for all the misfortunes of Italy, its worst enemy. To such a low plane was that institution brought that the Emperor Maximilian I. seriously considered having himself elected pope and combining in himself the two sovereignties of Church and state. That such a thought was possible is proof of the actual state of affairs. A most Catholic historian, Janssen (III. 77), says: "The court of Leo X., with its extravagant expenditure in card-playing, theatres and all manner of worldly amusements, was still more flagrantly opposed to the position of chief overseer of the Church than the courts of the German ecclesiastical princes, notably Albrecht of Mainz. The iniquity of Rome exceeded that of the ecclesiastical princes of Germany." And was not the chief idea, which some of the aspirants after the highest office in Christendom had in mind, well embodied in the words with which Leo followed his election, "Let us enjoy the papacy"? If the lives of these latter popes were unworthy, their treatment of the spiritual prerogatives was sacrilegious. Rome encouraged the Crusades but sent no Crusaders. In Rome everything was for sale. The forgiveness of sins itself was offered for money.

And, within papal circles, there was no movement towards reform. As well might men have looked for a burnt field to furnish food. It is not improbable that the very existence of the papacy was saved by the Reformation. This is the view to which Burckhardt chooses to give expression twice in the same work.[1] It discredited by its incumbents every high claim as-

---

[1] *Renaissance*, I. 136, II. 185. Ficker, p. 13, speaks of "the incalculable advantage which accrued to the Catholic Church from the Reformation."

serted for it. And yet, with abounding self-confidence, in the last hours of the Middle Ages, it solemnly reaffirmed the claim of supreme jurisdiction over the souls and bodies of men, the Church and the state. And after the Reformation had begun, Prierias, Master of the palace, declared the pope's superiority to the Scriptures in these words: " Whoever does not rest upon the doctrine of the Roman Church and the Roman pope as an infallible rule of faith, from which even the Holy Scriptures derive their authority, is a heretic." And to be a heretic meant to be an outlaw. Prierias was the man who spoke of Luther as " the brute with the deep eyes and strange fantasies."

Forces of another character were working. In quiet pathways, the mystics walked with God and, though they did not repudiate the sacramental system, they called attention to the religion of the heart as the seat of religion. The *Imitation of Christ* was written once, for all ages. The Church had found its proper definition as the body of the elect and that idea stood in direct antithesis to the theory the hierarchy worked upon. The preaching of the Waldenses had been condemned by the Fourth Lateran Council, but there was a growing popular demand for instruction as well as the spectacle of the mass, and the catechetical manuals laid stress upon the sermon. The Albigenses had been completely blotted out, but the principles of Lollardism and Hussitism continued to flow, though as little rills. The Inquisition was still doing its work, but in Germany schools for all classes of children were being taught. The laity was asserting its rights in the domain of learning and culture. These influences were silently preparing the soil for the new teachings.

In the 15th century, a potent force stirred Europe as Europe had never been stirred by it before, — Commerce. The industrial change, then going on, deserves more than a passing reference as a factor preparing the mind for intellectual and religious innovation. This, at least, is true of the German people. Explorations and the extension of commerce have, in more periods than one, preceded a revival of missionary enterprise. But, of all the centuries, none is so like the 19th as the last century of the Middle Ages, — vital with humanistic forces of all kinds.   It was a time of revolution in the methods of trade and the comforts and prices of living.   The world could never be again just what it had been before.   There was marked restlessness among the artisan and peasant classes. This industrial unrest was adapted to encourage and to beget unrest in things ecclesiastical and to accustom the mind to the thought of change there.

From Italy, whose harbors were the outfitting points for fleets during the Crusades, the centre of trade had shifted to the cities north of the Alps and to the Portuguese coast.   Nürnberg, Ulm, Augsburg and Constance in Southern Germany; Bruges, Antwerp and other cities along the lower Rhine and in Flanders; and the cities of the Hanseatic League were bustling marts, turning out new and wonderful products of manufacture and drawing the products of the outside world through London, Lisbon, Lyons and Venice.   Energy and enterprise were making Germany rich and her mercantile houses had their representatives and depots in Venice, Antwerp and other ports.[1]

Methods of business, such as to-day are suggesting grave problems to the political economist and moralist, were introduced and flourished.   Trading companies and monopolies came upon the stage and startled the advocates of the old feudal ways by the extent and boldness of their operations. Trusts flourished in Augsburg and other German cities.[2]   In-

[1] For the transfer of the centre of the Levantine trade from Venice to Lisbon at the beginning of the 16th century, see Heyd, II. 505–540.   Heyd says that the discovery of the route to India around the Cape of Good Hope by the Portuguese *hatte wie ein Donnerschlag am heiteren Himmel die Gemüther der Venetianer berührt.*   To counteract the stream of trade in the direction of Lisbon, the Venetians proposed a scheme for cutting a canal through the Isthmus of Suez in 1500 and, in the same interest, the Turks actually began that enterprise in 1529.   Manuel, king of Portugal, in 1505 stationed a fleet at Calicut to prevent the Venetians from interfering with the export of Indian goods to Portugal.   For the German Board of Trade at Venice, the *fondaco dei Tedeschi*, see Heyd, II. 520, etc.

[2] Writing in 1458, Æneas Sylvius said, "The German nation takes the lead of all others in wealth and power."   He spoke of Cologne as unexcelled in magnificence among the cities of Europe.   At Nürnberg he found simple burghers living in houses, the like of which the kings of Scotland would have been glad to house in.

dividuals and corporations cornered the import trade, the grain crop, the wine harvest, the silver, copper and iron product, sugar, linen, leather, pepper, even soap, for they used soap also in those days. The Höchstetters, the Ebners and the Fuggers were among the great speculative and trading firms of the age. They carried things with a high hand. Ambrose Höchstetter of Augsburg, for example, one season bought up all the ash wood, another all the grain and another all the wine. Nor was the art of adulteration left for these later, and often discredited, times to practice. They condescended to small things, even to the mixing of brick-dust with pepper. Commodities rose suddenly in price. In Germany, wine rose, in 1510, 49 per cent and grain 32 per cent. Imperial diets took cognizance of these conditions and tried to correct the evils complained of by regulating the prices of goods.[1] Municipalities did the same. Preachers, like Geiler of Strassburg, charged the monopolists with fearing neither God nor man and called upon the cities to banish them. Professors of jurisprudence, for there was at that time no department of social science, inveighed against monopolies as spiders' webs to ensnare the innocent.[2] It was a fast age. There was no precedent for what was going on. Men sighed for the good old times. Speculation was rampant and the prospect of quick gains easily captivated the people. They took shares in the investment companies and often lost everything. It was noticed that the directors of the companies were able to avoid

---

[1] So the Diet of Cologne, 1512. At the same time, however, it declared that its acts were not designed to prevent the association of merchants in trading companies. The Diet of Innsbruck, 1518, did the same, and complained of the trading companies for driving out the small dealers and fixing prices arbitrarily. Trithemius argued for laws protecting the people from the overreachings of avarice and declared that whosoever bought up meat, grain and other articles of diet to force up prices is no better than a common criminal. See Janssen, II. 102, sq.

[2] So Christopher Kuppner of Leipzig, in his tract on usury, 1508. He insists that magistrates should proceed against trading companies and rich merchants who, through agents in other lands, bought up saffron, pepper, corn and what not and sold them at whatsoever price they chose. According to the secretary of the firm, Conrad Meyer, the capital of the Fuggers increased in 7 years 13,000,000 florins.

losses which the common and unsuspecting investor had to bear. The confusion was increased by the readiness of town aldermen and city councillors to take stock in the concerns. It also happened that the great traders, whose ventures involved others in loss, were conspicuous in church affairs.

To the wealth, arising from manufactures and foreign commerce, were added the riches which were being dug up from the newly opened mines of silver, copper and iron in Bohemia and Saxony. Avarice was cried down as the besetting sin of the age and, in some quarters, commerce was denounced as being carried on in defiance of the simplest precepts of the Gospel.[1]

With wealth came extravagance in dress and at the table. Municipalities legislated against it and imperial parliaments sought to check it by arbitrary rules. Wimpheling says, table services of gold were not unusual and that he himself had eaten from golden plates at Cologne. Complaint was frequently made at the diets that men were being brought to poverty by their expenditures for dress upon themselves and the expenditures of the female members of their households.

In Germany, peasants were limited to a certain kind of cloth for their outer garments and to a maximum price.[2] The women had their share in making the disturbance and dignified town councils sat in judgment upon the number of gowns and other articles of apparel and ornament the ladies of the day might possess without detriment to the community or hurt to the solvency of their indulgent husbands. The council of Ratisbon, for example, in 1485 made it a rule that the wives and daughters of distinguished burghers should be limited to 8 dresses, 6 long

[1] A preacher in 1515 declared the spirit of speculation then prevailing to be of recent growth, only ten years old, and that it had not existed in former times. Janssen, II. 87.

[2] The diets of 1498 and 1500 forbade artisans to wear gold, silver, pearls, velvet and embroidered stuffs. They were forbidden to pay more than one-half a florin a yard for the cloth of their coats and mantles. Laws regulating dress were also passed in Italy. Elastic beds, false hair and other fashions came into vogue. Women sat in the sun all day to bleach their hair. In Florence, money was scented. See Burckhardt-Geiger, II. 87 sqq. John of Arundel, who was drowned at sea, 1379, had 52 new suits of cloth of gold or tissue. By a parliamentary act of 1463, no knight or other person might wear shoes or boots having peaks longer than two inches, *Soc. Engl.*, II. 426 sqq.

cloaks, 3 dancing gowns, one plaited mantle with not more than 3 sets of sleeves of silk velvet and brocade, 2 pearl hair bands not to cost more than 12 florins, one tiara of gold set with pearls, not more than three veils costing 8 florins each, etc.   But why enumerate the whole list of articles?   It is supposable the women conformed, even if they were inclined to criticise the aldermen for not sticking to their legitimate municipal business. Geiler of Strassburg had his word to say for these innovations of an extravagant age, the women with two dresses for a single day, their long trains trailing in the dust, the cocks' feathers worn in the women's hats and the long hair falling down over their shoulders.   The times were cried down as bad.   It is, however, pleasant to recall that a contemporary annalist commended as praiseworthy the habit of bathing at least " once every two weeks."

Among the artisans and the peasants, the unrest asserted itself in strikes and uprisings, strikes for shorter hours, for better food and for better wages.   Sometimes a municipality and a gild were at strife for years.   Sometimes a city was bereft at one stroke of all the workers of a given craft, as was Nürnberg of her tin workers in 1475.   The gilds of tailors are said to have been most given to strikes.

The new social order involved the peasant class in more hardship than any other.   The peasants were made the victims of the rapacity and violence of the landowners, who encroached upon their fields and their traditional but unwritten rights, and deprived them of the right to fish and hunt and gather wood in the forests.   The Church also came in for its share of condemnation.   One-fifth of the soil of Germany was in the possession of convents and other religious establishments and the peasant leaders called upon the monks and priests to distribute their lands.   In their marching songs they appealed to Christ to keep them from putting the priests to death.   The Peasant War of 1525 was not the product of the abuse of the principle of personal freedom introduced by the Reformation.   It was one of a long series of uprisings and it has been said that, if the Reformation had not come and diverted the attention of the people, it is likely Germany would have been shaken by such a social revolution in the 16th century as the world has seldom seen.[1]

In England, the restlessness was scarcely less demonstrative and the condition of the laboring classes scarcely less deplorable. Their hardships in the 14th century called forth the rebellion of Watt Tyler. The famous statute of laborers of 1350 fixed the wages of reapers at 3 pence a day; the statute of 1444, a century later, raised it to 5 pence. The laws of 1495, Cunningham says, were intended to keep down the wages of the daily toiler. English legislation was habitually bent on preventing an artificial enhancement of prices. At the very close of the Middle Ages, 1515, a regulation fixed the day's work from 5 in the morning until 7 or 8 in the evening in summer and during the hours of daylight during the winter. Legislation was sought to put a limit on prices against the inflation of combinations. Frauds and adulterations in articles offered for sale, bad work and false weights were officially condemned in 1504. Against the proclivity of the gilds to fix the prices of their wares at unreasonable figures, Henry VII. set himself with determination. With the development of sheep-walks, farm hands lost their employment.[2] To the author of *Utopia* the act of parliament in 1515, fixing wages, seemed to be " nothing else than a conspiracy of the rich against the poor," and " the laboring man was doomed to a life so wretched that even a beast's life in comparison seemed to be enviable."

The discoveries in the New World and the nautical exploits, which carried Portuguese sailors around the Cape of Good Hope, also stimulated this feeling of restlessness. While the horizon of the natural world was being enlarged and new highways of commerce were being opened, thoughtful men had questions whether the geography of the spiritual world, as outlined in the scholastic systems, did not need revision. The

---

[1] Ficker, p. 107 sq.; Müller: *Kirchengesch.* II. 196 sq. Among these peasant leaders, the piper of Niklashausen was one of the most prominent. In the last quarter of the 15th century, tracts were circulated among the peasants, calling upon them to resist the oppression of the ruling classes and demand the secularization of Church lands.

[2] Rogers, p. 143; Cunningham, pp. 399, 457 sq., 468 sqq., 476 sqq., 484.

resurrection of the Bible as a popular book stimulated the curiosity and questioning. The Bible also was a new world. The trade, the enterprise, the thought awakened during the last 70 years of the Middle Ages were incomparably more vital than had been awakened by the Crusades and the Crusaders' tales. When the Reformation came, the chief centres of business in Germany and England became, for the most part, seats of the new religious movement, Nürnberg, Ulm, Augsburg, Geneva, Strassburg, Frankfurt, Lübeck and London.

The Renaissance, as has already been set forth, was another potent factor contributing to the forward impulse of the last century of the Middle Ages. All the faculties of man were to be recognized as worthy of cultivation. Europe arose as out of a deep sleep. Men opened their eyes and saw, as Mr. Taine put it. The Renaissance made the discovery of man and the earth. The Schoolmen had forgotten both. Here also a new world was revealed to view and Ulrich von Hutten, referring to it and to the age as a whole could exclaim, " O century, studies flourish, spirits are awaking. It is a pleasure to live! "

But in the Renaissance Providence seems to have had the design of showing again that intellectual and artistic culture may flourish, while the process of moral and social decline goes on. No regenerating wave passed over Italy's society or cleansed her palaces and convents. The outward forms of civilization did not check the inward decline. The Italian character, says Gregorovius, " in the last 30 years of the 15th century displays a trait of diabolical passion. Tyrannicide, conspiracies and deeds of treachery were universal." In the period of Athenian greatness, the process of the intellectual sublimation of the few was accompanied by the process of moral decay in the many. So now, art did not purify. The Renaissance did not find out what repentance was or feel the need of it. Savonarola's admiring disciple, Pico della Mirandola, presented a memorial to the Fifth Lateran which declared that, if the prelates "delayed to heal the wounds of the Church, Christ would cut off the corrupted members with fire and sword. Christ had cast out the money-changers, why should not Leo exile the worshippers of the many golden calves?" In Italy, remarks Ranke, "no one

counted for a cultured person who did not cherish some erroneous views about Christianity."

The North had no Dante and Petrarca and Boccaccio or
Thomas Aquinas, but it had its Tauler and Thomas à Kempis
and its presses sent forth the first Greek New Testament. This
was a positive preparation for the coming age as much as the
Greek language was a preparation for the spread of Christianity through Apostolic preaching in the 1st century. German
printers went to Rome in 1467 and as far as Barcelona. In his
work on the new invention, 1507, Wimpheling [1] declared "that
as the Apostles went forth of old, so now the disciples of the
sacred art go forth from Germany into all lands and their printed
books become heralds of the Gospel, preachers of the truth and
wisdom." Germany became the intellectual market of Europe
and its wares went across the North Sea to that little kingdom
which was to become the chief bulwark of Protestantism. In
vain did Leo X. set himself against the free circulation of literature.[2]

The Greek edition of the New Testament and the printing-
press, — that invention which cleaves all the centuries in two
and yet binds all the centuries together — were the two chief
providential instruments made ready for Martin Luther. But
he had to find them. They did not make him a reformer, the
leader of the new age. Erasmus, whom Janssen mercilessly condemns, remained a moralizer. He lacked both the passion and
the heroism of the religious reformer. The religious reformer
must be touched from above. Reuchlin, Erasmus and Gutenberg prepared the outward form of the Greek and Hebrew
Bible. Luther discovered its contents, and made them known.

Such were the complex forces at work in the closing century of the Middle Ages. The absolute jurisdiction of the
papacy was solemnly reaffirmed. The hierarchy virtually constituted the Church. Religious dissent was met with compulsion and force, not by persuasion and instruction. Coercion
was substituted for individual consent. Popular piety re-

---

[1] *De arte impressoria.* The printer Gutenberg lived 1397–1468 and his son-
in-law, Schöffer, died 1502.

[2] In his bull of May 4, 1515. See Mirbt, p. 177.

mained bound in the old forms and was strong.   But there
were sounds of refreshing rills, flowing from the fresh fountain of the water of life, running at the side of the old ceremo-
nials, especially in the North.   The Revival of Letters aroused
the intellect to a sense of its sovereign rights.   The movement of thought was greatly accelerated by the printed page.
The development of trade communicated unrest.   But the
lives of the popes, as we look back upon the age, forbade the
expectation of any relief from Rome.   The Reformatory councils had contented themselves with attempts to reform the administration of the Church.   Nevertheless, though men did
not see it, driftwood as from a new theological continent was
drifting about and there were prophetic voices though the
princes of the Church listened not to them.   What was needed
was not government, was not regulations but regeneration.
This the hierarchy could not give, but only God alone.[1]

The facts, set forth in this volume, leave no room for the contention of the recent class of historians in the Roman Church,—
Janssen, Denifle, Pastor, Nicolas, Paulus, Dr. Gasquet — who
have devoted themselves to the task of proving that an orderly
reform-movement was going on when the Reformation broke
out.   That movement, they represent as an unspeakable calamity for civilization, an apostasy from Christianity, an insurrection against divinely constituted authority.   It violently
checked the alleged current of progress and popes, down to Pius
IX. and Leo XIII., have anathematized Protestantism as a poisonous pestilence and the mother of all modern evils in Church
and state.   In the attempt to make good this judgment, these
recent writers not only have laid stress upon "the good old
times," — a description which the people of the 15th century
would have repudiated,[2] — but have resorted to the defamation

---

[1] See Sohm's sententious words in closing his treatment of the Middle Ages,
Kirchengesch., 15th ed., 1907, p. 122 sq.   Colet, who was in Italy during the
rule of Alexander VI. said: "Unless the Mediator who created and founded
the Church out of nothing for himself, lay his hand with all speed, our most
disordered Church cannot be far from death. . . . All seek their own, not the
things of Jesus Christ, not heavenly things but earthly things, what will bring
them to death, not what will bring them life eternal." — SEEBOHM, p. 75.

[2] To the other testimonies in this vol. add Erasmus, *Enchiridion*, p. 11 sq.

of the German Reformer's character, setting aside the contemporaries who knew him best, and violently perverting Luther's own words. Imbart de la Tour, the most recent French historian of this school, on reaching the year 1517, exclaims, "The era of peaceful reforms was at an end; the era of religious revolution was about to open."[1]

Lefèvre d'Etaples was not alone when he uttered the famous words: —

The signs of the times announce that a reformation of the Church is near at hand and, while God is opening new paths for the preaching of the Gospel by the discoveries of the Portuguese and the Spaniards, we must hope that He will also visit His Church and raise her from the abasement into which she has now fallen.

The Philosophy of Christ, — the name which Erasmus gave to the Gospel in his *Paraclesis*, prefixed to his edition of the New Testament, — was to a large degree covered over by the dialectical theology of the Schoolmen. What men needed was the Gospel and the bishop of Isernia, preaching at the Fifth Lateran council in its 12th session, spoke better than he knew when he exclaimed: "The Gospel is the fountain of all wisdom, of all knowledge. From it has flowed all the higher virtue, all that is divine and worthy of admiration. The Gospel, I say the Gospel." The words were spoken on the very eve of the Reformation and the council of the Middle Ages failed utterly to offer any real remedy for the religious degeneracy. The Reformer came from the North, not from Rome and as from another Nazareth. The angel of God had to descend again and trouble the waters and a single personality touched in con-

---

[1] II. 579. An example of misrepresentation may be taken from Denifle, *Luther u. Luthertum* who picks out a single clause from one of Luther's sermons, *Die Begierde ist gänzlich unbesiegbar*, "Passion cannot be overcome," and holds it up as the starting-point for the Reformer's alleged profligate life. What could be more atrocious, unworthy of a scholar and a gentleman, when it was Luther's purpose in this very sermon to show that Christ imparts the power to overcome evil, which the natural man does not possess and calls upon men to flee to Christ's protection. In these last vols. Denifle outdid Janssen. Leo XIII. praised Janssen as a "light of historic science and a man of profound learning." Pius X. gave to Denifle the distinction of receiving the first copy of his book from the author's hand.

science proved himself mightier than the wisdom of theology and wiser than the rulers of the visible Church.

Remarkable the Middle Ages were for their bold enterprises in thought and action and they are an important part of the history of the Church.   We acknowledge our debt, but their superstitions and errors we set aside as we move on in the pathway of a more intelligent devotion and broader human sympathies, towards an age when all who profess the Gospel shall unite together in the unity of the faith in the Son of God.

INDEX